Gerd Fellermann

America's Mission

PRINCETON STUDIES IN

INTERNATIONAL HISTORY AND POLITICS

Series Editors
John Lewis Gaddis
Jack L. Snyder
Richard H. Ullman

———————————————

History and Strategy by Marc Trachtenberg (1991)

George F. Kennan and the Making of American Foreign Policy,
1947–1950 by Wilson D. Miscamble, c.s.c. (1992)

Economic Discrimination and Political Exchange:
World Political Economy in the 1930s and 1980s
by Kenneth A. Oye (1992)

Whirlpool: U.S. Foreign Policy Toward Latin America and the
Caribbean by Robert A. Pastor (1992)

Germany Divided: From the Wall to Reunification
by A. James McAdams (1993)

A Certain Idea of France: French Security Policy and the
Gaullist Legacy by Philip H. Gordon (1993)

The Limits of Safety: Organizations, Accidents, and Nuclear
Weapons by Scott D. Sagan (1993)

Mercenaries, Pirates, and Sovereigns: State-Building and Extraterritorial
Violence in Early Modern Europe by Janice E. Thomson (1994)

We All Lost the Cold War
by Richard Ned Lebow and Janice Gross Stein (1994)

Who Adjusts? Domestic Sources of Foreign Economic Policy during the
Interwar Years by Beth A. Simmons (1994)

America's Mission: The United States and the Worldwide Struggle for
Democracy in the Twentieth Century by Tony Smith (1994)

The Sovereign State and Its Competitors: An Analysis of Systems Change
by Hendrik Spruyt (1994)

Cooperation among Democracies: The European Influence on
U.S. Foreign Policy by Thomas Risse-Kappen (1995)

The Necessary War: An International History of the Korean War
by William Stueck (1995)

America's Mission

THE UNITED STATES AND THE WORLDWIDE STRUGGLE FOR DEMOCRACY IN THE TWENTIETH CENTURY

Tony Smith

A Twentieth Century Fund Book

PRINCETON UNIVERSITY PRESS

PRINCETON, NEW JERSEY

Copyright © 1994 by The Twentieth Century Fund, Inc.
Published by Princeton University Press, 41 William Street,
Princeton, New Jersey 08540
In the United Kingdom: Princeton University Press,
Chichester, West Sussex

All Rights Reserved

Library of Congress Cataloging-in-Publication Data

Smith, Tony, 1942–
America's mission : the United States and the worldwide struggle
for democracy in the twentieth century / Tony Smith.
p.   cm. — (Princeton studies in international history and politics)
"A Twentieth Century Fund Book."
Includes bibliographical references and index.
ISBN 0–691–03784–1   ISBN 0–691–04466–X (pbk.)
1. United States—Foreign relations—20th century.   2. World politics—20th century.
3. Democracy—History—20th century.   I. Title.   II. Series.
E744.S588   1944   327.73—dc20   94–11314   CIP

This book has been composed in Times Roman

Princeton University Press books are printed on acid-free paper
and meet the guidelines for permanence and durability of the
Committee on Production Guidelines for Book Longevity
of the Council on Library Resources

Second printing, and first paperback printing, 1995

Printed in the United States of America by Princeton Academic Press

10   9   8   7   6   5   4   3   2

*For my students and colleagues
at Tufts University*

y para mi compañero Jose David Ovalle

O, for a Muse of fire, that would ascend
The brightest heaven of invention,
A kingdom for a stage, princes to act
And monarchs to behold the swelling scene! . . .
But pardon, gentles all,
The flat unraised spirits that have dared
On this unworthy scaffold to bring forth
So great an object. Can this cockpit hold
The vasty fields of France? Or may we cram
Within this wooden O the very casques
That did affright the air at Agincourt?
Oh, pardon! Since a crooked figure may
Attest in little place a million,
And let us, ciphers to this great accompt,
On your imaginary forces work.
Suppose within the girdle of these walls
Are now confined two mighty monarchies,
Whose high upreared and abutting fronts
The perilous narrow ocean parts asunder.
Pierce out our imperfections with your thoughts.
Into a thousand parts divide one man,
And make imaginary puissance.
Think when we talk of horse that you see them
Printing their proud hoofs i' the receiving earth.
For 'tis your thoughts that now must deck our kings,
Carry them here and there, jumping o'er times,
Turning the accomplishment of many years
Into an hourglass. For the which supply,
Admit me Chorus to this history,
Who prologue-like your humble patience pray,
Gently to hear, kindly to judge, our play.

—Shakespeare, Prologue, *Henry V*

Contents

Foreword

WE IN THE WEST are still adjusting to the dawn of a world that suddenly lacks the fearful challenge of our most powerful communist rival. Policymakers in the United States sometimes seem almost wistful about the loss of the perfect clarity that characterized the missions and goals of foreign affairs during the cold war. And, of course, with the disappearance of a clear threat to national security, political leaders are uncertain about just what the public will support in terms of global strategy and action. In this context it is not surprising that students of international relations also seem perplexed, peering into a misty present for clues to a remarkably uncertain future.

Yet in the short run one thing is certain: the United States occupies a unique role in world affairs. In 1994, in a way that not even the most romantic nineteenth-century patriot could have foreseen, the destiny of the United States as leader of the planet's democracies has a touch of inevitability about it. We may be somewhat uneasy with this preeminence, but in any future competition with authoritarian or theocratic states that still resist the concept of government by the people, the first question will be how willing are Americans to fulfill their leadership role.

A new purity may emerge in the alignment of nations, with the common interests, aspirations, and constraints of the democracies representing the organizing principles for one bloc. While the evidence for such a development is only fragmentary as yet, it does seem that alliances of convenience with anticommunist states regardless of their political hues is a thing of the past. And, in the common principles of democratic nations, there are the beginnings of a credible agenda for foreign policy and national security affairs—an agenda built upon a foundation of continuing military strength as well as strong support for democratic movements everywhere. In some sense this approach derives from the fundamental lesson of the history of America in world affairs. It responds to the old question: can there be a world safe for democracy that is not dominated by democracies?

During and since the breakup of the Soviet empire, the Twentieth Century Fund has supported a number of works intended to help illuminate the near-term agenda of American foreign policy, including Richard Ullman's *Securing Europe*; Thomas Baylis's *The West and Eastern Europe: Economic Statecraft and Political Change*; Jeffrey Garten's *A Cold Peace: America, Japan, Germany, and the Struggle for Supremacy*; and James Chace's *The Consequences of the Peace: The New Internationalism and American Foreign Policy*. In addition, we have a number of studies of this critical subject under way, including Robert Art on America's grand strategy after the cold war; Monteagle Stearns on the American diplomatic method; Steven Burg on nationalism and the democratization of Eastern Europe; Anita Isaacs on building democracy in Latin America; David Calleo on rethinking Europe's future; and Henry Nau on American foreign policy after the cold war.

In the present volume, Professor Tony Smith of Tufts University offers a view that emphasizes the continuing central role of the global struggle for democracy as an abiding guide for U.S. policy over the years. Professor Smith traces the evolution of American policy, emphasizing the emergence of the United States as a significant global actor at the time of the Spanish-American War, through the era of Wilsonianism, World War II, and the cold war. Throughout this period, the growth in the United States' role in world affairs has roughly paralleled the spread of the struggle for democracy.

On behalf of the Trustees of the Twentieth Century Fund, I want to thank Tony Smith for this contribution to the literature of American diplomatic and political history. By emphasizing the democratic imperative, he has enriched the foundation for new thinking about America's place in the world.

Richard C. Leone, President
The Twentieth Century Fund
March 1994

Preface

THIS BOOK has a twofold purpose. The first is to recount the history of the various American efforts to foster democracy abroad and to evaluate the results of these attempts in terms of their own ambitions. The second is to ask how American foreign policy has contributed to the surge in the number, strength, and prestige of liberal democratic governments worldwide at the end of the twentieth century.

The first issue takes us through a hundred years of what this book will call American liberal democratic internationalism. Since 1898, when Americans had to decide what to do with their victory in the Spanish-American War—largely inspired by a determination to stop Spain's repeated abuse of human rights in Cuba—no theme has figured more prominently in the annals of American foreign policy than the repeated presidential calls to promote the creation of democratic government abroad. William McKinley's taking of the Philippines and Puerto Rico in 1898; Woodrow Wilson's interventions in Central America and the Caribbean before World War I, and his subsequent intention "to make the world safe for democracy" by reorganizing European politics thereafter; Franklin Roosevelt's concern for democracy in postwar Europe and Harry Truman's determination to democratize Germany and Japan during their occupation; Dwight Eisenhower's pledges to the "captive nations" of Eastern Europe; John Kennedy's ambitions in the Alliance for Progress in Latin America; Jimmy Carter's "human rights campaign"; Ronald Reagan's "democratic revolution"; George Bush's "new world order"; efforts by Bill Clinton to promote democracy in countries as different as Russia and Haiti—all of these were the product of an American conviction that if democracy were to spread, America's place in the world would be more secure. Surprisingly, no study exists examining the common purpose and ultimate consequences of these various related policies, a major gap in our understanding both of the character of American foreign policy and of its repercussions abroad. This book proposes to fill that gap by assessing the successes and failures of this country's democratizing mission and its impact on the national interest.

The second issue raised in this book involves the speculative question of the American contribution to the most critical political issue of the twentieth century: the need to create stable states and a stable international community in an era when the domestic basis of governmental authority has been radically changing, with profound repercussions on world affairs. The origin of the epochal change in the structure and legitimation of the state began in the eighteenth century with the industrial and American revolutions; it became a matter of international urgency with the French Revolution. Here demands for popular sovereignty were born; here modern nationalism had its beginning. The result was a crisis in political authority, which eventually spread worldwide.

The problem of taming nationalism politically by founding a stable form of mass-based state capable of participating in world affairs peacefully has been the chief political problem of the twentieth century. Nationalism, with its demands for international status and popular sovereignty, provided the major impetus for the Mexican, Russian, Chinese, Cuban, and Iranian revolutions while serving as a principal cause of the two world wars, European decolonization, the cold war, and the collapse of Soviet communism. Viewed in terms of the global history of this century, American liberal democratic internationalism becomes a force among many trying to shape nationalism politically in the modern world. How, then, has the United States contributed to the success of liberal democratic governments worldwide when fascism and communism were bidding ruthlessly for nationalist support and world supremacy in direct opposition to democratic movements? Is democracy's current victory limited and momentary, soon to be reversed by some new challenge, or can the momentum of liberal democratic internationalism be preserved? After two world wars and the collapse of Soviet communism, is the world finally safe for democracy?

For an academic audience, I hope this study will provide an historically based framework useful as the basis for further investigations of the ways in which international forces (not all of them American, to be sure) have promoted domestic political transformations favoring democracy. For a policy audience, I hope that it can help to show how the United States might most effectively foster democracy for others, while cautioning against unwarranted intervention abroad.

When I first approached the Twentieth Century Fund for support to write this book, its staff assumed that a shelfload of books already existed on the subject. There are, indeed, many superb studies of specific periods or policies, works whose arguments will be covered in the pages to follow. Still, the fact that no one has attempted to survey the overall history of American efforts to promote democracy worldwide is (as the Fund soon agreed) surprising. Where are the books that chronicle the general pattern of American initiatives since the late nineteenth century to promote democracy in specific countries or to affect the overall character of international relations? In the appendix, I have charted how fashions in social science research have managed to discourage investigation of a subject of central importance to our century.

Today, to be sure, the mood has changed. At the time my research began in 1988, a remarkable convergence of social scientists interested in America's sponsorship of democracy worldwide was starting to appear. In the political arena, a bipartisan consensus emerged even earlier, holding that the national security was enhanced by the expansion of democracy abroad. Since the mid-1960s, in reaction to Vietnam, the center-left had found all talk of the United States promoting democracy abroad to be hypocrisy masking aggression. But as early as 1973, in reaction especially to events in southern Africa, the mood in these circles began to change, culminating in the human rights campaign of the Carter presidency (1977–81). For its part, the center-right, which had been championing America's virtues to the world before the presidential campaign of Ronald Reagan in 1980, began to specify policies designed to promote democracy abroad as early as the summer of 1982. In the process, Reagan became the first Republican president emphatically to embrace the essential tenets of liberal democratic internationalism, or what might be called Wilsonianism: the conviction that American national interests could best be pursued by promoting democracy worldwide. Indeed, in some respects Reagan was more Wilsonian than any of his Democratic predecessors, including FDR, Truman, Kennedy, and Carter. That the Bush and Clinton administrations would follow in this tradition (even if they were more selective in their liberal democratic internationalism than were Carter and Reagan before them) indicates the enduring importance of this appeal in Washington at the century's close.

Many current policy questions hinge on understanding the logic of this century's political competitions. How important to the American national interest is it that in those regions of the globe traditionally most significant to the United States—Europe, Latin America, and the Far East—democracy is showing unprecedented strength? To what extent did American policy contribute to this reshaping of international affairs, and how important are these developments for world peace? When and how can American leaders preserve the momentum of democratic expansion, while at the same time recognizing the limits to their power—limits that if transgressed might convert these efforts into self-defeating crusades?

No analysis of the past can provide final answers to present and future problems, which are certain to have a logic of their own. Yet reflection on American policy over the twentieth century sheds considerable light on today's world and the possibilities for meaningful action.

Acknowledgments

WITH ITS many fine universities, the Boston area has been an excellent place to write this book. The libraries are unsurpassed and the Center for European Studies at Harvard University was helpful with the loan of an office. The Twentieth Century Fund was generous in its financial support, and Dean Mary Ella Feinlieb of Tufts University saw that securing release time was no problem.

My greatest debt is to colleagues far more expert than I on many of the complicated issues that this book addresses. Abraham Lowenthal, Jonathan Hartlyn, Fran Hagopian, Jorge Dominguez, and Howard Wiarda responded to a host of questions about Latin America. In the Dominican Republic, President Juan Bosch and Bernardo Vega were forthcoming on the character of American influence on their country, while in Jamaica, Prime Minister Edward Seaga was equally helpful. Klaus Schwabe closely reviewed my work on Woodrow Wilson and on the American occupation of Germany (reminding me that the German phrasing of the American saying that "God is in the details" holds that it is the devil who is there). Nicholas X. Rizopoulos corrected my account of American early postwar policy, especially with respect to Greece. Arthur Schlesinger, Jr., offered me his recollections on the Alliance for Progress and read my account of the Roosevelt years. Hideo Otake, Jeffrey Herf, David Blackbourn, and Tom Berger reviewed my study of the American occupations of Germany and Japan. Houchang Chehabi superintended my interpretation of American policy toward Iran under the shah and invited me to speak to a group of distinguished Iranian experts on the subject, while Vali Nasr took pains to correct my reading of American policy toward Iran in the 1950s. Tamsin Lutz facilitated my visit to Guatemala. Robert Pastor and Samuel Huntington critically read my chapters on the Carter and Reagan years, offering insights from their familiarity with Washington at that time. Scott Thompson reviewed my accounts of American policy in the Philippines and of the Reagan administration. Sally Terry, Grzegorz Ekiert, and Andy Markovitz shared their thoughts on American efforts to promote democracy in Eastern Europe since 1918. Pearl Robinson gave me abundant information on democratization in Africa, while Perrin Elkind shared her thoughts with me on American policy toward South Africa. Jeffrey Berry helped me study changes in domestic American political structure from Wilson to FDR. Rob Devigne discussed the historical character of Western liberalism and democracy with me. Tony Messina talked to me about British liberalism, while Myron Wiener discussed the impact of British imperialism on the democratic character of India today. John Jenke and Richard Eichenberg offered me their thoughts on the prospects for European integration and its relevance to liberal internationalism. Jaime Weinberg suggested the relevance of the Reconstruction experience in the American South following the Civil War. Robert Keohane, Jay Greene, and Eric J. Labs reviewed my account of the history of American social science methodology in comparative politics and international relations. David J. Hancock talked to me about American liberalism in the late eighteenth century. Lucian Pye and Larry Diamond supported the idea of this investigation early on, when others were skeptical it was worth pursuing. Ronald Steel, James Chace, and Miles Kahler talked with me endlessly about the various themes of the book. My greatest debts are to Don Klein and John Lewis Gaddis, who made suggestions for change in every chapter of the book.

As the academic reader may perceive, three types of analytical concern underlie this book, each of which may be traced back to a different thinker: an attention to the political importance of socioeconomic analysis, which stems from the work of Barrington Moore, Jr; a conviction as to the autonomous and important influence of political variables on historical developments, which comes from the work of Samuel P. Huntington; and a concern with the viability of liberalism in international affairs, long an interest of Stanley Hoffmann's. The inspiration of these three friends and colleagues should be apparent throughout the book.

Finally, my thanks to the Twentieth Century Fund, which generously supported my writing, and to Beverly Goldberg and Carol Kahn Strauss, my skilled and cheerful editors there. Without the Fund's financial and moral backing, this book might never have been written. It has also been a pleasure to renew my acquaintance with Walter Lippincott at Princeton University Press and to benefit from the able editing of David Blair.

America's Mission

CHAPTER ONE

The United States and the
Global Struggle for Democracy

> Whether the tremendous war so heroically fought and so
> victoriously ended shall pass into history a miserable failure,
> barren of permanent results—a scandalous and shocking waste of
> blood and treasure . . . of no value to liberty or civilization . . . must
> be determined one way or the other. . . . Slavery, like all other great
> systems of wrong, founded in the depth of human selfishness and
> existing for ages, has not neglected its own conservation. . . .
> Custom, manners, morals, religion are all on its side everywhere
> in the South; and when you add the ignorance and servility of the
> ex-slave to the intelligence and accustomed authority of the master,
> you have the conditions, not out of which slavery will again grow,
> but under which it is impossible for the Federal government wholly
> to destroy it . . . [unless we] give to every loyal citizen the elective
> franchise—a right and power which will be ever present, and will
> form a wall of fire for his protection.
>   —Frederick Douglass, December 1866

THIS BOOK explores the origins and the consequences of the central ambition of American foreign policy during the twentieth century: in Woodrow
Wilson's words, "to make the world safe for democracy." The book analyzes the origins of the effort to promote democracy abroad in terms of
Washington's definition of the American national security; it investigates
the consequences of the policies pursued with respect to individual countries the United States has sought to reform as well as with respect to the
changing character of the international system America has sought to reorder. The book thus tells a triple story, at once about the identity of America's self-assigned role in the world, the influence of America's democratizing mission on a selected group of countries, and the effect of America's
ambitions on the international system as a whole. The major countries analyzed are the Philippines, the Dominican Republic, Germany, Japan, and
Iran (although American influence in Chile, Guatemala, Mexico, Nicaragua, Poland, Czechoslovakia, Greece, South Africa, and Russia is also
considered). The chief presidential administrations reviewed in terms of
their frameworks for world order are those of Woodrow Wilson, Franklin

Roosevelt, Harry Truman, and Ronald Reagan. The book's primary focus is historical, but its account should help contemporary policymakers as they debate what more they might or should do to fulfill Wilson's famous injunction.

Until the 1990s, American scholarship neglected to investigate with any comparative framework or historical depth the consequences abroad of surely the greatest ambition of United States foreign policy over the past century: to promote democracy abroad as a way of enhancing the national security. Why has this subject not been investigated? The question leads to an exploration of intellectual currents in the American academic establishment, which is included in my appendix, "Notes on the Study of International Origins of Democracy." The aim of the book is to remedy the oversight, first by providing a historical account and a comparative framework for evaluating American successes and failures, then by assessing this undertaking's impact on world politics in the twentieth century.

Academic silence on the international origins of democracy abroad does not reflect a failure of American policy. The greatest success has been in Europe after 1945, where the democratization of Germany, the organization of the European Community, and the success of democracy in places like Poland and the Baltic and Czech republics depended in significant measure on American resolve. So, too, British policy has mattered. In Asia today, democracy exists most securely in areas once under British or American domination—India and Japan especially, but also the Philippines and Malaysia. In the Caribbean and Central America, the countries where democracy is most established are those that were once British colonies (with the notable exception of Costa Rica). In Africa, where the future of democracy today remains bleak, the most hopeful signs continue to come from areas formerly under British rule (except, perhaps, for the former French colony of Senegal)—especially in Botswana, Mauritius, the Gambia, and South Africa, and perhaps in due course from Nigeria and Kenya. Even in the many cases where American and British attempts to establish democratic government overseas failed, or where democracy is still fragile—most notably in the Hispanic Caribbean and Central America and in Africa—their respective efforts were nonetheless considerable and there is much to be learned from their inability to succeed.

Of course, the United States and Britain have not been the only actors attempting to promote democracy abroad. While French, Dutch, and Belgian colonialism failed completely in such undertakings (to the extent that it even tried), the consolidation of democracy in Greece, Portugal, and Spain beginning in the mid-1970s was due in substantial measure to the active role played by the European Community. Similarly, in recent years, nongovernmental agencies from Amnesty International to the Roman

Catholic Church have played critical roles in the rise of democratic movements in parts of Latin America, the Philippines, and Eastern Europe. Nevertheless, the principal disseminators historically of democratic institutions at the international level have unquestionably been the United States and Great Britain.

America launched itself upon a mission to promote democracy abroad somewhat accidentally. The Spanish-American War was fought for a variety of reasons, only one of which was to promote what today would be called human rights for Cubans suffering at the hands of the Spanish. Nor did concern for human rights mean Americans expected to see democracy flourish in Cuba once the Spanish left. When the American Congress declared in April 1898 that Cuba had a right to freedom and independence, it did not assume that this would readily translate into democracy for that island, much less for the Philippines.

Nevertheless, after the war, some kind of order had to established by the American occupiers. Annexation to the United States was at least a possibility; Hawaii had been annexed in July 1898, and the United States had by then long experience in granting statehood to peoples who organized themselves in ways compatible with established national practices. But for Cuba and the Philippines, Washington concluded instead that, for such numerous peoples so different from North Americans, eventual self-government was preferable. In these circumstances, trying to establish democratic government locally and then departing was all the Americans knew how to do, even if their way of providing it proved deficient in many respects.

The evident difficulties of fostering democracy in Cuba and the Philippines after 1898 did not dampen the American enthusiasm for such undertakings. When President Woodrow Wilson ordered the occupation of Veracruz, Mexico, in 1914, the intervention in Haiti in 1915, and the takeover of the Dominican Republic in 1916, he justified his actions as part of an effort to bring constitutional democracy to Latin America. In 1917, when the United States declared war on Germany, Wilson declared that America intended "to make the world safe for democracy" and subsequently issued his Fourteen Points dedicated to that end. His ambition at the Paris Peace Conference of 1919 to create a European order of democratically constituted, nationally self-determining states associated in the League of Nations, was the direct fulfillment of his pledge.

Again, when in the heat of World War II, President Franklin Delano Roosevelt asserted American support for "Four Freedoms" and signed the Atlantic Charter with British Prime Minister Winston Churchill, he reaffirmed American dedication to the goal of promoting a world order consisting of democratically constituted states. It was thus in keeping with

American policy that the United States interpreted Stalin as having aggressive designs on Europe when, in March 1945, he abrogated the "Declaration on Liberated Europe" he had signed a month earlier with Roosevelt and Churchill, promising free elections in Poland. And it was clearly in line with this tradition when, somewhat later in 1945, the administration of President Harry Truman instructed the American occupying authorities of Germany and Japan that their primary duty was to convert these two defeated, militaristic countries into stable democracies.

While the American occupations of Germany and Japan were the most concerted efforts mounted by the United States to promote democracy abroad, American ambitions did not cease with the end of these interventions in the early 1950s. Already the Marshall Plan of 1947 had repeated the American concern to support democracy throughout Europe, a theme heard again with the formation of the Organization of American States in 1948, reiterated toward Western Europe with the creation of the North Atlantic Treaty Organization (NATO) in 1949, and announced again by the administration of President Dwight Eisenhower after 1953 with respect to "the captive nations" of East Central Europe. In 1961, President John Kennedy expressed this determination anew with regard to Latin America in the Alliance for Progress. Even Southeast Asia was to be defended not simply to contain communism, but in the hope that these people too would become democratic.

By the mid-1960s, following the setbacks in Indochina and the evident failure of the Alliance for Progress, the voices calling for the promotion of democracy abroad were momentarily stilled. But by 1973, congressional opposition to what many termed the "amorality" of the foreign policy crafted by President Richard Nixon and his national security adviser, Henry Kissinger, led to demands that democratization be fostered in a variety of areas, most notably in southern Africa. Subsequently, there were additional initiatives to support democracy abroad: in President Jimmy Carter's human rights campaign, in the "democratic revolution" repeatedly called for by President Ronald Reagan, and in a variety of measures undertaken by President George Bush toward Eastern Europe, the former Soviet Union, the Philippines, and Central America beginning in 1989. President Bill Clinton's pledge to pursue this same goal demonstrates how firmly bipartisan it now has become to see American national security promoted by the expansion of democracy around the globe.

In the mid-1990s, Americans might well ask themselves how much the worldwide demand for democracy is the result of their century-old determination to promote this cause. Certainly the new global enthusiasm for democracy is the closest the United States had ever come to seeing its own traditional foreign policy agenda reflected on an international scale. The

American idea of a world order opposed to imperialism and composed of independent, self-determining, preferably democratic states bound together through international organizations dedicated to the peaceful handling of conflicts, free trade, and mutual defense (a package of proposals that may be called "liberal democratic internationalism") has been with us in mature form since the early 1940s.

Although the ingredients of this worldview had been put in place during the presidency of Woodrow Wilson (1913–1921)—so that "Wilsonianism" is a term synonymous with liberal democratic internationalism—its origins in American history lie even further back. Thus, Thomas Jefferson had been the first to insist that a peaceful world order in which America could fully participate needed to be one constituted by democratic states. Or again, support for the national self-determination of other peoples had its roots in the Monroe Doctrine of 1823, affirming an American commitment to an independent Latin America. For its part, the twentieth century call for free trade grew out of a preference for a nondiscriminatory international economic system as old as the Revolution of 1776, with its efforts to break out of British mercantilist control. And anti-militarism was evident in the Founding Fathers' fear that a standing army might threaten civilian government.[1]

The world of the mid-1990s therefore seemed to be asking for much the kind of global order that the United States has been proposing for three-quarters of a century (if not virtually since its Revolution). Throughout Eastern Europe, within much of the former Soviet Union, in most parts of Latin America, and along the Pacific rim of Asia, democracy is on the march, and with it calls for a liberal international economic order and increased cooperation through a multitude of international organizations, whose most important goal is the search not for competitive balance-of-power solutions to keep the peace, but instead inclusive, consensus building mechanisms of collective security. Indeed, the so-called new thinking of former Soviet leader Mikhail Gorbachev with respect to world order after 1986 seemed little more than a recognition of verities Wilson had set out seventy years earlier. Whatever his illusions as to the ease with which "right-minded men" might come to agreement, Wilson was the first world leader to respect the power of nationalism and to try to channel its great strength in the direction of democracy and international cooperation, beginning in Central and Eastern Europe but incorporating the rest of the world thereafter.

But this is not a book simply about American foreign policy told from the perspective of American actors. A principal reason that American liberal democratic internationalism had such an effect on world politics takes us from a study of the history of this country's foreign policy to the study of the evolution of political affairs worldwide. Since the late eighteenth century—beginning with the industrial, American, and French revolutions—a growing demand for popular sovereignty linked to the growth of nationalism has spread around the world. By its very nature, the demand challenged the traditional basis of authoritarian government, necessitating the development of new structures of mass participation through political parties and new modes of organizing power within the government that had never been seen. Correspondingly, the growth of nationalism took on international significance as states beheld the expanding capacities for action of early modernizers and sought to duplicate them, or as political movements within various countries began to recognize a common identity with the values and interests of parties and ideologies abroad.

By the early nineteenth century, this modern political consciousness had moved from Western Europe and North America to Latin America. Well before the end of that century, it had spread to Eastern Europe (including Russia), Turkey, Japan, and China. As it moved, the spirit of nationalism with its demands for popular sovereignty profoundly troubled international as well as domestic political stability.

Seen from this perspective, World War I was not only about how to handle the growth of German power in Europe; it was also about the proper organization of the state in an era of nationalism and the basis for a stable international order in the aftermath of the demise of so many authoritarian monarchies. Traditions of party government were weak to nonexistent in the regions left stateless by the collapse of the Ottoman, Austro-Hungarian, and Russian empires, and a shift in the relative power of states was accompanied during the interwar years by an ideological crisis unprecedented since the Reformation as communists, fascists, and democrats struggled with one another and against authoritarian holdouts to determine the fate of Europe.

Viewed from the vantage point of the international history of the twentieth century, American foreign policy was in keeping with the forces of the times as it sought to promote U.S. national security by encouraging likeminded democratic states to come into existence throughout the world. Nevertheless, much the same dilemma continued after World War II, despite fascism's defeat, as had occurred after World War I, despite the fall of three empires: class, ethnic, and interstate violence substantially intensified in those parts of the world where a stable modern state had not yet appeared. Now, however, the rising tide of nationalist demands were most evident outside Europe, in Africa, Asia, and Latin America, where debates over the proper organization of the state took on a new sharpness. In these circumstances, the cold war was not simply a bipolar conflict between Moscow and Washington to be studied strictly in terms of bilateral relations or of the systemic characteristics of such a world order; it was also a contest among nationalists within various countries, rivals holding different conceptions of the proper organization of the state who looked to the superpowers for example and support.

Whatever our collective relief at the end of the cold war, it is abundantly clear that the essential challenge of the century has not also ended. Nationalism and the call for an effective state resting on popular sovereignty remain demands that in many parts of the world are not fulfilled. Indeed, in many cases in Eastern Europe, Asia, and Africa, the end of the cold war has exacerbated nationalist conflicts as the political apparatuses that held states in place, largely by military power and secret police nourished by Washington or Moscow, have weakened or disappeared.

The American agenda calling for a world order of democratic states thus needs to be understood not only as an expression of the American national interest conducted with respect to individual countries, but also in the context of nationalist debates about state building in the twentieth century and American efforts to create a comprehensive framework for world order. Since Wilson's time, the most consistent tradition in American foreign policy with respect to this global change has been the belief that the nation's security is best protected by the expansion of democracy worldwide. His doctrine of liberal democratic internationalism has not always been predominant. It was notably absent in the Johnson, Nixon, and Ford years, for example, and it has never been without its internal debates. Nevertheless, as in 1918 and 1945, so in the 1990s after the cold war, Americans are asking what to do with their current preeminence in world politics, and many are finding that the traditional answer continues to ring true. Their assurance is sustained by the sight of so many movements and countries struggling to become democracies, and by the conviction that just as it has mattered to the United States that Germany and Japan became democratic, so it is of importance that Russia and Mexico today successfully democratize—with perhaps the democratization of other important lands such as Turkey and China to follow thereafter.[2]

AMERICAN TRIUMPHANT

If the United States had never existed, what would be the status in world affairs of democracy today? Would its forces based in France, Britain, the Low Countries, and Scandinavia have survived the assaults of fascism and communism, or would one of these rival forms of mass political mobilization have instead emerged triumphant at the end of the twentieth century?

The answer is self-evident: we can have no confidence that, without the United States, democracy would have survived. To be sure, London prepared the way for Washington in charting the course of liberal internationalism; and the United States was slow to leave isolationism after 1939, while the Red Army deserves primary praise for the defeat of Nazi Germany. Yet it is difficult to escape the conclusion that since World War I, the fortunes of democracy worldwide have largely depended on American power.

The decisive period of the century, so far as the eventual fate of democracy was concerned, came with the defeat of fascism in 1945 and the American-sponsored conversion of Germany and Japan to democracy and a much greater degree of economic liberalism. Here were the glory days of American liberal democratic internationalism (and not the 1980s, however remarkable that decade, as some believe). American leadership of the international economy—thanks to the institutions created at Bretton Woods in 1944, its strong backing for European integration with the Marshall Plan in 1947 and support for the Schuman Plan thereafter, the formation of NATO in 1949, the stability of Japanese political institutions after 1947 and that country's economic dynamism after 1950 (both dependent in good measure on American power)—created the economic, cultural, military, and political momentum that enabled liberal democracy to triumph over Soviet communism. Except perhaps for NATO, all of these developments were the product of the tenets of thinking first brought together in modern form by Woodrow Wilson, before being adapted to the world of the 1940s by the Roosevelt and Truman administrations.

In the moment of triumph, it should not be forgotten that for most of this century, the faith in the future expansion of democracy that had marked progressive thinking in Europe and America at the turn of the century seemed exceedingly naive. By the 1930s, democracy appeared to many to be unable to provide the unity and direction of its totalitarian rivals. Indeed, again in the 1970s, there was a resurgence of literature predicting democracy's imminent demise: its materialism, its individualism, its proceduralism (that is, the elaborate set of rules and institutions needed to make it function), its tolerance, not to say its permissiveness—the list could be extended indefinitely—seemed to deprive it of the toughness and confidence necessary to survive in a harsh world of belligerent, ideologically driven fascist and communist states.

Fascism was essentially undone by its militarism and its racism; Soviet communism by its overcentralized economic planning and its failure to provide a political apparatus capable of dealing with the tensions of nationalism not only within the Soviet empire but inside the Soviet Union itself. By contrast, however varied the forms of government may be that rightly call themselves democratic, they have demonstrated a relative ability to accommodate class, gender, and ethnic diversity domestically through complicated institutional forms centering on competitive party systems and representative governments. As importantly, the democracies have shown an ability to cooperate internationally with one another through a variety of regimes managing the complex issues of their interdependence, despite the centrifugal force of rival state interests and nationalism. Hence, at the end of the twentieth century, democracy is unparalleled for its political flexibility, stability, legitimacy, and ability to cooperate internationally.

Nevertheless, for three reasons it would be a mistake for American triumphalism to be excessively self-congratulatory. First, democratic values are no monopoly of the United States; second, it is not yet clear that democracy will necessarily dominate the future; and third, democracy has left quite a number of victims in its wake. The first point recalls that while democracy may not have survived without the United States, this country was not the sole repository of these values. Not only did the Scandinavians, Dutch, Belgians, and French share these values with Anglo-Americans, but so too did many in Germany, Italy, and Eastern Europe. More, these values are not simply Western but commend themselves in their own terms to other peoples establishing modern governments with party systems capable of mobilizing the mass of the population in durable political institutions.

Although it would be a substantial exaggeration to say that all societies must ultimately converge as democracies, it is nonetheless true that the flexible, decentralized accountability characteristic of democratic institutions, the virtues of a market economy, and the freedom of information and association characteristic of its practices appeal to many who study the reasons for democracy's success. If democracy was once "a leap in the dark," as Lord Derby told Prime Minister Benjamin Disraeli in the 1860s, it most certainly is no more. Democracy has demonstrated its ability (at least relative to rival forms of organization) to embody the nationalist demand for a state based on mass participation by incorporating the marginalized into political life and addressing the tensions of class and ethnic cleavage while preserving distinctions of social identity. Just as importantly, it has shown that its various peoples, despite their nationalist vanities and suspicions, can cooperate internationally in a variety of military, economic, and humanitarian endeavors in a way unparalled in history. These capacities reflect the values, practices, and institutions on which the United States alone has no monopoly.

A second, and more important reason to question American triumphalism is that it is by no means clear that democracy will dominate the future. A decade ago no one foresaw the speedy collapse of communism, while four decades back there were no end of discussions as to how peoples of Confucian culture were doomed to perpetual backwardness. Yet totalitarianism was defeated, and we now see the evidence that late-modernizers can outstrip early leaders by finding within their traditional systems ways to imitate the advances of others while avoiding the pitfalls of early success. The story of Germany relative to Britain at the turn of the century or the record of Japan after 1945 offer telling examples of the speed with which the international balance of power may shift.

In all, it must be recognized that liberal democracy appeals especially to Western peoples. If two great non-Western cultures have adopted liberal democratic ways—India and Japan—it was under the duress of direct British and American occupation. Without a feudal past, a strong and independent bourgeoisie, or the heritage of the Reformation, the Enlightenment, and the American and French revolutions, what reason is there to think others must necessarily follow in the Western mode? Perhaps in time, Confucian or Islamic societies will engender modern political orders more effective than those proposed by the West.[3]

Indeed, the possibility of an alternative development to liberal democracy growing from within currently democratic countries themselves should not be excluded. The tension between majority and minority rights; the danger of individualism to the common good; the threat of economic or environmental disaster combined with growing class and ethnic tensions over the next generation—all of these portend crises whose resolution might well not be in keeping with liberal democratic traditions and could eventually lead to the deterioration of these values and practices. The United States is certainly not immune to such seduction; virtually every presidential election turns up a messiah who earns some measure of popular appeal from an antidemocratic agenda. We would do well to keep in mind the foolish boasting of British and American imperialists of the nineteenth century who saw all the world progressively being raised up thanks to the blessings bestowed automatically by association with superior Anglo-Saxon ways. Pride cometh before the fall.[4]

The third reason to qualify our enthusiasm over liberal democracy's current victory is the many victims it has left in its wake. During the interwar period, the democracies had been pusillanimous in the face of fascist aggression; many could have been saved had the West had the courage of its convictions. The opposite problem occurred during the cold war. The most obvious victims were in Vietnam, where the trials of French colonialism were followed by the horrors of war with the United States. Vietnam was not an isolated incident; the general overmilitarization of the cold war involving the shoring-up of authoritarian governments from Guatemala to Iran, from South Korea to Zaire, should not be forgotten either.

These qualifications made, this book will maintain that liberal democratic internationalism, or Wilsonianism, has been the most important and distinctive contribution of the United States to the international history of the twentieth century, for this package of proposals has given political shape and direction to a variety of global forces in this period, which together have produced the current strength and prestige of democratic government worldwide.

Defining the Term *Liberal Democracy*

To this point, I have been using the term *democracy*, and more importantly *liberal democracy*, without defining either of these complicated and weighty words or explaining the significance of their association. To capture a fuller picture of Washington's operational code so far as its liberal democratic internationalism is concerned, we must probe more deeply the nature of American liberal democracy itself by seeing the way these values and practices have evolved historically in American life.

Fortunately, academics across the political spectrum have come to something of a consensus as to what they mean by the word *democracy*: free elections contested by freely organized parties under universal suffrage for control of the effective centers of governmental power. Of course there are differences on the best institutional form of democratic government—whether a presidential or parliamentary system is preferable, whether to establish a federal structure of rule, or how to organize an effective electoral competition. But on the most essential matter there is agreement: a democracy is a political system institutionalized under the rule of law, wherein an autonomous civil society, whose individuals join together voluntarily into groups with self-designated purposes, collaborate with each other through the mechanisms of political parties and establish through freely contested elections a system of representative government.[5] When most government officials speak of democracy in the pages to follow, it is something close to this notion of government that they have in mind.

The disputes begin when academics and government officials ask what *democratization* means, that is, what mix of cultural, economic, and social factors tend to initiate, consolidate, and perpetuate democracy. Is it enough to arrange for honest elections and then expect democratic ways to take root of themselves? (This was the American formula for Nicaragua in the 1920s, and it proved inadequate.) Or need one go further still, supervising the character of the constitution so that individuals selected will govern through an effective division of powers in government, while promoting civil liberties that include effective protection for freedom of speech and assembly? (This was the American agenda for the Philippines, where it has provided for a fragile democracy at best.) Or is it necessary to reform more deeply yet, to insist on labor's right to organize and on the right of the agrarian poor to gain land and credit? (This was the American approach to the democratization of Germany and Japan, the most critical and successful of such efforts.)

The best way to make sense of the various ways Americans have operationalized their concept of democracy is to turn to the term *liberal*—a word that has never been defined with the relative precision of *democracy*. Giovanni Sartori offers a helpful definition:

> [Liberalism is] the theory and practice of the juridical defense, through the constitutional state, of individual political freedom, of individual liberty. Two things will be immediately noted: a) I have not given prominence to "individualism," and b) I say "constitutional state" and not, as is at times suggested, "minimal state."[6]

Historically understood, liberalism has made a series of claims about the moral character of the individual and the state. Perhaps the most important contribution of liberalism to our day is its notion of constitutionalism or the rule of law: that duly established procedures—and not cliques or persons—should control the behavior of the state if authority is to be legitimate.

By the nineteenth century, liberalism's most distinctive influence on emerging democratic government had to do with its insistence on a limited state—a government constrained by the rule of law (subject to internal institutionalized checks and balances in the American case) and so weak relative to society that popular forces are capable of replacing it (in America, the presumption that the freedoms of speech, association, and election are so powerfully entrenched that no combination of governmental forces could subvert them before itself being ousted).

American liberalism is part of a tradition stretching back to England in the seventeenth century—especially to the Glorious Revolution of 1688–9, by which an aristocratic parliament established its authority relative to the monarchy, and to the writings of John Locke (1632–1704). In the eighteenth century, the arguments of the Enlightenment and the debates of the American and French revolutions nourished the liberal tradition, which was made relevant to the nineteenth century by such British thinkers as Adam Smith, Jeremy Bentham, Richard Cobden, and John Stuart Mill, as well as by William Gladstone, the great social and political reformer who was four times prime minister (for a total of fourteen years between 1868 and 1894) and who greatly impressed Woodrow Wilson.

The essential features of liberalism from the late seventeenth to the late nineteenth centuries were a defense of individual liberties and property rights, an appeal to reason over custom, and a demand for government limited under law and based on the consent of the governed. Liberals tended to be cosmopolitan in that they felt the principles they espoused to be universal; to insist on a secular state divorced from religious ties; to oppose militarism as the instrument of a despotic state; and (beginning in the late eighteenth century under the influence of Adam Smith especially) to favor free trade for the sake of limited government, prosperity, and peace.

For its time, and still for ours in many parts of the world, liberalism was a revolutionary doctrine. It combated religious intolerance, making society possible between groups holding to different ethical codes; it denied the blind dictates of custom, making government subject itself to law; and it insisted on reason and consent as the basis for an individual's submission to the dictates of authority. While its fortunes were tied to those of a rising bourgeoisie, liberalism's appeal depended as well on Western religious heterogeneity, the practices of certain Protestant sects, the character of some aristocratic groups, the relative role of the military in politics, and the rise of scientific thinking.

Revolutionary as this perspective was, most European liberals before the mid-nineteenth century were nonetheless not democrats; their claims were for liberty not for equality. Their opposition to democracy was based on fear of the mob—an aroused, uneducated public that knew not how to govern and so would deliver the state into the hands of a tyrant promising equality by dispossessing the holders of property. Their example: the Terror of the French Revolution (1793–4), in which a narrow clique of demagogic dictators unleashed the furies of mob violence on the land. Fearful of a repetition of these horrors, French liberals (and to a lesser extent their British counterparts) shied away from democracy before the 1880s. Even those who were democrats, however, usually did not call for a radical redistribution of property to favor society's disadvantaged. As a result, in Europe most democrats until the late nineteenth century tended to be socialists and considered the liberal insistence on the inviolability of property rights as a hindrance to democracy.

To be sure, liberalism had an affinity with democracy, which came from its belief that authority was legitimate only when it had the consent of the governed. Moreover, by calling for a weak state relative to society, and especially by opposing a strong military, liberals put themselves in the dangerous position of having the political order overwhelmed by mass discontent if somehow the working classes failed to see the government as legitimate. Finally, as nationalism appeared in the nineteenth century—whether in Greece, Italy, or Poland—liberals tended to support it, at first in opposition to absolutism but also in the name of self-determination and hence of popular democracy.

It was only in the 1860s in Britain, and the 1880s in France, that the marriage between liberalism and democracy began to be celebrated, to be consummated by World War I. Only then in Europe did liberal democracy appear in its modern form, wherein each tradition grafted to itself elements of the other. Democratic thinking adopted from liberalism a belief in

human fallibility, the need for reasoned discussion, the possibility for tolerance and thus for social diversity, and most importantly, a commitment to
the moral preeminence of the individual and of the group over the state
(reflected in institutionalized restraints on the power of government best
summed up as the rule of law). The difference between democratic socialism and communism lies in the latter's rejection of liberalism's restraints
on government in the name of its own democratic utopianism.

At the same time, liberal thinking (as in the writing of T. H. Green)
adopted from democratic arguments the need for universal suffrage (including the vote for women), labor's right to organize, and the notion that
the state might perform certain welfare functions and play a hand in regu-
lating the economy in circumstances where the natural workings of society
appeared unable to provide order. *Liberal democracy* is, then, a particular
form of democracy and a particular kind of liberalism, a matching of terms
(like *Marxism-Leninism*) in which each concept carries its own meaning
apart from the other, yet in which the fusion of the two creates a form of
government that is far richer and more complex than either term alone
suggests.[7]

While closely related to British liberalism ideologically and aware of the
excesses of the French Revolution, American liberal democracy has nonetheless had its own distinctive history. Lacking a feudal past and an aristocratic conservative tradition (though at times Alexander Hamilton and the
Federalists or thinkers in the South like John C. Calhoun might appear to
play the role), America has never had a powerful socialist tradition either.[8]
Consequently, liberalism has always been the dominant political creed in
the United States, even if it has been strikingly unself-conscious in the
positions it has taken. Americans might differ strongly among themselves,
but seen from the perspective of Western political thought in general, these
were family squabbles (the Civil War excepted, given slavery's incompatibility with liberal principles).

The most important statement on the uniqueness of American liberalism
remains Alexis de Toqueville's *Democracy in America* published in 1835
(a second volume appeared in 1840). Commenting that the United States
was "born free," that "the social state of the Americans is eminently democratic . . . even the seeds of aristocracy were never planted," Toqueville
continues:

> There society acts by and for itself. There are no authorities except within itself;
> one can hardly meet anybody who would dare to conceive, much less to suggest,
> seeking power elsewhere. The people take part in the making of the laws by
> choosing the lawgivers, and they share in their application by electing the agents
> of the executive power; one might say that they govern themselves, so feeble and
> restricted is the part left to the administration, so vividly is that administration

aware of its popular origin, and obedient to the fount of power. The people reign over the American political world as God rules over the universe. It is the cause and the end of all things; everything rises out of it and is absorbed back into it.[9]

Toqueville was correct to see how democratic the United States was by contrast with other countries in the 1830s, for with Andrew Jackson's election in 1828 it could rightfully call itself the first modern democracy. Yet it should be recalled that at the time of American independence there were property qualifications for the vote and that certain religious denominations, as well as women and slaves, were disfranchised. Had Toqueville arrived a decade earlier, his account might not have been so perspicacious.

As it was, Toqueville exaggerated the threat that as an unbounded democracy the United States might become a "tyranny of the majority" exercised through a despotic government against the independence of individuals and social groups. What he failed to see was that the call for a powerful state depended more on the existence of a conservative, aristocratic right or on a militant socialist left than on a liberal center of property such as predominated in the United States. The United States lacked the heritage of a centralized state that the tradition of a monarchy might have given it. And the early embrace of democracy (along with the expanding frontier and the competition among successive waves of immigrants) weakened the appeal of socialism, the other political creed to call for a strong state relative to society.

Thus, in theory as well as in fact, the distinguishing mark of American liberal democracy (even by comparison with other liberal democracies) has been a state limited by strongly organized social forces acting through freely organized political parties. Some of these social groups are religious, others ethnic, but the most serious debates have turned around property rights—whether private property rights are essential for the preservation of democracy, or whether they are an impediment to democracy's full realization. Accordingly, a fundamental divide in American political life is between liberals who borrow from socialist thinking the call for socioeconomic change that directly benefits the politically marginalized (although clearly there may be serious disputes over the nature of these reforms, and these debates have always been timid by socialist standards) and those who feel that reforms in political organization are enough in themselves (either because the state should not be given too much power or because market forces more effectively assure prosperity than state interventions in the economy). In sum, virtually all Americans are liberal democrats, but not all liberal democrats are the same.

It is inevitable that the meaning of liberal democracy in domestic American life should deeply mark the conduct of its foreign policy. When their policy intends to promote democracy abroad, Americans rather naturally tend to think in terms of a weak state relative to society. The result for others is a paradoxical form of "conservative radicalism": radical in that for many countries, democracy has meant an abrupt and basic political change away from the narrow-based authoritarian governments with which these people are familiar; conservative in that in fundamental ways, the Americans have not meant to disturb the traditional social power relations based on property ownership.

Here was the genius, and also the tragedy, of the American sponsorship of democracy abroad: it was genuinely innovative politically, but it was not profoundly upsetting socioeconomically. The genius of the approach was that it could be attractive to established elites abroad (provided that they had the wit to try to adapt), for whatever the hazards of introducing democracy, it promised to modernize and stabilize those regimes that could reform enough to be called democratic. The tragedy, especially in lands that were predominantely agrarian, was that these political changes (where they were accepted) were often not enough to create the cultural, economic, and social circumstances that could reinforce a democratic political order. As a result, American efforts either failed completely (as in Central America and the Caribbean during Wilson's presidency) or created narrowly based and highly corrupt elitist forms of democracy (as in the Philippines or more recently in the Dominican Republic).

It was different when the United States occupied Japan and Germany to promote democracy in 1945. But the men and women who undertook this mission were not liberal democrats of the traditional American sort. Instead, many of them were New Dealers, for whom the prerequisites of democracy included strong labor unions, land reform, welfare legislation, notions of racial equality, and government intervention in the economy. Moreover, they had the good fortune to be working with societies that already had centralized political institutions, diversified industrial economies, and (at least in Germany) many convinced democrats awaiting deliverance from fascism and communism alike. The Americans who conceived of the Alliance for Progress in Latin America were for the most part cut of the same cloth as the New Dealers. But their power in Latin America was not nearly so great as their predecessors' had been in Germany and Japan, and the socioeconomic structures of South and Central America lacked the inherent advantages for democratizers that the former fascist powers possessed. Hence the Alliance's failure.

This New Deal outlook was not typical of the Americans who took the Philippines in 1898 or who were in power under what was deservedly called the "progressive" presidency of Woodrow Wilson. These Franklin Roosevelt Democrats were also different from liberal reformers like Jimmy Carter, who favored a strictly human-rights approach to democratization. The most interesting contrast comes with Ronald Reagan, however, whose insistence on the contribution free markets could make to democratic government shared with the New Dealers the notion that political life depends in good measure on the structure of power socioeconomically (even if the two approaches differed on the need for governmental regulation and social redistribution).

As these cases suggest, American liberal democratic internationalism varied in its agenda over time. The continuity was such, however, that we can speak of a tradition in American foreign policy, one with an agenda for action abroad tied to a firm notion of the national interest that was to have momentous consequences for world affairs in the twentieth century.

A HISTORICAL EXAMPLE: POST–CIVIL WAR RECONSTRUCTION

If there are liberal democrats and liberal democrats in the United States, one can best sort out the distinctions among them not by further refining definitions but by providing an example that illustrates the spectrum of their thinking. No better study is at hand than that of the North's effort to "reconstruct" the South after the Civil War: to change the defeated Confederacy so that a democratic Union could be preserved. Here is the mirror of history in which Americans beheld themselves and self-consciously acted in the late nineteenth century, as they had during the late eighteenth, to establish their political identity. Here, too, one sees the repertoire of concepts that might be used later when American power in world affairs led it to contemplate democratizing other countries.

Of course, one must be careful not to push the comparison too far. Reconstruction was unique both in time (a quarter of a century before the taking of the Philippines) and in the issues it confronted: deep-set racism compounded by class differences, making reform especially bitter (a situation present in the Dominican Republic and Guatemala but not in the most important cases included in this book). The Northern obligation ultimately to reincorporate the South into the United States on the basis of constitutional equality also made the task especially delicate. More, the South could claim that it already was a liberal democracy; its government functioned democratically so far as white citizens were concerned—indeed with more civil liberties than in the North, its partisans could assert, since Lincoln suspended the writ of habeus corpus for disloyal activities. Finally, many aspects of what can be called liberal democratic internationalism in the twentieth century either go back to other events in the nineteenth century, or even to the Revolution of 1776 (which was far more radical politically than it was socioeconomically), or were invented in the twentieth century, such as a greater confidence in the government's ability to handle social issues, as Democratic administrations following FDR tended to believe. In short, analysis of Northern policy during Reconstruction serves more as an analogy than as a template for an understanding of the character of American liberal democratic internationalism in the twentieth century.

Nonetheless, the basic problem with the Confederacy (so the North felt) was that its very character had made a particularly deadly war unavoidable. How should the North act after its victory in order to create a more perfect union in a situation where differences that had for so long seemed so extreme had been further compounded by the deaths of 620,000 soldiers (including one-quarter of the South's white men of military age) and the destruction of two-thirds of the South's wealth? The challenge of remaking the South so that its reincorporation into the Union could create a stronger nation was the only occasion prior to the twentieth century when the United States would attempt to rebuild an entire society in such a way that its character was compatible with dominant American cultural, economic, social, and political values and institution.

Northern liberalism confronted three essential issues in dealing with the South both before the war and in rebuilding it thereafter, issues that would recur later in American thinking about foreign policy: the nature of interstate relations, as embodied in the question of whether a liberal democratic North could or should try to coexist in North America alongside a slave-owning South that gave no sign of being in decline; the nature of democracy, as embodied in black citizenship rights; the nature of property, as embodied in the rights of the defeated Confederate plantation owners to preserve their estates.[10]

With the surrender of the Confederacy, Washington had achieved the regional security it sought by reuniting the nation. But how was Washington to establish its legitimacy in terms of the people it reincorporated under its authority when it was pledged to rule by the consent of those it governed? The answer came as Northern military governors barred Confederate leaders from holding political office; called state constitutional conventions that ultimately included black voters, thereby profoundly changing the cast of Southern politics; and abolished slavery and destroyed plantation agriculture, a development that amounted to a social revolution. Yet despite these enormous changes, the South remained the South: it stayed agrarian economically, and hierarchical socially. So far as the third or more of its black citizens were concerned, it stayed undemocratic politically once the Jim Crow laws of the late nineteenth century ended their political participation. One might wonder sixty or seventy years after the war just what this terrible struggle had been about.

In fact, the war had been about many things worth fighting for. It had been about insuring the unity of the nation, so strengthening immeasurably the forces of liberal democracy worldwide. It had been about the definition of property, so that even if labor organization in the aftermath of the war proved exceedingly difficult to legitimate, property rights would never be defined as narrowly as they had been when slavery was defended by law. It had been about the character of democracy, so that even if the provisions of the Fourteenth and Fifteenth amendments designed to make African-Americans first-class citizens had been flagrantly denied in practice, the principle had been established for a later generation to build on. Thus, an examination of the stakes of this war are indeed relevant for our purposes, both as a way of studying the spectrum of American liberal democratic thought and as a case study of what happened to this thinking in practice.

While all Northerners in favor of the war were necessarily concerned to preserve the Union, deep differences existed on what further ends the struggle should serve. Not all agreed that victory should involve the emancipation of the slave from the tyranny of a monstrous definition of property rights; still more doubted that freedom meant the freedmen must be enfranchised and so incorporated into the greater American political community; and just a minority held that freedom could finally be brought about if the freedmen were socially empowered through economic reforms centering on the distribution of Southern plantations.

In practice, even when the need to preserve the Union was combined with a determination to end slavery, one or the other of these causes typically was emphasized. Abraham Lincoln stressed the former, for example, while the Abolitionist leader William Lloyd Garrison emphasized the latter. Moreover, many who would save the Union and free the slave did not call for extending political rights to blacks. Lincoln and Garrison were both reluctant to talk about political rights for the freedmen, unlike the majority of the Republican party. Still another great divide separated those who called for giving the vote to the freedman from those (like Frederick Douglass, Wendell Phillips, Thaddeus Stevens, and Charles Sumner) who stood for economic reforms as well, claiming that without them political freedom could not be maintained.

Ultimately, after an epic struggle, the Republican majority in Congress in 1866 passed the Fourteenth Amendment enfranchising the freedmen, and in 1867 made acceptance of this amendment a condition for Southern states to rejoin the Union. It was declared ratified in 1868. In effect, then, three war aims were gained: the preservation of the Union, the abolition of slavery, and the enfranchisement of the freedmen. The minority of American liberal democrats who supported economic rights for the freedmen saw their proposals soundly defeated by the Congress. A closer examination of the character of these various war aims may establish more clearly the principles and practices involved.

For some democrats, as for Abraham Lincoln, the cause of liberalism was inherent in the preservation of the Union. The president may not have been explicit in his reasoning, but the *Federalist Papers* (1787–88) had insisted seventy years before Lincoln that without an indissoluble union among the states, fragmentation would lead to a competitive climate like that in Europe and there would be war. With war would come internal oppression exercised by a strong state wielding an army. If the United States were to escape the pattern of European politics, it must be free of a military establishment and the inducements to war: hence, it must be united.[11] Accordingly, if a region were to secede and embolden others to follow its example, the result would be to endanger the liberties the Revolution of 1776 had fought to establish. In sum, the future of liberal democracy was linked to the future of the Union. As Lincoln implied in his Gettysburg Address of November 1863, the aim of this struggle was a war to end war in North America and in the process to make the region, if not the world, safe for democracy. It was to preserve the chances for the existence of a Union he called in 1862 "the last, best hope of earth."[12]

For a second group of democrats, the issue was not only the preservation of the Union, but the character of the South as a slave-holding region. Free labor, free soil, and democracy were incompatible with the South's "peculiar institution." The North therefore had a double obligation to fight: to end slavery as well as to save the Union and so create a firmer basis for freedom in America.

While it might be argued that slavery was sure to decline eventually due to the nature of economic development, slavery's energy in the 1850s seemed self-evident. Hence many Northerners had objected to the annexation of Texas in 1845 because it was a slave state; worried in the mid-1850s over Kansas and whether it would be free; opposed Southern calls to take Cuba and so extend slavery; and noted with alarm the enthusiasm with which the South welcomed the Supreme Court's Dred Scott decision of 1857, affirming that slaves were not citizens but property that could be taken into territories not yet granted statehood. It seemed, then, that not time but an act of will was required to settle the matter. In Lincoln's words of June 16, 1858:

> I believe this government cannot endure permanently half slave and half free. I do not expect the Union to be dissolved—I do not expect the house to fall—but I do expect it will cease to be divided. It will become all one thing or all the other. Either the opponents of slavery will arrest the further spread of it and place it where the public mind shall rest in the belief that it is in the course of ultimate extinction; or its advocates will push it forward, till it shall become alike lawful in all the states, old as well as new—North as well as South.[13]

It is worth repeating that while opposition to slavery was compatible with a determination to preserve the Union, these two liberal causes were not necessarily one and the same. Lincoln's reluctance to push too hard on the matter of slavery was in part tactical. He had not won a majority of the vote in 1860, but was made president by the electoral college. Once the war began, his problems remained tactical: how to keep the four slave states that stayed in the Union behind him, how not to awaken racist sentiment in the North against the war, and how to keep slave interests in the South as divided as possible. Despite his moral objection to slavery—"he who would be no slave must consent to have no slave" (1859)—he stressed his concern to preserve the Union, not his opposition to slavery. In 1862 he wrote:

> I would save the Union. I would have it the shortest way under the Constitution. . . . My paramount object in this struggle is to save the Union and is not either to save or to destroy slavery. If I could save the Union without freeing any slave I would do it, and if I could save it by freeing all the slaves I would do it; and if I could save it by freeing some and leaving others alone I would also do that.

But Lincoln's stance on slavery was not purely tactical. As he said in 1858:

> I am not, nor ever have been, in favor of bringing about in any way the social and political equality of the white and black races. . . . there is a physical difference between the black and white races which I believe will forever forbid the two races living together on terms of social and political equality. And inasmuch as the two cannot so live, while they do remain together there must be a position of superior and inferior, and I as much as any other man am in favor of having the superior position assigned to the white race.[14]

On January 1, 1863, Lincoln issued the Emancipation Proclamation, freeing the slaves in states at war with the North. But his Proclamation of Amnesty and Reconstruction announced in December 1863 for restoring the defeated Southern states to the Union was consistent with his concern to rally white opinion in the South to the Republican party. According to its terms, a Confederate state could rejoin the Union once 10 percent of its eligible voters (which did not include blacks) swore an oath of loyalty to the republic and agreed to the emancipation of the slaves, although Confederate military and civil officers might be liable to punishment.[15] In Louisiana and Arkansas, governments were created in line with these conditions, but the Congress refused to seat their delegates, claiming Lincoln's reforms were too superficial.

Like FDR at the end of World War II or Kennedy just before the war escalated in Vietnam, Lincoln died at a critical moment, leaving scholars to speculate over how his thinking would have evolved after the war. There is good reason to think that he was coming to realize the depth of white racism in the South and the need for the Republican party to enfranchise the freedmen if it had hopes of winning elections there. In his last public address, the president endorsed extending the vote to those blacks who were "very intelligent and [to] those who served our cause as soldiers."[16] Yet even if it is plausible that Lincoln would eventually have supported the Fourteenth Amendment (or its equivalent), it is understandable that Wendell Phillips might denounce Lincoln's program of amnesty for the South as one of "freeing the slaves and ignoring the Negro."[17]

Given the short distance Lincoln had traveled toward endowing the freedmen with political rights, his successor Andrew Johnson could say he was carrying out Lincoln's program when he issued a general proclamation of amnesty and pardon for most of the former Confederacy at the end of May 1865. Some Confederate properties were seized and its leading officials temporarily barred from office, but Johnson granted amnesties easily.[18]

Republican reaction was swift. In 1866 congressional Republicans tried to strengthen the conditions for Union by passing the Fourteenth Amendment to the Constitution, insuring the freedman the vote, and making its adoption by defeated states a condition of readmission. President Johnson campaigned against the amendment, which was defeated in every Southern states except Tennessee (which was thereupon readmitted to the Congress).

In the congressional elections of 1866, the Republicans emerged with large majorities in both Houses, and in 1867 they passed the First Reconstruction Act, designed to formulate an alternative to the president's conditions for a return to the Union. Congress divided the South into five zones, each with a military governor. Conditions for admission to the Union now included enfranchising blacks (that is, ratifying the Fourteenth Amendment), disqualifying from office past Confederate leaders, and certifying that 50 percent of those registered to vote had sworn an oath of past as well as future loyalty to the Union. Between July 1868 and July 1870, all the Southern states were readmitted to the Union in line with these provisions.

However, on another score, radical reformers in Congress were defeated: efforts to secure economic independence for the freedmen were repulsed. In March 1865 the Congress had established the Freedmen's Bureau designed to ease the transition from slavery to freedom by addressing the economic challenges confronting a community with few skills and no capital.[19] The bureau promoted education and public health, but the most important proposals were those heard in the Congress to distribute "forty acres and a mule" to families of freedmen from land taken from the wealthiest of Confederate plantation owners. Already some lands had been seized by freedmen (such as Jefferson Davis's holdings) or were given to them by Union military leaders (such as the forty thousand holdings given to freedmen on four hundred thousand acres along the Georgia and South Carolina coast by General William Tecumseh Sherman early in 1865).[20] W. E. B. Du Bois was exaggerating only somewhat when he wrote in 1935:

In the Freedmen's Bureau, the United States started upon a dictatorship by which the landowner and the capitalist were to be openly and deliberately curbed and which directed its efforts in the interest of a black and white labor class. . . . The Freedmen's Bureau was the most extraordinary and far-reaching institution of social uplift that America has ever attempted. It had to do, not simply with emancipated slaves and poor whites, but also with the property of Southern planters. It was a government guardianship for the relief and guidance of white and black labor from a feudal agrarianism to modern farming and industry . . . the greatest plan of reasoned emancipation yet proposed.[21]

By the amnesties he began to grant in May 1865, President Johnson nullified these transfers of property, and later in the year the Congress refused to consider proposals to expropriate Confederate plantations for the benefit of the freedmen. The general reasoning seemed to be that the slaves had acceded to the condition of free labor, and that now it was up to their own labor and the laws of the market to secure their livelihood. Such expropriation as occurred had already dealt a terrible blow to the political status of plantation owners; more social experimentation was uncalled for. Constitutional conservatism, also typical of liberal thinking, had its influence as well: where would the government stop if it took such a burden upon itself? As a result, most plantation land sold at depressed prices at public auction went to whites, often from the North, and virtually all estates were subdivided into sharecropping units on which the freedmen were now employed. In Georgia in 1874, where blacks constituted nearly half the agrarian population, they owned only 1 percent of the land.[22]

How fatal to the hopes for black freedom was the failure to secure for them a degree of economic independence after 1865 adequate to preserve them from the dictates of the white community? Certainly economic conditions explain a part of their predicament: agriculture entered into a depression after 1870, and hoped-for Northern investment did not arrive to industrialize the region for generations to come. Blacks remained trapped and squeezed by the general economic backwardness of the region. Yet if there is no guarantee that land redistribution would have been enough to insure the cause of black emancipation, surely it turned out to be a fundamental aspect of any such endeavor. Left without adequate community resources to defend themselves against the dominant white politicians, black liberty was at the suffrance of others.

It was not wholly unrealistic for Northern liberal democrats to believe in 1865 that political reforms alone might give freedom to the blacks; they could not foresee the future economic evolution of the South, and even their commitment to political reform came at a high price. The passage of the Fifteenth Amendment, adopted in 1870 as a reaffirmation of the blacks' constitutional right to the vote, followed Georgia's effort in the fall of 1868 to expel blacks from its legislature. But the more compelling argument, confirmed by subsequent events, was that basic economic change was needed sufficient to give the African-American community a measure of social as well as political independence from dominant white agricultural interests.

By 1890 the growing economic depression that began around 1873 was beginning to undermine such political freedoms as blacks were granted under the terms of the Fourteenth and Fifteenth Amendments. For roughly a decade (the timing varied from state to state), Northern troops had been in the South and Confederate leaders remained ineligible for public office, so that blacks came to enjoy many of the benefits of political citizenship. By 1877, these troops were gone, and for more than another decade, conservative white officials counted on black votes. The worsening economic downturn after 1890 and corruption in high office led to the toppling of these state governments and their replacement by Populist officials determined to disfranchise the black.

Populist objectives were achieved before the turn of the century, under the terms of what were known as Jim Crow laws. In Louisiana, for example, there were only 1,342 black voters registered in 1904, less than 1 percent the number that had been a few years earlier, in a state where blacks made up over 47 percent of the population of nearly 1.4 million.[23] Matters were not to change until the 1960s, under Presidents Kennedy and Johnson.

Despite these setbacks, 1865 was a victory for liberal democracy. The South lost the War. Mistaken are those who imply that the continued subordination of blacks to whites meant that liberalism secured no gains. Emancipation was better than slavery. African-Americans had the vote, although it took a century to begin to exercise it effectively. Despite a host of advantages held by capital in the definition of property rights, these rights were at least defined so that slavery did not figure among them; and the annihilation of plantation owners as a class deprived capitalist interests in the North of an ally that they might have had otherwise. But the greatest gain was to the future of liberal democracy as a world force: slavery as an agrarian system was destroyed and the threat that it might expand to the West (or even the Northwest) or to Cuba (and beyond) was ended. One can only speculate on the affinities in the twentieth century between the Confederacy, had it survived, and Germany in both World Wars. The Union was preserved, making the United States a potentially powerful nation internationally, a fact of enormous consequence for the fortunes of liberal democracy in the twentieth century. In Barrington Moore's words:

> German experience suggests that, if the conflict between North and South had been compromised, the compromise would have been at the expense of subse-

quent democratic development in the United States. . . . That the federal government was out of the business of enforcing slavery was no small matter. It is easy to imagine the difficulties that organized labor would have faced, for example, in its effort to achieve legal and political acceptance in later years, had not this barrier been swept away. . . . Striking down slavery was a decisive step, an act at least as important as the striking down of absolute monarchy in the English Civil War and the French Revolution, an essential preliminary for further advances.[24]

The victory of the Civil War by the North was indeed a victory. But it was just as assuredly not an unalloyed victory for democracy until more than three generations later for African-Americans.

CONCLUSION

For a study of American efforts to promote democracy abroad in the twentieth century, Reconstruction and its aftermath illustrate both the divisions among liberal democrats in the United States and the likely consequence of certain policies. In effect, the FDR, Truman, and Kennedy years bore some similarity to the thinking of those Radical Republicans whose ideas of emancipation involved socioeconomic reform directed at the disadvantaged sectors of society as a complement to political change. Correspondingly, the occupations of Japan and Germany and the plans (never realized) for the Alliance for Progress were relatively radical attempts by the United States to promote democracy abroad. By contrast, Wilson and Carter appear more closely related to the thinking of Northern liberals rather cautious in what they would force on the South and hence easily satisfied by an essentially political understanding of democracy. Wilson is the only one of the presidents to comment on Reconstruction, and his words published in 1893 reveal a great deal:

> [In 1876] normal conditions of government and of economic and intellectual life were at length restored. The period of reconstruction was past; Congress had ceased to exercise extra-constitutional powers; natural legal conditions once more prevailed. Negro rule under unscrupulous adventurers had been finally put to an end in the South, and the natural, inevitable ascendency of the whites, the responsible class, established. . . . At last the country was homogeneous and had subordinated every other sentiment to that of hope.[25]

Reagan falls in an anomalous position relative to other presidents, for while he stressed the importance of socioeconomic change, his antistatism in economic affairs was not of the sort that would have helped the blacks in the period under review. In debates today, the political impact of economic reform also remains of paramount concern, whether in speculation over what "shock therapy" has done or might do in Russia, or in arguing how the opening of markets and the ratification of the North American Free Trade Agreement may affect the prospects for democracy in Mexico.

As was already noted, Reconstruction offers no exact parallel to later American thinking about foreign affairs. As it came to be formulated by Wilson and his successors, liberal democratic internationalism had many aspects to it that were alien to debates over the former Confederacy after 1865—for example, free trade, collective security, and the value of international law and organizations. Nevertheless, insofar as the rooting of democracy is concerned, it is clear that even in the 1860s, there were liberal democrats in high office in the United States who believed that the task of promoting democracy for others involved more than political change alone. Other liberal democrats disagreed, seeing their job as strictly political. They secured passage of the Fourteenth and Fifteenth amendments, and it is conceivable that had the economic destiny of the South been more robust these reforms alone would indeed have been sufficient to achieve greater emancipation for African-Americans.

The root problem of the freedmen in the South once they had been given the vote was similar to that in agrarian countries around the world. Much as the North ultimately courted the whites in the South at the expense of the blacks, so in countries as different as the Philippines in 1898 or the Dominican Republic in 1916, or with the American policy toward Latin America under Presidents Carter and Reagan, the socioeconomic base of the dominant elite was not threatened. Indeed, in some cases it was reinforced as a means to secure American political interests.

In Germany and Japan after the war, the United States acted only somewhat differently. Fascists (like Confederates) were purged and socioeconomic reforms introduced. Yet even here the Americans did not push too far, especially when the struggle with the Soviet Union intensified in 1947. Many former elites survived with their positions eventually restored. The picture of Alfred Krupp von Bohlen und Holbach being released from jail in 1951, with his family properties (which had been the center of Hitler's armament industry) returned to him, mirrors in its way Confederate Vice President Alexander Stephen's release from prison and subsequent resurrection as United States congressman and governor of Georgia. As in the South, so in countries as different as the Philippines, the Dominican Republic, or Japan: local socioeconomic power structures, values, and political traditions proved strong enough to resist wholesale Americanization. Indeed, on balance, it is the strength of local ways relative to outside efforts to change them that deserves emphasis, as the fate of African-Americans in the South so vividly illustrates.

In different countries, American influence has counted in different ways. For example, Czechs and Slovaks today often gratefully acknowledge the American contribution to the establishment of their democracy in 1918–9 and consider Woodrow Wilson to be virtually a founding father of their republic. Nevertheless, Czechoslovak democracy during the interwar period was almost entirely the doing of its own people. So too, Germany might well have become a democracy even without the American occupation after 1945, though the character of its political order without Allied supervision might have made it less liberal than it is today, and the pace of European economic integration might have been altogether slower, with dramatic consequences for political stability on the continent. By contrast, Japanese democracy bears a more indelible American mark due to General Douglas MacArthur's assertive role in the establishment of its postwar order.

When we turn to the pre-industrial world, the impact of American policy changes dramatically. Thus, the Philippines is a fragile democracy, the American-inspired political institutions not having resolved fundamental issues of class power in this predominately agrarian country. So too in Latin America, the American contribution to democracy has been problematic, as in the case of Chile, or decidedly negative, as in Guatemala or in the Dominican Republic (before 1978, when for the first time a positive intervention occurred). Indeed, whatever its intentions, American policy on balance may have done substantially more to shore up dictatorships in the region than to advance the cause of democracy: the emergence of the Somoza and Trujillo tyrannies as the fruits of American interventions beginning with Wilson illustrates this clearly.

However, country studies alone do not tell us enough. After both the First and Second world wars, and again today in the aftermath of the cold war, America has formulated frameworks for world order in which the promotion of democracy played a conspicuous role. The emphasis on global security, the world market, and international law and organizations figure prominently alongside the call for national, democratic self-determination. The administrations of Wilson, Roosevelt, Truman, and Reagan emerge as particularly important in this context, where the focus is on the the ability of democratic countries to cooperate internationally.

Historical watersheds, such as we are now passing through, are moments when the study of the past is especially invigorating. The past is now securely the past: the actors and the consequences of their policies have less claim on the present and so can be studied with some dispassion. Simultaneously, the present is in search of its future and must take stock of how it arrived at its current position. The aim of this book is better to understand the past for its own sake and in order to serve the future.

As Americans ponder the challenges of world affairs at the end of the cold war, they may think back to other times when Washington's decisions were critical: not only to the end of the world wars in 1918 and 1945, but to the end of the Spanish-American War in 1898 and the Civil War in 1865 as well. What they will find is that in the aftermath of victory, Washington determined to win the peace by promoting a concept of national security calling ultimately for democratic government among those with whom the United States would work most closely.

Just how to achieve this end was never a clear matter, to be sure. As the North debated what to do with its victory over the South in 1865, so in 1898 American leaders were somewhat unsure what to do with their new role in the Far East and the Caribbean. The national debate in 1918–9 over Wilson's vision of a "peace without victory" so as "to make the world safe for democracy" was likewise raucous and uncertain. Only in the 1940s, in its planning for the postwar order, did Washington appear relatively clear in its thinking (and here too there were debates, contradictions, improvisations, and accidents aplenty as policy was made). Thus, when President Clinton, like Presidents Bush and Reagan before him, speaks of his conviction that no feature of U.S. foreign policy is more critical at the end of the cold war than helping the democratic forces in Russia, he may often be at a loss on how best to proceed. But he is articulating his concerns for peace in a recognizable way that stretches back across the generations, to American leaders in other times who have speculated on what to do in the aftermath of victory and who rightly concluded that the answer consisted in promoting the fortunes of democracy for others for the sake of American national security.

While this book was written for a general public concerned about the character of American foreign policy, it also seeks to establish a series of theoretical propositions for students of international relations, comparative politics, and American foreign policy, as well as for those interested in policymaking. While these points will be made at more length at various places in the text (especially in the appendix, but also in the concluding sections of most chapters), a summary statement here is in order.

For the student of international relations, this book's major finding is that the neglect of an appreciation of the United States' internally generated definition of national security, and of the importance of the intersection of this national security doctrine with major historical forces peculiar to the twentieth century, has created an overly abstract, ahistorical, rigid, and narrow field of analysis. Unable to understand liberal democratic internationalism as a historically constructed approach to American security interests defined by domestic political processes, and uninterested in seeing the specific challenges of international politics in the twentieth century in terms of the contending forces of nationalist ideologies, realism—the dominant school of international relations theory—has dealt mainly with strategic and diplomatic issues, treating the international system as a formal configuration of power whose properites can be studied ahistorically. However important realism's insights surely are, its contention that these are the only issues of importance needs serious reexamination.

The chief virtue of international relations theory is that it understands that political considerations are preeminent in the formulation of a state's foreign policy. That is, realism recognizes that power—most nakedly expressed in the threat of war—is the ultimate currency in world affairs; hence the state will by its very nature be fundamentally preoccuped by the question of how power is organized in the international system in terms of its own survival. The concept of national security as the organizing principle of a state's foreign policy is well articulated in realist theory.

Yet how a state views the organization of power in the international system may be far more complex than a simple rendering of formal models of bipolar, multipolar, or hegemonic configurations can provide. Security definitions arise out of particular domestically engendered perceptions of foreign affairs and are operationalized in an environment inhabited by the domestically engendered security pursuits of other countries. But realism has absolved itself of the need to investigate the historically constructed definition of national security, growing out of a country's cultural, economic, social, and political interests as formed into policy by its leaders and operationalized through the instruments of the state.

As economic theory posits a rational economic actor, so realism is satisfied by the notion of a rational actor in terms of power calculated in external terms alone. Yet by failing to see that the twentieth century has been an era of global political instability occasioned in good measure by the rise of nationalism and the search for mass-based states (and not typified simply by anonymous changes in the distribution of power in the international system), realism has discounted the critical ideological contest of this period, and so often overlooked the major stakes involved in world affairs in favor of what it simplistically sees as the eternal struggle of states for power. For example, it is as if the problem of German power relative to its neighbors is independent of the domestic constitution of the German state, as if any rational actor would operationalize German power (or react to it) in world affairs in the same way. Thus, whether Germany is governed by Wihelmine authoritarianism, Weimar democracy, or Hitler's Nazism becomes for the realist a secondary matter in explaining its behavior and that of its neighbors—a position that is absurd. These considerations are developed at more length in chapters four, five, eleven, and the appendix.

For students of comparative politics, this book insists on the importance of seeing the way in which international forces impinge on the evolution of the internal organization of states. Just as Confucian or Islamic systems of government have diffused over vast areas encompassing discrete peoples in the past (and may again in the future), so in this century communism, fascism, and democracy proposed blueprints for government capable of being adopted worldwide. Seeing how these global forces intersected with local interests in a way that sought to modernize governments by demonstrating how to create political parties and to attain nationalist governmental legitimacy in line with these highly charged proposals for state development should be a key concern of comparativists. Every chapter of the book illustrates this point, which is explicitly dealt with in terms of the academic literature in the appendix.

For students of American foreign policy, the need is to achieve a unified field of study based, as with international relations theory, on a history of this country's national security debate. Such a move should free the study of American foreign affairs from being overly descriptive and atheoretical (except for Marxist writing, which is not subject to these strictures), giving it a center of gravity in accord with which the multiple elements going into the national security debate—cultural, economic, political, and strategic—can find their respective places, not by crowding each other out, but by being understood in terms of one another.

At the same time, the study of American foreign policy must be accompanied by more careful attention to the logic of world history, especially to the structure of political development in foreign countries and in the international system. It is with these forces that American policy necessarily interacts, and a sense of the reciprocal character of the exchanges (for America, too, is a product of global developments) provides a necessary perspective from which to see the pattern in events. Chapters four, five, and the appendix elaborate on these points.

Finally, for policymakers, this book attempts to lay out the concrete national interests served by liberal democratic internationalism. It endorses the Wilsonian view that the promotion of democracy worldwide advances the national security of the United States, but it does so by arguing that such policy makes for better relations with other peoples and hence satisfies realist demands that the country think of its interests defined in terms of the international organization of power. While recognizing the important differences that have existed between realist and Wilsonian agendas for foreign policy, the following pages will insist that the two approaches are compatible. Liberal democratic internationalists should understand that democracy cannot be foisted upon a world that is unready for it, just as realists should grasp that the Wilsonian effort to provide stable, modern, democratic government to foreign peoples may well serve American security. The book endorses realism by offering repeated examples of unwise efforts by American presidents to force democratic government onto peoples unwilling or unready to accept it, with negative outcomes for American policy and with disastrous consequences for the peoples subjected to its influence. But more importantly (since such a case has not yet persua-

sively been made in the academic literature), it also endorses liberal democratic internationalism by insisting on the tremendous benefits that accrued
to the United States from the restructuring of Germany and Japan after
1945 into democratic states, while insisting that the national interest is also
served by the expansion of democracy today in Eastern Europe (including
Russia), Latin America (especially Mexico), and parts of the Far East.

PART I

Liberal Democratic Internationalism and American Foreign Policy, 1898–1921

CHAPTER TWO

Democracy in the Philippines

> It is in my judgment the duty of the United States to continue
> government [in the Philippines] which shall teach those people
> individual liberty, which shall lift them up to a point of civilization
> of which I believe they are capable, and which shall make them
> rise to call the name of the United States blessed.
>
> —William Howard Taft, first American governor
> of the Philippines, 1902

BEFORE 1898, when war with Spain broke out over Cuba, the United States had been reluctant to exercise dominion over foreign peoples. It was wary of being drawn into great power conflicts and unwilling to establish the kind of military institutions that might be a drain on its prosperity and a threat to democratic government. Without foreign entanglements, the country seemed virtually self-sufficient economically, protected from foreign attack by mighty oceans, and ill-suited to overseas conquests since only with great difficulty could non-European peoples be assimilated to American democracy.

To be sure, the United States had dealt roughly with its Indians and despoiled Mexico of half of its national territory in the 1840s. Yet these conflicts had not engaged the United States in struggles with European powers; they had not involved the conquest of relatively large populations (propositions to annex all of Mexico had been rebuffed by those who had no taste for trying to incorporate so large a non-European population); and they had not created much of a military establishment (in 1890 there were only thirty-nine thousand men in the Army and Navy combined).

At first reading the war of 1898 might not seem to have done much to upset this situation. The conflict itself was short—it lasted less than four months—with few casualties; 379 Americans died in combat (though some five thousand more died of diseases acquired while fighting). Moreover, by the terms of the Teller Amendment, added to the joint resolution of Congress giving President William McKinley the power to declare war on Spain, the United States disclaimed any "disposition or intention to exercise sovereignty, jurisdiction, or control over said Island [Cuba], except for the pacification thereof, and asserts its determination, when that is accomplished, to leave the government and control of the Island to its people." In congressional debates, it was clear that a vocal anti-imperialist minority had serious doubts as to the wisdom of this country taking on a new role in world politics and would hamper efforts to expand the American empire beyond the acquisition of the Philippines and Puerto Rico.

Yet despite the war's brevity, historians at the time and since have marked the Spanish-American War of 1898 as a watershed in the history of American foreign policy. By taking Puerto Rico and establishing a protectorate over Cuba, the United States established its dominion in the Caribbean. By seizing the Philippines, it became an Asian power with a role to play with respect to China and Japan. Most importantly, by breaking with an insular tradition, America was opening a new chapter in its relations with the rest of the world. Writing a decade before he was elected president, Woodrow Wilson summed up a common sentiment about the conflict, an opinion that has been generally shared by historians from his day to ours in thinking about American foreign policy prior to World War I: "No war has ever transformed us quite as the war with Spain transformed us. We have witnessed a new revolution. We have seen the transformation of America completed. . . . The battle of Trenton was not more significant than the battle of Manila. The nation that was one hundred and twenty-five years in the making has now stepped forth into the open arena of the world."[1]

The many motivations for war with Spain indicate the variety of forces driving the United States into the mainstream of world affairs. Business interests with a stake in Cuba called for the protection of trade and complained of investments destroyed or disrupted by the seemingly endless civil conflicts there, which had begun anew in 1895. Strategic thinkers were already forecasting the need for American control over a canal between the oceans through Central America (Nicaragua was seen as the probable site), which would result in a far greater presence of the United States in the Caribbean, whence an interest in Cuba. Proponents of social Darwinism were arguing that if this country were to be vigorous internally it needed to be active in international politics. Domestic tensions related to immigration, industrialization, and the final incorporation of the South into the Union were increasing, giving rise to a restless belligerence that could be channeled through imperialist ambitions. And humanitarian sentiments were outraged at the tremendous cruelty of the Spaniards: after the horrors of the Ten Years War of 1868–1878, which had killed perhaps two hundred thousand Cubans, Spain's policy of forced resettlement (after 1895) was taking another one hundred thousand Cuban lives, in a country whose population at the turn of the century had declined to under 1.6 million.[2]

Whatever the role of humanitarian concerns for Cuba, America did not go to war with Spain to make Cuba, much less the Philippines, into democracies. It was only after Spain had been defeated and the occupation of these foreign territories fell to the United States that attention was paid to their political development. Admittedly, the prospects for democracy did not appear favorable. Cuba was terribly poor. Its deep domestic divisions—racial issues aggravated class distinctions—had been worsened by thirty years of terrible civil war. But mainly, so most Americans felt, Cuba was weighed down by the legacy of hundreds of years of Spanish corruption and ineptitude compounded by Catholic dogmatism and the presence of many recently freed African slaves (at least one third of the population, who had been emancipated in 1886).[3]

There were calls for annexing Cuba; there was talk about preparing the island for stable republican government. In 1902 the United States accorded Cuba its independence, although the terms of the so-called Platt Amendment made Cuba an American protectorate, which meant Havana had to acknowledge Washington's right to intervene in its internal affairs should developments there threaten what Washington perceived to be its security interests. Unlike Puerto Rico, which was annexed in 1899 (its residents receiving American citizenship in 1917, its territory later being made a "commonwealth" with its own constitution), Cuba maintained a semisovereign status until 1934, when the Platt Amendment was rescinded. While American influence affected the island's political character, Cuba constituted nothing like the laboratory for democracy that the Philippines was to be.

The acquisition of the Philippines was something of an accidental conquest, a by-product of a war with Spain waged essentially for stakes in the Caribbean. Yet it was thousands of miles away, in a region that had never been of much concern to the United States, that this country for the first time in its history made a calculated effort to foster democracy abroad. The United States persisted in its undertaking longer than anywhere else (forty-eight years), during which time its sovereignty was uncontested, save for the period of Japanese rule during World War II. After the Philippines gained its independence on July 4, 1946, American efforts to stabilize democracy there continued. The United States worked to defeat the communist Huk rebellion in the aftermath of World War II, culminating with the election of Ramon Magsaysay as president in 1953. Later Washington supported Corazon Aquino's march to the presidency in 1986 and defended her power thereafter.

Today, nearly half a century after its independence, the Philippines is a troubled democracy, but it is a democracy nonetheless. From 1946 until 1972, the country held regular elections for the presidency and the congress. Despite election irregularities, the system allowed an alteration of parties in power until 1969, when Ferdinand Marcos became the first president in the republic's history to succeed himself. In September 1972, Marcos declared martial law, ruling the country with his cronies and military supporters (despite a token return to democratic forms in 1980) until the popular forces rallied behind Corazon Aquino drove him from office in February 1986. Subsequently, a new constitution was adopted, Aquino was confirmed in the presidency by a commanding vote of the electorate, and a new legislature was chosen and convened. Despite numerous attempts by the military to unseat her, Aquino remained in office until replaced by elections held in 1992.

Unlike Haiti, Iran, or Nicaragua, where a strong man's rule was followed by anarchy or revolution, enough of an institutional democratic base existed in the Philippines for democracy to survive fourteen years of betrayal under the Marcos dictatorship. Corazon Aquino and Catholic leader Jaime Cardinal Sin, whose steadfast determination may have been the single most important factor returning the country to democratic rule, often called their success in its early days a miracle, but the probability is that other factors better explain the dictator's fall and the resurgence of democracy. An economic crisis, the opposition of many of the great families of the country (and most interest groups), the militant stance of the Church, divisions within the ranks of the army—all these factors surely played their part in Marcos's collapse. Yet the fact that democracy ultimately prevailed when there were clear signs that the popular turmoil might be the prelude to a right-wing military coup (as in Haiti at this time) or to a left-wing insurgency (as in Nicaragua) raises the question of the character of Filipino democracy: its structure, its strength, its shortcomings.

To address this topic is to inquire into the dynamic of American imperialism in the islands since 1898 and the role the United States played in determining the values, practices, and institutions that constitute democracy in the Philippines today. It is a study in transplanting Western (or American-style) democracy to a distinctly foreign culture. Contemporary Filipino practices and institutions are an amalgam of American ways grafted onto local conditions in a unique manner that over time has become wholly Filipino.

THE DECISION TO SPONSOR DEMOCRACY

The United States did not conquer the Philippines in order to export the gospel of democracy there. Nevertheless, after sinking the Spanish fleet in Manila Bay on May 1, 1898, and assuming sovereignty over the islands, there was an implacable logic to fostering Filipino democratization.

Other alternatives included returning the islands to Spain after that country's defeat, but that was unthinkable given the hue and cry that had been raised against Spanish despotism in order to get the United States into war in the first place. The islands could be left to themselves, but Senator Henry

Cabot Lodge warned that if that happened they would become "like Haiti or Santo Domingo . . . with no Monroe Doctrine to prevent other nations from interfering"—by which he meant either Germany or Japan. Or the United States could keep Manila as a naval base and commercial entrepot, much as Britain held Hong Kong, but that seemed politically infeasible unless America took the entire archipelgo and established a serious foothold in the Orient. Should it make the archipelgo a colony, it would be the first time the United States had ever exercised sovereignty over a populous foreign people, raising difficult questions of how to rule them—to what end and with what means. America had entered the war with a pledge against foreign annexation; should that now be discarded?

Ultimately, the American decision was the last in this list: it would take the country as its first colony. But why? In most textbooks that recount President McKinley's deliberations over what was to be done with the Philippines, there is no ready answer. It is traditional to report that the president told a visiting group of clergymen that "late one night" he fell on his knees to ask for divine guidance on the matter, concluding "there was nothing left for us to do but take them all, and to educate the Filipinos, and uplift and Christianize them. . . . I went to bed . . . and slept soundly."[4]

Whatever McKinley's "humanitarian" sentiments, economic considerations also played a role. The islands were in proximity to southern China and seemed a logical extension of American possessions in the Pacific once the commitment to hold Hawaii had been made in the summer of 1898. Without denying the commercial lure of the islands and China, a strictly economic case for the conquest is difficult to make. Cheap Filipino labor and agricultural products put the islands in direct competition with domestic American unions and certain business interests, which early on opposed keeping the country under United States control. Unlike the Europeans, whose relatively limited natural resources meant that their imperialism almost always had a serious economic dimension to it, economic calculations carried far less weight for Americans. Nor did the economic promise of the islands ever in fact amount to much (although that does not mean that its mistaken overvaluation may not have been part of the American motive for control). The China trade was relatively minor and in any case did not depend on control of Manila for its fortunes; the United States Congress soon passed such a host of restrictions on American investment in the Philippines that corporate interests never saw involvement there as a lucrative undertaking.[5]

Certainly it was not strategic considerations that motivated the American conquest. Early on, it was recognized that sovereignty over such distant possessions could embroil the United States in conflicts it might better avoid. When the islands were seized by Japan in the aftermath of the attack on Pearl Harbor, these fears were realized.

Ultimately, it was considerations of national pride and purpose that were the primary (though not exclusive) motivations of American policy with respect to the Philippines. American leaders were engaging in the competitive, "manly" nationalist assertion that was sweeping Europe, as evidenced by the various scrambles of the European powers in Africa and the Far East. It was also a time of internal questioning as America experienced its coming-of-age as an industrial power. These were the days when Theodore Roosevelt could proclaim: "All the great masterful races have been fighting races. No triumph of peace is quite so great as the triumphs of war." Or as Senator Alfred Beveridge put it in a fashion more acceptable to traditional American moralism, God had "marked the American people as His chosen Nation to finally lead in the regeneration of the world."[6]

The result was an outburst of moralistic fervor in favor of holding the Philippines even though it was not at once evident that the effort to democratize the islands would take on the importance it eventually achieved. The Filipinos themselves first had to be subjugated in what turned out to be a bloody conflict (more than 4,000 Americans and 220,000 Filipinos died), and many Americans who cared about the values of democracy were convinced that the conquest of this distant land was a mistake. However, by virtue of the terms of the debate within the United States between imperialists and anti-imperialists, the importance of bringing democracy to the Philippines was soon established, even though neither party to the debate initially considered this to be a mission America should undertake.

At the time of the war, anti-imperialist forces in the United States had mounted a formidable campaign against taking over the Philippines. Some opponents of empire were isolationists worried about the strategic vulnerability of the islands and the involvement in international affairs their possession implied. Others feared the entry of cheap Filipino products that might compete with domestic output. Perhaps the most vocal feared the loss of American values that would come with ruling in an unaccountable fashion over a weak and distant people. Unless it intended one day to make a state out of the area, would the United States not involve itself in a form of despotism abroad that would ultimately corrupt democratic institutions at home? Yet how could the United States actually incorporate the Philippines? As the Americans had shown earlier in the century, when the annexation of Mexico was debated in the aftermath of its defeat in 1848, or when the annexation of the Dominican Republic was proposed in 1869, there was serious resistance to the idea of extending statehood, even after a probationary period, to people of a different ethnic stock than the majority of Americans. In 1898, there were more than 7 million Filipinos; their incorporation would have made them nearly 10 percent of the national population and the largest state in the Union.[7]

In these circumstances, the commitment to democratize the Philippines was a "second best" solution. It was a way of governing this possession on which both imperialists and anti-imperialists could agree. Imperialists could thereby tout the superiority of the Anglo-Saxon race, while anti-imperialists could reassure themselves that the ideals of self-government would not be endangered. All could agree that eventually the colony would be free to pursue its own destiny and hence be neither a threat to domestic economic interests nor a strategic commitment to be defended indefinitely. The result was important for the future of American foreign policy for the simple reason that American power now had a mission that justified its exercise—a mission that most assuredly did not mean that hopes for sponsoring democracy abroad were nothing but rhetoric camouflaging more serious reasons for action but instead that would make the United States a major force thereafter in the shaping of the domestic politics of foreign peoples, with enormous consequences for the structure of international relations as well.

Ultimately, therefore, the democratization of the Philippines came to be the principal reason the Americans were there; now the United States had a moral purpose to its imperialism and could rest more easily. The irony is that while many Americans ridiculed the Spanish for justifying their 333-year rule over the islands by bringing them Christianity (and suspected this was only a mask for power), so in a like manner, democracy would be the moving faith of the forty-eight years of American control. What other option was there? Not only did the United States lack the aristocratic, clerical, or military impetus to rule abroad—which characterized British, French, and German imperialism—but the nature of its own internal economic and political structure made democratization and the presumption of eventual self-government the only possible point of consensus on which to establish American rule.

As a result, while the lure of commerce and the lust for power had led to the American conquest of the Philippines in the first place, the United States had no choice thereafter but to govern with a serious commitment to the islands' democratization. Admittedly, this would take time. William Howard Taft—president of the Second Philippine Commission (1900), the first governor of the islands (1901–4), subsequently secretary of war (1904–8), then president of the United States (1909–13), and finally chief justice of the Supreme Court (1921–30)—declared in 1900 that Filipinos "need the training of fifty or a hundred years before they shall ever realize what Anglo-Saxon liberty is." And he continued:

> The incapacity of these people for self-government is one of the patent facts that strikes every observer, whether casual or close. The truth is that there are not in these islands more than six or seven thousand men who have any education that deserves the name, and most of these are nothing but the most intriguing politicans, without the slightest moral stamina, and nothing but personal interests to gratify. The great mass of the people are ignorant and superstituous.

Despite these reservations, Taft did hold out the promise of eventual self-government, as he explained to the Senate Committee on the Philippines in 1902:

> If I may say it personally, I did not favor going into the Philippine Islands. I was sorry at the time that we got into it. But we are there. I see no other possible means of discharging that duty which chance has put upon us than the plan I suggest. . . . We think we can help these people; we think we can elevate them to an appreciation of popular government. . . . My proposition is that it is the duty of the United States to establish there a government suited to the present possibilities of the people, which shall gradually change, conferring more and more right upon the people to govern themselves, thus educating them in self-government, until their knowledge of government, their knowledge of individual liberty shall be such that further action may be taken either by giving them statehood or by making them a quasi-independent government like Canada and Australia, or if they desire it, by independence.[8]

Within a few years of Taft's remarks—by the legislative elections of 1907, which saw the triumph of the Nacionalista party over the Federalistas, who had Taft's backing and who sought union with the United States—it became evident that the Filipinos would opt for independence. For many Americans, this decision was a relief. Filipino commercial development was in fact putting that land into direct competition with domestic American interests—from the sugar growers of Louisiana to the labor unions of California. Similarly, concern over foreign involvements, especially with Japan, had not disappeared. (The Depression of the 1930s and the Japanese invasion of Manchuria in 1931 and China proper in 1937 would later compound these concerns.) Nor were many Americans interested in extending statehood to the Philippines. As Secretary of War Elihu Root in 1901 told a visiting group of Filipino leaders who had come to Washington to request eventual statehood for the islands: "Gentlemen, I don't wish to suggest an invidious comparison, but statehood for Filipinos would add another serious race problem to the one we have already. The Negroes are a cancer on our body politics, a source of constant difficulty, and we wish to avoid developing another such problem."[9]

Yet while democracy was the governing principle of the American occupation, Republican Presidents Theodore Roosevelt and Taft refused to address the question of organizing Filipino independence. The Democrats had been talking of self-government since 1900, however, and the election of Woodrow Wilson in 1912 meant that their promise would have to be made more concrete. By the Jones Act, finally passed in 1916, the United States significantly extended the power of the Filipino electorate and its control over the islands' government. It also promised the islands their independence, but without fixing a date. In 1935 the Philippines gained commonwealth status, or full self-government for its internal affairs, with a promise of independence in ten years. In the process, Filipino political institutions came to resemble those in the United States, though with certain differences, such as a lack of a federal form of organization, somewhat greater powers for the president relative to the legislature, and the right to own national enterprises explicitly reserved to the state. While the war and a devastating Japanese occupation of the islands threatened to delay the American withdrawal, the Philippines became an independent democracy on July 4, 1946.

THE UNITED STATES AND FILIPINO DEMOCRACY: THE POLITICAL DIMENSION

The most important contribution the United States made to fostering the development of liberal democracy in the Philippines was indisputably the political system it set in place. In quick order, the Americans introduced all the trappings of modern government, from parties and elections to centralized governing institutions with a division of powers. As early as 1899 the Americans were conducting municipal elections to establish local councils with which they could deal on a host of issues, from preserving the civil peace to introducing public health and universal primary education. By 1907 elections were held to the national legislature, the first time such an institution had existed in that country.

It is a testimony to the fairness of the elections that the Federalista party, favored by Taft, went down to defeat at the hands of the Nacionalistas, headed by the two founders of the modern Philippines, Manuel Quezon and Sergio Osmena. While the bulk of power remained firmly in American hands, the United States oversaw the creation of an independent judiciary and, as noted, in 1916 and again in 1935 reorganized the central organs of government so as to devolve increasingly greater powers onto Filipino leaders. Baseball, a love of John Philip Sousa marches, and the proliferation of lawyers—all these were legacies of the American days. But equally enduring, and of far more importance, was the provision of a political framework for liberal democracy.

The Americans buttressed these political institutions in a variety of ways. Appreciating the role of education in the development of an effective citizenry and a united nation, the Americans had from the beginning emphasized the importance of schooling, which increased dramatically after 1900. Similarly, American recognition of the role of freedom of expression meant that a free press appeared early in the islands and for many decades was without rival in Asia. So too, the Americans saw to the creation of a modern legal code and a civil bureaucracy. By 1913, with Wilson's appointment of Francis Burton Harrison as governor, the Americans began the rapid Filipinization of the civilian bureaucracy. At Harrison's departure in 1921, this had been effectively accomplished, with Filipinos now in control. Of 13,757 government bureaucrats, 13,143 were Filipinos, who also occupied fifty-six of the sixty-nine top posts.[10] Finally, a sometimes neglected but fundamental contribution of American rule to the modernization of Filipino politics was to defuse the potential for a church-state controversy by disestablishing the Catholic Church: purchasing and redistributing Church lands, and ending the Church monopoly on education.

From the viewpoint of academic democratic theory stressing the sequences of political development favorable to the establishment of democratic institutions, the American efforts in the Philippines look like a textbook example of good government. The gradual expansion of democratic practices from the grassroots level to the center, on the one hand, and the gradual devolution of powers retained by the American authorities to Filipinos, on the other, correspond well to the findings of academic literature, which declares just such a process to be the most likely to create a durable democratic system. The basic reasoning is obvious: starting at the grass roots builds up a corps of public representatives who can then carry forward the business of government more effectively at the next level; for its part, incremental devolution allows for the measured expansion of governing capacities. The result upon independence is presumed to be a seasoned group of officials able to insure the viability of the institutions in which they have been reared professionally. Time is clearly an important element in the process: time for individuals to build coalitions and to elaborate operating norms. The result is a controlled pace of change, with the gradual emergence of institutions whose procedures prove able to accommodate new interests and demands and whose practices provide stability and an increasingly familiar and legitimate forum for individuals and groups to work out their differences and establish their common purpose. Compared to what the Dutch were doing in Indonesia, or the French in Indochina, or the British in Burma or Malaya, the American effort at promoting liberal political democracy in the first four decades of the twentieth century was without obvious parallel.

Was this contribution of the United States to the democratization of the Philippines an unmixed blessing, or were there perhaps indigenous Filipino roots to democracy that were stamped out in the process of imposing the American order? Were there powerful democratic currents in the values, practices, and relationship structures of late-nineteenth-century Filipino life such that reform under Spanish rule or independence under local leadership might have contributed effectively to the emergence of democratic government? Such a discussion is difficult because it must necessarily be hypothetical. Yet it cannot be avoided if we would have a just measure of the American role in establishing the character of Filipino democracy.

While the Spanish had provided the islands with centralized authority since their effective occupation began in 1565, their contacts with the indigenous population were strictly bureaucratic, and even this was relatively rudimentary, depending as it did on the cooperation of the Church and a handful of roving, local Spanish administrators. Political life was lively at the village level, but it was dominated by a narrow traditional elite—the *principalia*—whose authority was strictly local. In pre-Hispanic days, it appears that villages were based internally on extended kinship structures and on a rather rigid patron-client hierarchy with widespread debt peonage, so that social organization and hence power had both a horizontal and a vertical dimension. Except in the south, where Muslim influence had spread, there were no political structures above the village level. Under Spanish rule, the hierarchical structure of village life grew more rigid as the central authorities enrolled the local chiefs as tax collectors, and as these chiefs, in turn, took advantage of new laws vesting property in private hands to convert communal goods into their own possessions. In cultural terms, the Church operated in a parallel manner, adopting a paternalistic stance toward the population that had no shred of democratic practice to it.[11]

Hence, it is difficult to argue that the cultural values and practices of traditional Filipino life predisposed the people to democracy. Nonetheless, certain features of the pre-Hispanic organization do need mention in this respect. First, there was bargaining among members of the principalia to determine leadership roles, a procedure that was preserved by the Spanish. Secondly, the practice of *compadrazgo*, whereby individuals entered into a wide network of group-based rights and responsibilities based on blood and ritual exchange, allowed for a shifting system of allegiances whose flexibility might be thought a cultural precondition to mutual respect and compromise. This pattern has remained current in Filipino life even today. Finally, the rival patron-client networks might be thought of as contributing to a dispersion and balancing of power, what might be called a variant of feudalism, which has been argued by many as basic to the eventual emergence of democracy in both Japan and Britain.

These practices do not make the case that proto-democracy existed in traditional Filipino society. Individuals were obliged by the cultural system to place their extended kinship obligations above any allegiances to a greater group. The leaders of patron-client groupings were themselves above the law (in contrast to leaders in a Confucian system, where the existence of a rule of law could be said to provide a general framework of behavior and a restraint on arbitrary rule). And unlike Japan and Britain, there had never been a period in Filipino history when a king emerged with power on a par with that of the nobility, so providing the institutional framework and values that might later contribute to the emergence of a centralized state.[12]

It was well into the nineteenth century before popular agitation of a modern sort with national demands began to appear, and these protests were restricted to a small Manila-based elite. Analyses tend to divide popular agitation of the times into two kinds. The upper class Propagandists, an elite of *ilustrados* (the rich intelligentsia) whose wealth was largely based on land ownership and who, reacting to Spanish liberalism, wanted through peaceful reform to remake the Philippines along more open, secular lines under Spanish rule. The lower-class Katipunan, a more radical group organized in a secret society, was more egalitarian but also more mystical in its thinking, and it wanted independence—through violent means if necessary.

These late-nineteenth-century protest groups had little promise for democracy in their makeup. The Propagandists called for a secular, liberal state and, borrowing from contemporary Spanish liberalism, appeared to favor some form of democratic organization. Spanish repression effectively destroyed this movement; however, some members then joined the radical agitation for independence. Here the ideas were both vague and complex, the coalitions loose and fragile. But it seems highly unlikely that either of these movements, alone or in combination, was likely to bring forth democracy in the Philippines at the end of the nineteenth century had Commodore George Dewey simply sailed away after sinking the Spanish fleet on May Day 1898.

Certainly the forces under Emilio Aguinaldo, who finally prevailed in leading the struggle against the American occupation of the islands, gave little such indication. True, the first constitution proposed by Aguinaldo and written by Apolinario Mabini was democratic in most respects, though its insistence on a strong executive and a consultative congress (to hold the ilustrados at bay) indicates that it might well have developed into dictatorial rule.[13] Under the pressure of the American assault, however, Aguinaldo moved even more to the right, agreeing to restrict the franchise to landowners in order to insure his support from this class. The dominant forces now were essentially those of a new mestizo elite, its wealth based on the land and its control of a work force that was already in good measure either landless or sharecropping tenants (to be discussed below).

We cannot know what would have happened had the Americans not attacked Aguinaldo; perhaps the radical cast of the first constitution would have endured and laid the foundation of a democratic Philippines. Yet surely this would have been an extraordinary outcome, relatively unconnected as it was to the actual organization of power on the islands at the time: patron-client networks and extended kinship structures, where a few wealthy families with large landholdings wielded great influence. When we consider as well that the Filipinos had never had the slightest experience in government above the village level and that regional fragmentation was sharp, based on language and geography, skepticism as to the probability that democracy would have triumphed in 1898 is all the more justified.

More likely outcomes, assuming no foreign power invaded, would have been either strong-man rule and occasional civil war, or a confederation of oligarchs, or the fragmentation of the islands into different territories. Of the three, the most friendly to democracy (and the least likely to have occurred) would presumably have been the confederation of oligarchs with its separation of powers, preference for compromise over force, and country-wide political organization. In the sense of having only these likely nondemocratic options to choose from, the Philippines is strongly reminiscent of Latin America in the aftermath of its independence.

In fact, the American occupation permitted a confederation of oligarchs to rule in a constitutionally regularized manner, probably the most favorable outcome from the point of view of democracy of the various options open without American rule. Indeed, many of the most outspoken democrats of the islands came to welcome American sovereignty precisely because they saw in it the realization of their own ideals. The Federalista party, created by two ilustrados, Benito Legarda and Trinidad Pardo de Travera, favored universal education, the separation of church and state, a full panoply of civil liberties, and private property. The party was founded on Washington's Birthday 1901 and dedicated to the Filipinos "Americanizing themselves" so as to qualify one day for statehood. In Pardo's words, "I see the day near at hand . . . when it shall transpire that George Washington will not simply be the glory of the American continent, but also our glory, because he will be the father of the American world, in which we shall feel ourselves completely united and assimilated."[14]

The problem with such dreams was not so much what America then proceeded to do to them, but what these same indigenous oligarchs did with the democratization process: they used its political commanding heights, put at their disposal by the Americans, to modernize their control over the socioeconomic life of the country.

THE UNITED STATES AND FILIPINO DEMOCRACY:
THE SOCIOECONOMIC DIMENSION

During the nearly half century it controlled the islands, the United States put into place in the Philippines the full apparatus of democratic government. Political parties appeared, civil liberties were guaranteed, a free press flourished, the Church was disestablished, separate functions for the legislative and the executive were spelled out, a civil bureaucracy was created, and a judiciary set up. But the functioning of this democracy was plagued by division and corruption of such depth that the viability of the system left to its own devices seemed constantly in jeopardy. Many early Filipino nationalist leaders recognized the problem, calling in public for independence but constantly worried behind the scenes lest it be granted too quickly.

American officials ascribed the manifold problems they encountered in institutionalizing the rule of law to the racial character of the predominant Malay stock: they were superstitious, self-interested, unprincipled liars and thieves. A more persuasive explanation is that the influence of the country's enduring socioeconomic structure, resting on its land tenure system, was inhibiting the democratic functioning of its political system, as the interests of the rich and the obligations of extended family and patron-client loyalties outweighed by far abstract notions of the rule of law or appeals to the common interest.

As noted, before the American arrival, power in the Philippines—other than that possessed directly by the Spanish state and the Church—was structured horizontally through extended kinship structures and vertically through patron-client relations based on ownership of the land. During the nineteenth century, the importance of what we might call this socioeconomic power system had been greatly amplified by the effects of the introduction of commercial agriculture, which had begun in the late 1780s. Prior to this time, profit from agriculture had been relatively insignificant; wealth was largely in the hands of the Spanish, acting as the middlemen for trade between Mexico and China. But the decline of the China trade and the quickening pulse of the international market meant that for the first time capital might be accumulated in the islands through the export of such products as sugar, hemp, indigo, tobacco, and coconut, products that increasingly displaced the traditional staples of rice and corn. One account estimates that the value of agricultural exports rose thirty-six times over from 1820 to 1898.[15]

The chief beneficiaries of this new source of income were not the Spanish but foreign companies (British and American especially) and local middlemen. No complete history of the character of these Filipino middlemen has yet appeared, but presumably many of them came from the village principalia, whose control over the land had increased during the earlier period of Spanish rule thanks to the Spanish custom of recognizing individual title to land. However, there was a new group of landowner-middlemen which was not of the village elite: Chinese mestizos.[16]

The history of the Chinese in the Philippines is fascinating, yet for our purposes it is enough to say that after being merchants in Manila for many generations, they went on in the nineteenth century to establish country-wide trading networks carrying produce from the countryside to the ports

for export. In the process, those who became more Filipinized by birth—
and apparently marginalized from Chinese society as a result of Spanish
and Malay pressures—used their knowledge and contacts to acquire land,
which tenants would then farm to produce goods demanded by the international market. Many of today's greatest Filipino families trace their origins
back to such an ancestor. Thanks to local history and cultural values, as
well as to their real power, Chinese mestizos did not feel threatened by the
subsequent rise of Filipino nationalism.

The result was the emergence before the American conquest of an increasingly powerful new Filipino landed class whose wealth was based on
the production of export commodities. To be sure, the origins of this group
were recent and its numbers small.[17] Yet the decline of the economic livelihood of the Spanish (and their increasing divisions between peninsulares
and creoles), the influence of Spanish liberalism, and the accounts of the
independence of Spanish America meant that in due course this new class
of Filipinos would demand political power. In the Philippines as elsewhere, however, the Spanish stood firm, resisting any reform to their system of rule, and so provoking a series of nationalist outbursts until 1896,
when a planned insurrection finally broke out.

By the time Dewey arrived in Manila Bay, the uprising had been momentarily repressed and its leader, Aguinaldo, sent to Hong Kong with a
substantial payment from the Spanish treasury to keep him there. The
Americans engineered his return, however, in order to confront the Spanish
defenders of the islands with a native insurrection, except that in short
order the Americans found they could not dictate terms to the Filipino
forces they had allowed to organize. The result was a prolonged war, lasting until Aguinaldo's capture in March 1901.

Although the struggle against the United States had been fierce, it was by
no means unified. Like any such conflict, the Filipino patriots were divided
among themselves—by class interests, by ideological beliefs, by personalities. At the outset of his tenure, therefore, Taft set out on the time-honored
practice of divide and rule, what he called "a policy of attraction," and
looked about him for Filipinos with whom the United States could collaborate. It might come as no surprise that various leaders of the landed elite
were quite open to such a suggestion, for the United States represented not
only the liberal ideals many of them had espoused in their struggle against
Spain, but access to a broader international market for their goods as well.[18]

The Americans threw themselves as whole-heartedly into the economic
modernization of the Philippines as they did its democratization. Indeed,
the two were said to complement one another: a better educated public
made for a more informed and articulate citizenry while providing a better
work force. Or again, an improved infrastructure (necessary for economic
advancement) could contribute to a rise in the standard of living, offering

the citizenry more choices, more communication, more contact—all of which would break down the ways of the traditional world and prepare the Filipinos for life together in a democratic nation.

The problem with these American initiatives was that they did not succeed in breaking up the socioeconomic concentration of power held by the Filipino landed elite. Not simply was the democratic structure of politics unreinforced by a democratic structure of socioeconomic relations, but the elite could use the modern political and bureaucratic apparatuses set up by the Americans to expand their holdings and power.

In an agrarian society, a highly unequal pattern of landholding is fatal for democracy. The most obvious reason is that gross inequalities in wealth feed the fires of class conflict. Great wealth cannot exist alongside desperate poverty and assume that it can rely on the consent of the governed for such an arrangement to persist. While a landowning class that lives on its property and actively engages in the familiar practices of patronage may find its privileges better respected than a class that is absentee and interested in exacting the highest possible level of rents, in hard times, a sense of terrible need if not of acute injustice is likely to arouse the less privileged. In such circumstances, it is quite unlikely the landowners will permit the democratic process to proceed to their dispossession.

If there is unanimity about anything among those who write on the Philippines, it is on the depth of poverty of the rural population and on how the terms of tenancy have increasingly turned against the poor over the course of the twentieth century. Thus, one report has 3.5 million landless in a total population of 16 million in 1935, while another shows a rise in tenancy from 37 percent of the total agrarian population in 1938 to 58 percent by 1962. Analyses made in 1990, when 60 to 70 percent of the population was estimated to be rural, show no improvement whatsoever in tenancy. There is no doubt as to the misery this has created for the rural poor.[19]

But the intensity of class conflict in the Philippines was not the only socioeconomic factor that precluded the development of stable democratic government there. As a relatively undiversified economy, the islands did not require the kind of flexible, decentralized political institutions a more mature economy might need. Hence political institutions remain highly personalized and the rule of law practically impossible to base on social organization.

This consideration suggests that the most serious obstacle placed in the path of democracy by agrarian societies is their lack of an adequately complex division of labor able to furnish the medly of interest groups whose power checks one another socially and whose political accord requires both a party government and a state run by the rule of law. For a time, a powerful foreign presence may hold such a state in place; but once it departs, the battle of the oligarchs resumes, ultimately to be settled most commonly by some form of dictatorship.

The problem of the American presence from this perspective was that it did not pursue either of two courses of action to shore up democracy by changes in the Filipino socioeconomic system: either promoting family farms or industrializing the economy. Trade did increase handsomely between the islands and the United States once the Payne-Aldrich Tariff Law of 1909, providing for free trade, came into effect and the demand for goods in World War I was felt. In this process, however, Filipino industry was stifled and the islands were confirmed in their agricultural vocation. As late as 1969, one account of Filipino trade unions found them "fragmented and apolitical . . . organized labor does not play a prominent role in either the political or economic life of the country." If American rule did not stimulate industrial production, neither did it encourage the family farm. At the time of independence, the Philippines remained an overwhelmingly agricultural country, its political order dominated by landed oligarchs. Such a state of affairs did not bode well for democracy.[20]

In this respect, it matters little what crops are produced or what the precise tenure system be. Sharecroppers on small parcels of rice land (a staple crop) may be as desperate as hired labor on large sugar plantations. In this environment, the birth of a small, weak middle class in the urban areas does not constitute enough of a "third force" to dampen the political problem. Instead, this middle class is liable to invest whatever savings it achieves in land itself—and to let this out at as high a price as it can manage to an increasingly overpopulated countryside. The result is that the middle class comes to side with the rural oligarchy and in the process compromises what might otherwise be its commitment to democratic government.

The class of oligarchs who controlled society found that the Americans turned over to them control of the state. By controlling the state the class perpetuated its control of society. The process began with the municipal elections of 1899, which gave institutional form to a kind of elite contest and rule that had been on-going in the village since time immemorial. The American-imposed requirements for voting—tax payments or literacy— were such that basically only the principalia could vote; in any case not more than 3 percent of the population.[21] The expansion of the governmental system thereafter extended and modernized this elite's power.

Under American rule in the Philippines, the autonomy of the state from social forces was not attained. Instead, what Benigno Aquino called "the entrenched plutocracy" ruled in the form of the "sixty families" of the country: the Laurels in the Batangas; the Romualdezes in Leyte; the Rodriguezes in Rizal; the Somenas and the Cuencos in Cebu, and so forth.[22] Elections took place and power changed hands, but from one set of oli-

garchs who would turn the state apparatus to their advantage to another—
the frustrated electorate, at great effort, eventually chasing the latest gang
of rascals from office.

Thus the curse of a landowning oligarchy on democracy in a country like
the Philippines is not simply the destabilizing class conflict its relative monopoly of wealth engenders, but also, and even more importantly, the enforced institutional immaturity that its domination is sure to perpetuate.
The United States had done a great deal to prepare the Philippines to be a
democracy after its independence by the complex yet supple political
framework it left in place after nearly a half century of rule. Yet by actively
expanding the oligarch's power economically through the international
market system it opened to the islands and by modernizing the government
agencies through which this elite operated, the United States undermined
its otherwise exemplary achievements. It is as if the United States undid
with the one hand what it was doing with the other.

The Oligarchs and the State

The most important gap in the literature on the American occupation of the
Philippines is the lack of a detailed analysis of its effect on the land tenure
system. How exactly did the oligarchs turn American reforms to their benefit? How did Americans understand the changes they witnessed and of
which they were an indispensable part?

It would be erroneous to believe that American policy with respect to the
land was set up for the sake of private American economic interests. True,
Republicans of Taft's era wanted American investors to turn a profit in the
Philippines. President Taft encouraged private American investment to
flow to the islands and was disappointed when Congress refused to allow
generous mining and agribusiness concessions to United States corporations. When Harvey Firestone wanted to take the islands of Sulu or Mindinao for rubber plantations (along the lines of what the British were doing
in Malaya and the French in Vietnam), he was turned down. When Taft
wanted to allow twenty-five thousand acres per corporate tract, the Congress authorized only twenty-five hundred. Mining restrictions were such
that relatively little investment followed and the railway development Taft
hoped for was slow in coming. Taft's notion was not to plunder the Philippines for American profit, of course, but that the Filipinos too would benefit from the inflow of American capital, technology, and markets.

Part of the problem was that the Americans did not anticipate correctly
the way the islands would develop economically after 1900. They failed to
see the mechanisms by which the landowning interests would expand their
control in rhythm with the general expansion of the economy. In 1900, the
islands were underpopulated, so that by building a transportation infra-

structure the Americans might expect to open regions to farming that would be independent of the old centers of agriculture. From 1900 to 1946, the population grew from some 7 to 27 million, yet the vast majority of this increase became a poor workforce for the landlords and their middle class imitators rather than a small-holding population with an independent economic base.

The Americans did have plans to help increase the number of small farmers. When the United States purchased the 404,000 acres of Church lands in the Philippines from the Vatican in 1903, it planned to sell them to the 60,000 tenants who farmed them "at cost price, payable in long terms with moderate interest. The annual compounded sum will be only a trifle more than the rent hitherto paid." Similarly, the United States announced it would sell off the 16.6 million acres of public domain it had inherited from the Spanish crown in lots of forty acres modeled on the homestead provisions used at home. And in 1902 the Americans announced that they would register homestead deeds to tracts of forty acres that had been cultivated for at least five years upon payment of a $10 fee.[23]

However, these designs were frustrated by the ability of the Filipino rich to acquire large tracts of land. As early as 1908, the new Filipino legislature rescinded the American efforts to register homestead deeds, and wealthy individuals found ways to take over large blocks of friar lands, with momentous consequences for the future of democratic government there.

Two considerations appear to have predominated in American thinking. First, the conviction that small holders were the backbone of democracy did not mean that past certain limits an interventionist state should create such a class. A generation before the reforms of the New Deal, any other kind of talk smacked of socialism, seen by most Americans as a threat to democratic order. It could also be argued that larger holdings were more efficient, giving a greater impetus to economic modernization, which would be to the long-term benefit of the entire population.[24]

A second and doubtless more important reason for the Americans to acquiesce in the expansion of oligarchic holdings was that in line with Taft's "policy of attraction," the Americans had decided very early to base their rule on an alliance with this class. Once such a collaboration had transferred real power to the Filipino elites, it became progressively more difficult to dislodge them.

Hence the decision made in 1913 to place Filipinos in charge of the civil bureaucracy, intended to train local people in self-government, in effect allowed the oligarchy access to the execution of policy. By 1916, with the powers of the Filipino legislature expanded, the bureaucracy became a source of political patronage. Thus in 1918, the Philippine National Bank went into bankruptcy, the result of massive lending for fradulent or ill-conceived purposes to large landowners.[25]

By this time the momentum of political democracy was moving at sufficient speed that it was becoming increasingly unlikely that the Americans could regain the levers they would need to control developments in the socioeconomic domain. The compadrazgo system of extended kinship obligations with its corresponding ties of patron-client relations was reasserting itself over the very political institutions that the Americans were naive enough to believe could serve alone to insure the democratic character of the country.

Perhaps there was one moment when the United States might have regained the initiative: immediately after World War II, when General Douglas MacArthur returned to the Philippines. His father had been the first military governor of the islands, his own first appointment after West Point had been there, and he had returned as military commander in 1935 to prepare the defenses against a feared Japanese invasion. Moreover, MacArthur had a good appreciation of the importance of land reform. He had decided in his student days that the decline of Rome began when the small family farmers had been destroyed by wealthy, slave-owning landowners (with the assassination of Tiberius Gracchus in 133 B.C.), and he was to go on to Japan to oversee land reform as an integral part of bringing democracy to the defeated enemy (as not much later it would be used to help allies in Taiwan and South Korea). His basic learning experience had been in the Philippines: "If I worked in those sugar fields, I'd probably be a Huk myself," he once declared. In addition, MacArthur had sworn vengeance against those Filipinos—in effect, most of the oligarchy—who had collaborated with the Japanese after they seized the islands in December 1941, declaring he would "run to earth every disloyal Filipino." Here was the possibility of a purge of the landed elite by a man who had some inkling of the problems he was facing and whose prestige in the islands in 1944 was greater than that of any native Filipino.[26]

Why, then, did MacArthur not mandate land reform for the Philippines, the "citadel of democracy in the East," as he called it after his return to Manila in October 1944? He had the support from the president, of the new American high commissioner, Paul McNutt, and especially from the secretary of the interior, Harold Ickes, who wanted "to shoot or hang any Filipino who had anything to do with the puppet government, no matter what reasons they may have had for cooperating."[27] The most obvious answer is that as supreme allied commander in the Pacific his thoughts were focused almost exclusively on concluding the war with Japan. Even a man of MacArthur's prodigious energy could hardly be expected to undertake the reform of the socioeconomic structure of the Philippines at such a moment.

Another reason for his failure to act was that MacArthur had become more involved with Filipinos socially than was common in his set of Americans, and these were the very people who would lose most by reform. In the political struggle that followed the war, MacArthur backed Manuel Roxas, who had collaborated with the Japanese, against Sergio Osmena, who had been in Washington. Such a choice necessarily dictated a go-easy approach to the issue of collaboration and thus to any attack on the class interests of the oligarchs.[28]

A final argument against pushing reform was the threat of communism to the democratic government the Americans were preparing to leave behind. Peasant insurrections had begun as early as 1927, and by the mid-1930s communists had become active in the countryside following the Chinese model of organizing villagers. After 1941, the Filipino Resistance had included a powerful communist partisan group, the Huks, and in the aftermath of the war the communists had called for a purge of the collaborators in Manila and for land reform. MacArthur could reason that with the Americans departing, it was hardly the time to threaten the socioeconomic power structure that was expecting to take over an independent Philippines.

But if not then, when? In the aftermath of independence, American leaders lectured Filipino leaders in no uncertain terms as to the importance of land reform. During a visit of President Quirino in 1949, for example, President Truman, Secretary of State Dean Acheson, and the American ambassador to the Philippines warned that American credits "would be largely wasted" if Quirino did not find some way to get his house "in order."[29]

The year before, the Huk rebellion had broken out in earnest, and the Americans looked around for someone who might break the insurrection militarily and at the same time bring about the reforms necessary to preclude future problems.[30] Here was the commencement of America's two-track approach to communist insurgency, the one social reform, the other military force, which would be used from Asia to Latin America after 1945. Its result was the meteoric career of Ramon Magsaysay, promoted to defense minister in 1950, elected president in 1953—all at repeated urging by Washington.

But Magsaysay was no better able to bring about land reform than his predecessors. While a law mandating a reduction in agrarian rents was passed, the power of the landholders in the legislature, and thereby in the civil bureaucracy, simply short-circuited any serious effort at change. If the Americans, with their power base lying outside the islands, had not been able to bring about land reform, what realistic hope was there that a Filipino leader might succeed given the power of the oligarchy?

And so the problem of maintaining a democratic government in an agrarian order of highly concentrated land ownership persisted. The population continued to expand at a rate of some 2.5 percent annually; unclaimed land ceased to exist or seemed uninhabitable as in the case of Mindinao, where the Muslim population took up arms against the encroachments of Christian settlers; and the misery of the majority of the population grew. By

1976, the American government could publish an account of land reform efforts in this century showing no lasting accomplishments for any of them. Correspondingly, private armies under the control of the oligarchs prolifer- ated as a way to keep the rebellious peasantry in line.[31]

It is for this reason that the period of martial law declared by Ferdinand Marcos in September 1972 was at least initially so pregnant with possibili- ties. In short order, the dictator changed the economic orientation of the country from import-substitution industrialization to export-led growth. He ordered an end of private armies and built up the national military. And he decreed the most impressive land reform program in Filipino history, perhaps motivated in part by a desire to help the poor, but especially by an understanding that if he destroyed the power base of the oligarchy his own rule would be less contested. Had these reforms been even partially suc- cessful, they would have remade the socioeconomic landscape of the coun- try and in this respect at least created the possibility for a more effective democracy.[32]

The sorry story of the Marcos years needs no retelling here. In short order, his reforms failed, of course, but given the logic of Filipino history, one can appreciate the argument that an iron fist was called for. It is no discredit to the democratic reputation of Benigno Aquino to recall that in 1972, Aquino had said that the models of government he would follow if he came to power were those of South Korea and Singapore, where the state dominated society.[33] Indeed, Marcos's own dictatorship was sapped by the weak institutional structures he sought to work through; his reliance on cronyism mimicked rather than replaced the democracy he had sabo- taged. But despite his tale of greed and incompetence, Marcos was on the mark when he declared in 1971—in a book he ironically titled *Today's Revolution: Democracy*—that the "oligarchic elite manipulate and intimi- date the political authority . . . [through a] populist, personalist, and indi- vidualist kind of politics . . . [such that] corruption at the top is matched by social corruption below."[34]

It is for much this reason that many observers were disappointed by the Corazon Aquino government, in power from early 1986 to early 1992. By failing to order a land reform by decree as she had the power to do for over a year after taking the presidency, Aquino neglected to perform the sin- gle act that would most have aided the consolidation of democracy and "People's Power" in her country. Not surprisingly, analysis of the 1987–8 elections shows the continued grip of the oligarchic families on political life in the islands.[35] To be sure, the variety of groups mobilized in opposi- tion to the Marcos dictatorship may mean the beginning of a new day for Filipino democracy. Business, labor, students, and the Church have all dis- played a new awareness of the issues involved and a sense of their corpo- rate power. But these forces lack maturity. And both a communist insurgency and a mutinous military continue to endanger democracy, each blow they deliver further weakening democracy's chances. The future is impossible to predict. The political values and institutions of democracy left from the American days are doubtless precious assets in the struggle to preserve freedom in the Philippines. And the United States may continue to contribute to democracy in that country, whether by foreign aid packages or by the timely intervention of American forces. But the menace of antidemocratic forces, fed by the socioeconomic structures the Americans did nothing to correct, and in many ways modernized, remains very real as well.[36]

CHAPTER THREE

Wilson and Democracy in Latin America

> "When I go back to England I shall be asked to explain your Mexican policy. Can you tell me what it is?"
>
> "I am going to teach the South American republics to elect good men!"
>
> —President Wilson replying to an emissary of British Foreign Secretary Sir Edward Grey (who added on his return, "If some of the veteran diplomats could have heard us, they would have fallen in a faint.")

> "Suppose you have to intervene, what then?"
>
> "Make them vote and live by their decisions."
>
> "But suppose they will not so live?"
>
> "We'll go in again and make them vote again."
>
> "And keep this up for 200 years?"
>
> "Yes. The United States will be here 200 years and it can continue to shoot men for that little space until they learn to vote and rule themselves."
>
> —Exchange on Latin America between Grey and Wilson's ambassador to Great Britain, Walter Hines Page

THE ISSUE of how important it is for the United States to promote democracy abroad has been one of the major questions of twentieth century American foreign policy. From debates over Cuba and the Philippines in the late nineteenth century through the debates over the democratization of Eastern Europe and the former Soviet Union one hundred years later, Americans have argued the relevance to their own national interest of encouraging democracy for others, and the proper means for doing so where it has seemed appropriate. For this ongoing discussion, no period is more important to investigate than the presidency of Woodrow Wilson (1913–21), for it was his administration that first articulated a comprehensive agenda for American liberal democratic internationalism and that declared the promotion of constitutional democracy the world around to be the guiding principle of United States foreign policy—and this in areas as distinct as Latin America, the Philippines, and Central Europe. Of course other administrations, Republican as well as Democratic, both before and after

Wilson's tenure, have also expressed their dedication to the idea of further-ing democracy abroad. But none has more unreservedly dedicated itself to this mission, in deed as well as in word, than that of Woodrow Wilson.

The basis of Wilson's faith was a deep-set belief in the virtue and the efficacy of liberal constitutionalism for the promotion of justice, freedom, and political stability in the twentieth century. In most respects, Wilson was a traditional liberal democrat; his beliefs emphasized the need for a sense of public duty in the individual citizen and the fundamental impor-tance of institutions based on civil liberties and free elections to return able representatives to a government whose powers were constitutionally lim-ited. While no radical egalitarian, Wilson did become part of the Progres-sive movement and pressed particularly hard for the regulation of large concentrations of wealth held by corporate power and for the creation of more professional political structures, from the party system (where he de-nounced the bosses and their machines) to the civil service. He understood that as societies change so too must institutions, and he put his trust in constitutionalism, with its abiding dedication to a political system based on the rule of law, as the only proper way for reform to occur.[1]

While Wilson is properly called a liberal democrat, it is critical to see how he was also a "radical" and a "conservative" in terms of his beliefs and the temper of his times—especially when his ideas came to be formulated into a foreign policy. By virtue of his opposition to arbitrary, authoritarian governments as well as to large accumulations of private economic power, Wilson was something of a radical in world affairs, a man able to have sympathy for both the Mexican and Russian revolutions. In this respect, Wilson's commitment to democracy made him decidedly more radical abroad than he was at home. Yet by virtue of his belief in the need for a settled system of constitutional rule, Wilson's views appealed to conserva-tives, with their view that only institutions based on the rule of law can control the despotic use of power. In this latter respect, Wilson shared the British eighteenth century thinker Edmund Burke's distrust of the French Revolution. The strength of a perspective such as Wilson's was that it al-lowed him at one and the same time to support popular demands for liberty yet to insist on the need for ordered government. The weakness of such a perspective what is that it provided no sure guide for action as to when to salute populist uprisings, when to sound an alarm at their excesses.

Wilson's radical, populist spirit was evident in the way he championed the Mexican Revolution in 1914, declaring "my passion is for the sub-merged 85 per cent of the people of that Republic who are now struggling toward liberty":

> I challenge you to cite me an instance in all the history of the world where liberty was handed down from above. Liberty always is attained by the forces working below, underneath, by the great movement of the people. . . . It is a curious thing

that every demand for the establishment of order in Mexico takes into consideration not order for the benefit of the people of Mexico, the great mass of the population, but order for the benefit of the old-time regime, for the aristocrats, for the vested interests, for the men who are responsible for this very condition of disorder. No one asks for order because order will help the masses of the people to get a portion of their rights and their land; but all demand it so that the great owners of property, the overlords, the hidalgos, the men who have exploited that rich country for their own selfish purposes, shall be able to continue their processes undisturbed by the protests of the people from whom their wealth and power have been obtained. . . . They want order—the old order; but I say to you that the old order is dead.[2]

Moreover, Wilson saw a direct connection between his struggle against corporate interest in the United States and uprisings such as those in Mexico: "We have seen the hand of material interest sometimes about to close upon our dearest rights and possessions. We have seen material interests threaten constitutional freedom in the United States. Therefore, we will now know how to sympathize with those in the rest of America who have to contend with such powers, not only within their borders but from outside their borders also."[3]

Yet just as he could celebrate revolutionary change, so could Wilson celebrate law and order. He believed in the importance of international agreements and law as analogous to constitutionalism and thus as the foundation of collective cooperation to promote peace in world affairs; and he held that settled democratic governments were everywhere the best guarantee of domestic stability and the surest participants in organizations of international concord. Accordingly, through his support for the Pan-American League and the League of Nations, just as in his insistence on constitutional government in Latin America and self-determination in Eastern Europe, Wilson sought to promote the expansion of democracy and the rule of law worldwide. He maintained that America could contribute significantly to these developments and that American interests would be mightily served in the process.

Wilson's efforts "to make the world safe for democracy," acting mainly through international agreements and organizations, largely concerned Europe and occurred after 1917. That policy, its fate, and its message for our day is the subject of the next chapter of this book. The focus in this chapter is on Wilson's attempts to foster constitutionalism directly, through imperialist interventions that began shortly after he took office in 1913. They largely concerned Central America, Mexico, and the island of Hispaniola (composed of Haiti and the Dominican Republic) and have relevance for later generations.

Wilson's ideas about sponsoring the growth of constitutional government abroad long predated his search for public office. In essays written for

The *Atlantic Monthly* in 1901 and 1902, when he was president of Princeton University, Wilson put to himself "the intensely practical question" of the meaning of self-government. Wilson recognized clearly the uniqueness of the American democratic experience, but he insisted as well on the ability of others to learn the virtues of democratic government, and on the duty of America to engage in such instruction.

Wilson had welcomed America's entry into world politics in 1898, concluding that its domination of Central America and the Caribbean, and its presence in the Far East constituted a rightful coming-of-age for the country. While aware of the economic and strategic significance of the victory over Spain, Wilson's main focus was on the Philippines, seeing it as a training ground for Americans in moral development. In words that appear cribbed from Rudyard Kipling, Wilson announced:

> We must govern as those who learn: and they must obey as those who are in tutelage. They are children and we are men in these deep matters of government and justice. . . . But though children must be foolish, impulsive, head-strong, unreasonable, men may be arbitrary, self-opinionated, impervious, impossible, as the English were in their Oriental colonies until they learned. . . . It is plain we shall have a great deal to learn; it is to be hoped we shall learn it fast.

Whatever America's gains, the Filipinos too would benefit:

> We might not have seen our duty, had the Philippines not fallen to us by the willful fortune of war; but it would have been our duty to play the part we now see ourselves obliged to play. The East is to be opened and transformed, whether we will or no; the standards of the West are to be imposed upon it. . . . It is our peculiar duty, as it is also England's, to moderate the process in the interests of liberty; to impart to the peoples thus driven out upon the road of change, so far as we have opportunity or can make it, our own principles of self-help; teach them order and self-control in the midst of change, impart to them, if it be possible by contact and sympathy, and example, the drill and habit of law and obedience which we long ago got out of the strenuous processes of English history. . . . In China, of course, our part will be indirect; but in the Philippines it will be direct; and there in particular must the moral of our policy be set up and vindicated.[4]

Should it seem presumptuous that the United States felt itself able to give lessons to others, Wilson could rejoin that America itself had learned from a foreign power the virtue of its ways. On this basis, Wilson criticized those Americans who supported Emilio Aguinaldo's guerrilla struggle against American rule in the Philippines: "Liberty is not itself government. In the wrong hands—in hands unpracticed, undisciplined—it is incompatible with government."

> It were easy enough to give [the Philippines] independence, if by independence you mean only disconnection with any government outside the islands, the inde-

pendence of a rudderless boat adrift. But self-government? How is that "given"? Can it be given? Is it not gained, earned, graduated into from the hard school of life. . . . No people can form a community or be wisely subjected to common forms of government who are as diverse and as heterogeneous as the people of the Philippine Islands. They are in no wise knit together. They are of many races, of many stages of development, economically, socially, politically disintegrate, without community of feeling because without community of life, contrasted alike in experience and in habit, having nothing in common except that they have lived for hundreds of years together under a government which held them always where they were when it first arrested their development.[5]

In short, well before he came to power, Wilson was of the considered opinion that with time, firmness of purpose, and a steady hand, the United States could successfully promote the development of constitutional democracy abroad. That such a mission be carried forth would be in the interest of the United States as well as those "still in the childhood of their political growth."

As president, Wilson broke with Republican policy toward the Philippines by firmly committing the United States to its eventual independence. He appointed a liberal governor general to the islands, who rapidly carried out the Filipinization of the civil service. In 1916, Wilson signed into law the Jones Act, which provided for a reorganization of Filipino politics to the end of securing its internal self-government as a major step on its path to independence (as noted in the preceding chapter).

With respect to Latin America, the president's initiatives were equally bold, for within days of taking office he announced a radical new policy not to recognize those governments in the region that came to power by other than constitutional means. In short order, his nonrecognition doctrine was invoked with regard to Mexico. Not long thereafter, Wilson intervened forcibly in the Dominican Republic and Haiti and then in the several republics of Central America.

The vigor of Wilson's commitment to democracy abroad does not mean that he saw no other American interests at stake in Latin America or that his policy had no precedent in earlier administrations. In the case of Central America and the Caribbean, for example, Wilson understood clearly the strategic importance of the Panama Canal to the United States. And to gain his ends, he proved quite willing to use force and financial leverage, instruments of policy inherited from his Republican predecessors William McKinley (1897–1901), Theodore Roosevelt (1901–9) and William Howard Taft (1909–13). Moreover, his Republican predecessors had also made efforts to foster constitutional stability in Latin America, first in Cuba, then in Panama, finally in Nicaragua—leading to the sponsoring of the Central American Conference of 1907 and to the conclusion of a series of treaties whose intention was to provide an international mechanism for the peaceful resolution of disputes among countries in the region. Nevertheless, the presidency of Woodrow Wilson meant the triumph of a policy of principle over one of material or strategic consideration to a degree unparalleled in American history. Wilson would argue, of course, that a policy of principle was in the interest of national security. But his tendency was to appear disinterested in what America might gain from the spread of democracy in the hemisphere, to stress America's moral duty to promote, so far as it might, the growth of constitutional democracy worldwide—"to teach the South Americans to elect good men."[6]

THE PURSUIT OF DEMOCRACY IN LATIN AMERICA

Since 1823 and the announcement of the Monroe Doctrine, the United States had made it clear it would not tolerate a great-power sphere of influence in Latin America to rival its own there. The independence of this region from Spain (and later Portugal) was in the interest of American national security, and Washington committed itself to seeing that this situation remained undisturbed. To some extent, American thinking was based on commercial considerations. But Washington's primary concerns were geostrategic and related to national security. Should a hostile foreign power gain a foothold in this region, the defense offered by the Atlantic Ocean would be compromised. Not only would the southern United States be exposed to embargo or attack, but American control over an isthmus canal linking the East and West coasts of the United States might also be threatened. In a word, the Monroe Doctrine not only was a guarantee to Latin America that no European power would again subjugate the continent, but it was an equally clear statement that Washington regarded the region as its own sphere of influence, where American security concerns were to be respected by local parties.

Discussion of a canal had been growing since 1879, when Ferdinand de Lesseps, whose firm had constructed the Suez Canal (which opened in 1869), expressed an interest in duplicating his achievement across the isthmus of Panama. By the time of the Spanish-American War in 1898, it was clear to all that such a waterway could serve a vital military as well as commercial function, while the aftermath of that war gave the United States Puerto Rico and a protectorate over Cuba, whetting the appetite for a canal even more. In 1903 President Roosevelt engineered the separation of Panama from Colombia by sponsoring an uprising. In 1904 construction began. The canal opened in August 1914.

The principal reason to fear the expansion of European influence in proximity to the canal came from the long history of civil unrest in the region and the opportunity this offered to adventuresome outsiders to expand their influence. Ever since independence from Spain in the 1820s, Central America and the Dominican Republic had experienced domestic turmoil, as had Haiti, which had gained its independence from France in 1804. Stable governing institutions had not emerged from three hundred years of Spanish and French control. Instead, warring factions based more on wealth, territory, and military leaders (*caudillos*) than on ideology or class interest typically confronted one another in a seemingly endless cycle of conflict. In such circumstances, rival factions sometimes had an interest in appealing to foreign powers for help. The Dominican Republic, for example, had requested annexation successively from several powers in order to save itself from Haitian invasions in the mid nineteenth century. But in the decade before World War I, it was especially the Germans whom the Americans distrusted. First in Venezuela, later with respect to Nicaragua, Haiti, and the Dominican Republic, and finally—and most pointedly once war began—in relations with Mexico, Berlin made a bid for influence.[7]

By the turn of the century, the expansion of commercial agriculture and the extension of loans from European bankers opened the door to greater European involvement in Latin America. As in other parts of the world at the time, many Latin governments defaulted on their debts. The question was whether the Europeans would deal with them as they had dealt with the Egyptians, the Tunisians, the Ottomans, and the Chinese: threatening their sovereignty by taking over their finances or by annexing them outright.[8]

The issue became especially salient in 1902, when Venezuela defaulted on a foreign debt, which the British and German governments decided forcibly to collect. British and German gunboats blockaded and bombarded Venezuelan ports, provoking an urgent American effort to move the parties to arbitration. Although Washington was successful in this instance, President Roosevelt decided to announce a general policy for dealing with such matters when, in 1904, it became apparent that the Dominican Republic was in default and that European creditors would demand repayment.

The policy, known as the Roosevelt Corollary to the Monroe Doctrine, established that, with the prior agreement of the country concerned, American officials would take over the customs receipts of governments at risk to see that creditors were repaid. Since customs duties comprised 90 percent of the national budgets of most of the governments in question, the power wielded by American customs receivers was substantial, including American control of the size of the national budget, the rate of taxation—indeed, even access to the funds collected.

Washington expected that by administering the customs houses and establishing a sound financial system for these countries, it would contribute to their political stability as well as to their ability to resist European interventions. When the Taft administration added what was called "dollar diplomacy" to Roosevelt's initiative—by which it meant that American trade, investments, and loans should be seen as instruments contributing to stability—it was apparent that the United States had selected economic instruments as the primary avenue for the exercise of its influence.

Diplomatic initiatives complemented the exercise of economic power. As the Venezuelan Boundary Dispute of 1895–7 revealed (pitting Venezuela against Great Britain with respect to the former's border with British Guiana), or as the Central American Peace Conference and ensuing treaty of 1907 demonstrated, Washington hoped to manage conflicts through international agreement. Alternatively, the United States would wield Roosevelt's Big Stick: most notably in the use of force against Colombia in 1903, in the occupation of Cuba from 1906 to 1909, and in the dispatch of marines to Nicaragua in 1909.

Upon becoming president in 1913, Wilson thus found three policy instruments at his disposal for use in Latin America left by his Republican predecessors. In order of relative importance they were limited military occupation and control of customs houses; economic influence; and international agreements. The Democrats had long denounced Republican reliance on force in world affairs, and Wilson named as his first secretary of state William Jennings Bryan, a foremost pacifist. The new president also quickly made it clear that he intended to repudiate the practices of dollar diplomacy, which he claimed unacceptably compromised the sovereignty of governments. His most notable action in this respect was to force American banks to withdraw from the six-power consortium loaning funds to China; subsequently he refused to support American banks extending low-interest loans to Latin America in order to reduce European financial influence there.[9] It would therefore appear that Wilson intended to rely principally on the use of international agreements to secure American interests in the region.

In short order, Wilson reversed himself. He came to use American economic power as actively as the Republicans had, and he soon proved himself a determined practitioner of armed intervention in the region. Nevertheless, the focus of Wilson's policy was on changing the internal structure of the states in Central America and the Caribbean, in the expectation that this would provide the enduring political stability the United States needed of them. He would complement this policy by efforts to create a firmer basis for international law in the hemisphere. Here was the distinctive mark of much of what later would be called Wilsonianism.

As a demonstration of his good will, Wilson lobbied the Congress shortly after he took office against discriminating in favor of American vessels with respect to Panama Canal duties. He also indemnified Colombia for the loss of Panama and expressed an apology for American conduct in the matter (over Roosevelt's vociferous objections). In his dispute with Mexico in 1914, he accepted Argentine, Brazilian, and Chilean mediation (the ABC powers); and in 1915–6, he promoted the notion of a Pan-American Pact (a dress rehearsal for his later proposal for the League of Nations). Moreover, in virtually every initiative he undertook in foreign affairs, Wilson first formally justified himself by reference to international law. Such fastidiousness especially bothered imperialists of the Roosevelt school, who felt Wilson should show more backbone and give more red-blooded reasons for his actions. To others, such legalism appeared labored or hypocritical, whether as a justification for the occupation of Veracruz in 1914 or for the declaration of war against Germany in 1917.

But the most radical innovation in American policy in Wilson's hands concerned his determination that the internal political structures of Latin American countries needed to be reformed if a lasting solution to regional instability damaging to American security was to be found. Within days of Wilson's coming to power, Mexico and the Dominican Republic were to present him with the opportunity to define his views in terms of concrete policy. In both countries there were crises in government; political leaders looked to Washington to see how the new administration would react.

Wilson moved swiftly. Whereas previously the United States had recognized whatever government was effectively in control of a territory, Wilson announced a radically new policy of "nonrecognition" of regimes that had come to power by nonconstitutional means. Prior to Wilson, the United States—like the other world powers—acted in accordance with Secretary of State James Buchanan's words in 1848: "We do not go behind the existing Government to involve ourselves in the question of legitimacy. It is sufficient for us to know that a government exists, capable of maintaining itself; and then its recognition on our part inevitably follows."[10] Yet scarcely a week into his administration, Wilson issued what he rightly considered a landmark statement on relations with Latin America:

> We hold . . . that just government rests always upon the consent of the governed, and that there can be no freedom without order based upon law and upon the public conscience and approval. We shall look to make these principles the basis of mutual intercourse, respect, and helpfulness between our sister republics and ourselves. We shall lend our influence of every kind to the realization of these principles in fact and practice, knowing that disorder, personal intrigue and defiance of constitutional rights weaken and discredit government. . . . We can have no sympathy with those who seek to seize the power of government to advance their own personal interests or ambition. We are the friends of peace, but we know that there can be no lasting or stable peace in such circumstances. As friends, therefore, we shall prefer those who act in the interests of peace and

honor, who protect private rights and respect the restraints of constitutional provisions. Mutual respect seems to us the indispensable foundation of friendship between states, as between individuals.[11]

Whatever the possible ambiguities of this statement, events in Mexico were quickly to clarify Wilson's thinking.

Wilson and Mexico

In 1910, Mexico was swept by a revolution against the autocratic rule of Porfirio Diaz, who had monopolized power (except for a brief interlude in 1884) since seizing it in 1877. By May 1911 Diaz had resigned, and Francisco Madero, a democratic reformer much of the stripe Wilson wanted to encourage, was installed as president. Though a constitutional order was set in place, serious differences remained to plague the revolutionary forces. Finally, in February 1913, the forces of counterrevolution triumphed when General Victoriano Huerta murdered Madero and seized power. Ten days later, Wilson became president.

As the State Department informed Wilson, standard American procedure would be to recognize the Huerta government forthwith, for it seemed in effective control of the country. This policy was also advised by the American ambassador to Mexico (who had apparently conspired with Huerta in Madero's undoing) and by a number of American business leaders with large investments in Mexico, who looked upon Huerta as insuring a return to the days of Diaz, when their interests had prospered. The British and most other powers extended recognition to the new government at the end of March 1913.[12]

But Wilson would have none of it. By flouting any respect for constitutional rule, Huerta was setting a precedent for Mexico that Wilson believed could only perpetuate instability there, to the detriment of American interests, not to speak of the well-being of the Mexican people. As Wilson put it in a letter dated November 2, 1913: "I lie awake at night praying that the most terrible [outcome] may be averted. No man can tell what will happen while we deal with a desperate brute like that traitor, Huerta. God save us from the worst!" Three weeks later, Wilson sent a circular note to the powers declaring:

> Usurpations like that of General Huerta menace the peace and development of America as nothing else could. They not only render the development of ordered self-government impossible; they also tend to set law entirely aside, to put the lives and fortunes of citizens and foreigners alike in constant jeopardy. . . . It is the purpose of the United States, therefore, to discredit and defeat such usurpations whenever they occur. . . . Its fixed resolve is that no such interruptions of

civil order shall be tolerated so far as it is concerned. Each conspicuous instance in which usurpations of this kind are prevented will render their recurrence less likely, and in the end a state of affairs will be secured in Mexico and elsewhere upon this continent which will assure the peace of America and the untrammeled development of its economic and social relations with the rest of the world.[13]

Accordingly, the United States began to use every diplomatic means available to evict Huerta from power. At first Wilson offered to let the Mexican leader stand for office, should he agree to adopt a democratic constitution. But after Huerta's refusal, Wilson rescinded his offer and increased the pressure. Over a six-month period beginning in November 1913, Wilson secured British agreement not to aid the Mexican dictator with loans or munitions; sent American arms to Huerta's opponents, the Constitutionalists; and ordered the occupation the key port of Veracruz, thus denying Huerta important revenues. By August 1914, Huerta had fallen.

Given the power of domestic Mexican forces mobilized against Huerta, it is doubtful that Wilson's actions made more than a marginal difference to the dictator's ultimate downfall. And the Constitution of 1917, which finally ended the revolutionary period in Mexico and provided the country with remarkable political stability after 1920, was a wholly Mexican document. Nevertheless, from Wilson's point of view his policy had been vindicated: the United States stood for constitutional government in Latin America and would act with resolve to see it strengthened there. As he put it in an interview published in the *Saturday Evening Post* in May 1914, "They say the Mexicans are not fitted for self-government; and to this I reply that, when properly directed, there is no people not fitted for self-government."[14]

What Wilson also discovered, however, was the depth of Mexican nationalism, whose force was evident in the reaction to the American occupation of Veracruz in 1914 and again in response to the Punitive Expedition Wilson launched in the spring of 1916 against Pancho Villa in northern Mexico. Nor did lessons for Washington end here, for by Article 27 paragraph 4 of the Constitution of 1917, the Mexican government claimed national ownership of subsoil rights, which directly threatened American oil companies doing business there. In 1919, President Venustiano Carranza criticized the Monroe Doctrine as permitting interference in the internal affairs of sovereign states and reiterated Mexico's determination to prevent foreigners from gaining a preeminent role in its economy. Through the rest of Wilson's term in office, the oil companies and Mexico struggled for control, with the president refusing to intervene militarily and generally siding with the right of the Mexicans against American oil interests. (It was not until 1938 that the matter was finally resolved with the nationalization of all hydrocarbons by the government of Lazaro Cardenas.) Thus, in addition to the difficulties for his policy created by the Republicans, American oil companies, and the American Catholic Church, Wilson experienced the power of a populist revolution. The result—especially of dealings with the nationalist Carranza government after mid-1916—presumably tempered his later reaction toward the Russian revolutionaries who came to power amidst conditions of civil war in November 1917. Indeed, it was a learning experience for many Americans thereafter (and for none more than Franklin Delano Roosevelt, who as assistant secretary of the Navy initially supported Wilson's policies) that there were clear limits as to what kinds of domestic reforms Americans could introduce abroad through intervention.

Wilson and the Dominican Republic

From the point of view of this book, a more interesting test than provided by Mexico for Wilson's belief that the United States could promote domestic political change abroad came in the Dominican Republic. There occupation by American forces from 1916 until 1924 gave Washington direct control over the effort to promote constitutional rule for foreign peoples. Here was an example, if ever there was one, of Pascal's statement "Who would be an angel becomes a beast" (*Qui veut faire l'ange, fait la bete*), for a compelling case can be made that American ineptitude in realizing its ambitions left both the Dominican Republic and the reputation of the United States in Latin America worse off than had the occupation never been undertaken.

To be sure, the undertaking was a difficult affair, for the Dominican Republic did not enjoy virtually any of the preconditions for democratic government. Dominicans had seldom enjoyed stable (much less constitutional) rule, and the situation had grown unruly again late in 1911, when the Dominican president was assassinated. His replacement proved unable to restore order, and in the fall of 1912, the Taft administration obliged the country to accept the local archbishop as president in charge of a nonpartisan government. Within weeks of Wilson's inauguration, sickness forced the archbishop's resignation, and the Dominican congress named General Jose Bordas Valdes to a one-year term as president.[15]

Presumably, Washington would not have interfered in Dominican affairs had a constitutional process short of making the country a democracy confirmed the new regime. However, not surprisingly given the country's history, Bordas soon turned his office to his own account and gave clear signs that he meant to hold on past his one-year mandate. By September, civil war had broken out anew. In the name of constitutional order, Washington backed Bordas; but it also agreed to supervise elections in December 1913 for municipal councils and a constitutional convention. To no avail: no one showed much interest in playing by impartial rules, and in any case the United States itself seemed to have so little understanding of what it was doing (backing Bordas when his unconstitutional actions contributed directly to the unrest).

Free elections were finally conducted in October 1914 (some eighty thousand voted in a land of some 850,000 inhabitants), making General Juan Isidro Jimenez president. Washington expressed its ever more firm resolve to stand by the duly constituted authority. Ironically, however, the more the United States tried to help Jimenez—as by expanding the control of American officials into all aspects of the Dominican government's economic bureaucracies—the more nationalist sentiment rallied against him. Ultimately, revolt broke out afresh, Jimenez resigned, and no government would accept the terms of control the United States insisted upon. In November 1916, after its marines had occupied the capital Santo Domingo for six months, Washington installed its own military government to rule the country. American rule would last eight years.

The United States set to work in two primary domains to improve prospects for stable government in the Dominican Republic: it sought to modernize the agricultural system, and to reorganize government bureaucracies. To promote a more dynamic economy, the Americans sponsored the creation of a modern public transportation and communication system. They mandated the surveying of land and the registration of titles (a process that the Dominicans had begun in 1910) in the hope of promoting family farms and plantation agriculture.[16]

To modernize the operations of government, the Americans saw to the reorganization of the judiciary and the treasury, and to the creation of an agricultural service. But the most decisive American innovation came in the creation of a national constabulary, a National Guard. By disarming the caudillos and centralizing force within a newly constituted, nonpartisan group responsible to the duly elected civilian authorities, the Americans convinced themselves they were taking a major step toward insuring political stability.[17]

In 1922, their economic and bureaucratic reforms moving ahead, the Americans saw to the creation of a provisional government, which gradually assumed control of the country. After a constitutional convention and new elections, in July 1924, the United States withdrew from the Dominican Republic.

If the United States had been marginally successful in promoting constitutional rule in Mexico, it by no means could claim that its full-fledged intervention in Dominican affairs had reached the same goal. Soon after the American departure, civil strife broke out anew and was not ended until 1930, when Rafael Trujillo assumed power as president on the basis of his command of the National Guard. The United States now had the stability it had been seeking for the Dominican Republic—but at the price of a thorough-going dictatorship. Wilson's dreams of a constitutional order had become a nightmare.

The fate of the Dominicans suggests what happened elsewhere. In 1915, the United States initiated a twenty-year military intervention in Haiti. Once again, the economy and government bureaucracies were to some extent modernized and political power became more centralized. But constitutional democracy did not flower. (To the contrary, the violent nature of political life in Haiti offered an especially telling lesson to American observers—especially FDR—that there were clear limits on what America could hope for from the reforms it sponsored.)

Nor did American policy have a positive impact on the emergence of democracy in Nicaragua, where its most decisive legacy was in the Somoza dynasty, born of the American-sponsored National Guard. Nor in Costa Rica and Guatemala, where Wilson also admonished governments as to constitutional procedures, were the the fortunes of democracy noticeably improved.[18]

The Failure to Promote Democracy in Latin America

There is scarcely a writer on Wilson's efforts to promote democracy in Central America and the Caribbean who does not openly mock the effort.[19] The most common criticism is that the president and his various agents never understood the complexities of the situations confronting them in the region, so that their meddling only served in most instances to make a bad situation worse. Except in the case of the occupation of Veracruz in 1914, which hastened the fall of Huerta, there is no reason to think that Wilson contributed whatsoever to the emergence of constitutional democracy in the region.

What makes Wilson's policy even more annoying is that its primary motive seems to have been to reinforce the self-righteous vanity of the president. To be sure, American business saw that there were profits to be had from trade and investment in the area, and writers of a Marxist bent may assume that Wilson's major concern was to promote these interests. But Wilson repeatedly declaimed against the exploitive practices of big business in American domestic affairs as well as abroad. There is little reason to think that concern for American business interests motivated his interventionist policy.[20]

What, then, of the strategic importance of the Panama Canal? While this had been a legitimate concern of Roosevelt and of Taft, the war clouds hanging over Europe by 1914 meant that no foreign power was in a mood to dispute American hegemony in the faraway Caribbean (though subsequent German meddling in Mexico shows that the issue was not com-

pletely remote). In short, like commercial considerations, strategic thinking can explain only a part of Wilson's determination to bring stability
through constitutional regimes to the region.

The most important reason for American intervention, so the president's
critics insist, was psychological, or perhaps one might better say ideological and moral: Wilson felt the United States had a duty to perform. Wilson's claims of being "disinterested," giving "friendly advice," and representing "the interests of civilization" (as he repeatedly put it) seemed little
more than a love of power and self-righteousness decked out in solemn
pronouncements of altruism at just the moment when the conceits of Western civilization were going up in the flames of World War I.

The problem with all this criticism of Wilson, however, is that it fails to
take up the essential dilemma he faced: the serious question of whether the
United States had (and still has) a legitimate interest in the political stability of this part of the world; whether constitutional government might have
provided that stability (and could today); and whether a more judicious use
of American power could have brought about (or might yet do so) the flowering of democratic governments there, with direct benefit for American
security interests. Since his predecessors' policy of pursuing indirect, usually economic, means of influence had not worked, and since military intervention could not alone solve what was essentially a political problem,
Wilson proposed to address the matter of instability and the risk this posed
by going to the heart of the problem, insisting on constitutional governments as a permanent settlement to a recurrent threat to American national
security in this region. Since a number of later administrations (especially
those of Kennedy, Carter, and Reagan) have also sought to reform the domestic structure of states in the area as a way of serving the American
national interest, Wilsonianism—which for Central America and the Caribbean may be defined as making the pursuit of constitutional democracies
the unequivocal focal point of American policy—understandably remains
a vital strain in American foreign policy.

But if the appeal of Wilsonianism is obvious, so too is its problem. In a
word, what is desirable may not always be attainable. American power may
be too limited to promote democratic government for other peoples; or
Washington may not be aware of the best manner to proceed. In either case,
Wilsonianism may be a quixotic ambition, damaging not only to American
interests but also to the people on whom it is practiced.

The Philippines

Consider the case of the Philippines, a country in many respects comparable to Spanish America, and where Wilson himself initiated serious reforms once he took office. As noted in the preceding chapter, the fragility
of American-sponsored democracy in the Philippines stemmed from the

country's agrarian vocation and the ability of its socioeconomic elite to capture the political institutions that the United States began to create there within months of Spain's defeat in 1898. The oligarchy's personal domination of parties, bureaucracies, the executive, and the legislature (the courts seemed somewhat more immune) meant that Filipino political structures never attained a high degree of organizational autonomy, complexity, or adaptability.[21]

Lacking autonomy, Filipino political institutions were dominated by individuals and unable to set agendas of their own or to function for more than the narrow self-interest of those who ran them. Lacking complexity, these institutions were not able to check one another and so give authority to government. Lacking adaptability, they served only the interests of the oligarchy.

By contrast, a modern political system has institutional integrity. Stability is achieved when institutions can resist the usurpation of individuals through the rule of law, which sets official roles and forces change to occur in a regularized manner. However, where social forces are few and highly polarized, as in the Philippines, an autonomous state run by constitutional principles is difficult to conceive and democracy impossible to attain.

Wilson never perceived the difficulty of his ambition to bring constitutional government—not to say democracy—to an agrarian land such as the Philippines. Had he grasped how socioeconomic and political issues interact, he might have understood that only two avenues were open to democratize the country: its industrialization or a land reform creating family farms. In the absence of either, his Filipinization of the country's civil service and the devolution of power to a national legislature were too hastily implemented to serve the long-term interests of democratic stability. In essence, these political reforms benefited too narrow a segment of Filipino society, giving them the means to enhance their control over the country's economic base and its agrarian population. Certainly the problem was not created by Wilson alone, but with the "success" of the political reforms he implemented, it would have been terribly hard for later presidents to change the complexion of what was now coming to be the modern Philippines.

The Philippines offers an excellent comparison with Central America and the Caribbean, for each area had existed for some three centuries under Spanish rule so that an absolutist, centralized, hierarchical political life was the norm, and the influence of the Catholic Church was pervasive. In both areas, too, society was overwhelmingly agrarian and the extended family and elaborate patron-client networks defined political loyalties and rivalries.[22]

But the Philippines differed from Central America and the Caribbean in equally important ways. Such differences made it even more difficult to promote democracy in the latter than in the former. In ethnic terms, the

Philippines lacked the sharp-cut cleavages so typical in Latin America. Slavery had not been practiced in the Philippines, nor had an indigenous population been mercilessly exploited; and in terms of numbers, the Spanish presence had been much weaker than in Latin America. In class terms, the Philippines were again favored. Families of enough wealth existed there that they could exercise power through economic and not simply military instruments. Hence the stakes of power in the Philippines could be something more than military reputation, as they were in Central America and the Caribbean. Moreover, the Filipinos passed directly from Spanish to American rule; even if the oligarchs came to have armed retainers, they lacked the time to turn family feuds into full-scale military contests. In other words, the Filipinos were relatively unfamiliar with the caudillo (and with him the feudal and macho way of life known as *caudillismo*), that curse to political order that existed in Nicaragua and the Dominican Republic. In sum, difficult as the creation of stable democratic government may have been in the Philippines, it was substantially more difficult to contemplate in Central America and the Caribbean.

The Dominican Republic

The case of the Dominican Republic, where Wilson made his most sustained effort to introduce change in Latin America, serves well as an example of how difficult it could be to create a constitutional government. Freed from Spain in 1821, the country was quickly overrun by Haiti and ruled most cruelly until 1844, when at last the Dominicans fought their way free. Fear of a Haitian return put a premium on caudillo politics within the Dominican Republic, which in turn generated recurrent domestic strife quite in evidence when United States marines landed in 1916.

The turmoil prior to the American occupation was discussed earlier in this chapter, but several figures sum up the intractability of the situation in a striking manner. Between 1844 and 1916, the Dominican Republic had nineteen constitutions and twenty-three successful coups; only three of its forty-two presidents actually completed a term in office.[23] Despite the fact that some 70 percent of the government's budget went for military spending, the country was effectively controlled by various regional caudillos. Thus, in the days shortly before the American intervention, the major forces to rival General Bordas were labeled the Horacistas, the Jimenistas, and the Velasquistas—all in honor of the generals whom they followed. In due course, they changed their name, the Horacistas becoming the Partido Nacional, the Jimenistas the Partido Progresista. But the underlying reality of caudillo politics changed not a whit.

Caudillismo was the abiding curse of political life in the Dominican Republic, but ethnic and economic factors worked to aggravate the problem. As in the Philippines, political life in the Dominican Republic families and patron-client networks were the stuff of loyalty and hatred. Yet in the Dominican Republic ethnic cleavages complicated life even more: approximately 25 percent of the country was black, 25 percent white, and 50 percent mulatto—the legacy of slavery ran deep. So too did poverty. Dominican agriculture was too poor to sponsor the emergence of the kind of great families that existed in the Philippines, families who had tools of influence and interests at stake other than their reputation for military prowess.

Given, then, its caudillismo, its ethnic splits, and its relative poverty— all combined with the kinds of inherited values, practices, and institutions that typified the Spanish legacy—there is every reason to think that political conflict there would be more harsh than in the Philippines and democracy correspondingly more difficult to establish. Even Theodore Roosevelt, who had unequivocally championed the American conquest of the Philippines, said of the strategically important Dominican Republic, "I have about the same desire to annex it as a gorged boa constrictor might have to swallow a porcupine wrong-end-to."[24]

Not only were the obstacles to democracy greater in the Dominican Republic than they were in the Philippines, but the extent of American control there was far less and it was handled far less constructively. To be sure, American power permeated the region throughout the twentieth century, dominating it by economic, military, and cultural means. But without direct rule over an extended period of time, there have been equally clear limits on what the United States could accomplish.

The American impact on agriculture in the Dominican Republic is illustrative. As in the Philippines, the Americans believed that a modernized agricultural system would enrich the Dominican Republic and hasten its political development as well. Americans surveyed the land and registered ownership titles. Farm agents spread out over the country demonstrating new farming techniques. The expansion of road and port facilities extended the market throughout the country. Thanks to these improvements and the demand provided by the war in Europe, production grew rapidly until stopped by a sharp recession at the end of 1920.

But the political consequences of this economic modernization were less progressive. As in the Philippines, the Americans thought to help the small Dominican farmer to prosper by the measures they introduced. But those who did best by these developments were the big families and foreign investors. In the stimulus given to sugar production in the eastern part of the country, the changes the United States introduced made the poor even poorer, so stoking the flames of class warfare.[25]

In sum, American-sponsored economic development probably impeded the emergence of democracy in the Dominican Republic by facilitating the concentration of wealth in the country. Wilson may have understood that the agrarian question was the basis of the Mexican Revolution and needed to be settled equitably before stable constitutional government could emerge.[26] But this understanding remained intellectual; it did not translate into agrarian reform programs for Central America or the Caribbean of a sort that could aid the emergence of constitutional, much less democratic, regimes there. Latin America would have to await the Alliance for Progress in the 1960s before it would find Washington actively encouraging land reform abroad (though then too without notable success).

The single most important innovation introduced by the United States into Dominican political life came with the creation of a National Guard. The idea was to centralize legitimate force in the country and so to end caudillismo. The reform was successful; local chiefs were effectively disarmed and a national force was created to ensure public order. In the absence of deeply rooted and broadly based political institutions, however, civilian authorities proved unable to control the constabulary. Shortly after the American departure in 1924, the leader of the guard, Rafael Trujillo, emerged as the most powerful man in the country. By 1930, Trujillo was president—a position he was to retain until his assassination in 1961.

One could presumably argue that such tyrants might play the role absolute monarchs did in seventeenth century Europe, creating centralized bureaucracies, economic prosperity, and national sentiment where previously only the endless contests of feudal lords marked time. But the notion that the Trujillo or Somoza dynasties might require three centuries to fulfill their mission inspired few of their subjects with much hope for the future or much faith in the blessings of American democracy for themselves.

THE DILEMMA OF AMERICAN SECURITY IN LATIN AMERICA

Since at least the time of the Spanish-American War, the United States has had an abiding concern for political stability in Central America and the Caribbean. Economic interests (especially under Taft) and the psychological satisfaction of exercising power in a superior manner (especially under Wilson) were involved, but the strategic security of the United States was the primary reason for Washington's involvement in the region. The alternative—political instability—raised the specter of great-power intervention, which in turn posed real threats to American security from the Panama Canal to the cities on the Gulf of Mexico.

Presidents Theodore Roosevelt and William Taft had attempted to create order largely through designs to promote the economic modernization of the area—Roosevelt by taking over the customs houses, Taft by sponsoring American loans and investments—policies that had the additional attraction of serving the interests of American business and finance. Where these measures did not suffice, the United States used force. Results had not been encouraging. While Wilson continued the practices of his predecessors, he proved more ambitious as well, attempting to address the heart of the problem of political instability by direct efforts at promoting constitutional democracies in the region.

In light of the growing need worldwide in the twentieth century for the establishment of some form of party government to provide the political basis for economic development and for the expression of nationalist sentiment, Wilson's ambition was not vainglorious. Democracy was a modern form of the state, and in the liberal terms Wilson conceived it, democracy was a form of government that might indeed knit together the Western hemisphere.

But in Wilson's hands the application of American power did not achieve the ends for which it was intended. Indeed, by permitting the expansion of plantation agriculture with the concentrations of wealth this entailed, and by promoting national constabularies whose leaders soon seized power, American offered a textbook case of what not to do. Democracy was not born of these ill-informed attempts, which created a deep and long-lasting nationalist animosity toward the United States throughout Latin America.

The obvious lesson is that arrogant moralizing and abstract reasoning may easily run afoul of the constraints imposed by social reality. Wilson might have done well to have listened more carefully to his own words when he noted that democracy took root

> not because of its intrinsic excellence, but because of its suitability to the particular social, economic and political conditions of the people of the country for whose use and administration it had been framed. . . . No other people could expect to succeed by the same means [as the Americans] unless these means equally suited their character and stage of development. Democracy, like every other form of government, depended for its success upon qualities and conditions which it did not itself create, but only obeyed.[27]

What, then, should American policy be if it would promote stability in the area for the sake of national security? If intervention is so often counterproductive, is a hands-off policy clearly a better option? Washington seems damned if it intervenes (witness Wilson's legacy) and damned if it doesn't (witness the problems created for a later generation of American leaders by leaving dictators alone, or indeed by trying to get on with them, as in Nicaragua, Haiti, and Panama). The dilemma of American policy for the last century has been that neither a tactic of nonintervention (best known under FDR's label as the Good Neighbor Policy) nor various forms of intervention have succeeded in achieving the goal of providing political stability to this region.

Is the conclusion that no policy could have prevailed, that by virtue of its ethnic, class, political, and cultural character the region simply could not be democratized, nor in fact any other solution found to provide stability there? Perhaps, yet the evidence accumulated from other case studies in this book suggests that there was at least one promising avenue that was not taken that might have increased the prospects for democratic government in agrarian lands such as the Philippines and the Dominican Republic in the early twentieth century: remaking the socioeconomic power structure through effective land reform to create the local equivalent of families endowed with what Americans called forty acres and a mule. Education, credit, a transportation infrastructure, marketing facilities: all of these were necessary but not sufficient to achieve democracy in a context where the rich few dominated the poor many and neither could tolerate the political supremacy of the other.

To be sure, had such land reform been instituted there is no guarantee that democracy would have been its inevitable outcome. Mobilizing the poor into competitive parties and establishing governments based on the rule of law are obviously more complex developments than changes in the structure of land ownership could have produced. Yet failing such an undertaking or the wholesale industrialization of the area, whose complex division of labor might then have facilitated the emergence of democracy, there was little reason to think that American reforms would prove lasting. These lessons from American efforts to promote democracy in the Dominican Republic after 1916 are analogous to the lessons to be drawn from similar experiences dealing with the defeated Confederacy after 1865 and the Philippines after 1898, as the preceding two chapters described.

In a word, for intervention to produce democracy in agrarian lands long subjected to politically enforced hierarchies of race and class, far more radical measures were called for than the liberal United States was willing to contemplate during Wilson's presidency. While half a century had transpired between the end of the Civil War and Wilson's efforts to remake the Philippines and the Dominican Republic as democracies, not much had happened in the thinking of liberal democrats as to the responsible use of governmental power.

Perhaps the limits of Wilson's initiatives abroad were related to the way the Confederacy had been treated. Wilson was the first southern president since the Civil War. He was born in Virginia in 1856, the son of a Presbyterian minister who thought he had found scriptural authority for slavery. As a result of these roots, neither as president of Princeton nor as president of the United States did Wilson lift a finger to fight Jim Crow.[28] While not opposed to Emancipation, Wilson showed his sympathy for Southern whites confronted with the Fourteenth Amendment. As he put it in 1901:

> An extraordinary and very perilous state of affairs had been created in the South by the sudden and absolute emancipation of the negroes, and it was not strange that the southern legislatures should deem it necessary to take extraordinary

steps to guard against the manifest and pressing dangers which it entailed. Here was a vast "laboring, landless, homeless class," once slaves, now free; unpracticed in liberty, unschooled in self-control; never sobered by the discipline of self-support, never established in any habit of prudence; excited by a freedom they did not understand, exalted by false hopes; bewildered and without leaders, and yet insolent and aggressive; sick of work, covetous of pleasure—a host of dusky children untimely put out of school.[29]

As these lines indicate, Wilson never saw the plight of the black in American society as one to be addressed through socioeconomic change (or through sustained political initiative for that matter). If his horizon at home was so limited, how likely was it that it would be broader in the Dominican Republic or the Philippines? Whatever his sympathies for the down-trodden, his calls on occasion for socioeconomic reform, and his antipathy for authoritarian government, Wilson's essential belief was that the poor were best helped by the tutelage of their "betters"; true liberty required the discipline of order. The result is that toward Latin America, as toward Europe after the war, there is a certain justice to John Maynard Keynes fierce indictment of the president:

> [Wilson] had thought out nothing; when it came to practice, his ideas were nebulous and incomplete. He had no plan, no scheme, no constructive ideas whatever for clothing with the flesh of life the commandments which he had thundered from the White House. He could have preached a sermon on any of them or have addressed a stately prayer to the Almighty for their fulfilment, but he could not frame their concrete application when it came [time to act].[30]

In fairness to Wilson, his problem was more complicated. Wilson was a populist who believed in law and order. While there was an obvious tension in these two loyalties, the advantage of such a viewpoint is that he could sympathize with both the rebel and the guardian of the established order when its institutions were mature enough to be constitutional. On occasion, this perspective served him well, for it allowed him to champion both liberty and order, whose marriage in democratic government has been a supreme accomplishment of the West. Wilson's shortcoming was in his relative neglect of the socioeconomic dimension of democracy. It is true that he was a Progressive in domestic American politics and at time could recognize the need for economic reform abroad. But in practice, his reforms were essentially political not socioeconomic in content. In the context of agrarian societies, such a program for democracy was simply not sufficient to the task.

Since World War I, Washington has come forth with four distinct policies with respect to fostering political stability in Latin America and so ensuring that American security interests would not be threatened. The first has been intervention trusting to the power of essentially political reforms to gain democratic government, which would then provide the stability to guarantee American interests. This was Wilson's policy for Central America and the Caribbean, and it was Jimmy Carter's as well (though he was careful to avoid the use of force) more than half a century later. From this perspective, economic reforms were strictly ancillary to the dynamic of political change.

A second approach has been to come to terms with dictators in the region. Beginning with Wilson's successors Warren Harding (1921–3) and Calvin Coolidge (1923–9), Washington scaled down its interventions and became less single-minded about Wilson's doctrine of nonrecognition of undemocratic regimes. Under Herbert Hoover (1929–33), the United States repudiated the Roosevelt Corollary. With FDR came the Good Neighbor Policy, the essence of which was that the United States could live with authoritarian neighbors in the hemisphere so long as they had no allegiances to powers hostile to the United States in Europe, and provided that good economic relations could be set up. The idea that the United States should undertake prolonged and massive intervention in Latin America for the sake of political reform was frankly seen as quixotic. Under Eisenhower, Johnson, and Nixon, Washington actually went so far as to support authoritarians against constitutional leaders.

But just as Wilson was not able to bring stability to the region through democracy, so Eisenhower and Nixon were unable to bring stability through dictatorship for the simple reason that authoritarian governments were at odds with increasingly widespread demands locally for political participation.

A third approach, seen during the first two years of the Alliance for Progress (1961–3) was a throw-back to Wilsonianism in the sense of trying to promote democracy in Latin America. The Alliance's presuppositions differed critically from those of Wilson, however, and it tried to remake the socioeconomic system through directly empowering the poor. President Kennedy's idea was to steal the thunder of the Cuban Revolution's appeal in the hemisphere, but ultimately the Alliance lost the courage of its convictions as it recognized how stony the soil for democratic government was in the region, and it abandoned its commitment to land reform while agreeing to work with military governments.

A fourth way to address the task of democratization in Latin America appeared in the Reagan years, with a host of proposals to liberalize economic practices there. These reforms would bring about democracy by weakening the state's corporatist influence over business, labor, and the agrarian sector. The effort was Wilsonian in that Reagan thought to protect American security interests by fostering democracy, but it was like the Alliance for Progress in seeing an economic dimension to the political process. Reagan's approach differed greatly from the Kennedy's, however, by looking to reduce rather than to expand the state's involvement in the economy and so reassuring local elites that their privileges would be secure.

The dilemma for United States policy in Latin America is that it has no success story to guide its promotion of stable, pro-American governments there. FDR, Eisenhower, Johnson, and Nixon expressed a willingness to work with whatever regimes emerged so long as they were friendly to American interests. The difficulty with this policy was that it made American interests hostage to cruel and weak authoritarian governments in the region. By contrast, liberal democratic internationalists (in their very different guises from Kennedy and Carter to Reagan, Bush, and Clinton) suspect that only enduring constitutional democracy in the region will finally guarantee the safety of American interests. In their hands, the Wilsonian legacy remains very much alive in the United States as the century comes to its end.

CHAPTER FOUR

Wilson and a World Safe for Democracy

> We are glad . . . to fight thus for the ultimate peace of the world and
> for the liberation of the peoples, the German peoples included;
> for the rights of nations great and small and the privilege of men
> everywhere to choose their way of life and of obedience. The world
> must be made safe for democracy. Its peace must be planted upon
> the tested foundations of political liberty. We have no selfish
> ends to serve. We desire no conquest or domination. We seek no
> indemnities for ourselves, no material compensation for the
> sacrifices we shall freely make. We are but one of the champions
> of the rights of mankind. We shall be satisfied when those rights
> have been made as secure as the faith and freedom of the nations
> can make them.
>
> —Woodrow Wilson requesting that the Congress
> declare war on Germany, April 2, 1917

ALTHOUGH AMERICAN EFFORTS to promote democracy abroad have often
focused on a single country (as in the case of the Philippines or the Dominican Republic discussed in earlier chapters), the presidency of Woodrow
Wilson had far more ambitious objectives. His policy toward Latin America had been regional in scope, but with the entry of the United States into
war against Germany in 1917, his horizon expanded to Europe, and Wilson
stepped forward with specific proposals for a global system of peace and
security.

Wilson's recommendations marked the first time that the United States
had elaborated a framework for world order. It proposed that governments
recognize each others' legitimacy when they were constitutional democracies, and that they should maintain the peace through a system of collective
military security and liberal economic exchange. Envisioned as a comprehensive framework for world order, Wilson's program constituted the
foundation of what afterward could be called American liberal democratic
internationalism or, more simply, Wilsonianism.[1]

Wilson's liberal democratic internationalism was not a radical departure
from traditional American national security policy. Thomas Jefferson had
insisted that the United States could only participate in a world community
dominated by democratic states. With the Monroe Doctrine in 1823, the

United States had declared itself opposed to the reimposition of European rule in the Western Hemisphere and so aligned itself with nationalist forces in Latin America, whose states Washington would recognize as sovereign. With the Open Door Notes of the turn of the century, Washington reaffirmed its commitment (as old as the Revolution) to a nondiscriminatory international trading system, hostile to mercantilism and imperialism alike (a position used again in the 1930s, especially to protest Japanese incursions on Chinese sovereignty). While Wilson's proposals to restructure world politics were far more bold than any American leader had ever before laid out, they were nonetheless quite in line with basic propositions of United States foreign policy set long before his time.

Today we can appreciate more clearly than was possible in 1917–9 the enormous stakes involved by the entry of the United States on the central stage of world history under Wilson's leadership. Nationalism, which had begun to affect world politics in the late eighteenth century with the French Revolution, was now a global force, fueling not only the animosities of World War I but also the breakup of the Russian, Ottoman, and Austro-Hungarian empires thereafter. New states were emerging, struggling to achieve support from their populations through mass based political parties. With the victory of the Russian Revolution in 1917, communism offered itself as an ideology of state building and nationalist consciousness at the very moment Wilson was proposing liberal democracy to the same end. In short order, Mussolini and Hitler would offer yet a third modern alternative with fascism.

Wilson was not fully aware of the magnitude of his undertaking, of course. Like Lincoln during the Civil War, Wilson could only sense that the struggle he was engaged in concerned more than the traditional ends of state policy, and that the character of the peace to be established after the war would be critical to world affairs in a more lasting way than victory in battle often entailed. His reaction to the Bolshevik Revolution was hesitant, and he had left office before fascism took power in Italy. Nonetheless, in his ambitious initiatives of 1917–9, Wilson laid the groundwork for many of the fundamental tenets of American national security policy for the rest of the twentieth century: that nationalism should be respected as one of the most powerful political sentiments of our times; that democracy is the most peace-loving and only legitimate form of modern government, and that the United States has a self-interested as well as a moral obligation to further its prospects abroad; that democracy and capitalism are mutually reinforcing systems of collective action so long as large accumulations of wealth do not control the political process; that in a world destined to be composed of many states, the need for mutual understanding and common purpose calls for a new respect for international law sustained by multilateral institutional arrangements; that a nondiscriminatory world economic system that is antiprotectionist and antimercantilist promotes general prosperity and peace; and that a global system of collective security is necessary to stop aggression.

Then as now, however, two obvious questions arise. The first was whether a world order dominated by democratic states could, in fact, be established. If democracy's prospects for sinking roots abroad were dim, would America not be better advised to follow the practices of traditional statecraft, which dictated working with foreign governments as they were rather than becoming engaged in difficult and protracted struggles to change their domestic character? The second question was whether, once in place, a world community of democratic states would in fact operate any differently than other state systems had in the past. If Christian and Muslim states went to war with their own kind, why not democracies?

The first question asks whether there are boundaries set by culture and history to the expansion of democratic government. Perhaps one could dispense with the requirement that agrarian societies become democratic. Their predisposition to authoritarianism was strong, their ability to disrupt the peace of the world minimal, and it was only at a later stage in their political development that a choice for democracy would be possible. But why assume that other industrial countries must become democratic before the United States could rest easy? If liberal democracy had less than universal appeal, might not the United States be well advised to avoid pushing its ways too hard, both for the sake of peace and for the purpose of safeguarding democratic government where it had naturally developed? The first argument against Wilson's hope to make the world safe for democracy—whether in 1919, 1945, or 1995—is that it misdirects American attention from the essential question with respect to the conduct of states in the international arena—are they hostile to the United States or not?—to questions of their internal order. It incites an antipathy toward nondemocratic governments, which may be ill-advised. It indulges the country in a moralistic and self-righteous missionary crusade, which is a quixotic use of power that can be cruel and self-defeating.

Even should an order of democratic states in fact be created, the second question asks why we should assume it could indeed be organized so as to operate for the sake of the common good. What reason is there to assume some special dispensation for democracy to redeem the world when no other common code, be it monarchical, Christian, or Islamic, had succeeded before? Why should democracies necessarily be more cooperative and peace-loving than empires, for example? May not popular passions be as easily aroused as those of an aristocracy? Will the modern world with its economic and environmental interdependencies not breed as many sources of conflicting interest as at any time in the past, perhaps more? Might not the ensuing struggles between peoples rather than princes be especially cruel?

The questions surrounding Wilsonianism therefore concern not only his administration, but the conduct of much of American foreign policy in this century. The answers to these questions remain as urgent for our times as for the world of 1919.

WILSONIANISM IN THEORY

The essential genius of Wilson's proposals for a new world order after World War I was that it had a vision of the proper ordering of domestic as well as international politics that was well suited to the development of political and economic forces worldwide in the twentieth century. Here was a period in Germany, Russia, and Eastern Europe where social forces were struggling over the modernization of the state, where rival conceptions of national unity were trying to make government responsive through party government to nationalistic appeals for popular sovereignty. In domestic terms, Wilson respected the power of nationalism and favored national self-determination. States were presumed to be legitimate when they were democratically constituted, and it was expected that in most instances ethnic boundaries would make for the frontiers of countries. In the context of the world of 1918, such a proposal was radical; it accepted the dismemberment of empires (those of Austria-Hungary, Russia, and Turkey immediately; those of the Western European powers by implication thereafter), and it worked for the replacement of autocracies with democracies in Germany and the new nation-states to the East.[2]

For international relations, Wilson called for a liberal economic regime and a system of collective security designed to preserve the peace. Again, his initiative was radical for it challenged the competitive mercantilistic practices that dictated much of world commerce with a more open trading system, just as it proposed to replace competitive balance of power thinking politically with what he called "a convenant of cooperative peace."

In short, the foundation of Wilson's order was the democratic nation-state; its superstructure was an international order of economic, military, and moral interdependence. Nationalism wed to democracy; democracies wed in peace, prosperity, and mutual respect embodied in international law and institutions: such was Wilson's essential vision, a form of liberalism he felt to be both necessary and appropriate for his era and essential to guarantee American national security. Each of these interlocking propositions deserves a closer look.

In his views on the proper organization of domestic affairs, Wilson was a man of 1848. That year marked the first flowering of that "springtime of nations" when, following upheavals in Paris, populist uprisings confronted the German and Austro-Hungarian monarchies with demands democracy and national self-determination. Over and again, Wilson insisted that the peace treaties signed in Paris in 1919 had as their "central object . . . to establish the independence and protect the integrity of the weak peoples of the world."[3] Or again, "The heart and center of this treaty is that it sets at liberty people all over Europe and in Asia who had hitherto been enslaved by powers which were not their rightful sovereigns and masters."[4] As he declared in a celebrated address to the American Congress in January 1917:

> No peace can last, or ought to last, which does not recognize and accept the principle that governments derive all their just powers from the consent of the governed, and that no right anywhere exists to hand peoples about from sovereignty to sovereignty as if they were property. I take it for granted . . . that statesmen everywhere are agreed that there should be a united, independent, and autonomous Poland, and that henceforth inviolable security of life, of worship, and of industrial and social development should be guaranteed to all peoples who have lived hitherto under the power of government devoted to a faith and purpose hostile to their own. . . . I would fain believe that I am speaking for the silent mass of mankind everywhere who have as yet had no place or opportunity to speak their real hearts out. . . . no nation should seek to extend its polity over any other nation or people, but every people should be left free to determine its own polity, its own way of development, unhindered, unthreatened, unafraid, the little along with the great and powerful.[5]

As these lines suggest, Wilson was a friend to nationalism everywhere. He endorsed the Balfour Declaration, promising the Jewish people a place in Palestine. He was sympathetic to the needs of the Armenians (and deliberated whether the United States should exercise a mandate over this people). He gave repeated assurances to the Germans that, once their autocratic leaders were deposed, their national integrity would be respected. Czechoslovak patriots quoted Wilson's words of 1898 as their organizing slogan in the United States during World War I: "No lapse of time, no defeat of hopes, seemed sufficient to reconcile the Czechs of Bohemia to incorporation with Austria. Pride of race and the memories of a notable and distinguished history kept them always at odds with the Germans at their gate and the government over their heads."[6] As the president put it in 1919, "self-determination is not a mere phrase. It is an imperative principle of action, which statesmen will henceforth ignore at their peril."[7]

Respect for nationalism was not enough, however. Nations needed to be organized democratically. From Wilson's perspective, a major advantage of democratic government aside from its moral appeal was that it was more stable and less predatory than autocratic government. Democracy was more stable because it provided a formula that could accommodate contending social forces by providing for orderly change under the rule of law; it was thus a form of government appropriate to the increased specialization and interdependence of modern life. Democracy was less predatory because public opinion could supervise official decision-making and prevent the kind of aggressions abroad that served selfish private interests. A constitutionalist for domestic matters, Wilson was a constitutionalist for the world community as well. Because no nondemocratic constitutional government had established the rule of law to the degree of the democracies, democracy's internal procedures for conflict resolution and compromise—for providing unity while respecting diversity—might be transferred to institutions governing world affairs.

Wilson's faith in popular sovereignty made him the enemy of monarchical rule. In the case of Germany, Wilson repeatedly distinguished between the German people and their government. As he put it to the Congress in his request for a declaration of war:

> We have no quarrel with the German people. We have no feeling toward them but one of sympathy and friendship. It was not upon their impulse that their government acted in entering this war. It was not with their previous knowledge or approval. It was a war determined upon as wars used to be determined upon in the old, unhappy days when peoples were nowhere consulted by their rulers and wars were provoked and waged in the interest of dynasties or of little groups of ambitious men who were accustomed to use their fellow men as pawns and tools.[8]

Or again: "German rulers have been able to upset the peace of the world only because the German people were not suffered under their tutelage to share the comradeship of the other peoples of the world either in thought or in purpose. They were allowed to have no opinion of their own which might be set up as a rule of conduct for those who exercised authority over them."[9] Thus, as the war neared its end, Wilson indicated that the German surrender should come from representatives of the people; in other words, that the Kaiser be deposed and the way cleared for democracy before peace could be concluded.

Similarly, Wilson welcomed "the wonderful and heartening things" that transpired in Russia during March, 1917, when the Czar was forced to abdicate to republican forces:

> Russia was known by those who knew it best to have been always in fact democratic at heart, in all the vital habits of her thought, in all the intimate relationships of her people that spoke their natural instinct, their habitual attitude toward life. The autocracy that crowned the summit of her political structure, long as it had stood and terrible as was the reality of its power, was not in fact Russian in origin, character or purpose; and now it has been shaken off and the great, generous Russian people have been added in all their naive majesty and might to the forces that are fighting for freedom in the world, for justice, and for peace.[10]

The marriage of democracy to nationalism was not at all a foregone conclusion in Wilson's thinking. In Eastern Europe, the prospects for democracy varied with the country. As Wilson's experience with Polish nationalists during the war taught him, not all were so favorably disposed as the Czechoslovaks for a postwar consolidation of republican government.[11] Throughout much of Central and Eastern Europe were the old right-wing militaristic "forces of order" embodied in the aristocracies and autocracies that Wilson so much deplored, against whom America had gone to war.[12] The war over, these reactionaries would scheme once again to take power and wage war. And on the left were the new "forces of movement" embodied in the Bolshevik Revolution of November 1917. Here Wilson perceived an energy born of oppressions centuries old, now demanding "world revolution," which threatened to bring struggle and suffering to the peoples of East and Central Europe—and perhaps beyond, into Asia—in the disorder following the destruction of war. Isaiah Bowman, a chief adviser to the president in 1918–9, cites Wilson saying that "the poison of Bolshevism was readily accepted by the world because 'it is a protest against the way the world has worked.' It will be our business at the Peace Conference to fight for a new order, 'agreeably if we can, disagreeably if necessary.'"[13]

In these politically polarized circumstances, Wilson preached the doctrine of the liberal democratic alternative to reaction and to revolution, a third way forward, which called for clear resolve. In some measure, Wilson understood the full scope of his enormous ambition: "The conservatives do not realize what forces are loose in the world at the present time," he observed in January 1919. "Liberalism is the only thing that can save civilization from chaos. . . . Liberalism must be more liberal than ever before, it must even be radical, if civilization is to escape the typhoon."[14]

Liberalism: here was the touchstone on which Wilson based his hopes for a new order of world peace. Following in the footsteps of British and American liberals before him, Wilson viewed himself as a cosmopolitan as well as an American, a man able to understand and respect the interests of others and to look forward to a structure of world order that would permit nations to work together cooperatively in a system where the self-interest of each would be realized in terms of the common interest of all. Nationalism and democracy were not enough. Only international economic and political cooperation could preserve the peace. "Unless all the right-thinking nations of the world are going to concert their purpose and their power, this treaty is not worth the paper it is written on," he warned in 1919, "because it is a treaty where peace rests upon the right of the weak, and only the power of the strong can maintain the right of the weak."[15]

The economic dimension of the new democratic world order would be modeled on the kind of multilateral, nondiscriminatory system the British had promoted since the first half of the nineteenth century—a set of measures known as international economic liberalism. The United States had backed such procedures earlier, most vigorously in international affairs by the Open Door Notes of 1899–1900, when Washington asked that China be permitted to adopt a uniform stand with respect to trade and investment, equal with regard to all with whom it treated. America did not endorse free trade, but it was most decidedly liberal and anti-imperialist in that, as the name Open Door suggested, states would deal with one another economically in uniform terms without special favors (so-called most favored nation treatment, by which all trading partners would be extended the most generous terms provided any of them).

The political significance of this policy was even more important than its economic promise. The Open Door Notes were the functional equivalent of the Monroe Doctrine for the Far East, since Washington sought to preserve the political integrity of China against demands that it be divided into spheres of influence based on European and Japanese economic interest.

Accordingly, in September 1916, speaking of the American business stake in the Panama Canal, the president declared:

> Here is the loom all ready upon which to spread the threads which can be worked into a fabric of friendship and wealth such as we have never known before! The real wealth of foreign relationships, my fellow-citizens, whether they be the relationships of trade or any other kind of intercourse, the real wealth of those relationships is the wealth of mutual confidence and understanding. If we do not understand them and they do not understand us, we can not trade with them, much less be their friends, and it is only by weaving these intimate threads of connection that we shall be able to establish that fundamental thing, that psychological, spiritual nexus which is, after all, the real warp and woof of trade itself. We have got to have the knowledge, we have got to have the cooperation, and then back of all that has got to lie what America has in abundance and only has to realize, that is to say, the self-reliant enterprise.[16]

Given these liberal assumptions, Wilson opposed German mercantilist principles, which implied the necessity of political control over foreign peoples for the advancement of German industry. Speaking before the American Federation of Labor in November 1917, Wilson praised the German success: "The whole world stood at admiration of her wonderful intellectual and material achievements. . . . She had access to all the markets of the world. . . . She had a 'place in the sun.'" But given the structure and attitudes of German business, the president continued, "the authorities of Germany were not satisfied":

> There is no important industry in Germany upon which the Government has not laid its hands, to direct it and, when necessity arose, control it. . . . You will find that they were the same sort of competition that we have tried to prevent by law within our own borders. If they could not sell their goods cheaper than we could

sell ours at a profit to themselves they could get a subsidy from the Government which made it possible to sell them cheaper anyhow, and the conditions of competition were thus controlled in large measure by the German Government itself. But that did not satisfy [them]. All the while there was lying behind its thought in its dreams of the future a political control which would enable it in the long run to dominate the labor and the industry of the world. They were not content with success by superior achievement; they wanted success by authority . . . [thus] the Berlin-Baghdad Railway was constructed. . . . I saw a map in which the whole thing was printed in appropriate black the other day, and the black stretched all the way from Hamburg to Baghdad—the bulk of German power inserted into the heart of the world.[17]

The point is worth emphasizing, for it would reappear in American conduct toward Germany after 1945: German capitalists were to be obliged to see the world from a liberal Open Door perspective, not from a mercantilist point of view, which implied the necessity of political control over foreign peoples for the advancement of German industry.

Wilson was also outspoken in his distrust of unregulated American trusts. Politics, not economics, should command. Sounding every bit the Progressive, Wilson warned: "Men who are behind any interest always unite in organization, and the danger in every country is that these special interests will be the only things organized, and that the common interest will be unorganized against them. The business of government is to organize the common interest against the special interest." The same logic applied abroad. He broke with Taft's dollar diplomacy, forced American banks out of China, and resisted loans to Latin America, which he felt might compromise national sovereignties in the region. Similarly, writing of the Russian Revolution toward the end of his life, Wilson remarked "that great and widespread reaction like that which is now unquestionably manifesting itself against capitalism do not occur without cause or provocation":

... before we commit ourselves irreconcilably to an attitude of hostility to this movement of the time, we ought frankly to put to ourselves the question: Is the capitalistic system unimpeachable? ... Have capitalists generally used their power for the benefit of the countries in which their capital is employed and for the benefit of their fellow men? Is it not, on the contrary, too true that capitalist have often seemed to regard the men whom they used as mere instruments of profit? ... if these offenses against high morality and true citizenship have been frequently observable, are we to say that the blame for the present discontent and turbulence is wholly on the side of those who are in revolt against them?[18]

One body of literature has seen Wilson's primary postwar project as the creation of a liberal international economic order, with the League of Nations serving as its guarantor. By these lights, Wilsonianism is essentially synonymous with "liberal capitalist (not democratic) internationalism," and this material and class interest, not the political rhetoric of democracy, is the heart of his appeal to later American leaders.[19]

The problem with this interpretation of Wilsonianism is that it takes an aspect of Wilson's agenda and mistakes it for his whole program. Certainly Wilson was an international economic liberal; that point is not in doubt. But Wilson's primary concerns were political. Aside from sponsoring democratic national governments, his first priority was the League of Nations, whose basic mandate he saw as providing collective military security; economic issues were secondary in its functioning (and even then included the creation of the International Labor Organization, which might be seen as a constraint on liberal capitalism). Nor did the Peace Conference engage in prolonged deliberations on a new world economic order. Germany was not ushered into a liberal economic order internationally; the closed new states of Eastern Europe were no better suited for such an arrangement. More, the United States was adamant that interallied loans be repaid, putting a serious strain on global finances. In fact, Wilson's shortcoming was that he did not stress enough the economic dimension of his agenda for world order. John Maynard Keynes may have clearly seen at the time the need for an economically integrated Europe in cooperation with the United States, but it was precisely because Wilson did not fully understand what was needed that Keynes became such a harsh critic of the president.[20]

What mattered far more to Wilson, and where his thinking was more original, was in his ambition to build a liberal collective security system centered on Europe after 1918, an idea that was embodied in the League of Nations.[21] As Wilson accurately perceived, the prospects for the survival of the young democracies of Eastern Europe he was working so hard to establish would be greatly enhanced if they could have cooperative relations with a fully democratized Germany and with the more established democracies of Western Europe and the United States in the League. As the president put it early in 1919:

> Do you realize how many new nations are going to be set up in the presence of old and powerful nations in Europe and left there, there, if left by us, without a disinterested friend? Do you believe in the Polish cause as I do? Are you going to set up Poland, immature, inexperienced, as yet unorganized, and leave her with a circle of armies around her? Do you believe in the aspirations of the Czecho-Slovaks and Jugo-slavs as I do? Do you know how many powers would be quick to pounce upon them if there were not guarantees of the world behind their liberty? Have you thought of the sufferings of Armenia? You poured out your money to help succor Armenians after they suffered. Now set up your strength so that they shall never suffer again.[22]

The general premise on which Wilson's argument depended was to be repeated time and again in words similar to those he used in January 1917:

> The question upon which the whole future peace and policy of the world depends
> is this: is the present war a struggle for a just and secure peace, or only for a new
> balance of power? If it be only a struggle for a new balance of power, who will
> guarantee, who can guarantee, the stable equilibrium of the new arrangement?
> Only a tranquil Europe can be a stable Europe. There must be, not a balance of
> power, but a community of power; not organized rivalries, but an organized com-
> mon peace.[23]

Three basic assumptions undergirded Wilson's notion of the League.
First, it was to be composed of democratically constituted states. "A steadfast concert for peace can never be maintained except by a partnership of
democratic nations. No autocratic government could be trusted to keep
faith within it or observe its covenants. It must be a league of honor, a
partnership of opinion. . . . Only free peoples can hold their purpose and
their honor steady to a common end and prefer the interests of mankind to
any narrow interest of their own."[24] Subsequently, the stricture on the need
to be democratic was loosened in favor of admitting states that were simply
"fully self-governing," while the mandate system pledged the League
eventually to welcome other peoples under foreign control to a club of
self-determining countries. Of the thirty states that signed the original instrument creating the League in 1919, fewer than half were democracies.
In 1938, when League membership had increased to fifty-seven states, the
proportion was smaller still.[25]

Wilson's second assumption was that these self-governing peoples
should be capable of disinterested moral judgment and should recognize
that henceforth their individual interest would best be served by pursuing
the common good enshrined in international law and organization. "The
nations of the world have become each other's neighbors," he declared in
May 1916. "It is to their interest that they should understand each other. In
order that they may understand each other, it is imperative that they should
agree to cooperate in a common cause and that they should so act that the
guiding principle of that common cause shall be even-handed and impartial
justice."[26] The Fourteen Points, announced in January 1918, were to be a
statement of general rules as well as specific terms for peace in Europe.
Beyond this, Wilson did not go, assuming that the League should work out
its mechanism of interaction experimentally as it dealt with issues of world
order. His presumption was that once a commitment had been freely undertaken by member states to live internationally under a rule of law, it was up
to the League to prescribe the details of its conduct as it faced the challenges to its mandate.[27]

Wilson's third assumption was that while the world desperately needed to end arms races, the League must recognize there would be occasions on which it might be obliged to use force. "Mere agreements may not make peace secure," he observed in January 1917. "It will be absolutely necessary that a force be created as a guarantor of the permanency of the settlement so much greater than the force of any nation now engaged or any alliance hitherto formed or projected that no nation, no probable combination of nations could face or withstand it. If the peace presently to be made is to endure, it must be a peace made secure by the organized major force of mankind."[28] Later, Wilson was to retreat from such a radical suggestion, with its implication that a supranational government would have at its disposal forces so powerful. The League was not to have an independent military force nor its own financial resources, and its Council had to be unanimous for collective deterrence of aggression to take place. The League was not a world government.[29]

WILSONIANISM IN PRACTICE

Nationalism, democracy, a liberal world economic order, a system of collective security, a moral commitment to leadership in such an arrangement on the part of the United States: this was the Wilsonian project of liberalism for world order after 1918. In the interwar years these ambitions came to naught. No way was found to integrate the Soviet Union, born of that war, into the European balance of power, while the threat of communism domestically put a heavy strain on democratic forces throughout the continent. Except in Czechoslovakia, democracy was unable to find fertile soil in Eastern Europe, where a zone of weak states looked with fear alternatively at Berlin and Moscow. After 1929, a weakly structured system of international trade and finance buckled under the weight of the Depression. After fourteen years of effort, democracy collapsed in Germany in 1933 with the rise of Hitler. Democratic forces in France and Britain lost their self-confidence. The United States refused to join the League of Nations and lapsed again into isolationism.

During the 1920s, a leading explanation of the failure of Wilson's ambitions had to do with the conduct of the president himself. Wilson abandoned his principles, the argument went, and in the process betrayed the hopes of those European democrats who held to them, the Germans most of all. The president then compounded his mistakes in Paris by failing to convince his fellow Americans of the importance of his program. America's subsequent isolationism—the Senate's rejection of the Paris Treaty, the Republican victory in the presidential election of 1920, Washington's inability to stop the economic crisis in Europe thereafter or to counter the rise of fascism—was certainly not the intended consequence of Wilson's policies. Nevertheless, isolationism was the regrettable but not surprising result of a style of leadership that was too abstract and too moralistic to anticipate the difficulties of implementing such a visionary policy. This was the essential charge of influential commentators at the time, such as John Maynard Keynes, Harold Nicolson, and Walter Lippmann, all devoted Wilsonians in 1918, who were sorely disappointed by the peace settlement. Keynes's indictment is the most trenchant and famous ever made of Wilson. Under the pressure of quicker, sharper men in Paris who fought for national interests only (especially French Prime Minister Georges Clemenceau), Wilson lost his balance, so Keynes maintained, and permitted a "Carthaginian Peace: . . . if ever the action of a single individual matters, the collapse of the President has been one of the decisive moral events of history."[30]

The most obvious way to criticize Wilson in terms of his own principles was to cite the conditions imposed on the defeated Germans at Versailles. In 1917 Wilson had made a critical distinction between the German militaristic autocracy and the German people. But the peace settlement forced the new republican government of Germany to sign a "war guilt clause" assuming Germany's sole moral responsibility for the war, saddled that country with reparations on a scale that appeared ruinous, and deprived it of territories while forbidding its unification with Austria in a way that goaded to anger German nationalism. What had happened to Wilson's call in 1917 for a "peace without victory?"

> Victory would mean peace forced upon the loser, a victor's terms imposed upon the vanquished. It would be accepted in humiliation, under duress, at an intolerable sacrifice, and would leave a sting, a resentment, a bitter memory upon which terms of peace would rest not permanently, but only as upon quicksand. Only a peace between equals can last. Only a peace the very principle of which is equality and a common participation in a common benefit.[31]

Wilson may have thought to save himself from the brutality of the peace with the promise of the League. Yet according to Lippmann, Nicolson, and company, not only was this a doubtful gamble given the compromises he had to make to achieve it and the volatile tempers of the times, but the president made repeated mistakes in his efforts to persuade the American public of the wisdom of the accords. Thus, Wilson should not have made the congressional elections of November 1918 a test of loyalty to his program. Or he should have taken a bipartisan delegation with him to Paris in January 1919 (prominent friendly Republicans such as Taft or Root, for example). Most importantly, when the treaty came up for Senate ratification in November 1919 and again in March 1920, he might have accepted reservations to the provisions for the League that would not have substantially compromised its operations. In all of these respects, Wilson significantly damaged the prospects that his fellow citizens would willingly engage themselves in a dramatic shift in American foreign policy toward a prominent and permanent engagement in European politics.

Was the president's stubbornness due to his Calvinism, as many have maintained; to his shaken physical state and the toll this took on him psychically, as more recent work has suggested; or again, to the changing role of the presidency in American life?[32] Whatever the verdict, Wilson could have promoted his policy far more skillfully than he did.

Yet, suppose that Wilson had been in full possession of his faculties and had built a bipartisan consensus around his ideas. Would the world then have been made safe for democracy? To put the question of Wilsonianism in these terms is to shift the focus of analysis from the president and his program to the world in which it was to operate.

Circumstances in Europe created four major categories of objective difficulties for Wilson's plans: the character of Allied (and especially French) demands for the postwar settlement; the impact of the Bolshevik Revolution on class tensions in Europe (even more than on relations among states); the prospects for democracy over the medium term in Germany; the situation politically in Eastern Europe, a largely agrarian region with ethnically mixed peoples.

The first of these obstacles to Wilson's vision—French security concern with respect to Germany—was the most politically charged matter at the Peace Conference.[33] The determination of America's allies—and the French in particular—that Germany would be made to pay dearly for the war proved tremendously costly to Wilson. Without Franco-German reconciliation, what chance could there be for liberal democratic forces to join hands across national boundaries? How could a liberal economic order be maintained; how could the League function effectively? Under Georges Clemenceau's leadership, the French were working to divide and bleed Germany to such an extent that its preponderance over France would forever be ended. Whereas Wilson proposed to control German power by integrating it into a more united Europe, the French proposed to deal with the problem by dismembering the country.

Clemenceau's war aims (not the most radical expressed in France) made short shrift of Wilson's call for "peace without victory." In the east, in addition to favoring maximum boundaries for Czechoslovakia in the peace settlement, the French supported maximum Polish claims (for Upper Silesia and Danzig especially, as well as for eastern Galicia)—all to have strong allies against Germany in the region. To the south, the French prevented Austrian unification with Germany. In the west, the French not only expected the return of Alsace and Lorraine but also coveted the Saar and influence over an autonomous Rhenish state on the left bank of the Rhine.

So much for Wilson's ideas of Franco-German rapprochement or his notion of extending the principles of national self-determination to the Germans and Austrians.[34]

As for reparations, the Germans would pay dearly. So much for the ideas of an integrated European economic system where the advantage of each is maximized by the advantage of all. Even if Clemenceau was only thinking defensively, and even if later economists were skeptical as to how damaging the reparations actually were, here was the old-fashioned world of power politics of a direct and brutal sort.[35]

Wilson's problem with the French was aggravated by a negotiation process at the Peace Conference, where the French could find support from the British or the Italians on specific matters. In addition, the complexity of the issues, the time involved, the calls for revenge in the United States as well as among the allies—all of these wore down an already physically exhausted Wilson. "Hang the Kaiser;" "squeeze the orange til the pips squeak": this was the mood outside the conference walls. And what were Wilson's alternatives? As even his critics have conceded, had he walked away from the conference the British and French positions might have hardened and the new democratic leaders in Germany been handicapped even more in their functions.[36] Perhaps the League could set right what the peace settlement had so badly compromised, or so Wilson must have hoped.

A second obstacle to Wilson's liberal democratic internationalism outside his power to control came from the triumph of Lenin in Russia. Wilson had welcomed the fall of the Czar in March 1917, but he did not approve of the Bolshevik Revolution that November. Yet he kept a careful distance, justifying the small number of troops he sent to the Soviet Union in terms of continuing the struggle against Germany. "The word 'Bolshevik' covers many different things," he declared at the Peace Conference in March 1919. "In my opinion, to try to stop a revolutionary movement is like using a broom to sweep back a spring tide. . . . The sole means of countering Bolshevism is to make its causes disappear. Moreover, it is a perilous enterprise; we don't even quite know what its causes are."

Given this caution, Wilson temporized, apparently hoping either that the Revolution would turn more moderate or that it would collapse due to internal conditions. Although the president wanted the Soviets to be invited to the peace conference, the United States had no fixed policy toward the Soviet Union during its critical deliberations. As his comments of May 1919 reveal, his overtures were based on caution: "We can recognize none of these [rival] governments as the government of Russia, and we must bind them to a procedure which will lead to the formation of a regular democratic government. If they resist, we can break off relations with them."[37]

The French deplored Lenin's success for the fact that the revolution had expropriated important French investments and denied Paris the reassurance of an ally to the east to counter Germany. Whereas this concern might have reconciled them to closer relations with Berlin, the French were not to be moved.

Perhaps most importantly, by splitting the left and by terrifying the right, the Russian Revolution dimmed the prospects for democracy in Germany and Eastern Europe even more, while complicating political matters in France, Spain, and Italy. In Germany, the right became more assertive, the democratic left more moderate. In Eastern Europe, the new democratic regimes installed from the Baltic to the Adriatic and the Black Sea were soon swept from power as the region deliberated its predicament between Moscow and Berlin.[38] In short, the consequences of the Bolshevik Revolution seriously complicated Wilson's hopes for a peace based on democratic regimes in Europe by weakening the ranks of the democrats, who experienced a new wave of assaults from extremes to their right and left.

The third obstacle to Wilsonianism in the interwar period came from the prospects for democracy in Germany. Wilson had wanted the Kaiser to abdicate and representatives of a new German republic to negotiate the surrender, which the Germans understood would be based on the Fourteen Points. Had the settlement followed these expectations, might the democratic promises of 1848 finally have been realized for Germany? Certainly the democratic parties there would have received a bigger boost: the German right would not have been able to lay so much blame on republican forces for the defeat; important bourgeois interests might have viewed the new regime more favorably; the tensions involved with the hyperinflation of the early 1920s, incurred while making reparation payments, would have been avoided; immediate membership in the League would have prompted a greater sense of democratic comradeship. Hence the poignancy one feels in the words of the final capitulation of the newly formed German republican government to the stiff ultimatum of the victors:

> The German people, after their terrible sufferings of these last years are without means of defending their honor against the outside world. Yielding to overpowering might, the government of the German Republic declares itself ready to accept and to sign the peace treaty imposed by the Allied and Associated governments. But in so doing, the government of the German Republic in no wise abandons its conviction that these conditions of peace represent injustice without example.[39]

Yet it is difficult to make an unequivocal argument that a "peace without victory" would have guaranteed the consolidation of democracy in Germany. It should be remembered that in the late 1920s, "the spirit of Locarno" spelled a period of rapprochement among the democrats of Britain,

France, and Germany, when for a time it appeared the curse of the Great War had been lifted. Democracy did sink roots in German soil before 1933, but not deeply enough to hold the spectre of Hitler at bay; probably not deeply enough even had the peace been on generous terms.[40] Wilson never proposed to dispossess the old German ruling class of their privileges. Although the Kaiser went to live out his days in Holland and the aristocrats' undisputed political preeminence was now clearly over, the social heart of German militarism continued to beat. Irredentist claims persisted to the east with millions of Germans living in Poland and Czechoslovakia especially. Economic affairs remained dominated by mercantilist cartels. And the Depression still fell in all its fury on a frightened people, where a militant left aligned with Moscow had broken with the democratic left, and where an unrepentant right used the threat of a communist revolution to justify its own outrages against the democratic order.

A fourth and final major obstacle to liberal democratic internationalism in the postwar era comes from an assessment of the prospects for democracy in Eastern Europe in the belt of states from the Baltic in the north to the Black Sea and the Adriatic in the south. In this largely agrarian region, democracy alarmed the traditional elites almost as much as Bolshevism, while economic difficulties and ethnic and border tensions resulting from the peace settlement increased tensions markedly. Authoritarianism was an ever-present temptation, often to preempt attempts to seize government by the extreme right. All the states of the region began the interwar period as democracies; by the early 1930s only one remained.[41]

Czechoslovakia was the single exception, the one country where Wilson's ideas bore fruit. A democratic government was recognized by the Allies in October 1918 and stayed in power until the final German onslaught in 1939. Czechoslovakia is an interesting example of the kind of circumstances where liberal democratic internationalism did provide a practical framework for American foreign policy.

The most important factor explaining the success of democracy in Czechoslovakia in the interwar period is that there was no traditional right there and no obvious social base for an authoritarian reaction. The country was born from a fragment of an empire and thus there was no native monarchy—the Slovaks having been under Hungarian rule, the Czechs under Austrian. Nor was there a Czech or Slovak landed elite with which the new republic had to deal. Instead, most of the large land owners were Germans or Magyars. By 1920, a reform bill had provided for the redistribution of these lands to small farmers, who became enthusiastic supporters of the republic and whose Agrarian party combined elements of both the Czech and Slovak populations (as well as some Magyars and Ruthenians— a Ukrainian people—aware that conditions then became better for them than for their bretheren in other lands).[42]

By historical coincidence, then, Czechoslovakia came into being as a "bourgeois" republic. A Social Democratic movement had an established pedigree before independence and was solidly republican. The Communist party harbored no revolutionary illusions but cooperated with the new democratic order. It helped that the country was rich—in 1937, the Czech regions enjoyed a per capita income higher than France. A solid middle class had the skills to administer the government ably, under the leadership of such outstanding democrats as Thomas Masaryk and Eduard Benes. When the farmers rallied to the republic, the democratic consensus was firmly established. In addition, the country was economically balanced between agrarian and industrial activities, which helped to mitigate the economic difficulties that beset the area generally during the interwar years.

Tensions between the country's ethnic groups did seem at times to threaten political stability. Of its population of 14 million, more than 3 million were German, seven hundred thousand were Hungarian, and three hundred thousand were Ruthenians. The Germans and Hungarians were accustomed to belonging to the dominant ethnic group under the former imperial system. They did not reconcile themselves easily to Czechoslovakian sovereignty and could complain that the Paris settlement had deprived them of the right to the national self-determination that had been afforded to others.

Nor were relations between the dominant Czechs and Slovaks smooth (as their separation in 1992 into two countries was to demonstrate). Historically, they had lived separate political lives; their first joint association was in the state founded in 1918. Moreover, the relative economic backwardness of the Slovaks and their cultural provincialism meant that they resented the more prosperous and secular Czechs and their leading role in the affairs of the new regime. Whatever the Czech efforts, they were never able to overcome a tendency on the part of many Slovaks to want more autonomy—and a corresponding willingness of some Slovaks to flirt with right-wing ideologies when the temptation arose.

Nevertheless, it is possible to speculate that these very tensions helped Czechoslovakian democracy. A single dominant ethnic group could have proved more hostile to minorities; it might have sacrificed certain democratic freedoms for the sake of ethnic advantage. By having to bid constantly for Slovak support, the Czechs had to ensure the viability of a system of mutual understanding and compromise. Meanwhile, both communism and fascism could be seen as foreign to the democratic cast of Czechoslovakian nationalism.

This ethnic compromise was worked out within a political system borrowed in part from the French Third Republic. The president was elected by the legislature, which also selected a cabinet. Thanks to proportional representation, Czechoslovakia had a multiparty system—cabinets typically counted the participation of five parties. In other Eastern European countries (and in France) such a party system made governing coalitions difficult to sustain. In Prague the cooperation of Czechs and Slovaks proved crucial. Though there were fourteen different cabinets in power between 1920 and 1938, multiparty democracy survived. When the country fell to Germany it was a moral loss of the first order to the West.

Wilson's relationship to Czechoslovakian democracy began with diplomatic support for that country's creation in 1918, and with his call for secure borders for it in 1919. As statements by the republic's foreign minister and later President Eduard Benes demonstrate, Wilson's League of Nations was indeed the kind of international guarantee a vulnerable democracy such as Czechoslovakia needed after 1920. But the achievement of Czechoslovakian democracy was fundamentally an act of these peoples themselves. At certain moments, Wilson's efforts were critical, but far from decisive. Similar ambitions along the length of Eastern Europe—in Poland or Yugoslavia, for example—fell on far less fertile soil.

To recapitulate: Wilson's effort to create a liberal democratic alternative to the forces of reaction and revolution foundered not so much on his style of leadership as on the social and political reality he faced in Europe. No observation about Eastern Europe could have been more mistaken than that of Thomas Masaryk, saying the war had left the region "a laboratory atop a vast cemetery."[43] Despite the upheavals of the war, Europe was not a tabula rasa, but a continent of social and political forces and in fierce contention. Hence, Wilson's project was thwarted by a French determination to be done with the German menace, by the Bolshevik Revolution, by splits on the left and the resurgence of the right in Germany, by the agrarian social structures of Eastern Europe with class and ethnic antagonisms of great intensity, and by an American nationalist opinion reluctant to see its national security involved in dangerous new foreign entanglements.

THE DILEMMA OF AMERICAN POLICY IN EUROPE

As with his policy toward Latin America (reviewed in the last chapter), so too with his policy toward Europe, Wilson failed in his efforts both to root democratic forces in countries where they were struggling to take power and to establish a stable new configuration of power among the states of the continent. German democracy was not robust; Franco-German rapprochement did not occur; outside Czechoslovakia, democratic forces were weak in Eastern Europe; the Russian Revolution remained militant; communist parties in Western Europe sapped democratic forces; fascism came into power in Italy in 1922, encouraging like-minded movements to duplicate its success; no way was found to counter economic nationalism and the destructive impact of the Depression that began in 1929; collective security proved unable to halt Italian aggression in Ethiopia or Japanese attacks on

China; and the American people and Congress refused to identify the national security with an active hand in the protection of liberal democracy in Europe.

Was there a better guide than Wilsonianism as to how America should defend its legitimate concerns in the founding of a stable European order friendly to this country's interests? Between 1940 and the early 1950s, the most influential thinkers in this country on the proper conduct of American foreign policy—Walter Lippmann, George Kennan, Hans Morgenthau, and Reinhold Niebuhr—took special pains to use Wilson as a negative example, a textbook study of how foreign policy should not be formulated. For these analysts, Wilsonianism stands for the American penchant to conduct its foreign conduct by moralizing about it, by assuming that somehow democracy is a panacea for the world's problems. In their eyes, liberal democratic internationalism betrays a vein of naive and utopian idealism ill-fitted to effective participation in global politics. The affliction did not start with Wilson nor end with him, but his presidency marks its high-water point. Realism, the dominant school of international relations theory in the United States, was founded at this time by these men and built its concepts by consciously pitting itself against the basic tenets of Wilsonianism.

Thus, referring to the settlement of 1919, George Kennan wrote:

> This was the sort of peace you got when you allowed war hysteria and impractical idealism to lie down together in your mind, like the lion and the lamb; when you indulged yourself in the colossal conceit of thinking that you could suddenly make international life over into what you believed to be your own image; when you dismissed the past with contempt, rejected the relevance of the past to the future, and refused to occupy yourself with the real problems that a study of the past would suggest.[44]

In Hans Morgenthau's words:

> In the end, Wilson had to consent to a series of uneasy compromises, which were a betrayal of his moral principles—for principles can, by their very nature, not be made the object of compromise—and which satisfied nobody's national aspirations. These compromises had no relation at all to the traditional American national interest in a viable European balance of power. Thus Wilson returned from Versailles a compromised idealist, an empty handed statesman, a discredited ally. In that triple failure lies the tragedy not only of Wilson, a great yet misguided man, but of Wilsonianism as a political doctrine.[45]

Walter Lippmann's charges were even harsher, for they allege that Wilson's mistakes set the stage for the rise of fascism and the inability of the democracies to rally effectively to the challenge:

> To end the struggle for power, Wilson sought to make the nations powerless. The Wilsonian principles stipulate that the nations should disarm themselves physi-

cally and politically and then entrust their independence and their vital interests to an assembly of debating diplomats. . . . The cynicism which corroded the democracies in the interval between the two German wars was engendered by a moral order which was in fact a moral frustration . . . which, insofar as its prohibitions had influence in disarming the nations, disaggregating alliances, and disrupting great states, was a preparation not for peace under the law but for aggression in the midst of anarchy.[46]

How, then, should American foreign policy have been formulated? These writers consider themselves realists. They insist that the national interest should be determined rather strictly by calculations of the relative amount of power among states, with a view of preventing threats to the existence or independence of the United States. Seen from this perspective, the only obvious antagonist of the United States in world affairs at that time was Germany, which Washington should forthrightly have mobilized to contain. They have no patience with the "idealism" of a "utopian," "moralistic" crusade to change the character of international relations by making states democratic, such as Wilson advanced, for this talk only put a smokescreen over the essential matter of dealing with German power.

Lippmann put the argument first and best, declaring in 1943, in words that he meant to apply to Wilson, that Americans

> have forgotten the compelling and, once seen, the self-evident common principle of all genuine foreign policy—the principle that alone can force decisions, can settle controversy, and can induce agreement. . . . [Hence] a policy has been formed only when commitments and power have been brought into balance. This is the forgotten principle which must be recovered and restored to the first place in American thought if the nation is to achieve the foreign policy which it so desperately wants.[47]

Morgenthau insisted on much the same point when he wrote:

> What passed for foreign policy was either improvisation or—especially in our century—the invocation of some abstract moral principle in whose image the world was to be made over. . . . embracing everything, it came to grips with nothing. In part, however, it was a magnificent instrument for marshaling public opinion in support of war and warlike policies—and for losing the peace.[48]

In a word, the realists maintained that Wilson did not adequately appreciate the character of "power politics" or the "balance of power" in his deliberations, by which they meant the need to contain German power so that it would not dominate the continent, a turn of events that would have been seriously threatening to American national security. In Lippmann's view, for example, Wilson failed to explain to the American people why the country went to war: "The reasons he did give were legalistic and moralistic and idealistic reasons, rather than the substantial and vital reasons that the security of the United States demanded that no aggressively expanding imperial power, like Germany, should be allowed to gain the mastery of the Atlantic Ocean."[49]

These charges ask for an indictment that the evidence does not warrant. Thus, Wilson was not a pacifist, and his proposals for disarmament are best understood as confidence-building measures among states, not as a reluctance to back commitments with force, as Lippmann suggested. Again, the League of Nations was not to have either financial or military resources independent of the states that participated in it, and its Council had to act by unanimous agreement; the League was not to be a world government. More, the call for self-determination was not intended as a blank check for secessionist movements. Wilson respected economic, strategic, and historical considerations that had to be weighed against nationalist feelings; it was only toward the end of the war that he finally resigned himself to the dismemberment of the Austro-Hungarian empire rather than to seeing it reconstituted as a democratic federalist structure.

But most importantly, Wilson intended the League to be the vehicle to bind the United States permanently to a management role in world affairs. Whatever the shortcomings of the details in his plan, American membership in the League might well have provided the check on Germany that Wilson's critics allege his naivete and moralizing prevented him from establishing.

For Wilson, the vital issue at the Peace Conference was the League; for his critics, it was Germany. Yet the League's very existence implicitly addressed the essential issue for Europe from 1871 until 1945 (and perhaps once again today): the German question. Given Germany's population, economic strength, militaristic history, political structure, and geography, could it live peacefully with its neighbors? Were the only alternatives to destroy it or be conquered by it? American leadership of the League portended that Germany might be contained by American power. Once contained, domestic reforms might be consolidated so that Germany could live with its neighbors by progressively shedding its militaristic elements in favor of developing itself as a democracy capable of interacting peacefully with the other states of Europe. But even without German reforms, membership in the League would automatically tie America into the European balance of power and so safeguard American national security.

Wilsonianism did, therefore, meaningfully address the critical issue of what to do about Germany. If the League's fundamental purpose was to check aggression against weaker states created by the dismemberment of the Russian, Ottoman, and Austro-Hungarian empires after 1918, if its collateral ambition was to foster democratic government and liberal international economic exchange, then what better safeguard could be put on German power? As a way of addressing the growing presence of the Soviet Union in world affairs, it offered a useful forum as well.

In addition to the League, Wilson had two other ways of influencing Germany. His preferred approach was to control German power by absorbing it into a liberal economic, political, and military arrangement that would effectively integrate Germany with its neighbors (especially France) and the United States. Here was the germ of the American idea after 1945 to push for European integration based on Franco-German rapprochement. Wilson also agreed to join the British in guaranteeing France against German attack in a treaty independent of the League. The Senate defeated this latter project along with barring American membership in the League.

It is true, of course, that the failure to deal generously with Germany in 1919 meant there was a sympathy on the part of many European liberals for German displeasure with the peace settlement. In turn, this sympathy, in combination with an antimilitarist prejudice, contributed to a liberal inability to deal with the rise of Hitler. But to suggest, as Walter Lippmann did, that the entire liberal peace program was actually little more than an exercise in fomenting the next war is to lay far more of a charge on Wilson's shoulders than is deserved. It is as if the impact on German politics of the Russian Revolution or the Depression of the 1930s were somehow of trivial importance given the blinders Wilson allegedly placed on liberals' appreciation of the German question. In fact, it is precisely the antidemocratic, mercantilist, and militaristic Third Reich that a proper Wilsonian should be primed to oppose from the first. (The same point can be made against those who allege that FDR's willingness to try to work with the Soviet Union was Wilsonian.)

Nor do Wilson's critics—the unreconstructed advocates of balance of power thinking—demonstrate how they would have handled European affairs better. What reason is there to think that a Germany dismembered in 1919 might not have found a way to rise and avenge itself (perhaps in league with the Soviet Union)? Within a few years, the British were beginning to suspect France of hegemonic ambitions in Europe, while no way was found to work with the Soviet Union—tinder enough for another war, one might say, had Wilson's liberal peace program never been mooted. Would a world that denied the power of nationalism, spurned the appeals of democracy, been uninterested in liberal international economic practices, and made a recourse to arms the first duty of states been such an attractive alternative to Wilson's vision? In short, it is far from obvious that Clemenceau's formula for handling Germany was more farsighted than Wilson's. Wilsonianism may have been a failure after 1919, but the realists indicate no more realistic way to proceed.

Fail though it did at the time, the virtues of Wilson's policy for the post-war world were threefold. First, it acknowledged the fundamental political importance of nationalism, seeking to direct rather than to repress its energy. Second, it sought to channel the demands for popular sovereignty contained in nationalism in the direction of democratic government, and away from authoritarian or totalitarian regimes (though the latter—a particular curse of the twentieth century—was not yet clearly visible when Wilson was in office). Third, it attempted to provide a structure of international institutions and agreements to handle military and economic affairs among democratically constituted, capitalist states. In all of these respects, American national security thinking followed Wilson's lead after 1945. Again today, in the aftermath of the cold war, we can see the prescience of his proposals as we deliberate the problems of nationalism in Eastern Europe, the course of Western European integration based on Franco-German understanding, and the need for organizational mechanisms to provide for the peaceful formulation of a gamut of issues from the economic to the military.[50]

It is commonly observed that politics as an art requires pursuing the desirable in terms of the possible. The dilemma of leadership is to decide when it is weakness to fail to exploit the inevitable ambiguities, and therefore possibilities, of the historical moment, and when it is foolhardy to attempt to overcome immovable constraints set by a combination of forces past and present. Since options are always open to some extent, greatness requires creating opportunities and taking risks within the limits set by history.

While the constraints of history nullified Wilson's hopes, his efforts did not totally contradict the forces of his time. Democratic nationalist forces did exist in Germany and parts of Eastern Europe. If it was unlikely that the Bolshevik Revolution would ever have turned in a democratic direction, it was not until 1921 (with the Tenth Party Congress, which established iron discipline within the Communist party, and with the crushing of the Kronstadt mutiny, a sailors' uprising against Lenin's rule) that its totalitarian cast was definitely set. If it was unlikely that democracy would consolidate itself in Germany given the rancors of the right, the splitting of the left, and the rigors of the Depression, it certainly was not until after 1930 that this became manifestly evident. Again, although the Senate had repudiated the League in 1919–20, it could reconsider its position, as at times the American government seemed interested in doing. In short, Wilson's gamble on the forces of democracy and collective security (which in practice would have been the balance of power under another name) was not totally unrealistic. And what were his other options? Indeed his greatness as a visionary comes from how close to success his program came. Suppose America had joined the League in good faith, an organization basically of his devising? By that single act, the course of history might have been changed, for it would have committed the United States to the maintenance of a European equilibrium containing Germany.

The best evidence of the power of Wilsonianism, however, comes from its resurgence in American foreign policy in the aftermath of World War II. Bretton Woods, the initial plans for the United Nations, the hopes for Western European integration that lay behind the occupation of Germany and the Marshall Plan—all this was essentially Wilsonian in inspiration (even when operationalized by people like Keynes and Kennan who saw themselves as opponents of Wilson's position in Paris in 1919).[51] In the late 1940s, Wilsonianism was thus to have a success that it was denied in the early 1920s. But it was in the late 1980s that Wilson's time truly arrived. Of all the extraordinary developments connected with the end of the cold war in 1989, surely one of the most noteworthy was the way Soviet leader Mikhail Gorbachev's "new thinking" for Europe—with its insistence on the importance of national self-determination, democratic government, and collective security—echoed Wilson's appeals of seventy years earlier.

Accordingly, when Czechoslovakia's President Vaclav Havel addressed an emotional joint meeting of Congress on February 21, 1990, the first American he mentioned was Woodrow Wilson, whose "great support" in 1918 for Czech and Slovak nationalists had meant that they "could found our modern independent state." Havel acknowledged the spirit of Wilsonianism as well: that small nations deserve to be free; that their sovereignty should be based on national self-determination, which in turn implies the establishment of constitutional democratic government; that the intercourse of nations should be based on nondiscriminatory, liberal economic arrangements; and that democratic states should defend their common interest against the threat of selfish aggrandizement and war. Finally, he declared:

> Without a global revolution in the sphere of human consciousness, nothing will change for the better in the sphere of our being. . . . We still do not know how to put morality ahead of politics, science and economy. We are still incapable of understanding that the only genuine backbone of all our actions, if they are to be moral, is responsibility—responsibility to something higher than my family, my country, my company, my success.[52]

It was in recognition of Wilson's spirit—and not simply his actions—that during the interwar years so many boulevards, statues and parks in Rumania, Poland, Yugoslavia, and especially Czechoslovakia were named after him. In the aftermath of the most terrible war the world had seen, many of the peoples of Eastern Europe regarded Wilson as a liberator, indeed as a founding father of their new-born states.[53]

Unlike most statesmen, then, Wilson deserves to be measured not on the basis of achieving the ends of his policy in their time, but by the magnitude of his efforts and the influence they continued to have in later years. Seen from the perspective of the mid-1990s, three-quarters of a century since he left office, Wilson's concern that nationalism abroad be turned in the direction of democratic government for the sake of the American national interest seems soundly conceived. Writing in 1889 on "Leaders of Men," Wilson had declared:

> Great reformers do not, indeed, observe time and circumstance. Theirs is not a service of opportunity. They have no thought for occasion, no capacity for compromise. They are early vehicles of the Spirit of the Age. They are born of the very times that oppose them. . . . Theirs to hear the inarticulate voices that stir in the night-watches, apprising the lonely sentinel of what the day will bring forth.[54]

PART II

Liberal Democratic Internationalism, 1933–1947

CHAPTER FIVE

FDR and World Order:
Globalizing the Monroe Doctrine

> We owe it, therefore, to candor and to amicable relations existing
> between the United States and [the European powers] to declare
> that we should consider any attempt on their part to extend their
> system to any portion of this hemisphere as dangerous to our peace
> and safety. . . . with the [Latin American] Governments who
> have declared their independence and maintained it, and whose
> independence we have, on great consideration and on just
> principles, acknowledged, we could not view any interposition for
> the purpose of oppressing them, or controlling in any other manner
> their destiny, by any European power in any other light than as the
> manifestation of an unfriendly disposition toward the United States.
> —James Monroe, 1823

> I am proposing, as it were, that the nations should with one accord
> adopt the doctrine of President Monroe as the doctrine of the world:
> that no nation should seek to extend its polity over any other nation
> or people but that every people should be left free to determine its
> own polity, its own way of development, unhindered, unthreatened,
> unafraid, the little along with the great and powerful.
> —Woodrow Wilson, 1917

> The establishment of order in Europe . . . must be achieved by
> processes which will enable the liberated peoples to destroy the
> last vestiges of Nazism and Fascism and to create democratic
> institutions of their own choice. This is a principle of the Atlantic
> Charter—the right of all peoples to choose the form of government
> under which they will live—the restoration of sovereign rights
> and self-government to those peoples who have been forcibly
> deprived of them by the aggressor nations.
> —Franklin Delano Roosevelt, 1945

IN THE MONROE DOCTRINE of 1823, the United States gave official notice
of its determination to prevent the reimposition of European rule in Latin
America once popular forces secured the continent's independence from
Spain. In the years 1941–7, the United States gave notice that it intended,
in effect, to globalize the Monroe Doctrine in the aftermath of the Axis

defeat. Peoples liberated from German, Japanese, or Italian control by Allied armies were to establish their own sovereign governments, not become dependents of new empires. West European colonies were to receive their independence in due course. Moscow was put on notice to limit its postwar territorial demands. Calling variously for "self-government," "self-determination," and "democracy," the United States opposed what it repeatedly referred to as great power "spheres of influence." Here was the high-water mark of American liberal democratic internationalism, a time when the United States put isolationism behind it and, keenly aware that the country's national interest required it to play a major and permanent role in international affairs, stepped forward with a group of proposals that amounted to a comprehensive program for world order.

To be sure, Washington recognized that a powerful government might have "legitimate" security concerns with respect to the conduct of a weaker neighbor; since 1898, America itself had intervened repeatedly in Latin American affairs, and Washington was realistic enough by the 1940s to understand that other powerful states might also insist on having their interests respected in regional matters. Nevertheless, since the inception of the Good Neighbor Policy toward Latin America in 1933 (the substance of which had actually been practiced since the last years of the Wilson presidency), the United States had announced curbs on its own interventionism and it felt a similar restraint was incumbent on other great powers. The result was an American foreign policy favorable to the growth of nationalism and hostile to imperialist ambitions. Britain and France greeted the American proposals with almost as much resentment as the Soviet Union.

Washington was aware that its policy could lead to the proliferation of states in the world and sought to create new mechanisms to coordinate their relations. The United States favored a system of collective security to preserve the peace, an open international economic system to promote general prosperity, and a shared political consensus to preserve this equilibrium maintained through a network of international institutions. The Wilsonian cast of such an endeavor is apparent.

Franklin Delano Roosevelt, thirty-second president of the United States (1933–45), was the modern embodiment of traditional American liberal democratic internationalism. In economic matters, following especially the counsels of his secretary of state, Cordell Hull, the chief American architect of the postwar economic order, the longest serving secretary of state in American history (1933–44), and a Wilsonian through and through, FDR stood four-square for a liberalizing, nondiscriminatory, international system of trade and investment. First with the Reciprocal Trade Agreements Act of 1934, then (and far more importantly) with the creation of the Bretton Woods system in 1944, the United States established the chief principles and mechanisms responsible for the most extensive and successful expansion of international commerce and finance in world history.

Hull's particular concern had always been foreign economic relations. He saw peace and prosperity as working together, just as he attributed the impetus to war in good measure to protectionist, competitive economic practices. As a result he favored lowering tariffs and making them equal to all, an approach he expected to stimulate economic growth and to foster international political cooperation. Hull's first great triumph came with the Reciprocal Trade Agreements Act of 1934. As he put it later:

> Economic warfare . . . foments internal strife. It offers constant temptation to use force, or threat of force, to obtain what could have been got through normal processes of trade. . . . The basic approach to the problem of peace is the ordering of the world's economic life so that the masses of the people can work and live in reasonable comfort. . . . The principles underlying the trade agreements program are therefore an indispensable cornerstone for the edifice of peace. . . . it is a fact that war did not break out between the United States and any country with which we had been able to negotiate a trade agreement. It is also a fact that, with very few exceptions, the countries with which we signed trade agreements joined together in resisting the Axis. The political line-up followed the economic line-up.

In a like manner, Roosevelt insisted in his message to Congress in February 1945, asking it to ratify the agreements reached at Bretton Woods: "The point in history at which we stand is full of promise and of danger. The world will either move toward unity and widely shared prosperity or it will move into necessarily competing economic blocs."[1]

In military affairs, Roosevelt initially looked forward to cooperation rather than competition among what he called "Policemen" (the United States, the Soviet Union, Great Britain, and China), which together might manage global security concerns. Later he put his trust in the United Nations, originally conceived in collective security terms as the modern embodiment of the League of Nations. In each case, FDR was hoping to maintain the wartime cooperation of the great powers. He was thinking as a Wilsonian in collective security terms, which distrusted competitive balance of power relations. It was only well after FDR's death in April 1945 that the United States responded to the growing Soviet-American rivalry by entering into a military alliance with Western Europe, creating the North Atlantic Treaty Organization (NATO) in 1949.

While FDR was committed to the defense of democracy in Europe, sponsoring democratic government everywhere was not the be-all and end-all of his policy. In circumstances where the prospects for democracy seemed dim, Roosevelt was satisfied with simply opposing great-power spheres of influence, defending undemocratic governments from Turkey to

China from the encroachments of their imperialist neighbors. It was enough, in these circumstances, that states be self-governing in the sense of being independent from direct foreign control. As FDR understood, nationalism was at least as powerful a force as imperialism. FDR had come to appreciate the strength of Latin American resistance to Wilson; Japanese and German militarism had made potent use of nationalist passions; and the history of Eastern Europe during the interwar years could be cited to demonstrate the follies of nationalist jealousies.

Harry S. Truman, who succeeded Roosevelt in April 1945 and remained in office until 1953, continued in this liberal tradition. The distinguishing mark of the Truman administration, beginning especially in 1947, was a more focused effort to influence the internal political lives of peoples abroad, as America moved from a multilateralist or one world approach in international affairs to a policy known as containment.

Containment was the strategy designed to meet the challenge of international communism backed by the might of the Soviet Union. As authored by State Department official George Kennan in 1946, containment put a priority on denying the Soviets control of Western Europe and Japan, areas vital for economic power. Kennan expected the Soviet regime then to change from within and eventually to moderate its foreign policy.

In short order, two contentious issues confronted the containment doctrine. The first was that to safeguard the core areas of world power, additional territories might need protection, whether that be Greece in the case of Europe or South Korea in the case of Japan. How was the extent of these collateral commitments to be defined? The second was that Soviet power could be exercised through "fraternal parties" to be found virtually everywhere in the world. It was not enough to counter the Soviets diplomatically and militarily as in traditional international relations. Instead, the United States had to involve itself in the domestic politics of the states with which it had relations to an extent unprecedented in world affairs.

Each of these issues had an answer in the Truman Doctrine of March 1947, which extended American political and military support for the Greek and Turkish governments (and, by extension, for others thereafter). It also dedicated itself "to help free peoples to maintain their free institutions and their national integrity against aggressive movements that seek to impose upon them totalitarian regimes." Castigating the actions of a "militant minority," "the terrorist activities of several thousand armed men," Truman insisted, "This is no more than a frank recognition that totalitarian regimes imposed on free peoples, by direct or indirect aggression, undermine the foundations of international peace and hence the security of the United States."

What the Truman Doctrine was militarily and politically, the Marshall Plan was in economic terms. Announced in June 1947, the European Recovery Program, as it was formally called, authorized large loans to European programs for economic repair and reform. "Its purpose," Secretary of State George Marshall declared, "should be the revival of a working economy in the world so as to permit the emergence of political and social conditions in which free institutions can exist." One may debate just how critical the sums disbursed actually were, but there is no doubt that the reforms they promoted were basic to the recasting of postwar politics in Western Europe, both at the domestic level and with respect to the longer-term prospects for regional integration. In good measure, the Marshall Plan was the foreign policy dimension of the New Deal, applied now for the sake of national security. Both programs reflected a commitment to government's responsibility for "economic democracy" and economic growth, and both tied these ambitions to an increasingly open and interdependent world economic order free of communist control.[2]

Much as the Soviet Union and the United States had fundamentally opposed designs for domestic governments and the structure of international affairs, so they had different ways of instrumentalizing their policies: the United States depended on economic might and appeals to dominant socio-economic elites, while the Soviet Union relied on disciplined Leninist party organization and Marxist appeals to those marginalized by the established order. With the presence of the Red Army in Eastern Europe, the existence of strong communist parties in much of Western Europe, and the apparent strength of communist revolutionary movements in China, Greece, the Philippines, and Vietnam in the late 1940s, it was apparent that Marxism-Leninism had a worldwide ideological and institutional appeal to rival that projected by the United States with its liberal democratic internationalism.

While the confrontation between the United States and the Soviet Union might be said to have begun in 1945 over the fate of Poland, it was only in 1947 that its full scope became generally apparent. As it did, American policymakers discovered that compromises had to be made with principle. As a result, American liberal democratic internationalism necessarily became more defensive, more divided internally, and more contradictory in its implementation.

Nowhere was the change in American policy more evident than in the priority it assigned to promoting democracy abroad. Explicitly dedicated to the defense of the "free world," the United States nonetheless found itself defending authoritarian governments that were struggling against communism. On occasion such policies led it to oppose even democratic forces, where they appeared weak and willing to cooperate with local communists. Formerly opposed to great power spheres of influence, the United States now acknowledged its need to act in just such terms abroad. While these policies flowed from a logical evolution of American security concerns, they nevertheless amounted to a substantial change away from Wilsonianism, at least so far as the dedication to promote democracy abroad was concerned.[3]

THE NEW REALISM

Faced with global responsibilities in the aftermath of the Second World War, the goal of encouraging democracy abroad now became but one ambition among many in the nation's foreign policy, to be supported in many instances only after other problems had been resolved. To be sure, Washington would tolerate nothing less for Germany and Japan than that they be reconstituted as democratic polities. The importance of the decision means that an entire chapter of this book is devoted to it. But America's most basic political demand for the postwar world was that it be composed of independent (that is self-governing or self-determining) states; that these governments should be democratic was an important, but second-order, concern.

While the most famous of Roosevelt's initiatives during the war with respect to the postwar political order—from the Atlantic Charter in 1941 to the Declaration on Liberated Europe in 1945—seemed to pledge America to support democracy when it spoke of self-government and self-determination for the peoples overrun by Axis aggression, in fact these terms were not synonymous with democracy. In circumstances from China to Turkey to Latin America, where the prospects for democracy seemed dim, the Roosevelt administration insisted only that these states be independent of foreign control. Eventually they might become democratic as well—a development to be valued in its own right and as an additional guarantee of a more stable world order. But operationally, the call for democracy was often no more than a code word meant to keep rival great powers from trying to carve out spheres of imperial control for themselves over the weaker peoples of the world.

Take the example of the Atlantic Charter, the statement issued by Roosevelt and British Prime Minister Winston Churchill in August 1941 and reconfirmed by the Declaration of United Nations, signed by the Big Four on January 1, 1942, and subsequently by forty-seven other heads of government. The Charter instantly became sacrosanct as a basic statement of purpose, a pledge to the future, on the part of the Allies. The third of its eight points did not use the term *democracy*, yet its meaning seemed clear: the signatories declared that "they respect the right of all peoples to choose the form of government under which they will live; and they wish to see sovereign rights and self-government restored to those who have been forcibly deprived of them."[4]

However, many of the countries that subscribed to the Charter were not themselves democracies and gave no indication that they intended to undergo such a transformation. In addition, the famous Charter was never even signed by Roosevelt and Churchill but had been left as simply a memorandum of agreement. The essentially pragmatic spirit of Roosevelt's attitude is well conveyed at his 985th press conference in December 1944, when he was asked to elaborate on the purpose of the Atlantic Charter:

> There are a lot of people who say you can't attain an objective or improvement in human life or in humanity, so why talk about it. Well, those people who come out for the Ten Commandments will say they don't live up to the Ten Commandments, which is perfectly true, but on the whole they are pretty good. It's something pretty good to shoot for. The Christian religion most of us in this room happen to belong to, we think it is pretty good. We certainly haven't attained it. Well, the Atlantic Charter is going to take its place, not comparing it with the Christian religion or the Ten Commandments, but as a definite step, just the same way Wilson's Fourteen Points constituted a major contribution to something we would all like to see happen in the world. Well, those Fourteen Points weren't all attained, but it was a step toward a better life for the people of the world.[5]

As FDR's words suggest, by the early 1940s, American liberalism had been leavened with a healthy dose of realism. As a result, liberal demands came to be put forward selectively and incrementally, in such a fashion that sponsoring democracy did not seem so singularly important or so urgent as it might have appeared to an unreconstructed Wilsonian.

Hence Roosevelt had established diplomatic relations with the Soviet Union late in 1933 without the expectation that democracy would soon flower there. True, in December 1943 the president assured the American people: "Stalin is a man who combines a tremendous, relentless determination with a stalwart good humor. I believe he is truly representative of the heart and soul of Russia; and I believe we are going to get along very well with him and the Russian people—very well indeed." Yet we may confidently assume FDR did not think the Soviet dictator had been democratically selected to represent his people's wishes. So, too, at Yalta, when Roosevelt insisted upon Stalin signing the Declaration on Liberated Europe, which pledged the Big Three to hold free elections to establish postwar governments in the countries they liberated from the Nazis, his realism was packaged as idealism: democratic government was not so much an end in itself as a way to limit Soviet expansion. What other recourse did the president have? To threaten war over Poland would have been to bluff. Soviet aid was still needed in the fight against Japan, and Roosevelt could conclude that Stalin was more likely to limit Soviet territorial claims if he were reassured of American noninterference in a region of obvious importance to Soviet security than if the United States threw down the gauntlet there before Germany had even surrendered.

Perhaps it was another example of his irrepressible bonhomie when in 1943 Roosevelt introduced Madame Chiang Kai-shek as representative of "one of the great democracies of the world." Given that official Washington was well aware of the corruption, incompetence, and brutality of her husband's regime, surely there was little truth (perhaps even some irony) in his remark on the same occasion that "I feel that we in this country have a great deal more to learn about China."[6] A stable, independent China working with the United States, yes; but it is hard to believe Roosevelt put much stock in the future prospects for democracy there.

With respect to Turkey, the State Department was candid, declaring that American policy was "live and let live," based on the principle of "the right of peoples to choose for themselves without outside interference the type of political, social, and economic systems they desire."[7] Whether Turkey was a democracy was not an issue that much perturbed Washington in 1945; whether it was stable, independent, and reliably pro-Western mattered very much indeed. The same determination was evident in Truman's sharp reaction to Soviet encroachments on Iranian and Turkish sovereignty in 1945–6. Hence in 1947, when Truman called for aid to Greece and Turkey to protect them from the threat of communism, he called the former a democracy (although admitting, "The government of Greece is not perfect. . . . It has made mistakes"), but he in no way implied that such a term suited Turkey. Similarly, with respect to Iran in the summer of 1941, the State Department insisted that Britain and the Soviet Union give public assurances that their joint occupation of the country would not be permanent. But Secretary of State Hull labored under no misconception that democracy might come in the wake of the Anglo-Soviet occupation. It was quite enough that Iran regain its status as an independent country. In 1942 FDR had quoted a Balkan proverb to Churchill, whose message now outlived the war: "My children, it is permitted you in times of grave danger to walk with the devil until you have crossed the bridge." Whereas previously this had implied cooperating with Moscow, now the same adage could be used in the struggle against world communism.[8]

The most important source of this new realism about the appropriateness of democracy for other peoples most likely came from the Roosevelt administration's analysis of the fate of Wilson's interventions in Latin America a generation earlier. FDR had been assistant secretary of the Navy under Wilson, and he had enthusiastically endorsed Wilson's interventions in Central America and the Caribbean. He had come to appreciate the difficulties for American intervention in Haiti, Nicaragua, and the Dominican Republic, however, and the animosity these efforts raised throughout Latin America.

Hence in an address to the Pan-American Union less than six weeks into his first term as president, Roosevelt omitted speaking of democracy when he talked of the "inspiration" to be derived from reflecting on the "common ties—historical, cultural, economic and social" binding together the peoples of the Western Hemisphere. Then in December 1933, speaking more pointedly at the Woodrow Wilson Foundation, Roosevelt spelled it out concretely, declaring: "The maintenance of constitutional government in other nations is not a sacred obligation devolving upon the United States alone. . . . the definite policy of the United States from now on is one opposed to armed intervention."[9]

Already at the Seventh Pan-American Conference in Montevideo earlier in December 1933, Secretary Hull had agreed to sign a Convention on the Rights and Duties of States, by which the United States revoked the Roosevelt Corollary of 1904 to the Monroe Doctrine, which had given the United States a unilateral right to intervene militarily in the affairs of other states in the hemisphere. According to Article 8 of the Convention, "No state has the right to intervene in the internal or external affairs of another."[10] Subsequently, the United States also renounced its right to intervene under the terms of established bilateral treaties. In May 1934, the United States abrogated the Platt Amendment giving it authority to act in Cuba, and thereafter, in the same spirit, it withdrew American troops or ended similar treaty rights in Haiti, the Dominican Republic, Nicaragua, and Panama. So long as governments did not come under the domination of a foreign power, the United States would pledge itself not to interfere in their domestic affairs. (The one reservation to this pledge came in an assertion that should the countries of the hemisphere act in concert, then intervention might be justified.)[11]

However well this Good Neighbor Policy may have been received domestically and in Latin America, it was not a boon to democracy in the region. With the withdrawal of American customs agents from the Dominican Republic, Rafael Trujillo was in a better position to consolidate his dictatorship in that country. So too, within a year of the withdrawal of American marines from Nicaragua, Anastasio Somoza had killed Augusto Sandino and emerged as the undisputed king-pin of the land. And in Cuba, Fulgencio Batista moved into position to control the island, reassured that Washington would not look too closely at how affairs there were managed so long as order was assured.[12] Thanks to Wilson, governmental functions in the region had become more centralized; under Roosevelt, the dictators who emerged in good measure from the forces put in motion by these earlier interventions were left to manage affairs as they saw best.

True, the United States continued to work diplomatically for the promotion of constitutional government in the region. By refusing to intervene in

Mexico on behalf of the Catholic Church in 1934, for example, and by allowing Mexico to expropriate American oil concessions there unchallenged in 1938, FDR avoided a confrontation with the government of Lazaro Cardenas in a manner that not only helped Mexican-American relations but that also contributed to the consolidation of the Mexican government. In other circumstances, even if governments might not reflect the will of the governed, they nonetheless were expected by Washington to have enough institutional integrity to assure stable rule. So in the spring of 1935, when Guatemalan President Jorge Ubico acted to amend his country's constitution in order to extend his rule, Secretary Hull instructed the American ambassador to point out to the president the adverse repercussions his actions would have elsewhere in Central America:

> If the tendency referred to is continued and Central America reverts to a system of personal rule, there is foreseen a return to the conditions of permanent intranquillity and frequent international conflict which characterized the period prior to 1907–1923, when constitutional government was practically unknown in Central America.[13]

Still another American goal for the region—indeed, by far the most important—was to knit it together in ties of economic interdependence. The Reciprocal Trade Agreements, which Washington began to negotiate with various countries in 1934 (the same year the Export-Import Bank was founded to facilitate American foreign trade), were intended as an integrative glue that would hold together the politically independent states of the Western Hemisphere (and beyond). The argument was largely Cordell Hull's, who rightly saw the effort to set in place an increasingly dense structure of economic interdependence as one of the most ambitious projects the United States had ever engaged in to promote harmony among states. In the process increased American influence with its smaller economic partners might well have positive repercussions on the prospects for democracy in the region.[14]

Whatever the American intentions with respect to economic ties, the consequences were on balance unfavorable to the emergence of democratic regimes in the Western Hemisphere. The impact of economic dynamism ignited by increased trade in the region led largely to the expansion of plantation agriculture, with the concentrations of wealth and the polarization of classes this implied. If sugar and cattle were forms of livelihood that were inimical to democracy, then so were the Reciprocal Trade Agreements.

Hence, in a country like Nicaragua or the Dominican Republic where a dictator ruled, the infusion of new economic strength (thanks to a closer American connection) tended to consolidate the tyrant's hold. By contrast, in Cuba, where a progressive authoritarian who wanted to steal the thunder of the left was in charge, the long-term consequence of the American stimulation of sugar production may have helped the emergence of middle-class forces potentially sympathetic to democracy.[15] In still other lands, oligarchic control or a more egalitarian distribution of economic power may have been the result of the opening of new foreign markets, but the outcome depended on the prior structure of socioeconomic power, which varied widely from El Salvador (oligarchic) to Costa Rica (where small holders were more numerous).

The political impact of increased trade and investment in the region thanks to the American connection depended, in short, on how it affected the class structures of these countries. There was no reason to assume that democracy would necessarily be promoted by American economic influence. Had Roosevelt forgotten his own brave words? In 1936 he had warned against "the evils of farm tenancy":

> In our national life, public and private, the very nature of free government demands that there must be a line of defense held by the yeomanry of business and industry and agriculture. I do not mean the generalissimos, but the small men, the average men in business and industry and agriculture. . . . Any elemental policy, economic or political, which tends to eliminate these dependable defenders of democratic institutions, and to concentrate control in the hands of a few small, powerful groups, is directly opposed to the stability of government and to democratic government itself.[16]

In considering the likely political impact on the small agrarian countries of Central America and the Caribbean of the economic elements of his Good Neighbor Policy—which in most instances increased not only output but also concentrations of land and wealth, and so was detrimental to the prospects for democracy there—Roosevelt would have done well to keep his own admonitions in mind.

The main lesson to be drawn from the American experience with the Good Neighbor Policy was that it demonstrated the Roosevelt administration's awareness that the prospects for democracy depended in good measure on time and place. It could not be mandated from Washington, and the effort to do so could actually destabilize the region and create anti-American sentiment. A decade after the Good Neighbor Policy began, as the United States prepared to globalize the Monroe Doctrine, Americans could recall what they had learned from their experience with Latin America: opposition to spheres of influence in international affairs did not necessarily mean a commitment to democracy. A new liberal realism had replaced the relative simplicity and the naivete of Wilson's worldview. But at a price.

Democracy and Anti-Imperialism

Despite the evidence that the Roosevelt administration was realistic about
the prospects for democracy in much of the world, Washington nonetheless
sounded the theme loudly, in good measure to enlist the commitment of
American public to move from isolationism toward a leading role in world
affairs. Even before Pearl Harbor, Roosevelt had labored to make American patriotism synonymous with the defense of democracy: "I tell the
American people solemnly that the United States will never survive as a
happy and fertile oasis of liberty surrounded by a cruel desert of dictatorship," the president declared in the middle of 1941. And later that year,
"There must be liberty, worldwide and eternal"; "The American people
have made an unlimited commitment that there shall be a free world."[17]
The appeal to rally 'round the flag in the name of democratic values became a way to incite a patriotic crusade, which could only intensify as the
nation was swept into the conflict at the end of 1941.

In his efforts to move the world in a more liberal direction, FDR described his goals in ways that generally seemed compatible with common
sense and decency. But the amiable tenor of the president's words should
not disguise the extraordinary extent of the postwar American ambition,
which in effect was to replace great power spheres of influence with a more
integrated and centralized world system resting in good measure on American power.

But for the devastation of the war, American notions of the proper organization of the international system would have been supremely irrelevant
to world affairs, as fated for disaster as Wilson's plans for the peace after
1919. They would have been strongly resisted by France and Britain, and
rejected out of hand by Germany, Japan, and the Soviet Union. Only the
weaker peoples of the world would have welcomed such initiatives, for
they promised to enlarge significantly their margin of political maneuver.
Given the relative power of the United States in 1944–5, however, a major
restructuring of world politics was potentially at hand. FDR's good-
natured manner should not for a moment obscure the boldness of the American liberal democratic internationalist vision.

While American opposition to a Soviet sphere of influence in Eastern
Europe was to have momentous consequences for the postwar order, initially Washington was especially concerned with dismantling the British
Empire. That is, anti-imperialism, not anticommunism, was the first com-
mandment of American policy. Given their established position in world
politics, the British were the first to infringe on the American-inspired
order and so the first to be dealt with accordingly.[18]

Well before the war, Secretary Hull had set to work to break the tariff
wall set up by the British imperial preference system in 1932 by the Ottawa

Agreements. He complained that these agreements were "the greatest injury, in a commercial way, that has been inflicted on this country since I have been in public life." Nevertheless, Hull wanted Britain to be "the apex of the arch" of the economic liberalization measures he envisioned when he entered office in 1933.[19]

Friction over Article 4 of the Atlantic Charter was therefore a foregone conclusion, since it pledged the signatories "to further the enjoyment by all states, great or small, victor or vanquished, of access, on equal terms, to the trade and to the raw materials of the world which are needed for their economic prosperity." To Hull's dismay, Churchill qualified his acceptance of these provisions with a statement that the countries involved must pay "due respect to their existing obligations," by which he meant to exempt Britain's imperial preference system from compliance. Hull immediately counterattacked. As early as the spring of 1942, using American aid to Britain through Lend-Lease as an instrument of policy, Hull began to win acceptance in London of the American view of postwar international economic relations.[20] The repercussions such concessions would have on the integrity of the British Empire were manifest to all. Foreign Minister Anthony Eden speculated that FDR hoped that the colonies "once free of their masters will become politically and economically dependent upon the United States."[21]

The Americans could also be directly political in their demands. Accordingly, Great Britain repeatedly sought assurances that the trusteeships Roosevelt wanted established under the United Nations after the war (much like the Mandate system under the League) were not to be mechanisms to deprive them of their colonies. When reminded by Churchill that the British had no intention in "scuttling" their empire, Roosevelt would characteristically seek to reassure the prime minister. But just as characteristically, the president would eventually return to his theme (much as he was repeatedly reassuring to Stalin with respect to the future friendship of Eastern Europe for the Soviet Union, yet insistent that this cooperative spirit be demonstrated through free elections).

At one point at Yalta, the dispute between Roosevelt and Churchill broke out in front of Stalin, a development the two Western leaders usually worked to avoid. The outburst came as Secretary of State Edward Stettinius made reference to the trusteeship arrangement to be supervised by the United Nations after the war. At this point, the American minutes report, Churchill

> interrupted with great vigor to say that he did not agree with one single word of this report on trusteeships. . . . He said that under no circumstances would he ever consent to forty or fifty nations thrusting interfering fingers into the life's existence of the British Empire. As long as he was Minister, he would never yield one

scrap of their heritage. He continued in this vein for some minutes. . . . He asked how Marshal Stalin would feel if the suggestion was made that the Crimea should be internationalized for use as a summer resort.[22]

According to Harry Hopkins, Churchill spoke in such a rapid and excited manner that his words were sometimes hard to follow, except that he repeatedly muttered "never, never, never." During this tirade, it is worth noting, a pleased Stalin "got up from his chair, walked up and down, beamed, and at intervals broke into applause."[23]

Washington was not to be moved. Given the friendship between the United States and the imperial powers of Western Europe, as well as the need for postwar stability, the best the Americans were willing to allow the Europeans was an orderly retreat from empire. Secretary Hull rightly notes: "At no time did we press Britain, France or The Netherlands for an immediate grant of self-government to their colonies. Our thought was that it would come after an adequate period of years, short or long, depending on the state of development of respective colonial peoples, during which these peoples would be trained to govern themselves."[24] But in the case of India, the United States was convinced that Britain would find the subcontinent ready to revolt if London did not assure Indian nationalists of independence after the war. And in Southeast Asia, where Britain, France, and the Netherlands all had important colonial possessions, Hull reports that in September 1944, Roosevelt "warmly approved" a memorandum stressing the value of

> early, dramatic, and concerted announcements by the nations concerned making definite commitments as to the future of the regions of Southeast Asia. . . . It would be especially helpful if such concerted announcements could include 1) specific dates when independence or complete (dominion) self-government will be accorded, 2) specific steps to be taken to develop native capacity for self-rule, and 3) a pledge of economic autonomy and equality of economic treatment toward other nations. . . . In addition to their great value as psychological warfare [against the Japanese] such announcements would appear to be directly in line with American postwar interests.[25]

In due course, Hull's proposal was transmitted to the European governments concerned. Churchill, who had earlier declared that he had "not become His Majesty's Prime Minister in order to preside over the liquidation of the British Empire," replied with characteristic verve:

> There must be no question of our being hustled or seduced into declarations affecting British sovereignty in any of the Dominions or Colonies. Pray remember my declaration against liquidating the British Empire. If the Americans want to take Japanese islands which they have conquered, let them do so with our blessing and any form of words that may be agreeable to them. But "Hands Off

the British Empire" is our maxim and it must not be weakened or smirched to please sob-stuff merchants at home or foreigners of any hue.[26]

As Churchill's words illustrate, the British saw the American opposition to great-power spheres of influence as a disguised effort to take over the entire globe for itself. American anti-imperialism appeared to them to be little more than imperialism in new dress. In this respect, Churchill had more in common with Stalin than with Roosevelt, for the British leader had no doubt as to Soviet imperial designs, which he was prepared to block when he could but accept when he must. All this American talk about democracy and independence was rhetoric the British would engage in only when it served a purpose, which they understood to be the classic gambit of great powers maneuvering to secure spheres of interest for themselves. So they would suffer the Americans by turn to be naive or windbags, until their own interests were attacked. An amusing example of such a run-in came in a discussion between the president and British Colonial Secretary Oliver Stanley in January 1945:

> Roosevelt: I do not want to be unkind or rude to the British, but in 1841, when you acquired Hong Kong, you did not acquire it by purchase.
> Stanley: Let me see, Mr. President, that was about the time of the Mexican War, wasn't it?[27]

Here, then, with respect to its closest ally, Washington declared Britain's imperial days to be drawing to an end. In due course, and with a change in government from Tory to Labour, the British came to be of a like mind. In 1947, they granted independence to India and asked the United States to inherit their role as paramount power in the eastern Mediterranean (an offer accepted by the United States in the Truman Doctrine). But while the war was on and Churchill in command, the British remained firmly committed to the defense of their empire and opposed to many basic features of the American scheme of things.

The French were equally resolved to resist efforts to dismantle their empire. Indeed, the later tragedy of Indochina was directly linked to General Charles de Gaulle's unwavering determination that France must reimpose its sovereignty on Indochina after the war, lest France lose the greatness he was so certain it needed and deserved. As a result, de Gaulle was unalterably opposed to what he correctly sensed were American efforts to consign his country to second rank status in world affairs.[28]

While the British supported a reestablishment of French power in Europe as a counter to German and Soviet strength, and opposed the dismantlement of the French Empire as a threat to their own, Stalin and Roosevelt were in agreement that France was, and would remain, a weak actor on the world stage. In this spirit, Roosevelt repeatedly speculated on how various parts of the French empire might be apportioned as trusteeships: Indochina to China, Senegal to the United States, North Africa to Great Britain, and New Caledonia to Australia.[29]

The immovable obstacle to such speculation was de Gaulle. Commenting on Roosevelt's proposal for the United Nations, de Gaulle noted, "As was only human, his will to power cloaked itself in idealism." And the General reports he admonished the president directly:

> It is the West that must be restored. If it regains its balance, the rest of the world, whether it wishes to or not, will take it for an example. If it declines, barbarism will ultimately sweep everything away. . . . This is true of France above all, which of all the great nations of Europe is the only one which was, is and always will be your ally. . . . But it is in the political realm that [France] must recover her vigor, her self-reliance and consequently, her role. How can she do this if she is excluded from the organization of the great world powers and their decisions, if she loses her African and Asian territories—in short, if the settlement of the war definitively imposes upon her the psychology of the vanquished?[30]

What the general did not know at the time was that Roosevelt, in his dislike for this obstreperous Frenchman, had once sarcastically proposed to Churchill that de Gaulle be made governor general of Madagascar when the war was over.

DEMOCRACY AND SOVIET IMPERIALISM

Of course, the most important question for the structure of the international system after the Axis defeat was not so much what would happen to the French and British empires, but what the Soviet Union would insist on for itself either in imperial terms or with its own vision for the proper ordering of world affairs. Would Moscow demand spheres of influence in Eastern Europe, Turkey, Iran, northern China, and Korea; would it actively support communist takeovers in a host of countries in Latin America and Asia; or would it abide by the American plan for a postwar order of politically independent states bound together by ties of collective security in the United Nations and of economic interdependence in the manner of the Bretton Woods Agreements?

Internal discussions among American officials conceded that some spheres of Soviet influence would surely exist after Germany and Japan's defeat. Countries like Poland would presumably be deferential to Soviet foreign-policy concerns, something like Finland later was to exemplify, or much like most of Latin America was in relation to the United States. As with the term *self-determination*, so the meaning of *sphere of influence* was ambiguous.[31] What at no time the Americans deemed permissible was that the Soviet Union would annex these lands to itself (with the exception of the territorial adjustments of 1939, and even here FDR expected local populations to ratify the transfers by plebiscite), or that governments depending ultimately on Soviet force of arms would continue to rule these lands indefinitely after the defeat of fascism.

From an early point in the war, serious tensions on this question surfaced. When British Foreign Secretary Anthony Eden visited Moscow in December 1941, Stalin grimly asked him whether the Atlantic Charter, signed but four months earlier with its implicit condemnation of postwar spheres of influence, was directed against Germany or the Soviet Union. Certainly the Soviet Union expected to keep the territories it had gained through its 1939 nonaggression pact with Germany: the Baltic states and parts of Finland, Rumania, and Poland. While the Americans continued to insist that it was premature at that juncture to decide further territorial settlements until victory was in sight, this initial encounter pointed up the serious interests and suspicions that discussions of postwar spheres of influence were sure to raise. Here, as later, Washington insisted that self-determination be the rule.

But Stalin would not concede the principle or postpone the matter. During Eden's visit, Moscow indicated that its willingness to sign an Anglo-Soviet treaty directed against Germany depended on British willingness to ratify Soviet boundaries as they were in September 1939. Britain's initial reaction was to reject the Soviet proposal and to cite the Atlantic Charter as the basis for its position. Moscow insistently repeated its demand. By March 1942 London had decided that the need for an accord with the Soviets was so great that it should comply.

At this juncture, the Americans made their displeasure fully apparent. The president reacted negatively to the proposal, then suggested as a compromise that the inhabitants of the areas affected be permitted by the Soviets to leave with all their possessions if such were their wish. Meanwhile, Assistant Secretary of State Adolf Berle vigorously denounced the entire proposed Anglo-Soviet agreement as a "Baltic 'Munich,' " unjust in itself and a prelude to later Soviet takeovers elsewhere. Under-Secretary of State Sumner Welles declared himself "in full accord," with Berle, as did Secretary Hull. Ultimately, the United States reiterated its insistence that the question of frontiers must be postponed until the close of the war. In the Anglo-Soviet Treaty, finally signed at the end of May 1942, there was no mention of the Soviet demand. The American position that self-determination be the established rule of the postwar order had not been generally accepted, but neither had it been sacrificed to Soviet displeasure.[32]

At Tehran in December 1943, the question of the future of the Baltic republics once again came up. American minutes for a meeting between Roosevelt and Stalin report that FDR declared that "he fully realized the three Baltic Republics had in history and again more recently been a part of Russia and added jokingly that when the Soviet armies reoccupied these areas, he did not intend to go to war with the Soviet Union on this point." Characteristically, what he had given with one hand, the president promptly took back with the other, announcing that "the big issue in the United States, insofar as public opinion went, would be the question of referendum and the right of self-determination. He said he thought that world opinion would want some expression of the will of the people, perhaps not immediately after their reoccupation by Soviet forces, but someday, and that he personally was confident that the people would vote to join the Soviet Union."[33]

The fate of the Baltic republics was only one salvo in the American opposition to a Soviet sphere of influence exercised by direct political control from Moscow. The United States vigorously protested Churchill's agreement with Stalin in October 1944 to divide Eastern Europe (with the exception of Poland and Czechoslovakia) into spheres of influence, the British predominant in Greece while Soviet influence would be recognized in Rumania and Bulgaria (and to a lesser extent in Yugoslavia and Hungary).[34] Months before Churchill's famous meeting with Stalin, the State Department had implicitly invoked the American doctrine of self-determination to the British embassy in no uncertain terms with respect to the Balkans:

> Special efforts are being made for concerted action in laying the foundations of a broader system of general security in which all countries great and small will have their part. Any arrangement suggestive of spheres of influence cannot but militate against the establishment and effective functioning of such a broader framework.

Accordingly, when for once Roosevelt gave in to Churchill's insistence that Britain must exercise control in Greece for a period after its liberation from Nazi forces, the American president insisted it should not be for more than three months stating: "We must be careful to make it clear that we are not establishing any postwar spheres of influence."[35]

As this account indicates, the Declaration on Liberated Europe signed at Roosevelt's instigation at Yalta in February 1945 was no face-saving device behind which he intended to concede Soviet control in much of Eastern Europe. A reading of the documents before and after this conference, and its sequel at Potsdam that July, gives no reason to doubt the seriousness of the American commitment to the terms of the declaration. Twice the declaration evokes the Atlantic Charter, and it associates the Big Three in a guarantee to assist the peoples they free from Axis control "to solve by democratic means their pressing political and economic problems."

> The establishment of order in Europe and the rebuilding of national economic life must be achieved by processes which will enable the liberated peoples to destroy

the last vestiges of Nazism and Fascism and to create democratic institutions of their own choice. This is a principle of the Atlantic Charter—the right of all peoples to choose the form of government under which they will live—the restoration of sovereign rights and self-government to those peoples who have been forcibly deprived of them by the aggressor nations.

To foster the conditions in which the liberated peoples may exercise these rights, the three governments will jointly assist the people in any European liberated state or former Axis satellite state in Europe where in their judgment conditions require a) to establish conditions of internal peace; b) to carry out emergency measures for the relief of distressed people; c) to form interim governmental authorities broadly representative of all democratic elements in the population and pledged to the earliest possible establishment through free elections of governments responsive to the will of the people; and d) to facilitate where necessary the holding of such elections.[36]

The declaration was not to be quickly forgotten. In meeting after meeting, Americans would invoke it. Ultimately, in May 1945, Truman refused to sign peace treaties and thus to recognize the governments of Rumania, Bulgaria, and Hungary because their composition and conduct did not correspond to the assurances of the declaration.[37]

In effect, what Truman was proposing for Europe was Wilson's original doctrine of nonrecognition of regimes in Latin America that could not justly claim democratic legitimacy. By contrast, the British felt that once these governments were recognized and the Red Army withdrawn, the terms of the declaration had more chance of being implemented. The Americans were far more skeptical. Although the United States finally decided to recognize the Polish Provisional Government of National Unity at the end of June 1945, Washington tied its recognition to that regime's obligation "to hold free and unfettered elections on the basis of universal suffrage and secret ballot."[38]

In the Far East as well as in Eastern Europe and the Balkans, American policymakers were faced with handling the political reconstruction of the Axis countries and those that the Axis powers had occupied. The most intricate problem concerned the character of the domestic political forces that surfaced after the fascists' defeat and whether they would respect the terms of the declaration calling for democratic self-determination.

In some countries, local forces made the transition to stable governments relatively quickly. In Western Europe—France, Italy, the Low Countries, and Scandanavia—democratic forces were soon ascendant. In Yugoslavia, by contrast, Joseph Tito's communist Partisans quickly seized power, so violating Tito's engagement to see a government in Belgrade established according to democratic procedures. The State Department identified his movement as "thoroughly totalitarian."[39] Spain chose a third alternative—

continued rule by the right. Given Franco's help to Germany, Stalin called for his overthrow, but Roosevelt and Churchill resisted, preferring to deny the country membership in the United Nations and to wait for the Spanish people themselves to deal with the caudillo.[40]

Elsewhere it was not the local popular forces but the occupying armies of the victorious Allies who set the framework for the postwar political succession. In these cases they became important actors. The conquering armies worked to leave behind them a political system that corresponded to their interests. "Whose rule, his religion" (*cuius regio, eius religio*)—the formula that settled the religious wars in Germany in 1648—was to become the de facto procedure by which the British, American, and Soviet occupying authorities tried to arrange matters politically in the wake of the Axis defeat.

While official American discussions of communism in the postwar world generally assumed a common interest between Moscow and local communist movements, in practice, the United States made country-by-country distinctions. Whatever his connections in Moscow, Ho Chi Minh was not considered an instrument of Soviet foreign policy, and at first the United States did not flatly oppose his declaration of an independent Vietnam in the wake of the Japanese occupation of that country. So too, Mao Zedong's forces in China were initially seen as relatively independent of Moscow's control; Chiang Kai-shek was encouraged to cooperate with them.[41] Nevertheless, an affinity was assumed to exist between the different communist movements, a solidarity reinforced by the mechanisms of the Cominform (the renamed Communist International), and by a common antagonism to the basic values and interests of the democratic-capitalist West.

In Italy, the communists were relatively weak after the war. But twenty years of fascist rule had polarized politics between the left and the right, making it far from certain that a viable centrist option would materialize. The State Department's Briefing Book Paper on Italy for Truman at Potsdam noted America's strategic interest in Italy, and warned explicitly against "a new totalitarianism" that might arise there given "the power and will of the USSR . . . ; internal political confusion and a well organized Communist party; the absence of any machinery for, and indeed any real experience of, democratic government; the knowledge that American troops are being withdrawn and with them the assurance of disinterested protection." However, if the economy could be reinvigorated, sound government provided, and "fair treatment by the victorious powers" be demonstrated, "a violent ideological swing to right or left could be discounted. A moderate left movement is not only inevitable but should be encouraged so as to give scope to the essentially sound peasant and laboring classes and in order to avoid exasperating by vain opposition a natural trend."[42]

Unlike Vietnam, where Washington could look with at least some equanimity on a communist takeover, the emergence of such a government in Western Europe was far more troublesome.[43] As seen by Rear Admiral Ellery Stone, chief commissioner of the Allied Commission for Italy:

> [Italy] is split into eight conflicting political parties with membership of less than 10 per cent of the population and no outstanding leader to come to the fore; she has had five Governments [in the preceding 21 months]; a million of her men have been in exile either as slave labor or as prisoners of war. . .her economy has been totally disrupted. . .without coal and raw materials she faces unemployment amounting to several millions; the country is full of arms illegally held. Like other European countries devastated by the war, the ground in Italy is fertile for the rapid growth of the seeds of an anarchical movement fostered by Moscow to bring Italy within the sphere of Russian influence. Already there are signs that, if present conditions long continue, communism will triumph—possibly by force.
>
> The great majority of Italians desire to see a democratic Italy. They will only permit communism to take hold because of fear—since that party is the best organized and best armed in the country—or because of apathy arising from a generation of non-participation in democratic political life, the shame of defeat, and the results of privation. . . . unless they receive help and guidance from the democracies . . . they will inevitably turn to the USSR and join the group of "police" states united by communism, which is extending westward from Russia.[44]

Ultimately, American hopes were realized for a stable center government in Italy. In December 1945, the Christian Democrats first came into power under the leadership of Alcide De Gasperi. In June 1946 a referendum repudiated the monarchy in favor of a republic and elected a constituent assembly. A new constitution came into effect in January 1948, and that April the Christian Democrats won a majority in Parliament. Whatever its vicissitudes subsequently, the basis of Italian postwar democracy had been firmly laid.

Poland, however, was the country that would serve as the best gauge of Soviet intentions toward the postwar international order. The world had gone to war over Hitler's invasion of it, and its size and strategic location (between Germany and the Soviet Union), the existence of more than 6 million Polish Americans, as well as the country's liberation by the Red Army in January 1945—which gave Stalin direct control over its political future—meant that in American thinking the fate of Poland was particularly important.

There was little reason to think that in 1944–5 the Soviet Union was at all inclined to tolerate an independent Poland. Memories of centuries-old conflicts were made still more vivid in Russian minds by recollections of their loss of territory to Poland in the conflict of 1920–1, while Stalin's crimes against the Polish people during the war were far too serious to suppose that an independent Warsaw would be other than hostile to Moscow's influence. Foreign Minister Vyacheslav Molotov had contemptuously dismissed the country in October 1939 as "this ugly offspring of the Versailles Treaty," and whatever verbal reassurances Stalin may have given Churchill and Roosevelt, his actions in Poland were unmistakably intended to secure indelible communist rule and Soviet influence there.[45] There was little likelihood that the Polish government-in-exile in London and the Soviet Union could freely come to a meeting of minds on their mutual respect for one another.

A reading of the background papers and minutes of the various Big Three meetings during the war suggests that no issue so preoccupied the Americans with respect to the Polish question as that "free and unfettered elections" be held there in due course after Germany's surrender. Indeed, the issue is brought up so frequently that one may doubt whether any other single item of business at Yalta in February 1945 received more attention. The United States did not argue strongly over the postwar borders of Poland, nor over the precise modalities of the formation of a coalition-transition-provisional government (although obviously it had opinions on all these matters). Where the Americans dug their heels in was on elections. Stalin may well have suspected that the United States hoped to reduce Soviet influence in Poland through the outcome at the polls, but he could not have been in doubt that Washington was serious on the matter. Roosevelt may have been as naive on the prospects for Polish-Soviet understanding as he was on the likelihood that Nationalists and Communists in China could come to a working arrangement, but he did not give Poland away at Yalta.[46]

However overoptimistic Washington's perception of Polish-Soviet relations may have been, without the benefits of hindsight it is not self-evident that a more aggressive posture on Poland would have been more successful. Roosevelt's policy represented a realistic appraisal of the situation, not—as some have charged—a Wilsonian belief (if indeed trying to cooperate with a dictatorship such as Stalin's had anything Wilsonian about it) that one good turn would deserve another. Moreover, the Americans were not mistaken to believe that domestic conditions in Poland were favorable for the emergence of stable democratic government after 1944. To be sure, during the interwar years, Polish democracy had been a fragile arrangement, finally ended by left-leaning General Joseph Pilsudski in 1926, who permitted only a modicum of parliamentary power thereafter. Pilsudski may not have ruled democratically, but he was seen as a national hero who paid more than lip service to the values of democratic government. However, class and ethnic cleavages cut deeply into the political landscape, and Poland's geographic location between two far more powerful dictatorships heightened domestic tensions immeasurably. In comparison with Czechoslovakia, Poland's democratic forces were weak.

Yet by 1945, the prospects for democracy had noticeably improved. Perhaps the most decisive factor was the weakness of the Polish Communist party. Ironically, its most severe blows had been delivered in the late 1930s by Moscow. In 1938, the party had been brutally purged and twelve members of its Central Committee executed by Stalin. Given traditional Polish antipathy toward the Soviet Union, the Communist party could not recover easily from this trauma. Thus, unlike elsewhere in occupied Europe, where the local communist party played a leading role in domestic resistance forces, its role in Poland was relatively marginal. The noncommunist resistance, the Home Army, had no trouble maintaining its independence from communist efforts to capture the leadership of the resistance forces. After the war, then, it was not likely that Polish communists would have fared well at the polls in a free election, even if they had benefited from the short-term aid of the Soviet army of occupation.

Nor was a rightist authoritarian government a serious probability. Neither the social base nor the ideological appeal of the right existed in any strong measure in postwar Poland. The powerful Polish landlord class was virtually destroyed when the Soviet Union annexed its holdings to the East, where it had ruled over predominately Ukrainian and Belorussian peasants. And any temptation to imitate German authoritarianism had been extinguished in the inferno of the war.

If the right- and left-wing enemies of democracy were relatively weak in 1945, what of the forces of the center? Given the impeccable democratic credentials of Poland's first postwar premier, Stanislaw Mikolajczyk, and his leadership of the strongest political movement in the country, the Polish Peasant party, as well as the existence of a strong Social Democratic party, there is good reason to think that Poland, left to its own devices, might have become a vigorous democracy. Roosevelt's confidence in a democratic future for Poland was well placed, and his willingness to believe the Soviets understandable: "At Tehran, I was very glad to hear Marshal Stalin say, not once but several times, that he did not desire Poland to be an appendage of the Russian Soviet Republics, but should, on the other hand, be a completely self-governing, large and completely independent nation."[47] Unfortunately, at Yalta, Stalin began to sound a different note. The exchange is memorable:

> President: I want this election in Poland to be the first one beyond question. It should be like Caesar's wife. I did not know her but they said she was pure.
> Stalin: They said that about her but in fact she had her sins.[48]

The fate of Poland was sealed by Stalin's decision to install a communist regime in power; unless the United States wanted to go to war over the matter, there was little Washington could do directly. In terms of active decision-making, Greece therefore represented the first difficult situation for the postwar American officials, for more than in either Italy or Poland Washington's role in the course of events was critical.

The major political concern confronting the Americans was the power of the Greek Communist party (KKE). The party controlled the major resistance force in Greece, the National Liberation Movement (EAM) and its armed wing (ELAS). In October 1944, when the Germans departed, the communists alone had the capacity to rule the country.

But as the Germans withdrew, a British army of occupation arrived to assure Greek reconstruction. At Moscow in October 1944, Churchill had negotiated for Greece to remain a British sphere of influence. His intention was to impose British authority until the Greek monarch, George II, returned from exile in London.[49]

Stalin kept his word to abandon support for the KKE, but communist power in the country nonetheless remained formidable. Churchill was very much of the opinion that a communist government in Athens would mean the end of British influence in this critical region of the world and the corresponding expansion of Moscow's power there. He therefore decided to use force against a communist uprising that began in December 1945. By February 1946 the British effectively controlled Greece.

The question thereafter was how Britain would restructure a government for Greece, which had been without a parliament since the 1936 coup of General John Metaxas. The material the British had to work with was not promising. Republican forces were divided among themselves despite the emergence of George Papandreou as their leader, while being opposed by both a revolutionary communist force on the left and an antidemocratic right based on the monarchy, the military, and those who had collaborated with the Germans.

In these trying circumstances, Lincoln MacVeagh, the American ambassador to Greece since 1933, tried to foster the strength of the republican forces while holding in check the extreme right. He recognized that important preconditions for democracy were in place; many Greeks who supported the EAM did so for lack of a better alternative. Given the opportunity to join other parties, the likelihood is that they would desert the communists. Republican values appealed strongly to a sizeable portion of the Greek electorate: Greece had experimented with liberal democracy intermittently from 1910 to 1936, under the leadership of Eleftherios Venizelos, during which an effective land reform had been implemented. Thanks to its dynamic mercantile class (with its important foreign connections), a bourgeoisie existed that could benefit from stable, democratic rule (although many of the cosmopolitan Greeks were royalists).[50] MacVeagh's wrote in December 1944: "The truth is that neither pure royalism nor pure communism has many followers in Greece today, while each enjoys accretions of strength, none the less dangerous for being fundamentally fictitious, from suspicions which are rife and growing among democrats with possessions, on the one hand, and among democrats without possessions but hungry, homeless and armed on the other."[51]

Accordingly, MacVeagh worked to support the Greek center. In January 1946 he encouraged increased financial aid for Athens, writing that without help, "the present democratic government will certainly fall and probably be succeeded by a regime of the extreme right, which in turn could scarcely fail to produce in due course a communist dictatorship."[52]

In these circumstances, the parliamentary elections of March 1946 were of great importance, for they established the first postwar government of Greece. Unfortunately, the left called for a boycott and a right-wing majority was returned by the electorate. That September, a plebiscite restored the monarchy.

Students of this period have not come to a consensus on how representative either the elections or the plebescite actually were, nor on whether these votes should have been held when they were from the point of view of providing stable government for Greece. Critics of the elections have argued that the elections were held too early, under conditions that facilitated fraud and intimidation by the right. British and American officials wanted the elections so that the British army could depart and the Greeks could begin the job of self-government. While acknowledging that Greek government forces "exercised undue influence" in the voting, American observers nonetheless concluded that even "without that influence we are satisfied that a majority of votes for the King could still have been obtained."[53]

If a king there had to be, then an important ingredient for a stable noncommunist government in Greece lay in a constitutional monarchy of clearly defined and limited powers. Repeatedly, MacVeagh used the term *fascist* to describe some of those in power, calling for the removal of "certain notoriously reactionary rightists," denouncing the "lawlessness of extreme right groups" and warning the monarch directly that "what seems to be needed now is that King and Government should work together in creating here such a liberal democracy as the Western Powers can support."[54] At the same time, MacVeagh criticized what he saw as the blind support the British gave the throne, including its protection of right-wing death squads organized earlier under German auspices, whose "white terror" against the left was damaging to the prospects for a responsible democratic center government.[55]

Elections did not stabilize the political situation in Greece, nor did the return of George II. In the fall of 1946, the communists launched a bitter civil war, which lasted until late in 1949. American support for the Greek government during these trying years was decisive in preventing a communist seizure of power. What it was less able to do was to restore democracy in Greece.

Many writers on Greek-American relations complain that the United States saw that country, in the words of one analyst, "as little more than a battlefield of the Cold War," and that subsequently the real problems of Greece were ignored, a tilt toward the right "stifling all chance for desperately needed social reform and political development."[56] The charge is hard to accept unconditionally.

It was, after all, the left that decided to boycott the March 1946 elections, in what can only be judged a serious tactical mistake, and then to launch a full-fledged civil war with foreign (largely Yugoslav) assistance. Nor could the United States be held responsible for the irresponsible behavior of George II. As MacVeagh's comments indicate, though the communists were beaten, the task nonetheless remained of consolidating a stable constitutional order in an environment where the King and the military had gained the upper hand. Keeping the army in the barracks and the king in the palace was no easy feat. The fragmented character of the centrist parties, the historically inherited animosities between republicans and royalists, the traditional importance of charismatic leaders and patron-client relations, and the active part played in Greek politics by the military added up to a situation in which the prospects for stable democratic government certainly did not look too promising despite the victory over communism. How the United States could have managed affairs so as to rescue republicanism in a way dramatically different than it did is never indicated by these authors, except for those who openly suggest that Greece should have been allowed to fall under communist rule.[57]

It is beyond the scope of this chapter to review the vicissitudes of republicanism in Greece in the difficult years between 1949, when the communists were finally defeated, and 1974, when the colonels' military government, which had ruled since 1967, finally gave way to democracy. At times, American policy surely aided the republican forces, at others their reactionary enemies. But on balance, Greece's failure to develop stable democratic institutions had far more to do with Greek internal politics than with Anglo-American imperialism.

For American policymakers, Greece represented the need to compromise the American commitment to foster democratic government for the sake of the struggle against communism by working closely with authoritarian leaders. America hoped that Greece would be a democracy; it insisted that Greece be independent of communist control. For the first time after 1945, the Americans came up against what would soon be a classic cold war dilemma: in a situation where the democratic center was weaker than the authoritarian right, while the radical left was potentially strongest of all, what should American policy be? Since the first order of business was to block a probable communist takeover, the Americans faced up to political reality. From Latin America to Turkey to China, the Americans had established their priorities: regional stability and independence were more important than democracy. But now they found themselves in the uncomfortable position of actively supporting authoritarian regimes, and this in the name of fostering a liberal democratic world order. The irony and the contradiction were not lost on the internal debate within the United States.

THE LIBERAL DEMOCRATIC INTERNATIONALIST IMPERATIVE

The intellectual debate trying to determine how the cold war began is now more than forty years old. In the 1950s, the dominant perspective blamed Soviet imperialism for the struggle. Had Stalin not taken Eastern Europe and tested Western intentions in Turkey and Iran, the cold war might have been avoided. By contrast, a decade later, revisionist historians found the United States to be primarily at fault. Failing to understand legitimate Soviet security interests, the United States had interpreted Stalin's defensive moves as expansive; meanwhile domestic economic interests were clamoring for greater access to the world markets. The result was a series of American initiatives centered on the reunification of Germany, the economic revitalization of Western Europe, and the creation of NATO, decisions that set off the cold war.

By the 1970s, commentators were tending to shift from laying responsibility on one of the two major parties to the struggle to the structure of the contest itself. Now the cold war was seen as in good measure unavoidable, given the very different security concerns and operational codes and capacities of the two superpowers, the power vacuum in Europe and the unresolved dilemma of what to do about Germany, and the momentum of the arms race, which had developed a deadly logic all its own. At roughly the same time, post-revisionist accounts attempted a blend of the various schools of analysis into an integrated explanation of the origins of the cold war.[58]

In four respects, this chapter agrees with arguments advanced by the revisionists. First, the activist, as opposed to reactivist, character of the United States in world affairs after 1944 needs to be clearly set forth in any account of the postwar period. The United States had an essentially Wilsonian design for world order set out in terms of international economic and security agreements that it envisioned would be subscribed to by a community of states formed on the basis of nationalist, democratic self-determination. Thus, for example, before the cold war began, Washington was already pushing the French and British to decolonize and making it clear to the Soviets that they should limit their territorial expansion after Germany's defeat. Second, the rhetoric of liberal democratic internationalism was to an extent symbolic and manipulative, crafted as much to rally a moralistic but inexperienced American public into an expensive, dangerous, and prolonged involvement in world affairs as to secure the blessings of liberty and justice for other peoples of the world. No more able practitioner need be cited than President Roosevelt. Third, an important part of the impetus for an activist role in international relations was economic. Whether it was special interests or the national security that concerned them, American leaders understood as they never had before the priority of an international economic order constructed under their auspices. Finally, American policy cannot be studied in its own terms alone, but must be seen in conjunction with the overall cast of world forces. Seen from the viewpoint of international history, the particular way the United States appealed to class, nationalist, and political interests around the world in large measure determined America's successes and failures in international affairs.

The problems with the revisionist approach are nonetheless substantial. One major shortcoming is that revisionists show little appreciation of the expansionist potential of Stalin's communist system or the baleful consequences its success would have had on world affairs. Like Wilsonian America, the Leninist Soviet Union had an agenda for the reordering of domestic and world political structures. Lenin's "dictatorship of the proletariat" was imitated successfully enough in countries as diverse as China, Cuba, Nicaragua, Ethiopia, Yugoslavia, and North Korea. Even where the Soviet Union imposed these governments by force, they could come to have a life of their own, whether in East Germany or Rumania. The picture emerging now from Soviet archives of Stalin's behavior indicates that his was no ordinary government seeking accommodation with the West on the basis of reasonable security considerations. John Lewis Gaddis remarks that the evidence includes "stories more horrifying than most of the images put forward . . . by the Soviet Union's most strident critics while the Cold War was still going on." And he cites Milovan Djilas's interview with Stalin, where the Soviet dictator reportedly declared: "The war shall soon be over. We shall recover in fifteen or twenty years, and then we'll have another go at it." Or as Soviet Foreign Minister Molotov put it: "Stalin looked at it this way: World War I has wrested one country from capitalist slavery; World War II has created a socialist system; and the third will finish off imperialism forever."[59] In short, revisionism steadfastly refuses to see the Soviet Union's leading role in the cold war or to assess that country with the same high moral tone it reserves for its study of American affairs, and this failure makes it no more than a partial account of events.

Just as seriously, revisionism neglects to explore the reasons that the cold war began in the structure of international politics after 1945. The superpowers found means apart from their formidable military might (the essential factor of their status as superpowers) to exercise influence. The United States appealed to other countries in terms of its economic strength and political system, while the influence of the Soviet Union was largely exercised through "fraternal" communist parties. In the numerous power vacuums created after the war, each country might defensively define its own security needs in a way that seemed to the other like an offensive action. So the Truman administration interpreted Soviet moves in Iran and Turkey as expansive, while Stalin's government saw the efforts to install democratic government in Poland as a threat to its necessary sphere of influence. As tensions grew over the postwar organization of Germany, recognized by both sides to be the key to predominance in Europe, it was virtually inevitable that relations would worsen markedly. Finally, the arms race itself created a momentum terrifying to contemplate yet difficult to control. In short, there were reasons rooted in the structure of international affairs for the cold war to break out, which revisionist accounts of the period refuse to acknowledge.

Finally, and for our purposes most importantly, by laying primary emphasis on the economic motivations of American foreign policy, revisionism necessarily understates the preeminence in Washington's calculations of political concerns expressed in terms of preserving the national security. One can (and should) meld political and economic explanations of the basis of American foreign policy into a compelling synthesis. What nonetheless needs to be recognized in such undertakings is the ultimate predominance of political considerations in determining the logic of Washington's positions.[60]

Admittedly, a part of the reason for Washington's effort to create a plural world political order was surely economic interest. The United States was born of a revolt against mercantilism and, despite enormous changes in its economic structure thereafter, has generally favored a nondiscriminatory multilateral international economic order thereafter for the sake of its agrarian, corporate, and financial interests. But such a world economic system has also favored America's security interests, which in any case were the predominant consideration when the character of the country's foreign policy was being established. Witnesses to the Depression and the rise of fascist militarism in the 1930s, American leaders in the 1940s were persuaded that competitive scrambles for access to resources and markets were a leading cause of war. Hence their determination to set up a framework of international institutions to regulate a nondiscriminatory world economic order served not only domestic economic constituencies but, far more critically, national security as well.[61]

Since its independence—and especially after the settlement of its continental frontiers in the 1840s—the leitmotiv of American foreign policy has been its support for the creation of a politically plural world order, that is, a community of sovereign states opposed to imperialism and pledged to mutual nonaggression. The motivation for this policy was national security: no foreign power should have the ability to threaten the existence of the United States.

Defining *the national security* is a contentious issue, related to the definition of that other vague concept, *the national interest*. What the concept of national security nonetheless points to is a concern by a government for its own survival as an independent, self-determining agent in world affairs, a concern defined politically as a state's preoccupation with its position in a configuration of power in the world arena. The idea presupposes, then, an inventory of threats to sovereignty, of which the most obvious is military, but where economic, geostrategic, or cultural considerations most certainly may play their part as well as they are melded together through the perceptions of leaders influenced by their culture, their times, and their own distinctive personalities.

In the more than two centuries of American history, the sense of threat to the national security has necessarily expanded with America's role in the world. At first, American concerns were limited to the Western hemisphere, hence the Monroe Doctrine of 1823. By the end of that century, the Open Door Notes announced an extension of American security concerns to the Far East. (Thereafter, the Open Door served as the basis for policy in the Far East, especially as a way to protest Japan's encroachments on China, most notably as reaffirmed by the Stimson Doctrine—named after Secretary of State Henry Stimson—in 1932.) After World War I, Wilson understood that the country's national security required it to play a leadership role in European affairs, now infusing the call for self-determination with an explicit recognition of the power of nationalism and of the desirability of democratic government where possible—a package of reforms that constituted what this book calls liberal democratic internationalism or Wilsonianism.

With the rise of fascism in the 1930s, Washington's geopolitical thinking became truly global in scope. Were Eurasia dominated by the Axis powers, Roosevelt worried, American life would become regimented politically and economically, destroying what was vital and great about the United States, until finally its enemies felt powerful enough to attack. Accordingly, fascist successes in Latin America were also a matter for concern.[62]

With the defeat of fascism, these geopolitical concerns regarding the national security switched to the threat posed by another international totalitarian movement led by the Soviet Union. Much as Lincoln had doubted that a democratic North could live alongside a slave-owning Confederacy, much as Wilson had been concerned about those structures of world order that would make the world safe for American democracy, much as FDR contemplated America's fate in a world dominated by fascism, so Truman worried:

> If communism is allowed to absorb free nations, then we would be isolated from our sources of supply and detached from our friends. Then we would have to take defense measures which might really bankrupt our economy, and change our way of life so that we couldn't recognize it as American any longer. . . . It would require a stringent and comprehensive system of allocation and rationing in order to husband our smaller resources. It would require us to become a garrison state, and to impose upon ourselves a system of centralized regimentation unlike anything we have ever known.[63]

The result by the late 1940s was that the United States expanded its security perimeter in the Eastern Mediterranean and then in the Far East, and added control over foreign oil reserves to its security considerations. With the outbreak of the Korean War in 1950, such geopolitical thinking took hold with exaggerated force, as events in every corner of the world became defined in terms of American security concerns, with particularly deadly results in Vietnam.[64]

The result was a bid for international hegemony that in certain instances involved imperialist efforts to control the domestic organization of foreign states. The distinctive mark of American imperialism, however, was its dedication to the self-determination of other countries, which by Wilson's time meant a preference for democratically constituted nationalist states. That is, American hegemony constituted a form of anti-imperialist imperialism, aiming to structure other countries economically, socially, and politically so that they would presumably be part of a peaceful world order congenial to American interests. The problem, of course, was that many peoples did not lend themselves to the American vision, either in the interwar period, after 1945, or again after the fall of the Berlin Wall in 1989. In these circumstances, the result of American imperialism was often terribly damaging to foreign peoples whose nationalist identity refused to be subjected to American pressure—as in Vietnam or Iran—or who suffered under authoritarian governments supported by Washington.

Seen from this perspective, *realism* and *idealism*, as they are discussed in academic debates about the political character of American foreign policy, have been complementary rather than opposed approaches to furthering American interests in the world. As realists, American leaders have shown themselves to be practitioners of the balance of power, mindful to fend off the expansion of powers that might threaten American security. Yet rather than annex foreign territories to its own imperial control, the

United States, for reasons peculiar to its own national identity (including its geostrategic reasoning, its culture and ideology, and especially its economic and political structures) has favored measures to reinforce the independence of states whose incorporation under the control of another great power might threaten American national security.

Put differently, liberal democratic internationalism has been the American way of practicing balance-of-power politics in world affairs. Wilsonianism has been an operational code giving continuity to American policy not only because it expresses American interests but also because in an era of nationalism and mass government—the demands for which have grown in urgency since the late eighteenth century—America's traditional goal of a plural world political order met with a relatively sympathetic reaction on the part of other major forces in world affairs.

To be sure, realism and idealism could at times be at loggerheads, so fueling the endless debates about the proper course of American foreign policy. The disregard in realist thinking for the domestic bases of the state could lead the United States to heavy-handed interventions when political, not military, reasoning would have been more appropriate. (Such, for example, were the shortcomings of Eisenhower in Guatemala and Iran, Nixon and Kissinger in Latin America, and Johnson in Vietnam.) By contrast, Wilsonians might exaggerate the appropriateness of democracy for all peoples, so introducing a self-defeating, moralistic quality into American policy. (Such, for example, was the problem of Wilson's policy toward the Dominican Republic or Carter's policy toward Iran.) But at a deeper level of action, realism and liberal democratic internationalism could work in tandem, the former identifying America's natural allies in balance of power terms, while the latter built up the strength of these allies by indicating ways to reinforce their domestic political bases in ways congenial to the American national interest. Properly conceived, Wilsonianism was an indispensable weapon in the realist's doctrine of containment. Power and principle could on many occasions be as one.

The dominant logic of American foreign policy was dictated by concerns for national security; and the dominant way Washington saw to assure this security in terms of the construction of a stable world order congenial to America's way of life was that democratic governments be promoted worldwide. Nowhere can this abiding American concern better be seen than in a review of American occupation policies in Germany and Japan at the close of World War II. Here American energies were focused with special intensity. Whatever the outcome of American-Soviet relations, it was widely perceived in Washington that in due course Japan and Germany would again be major actors in world events. A primary question for American officials was, therefore, the future international conduct of these two defeated powers.

World War I had been called by Wilson "a war to end wars" and had manifestly been an utter failure in that regard. Could the United States propose a reconstruction of Japan and Germany domestically that would curb their military ambitions? What kind of international system would be best suited to aid in this task? If these two countries could in fact be liberalized economically and democratized politically, what would the repercussion be on world affairs?

Until recently, the most common topic to consider when thinking back on the period 1945–50 has been the origins of the emerging worldwide Soviet-American rivalry. Since this confrontation was the decisive event in international affairs for more than four decades, it is understandable that establishing the character of its origins has been an absorbing occupation. But for American leaders in 1944–5, the sense of this impending rivalry was less pressing than their concerns about the eventual place of Japan and Germany once the trauma of the war had passed. From the perspective of the mid-1990s, when the cold war is behind us and the strength of these two defeated powers is once again so evident, we may be especially interested to see what American leaders felt should be done half a century ago to render Japan and Germany constructive members of the international order. It is to an investigation of these questions that we now turn.

CHAPTER SIX

Democratizing Japan and Germany

> Japan had become the world's great laboratory for an experiment in
> the liberation of a people from totalitarian military rule and for
> the liberalization of government from within. It was clear that the
> experiment in Japan must go far beyond the primary purpose of
> the Allies—destruction of Japan's ability to wage another war and
> the punishment of war criminals. Yet history clearly showed that
> no modern military occupation of a conquered nation had been a
> success. From the moment of my appointment as supreme
> commander, I had formulated the policies I intended to follow. . . .
> First destroy the military power. Punish war criminals. Build the
> structure of representative government. Modernize the constitution.
> Hold free elections. Enfranchise the women. Release the political
> prisoners. Liberate the farmers. Establish a free labor movement.
> Encourage a free economy. Abolish police oppression. Develop a
> free and responsible press. Liberalize education. Decentralize the
> political power. Separate church from state.
> —General Douglas MacArthur,
> Supreme Allied Commander in Japan

> [Being military governor] was the nearest thing to a Roman
> proconsulship the modern world afforded. You could turn to your
> secretary and say, "Take a law."
> —John McCloy, American High Commissioner in Germany

> The pine is brave
> That changes not its color,
> Bearing the snow.
> People, too,
> Like it should be.
> —Hirohito, Emperor of Japan, 1946

IN LIGHT of the decline of communism at the end of this century, the historical meaning of World War II has begun to assume a new importance.
Today we can see more clearly than before that the Second World War not
only marked the defeat of fascism as a viable form of political organization;
it also opened the possibility of fostering democracy in Germany and
Japan. It thereby created the conditions for a liberal world order that could

contain and ultimately eclipse communism's pretension to world revolution. Seen from the perspective of the 1990s, World War II thus marked the defeat—one immediate, and the other after four decades—of both totalitarian rivals of democracy. As such, it stands as one of the great watersheds in human history.

Some observers have marked the conflict of 1914–8 as the epochal event of our century. They contend that the questions of German and Soviet power in European affairs, issues initially raised during the First World War, remained the defining themes of world politics thereafter.[1]

But such an interpretation does not sufficiently credit fascism with the serious moral and practical challenge it presented as an alternative form of political organization to communism and democracy. Nor does it recognize that with World War II, a new chapter was being opened in Germany's historical role (and not simply an old one closed). As with Japan, it became an active participant in a liberal world order run by Washington, an order whose success would eventually lead to the decline of Soviet power.

Today we can appreciate how momentous the victory over fascism truly was. It was not simply that the United States and Great Britain triumphed over Germany and Japan; it was that one form of government and one proposed structure of world order won out over another. Of course, Soviet power was the single most decisive factor bringing about Germany's defeat. Indeed, at first it might appear that Moscow was the principal victor in this war, for the struggle against the Nazis seemed to fuse nationalism with communism in the Soviet Union, gave the Red Army control of Eastern Europe, and greatly facilitated the eventual triumph of communism in China. From the perspective of the 1990s, however, it was the democracies that were its victors. This judgment rests less on what the democracies won during the war than on what they accomplished with the peace.

For the war to matter so decisively in the ensuing contest between the United States and the Soviet Union, America had to restructure Japan and Germany so that they would lend support to Washington's leadership of world affairs after 1945. The question, then, was whether these countries could be converted to liberalism, a set of institutions and practices that may be defined as democratic in terms of domestic politics; nondiscriminatory, antimercantilist, and open in terms of international economic policy; and antiimperialist (or antimilitarist) in terms of foreign policy.

The American determination that postwar Germany and Japan be demilitarized, that their political orders be democratized, and that their economic systems be liberalized so that they might be integrated into a global economy, constitutes the most ambitious program American liberal democratic internationalism has ever undertaken. Utterly defeated though both countries were, their modern character as industrial societies had already been established. Could the United States expect to foster basic developmental changes there when it had failed to do so in seemingly more malleable countries like the Philippines and the Dominican Republic? Could Washington expect Germany and Japan's neighbors, victims of these countries' aggression and aware of their future capacity to regain power, to trust them enough to cooperate with them in consolidating a liberal world order? Indeed, how did a consensus in favor of promoting liberalism win out in the United States, where other proposals existed, either permanently to cripple these militaristic peoples or, alternately, to allow them to regain a healthy measure of economic vitality, without insisting on their liberalization so long as they could be counted as dependents of the United States in the contest with the Soviet Union?

Most reservations as to the likelihood of transforming these countries stemmed from a consideration of their deeply authoritarian character. Despite their great differences culturally, Germany and Japan were remarkably similar in the reasons for their historical aversion to liberalism. Possessed of a sense of weakness and worried about the encroachments of Western powers, each country had unified and set up a strong central government supported by a resolute military at about the same time—Japan in 1868, Germany in 1871. Under the auspices of a powerful current of nationalism, whose tenets served to extol the superiority of national ways to those of a dangerously liberal West, the Japanese launched a program of rapid national industrialization, while by the late 1870s, German industrialization (which had begun twenty years earlier) took a protectionist turn that could eventually be labeled neomercantilist.

Although economic modernization necessarily involves substantial changes in social structure and activity—more specialized and interdependent division of labor, urbanization, an expanded educational system, and larger state bureaucracies, for example—the process does not necessarily involve a convergence of political types. In a word, democratic political institutions characterized by popular control of parties and party control of government, a preference for an open world economic order, and a relatively weak military establishment such as typified the United States and Great Britain in the nineteenth century need not be the automatic consequence of the industrial revolution.

Germany and Japan constitute cases in point. Here, conservative, authoritarian states survived the transition to economic modernization by a variety of procedures that at once preserved the allegiance of traditional groups, gained the loyalty of new economic elites, and effectively excluded from power the workers, peasants, and new middle class. In the process, the social and intellectual forces that had brought about democracy in the United States and Great Britain found themselves stunted.

Thus, while some of the traditional social elites in Germany and Japan were dispossessed in the process of change—a good part of the samurai or warrior class in Japan fell on hard times, for example—others maintained a firm grip on power. Both the landowning Junkers in Germany and the oligarchs in Japan manned key bureaucracies and the highest levels of the military, thereby keeping great power for themselves while struggling against demands for a transfer of power to parliamentary government.

Moreover, new economic elites—big business interests in both countries or the new class of landlords in Japan—also identified with a strong government. Beginning in the late nineteenth century, the state provided emerging big business with subsidies and protection. By the twentieth century, with an increase in peasant discontent and the beginning of labor organization, big business, joined in Japan by a new landed elite, looked for an authoritarian state to protect their interests against popular discontent. Although the social origins of the new capitalist class in Japan and Germany may have consisted of what the aristocracy would call parvenus, this elite of new money deferred to a repressive political order.

To be sure, there were significant differences between the two countries. Although Japanese business and landed elites supported a strong state, they did not combine as they did in Germany (the "marriage of iron and rye") to repress popular forces. Nevertheless, the prospects for economic liberalism in foreign affairs remained dim, since each country in its pursuit of foreign markets and raw materials developed an integrated industrial and financial network (cartels in Germany, zaibatsu in Japan) supported by a range of state initiatives to an extent that was neomercantilist. Given the success of these undertakings as measured by the economic performance of both countries, authoritarian governments found new ways to claim legitimacy for their rule. The price, however, was a state pledged aggressively to defend what increasingly appeared to be an autarkic domestic economy.

The extent to which these developments, especially in Germany, were distinctly different from events in Britain or France has been debated hotly in recent years. Although critics of the notion of a German special way (*Sonderweg*) have demonstrated the survival of traditional elites in political life in France and Britain while pointing to the strength of the German bourgeoisie, one should not conclude that Germany (much less, Japan) experienced a form of political development similar to Britain or France (much less the United States).[2]

To be sure, there were democratic developments in both Germany and Japan. Both eventually adopted constitutions that allowed popularly elected parliaments to have some control over the executive. In Germany, where democratic forces came into power in 1919, an unstable coalition of democratic parties managed to rule for fourteen years—the country's first democratic regime, the Weimar Republic. However, authoritarian forces rooted in the state bureaucracy, military, big business, and landowning circles never accepted democracy's mandate. New totalitarian groups on the left and the right—the communists as well as the Nazis—began to undercut democracy's strength as well. Finally in 1933, parliamentary government collapsed under the weight of these continuing divisions, the Depression, and Hitler's demagoguery.[3]

While there are historians who feel that Weimar democracy might have survived had, for example, the peace terms laid down in 1919 been more generous or had the new German government aggressively purged the bureaucracy and military of its authoritarian leaders in 1919, few argue that Japanese liberals could have expanded their hold on power in the 1920s. Political factions that became parties appeared in Japan in the early 1880s, and after the promulgation of a constitution creating the Diet in 1889, increasingly gained power over decisions made by the state. The emergence of a stronger parliament had to be at the expense of the throne and the military. During the 1920s, reacting favorably to Wilsonian proposals for reducing armaments and increasing international cooperation of economic and political matters, the Diet cut military budgets, and prominent ministers opposed the military's expansionist designs, often at the price of their lives. Indeed, as late at 1936, one party received a plurality in national elections campaigning under the motto "Will it be parliamentary government or fascism?"[4]

Yet despite progress toward becoming more effective representatives of popular opinion and wielding effective influence in government, Japanese political parties remained weak even by German standards, both in their ability to organize popular opinion and relative to the power wielded by the state and the military. Beginning in 1931, when the Army engineered the Manchurian crisis so as to take over that part of China, the military started to displace parties and parliament in domestic politics, just as it began to eclipse the throne. The military could point to its earlier role of defending the state before the Meiji Restoration of 1868, to its contribution to imperial authority thereafter, and to its victories in the name of national security in wars with China (1894–5), and Russia (1904–5), and to its part in the annexation of Korea in 1910. After the invasion of China proper in 1937, and the moves against Indochina in 1940–1, the military finally became the undisputed center of power in Japan.[5]

As the role of the army in promoting fascism in Japan indicates, Germany and Japan had their important differences. In Japan the position of the throne, the role of Shintoism in political life, and the evolution of the military's role in politics meant that there was no mass fascist party like the Nazis and no demagogue like Hitler. In Japan constitutional forms could be kept, traditional values invoked in the name of a Greater East Asian Co-Prosperity Sphere. Whatever the wanton ruthlessness of its leaders (in China and Korea especially), Japan perpetrated no Holocaust.[6]

Despite these differences, in three key respects these countries were not liberal: except during the Weimar years, parliaments did not control governments (that is, democracy was weak); mercantilist policies of national economic development were pursued (that is, capitalists predominately tended to think in competitive, nationalistic terms that were implicitly expansionist, a condition that remained true also under Weimar); and militarism was the primary instrument of foreign policy. With the triumph of fascism (in 1931 in Japan, in 1933 in Germany), Germany and Japan became thoroughly antiliberal—and they were proud to trumpet the distinction.[7]

A comparison of the authoritarian character of Germany and Japan in the twentieth century with democratic Great Britain and the United States may clarify these distinctions. Britain and the United States had fairly weak states relative to organized groups in their societies, in good part because of the timing of their industrialization and their geographical position. Britain's island status reduced the need for a standing army; its feudal past reduced the power of the central executive; and its early industrialization lessened the dependence of leading economic forces on the state. The United States had a British constitutional heritage, no feudal aristocracy, geographical richness, and continental isolation. During the nineteenth century, governing power in both countries came to be lodged in institutions controlled by parties that were responsive to civil society. Both states thus entered the twentieth century without the unaccountable authority the executive possessed in Germany and Japan.

Again in contrast to the fascist powers, British and American industrialization had come about with capitalist forces championing a weak state and a nondiscriminatory international economic system (although the United States remained protectionist until FDR's election). Important as the state may have been to capitalist fortunes at home and abroad, American and British capitalists never depended on government support and mercantilist practices to the extent of their German and Japanese counterparts.

Most significantly, perhaps, the military establishments in Britain and the United States were altogether weaker in political affairs, lacking the size, independent social base, constitutional privileges, ideological mission, and historical cachet of their German and Japanese counterparts. In the United States especially, civilian control of the military had been a liberal democratic article of faith since the republic's founding.[8]

Democracy's inherent differences from fascism need not have meant that the United States would have sought after the war to remake Japan and Germany in a liberal image. One possibility was simply to destroy the warmaking ability of these defeated lands once and for all, making them into agrarian-pastoral nations, as Secretary of the Treasury Henry Morgenthau proposed for Germany, a warning to others who might follow their example. In a poll taken in 1944, 13 percent of the American public favored exterminating all Japanese; in 1945, 33 percent called for the summary execution of the emperor; and President Franklin D. Roosevelt showed interest in a plan to mate Japanese to more docile Polynesians in order to pacify the race.[9]

Still another possibility was to use the enormous potential power of Japan and Germany in world affairs to contain the Soviet Union without making much effort to reconstruct them as democracies, an option favored early on by the prominent State Department official George Kennan. That a determined effort to liberalize these two countries would be undertaken after their defeat was by no means a foregone conclusion.

Thus, when FDR first considered the postwar reorganization of Germany, it was not the country's democratization but its dismemberment that he favored. At the Tehran Conference in November 1943, the president announced a plan that he "had thought up some months ago for the division of Germany in five parts" that were to be self-governing, plus two regions under international control. Prime Minister Winston Churchill, whose views on dismemberment were the most restrained of the postwar leaders, called for "seeing Prussia, the evil core of German militarism, separated from the rest of Germany." Foreseeing a conflict between Russia and the West, aware of Western Europe's need for a revitalized Germany economically, and fearful of a balkanization of central Europe that could only increase Soviet influence, Churchill proposed replacing German power with a "Confederation of the Danube," wherein parts of southern Germany would be combined with part of the former Austro-Hungarian empire. Roosevelt remarked that Germany "had been less dangerous to civilization when in 107 provinces," while Stalin noted that "if Germany was to be dismembered, it should really be dismembered." Sitting at this point on the sidelines of great-power activities, the French could only nod agreement, suggesting which parts of Germany they might annex, which parts they could control more informally.[10]

Punitive measures contemplated against Germany included far more than reparations. Deindustrialization as well as dismemberment were envisaged. Late in 1944, Roosevelt endorsed limits to be placed on Germany's postwar industrial output, while certain sectors, such as synthetic rubber and airplanes, were to be banned altogether. For a time the president even favored Secretary Morgenthau's proposals to make Germany an agrarian society:

> It is of the utmost importance that every person in Germany should realize that this time Germany is a defeated nation. I do not want them to starve to death but, as an example, if they need food to keep body and soul together beyond what

they have, they should be fed three times a day with soup from Army soup kitchens. That will keep them perfectly healthy, and they will remember that experience all their lives. The fact that they are a defeated nation, collectively and individually, must be so impressed upon them that they will hesitate to start any new war. . . . Too many people here and in England hold to the view that the German people as a whole are not responsible for what has taken place—that only a few Nazi leaders are responsible. That unfortunately is not based on fact. The German people as a whole must have it driven home to them that the whole nation has been engaged in a lawless conspiracy against the decencies of modern civilization.[11]

As a result, American position papers prepared for Yalta in February 1945 advocated "the lowest standards of health, diet and shelter compatible with the prevention of disease and disorder . . . a rock-bottom standard of living for the Germans."[12] According to Joint Chiefs of Staffs (JCS) Directive 1067, of April 26, 1945, which later served as the document guiding American occupation policy:

Germany will not be occupied for the purpose of liberation but as a defeated enemy nation. . . . The principal Allied objective is to prevent Germany from ever again becoming a threat to the peace of the world. . . . you will take no steps a) looking toward the economic rehabilitation of Germany, or b) designed to maintain or strengthen the German economy.[13]

While the notion of a punitive peace for Germany had strong public advocates for more than a year after that country's surrender, and even longer for Japan, there were others calling for their reconstruction. Some were realists like George Kennan or Winston Churchill, who saw even before the end of hostilities that the economic revitalization of Europe and its ability to face down domestic communist challenges, as well as the threat posed by the Soviet Union, required a rebirth of German and Japanese power. Their hope was to control this process through organizing the reliance of both countries on the international predominance of the United States, augmented in the case of Germany by a process of European economic and even political integration. But their thinking was not essentially Wilsonian: they did not contemplate remaking the domestic life of these two countries with a view to their conversion to democracy. Given his concern with blocking the expansion of Soviet power, Kennan, for example, found much to respect in Antonio Salazar's authoritarian regime in Portugal, and he wasted no time lamenting the failure of self-determination in Eastern Europe on grounds of Wilsonian idealism.[14]

Others who advocated the reconstruction of Germany and Japan were more pragmatically liberal, men like Secretary of State Cordell Hull or General Lucius Clay, the commander of the American zone in Germany.

These men were committed to reworking German and Japanese domestic structures in the direction of democracy and economic liberalism in the expectation both that their militarism could thereby be controlled and that communism held at bay. Unlike the realists, they recognized that German and Japanese democratization might be an aspect of Soviet containment.[15] In this respect, they were what might be called Wilsonian realists like General Douglas MacArthur, supreme allied commander in Japan, who championed both liberalism and anticommunism at once—determined that Japan should be liberalized and join the struggle against communism, but unwilling to subordinate either goal to the other.

There could be serious differences between realists and liberals over occupation policy. For example, Kennan disliked the purges and economic deconcentration measures undertaken by MacArthur in Japan.[16] Nevertheless, realists and liberals could agree on a medium-term goal of revitalizing the two countries so as to put them in concert with the United States in what increasingly came to be seen as the need to contain the Soviet Union. And on matters such as the need to integrate Germany into a new European economic and political order, these two groups could be in near-perfect accord. While the desire to punish Germany and Japan survived Roosevelt's death, it quickly lost force when realists and liberals agreed on a policy designed to revitalize both countries in the face of the Soviet challenge.

A useful way to study American efforts to liberalize Germany and Japan is to analyze the fate of what the American Army called the Four D's for Germany (a terminology which also fits the goals in Japan reasonably well): demilitarization, democratization, decartelization, and denazification (better referred to for comparative purposes as deprogramming). Obviously, these goals to some extent overlapped—usually in a mutually reinforcing manner, though sometimes in contradiction to one another.

Of the four goals, the Americans considered demilitarization as the most important: an end had to be put to the expansionist ambitions of Germany and Japan. Democratization, decartelization, and deprogramming were means to this end.

DEMOCRATIZATION

It should be recalled that democratic forces in Japan and Germany had generally favored cooperation with the West during the interwar years and had explicitly opposed the racist and militaristic slogans of their ultranationalist opponents on the right (although in Germany they, too, wanted to "reverse Versailles"). The triumph of fascism in these two countries therefore involved the destruction of their democratic movements. The American effort, first to revive democratic politics in Germany and Japan, then to ensure that such practices would continue to hold sway, was not simply an act of utopian idealism but had a solid historical argument to support it. To demilitarize these countries, the best tactic was to democratize them.

The process of imposed political reorganization differed in important respects in Japan and Germany. In Germany, the Nazi regime simply collapsed: Allied military commanders took over control of the country, which had previously been divided into four separate zones (American, British, Soviet, and French), in each of which the military governor had final authority, working through his own bureaucracies (with extensive German help, to be sure). In Japan, MacArthur had final authority undivided with other Allied officials, and exercised it primarily through the maintenance of the Japanese throne, Diet, and bureaucracy.

Although the situations were different, occupation authorities had a shared understanding that political reform was the heart of the democratization process. As we have seen in earlier chapters, Americans conceived of legitimate, stable government as a process of self-determination. The process was to be carried out by organized civic interest groups, usually of a class, ethnic, or religious kind. A party system would then steer these groups toward competitive elections whose winners would control government. A wide range of civil liberties would allow citizens to assemble, articulate their interests, and elect their candidates. Constitutionally established checks and balances designed to monitor state officials in the exercise of their functions were mandated. Of course, the particular structure of these functions might vary according to time and place. There could be differences as to whether it was better to have a two- or multiparty system, whether it was preferable that a parliamentary body select the chief executive or a separate election determine a president. Whatever the variations, the Americans were determined to make government in Germany and Japan function democratically.

In April 1945, JCS 1067 set out Washington's instructions to Clay in Germany:

> The principal Allied objective is to prevent Germany from ever again becoming a threat to the peace of the world. Essential steps in the accomplishment of this objective are the elimination of Nazism and militarism in all their forms, the immediate apprehension of war criminals for punishment, the industrial disarmament and demilitarization of Germany, with continuing control over Germany's capacity to make war, and the preparation for an eventual reconstruction of German political life on a democratic basis.[17]

At Potsdam in July-August 1945, the Allies confirmed this mission in a Declaration on Germany, announcing their intention "to prepare for the eventual reconstruction of German political life on a democratic basis and for eventual peaceful cooperation in international life by Germany." With respect to changing the educational system, the declaration called for efforts "to make possible the successful development of democratic ideas," while it mandated reforming the judicial system "in accordance with the principles of democracy, of justice under law, and of equal rights for all citizens without distinction of race, nationality, or religion."[18]

Again in July 1947, when JCS 1067 was replaced by JCS 1779 as the document stating basic American policy, the United States once more defined its political objective as "fundamentally that of helping to lay the economic and education bases of a sound German democracy, of encouraging bona fide democratic efforts and of prohibiting those activities which would jeopardize genuinely democratic developments."[19] The degree to which Washington decided virtually spontaneously that the only governmental form which it could wholeheartedly support in Germany and Japan would be democratic is an impressive demonstration of the powerful cultural biases working on American decision-makers, for their conviction existed in good measure independently of any deliberate calculation of historical, economic, or geostrategic reasoning.

With respect to Japan, the Allies at Potsdam declared that they looked forward to

> a peacefully inclined and responsible government. . . established in accordance with the freely expressed will of the Japanese people. . . . The Japanese government shall remove all obstacles to the revival and strengthening of democratic tendencies among the Japanese people. Freedom of speech, of religion, and of thought, as well as respect for the fundamental human rights shall be established.[20]

Similarly, the American Initial Post-Surrender Policy for Japan, dated August 29, 1945, and intended as MacArthur's charter for governing, declared as the country's "ultimate objectives":

> a) to insure that Japan will not again become a menace to the United States or to the peace and security of the world; b) to bring about the eventual establishment of a peaceful and responsible government which will respect the rights of other states and will support the objectives of the United States as reflected in the ideals and principles of the Charter of the United Nations. The United States desires that this government should conform as closely as may be to principles of democratic self-government, but it is not the responsibility of the Allied powers to impose upon Japan any form of government not supported by the freely expressed will of the people.[21]

In the process of passing from principle to practice, the Americans engaged in a panoply of activities aimed at creating the conditions for democratic organizations to flourish. In both countries, individuals (including communists) who had been political prisoners under the former regimes were released, civil liberties necessary for a functioning democracy were proclaimed, and parties were invited to organize in a democratic manner. Once occupation officials authorized parties to function, they announced schedules for election following a full and free deliberation of the issues (allowance made for the exclusion of rightists, discussed below).[22]

In Germany and Japan, the Americans made no effort to impose their own style of presidential or party system as they had in places like the Philippines and Central America. Instead, both countries were permitted to develop more in line with their own democratic traditions, which resembled British far more than American ways. Accordingly, parties had fixed programmatic concerns and substantial powers to insure internal discipline; for example, they could appoint members to run in specific electoral districts and expel them when they broke ranks in parliamentary voting. None of this was characteristic of American parties, which have traditionally been relatively loose coalitions of interests structured around pragmatic rather than ideological programs and without extensive disciplinary means of controlling their members. Similarly, the American occupiers did not insist on a presidential system, but instead endorsed an executive selected by parliamentary procedures. Not only did this correspond more closely to German and Japanese prewar practices, but it also presumably made for a somewhat weaker executive, which is what the Americans preferred.

In the process of organizing a new political framework for Germany and Japan, the Americans explicitly banned from political and bureaucratic life, as well as high corporate position, those individuals who had played an active role in wartime affairs. JCS 1067 ordered that "all members of the Nazi party who have been more than nominal participants in its activities, all active supporters of Nazism or militarism and all other persons hostile to Allied purposes will be removed and excluded from public office and from positions of importance in quasi-public and private enterprises."[23]

Initial estimates were that at least 2 million Germans would be subject to these strictures (in all four zones), while in Japan (which had no equivalent to the Nazi party) the purge would fall most directly on the military. War crimes trials (at Nuremberg and Tokyo, most prominently) resulted eventually in nearly five hundred executions in Germany, nearly nine hundred in Japan. Thousands more were imprisoned. Tens of thousands more were barred from high public or private office. In both countries, occupation authorities ordered state debts to be repudiated thereby impoverishing those individuals or firms that had financially supported the war. In Germany, property belonging to Nazis convicted of personal complicity in the prosecution of the war was confiscated, while in Japan the profits of firms and families that had benefited from the war were likewise seized. Occupation authorities banned parties and societies that had supported the wartime governments from political participation. American rules mandated a party system "constituted by voluntary associations of citizens in which leaders are responsible to the members." But it specified to Clay that if "an authorized party is adopting or advocating undemocratic practices or ideas, you may restrict or withdraw its rights and privileges."[24]

Despite these efforts, students of the purges are nearly unanimous in pointing out their failures (with respect to Germany more than to Japan). Except for the cases conducted before the highest tribunals, punishments were inconsistent or nonexistent. Those purged often returned to power (especially after the occupations ended), apparently little chastened by the experience.[25]

Many see little reason to lament these facts. To them, purges were obstacles to rebuilding these countries, which was more important than weakening them through decapitating their leadership. But even for those who deplore the failure to conduct the purges more thoroughly, the fact remains that barring individuals from political and economic life, like preventing the organization of parties championing the old regime, contributed more than marginally to the promotion of democracy in both countries. The purges allowed new elites to arise and new parties on the democratic right to woo voters who might otherwise have adopted extremist positions away from their wartime sympathies. Certainly by dissolving the military in Japan, disbanding the ministries of the army and the navy, and barring some 117,000 of its officers from high public or private office, the United States effectively broke the power of that institution in Japanese life which was most responsible for that nation's ultranationalism and expansionism.

In the case of Germany, the emergence of a newly constituted national government proved a laborious project. Elections were held in January 1946 in the American zone for local governments, and thereafter throughout the year for constituent assemblies to write the constitutions of the three states (*Laender*) the Americans controlled. During the process, the Americans insisted that the Germans themselves write their constitutions. When later it became time to establish a federal constitution, the Germans, working from domestic tradition, decided to keep the parliamentary system characteristic of Weimar, diminishing, however, the powers of the president and amending such matters as the character of proportional representation so as to reduce the number of parties in the Bundestag. Thanks in good measure to American influence, federalism was introduced (with an eye to eliminating the power of Prussia, while limiting the national government), and Supreme Judicial Courts were established as an additional check on the power of the central government.[26]

Moving to integrate the four zones was far more difficult than providing a political structure for the American zone alone: first the French, then the

Soviets raised objections to the reconstitution of a German state. But by May 1949, after endless difficulties that involved debates over both the economic integration of Europe under the auspices of the Marshall Plan as well as the nature of the response to the Soviet threat in Europe, the three Western zones were finally politically merged under the terms of a new constitution (called the Basic Law). Bundestag elections were held in August, and on September 20, 1949, Konrad Adenauer of the Christian Democratic party was elected (by a one-vote majority) the first chancellor of the Federal Republic of Germany, with its capital in Bonn.[27]

In Japan, by contrast, the process of forming a new national government moved more quickly. A Japanese government remained in place, federalism was not contemplated (though in April 1947, the Americans replaced the appointed heads of the prefectures by elected governors), and, most importantly, MacArthur did not have to work with other Allied commanders to come to an agreement on how the new system should be organized.

On the other hand, Japan's weak democratic tradition meant that far more American intervention was called for than in Germany. The cabinet committee first designated to rewrite the country's constitution failed to meet American expectations. With the assistance of an able staff, MacArthur set out himself to draft a text, one which the Japanese finally adopted with few revisions. The new constitution converted the emperor into a constitutional monarch and abolished the peerage. It vested supreme power in the Diet, now made wholly responsible to the people organized by competitive party elections. A bill of rights was formulated, whose assumptions of individual and group freedom clashed with basic collectivist values enshrined in Japanese tradition. Indeed, with its measures to provide equality for women and collective bargaining for labor, the civil liberties promised the Japanese were more advanced than American domestic legislation at the time. Finally, MacArthur insisted on the famous Article IX of the new constitution, by which Japan pledged itself never again to go to war:

> Aspiring sincerely to an international peace based on justice and order, the Japanese people forever renounce war as a sovereign right of the nation. . . . Land, sea and air forces, as well as other war potential, will never be maintained. The right of belligerence of the State will not be recognized.[28]

National parliamentary elections were first held in April 1946. As in Germany, the Americans were reassured that few votes were cast for the communists or groups that could be construed as representing the extreme right (a combined total for the far left and far right of less than 20 percent in each country). Also as in Germany, although with a far stronger mandate, the conservatives dominated the Diet. (The Liberals and the Progressives—renamed the Democrats in 1947—won just over 50 percent of the vote in 1946; in 1955, they united in the Liberal Democratic party, which ruled Japan until 1993.)

Scholars who have studied these new political systems have been nearly universal in their praise for the American accomplishment. Of course, some problems were not handled well (for example, the organization of electoral districts that favored rural districts in Japan). And there should be no effort to minimize the contribution of Japanese, and especially German, leaders to the success of the undertaking. The powerful roles of leaders such as Konrad Adenauer, Kurt Schumacher, Yoshida Shigeru, and Emperor Hirohito were of fundamental importance from the first days of the occupations. Finally, democratization occurred through a framework sanctioned by tradition; the choice of a party and parliamentary system similar to those of the prewar order in Japan and Germany clearly represented a return to a national type of democratic political organization. That said, the American contribution to German democratic political organization was substantial; to the new Japanese order it was fundamental. Of the three D's to be analyzed, the Americans were considerably more successful in their efforts to rework the political system in accordance with their aims than they were in the two other spheres.

DECARTELIZATION

In earlier chapters, we have seen that the primary obstacle to the success of American efforts to promote democracy abroad lay in the failure to address the socioeconomic structure of power on which political life in good measure depended. In the case of the Philippines or Central America, for example, the Americans were content to establish a free press, permit parties to organize, and supervise elections to the offices where power was effectively located. But they would leave basically untouched (or actually reinforced) economic interests and social arrangements that heavily concentrated wealth and power. Much the same could be said for Northern policy toward the Confederacy after the Civil War. As a consequence, once the Americans (or Northerners) had departed, the local socioeconomic elite would turn the political system to its advantage with the result that democracy either remained quite fragile (as in the Philippines) or ceased altogether to exist (as in the Dominican Republic).

Toward Germany and Japan in 1945, American thinking was more sophisticated. At the end of the war, in line with much of New Deal thinking, the dominant (though far from universal) opinion in the United States was that breaking up the industrial and financial combines that dominated the economic life of these countries would contribute to their demilitarization as well as to their democratization. The essential notion was that the economic elites of these countries had favored war and helped to wage it effectively. As late as July 1947, the Americans could still state as official policy with respect to Germany that they wanted "a dispersion of ownership and control of German industry through the dissolution of such combines, mergers, holding companies and interlocking directorates which represent an actual or potential restraint of trade or may dominate or substantially influence the policies of government agencies."[29] So far as Japan was concerned, MacArthur put the thinking with characteristic bluntness:

> Japan has long had a system of "private enterprise"—but one which permitted ten family groups comprising only fifty-six Japanese families to control, directly or indirectly, every phase of commerce and industry; all media of transportation, both internal and external; all domestic raw materials; and all coal and other power resources. The "private enterprise" was thus limited to a few of feudal lineage, who exploited into virtual slavery the remainder of the Japanese people, permitted higher standards of life to others only through sufferance, and in search of further plunder abroad furnished the tools for the military to embark upon its ill-fated venture into world conquest. The record is thus one of economic oppression and exploitation at home, aggression and spoliation abroad.[30]

American attempts to address socioeconomic obstacles to democratization, encountered some serious problems: trust-busting, reparations, and purges in Japan and Germany so disrupted economic life that the population grew discontented, which in turn threatened efforts to bring about stable democratic political life. General Clay declared that JCS 1067 had been written "by economic idiots," for democracy "could not be taught or learned on empty stomachs."[31] While Clay nonetheless carried forward with the dissolution of some German trusts, his reforms did not substantially transform the character of economic concentration in the country. By the fall of 1946, when Secretary of State James Byrnes was publicly calling for the recovery of German industry for the sake of general European economic rehabilitation, Washington began shelving its own directives on decartelization.

Much the same process occurred in Japan, though far more slowly. While Japan's economic difficulties mattered less to regional or world affairs than Germany's, and while MacArthur recognized the contradiction between democratization and decartelization, he persisted through 1947 in trust-busting. Washington ordered a "reverse course" in 1947, however, a move formalized with the publication in October 1948 of National Security Council document 13/2.[32]

Another problem with American thinking about decartelization was the exaggerated responsibility it assigned to German and Japanese industrial and financial firms for their countries' rapacious militarism. It is true that big business in Germany was for the most part hostile, or at best indifferent, to the fate of democracy in the interwar years, that both German and Japanese corporate leadership worked closely with their respective militaries, and that both extorted the most they could (which was a great deal) from the peoples subjugated. It is nevertheless difficult to maintain that big business in Japan had been fundamentally antidemocratic (its influence in the Diet was perhaps its most effective access to governmental power in the 1920s) or that in either country the economic community favored war.[33]

Despite its inaccurate beliefs, the United States reformed the economic practices of these countries in three critical ways that greatly reinforced democracy and liberalism. First, the Americans insisted on the right of labor to organize freely and to enter into collective bargaining agreements with management. Some criticized American policy for not going far enough: for inhibiting the socialization of the means of production, for example, or in taking initiatives (in Japan especially) to counter communist influence in the union movement, which compromised their freedom of action. Whatever the merits of these charges, American achievements remain impressive. In West Germany, where unionism already had a distinguished history, business finally accepted unequivocally the right of labor to organize and be represented both in domestic politics and at the work place (with results beneficial to German economic expansion thereafter and from which the Americans themselves might have learned something for their own relations among management, unions, and the state). In Japan, where unionism had always been weak, union membership increased eleven-fold by 1946 above its high point before the war, and labor's rights politically and with respect to management were expanded and more secure.[34]

A second basic socioeconomic transformation engendered by the American occupation was enforced only in Japan: a thorough-going land reform program altered the pattern of ownership in the countryside and removed the major social pillar of traditional authoritarianism and militarism. Japanese village life had been one of the chief bases of the romantic conservatism of modern ultranationalism; its economic poverty had been an obstacle to the creation of a larger national market; and the sons of landlords and well-off peasants had formed the bulk of the junior officer corps while the peasants themselves constituted the better part of the conscripts. (A somewhat analogous system existed in prewar Germany, where the landed elite, the Junkers of Prussia, held powerful positions in the state bureaucracy and the military. The Soviets had conquered this area and proceeded with the speedy expropriation of the seven thousand large estates there, taking without compensation all properties over one hundred hectares, converting them to small-holdings or state-owned collectives.)[35]

In Japan almost half the population lived on the land, with some two-thirds being either wholly or partially tenant farmers. The land reform law of October 21, 1946, placed limits on the maximum amount of land a family could own. Long-term government bonds paid for the expropriated land, which in effect meant they were seized without adequate compensation. The tenants-turned-owners were provided with sufficient credit to take over the land they were awarded, so that the rate of tenancy fell dramatically from perhaps 70 to 10 percent of the rural population, and the rents on the let land that remained had been lowered. Most importantly, the new farmers were mobilized into politics under the auspices of their own interest groups and the conservative parties.[36] MacArthur was correct when he counted this reform one of the two greatest accomplishments of his administration (the other being the Japanese constitution). He remarked: "The redistribution formed a strong barrier against any introduction of communism in rural Japan. Every farmer in the country was now a capitalist in his own right." He might have added that by the same token, he had also destroyed the most important social base for relaunching fascism.[37]

The third major liberalizing impact of the American occupation from a socioeconomic point of view was to break down Japan and Germany's nation-centered, neomercantilist form of economic organization, which depended on state sponsorship of the country's economic growth through aggressive moves in world affairs. In its place, Washington proposed a world economy sustained by principles of economic openness and interdependence.

The importance of American initiatives in this respect must be emphasized. While international trade was as old as world history, the energy of the industrial revolution produced inevitable clashes over preferential access to materials and markets. Since the early nineteenth century, Great Britain had sought to regulate this competition through international practices of free trade or, if this were not obtainable, through nondiscriminatory practices where commerce moved without the need of governmental protection. But as the new imperialism of the late nineteenth century had demonstrated—when Africa was partitioned, the Ottoman and Chinese empires weakened—establishing such an order seemed a large, if not impossible, undertaking.[38]

Britain's liberal program was self-serving. As the first industrial country, its goods could presumably undersell the competition without the need for political control. Eventually, as their power declined, the British came to change their outlook and by the 1930s had constructed an imperial preference system. By the time of the Roosevelt administration, however, the United States had come to champion much the same international economic system the British had earlier favored and for much the same reasons.

The liberal international economic order that the Americans tried to impose on Japan and Germany in 1945 thus had a venerable pedigree. But these two countries had industrial and financial systems that were tightly integrated along national lines and that had performed remarkably well. There is little reason to think they would have transformed themselves without determined American insistence. The struggle over the form capitalism should take in Germany and Japan was thus a key element of American occupation policy. Wilson had recognized the problem in 1917; the Truman administration decided to address it.[39]

American ambitions to convert West Germany to a more liberal orientation ultimately bore fruit in the 1950s, thanks largely to the tremendous innovations in regional and world economic integration prepared for by the Bretton Woods Agreements of 1944 and even more by the direct aid and planning contained in the Marshall Plan in 1947. Thereafter, the initiative was seized (as the Americans had hoped) by the Europeans themselves. In 1949 Western powers negotiated the entry of the Federal Republic into the Council of Europe and the Organization of European Economic Cooperation, in return for a German agreement to relax exclusive sovereign control over its economic policy. In 1951, the Schuman Plan succeeded in integrating major aspects of French and German industry through the creation of a joint High Commission in charge of coal and steel production (the European Coal and Steel Community). In 1957, with the signing of the Declaration of Rome creating the European Economic Community, Europe entered formally into what must be considered one of the greatest economic undertakings in history: the effort (still not achieved) to overcome national rivalries and divisions through the creation of an economic structure so interdependent that the interest of each of its members can only be pursued in ways commensurate with general agreement among partners.[40]

In important respects, the political consequences of this economic integration are that sovereignty in Western Europe is today in the process of being pooled; the problem of Germany's relative power is being addressed by a process of mutual economic and political assimilation. More than four decades after the announcement of the Schuman Plan, European integration is far from complete. Yet there has been enough success to bring about a fundamental reordering of the political character of Europe. The achievements of integration—the strength of democracy, the openness of markets, the elimination of internal military suspicions—must be counted the greatest accomplishment of liberalism on historical record.

There are writers who suggest that these developments only began in 1947 and then largely by accident. Yet American planners had anticipated some kind of integration years earlier. In 1944 Secretary Hull had noted, "the primary and continuing objectives of our economic policy are: 1) to render Germany incapable of waging war, and 2) to eliminate permanently German economic domination of Europe." The aim was to "eliminate self-sufficiency by imposing reforms that will make Germany dependent upon world markets."[41] The policy was quintessentially liberal in inspiration: German economic strength would be maintained, but restructured for the common good. A State Department memorandum spelled out the idea in more detail, concluding:

Elimination of German economic domination over Europe requires the prohibition of all discriminatory trade controls, clearing agreements and international cartel arrangements. . . . [This policy depends] upon our general success in achieving world trade expansion under liberal conditions of trade.[42]

It was equally important to provide Japan with access to the world market. Since the 1890s, Japanese militarism had depended in part on the feeling that the country must expand abroad economically or die. Part of the problem was obtaining raw materials in which the Japanese islands themselves were so deficient. Part of the problem was felt to be population pressure: the number of Japanese had increased from about 30 to 65 million between 1868 and 1930. Thus, the conquest of Manchuria in 1931 had been part of a plan to settle some 5 million Japanese there over a twenty-year period, where they would farm and oversee the export to the homeland of abundant, critical raw materials (iron and coal especially) lacking in Japan. The pressures were so acute that Akira Iriye sees the failure of Japan to obtain adequate assurance of equal access to world markets as the principal cause of its belligerence from 1931 to 1941:

[Militarism was] the antithesis not of pacifism but of peaceful expansion. Militarism triumphed not as a goal but as a means for obtaining the same ends which the diplomacy of the preceding era had unsuccessfully sought. . . . The dilemmas of modern Japan were the world's as well as Japan's. They were an expression not only of the pathology of the modern Japanese mind but also of the inherent contradictions and irrationalities of the modern world.[43]

Japan's sense of economic encirclement may have been exaggerated, but it was real. Its desperate search for markets and resources led to a bid for direct control over Asia from Indonesia to Korea, including China. As a result, American diplomacy in Asia before the war centered largely on trying to accommodate Japan's perceived economic needs without permitting rampant imperialism.[44]

For the Americans in Japan after 1945, the job appeared much as it had before 1941: to persuade the Japanese that their interests would be served by a liberal, nondiscriminatory international commercial system. Secretary Stimson, who had had first-hand experience dealing with Japanese expansionism in 1931–2, declared in 1945 (in words that would have suited Secretary Hull equally well), "We have a national interest in creating, if possible, a condition wherein the Japanese nation may live as a peaceful and useful member of the Pacific community." Perhaps this was MacArthur's meaning at the surrender ceremonies of September 2, 1945, when he declared, "The energy of the Japanese race, if properly directed, will enable expansion vertically rather than horizontally."[45]

There was good reason to think the Japanese would accept a renewal of the prewar offer. Important business interests before the war had favored the Anglo-American approach to an open global economic system. Not surprisingly, in August 1945, according to the report of a former president of the Japanese National Chamber of Commerce and Industry, leading business leaders contemplating the forthcoming American victory "uncorked their champagne bottles and toasted the coming of a new 'industrialist' era."[46]

The question was whether the Americans could deliver on their promises of economic liberalism. Japan's neighbors could not be expected to work with it as Germany's might. By creating a global commercial system, and by establishing preferential relations with the United States, Washington hoped to meet Japan's needs.[47]

Japan's economic recovery began in earnest in 1950, in some measure on the rush of orders from the United States after the Korean War broke out. Since then, Japan has found its need for foreign markets and raw materials amply satisfied by the liberal postwar world economic system. A half century later, although there are signs on every side that the system may not hold, it has functioned admirably so far as Japanese interests are concerned.

Despite this success, Japan's economy continues to strive to be self-reliant while remaining dependent on open world markets. Japan is self-reliant in that its constant primary concern remains the strength of its own economy seen in narrow national terms; and it is dependent to the extent that it must rely on a high level of foreign trade with countries over whom its political influence is relatively minor for markets and raw materials. Of course, one must not make the distinction too categorically; all countries are in some measure self-reliant yet dependent. Yet while the Americans obtained a limited restructuring of both German and Japanese capitalism, replacing state-protected cartels with competitive oligopolies (so making them more efficient), the critical difference lies in the extent of German economic integration with the rest of Western Europe and the closeness of this association, in turn, with the United States. While Japan remains the second most important trading partner of the United States (after Canada), it nonetheless remains true that the place of Japan in the world economic system is not so secure as that of Germany. Many observers with a memory of the past find this lack of a firmer resting place most disquieting.

PSYCHOLOGICAL DEPROGRAMMING

Since the conquest of the Philippines, Americans have generally held that the promotion of democracy requires the development of what has been called a civic culture: attitudes and values that promote participation by the citizenry in political matters led by government leaders who feel accountable to an informed electorate. An interest in public affairs, membership in political organizations, respect for differing points of view, an ability to compromise through an impartial system of rules on which disputes may be joined—such are some of the attitudes deemed essential to democratic citizenship. Presumably, authoritarian-militaristic societies have a different kind of political culture, whose characteristics include conformity to group expectations, unquestioned obedience to traditional authority, personal dogmatism and intolerance, and a willingness to settle disputes by force.

To be sure, in practice these distinctions are not quite as evident as in theory. Speaking of the frequent allusions he heard about "the German mind," General Clay remarked, "If it did exist, we never found it; German minds seemed to us to be remarkably like those elsewhere."[48] General MacArthur, on the other hand, frequently evoked "the Oriental mind," and claimed he had special insights into its nature. But he was careful to treat it respectfully in public:

> I carefully abstained from any interferences by edict with the cultural traditions or the personal Japanese way of life. In frequent public statements I advised the Japanese people to seek a healthy blend between the best of theirs and the best of ours. . . . this mutual respect became the foundation of the basic esteem our two peoples came to have for one another—and enabled the occupation to write a unique and warmly human chapter in world history.[49]

Such noble sentiments notwithstanding, Clay was enthusiastic about "our efforts to reorient the thinking of the German people."[50] And MacArthur was outspoken in his assaults, calling Japanese social organization "feudal," a "theocracy," and complaining: "There was no such thing as civil rights. There were not even human rights." So too, he lambasted their "almost mythological belief in the strength and wisdom of the warrior caste. It permeated and controlled not only all the branches of government, but all branches of life—physical, mental, and spiritual. It was interwoven not only into all government processes, but into all phases of daily routine. It was not only the essence, but the warp and woof of Japanese existence." As a result, he felt, it was the American mission to liberate the Japanese from "this condition of slavery."[51]

From the American perspective, both countries were ready for what today might be called "psychological deprogramming," whereby the closed and authoritarian ways of the past would be replaced by a more democratic set of values and style of behavior. In Germany, there was frequent reference to what was called Stunde Null (zero hour), the mental and institutional vacuum created by the defeat. As Washington informed Clay in 1947:

> Your Government holds that the reeducation of the German people is an integral part of the policies intended to help develop a democratic form of government. . . . it believes that there should be no forcible break in the cultural unity of Germany, but recognizes the spiritual value of the regional traditions of Germany

and wishes to foster them; it is convinced that the manner and purposes of the reconstruction of the national German culture have vital significance for the future of Germany. . . . you will expedite the establishment of those international cultural relations which will overcome the spiritual isolation imposed by National Socialism on Germany and further the assimilation of the German people into the world community of nations.[52]

Similarly, MacArthur declared that Japan's defeat involved

not merely the overthrow of their military might—it was the collapse of a faith, it was the disintegration of everything they had believed in and lived by and fought for. It left a complete vacuum, morally, mentally, and physically. And into this vacuum flowed the democratic way of life. . . . A spiritual revolution ensued which almost overnight tore asunder a theory and practice of life built upon 2000 years of history and tradition . . . an unparalleled convulsion in the social history of the world.[53]

At the onset of the occupations, purges of former leaders were undertaken (as we saw above) in part to educate the populations about the crimes of their rulers. The Nuremberg and Tokyo war crimes trials were the most celebrated of these efforts. But long-term education to change the thinking of the subject populations was needed as well. The two major vehicles for accomplishing this reform were the educational system and the media.

Educational reform presented the triple problem of revising the curriculum, the character of the instructors, and the organization of the school system itself.[54] As Washington's instructions to Clay read:

In recognition of the fact that evil consequences to all free men flow from the suppression and corruption of truth and that education is a primary means of creating a democratic and peaceful Germany, you will continue to encourage and assist in the development of educational methods, institutions, programs and materials designed to further the creation of democratic attitudes and practices through education.[55]

With respect to the curriculum, the United States ended instruction designed to promote militant nationalism as well as rote learning, deemed to create a passive citizenry. Courses of instruction in social studies and (at the university level) political science were introduced for the first time. The success of these efforts is debatable. At the end of the occupations, Japan and Germany revised the American-inspired curriculum, although starting in the 1960s, the Germans began to make serious efforts to understand their own history more thoroughly and critically. The same cannot be said for Japan.

The teaching corps also needed reform. In Germany, it was estimated that perhaps 80 percent of the teachers were Nazi party members. It was in this domain that American efforts probably had their least impact, it being left to the national authorities to deal with instructor certification in their own ways.

Finally the Americans tried to open the educational system. Councils of parents were formed in Japan, schools became coeducational and free, and the Ministry of Education found its powers reduced. In Germany the Americans tried to discourage the early tracking of students, which tended to preserve class inequalities, by opening schools to students from all backgrounds. Again, with the idea that a new, educated elite was called for, the Americans encouraged the expansion of higher education. In Japan the number of those attending universities increased many times over.

The other major vehicle through which the Americans hoped to reorient public opinion toward democracy was through journalism and radio. There were major changes in the ways communications were handled. Investigative reporting was introduced to the press; radio programming stressed diversity of opinion. On the whole, American-inspired reforms in these fields fundamentally changed the national media as intended.[56]

Additional American efforts to make the subject populations more supportive of democratic procedures took many forms. For example, Clay set up America Houses, where American books, magazines, and cultural accomplishments were publicized. He also practiced what was known as a "goldfish policy," making his activities public and accessible as a lesson in how to govern. MacArthur had different concerns. He was especially interested in promoting the place of women in Japanese life—both because of his respect for them and out of his belief that they were pacifists by nature—and he insisted that the state religion, Shintoism, be disestablished. Instead, he promoted Christianity, arranging for 10 million Bibles to be imported (and claiming that 2 million Japanese had converted).

It is difficult to know the extent to which American efforts were effective. Public opinion polls taken over a period of decades indicate that the populations of both countries are increasingly concerned to think critically about political issues and look with growing skepticism on forms of political behavior that might be labeled authoritarian. The results did not come immediately. Only a small minority of Germans in 1946—about 5 percent of respondents—felt the Nuremberg trials were unfair; 72 percent would have liked to have seen Hitler prosecuted. Presumably these opinions are explained by a finding that 92 percent of the population rejected the notion of collective guilt. But when asked whether National Socialism had been a good idea badly executed, 40 percent agreed in 1946, a number that grew to over 50 percent a year later.[57]

Other figures show positive developments over longer stretches of time. In 1951 only 32 percent of the German population accepted Germany's sole responsibility for the war; by 1967 this figure had increased to

62 percent. Perhaps the most encouraging evidence comes from a question asked repeatedly between 1951 and 1978[58]:

Question: When in this century do you think Germany has been best off?

	1951	1959	1963	1970
Federal Repbulic (1949–)	2	42	62	81
Prewar Third Reich (1933–9)	42	18	10	5
Weimar Republic (1919–33)	7	4	5	2
Empire (pre-1914)	45	28	16	5
Other	4	8	7	7

A roughly comparable survey of the Japanese reports[59]:

Question: Some people say that if we get good political leaders, the best way to improve the country is for the people to leave everything to them, rather than for the people to discuss things among themselves. Do you agree or disagree with this?

Those who disagree as a percentage of respondents:

1953	1958	1963	1968	1973
38	44	47	51	51

As for their reaction to the American occupation, 49 percent of Germans in 1950 thought of it as poorly done and only 15 percent viewed it as positive (though in the Soviet zone, the figures were 95 percent and 1 percent respectively). By contrast, in Japan, a survey conducted just after MacArthur was relieved of his command in 1951, asked "Do you think the occupation has been beneficial to Japan?" A total of 92.8 percent replied affirmatively, with only 1 percent saying no.[60]

What we may cautiously conclude is that some change in the intended direction toward democracy has occurred over the last four decades. How deep the change goes, how meaningful it is in terms of the range of factors that must go together to keep democracy functioning, and how significant American reforms were to all of this are questions that no one has yet explored in any depth.

Two Reflections on the American Legacy

The foregoing discussion raises two final questions: first, to what extent do the actions of German and Japanese domestic political forces explain better than occupation policy the eventual democratization of these two countries; and second, to what extent did these reforms ultimately help create a more powerful liberal world order?

One may certainly doubt how considered American occupation policy actually was. Robert E. Ward, a long-time student of the occupation of Japan, suggests how free-floating American reformism was.

This self-righteous bias in favor of American political institutions and practices may well have been reinforced by the ignorance of most higher ranking occupation officials where Japanese history, society, and politics were concerned. . . . The presurrender plans display a far greater consciousness of the obstacles to the successful democratization of Japan posed by Japan's past experiences and culture. They were in this sense more diffident, more limited, and less optimistic. The SCAP staff, on the other hand, might with only slight exaggeration be characterized as "rushing in where angels fear to tread." It might equally be said, however, that had they known more, they might have accomplished less.[61]

In the case of Germany, Clay's political adviser Robert Murphy similarly reports:

We had to improvise as we went along. . . . I was rather dismayed to learn that [Clay] knew virtually nothing about Germany. . . . Information about Germany's history, its former financial and industrial ramifications, its prewar personality, and so forth might have cluttered the mind of a deputy military governor.[62]

Such remarks could be multiplied; there were changes, contradictions, hesitations, and improvisations as the occupations continued. But these observations should not disguise the essential liberal democratic internationalist premises on which America acted in Germany and Japan, and that remained relatively constant throughout. Continuity was provided, on the one hand, by a Wilsonian agenda that effectively fostered national security in terms of the promotion of economic liberalism and democracy abroad, and, on the other, by a succession of political leaders and public servants who were the direct legatees of the Wilsonian tradition.[63]

To assert a deliberate and important American role in the creation of liberal democratic governments in Japan and Germany is not to deny the indispensable part played in these developments by local actors. The problem is how to assess the contribution of the Americans and relative to that of German and Japanese leaders.

Germany had a long constitutional heritage, a liberal tradition that can be traced back to the early nineteenth century, and a domestic democratic movement that had grown from the turn of this century until it was in power during the Weimar years. Both Konrad Adenauer and Kurt Schumacher—leaders of the democratic right and left respectively in the postwar era—were authentic products of German history, not men created by American fiat. Again, the "social market economy" fathered in good measure by Ludwig Erhard and the Christian Democrats represented a German, not an American, approach to business-labor relations and the welfare state. These individuals were the actual makers of a stable democratic order in Germany, and they reached out to other Europeans to effect a change in German relations with the rest of the continent.[64]

Throughout Western Europe, leaders were coming to a similar conclusion: that the continent needed to be integrated through liberal economic practices and through democratic political agreements so as to give peace and prosperity to the region. De Gasperi, Spaak, Monnet, Schuman, Bevin, Churchill, Adenauer, Christian Democrats in every country: these were Europeans whose vision of a liberal postwar order existed quite independently of the will of Washington.[65] Indeed, John Lewis Gaddis has persuasively argued that European leaders successfully maneuvered to draw an often reluctant United States much more deeply into a commitment to the region than Washington alone would have contemplated.[66]

Striking a neat balance between the American and the European contribution to the political evolution of that region is no easy matter. What is certain is that we cannot stop with American efforts alone. Nevertheless, it is likely that the rule of Adenauer's Christian Democratic party might not have lasted so long or run so smoothly (or, indeed, happened at all) had the Americans not been there. In at least two respects, Schumacher's Social Democrats presumably represented a fundamental alternative to the Christian Democrats: they might have opposed a liberal economic opening to the West in favor of state ownership of production; and they might have insisted on a more neutral orientation to German foreign policy as part of an effort to conciliate Moscow. It was with good reason that the Social Democrats taunted Adenauer as "Chancellor of the Allies."[67] To the extent, then, that the American presence in Germany tilted domestic politics toward the conservatives, and this in turn contributed both to the character of the cold war and to the identity of the European Community, then the American impact on German politics was important over and above the various policies reviewed in the preceding pages.

But the American project did not depend on German Christian Democrats alone. Many Americans expected socialism to be far stronger in Western Europe after the war than it was, and they were quite prepared to work with it. In fact, many of those Americans responsible for the Marshall Plan would actually have preferred socialist governments in the area, thinking them particularly amenable to a fresh start in regional affairs and able to commit their governments more easily to planned schemes of integration. Ironically, the greatest outside force working against the socialists in West Germany was not the Americans but the Soviets. By refusing to integrate their zone with the rest of Germany, Moscow was depriving German socialism of one of its strongest bases of support in prewar German elections.

Where American policy was probably most decisive was not within West Germany but between Bonn and its neighbors. Through the Marshall Plan in 1947, and NATO in 1949, the United States demonstrated its commitment to the peace, prosperity, and integration of Western Europe, thereby seeking to end what for three-quarters of a century had been the

German question. Without this commitment and the explicit definition of its intentions, there is reason to think that the stability Europe today enjoys would be far less sure than it is and that the cold war might not have ended on terms as favorable as it did.[68] In fact, through the mid-1990s, many European voices were raised to insist that the United States must continue to play a leading role in NATO: not because the Russian threat might yet recur, so much as out of continued concerns about German "reliability."

The American impact on the course of events in Japan bears some of the same features one sees in West Germany. Both in economic policy and in foreign affairs, Yoshida Shigeru, conservative prime minister from 1946 to 1954 (except for an interlude from May 1947 until October 1948) seemed to be a willing collaborator with the United States, much as Adenauer was in Germany. Nevertheless, MacArthur tended to favor the democratic socialists; and until the "reverse course" of 1948, they, in turn, were more genuinely enthusiastic about virtually the entire range of American-sponsored reforms than were their conservative counterparts.

In economic matters, for example, American efforts to break up the zaibatsu were largely unsuccessful. Socialists in power might have suited MacArthur better. Despite praise of MacArthur at points in his memoirs as "a great statesman" (and the occupation being carried out with "far-sighted vision and consummate tact"), Yoshida concludes his reminiscences inveighing against the "prejudice" of "over-zealous" Americans, who,

> dedicated to 'new-deal' idealism, often went to extremes, in complete ignorance of the complex realities then prevailing in our country. . . . [Remember] how a purge was enforced which deprived our nation of a trained body of men at a crucial moment; how the financial concerns were disintegrated through the complete break-up of zaibatsu and by the institution of severe anti-monopoly measures, gravely retarding our economic recovery; how notorious communist leaders were released from prison and praised for their fanatical agitation, causing untold injury to our body politic; how organized labor was encouraged in radical actions thus endangering law and order; how education was reformed, sapping the moral fibre of our bewildered youth. Besides, our politics were so disorganized that militant unions, heavily infiltrated by communism, ran amok in defying the authority of the government.[69]

It is reasonable to conclude that the American impact was greater on democratization in Japan than in West Germany. Left to its own devices, Japan probably would not have undertaken comprehensive land reform, abolished its military ministries, or reworked its constitution—either to provide the range of civil liberties dictated by the Americans or to restrict the throne so completely to ceremonial duties. These policies were of the utmost importance in determining the character of postwar Japan. Whatever the flaws in the purges or in the efforts to deconcentrate economic holdings, the impact of American restructuring today, continues to mark profoundly Japanese political life, more than four decades after the end of the occupation in April 1952. By contrast, the strength of democratic forces in West Germany was such that the American contribution appears relatively marginal.

In the domain of international politics, however, America did more to integrate Germany with its neighbors than it could do for Japan. Part of the problem is that Japan has lacked the ability to integrate itself regionally in the manner of Germany. But part of the problem is Japan's self-defined relationship to the international economic order. There are persuasive arguments to the effect that Japan does not play by the rules; that it acts in a manner that favors its commerce unduly while overly discriminating against those of its neighbors relative to the practices of the United States or the European Community. Nor is there full confidence that the Pacific rim markets (which include the United States) will continue to provide Japan with the economic exchanges it requires. Given the country's record of self-righteousness, many observers worry about the future.[70] Perhaps these concerns are exaggerated; but it is notable that parallel concerns about Germany are much more muted.

We may therefore conclude that in different ways American liberal democratic internationalism profoundly marked the postwar life of Germany and Japan. American influence over Germany was most important with respect to that country's relations with the rest of Western Europe and hence to the prospects for democracy in Europe. With regard to Japan, American influence was critical in overseeing internal political reform and providing access to a global market.

A second issue takes us away from what American policy accomplished domestically or regionally to what this meant globally and historically. Was there a price to be paid for accomplishments as significant as these? Is it possible Washington oversold the cold war to Japan and Germany in order to encourage their domestic elites to reform along American lines? Did Washington use the Korean War to exaggerate the Soviet danger to Europe and the Chinese danger to Japan? Was George Kennan perhaps correct in the early 1950s when he counseled against becoming ideologically pitted against the Soviet Union and overmilitarizing relations with Moscow? Did the preoccupation with Japan and MacArthur's outspoken anticommunism lead directly to a sterile China policy and to intervention in Vietnam? Was the rise of McCarthyism in the United States a price paid for the crusade for democracy in Europe and Japan?

Surely the cold war was a godsend for American purposes, thanks to which conservative forces in both Germany and Japan were ready to make their break with the past and to throw their lot in with the American order. "I think you could say that it probably took the Cold War and fear of the

Russians to make the Germans accept the occupation so well," declared Clay. "We began to look like angels, not because we were angels, but we looked [like] that in comparison to what was going on in Eastern Europe."[71] Much the same holds true for Japan, where conservatives may have exaggerated the threat of communism in Asia as a way of manipulating American authorities, but where these same leaders were in turn manipulated by Washington and in their fear of world communism were all the more willing to comply with American suggestions. If playing by liberal rules was the price for being saved from communism, then small price it was indeed.

These considerations suggest that American success was not cost free. And yet a success the policy nonetheless was. In late 1944 a State Department planning document had phrased the American hope clearly:

> In the long run, the best guarantee of security, and the least expensive, would be the assimilation of the German people into the world society of peace-loving nations. These considerations urge the search for a continuing policy which will prevent a renewal of German aggression and, at the same time, pave the way for the German people in the course of time to join willingly in the common enterprises of peace.

While European economic integration might be one means to this end, the State Department insisted especially on the force of democracy domestically:

> Germany's repudiation of militaristic and ultranationalistic ideologies will in the long-run depend on the psychological disarmament of the German people, tolerable economic conditions, and the development of stable political conditions. The most plausible hope for lasting political reconstruction and orderly development lies in the establishment of democratic government.[72]

From today's perspective, the self-congratulatory words of John McCloy, U.S. high commissioner in Germany, seem vindicated: "We made unthinkable another European civil war. We ended one of history's longest threats to peace."[73]

MacArthur was equally convinced of the contribution of the American occupation of Japan to that country's future:

> History records no other instance wherein the military occupation of a conquered people has been conducted with the emphasis placed, as it has been here, upon the moral values involved between victor and vanquished. Right rather than might has been the criterion. The fruits of this policy are now self-evident.[74]

Whatever reservations might rightly be expressed to these sentiments, they should not blind us to liberalism's substantial victory. By fostering democratic governments in Germany and Japan and by making these two countries into willing participants in a liberal economic world order, the United States achieved the power to face down the Soviet Union and to promote the eventual collapse of the communist promise. The liberal consequences of the peace fulfilled enough of their promise to be worthy of respect even if there was a price to be paid. In the following chapter, which turns to the evolution of the cold war, we will see what that cost entailed.

PART III

Liberal Democratic Internationalism and the Cold War, 1947–1977

CHAPTER SEVEN

Eisenhower and His Legacy, 1953–1977

> We cannot be too dogmatic about the methods by which local
> communists can be dealt with [in Latin America] . . . where the
> concepts and traditions of popular government are too weak to
> absorb successfully the intensity of the communist attack, then we
> must concede that harsh governmental methods of repression may
> be the only answer; that these measures may have to proceed from
> regimes whose origins and methods would not stand the test of
> American concepts of democratic procedure; and that such regimes
> and such methods may be preferable alternatives, and indeed the
> only alternative, to further communist successes.
>
> —George F. Kennan, memorandum to the secretary of state
> on U.S. policy toward Latin America, March 1950

> I know of no evidence that "democracy," or what we picture to
> ourselves under that word, is the natural state of most of mankind.
> It seems rather to be a form of government (and a difficult one,
> with many drawbacks, at that) which evolved in the 18th and
> 19th centuries in northwestern Europe . . . and which was then
> carried into other parts of the world, including North America,
> where peoples from that northwestern European area appeared as
> settlers. . . . Democracy has, in other words, a relatively narrow
> base both in time and in space; and the evidence has yet to be
> produced that it is the natural form of rule for peoples outside those
> narrow perimeters.
>
> —George F. Kennan, *The Cloud of Danger*, 1977

GIVEN THE RECORD of American accomplishment in Germany and Japan
during the occupation period following World War II, it is tempting to
exaggerate the power of Wilsonianism itself to protect the national interest.
If America's earlier ambitions to foster democracy had not worked out
terribly well for the Philippines or the Dominican Republic, perhaps these
failures could be accounted for by their simple agrarian character and their
Spanish heritage rather than on anything the Americans had neglected to
do. Given better material, such as Germany and Japan, the project to promote democracy could be more successfully realized.

Yet such observations fail to appreciate the extent to which America's efforts were stymied by the internal contradictions of American liberal democratic assumptions themselves. For reasons of political expediency (which dictated assuring control in the most direct manner possible) as well as out of liberal democratic convictions (which enshrined the rights of private property and the need to limit the state's power relative to society), Washington's prescription for change was a "conservative radicalism": radical in its insistence on political democracy; conservative in safeguarding the socioeconomic privileges of the established order.

From the defeat of the Confederacy in 1865 and the subsequent Reconstruction of the South, to the taking of the Philippines in 1898 and the occupation of the Dominican Republic in 1916, the United States showed a decided preference for achieving political change favorable to democracy by working through the established socioeconomic power structure. Whatever the talk about forty acres and a mule being the well-spring of civic virtue, whatever the warning by Wilson's time of the danger of large concentrations of wealth to democratic government, faced with the challenges of ruling abroad, the Americans invariably co-opted local elites in a bid to make them the agents of reform in their own lands—be they white plantation owners in the South after 1865, landed oligarchs and the "ilustrados" in the Philippines after 1898, or *la gente de primera* (the landed elite) of the Dominican Republic after 1916.

At times, to be sure, a more radical socioeconomic bid might be made: at the inception of the Alliance for Progress toward Latin America in the early 1960s (reviewed in the next chapter), just as in the occupations of Germany and Japan. Nevertheless, the Alliance quickly backed down from its insistence on wide-scale reform when it discovered the depth of Latin American resistance to such efforts, and occupation policy became less experimental as the cold war intensified.

Hence, from William Howard Taft's "policy of attraction," designed to win over the elite of the Philippines to American rule at the turn of the century, to Ronald Reagan's policy of "constructive engagement" in the 1980s to get foreign governments to reform themselves, Washington indicated it understood the limits on its power and the need for local cooperation (some might prefer to say collaboration) to effect the changes it could. Given this approach, the varying fortunes of American attempts to transplant democratic institutions rested in large part on the character of the peoples they tried to influence.

As noted in chapter five, Franklin D. Roosevelt recognized that the expansion of democracy abroad was not an end that the United States should pursue everywhere. As the Good Neighbor Policy toward Latin America demonstrated when it implicitly recognized that democratic government was unlikely in this region, an explicit commitment not to intervene sometimes better served the national security, even if dictators flourished as a result. Washington therefore worked for democracy where it could (as in Japan and Western Europe), called for it where it might (as in Eastern Europe), but realistically accommodated itself to working with authoritarian governments in other areas, from Turkey to China, when the pursuit of American interests required such flexibility.

The policy that resulted may be called *selective* liberal democratic internationalism. Despite a primary mission of the American occupations of Germany and Japan to transform these two defeated militaristic states into peaceful democracies, outside Western Europe and Japan, American power was seen as too limited, the appeal of democracy in many places too foreign. The goal of making the world over in the democratic image seemed unrealistic as guide for policy. In Asia, Latin America, and Africa—the so-called third world (to indicate its position between East and West)— American leaders felt that by respecting the power of nationalism, and calling for "self-determination" (which in practice meant accepting states whose authority was based on locally mustered forces), they could secure their fundamental objectives: a world order composed of sovereign states, interrelated through a nondiscriminatory international economic system and a host of international organizations for conflict resolution, of which the United Nations was the most important.

The result was to be a global system hostile to imperialism (or to great power spheres of influence that involved direct political control of the sort the Soviet Union proposed for Eastern Europe) and friendly to nationalism. While the prospects for democracy were not perceived to be dimmed by such arrangements, neither was democracy to be forced upon an unwilling world. In all, the Americans could think of themselves as *realistic liberals*, a term that might be related to the presumed American virtue of pragmatism, and that, enshrined by academics as *realism* (discussed in the appendix), could be elaborated into a formal framework for the analysis of foreign policy. The result was a bipartisan foreign policy (where *bipartisan* means liberals and realists as well as Democrats and Republicans) wherein everyone could agree, even if for different reasons, that communism worldwide had to be opposed (realists seeing Marxist-Leninist ideology as a cover for the power of the Soviet state, liberals taking the ideology at face value and seeing it as a threat to liberal democratic values).

Notwithstanding American optimism that working with authoritarian regimes would not damage the prospects for democracy in the long run, in fact this new atmosphere encouraged practices that could indeed jeopardize democracy's chances. As the three-cornered struggle for power in Greece among royalists, republicans, and communists demonstrated as early as 1945, Washington might well be presented with situations where it risked allowing a communist takeover if it backed republican against rightist forces. With the tensions of the cold war intensifying in 1947, American interest in gambling on democratic forces abroad steadily diminished. Faced with a situation in which right-wing authoritarians seemed more likely to block the rise of communists than republican constitutionalists, Washington might actually oppose apparently democratizing movements abroad.

The result was a policy that Washington never considered before: direct support for practices and institutions abroad fundamentally hostile to democracy. Washington had progressed from intervention for the promotion of democracy under Wilson, to nonintervention under FDR (which in practice put Washington's blessing on authoritarian governments), to interventions deliberately favoring authoritarianism. In the process, the rhetoric of democratic internationalism was debased as it was used to disguise policies frankly premised on using authoritarian means to secure anticommunist ends: first in Iran following the CIA-engineered coup of August 1953, then in Guatemala in conjunction with the CIA coup of June 1954, and finally, and with the most disastrous consequences, in Vietnam after the Geneva Conference in July 1954, when the French began their staged withdrawal from Southeast Asia and the United States stepped in. Such a process of change did not mean that furthering democracy abroad was not in the American national interest, but rather that time and place determined when Washington would back it seriously.

Although the date of the beginning of the cold war is arguable, its impact on American thinking about democracy abroad is clearly visible by 1947, when there was a change away from promoting reform and toward building up stable governments committed to the struggle against communism. With the Korean War in June 1950, tensions increased further. In the hysteria surrounding Senator Joseph McCarthy's charges beginning in February 1950 that communists had infiltrated the American government, even democracy at home became more precarious. Few dared point out the irony that in the name of defending democracy, Washington was dictating infringements on democratic values at home and abroad.

The change in American policy toward Latin America was indicative of this evolution. In November 1945, in the enthusiasm of the victory over fascism, Secretary of State James Byrnes had seconded the proposal of Uruguayan Foreign Minister Eduardo Larreta that "'the parallelism between democracy and peace must constitute a strict rule of action in inter-American policy.'" Brynes's statement (at times citing Larreta's) was pure Wilsonianism:

> The established principle of non-intervention by one state in the affairs of another should not shield "the notorious and repeated violation by any republic of the elementary rights of man and of the citizen. . . ." Violation of the elementary rights of man by a government of force and the non-fulfillment of obliga-

tions by such a government . . . justifies collective multilateral action after full consultation among the [American] republics in accordance with established procedures.[1]

Such a mood was short-lived. With the well-publicized failure of Ambassador Spruille Braden (later undersecretary of state for Latin American affairs) to move Argentina—which had been sympathetic to Hitler and hostile to the Allies—toward democracy in 1945, and with the intensification of the cold war, embodied in Latin America by the collective security treaty known as the Rio Pact, signed in September 1947, the Truman administration returned to the noninterventionist practice of the Roosevelt years. In 1947 Byrnes and Braden resigned, and what the administration considered to be a more realistic policy—best witnessed in efforts to secure a rapprochement with Peron's Argentina—came into being in the effort to check communism in the hemisphere.[2]

By March 1954, at the Tenth Inter-American Conference, the new Eisenhower administration made it clear that Washington would intervene—not so as to aid democratic forces in a Wilsonian manner, but to stop communism even at the price of reinforcing authoritarian regimes. The choice of the conference site in Caracas, Venezuela, then under the control of the anticommunist dictator Marcos Perez Jimenez, made the tilt of American policy all the more apparent. An armistice had been signed in Korea in July 1953, and by the summer of 1954 the Eisenhower administration had faced down Senator McCarthy, but a cold war consensus had meanwhile consolidated itself in Washington joining liberals and realists as anticommunists in determined oppostion to the expansion of Moscow's power.

American reactions to Iranian demands in 1951 for control over British petroleum concessions in Iran were indicative of this Rooseveltian realism as to democracy's prospects. Secretary of State Dean Acheson was quick to denounce what he called the "persistent stupidity" of the British owned Anglo-Iranian Oil Company, and acknowledged Iran's sovereign right to nationalize what it could. But he was equally clear that he felt it an "illusion" of "American liberals" to think that there was any possibility that "a moderate leadership existed between the Tudeh party communists and the feudal reactionaries and mullahs." Only the shah could give Iran the kind of stability American interests in the region required.[3]

Acheson's perspective on Iran in the early 1950s could be taken as a judgment on the prospects for democratic rule practically anywhere in the third world. Throughout these regions, democratizing forces appeared weak: divided among themselves, ideologically uncertain, often anti-American, and overly willing to work with local communists in the pursuit of common objectives. Seeing the world increasingly through the lenses of the cold war, official Washington tended to reduce the main political players in the third world to the traditional conservative elites and the communists aligned with Moscow who terrified them. In such circumstances, Washington would work with the right.

In an era of nationalism and popular sovereignty, the decision to work with authoritarian governments was fateful, for it involved the United States in shoring up authoritarian regimes based on fragile political coalitions at home in a manner that was becoming frankly reactionary. Until 1947, the choice for policymakers had been between a Wilsonian advocacy of democracy and a Rooseveltian preference for nonintervention. Now a third option gained favor: intervention for dictatorships, even against indigenous political forces that might be bent on creating constitutional, democratic regimes.

AMERICAN REALISM AND MASS POLITICS IN THE TWENTIETH CENTURY

In the aftermath of the Vietnam War, it became standard fare for many students of American foreign policy to point out that in its concern with "international communism," Washington failed to appreciate the power of nationalism in determining regional struggles. The third world was not a row of "falling dominoes," to quote President Dwight D. Eisenhower's celebrated phrase, but an area for the most part able to fight off the domination of either superpower. In these circumstances, America's task was to make common cause with popular forces. Where this was not possible, the success of communism in a nonstrategic area should not be a threat to a superpower. The most farfetched (and widely cited) misperception confusing local events with the bipolar struggle is surely the observation made before the China Institute in America on May 18, 1951, by Dean Rusk, then assistant secretary of state for Far Eastern affairs (later Kennedy and Johnson's secretary of state): "The Peking regime may be a colonial Russian government—a Slavic Manchukuo on a larger scale. It is not the government of China. It does not pass the first test. It is not Chinese."

The crux of the problem for American policymakers lay in the great transformations that were taking place around the world as states struggled to control the mass of the population, which for the first time in most places was being mobilized into politics. Traditional authoritarian regimes had somehow to establish direct political links with the entire citizenry. Agrarian elites invariably resisted such developments for fear of losing their control over the land, just as business elites opposed the organization of labor for fear losing control over their enterprises. For governments the problem was one of developing norms and institutions that would incorporate the bulk of the population into the life of government in a stable manner. New legal systems and titles of legitimacy; new groups organizing and pressing new demands; competitive parties arising for the first time, whose officials had never had to maintain their rule through party procedures: such were the manifold problems of political order over most of the globe in the twentieth century, a world order where the membership of the United Nations increased from 51 to 126 members between 1945 and 1968.

Seen from this perspective, the modernity of fascism, communism, and democracy lay in the fact that each accepted the challenge of organizing mass political participation. A three-cornered competition at once domestic and international thereupon ensued for the allegiance of hitherto excluded workers, peasants, and marginalized ethnic groups.

Fascism's particular solution to the class and ethnic tensions of modernity came in the form of highly charged, militaristic, racist nationalism combined with a totalitarian effort to organize the population through tightly controlled, hierarchical political mechanisms subservient to a single leader. Its promise to traditional elites was to allow them to continue to run their affairs with respect to an obedient class of workers and peasants, although in Germany the Nazi party, and in Japan the military, replaced these older elites politically and took command of the state.

Fascism's inherent racism and militarism led it to disaster in World War II, but watered-down versions of fascistic states continued to exist after 1945 in such places as Argentina and Spain. The temptation to solve the problem of the incorporation of the masses into politics in a manner similar to fascism has recurred elsewhere in more recent times, as in the Ba'ath movement in Syria and Iraq.

By contrast, communism's solution was to organize a revolution based on the exploited sectors of the population, led by a disciplined Leninist party. The genius of the party was its ability to harness nationalism and the class demands of what was often a substantial majority of the population into a coalition led by a revolutionary organization willing to work through whatever institutional means were available in its pursuit of power. Once in control, the "dictatorship of the proletariat" pledged to serve the needs of the workers and peasants (symbolized by the hammer and sickle displayed on the Soviet flag), whom it mobilized in military fashion under party control. Traditional elites could expect nothing but death, exile, or painful "reeducation."

In addressing itself to claims of social justice for the marginalized majorities in the agrarian world, the communists were advancing an appeal that liberal democracy had traditionally been slow to understand. While American liberal democrats associated with the New Deal were, by the 1930s, finally able to assert the need for political intervention to right the injustices of a free market, any talk of socialism remained taboo. With its connotations of a state gradually extending control over social forces ever less able to influence their government, socialism in America remained weak.

The paramount American virtue was freedom; justice was expected to flow naturally from liberty's triumph. The appeal of American democracy abroad was thus better suited to the middle-class forces and to those progressive elements among the traditional elite that understood the need to gamble on reform in order to preserve their socioeconomic privileges. If America would back their efforts in favor of democracy, it was not at all prepared to battle the socioeconomic pyramids of power and privilege built on distinctions of race and class.

It was precisely in addressing the volatile emotions linked to social and economic justice that the communists were most effective. "Colonial slaves of Africa and Asia: the hour of proletarian dictatorship in Europe will also be the hour of your own liberation," the Third [Communist] International declared when it announced its goal of "world revolution" at its First Congress in Moscow in 1919. As the International instructed its Chinese comrades in 1923: "The national revolution in China and the creation of an anti-imperialist front will necessarily coincide with the agrarian revolution of the peasantry against the survivals of feudalism. . . . the central question of all policy is the peasant question."[4]

The struggle between the Soviet Union and the United States after 1945 was therefore more than a traditional struggle between two great powers jockeying for position among the many power vacuums that opened around the world in the aftermath of World War II. Each power had to be concerned not only about the behavior of client states in the international arena but also about their domestic base of support. As with fascism, the struggle was at once international and domestic, as rival groups organizing mass political bases sought to protect their interests by allying themselves with strong forces abroad.

With the expansion of Soviet control over Eastern Europe and the triumph of communism in China by 1949, the communist system seemed a viable form of political modernity, as significant a threat to democracy as fascism had ever been. With an international headquarters in Moscow and "fraternal" parties active in most countries of the world, Washington was well advised to consider the communist challenge to be global in scope.

At the end of the twentieth century, there is a greater understanding of the strength democratic political systems and market economies possess. Democratic mechanisms that involve the entire citizenry in politics, that build different coalitions on different issues, and that provide for the accountability and rotation of leaders have created flexible yet stable governments—at least by comparison to alternative forms of rule. Perhaps democracy's greatest strength lies in its compatability with a market economy. By protecting capitalism itself, as well as the citizenry at large, from the dangers of unregulated competition, by insisting on a degree of government intervention favorable both to economic growth and to social stability, democracy had managed by the 1940s to ensure high degrees of prosperity as well as historically unmatched levels of political freedom and justice.

Nevertheless, the obstacles to creating such a system, as opposed to having the benefits of one already in place—the problems of democratization in an authoritarian context—are considerable. Traditional elites resist the diminution of their power; excluded sectors of the population rise up in long-repressed indignation at the established order; powerful foreign influences are targeted for nationalist attack. The process that introduces democracy and incorporates the mass of the population into representative institutions is not an easy affair.

In short, in its formative phase, democracy is particularly weak. Unlike its totalitarian rivals, democracy cannot organize its strength through a single-party structure; it cannot provide its supporters the euphoria of a particularly militant ideology; it cannot guarantee to traditional elites the preservation of their privileges any more than it could assure the mass of the population full justice for the wrongs they have endured; and it cannot promise its followers the leadership of a strong state. As a way of respecting (indeed encouraging) diversity; as a procedure for securing compromise (not hard decision); as an ethic of toleration (which discourages militancy); as a limited (rather than absolute) state, its appeal is naturally restricted to the middle sectors of society: those with something to lose from revolution but with something to gain from reform. Where these groups are weak or terrified by threats from above or below, the appeal of some form of either communism or fascism is more likely to hold sway.

These generalities may help to clarify why the Americans came to choose stability over democracy (and not stability through democracy) as the cold war intensified. At a critical moment in 1949, there was a momentous hesitation on Washington's part. Should the United States recognize the victory of Mao Zedong's forces in China (as the British, among others, were counseling the United States to do)? Unsure of the geopolitical tack to take given China's announced hostility toward the United States, and afraid of domestic opposition, the Truman administration waited to see how Sino-Soviet relations would work themselves out. It is conceivable that had Sino-American relations improved at this critical juncture, the United States would not have seen the expansion of communism in parts of Asia or Latin America as inherently threatening developments.

But in February 1950, Senator Joseph McCarthy made his entrance on the stage of American politics, and in June the Korean War began, which was ultimately to involve armed conflict between American and Chinese troops. The unfortunate result was the widespread conviction in Washington that the struggle against communism in Asia and Latin America was directly linked to the struggle against Soviet power in Europe. From June of 1950, when the Korean War began, to sometime in the mid- to late 1960s, when more and more observers came to see the war in Vietnam as a mistake, mainstream realist and liberal thinking in the United States was in agreement on the need to stop communist advances in Asia and Latin America.

The most common practice for Americans engaged in countries where a communist threat was perceived was to build up a client military (augmented by a secret police). At one stroke, the Americans helped to strengthen an organization capable both of rooting out local communists and, in some instances, of blocking direct Soviet or Chinese expansion. Usually, the military was already an important actor in local politics: in Latin America and the Middle East, for example, the military's role in government had long been a central fact of political life (to such a point that its "guardian" role was formally recognized in some Latin American constitutions). At times, the military was in league with the traditional order through its officer corps; at other moments, it might possess enough organizational strength to constitute a new elite, promoted from the people, based on their own resources. In either case, the risk was that the military would become a self-serving interest with the means to seize power.

American support for foreign militaries therefore did not create a political role for them, but it did augment their power and intensify their confidence relative to other forces in society. In theory, one could make the case for the military as a modernizing force, the founder of stable political institutions built on civilian rule. Turkey or Mexico might be cited as cases where such a transition to modern politics had occurred. But in practice, the military as a progressive force was more rare. Instead, states in the 1950s and 1960s made more autonomous by the presence of strong militaries were likely to strike bargains with the traditional elites and, with American support, block the mobilization of the mass of the population into politics. In a word, by militarizing the cold war beyond Europe, the United States usually became reactionary so far as the twentieth century's move toward some form of popular sovereignty was concerned and so turned local nationalist forces in an anti-American direction. The dilemma for Americans about how to proceed in a more constructive way was real, and the debate over proper policy persisted over four decades, from the argument about Greece in the late 1940s to that over Nicaragua in the late 1980s.

THE EISENHOWER YEARS

President Dwight D. Eisenhower (1953–61) and his activist secretary of state, John Foster Dulles (1953–9), engaged in ceaseless talk about the American duty to protect the "free world" from communism. At times, it sounded almost as if Woodrow Wilson had been reincarnated in the person of Dulles, with his moralistic crusading against iniquity under the banner of Old Glory. As Dulles told *Life* magazine before the presidential election of 1952:

There is a moral or natural law not made by man which determines right and wrong and in the long run only those who conform to that law will escape disaster. This law has been trampled by the Soviet rulers, and for that violation they can and should be made to pay. . . . We should be dynamic, we should use ideas as weapons; and these ideas should conform to moral principles. . . . We have always been, as we always should be, the despair of the oppressor and the hope of the oppressed.

Accordingly, as the 1952 Republican party platform put it in words written by Dulles:

We shall again make liberty into a beacon light of hope that will penetrate the dark places. It will mark the end of the negative, futile, and immoral policy of 'containment,' which abandons countless human beings to a despotism and godless terrorism, which in turn enables the rulers to forge the captives into a weapon of our destruction. . . . the policies we espouse will revive the contagious, liberating influences which are inherent in freedom. They will inevitably set up strains and stresses within the captive world which will make the rulers impotent to continue their monstrous ways and mark the beginning of the end.[5]

The Wilsonianism of such phrases was not accidental. Both men were the sons of Presbyterian ministers, and Dulles had been Wilson's student in a course on political ethics at Princeton. Dulles's uncle, Robert Lansing, was Wilson's secretary of state; and Dulles had accompanied Wilson to the Paris Peace Conference in 1919, after World War I. Both men were described by their contemporaries as rigid, Old Testament characters, believers in a stern God and certain that the United States had a mission of the highest moral importance in international affairs.

Yet the world Dulles lived in was not Wilson's, and the secretary had imbibed enough realism in his many years of experience in foreign affairs to know the difference between word and deed. Dulles's passionate rhetoric therefore was not always matched by action. In the case of Eastern Europe, Dulles followed the precedent of the Truman administration and worked to encourage the example of Yugoslavia's independence from Moscow. The fact that Yugoslav leader Josef Tito was a communist who was thoroughly opposed to democracy was not the issue. Priority should be given to breaking up of the Soviet empire, if not through democracy then by encouraging the self-determination of the nations of Eastern Europe. As Dulles put it in an interview in October 1956, speaking of "the liberation of the satellites":

Anything which weakens this great structure [the Soviet empire] and leads to its breaking up into its constituent parts, its natural constituent parts, so that these countries can exercise their own independence and their own freedom, that we favor. . . . Now, what they do with their freedom after they get it is a second problem. We naturally would like them to have the same kind of freedom and exercise it the way we do, with our same democratic processes. We believe that's the best system that there is, but that is a system which can only be spread throughout the world gradually, and as I say, today there are not many parts of the world where that particular system prevails.[6]

Hence, while "the static doctrine of containment" was to be replaced by "roll-back" and "liberation" for the "captive nations" of Eastern Europe, Dulles was careful to caution against war. As he declared in his 1952 *Life* article, "We do not want a series of bloody uprisings and reprisals [in Eastern Europe]. There can be peaceful separation from Moscow, as Tito showed . . . and we can be confident that within two, five, or ten years substantial parts of the present captive world can peacefully regain national independence."[7] He insisted his confidence was well-founded:

> Some say that it is unrealistic and impractical not to recognize the enforced "incorporation" of Estonia, Latvia, and Lithuania into the Soviet Union. We believe, however, that a despotism of the present Soviet type cannot indefinitely perpetuate its rule over hundreds of millions of people who love God, who love their country, and who have a sense of personal dignity. The Soviet system, which seeks to expunge the distinctive characteristics of nation, creed, and individuality must itself change or be doomed ultimately to collapse. . . . The captive peoples should know that they are not forgotten, that we are not reconciled to their fate, and above all, that we are not prepared to seek illusory safety for ourselves by a bargain with their masters which would confirm their captivity. . . . We have not forgotten the Atlantic Charter and its proclamation of "the right of peoples to choose the form of government under which they will live." We still share the wish expressed in that Charter "to see sovereign rights and self-government restored to those who have been forcibly deprived of them."[8]

President Eisenhower, who sometimes deplored the "purple prosecuting-attorney style" of his secretary of state, nonetheless shared much the same worldview as Dulles. Campaigning in October for the 1956 presidential elections, Eisenhower saluted those Poles and Hungarians "willing to die" for freedom. Yet only weeks later, after the Hungarian uprising had been crushed, the president declared:

> Our hearts have gone out to [the Hungarian insurgents] and we have done everything it is possible to, in the way of alleviating suffering. But I must make one thing clear: the United States doesn't now and never has advocated open rebellion by an undefended populace against force over which they could not possibly prevail. We, on the contrary, have always urged that the spirit of freedom be kept alive, that people do not lose hope. But we have never in all the years that I think we have been dealing with problems of this sort urged or argued for any kind of armed revolt which could bring about disaster to our friends.[9]

In short, despite the talk about "brinkmanship," the administration was realistic enough to understand the limits of American power and the high cost that any effort to liberate the satellite countries by force would entail. Its first concern was to encourage nationalism of the Titoist sort in the region as a solvent of Soviet power. In such circumstances, the fate of democracy would depend on later developments.

Historians have found reason to commend Eisenhower for his restraint with respect to Eastern Europe—his understanding that whatever the crimes of the Kremlin, they could not be corrected by force.[10] Such restraint was again apparent in 1954, when the French asked Eisenhower to come to their assistance in Vietnam and the president refused. What, then, of the promotion of democracy in the third world?

A National Security Council meeting early in 1955 offers an illustration of the disagreements among top government officials over the relative merits of supporting democracy abroad. At the session, Secretary of the Treasury George Humphrey argued that "the U.S. should back strong men in Latin American governments [because] whenever a dictator was replaced, communists gained." Nelson Rockefeller, then special assistant to the president, disagreed: "It is true, in the short run, that dictators handle communists effectively. But in the long run, the U.S. must encourage the growth of democracies in Latin America if communism is to be defeated in the area." Eisenhower sided with Rockefeller: "In the long run, the United States must back democracies."[11]

The problem, however, was preparing for the long run while living in the present. If democracy could be established, it might indeed stop communism's advance in many countries of Asia and Latin America. But democratization as a process was an uncertain undertaking at best and might result in a communist takeover. What must be done? Eisenhower's actions spoke for themselves. Seven months before he privately affirmed his faith in democracy in the lines cited above, the president had used the CIA to topple what appeared to be a democratizing government in Guatemala. Ten months before that, he had approved the overthrow of a constitutional regime in Iran. If Washington could think in the long run, it lived in the short term. Whatever the obstacles authoritarianism placed in the path of eventual democratic government, Washington would rather gamble on right-wing forces than on working with republican forces, which might give way to a communist victory.

IRAN AND GUATEMALA, 1953–1954

Aside from Vietnam, the two most important American policy decisions with respect to working with alternative kinds of governments in the third world during the Eisenhower years concerned Iran, under Prime Minister

Mohammed Mossadegh (1951–3), and Guatemala, under President Jacobo Arbenz (1951–4). In each country, for the first time in its history, a constitutional regimes had emerged whose leaders were pledged to extend the democratic government. In each country, reformist leaders sought to expand their appeal by enlisting nationalist support for their programs through efforts to expropriate a major part of the holdings of foreign investors critically important to the national economy: the Anglo-Iranian Oil Company in Iran; the United Fruit Company in Guatemala. In each country, these constitutional, potentially democratizing regimes faced stiff opposition from a traditional, authoritarian right, while an indigenous communist party with links to the Soviet Union tried to turn the momentum of reform to its own ends of taking power. And in each country, the United States utterly disregarded the prospects for the long-term development of democracy and, in the name of stopping communism, covertly organized a successful strike against their governments through the auspices of the Central Intelligence Agency (CIA), headed by Allen Dulles, brother of the secretary of state. Finally, in each case the direct beneficiaries of American action were domestic forces implacably hostile to both constitutionalism and democracy, which with American support were able to eliminate all rivals from power, so leading their countries into the inferno.

An argument can surely be made for Eisenhower's skepticism as to the strength of moderate political forces in either country. While there are experts on both Iran and Guatemala who appear to believe that the Mossadegh and Arbenz governments might have successfully consolidated democratic political systems in their respective countries with relative ease had the United States not overthrown them, it nonetheless remains difficult to find reasons to think that the prospects for democracy in the early 1950s were particularly favorable in either place.

In Iran, Mossadegh's National Front had been created in late 1949 as a coalition of factions that gravitated to his forceful personality. It was a young and weakly organized liberal nationalist movement that would eventually—regardless of American policy—have been faced with serious challenges from the communist left (the Tudeh party) and, more importantly, from the conservative elements of the population organized around the shah. There are those who believed Mossadegh to be emotionally unstable. He warned himself that if his reforms failed, the communists would take power. Were these problems not enough, the British determination to make an example of him put pressures on his young and fragile political coalition, which were difficult to parry. But surely the most serious issue had to do with the immaturity of the Iranian party system, which was unable to buckle together the forces of reform. As Mossadegh himself put it in 1962, "The backwardness of Iran is due to the absence of political and social organizations and it was because of this defect that our beloved Iran lost its freedom and independence without anyone being able to make the slightest protest."[12]

In these circumstances, taking seriously a communist bid for power, as the Americans did, made sense. The Tudeh's inroads into the blossoming trade union movement and its open ties with the Soviet Union made it a force to be reckoned with as early as 1946. A year after Mossadegh's overthrow, the shah's security apparatus uncovered a Tudeh network in the armed forces comprising at least 458 officers, organized independently of the main party structure and reporting directly to an intelligence officer at the Soviet embassy. Even greater power was arrayed against Mossadegh on the right: the traditional landed elite, the throne, and the military. Recently analyzed evidence has suggested that these forces, organized behind General Fazlollah Zahedi, who eventually led the coup, were determined to preserve their interests from reform and played a more important role (relative to the CIA) than is usually credited them in ousting the National Front from power.[13]

Skepticism as to the strength of democratic forces was also warranted in the case of Guatemala. There, the Revolution of 1944 (as it called itself in honor of the overthrow of long-term dictator Jorge Ubico) faced both a conservative opposition, which stood to lose through political and economic reforms, and more importantly, communist efforts to dominate the government from within. The country's first postrevolutionary president, Juan Arevalo (1945–51), had kept his distance from local communists as he introduced his reforms. In the elections of 1951, universal suffrage was introduced, and Arevalo's reformist successor, Jacobo Arbenz, did well, gaining 60 percent of the vote against two conservative opponents.

But Arbenz was closely associated personally with Guatemalan communists who were in contact with Moscow, and he relied on them for his most important reform effort, the redistribution of land. In addition, the president was willing to split with the United States on what Washington felt were key matters of international security: a refusal to approve American involvement in the Korean War or to agree to American proposals to block communist regimes in the Western hemisphere. Matters grew all the more serious when a secret shipment of arms to Guatemala from Czechoslovakia was uncovered.

In the most authoritative account of the Arbenz years yet published, Piero Gleijeses writes:

> By late 1952, President Arbenz had chosen the stand from which he would not deviate. His closest political friend was the PGT [the Guatemalan Communist party], and his closest personal friends were its leaders. Arbenz continued to read. "He read books on the Russian revolution, the history of the USSR, the military strategy of the Soviet generals in WWII. All this molded his way of looking at the

world," observes [Guatemalan Communist head Jose Manuel] Fortuny. By 1952, "through all this reading," adds his wife, "Jacobo was convinced that the triumph of communism in the world was inevitable and desirable. The march of history was toward communism. Capitalism was doomed." . . . in the last two years of his administration [Arbenz] considered himself a communist, and with his few confidents, he spoke like one. The PGT leaders formed his "kitchen cabinet," and with them he took his most important decisions.[14]

In sum, the evidence indicates that the Eisenhower administration was not mistaken in seeing communist movements in Iran and Guatemala as growing in power, or to doubt the ability of centrist governments to stem the tide. Given the recent Korean War and the aftershocks of McCarthyism at home, there is little wonder that the United States took seriously the possibility of communist takeovers and took action to block it. The geostrategic importance of both Iran and Guatemala was arguably great enough, and communist strength so real, that Washington had a right, based on a compelling sense of national security, to work to deny the Soviet Union greater influence either place.[15]

Two pertinent objections to the policies of the Eisenhower administration are nevertheless possible—one questioning the means Washington used, the other the American ends. The first maintains that with proper American assistance, the Arbenz or Mossadegh regimes might have had the capacity to hold communist influence at bay. These constitutionalist governments might have been converted into democratizing governments capable of honoring American security concerns.

The other objection maintains that if the effort to promote democracy failed, it did not matter if these governments became communist. In a bipolar world, as the containment doctrine itself had once clearly held, only the fortunes of Western Europe and Japan were of basic strategic importance to the United States. A communist success in a country as insignificant to the balance of power as Guatemala or Vietnam or perhaps even Iran was not an issue that called for the kind of counterrevolutionary agitation manifested by Washington.

We may leave it to geopolitical theorists to argue what might have happened to the international balance of power had countries such as Guatemala or Iran become communist in the 1950s. Surely Iran mattered more in geostrategic terms than Guatemala or Vietnam. Suffice it to say that the Eisenhower administration simply assumed that any such development would mean a critical setback for American power in the world. China had become communist in 1949. An uneasy armistice was signed in Korea in July 1953. These were not times that encouraged fine distinctions as to whether it mattered where communists might elsewhere come to power.

The end of blocking such a development everywhere was accepted without debate.

Also beyond debate were the means to be employed—support for authoritarian forces against constitutional governments. The administration never seriously explored the possibility of reinforcing and redirecting potentially democratizing reformers like Arbenz and Mossadegh in a constructive manner. Whatever the sincerity of Eisenhower's statement that in the long run America must back democracy, in the short run, Washington opted for a simpler and more direct tactic: using the CIA to work with traditional authoritarian forces. By failing to engage in the complex, difficult, time-consuming, and undoubtedly risky attempt to promote constitutionalism, the United States not only exposed itself to serious moral criticism for becoming a party to cruel authoritarian rule over the peoples of Iran and Guatemala, but it also opened itself to the practical objection that its reactionary policies led to the creation of powerful nationalist forces in these regions that ultimately lashed back at the United States in the form of the Cuban Revolution of 1959 and the Iranian Revolution of 1979.

To make a case that the administration might have acted more progressively involves demonstrating that a reformist option existed in Iran and Guatemala to parry the communist threat. Obviously such an argument cannot be made definitively; we can never know what the United States might have achieved had it acted differently. But an argument can be made.

The catalyst for action in Iran and Guatemala was the decision by both governments to nationalize major foreign investments that dominated national economic life. From Washington's perspective, both the United Fruit Company and the Anglo-Iranian Oil Corporation were vast enterprises, whose expropriations might well have triggered a host of similar measures in other countries in Latin America, the Middle East, and Africa had they gone uncontested. The State Department and the companies concerned were keenly aware of this. Nevertheless, there was already clear precedent in American foreign relations to permit foreign countries to expropriate American investments with full, prompt compensation. For example, in the late 1930s, Mexican President Lazaro Cardenas had managed the expropriation of American petroleum and hacienda properties in his country in a move Washington eventually accepted.

Still more important, it is ironic that the United States Justice Department was preparing antitrust cases against both United Fruit and the American oil company cartel in the early 1950s, suits that could have been used to justify Washington's decision to back Iranian and Guatemalan demands. The Eisenhower administration would have paid a political price for such a course of action; American business would not resign itself happily to expropriations abroad. Yet it is conceivable that a compromise solution might have been found, leaving intact the ability of American companies to be protected from unregulated seizure overseas. The willingness of the American-Arabian Oil Company (Aramco) in Saudi Arabia to increase Riyadh's share of petroleum profits had been a key factor in the Iranian demand for more control over British operations. As such, it constituted an example of what might have been worked out.[16] In Guatemala, the difference between American and Guatemalan negotiators with respect to adequate compensation for United Fruit amounted to less than $15 million.

However, relations between host countries and foreign investors was not the most serious issue facing the Eisenhower administration. As Dulles put it, "If the United Fruit matter were settled, if they gave a gold piece for every banana, the problem would remain just as it is today as far as the presence of communist infiltration in Guatemala is concerned."[17] The problem was political: how could the avalanche of changes surrounding reform be guaranteed not to turn to the advantage of the communists?

In Iran, the intelligence evidence available to Eisenhower did not say Mossadegh was a communist or under their influence. His independence of both the party and the Soviet Union was well established.[18] Hence, a key to success in Iran might presumably have been for the United States to induce the shah to rally the army and such conservative forces as he could behind constitutional reform. The result would have been an alliance of the center and right against the Tudeh (communist) party—which had already lost popular support for its obvious subservience to Soviet interests in Iranian Azerbaijan—as well as against those elements on the right worried by secularism and the empowerment of the masses.

Admittedly, such an alliance would have been difficult to achieve. The Americans tried—unsuccessfully—to produce just such a coalition in the late 1940s in Greece. But the shah might have been persuaded to become a constitutional monarch, interested as he was in American advice, which could have stressed the nationalist appeal the throne would gain from appearing to lead the effort to nationalize the country's petroleum resources.

Washington's concern that communists were taking over the reform process in Guatemala was better founded. Arbenz was quite sympathetic to communism. Although no communist held a cabinet position, communists were his closest advisers and were especially powerful in the agrarian reform bureaucracy. Yet had the United States backed Arbenz's reforms and exacted from him an agreement to allow noncommunists to organize the peasant beneficiaries of the land distributed, these new recruits to the system of private property might have been organized within a democratic party system.

National Intelligence Estimates at the time put the number of communist party members at only five hundred in 1952, and fewer than one thousand a year later. Given the power of the Church and the army, the absence of any communists in the cabinet, and the fact that only four of the fifty-six members of Congress were communists—all of which were pointed out to the administration by the American intelligence community—there is at least some reason to think that American-backed reform might have succeeded.[19]

By 1954 government reform programs had distributed land to some one hundred thousand landless families, perhaps half a million people, in a country of some 3 million. By making property owners out of such a large percentage of the population, and then organizing support for the government that brought it about through an expanded political party system, democratic forces might conceivably have consolidated themselves. But such a policy would have required support for the expropriation of some four hundred thousand acres of land taken from the country's largest landowner, United Fruit (whose total holdings were about 550,000 acres). The Guatemalan government had offered the American corporation about $1.2 million as compensation for its losses, a sum established on the basis of the taxed value of this land. Washington insisted on behalf of United Fruit that the value was $15.9 million, that the company be reimbursed immediately and in full, and that Arbenz's insistence on taking the land was clear proof of his communist proclivities.

In sum, there is reason to think that the Eisenhower administration might have backed effective constitutionalist movements in Iran and Guatemala, yet the United States never considered supporting the reformist ambitions of either the Mossadegh or Arbenz governments. There were massive Western investments that would be lost should these regimes be given a green light; and there was the likelihood that other governments would act similarly once the example had been set. Moreover, Washington could not be sure that American oil companies would secure a place in the production of Iranian petroleum, where they ultimately acquired a 40 percent share. The payoff to American interests by the overthrow of these regimes was in this respect immediate, direct, and substantial to a group that generally supported the Republican party.

But the decisive thinking was political: aside from isolated voices like Nelson Rockefeller's, no one believed that centrist, nationalist reforms could stop communism. Traditional elites and the military seemed better equipped for the job than reformers, with their anti-Western, or at least neutralist, sympathies and their well-founded suspicion of their domestic military establishments. In Iran, the Americans hoped to gain an additional benefit as a militarily reinforced shah joined the United States in containing the Soviet Union on its southern flank.

Given the failure to explore the possibility that reformist regimes might have emerged in Iran and Guatemala in the mid-1950s, it might seem beside the point to criticize the Eisenhower administration for the inflated rhetoric it used to trumpet its victories. Yet the debasement of the terminology of democratic internationalism was critical to the willingness of the American public to be led into future adventures, of which Vietnam was the most notable.

Thus in Guatemala, the Castillo Armas government, which came to power with the coup, repossessed the land earlier distributed to one hundred thousand families. Dulles could nonetheless declare in words cited approvingly by Eisenhower: "Now the future of Guatemala lies at the disposal of the Guatemalan peoples themselves." Apparently there had been no other choice:

> [Guatemala] is the scene of dramatic events. They expose the evil purpose of the Kremlin to destroy the inter-American system, and they test the ability of the American States to maintain the peaceful integrity of this hemisphere. For several years international communism has been probing here and there for nesting places in the Americas. It finally chose Guatemala as a spot which it could turn into an official base from which to breed subversion which would extend to other American Republics. This intrusion of Soviet despotism was, of course, a direct challenge to our Monroe Doctrine, the first and most fundamental of our foreign policies.[20]

By the middle of 1958, the Eisenhower administration was coming to believe that stability in Latin America called for an effort at socioeconomic reform. In its political calculations, there was growing concern over American support for Cuban dictator Fulgencio Batista and even thought of covert action to overthrow Dominican dictator Rafael Trujillo.[21] Such thinking may have eased the introduction in Washington of the Alliance for Progress in 1961, but so far as Guatemala was concerned the damage done to constitutional government was irreparable for more than a generation, bequeathing to that country a succession of oppressive military regimes.

Washington also saw events in Iran in geopolitical terms. Exploiting this thinking, the shah spoke of his concern over "international communism" and of his determination to contain the Soviet Union on its southern flank. American support for the throne and a rise in oil profits increased the power of the Iranian state in that country relative to society. Eisenhower took pride in his accomplishment: "We as a nation . . . have a job to do, a mission as the champion of human freedom . . . to conduct ourselves in all our international relations that we never comprise the fundamental principle that all peoples who have a right to an independent government of their own full, free choice." Asserting that "the cold war is the central fact of our time," stressing its character as "the conflict between liberty and slavery," the president declared:

> For some decades our purposes abroad have been the establishment of universal peace with justice, free choice for all peoples, rising levels of human well-being,

and the development and maintenance of frank, friendly, and mutually helpful contacts with all nations willing to work for parallel objectives. . . . Manifestly we cannot counter communist tactics with their own weapons; with free speech and a free press established in most of the important nations of the West, there is no possibility of employing the big lie, often repeated, as a means either of unifying our own people or influencing others. Any attempt to do so would be futile, foolish, and, for us, immoral, and lies so employed would bewilder and divide the nations of the West. . . . Credibility in our informational programs is the first essential, and it cannot be achieved by falsehood and hypocrisy.[22]

Today it is permissible to doubt that America was truly innocent of "employing the big lie," whether its objectives could indeed be "achieved [without] falsehood and hypocrisy," whether Washington's conduct in much of the third world might not in fact "bewilder and divide the nations of the West." Certainly many of the peoples of these areas felt that Washington was guilty of precisely the evils Eisenhower assured his public he abhorred. In 1959, the strength of the Cuban Revolution came in part from the widespread hostility to American interventions in Latin America, but especially in reaction to events in Guatemala. In 1979 revolution in Iran brought to power forces angry in their denunciation of America as "the Great Satan." While neither of these events could have been predicted in 1953–4 and both depended on a history of American interventions far more complex than CIA interventions in just Iran and Guatemala alone, still both revolutions represented consequences that Washington had failed to evaluate when it dismissed nationalist sentiment in Iran and Central America as a force to be reckoned with.

It was in Southeast Asia, however, that America paid the highest price for its disregard in the Eisenhower years of the need to come to some understanding of what strong reformist governments might look like in the effort to stop communism. What the apparently easy successes in Iran and Guatemala seemed to demonstrate was that the United States could do as it would in the third world, and hence that in Vietnam too, where the French suffered a defeat at the hands of Ho Chi Minh's communist forces in the spring of 1954, American power might make a decisive difference without paying too much attention to the complexity of local forces and events.

Vietnam

Conventional wisdom about Vietnam holds that Washington's primary concerns in Southeast Asia were geopolitical—to contain the expansion of communism by demonstrating a resolve not to abandon a potentially "salvagable" country such as Vietnam to communist aggression. Most policymakers in Washington believed that the entire structure of containment Washington had put together the world round since 1947 depended on this commitment. Incredible as it may seem, the national security of the United States in a bipolar world had been made to rest on the international orientation of a small country far from any center of world power.[23]

The Korean War was doubtless the key factor in making Washington think of Vietnam geopolitically (and Iran and Guatemala as well). But there was a component of Wilsonianism as well. As President Truman put it in October 1950, the American purpose in Korea was to fight "to establish the rule of law in the world" and promote the establishment there of a "unified, independent, and democratic government":

> Today we face a violent and cynical attack upon our democratic faith, upon every hope of a decent and free life—indeed, upon every concept of human dignity. Those who support this evil purpose are prepared to back it to the limit. . . . The Soviet Union and its colonial satellites are maintaining armed forces of great size and strength, in both Europe and Asia. . . . [We] must oppose strength with strength.
>
> Our national history began with a revolutionary idea—the idea of human freedom. . . . We are strong because we use our democratic institutions continually to achieve a better life for all the people of our country. This is the source of our strength. And this idea—this endlessly revolutionary idea of human freedom and political equality—is what we held out to all nations as an answer to the tyranny of international communism. We have seen this idea work in our own country. We know that it acknowledges no barriers of race, or nation, or creed. We know that it means progress for all men.[24]

In due course, the struggle in Korea became linked to that in Vietnam. In March of 1952, a National Security Council paper speculated that if communists came to power in Vietnam, they might soon take over in Burma and Thailand, and quite possibly in Malaya and Indonesia as well. Were that not bad enough:

> South Asia certainly, and possibly important areas of the Middle East would be influenced toward alignment with the communist bloc. Japan, economic pressures aside, would be more disposed to accommodate itself to the communist bloc by reason of its altered evaluation of the relative balance of power. Western European confidence in the strength and future of the West would be further undermined.[25]

Eisenhower saw the stakes in Vietnam in a similar geopolitical light. In April 1954 the president wrote to Churchill comparing the French stand at the critical fort of Dienbienphu to the bravery shown at Thermopylae, Bataan, and the Alamo, stating that if "Indochina passes into the hands of the communists, the ultimate effect on your and our global strategic position with the consequent shift of power ratios throughout Asia and the Pacific could be disastrous." Nevertheless, Eisenhower was well aware of the limitations of military action; he refused the French request for military assistance to relieve their beseiged garrison (the surrender of which in May 1954 signaled the French defeat). Among the president's considerations were the French reluctance to concede real power to local nationalist forces, the opposition of American allies to military action in Southeast Asia, and his own recognition that American involvement there could lead to "a succession of Asian wars, the end result [being] to drain off our resources and to weaken our over-all defensive position."[26]

If a military solution was not the preferred way of securing what was commonly referred to in those years as "Free Vietnam," what was? With South Vietnam split from the North by the terms of the Geneva Conference concluded in July 1954, the Americans set to work to establish a government in Saigon that would be immune to communist takeover. A part of their plan was military: through direct aid to the South Vietnamese government and through the Southeast Asian Security Treaty (SEATO), a multilateral security treaty approved by the Senate early in 1955 by a vote of 87–1, Washington would see that the North was held at bay. Korea had demonstrated that it was fundamental to show such resolve.

But a critical part of their plan was political: by building up a stable noncommunist force in the South, Washington hoped to avoid the incorporation of this area into the North through elections scheduled for 1956, which Eisenhower acknowledged the popular communist leader Ho Chi Minh was sure to win. With American support, Saigon refused to participate in these elections. It was now up to the United States to see that an effective national government be set up in the South.

One strong voice in Washington spoke out with special clarity in favor of seeing the contest in Southeast Asia primarily in political, not military, terms. As early as 1951, Senator John F. Kennedy had argued:

> To check the southern drive of communism makes sense, but not only through reliance on the force of arms. The task rather is to build strong native non-communist sentiment within these areas and rely on that as a spearhead of defense. . . . Without the support of the native populations there is not hope of success in any of the countries of Southeast Asia.[27]

Kennedy remained true to his vision of a political rather than a military approach to the struggle in Southeast Asia. Speaking to a conference of the American Friends of Vietnam in the summer of 1956, he stepped forward as a neo-Wilsonianism, using prose that his supporters found as inspiring as his critics found florid:

> Vietnam represents the cornerstone of the Free World in Southeast Asia, the keystone to the arch, the finger in the dike. Burma, Thailand, India, Japan, the Philippines obviously Laos and Cambodia are among those whose security

would be threatened if the red tide of communism overflowed into Vietnam. . . . Vietnam represents a test of American responsibility and determination in Asia. If we are not the parents of little Vietnam, then surely we are the godparents. We presided at its birth, we gave assistance to its life, we have helped to shape its future. . . . this is our offspring—we cannot abandon it, we cannot ignore its needs. And if it falls victim to any of the perils that threaten its existence—communism, political anarchy, poverty and the rest—then the United States, with some justification, will be held responsible, and our prestige in Asia will sink to a new low.

Faithful to his 1951 message, which saw a political solution that allied Vietnamese nationalists with the West, Kennedy appealed for American support in Vietnam for "a revolution of their own making, for their own welfare, and for the security of freedom everywhere":

Vietnam represents a proving ground for democracy in Asia. . . . Vietnam represents the alternative to communist dictatorship. If this democratic experience fails . . . then weakness, not strength, will characterize the meaning of democracy in the minds of still more Asians. The United States is directly responsible for this experiment—it is playing an important role in the laboratory where it is being conducted. We cannot afford to permit that experiment to fail.[28]

Despite a disregard for the prospects of democratic "nation-building" in Iran and Guatemala, the Eisenhower administration assembled an impressive array of American talent to bring political order to South Vietnam. Among others, Wolf Ladejinsky, who had overseen Japanese land reform during the American occupation, was made a special adviser to the president of Vietnam, while Edward Lansdale, who had recruited Ramon Magsaysay in the Philippines to put down the communist Huk insurgency, arrived with ideas on counterinsurgency and how to find a "Vietnamese Magsaysay."

Lansdale's formula for nation-building, expressed in a lengthy memorandum circulated in January 1955, read like many more that would follow. Essentially, it proposed a Madison Avenue–type strategy to market a product called democracy. (This approach reached its height during the Kennedy years, when the determination to "win the hearts and minds" of the people was expressed as a project with the acronym *WHAM*.) For Lansdale, the three "elements we need for winning" were successful teamwork; stronger free Vietnamese; and a population largely "willing to risk all for freedom." He listed a host of platitudes to achieve these aims: an "operating philosophy of helping the Vietnamese to help themselves;" an approach "as friends (not as bossy supervisors . . . not as dressed up speech-makers;" an assurance "that their own future (and that of their children and their children's children) will be more rewarding under our system than under communism—more rewarding politically or socially, economically, and spiritually." Lansdale found it "critical" to give "the people a truly representative government" complete with a constitution modeled on that of the United States.[29]

The man chosen by the Americans to give programmatic form to such an ambitious political undertaking was Ngo Dinh Diem, a Catholic mandarin who had resisted earlier attempts by both the Japanese and the communists to include him in their governments for Vietnam. He appeared to be a firm leader and a proven nationalist. Washington committed itself to the support of Diem's government by a letter from Eisenhower dated October 1, 1954, and was to maintain its allegiance, despite serious doubts about the wisdom of its decision, until it finally acquiesced in his forced removal from power (although apparently not in his assassination) on November 1, 1963.

Whatever the firmness of Diem's commitment to fight communism, his abilities at nation-building were so limited that his years in office constitute something of a textbook example of how not to go about it. The crux of the problem was that Diem personalized his rule, showing a stubborn unwillingness to give any institutional form to political power in Vietnam that he or his closest associates could not control directly. While Diem justified his practice in terms of Confucian ethics that he assumed Americans could not understand, and while Washington was pleased to see that he would not shrink from the use of force to impose his rule on the country when first he had seemed unable to do so, the result was a disaster. Rather than dealing with any of the organized groups in South Vietnam (other than the Catholics) except as obstacles to his rule, Diem in short order created a political wasteland that played into communist hands. Ironically, in the process Diem both deprived the Americans of the ability to replace him (since no recognized noncommunist civilian leaders survived his repressions) and opened the door to communist efforts to recruit Vietnamese nationalists to a united front coalition designed to end his rule and push his American sponsors out of the country.

Some American officials in Vietnam, like Ambassador Elbridge Dubrow, appreciated the need for an effective noncommunist political coalition there. But no plan was ever devised on how to proceed in a comprehensive, coherent, or compelling way. No effective land reform or political coalition building was proposed, much less implemented, during the nine years Diem was in charge in Saigon.

The absence of a serious political plan did not mean the Americans were not busy on other fronts: military advisers expanded Diem's army; technical advisers began to flood the country with goods, and "civic action" programs tried to improve health and agricultural output. Political advisers served only to evaluate the strength of the communist movement and monitor Diem's personal commitment to the struggle. None of these measures produced either social justice or an effective political coalition to stop the communists. But the rhetoric of democratic government could still be used. For example, in 1961, when Vice President Lyndon Johnson visited Saigon, he saluted Diem as "the Churchill of the decade . . . in the vanguard of those leaders who stand for freedom." But when asked later by the journalist Stanley Karnow if perhaps he had not been swept away by the occasion, Johnson replied, "Shit, Diem's the only boy we got out here."[30]

Meanwhile, Washington's concern with the military aspect of the war took a new turn as the Kennedy administration looked more closely at Chinese insurgency tactics after Nikita Khrushchev told Kennedy at the Vienna Summit in June 1961 that "wars of national liberation" were legitimate and that the young American president should expect to see them spread in coming years. The result was a vogue of counterinsurgency thinking in Washington, which without doubting the need for a political solution in South Vietnam, stressed the necessity of a strictly military response to the communist bid for power such as had already occurred in Greece, Malaysia, and the Philippines. Moreover, in the context of the failed attempt to overthrow Castro at the Bay of Pigs and a renewed Berlin crisis, whereby the Soviets appeared to be trying to neutralize Germany and so destroy the Atlantic Alliance, a demonstration of resolve to act militarily seemed incumbent on Washington.[31]

The result was that the Kennedy administration reduced its pressures on Saigon for meaningful socioeconomic or political reform. Determining when Diem's crackdowns had irreversibly damaged the ability of non-communist forces to form an effective government in South Vietnam is difficult, but surely it had occurred by the end of the 1950s, before North Vietnam (in the summer of 1959) decided to sponsor an uprising in the South against his regime. For most Americans, however, even those interested in domestic Vietnamese politics, that country was the far side of the moon. As late as 1960, Senator Kennedy was still able to laud the choice of Diem's leadership: "We saw a miracle take place. I should have had more faith in my own propositions about the potential power of free Asian nationalism."[32]

How naive Kennedy actually was as to Diem's political abilities may be disputed, but certainly Frederick Nolting, whom Kennedy later appointed as ambassador to South Vietnam, was a model of ignorance when it came to understanding the political challenge of stopping the communist advance. After he became president, Kennedy dated the disorders that ultimately brought Diem down to the Buddhist riots that began in the spring of 1963. As he put it in September 1963, "We are prepared to continue to assist [the South Vitnamese], but I don't think that the war can be won unless the people support the effort and, in my opinion, in the last two months, the government has gotten out of touch with the people." A few days later, he elaborated:

Our object [is] to bring Americans home, permit the South Vietnamese to maintain themselves as a free and independent country, and permit democratic forces
within the country to operate—which they can, of course, much more freely
when the assault from the inside, and which is manipulated from the North, is
ended. So the purpose of the [upcoming meeting on Vietnam] in Honolulu is how
to pursue these objectives.[33]

One may well doubt that Diem had lost touch only in the spring of 1963,
much less that the United States at this late date could contemplate a military withdrawal leaving behind a functioning democracy in Vietnam. In
political terms, Diem had never established any political institutions that
extended beyond himself, his families, or his closest collaborators; this was
evident years before Kennedy became president. Diem's other failure, not
to institute land reform, added to the communists' appeal in the countryside. Indeed, such changes as occurred in Vietnam's land tenure system
tended to worsen matters so far as popular rebellion was concerned, driving
peasants even more into the arms of the communist forces.[34]

Once Diem was removed from power in November 1963, the hopelessness of the political situation became vividly apparent as a succession of
generals underscored the strictly military character of the government
there. In 1964 there were seven military governments in Saigon. But the
Americans did not stop trying. As Ambassador Henry Cabot Lodge put it
that year, the United States had "to saturate the minds of the people with
some socially conscious and attractive ideology which is susceptible of
being carried out." Or in Ambassador Ellsworth Bunker's words in 1967,
the need was to give the Vietnamese government "an idealistic appeal, or
philosophy, which will compete with that declared by the Vietcong."[35]

Was there ever a time when things might have turned out differently,
when the United States might have helped to build a strong noncommunist
government in Saigon, the equivalent to what it had to work with in Manila, Athens, or Seoul? Probably there was not: as early as 1945, the communists had won the political battle in Vietnam and only a massive military
attack against them—involving destruction quite out of proportion with
any American interest to be served in preventing their victory—could deny
this fact.

The argument for this conclusion takes us back to the 1930s, when
French repression broke the back of the noncommunist nationalist movement in Vietnam, allowing Ho Chi Minh's forces to capture the nationalist
flag. Thereafter, the Japanese takeover of Indochina facilitated communist organizing. Elsewhere in Southeast Asia where they seized European
colonies—as in the Philippines, Indonesia, and Malaya—the Japanese encouraged the collaboration of noncommunist nationalist groups to work
with them. But in Vietnam, the Japanese worked through collaborationist
French forces, thereby indirectly augmenting Ho Chi Minh's nationalist

appeal. Once the French returned in 1945, their intention to reassert control over the region only furthered the fusion of nationalist and communist forces.[36]

Perhaps this argument underestimates the possibilities after the Geneva Conference in 1954 to build a stable noncommunist government in Saigon. Perhaps in the five-year interlude before the North decided to resume the conflict against American imperialism something in fact could have been done, as Senator Kennedy believed, to deny the communists a victory by building the functional political equivalent in South Vietnam of the governments in the Philippines, South Korea, or British-influenced Malaya. To the extent this is true, the fault lies with the Eisenhower administration, which in South Vietnam was demonstrating the same lack of interest in finding an effective political solution to the communist challenge that it had so conspicously demonstrated earlier in Guatemala and Iran when it had insisted on the primacy of force.

Given the panoply of families with whom American imperialism has worked—the Somozas, the Trujillos, the Pahlavis, the Marcoses, and others—the Ngos were neither particularly corrupt nor cruel. But as was abundantly clear by 1959, the Ngos had no effective political organization to counter the communists. Yet in the mid-1950s, Kennedy had staked his position to the argument that America must stand firm for geopolitical reasons against communism in Indochina, and that the proper vehicle for this struggle was a "democratic experiment" centered on Ngo Dinh Diem. In his Inaugural Address of January 20, 1961, President Kennedy persisted in fostering his neo-Wilsonian ambitions on parts of the world where in many instances they were tragically inappropriate:

> Let every nation know, whether it wishes us well or ill, that we shall pay any price, bear any burden, meet any hardship, support any friend, oppose any foe to assure the survival and the success of liberty. This much we pledge—and more. . . . To those new states whom we welcome to the ranks of the free, we pledge our word that one form of colonial control shall not have passed away merely to be replaced by a far more iron tyranny. . . . to those peoples in the huts and villages of half the globe struggling to break the bonds of mass misery, we pledge our best efforts to help them help themselves, for whatever period is required—not because the communists may be doing it, not because we seek their votes, but because it is right.[37]

REALISM REASSERTED

Evaluating the experience of American foreign policy from the early 1950s through the early 1960s can to lead to apparently contradictory conclusions: the Americans are to be damned when, as in the Eisenhower years, they failed to be serious Wilsonians and abandoned the ambition to encourage constitutional government in Iran, Guatemala, and South Vietnam and relied on authoritarians instead; but they are also to be damned when they talk about undertaking such efforts, as in Vietnam during the Kennedy years, in blind disregard of how anachronistic their calculations were.

The answer to this apparent contradiction is simply that good long-term policy could not be made in disregard of the challenge of the twentieth century: to organize nationalist sentiments into a mass-based state. To fail to support reformist governments when they have a chance of succeeding is mistaken (as the Guatemalan and Iranian cases illustrate) because of the weakness of authoritarian regimes and the danger to American interests when Washington opposes strong nationalist forces abroad. But it may be equally mistaken to insist that a democratizing experiment can prevail when it is abundantly apparent that nationalist mass-based forces have taken a country in another direction, with little likelihood they can be stopped short of extraordinary military intervention (as the story of Vietnam indicates). What we see in all these instances is a reckless disregard for local circumstances based on dubious geopolitical concerns clothed in the heady rhetoric of liberal democratic internationalism.

Does this account of the decade of 1953–63 depend too heavily on a criticism of the worldview of American decision makers and not enough on the influence of domestic considerations? American presidents had to win elections, after all, not satisfy the critical demands of writers a generation later. In these years, the surest way to lose an election was to be accused of being "soft on communism," especially by losing another outpost to world communism. Kennedy was just as ready to attack Eisenhower and Nixon for their "loss" of Cuba or for the "missile gap" allegedly favoring Moscow, as the Republicans had been to pillory the Democrats for the "loss" of China in 1949 or the "loss" of Poland at Yalta in 1945. Since it seemed apparent that intervention had worked in the Iran and Guatemala, why should it fail in Southeast Asia? Had the British not also mistakenly reasoned from what they believed to be their success with Mossadegh in 1953 that they could handle Nasser in the same way in 1956, so provoking their debacle at Suez?

Given the hypocrisy about promoting democracy abroad during the Eisenhower years, and the intoxicating idealism of Kennedy's liberal democratic internationalist message, it was initially refreshing that the administrations of Richard Nixon (1969–74) and Gerald Ford (1974–7) made it a matter of public record that they would not trade in such rhetoric. Acting in concert with President Nixon, Henry Kissinger (as national security adviser, then as secretary of state) orchestrated a foreign policy for the United States based on the European realist tradition, which holds that a country's interests should be "unsentimentally" assessed and promoted. Of course, such thinking had been current in Washington since the days of Theodore Roosevelt and had been most recently heard during FDR's presidency, which had recognized the Soviet Union and inaugurated the Good Neighbor Policy toward Latin America, whatever the moral objections to either action. But since the onset of the cold war in the late 1940s, a moralistic tone had come to prevade foreign policy discourse in the United States in a way that often made sensible policies in terms of national security difficult to pursue.

According to Kissinger, as to realist thinkers before him, undue concern for democracy abroad was to be deplored as the manifestation of a dangerously mistaken way of furthering American interests. Kissinger's arguments in this respect rationalized Nixon's conviction that world affairs must be seen exclusively in terms of the East-West struggle, a view the president had held even before becoming Eisenhower's vice president more than a decade earlier. The hypocrisy of Eisenhower and Dulles and the misplaced idealism of Kennedy was now superseded by a frank honesty that called itself realism (even if it was seen by others as cynicism). The United States would work with such governments as it could in world affairs; whether these states were democratic was a strictly second-order concern. Working from such a perspective was all the more important by the early 1970s, when American power relative to the Soviet Union appeared to be in decline as Moscow reached nuclear parity with the United States, the war in Vietnam drew to a close, and the militancy of the Organization of Petroleum Exporting Countries became evident.

The result of working with states on the basis of their posture toward the United States rather than with regard to their domestic form of government, Kissinger could argue, should be a more effective foreign policy, which in turn might better serve such moral goals as were possible to attain. In a book published in 1960, Kissinger had recognized the desirability of the spread of democratic governments worldwide. But he was skeptical that such a development was likely in the forseeable future or that there was much that the United States could do to further the process.

Instead, Kissinger favored working for reform where it was possible, given the limits on American power and the interests that might be damaged in the pursuit of unreachable goals. For example, Kissinger could maintain that his opposition to the Jackson-Vanik amendment to the Trade Reform Bill with the Soviet Union in 1973 was well-founded. While Jackson-Vanik tried to tie most-favored-nation trading status for the Soviet Union to Moscow's willingness to permit emigration of its citizens to other countries (especially of Jews to Israel), Kissinger could assert with good reason that such a stand not only endangered the entire structure of detente he had worked to elaborate—and hence complicate the American withdrawal from Vietnam and upcoming arms control agreements—but that it would also provoke a Soviet reaction that would actually diminish the number of its citizens allowed to emigrate. In short, to be rigidly self-righteous in crusades for moral improvement abroad could be self-defeating. Better, then, to work with states as Washington could for objectives that were possible to achieve—and here the opening to China was of particular importance, whatever China's form of government—rather than pursuing the goals of liberal democratic internationalism without regard for their practicality.[38]

The operational logic of "geopolitical" thinking, as Kissinger labeled the Nixon administration's approach to world affairs, consisted in viewing foreign relations as integrated, where events anywhere would have consequences for the balance of power between East and West and so affect American national security. The cost of failing to see the gravity of what might seem isolated or minor events in terms of the "equilibrium" in the balance of power could be high, especially now that the balance of power in world affairs appeared to be shifting against the United States. For example, if Soviet and Cuban-backed forces seemed to be winning a civil war in Angola (which broke out as the Portuguese were departing in 1974), the United States needed to block their success. In Kissinger's words:

> When one great power tips the balance of forces decisively in a local conflict through its military intervention—and meets no resistance—an ominous precedent is set, of grave consequence even if the intervention occurs in a seemingly remote area. Such a precedent cannot be tolerated if a lasting easing of tensions is to be achieved. And if the pattern is not broken now, we will face even harder choices and higher costs in the future. . . . To claim that . . . the United States has no important interests [in Angola] begs the principal question. If the United States is seen to waver in the face of massive Soviet and Cuban intervention, what will be the perception of leaders around the world as they make decisions concerning their future security?[39]

While in theory support for democratic movements abroad was not automatically ruled out by geopolitical realism, in practice, special emphasis on such matters could be seen as prima facie evidence that one did not understand that "scientists of equilibrium, artists of relativity . . . coldly and unemotionally assessed the requirements of the balance of power little influenced by ideology or sentiment."[40] Indeed, such an approach to foreign policy was necessarily dismissive of liberal democratic internationalism by virtue of its central focus on how a state acted in world affairs, not on its domestic system of government. Certainly, Kissinger was not interested in how to channel the force of nationalism abroad into domestic governments compatible because of their structure and values with the United States. Accordingly, Washington would maintain good relations with the authoritarian government of the Greek colonels, however the Greek populace reacted. Nor was a word heard when, in 1972, a military coup toppled a fledgling constitutional government in El Salvador, or when again, in 1972–3, Ferdinand Marcos in the Philippines and Anastasio Somoza Debayle in Nicaragua, rewrote the constitutions of their countries in an effort to make themselves presidents for life. The weakness of these dictatorships in domestic terms was not a matter to concern geopoliticans for the simple reason that they do not normally weigh such factors. So, too, many feared that Kissinger was prepared to deliver Eastern Europe definitively to the Soviet Union at the Helsinki Conference on Security and Cooperation in Europe in 1975, abandoning support for democratic and nationalist forces there in return for a free hand for the United States elsewhere in world politics.

Kissinger's supporters may later have claimed that he had supported the Helsinki process, which led to the erosion of Soviet power in Eastern Europe by endorsing human rights and pledging the signatories "nonintervention in the internal affairs" of other states (and so might be seen as a repudiation of the Brezhnev Doctrine, which since the 1968 Soviet invasion of Czechoslovakia had guaranteed the integrity of the Warsaw bloc). Kissinger's critics, by contrast (and they included many prominent Republicans, such as Ronald Reagan), saw the Helsinki accords as finally ratifying the interpretation of Yalta giving Moscow control over Eastern Europe. For them, granting the Soviet Union a stable sphere of influence in this region looked like appeasement. It was far too high a moral price to pay for an intangible process called detente, which the Soviets might eventually turn to their advantage.[41]

In contrast to the silence in his lengthy memoirs on the position the United States took on the abrogation of constitutional government in the Philippines and Nicaragua, Kissinger wrote at length on American intervention in Chilean affairs after 1970, when Salvador Allende was elected president. He reports that his concern was strictly to prevent a communist takeover in that country, a development he saw as dangerous to America geopolitically. The intervention's impact on the constitutional tradition of Chilean politics was not a matter to detain him, the immediate threat from the Chilean left being infinitely greater.

> Allende's election was a challenge to our national interest. We did not find it easy to reconcile ourselves to a second communist state in the Western hemisphere. We were persuaded that it would soon be inciting anti-American policies, attacking hemisphere solidarity, making common cause with Cuba, and sooner or later establishing close relations with the Soviet Union. . . . Chile bordered Argentina, Peru, and Bolivia, all plagued by radical movements. Allende's success would have had implications also for the future of Communist parties in Western Europe, whose policies would inevitably undermine the Western Alliance.[42]

With respect to the shah of Iran, Kissinger similarly believed that America had no alternative to offering its support. Commenting that, "the concept of representative democracy requires a social cohesiveness unattainable in many developing societies," Kissinger argued:

> Assuming we had understood the peril [to the shah], what should the United States have advised? Do we possess a political theory for the transformation of developing countries? Do we know where to strike the balance between authority and freedom, between liberty and anarchy in feudal, religious societies? It is easy to argue that a more rapid liberalization would have saved the Shah; that moves toward parliamentary democracy to broaden political participation would have defused the pressures . . . [but] it is likely that these "enlightened" nostrums would have speeded up the catastrophe. . . . His truly implacable enemies were the conservative, feudal groups deprived of their social privileges; or radical leftists. Neither was remotely interested in parliamentary democracy.[43]

In short, in El Salvador, Nicaragua, the Philippines, Chile, or Iran, no viable third force existed between the authoritarian right and the revolutionary left, so far as Kissinger was concerned. America would act in terms of the law of the jungle, cooperating with whom it had to cooperate to preserve the substantial interests that it had at stake. Only in the last months in office did Kissinger alternate his position on this matter. In April 1976, on a trip to Africa, he reversed what had earlier been his support for white minority governments in southern Africa and declared instead that "racial justice . . . is a dominant issue of our age. . . . Our support for this principle in southern Africa is not simply a matter of foreign policy but an imperative of our own moral heritage."[44] Cynics might be forgiven for thinking that this represented less a conversion to Wilsonianism on Kissinger's part, than his conclusion that black governments would remain in Africa and had strong supporters in the United States, so that Washington was well-advised to make common cause with them.

If American democratic internationalism had its shortcomings in the 1950s and 1960s, how much more successful was Kissinger-style realist leadership, with its penchant for working with dictatorship abroad? Kissinger's conviction that only the struggle with Moscow mattered meant that no serious thought was given to influencing the growing forces of nationalism and mass politics that typified the twentieth century. Geopolitical thinking put the emphasis on working with states, not with analyzing their social bases of support, and so found arguments for working with governments shallowly rooted in domestic social forces. Seen from the perspective of the changes in domestic politics worldwide in the twentieth century, it was a reactionary policy with a built-in flaw that could lead to serious reversals.

Thus, in Iran, the disregard of the prospects for constitutional government in the 1950s left in power a monarch, not any promise of an institutionalized political process. A highly centralized state—dependent on oil profits and the strength of its military and secret service, all supported by the United States—ultimately proved a fragile arrangement arrayed against a popular, nationalist revolution (see chapter nine). Kissinger may be correct that by the early 1970s, the die was cast and nothing could have been done to save the shah. But what of the missed opportunities of the early 1950s, a matter Kissinger ignores, or in the early 1960s when, at Washington's urging, the shah initiated a series of reforms that might have transformed him into a constitutional monarch? By its support for the shah, the United States got twenty-five years of good relations with Iran. In the fifteen years since he fell, Washington has felt the full blast of outraged Iranian nationalism.

So too in Latin America, the legacy of the Guatemalan intervention damaged American influence and played a part in the destructive polarization of politics throughout the continent, especially after the triumph of the Cuban Revolution in 1959. Here, much more than in Iran, Nixon and Kissinger had the opportunity to promote democracy but scorned the chance. In Nicaragua in 1973–4, Somoza was weak. So were the Sandinistas, and the democratic movement was growing in strength, but Washington was totally uninterested in domestic developments in that country. The failure to act opened the door to a Sandinista victory in 1979 (see chapter nine). As with Iran, a disdain for thinking in terms of domestic political forces meant a setback for American interests in a sensitive region.

The dilemma for American policy from 1947 to the end of the cold war in 1989 was that neither Wilsonianism, with its emphasis on domestic political reforms in countries where America had an interest, nor realism, with its willingness to work with whomever was in power provided they were anti-Soviet, proved itself to be a fully adequate guide for foreign policy. Each was better at uncovering the weaknesses of the other than in showing its own strength. Realists like Kissinger might have been right that in many cases it was premature to push for democracy, indeed that the very effort could prove damaging not only to American interests but even more to foreign peoples themselves. But realists were wrong in their failure to see that American national security at times required analyzing the domestic base of governments with which Washington would work. This was the Wilsonian argument: American support for authoritarian regimes based almost solely on military force could create unstable governments and breed the very anti-American nationalism that Washington sought to discourage, while political reform could generate domestic stability and workable ties with the United States that would enhance the national security.

Perhaps this is why Franklin Roosevelt looks strong in historical perspective: though not immune to failure, his effectiveness as a selective liberal democratic internationalist was that he was likely to be realistic without being cynical, and to be idealistic without being self-defeating. Here was a reason that President Kennedy and his advisers harkened back to FDR when they introduced the Alliance for Progress for Latin America in 1961. Just as the New Dealers took a comprehensive agenda of reforms to Germany and Japan in 1945, so the Kennedy administration could think in terms of the socioeconomic requirements of democratization for Latin America. And just as Roosevelt could be prudent about the terms of his involvement for the sake of promoting democracy abroad, so too the Kennedy administration would have its reserve. In the survey of the first thirty years of the cold war—from the Truman Doctrine in 1947 until the inauguration of Jimmy Carter as president in 1977—the Alliance is the most important instance of a sustained American effort to foster democracy overseas aside from occupation policy in Germany and Japan. It is to that experience that we now turn.

CHAPTER EIGHT

Kennedy's Alliance for Progress, 1961–1965

> We propose to complete the revolution of the Americas, to build
> a hemisphere where all men can hope for a suitable standard of
> living, and all can live out their lives in freedom and dignity.
> To achieve this goal political freedom must accompany material
> progress. . . . Let us once again transform the American continent
> into a vast crucible of revolutionary ideas and efforts.
> —John F. Kennedy, March 13, 1961

> Democracy is the destiny of humanity. . . . our moral obligations
> as a wise leader and good neighbor in an interdependent community
> of free nations, our economic obligations as the wealthiest people in
> a world of largely poor people . . . and our political obligations
> as the single largest counter to the adversaries of freedom
> [means that our] fundamental task is to help make a historical
> demonstration that . . . economic growth and political democracy
> can develop hand in hand.
> —John F. Kennedy, March 22, 1961

OF ALL THE NORTH AMERICAN EFFORTS to bring democracy to Latin
America, none has ever been even remotely so ambitious as the Alliance
for Progress. In the more than 170 years that have passed since the Monroe
Doctrine of 1823, only the Kennedy administration (1961–3) proposed to
interrelate explicitly the variety of problems plaguing the region—its economic poverty, social inequality, and political oppression—and to insist
that all needed to be addressed simultaneously. With the full backing of the
president, some of the best minds in Washington outlined the far-reaching
terms of a proposal to foster both democracy and social justice in Latin
America and saw that the Alliance had its own separate bureaucratic structure closely related to the State Department and the Agency for International Development.[1] Kennedy called for committing $20 billion over
ten years; in fact, $22.3 billion was disbursed to Latin America under the
program.[2]

Previous attempts by Washington to foster democracy in the region had
been limited to essentially political matters: mediating among factions,
monitoring free elections, supervising civilian administration (especially
in finance), and assisting in the formation of a national constabulary.[3] On

occasion, American authorities appeared to recognize the importance of landowning arrangements and sought to modernize land tenure systems. For example, by 1914 Woodrow Wilson had come to feel that social and economic reform were essential to the eventual consolidation of democracy in Mexico (just as he had heard from Felix Frankfurter that the dilemma for American power in the Philippines was to provide a social basis for democracy after the islands' eventual independence).[4] But neither in the Philippines nor in Latin America did Wilson propose such reforms while in office. What was not appreciated in any depth was that without a determined commitment to change, the traditional predominance of the landed elite would reproduce itself rather automatically when it was given access to larger markets in the United States. The political results of these economic developments were strongly adverse for the fortunes of democracy.

Distinct as the Alliance for Progress is in the history of relations between the United States and Latin America, it was no maverick idea. Prominent liberal Latin American leaders had proposed in the mid-1950s that Washington undertake a variety of projects that later materialized in the Alliance. The Eisenhower administration itself had begun to act on some of them by 1958, responding to the advice of the president's brother, Milton Eisenhower, as well as to the Latin leaders, and to Vice President Richard Nixon's disastrous tour of the region that May, when hostile crowds revealed the depth of popular antagonism toward the United States. More, the Alliance could be seen as something of a hybrid program faithful to the tradition of American liberal democratic internationalism, mating Wilson's insistence on the necessity for democracy in the hemisphere with FDR's conviction that socioeconomic reforms must undergird democracy.

While related to these antecedents, the boldness of Kennedy's initiative should nevertheless be emphasized. Under the terms of the Good Neighbor Policy, Roosevelt had stepped away from Wilson's ambition to promote democracy in the Americas. Under Eisenhower, the United States had actually overthrown a constitutional government in Guatemala bent on land reform. By 1961 the notion that the world outside Europe and Japan might be ready for democratic government was not one that had been heard in Washington for a long while.

The genesis of the program was not abstract and intellectual, however, but historical and political and clearly vital to the national security: how to deal with the Cuban Revolution of 1959 and its ambition to export anti-American, communist takeovers throughout the hemisphere. Americans feared a "second Cuba," and were determined that Che Guevara's threat to launch "two, three, many Vietnams" by opening new guerrilla offensives throughout Latin America would not succeed.

One tactic Kennedy inherited from his predecessor was forceful confrontation against Havana. But the ignominious defeat of American-backed

Cuban rebels at the Bay of Pigs in April 1961 put an end to the thinking that the CIA could deal with communism in Cuba as easily as it had in Iran and Guatemala during the Eisenhower years. The CIA did not end its efforts to rid Cuba of Castro after April 1961, but its manifest failures did turn serious attention to dealing with the communist challenge to established governments in the hemisphere by political, rather than by covert or military, means.

Indeed, even had the Bay of Pigs been successful, it appeared to Washington that a program like the Alliance was the order of the day. For the liberal democratic internationalists now in power there, the root problem of communism in Latin America was not Cuba and Castro so much as poverty and oppression. Rather than acting as if Havana alone was the issue, the Kennedy administration faced up to the fact that Castro's success was symptomatic of a crisis throughout the area. The result was a policy to promote the democratization of the authoritarian states in the region as the most effective way of keeping the communists at bay, thereby promoting American national security.

Such neo-Wilsonian thinking had long been absent in Washington. During the Roosevelt and Truman years, America had tolerated authoritarian regimes in Latin America, convinced that the stability they provided was the best way to protect American security. Under Eisenhower, Washington had served notice it would aid authoritarians even against constitutional governments if to do otherwise risked a communist takeover. But as Kennedy judged when he assessed the consequences of the Chinese and Cuban revolutions, authoritarian governments were politically weak and so could be subverted by insurgency tactics dubbed "wars of national liberation." The problem was not to stop the Red Army but to block domestic Leninist parties from taking power. As the terrain of the East-West conflict became fundamentally political, the reform of authoritarian systems seemed the only enduring answer to the challenge of communism. As in Wilson's time, the expansion of democracy in Latin America seemed in the national interest.

Kennedy was the man for the job. In the early 1950s, he had distinguished himself in the Senate by recognizing the potent force of nationalism in the decolonization process, saying that the United States should put itself on the side of nationalist forces in places as different as West Africa, North Africa, and Southeast Asia. As early as the mid-1950s, Kennedy argued that the best way to block the advance of communism in Indochina was to harness nationalism to democracy. If such thinking seemed appropriate for faraway South Vietnam, how much more relevant it must appear to political conditions in Latin America, where a series of distinguished leaders from Puerto Rico and countries as different as Venezuela, Costa Rica, Chile, and Brazil spoke up in these terms.

The Alliance as a Reform Program

The Charter of Punta del Este, which formalized the Alliance for Progress, was made public on August 17, 1961. Today, more than thirty years later, the document and its attendant declarations still are compelling in the way they link socioeconomic to political reform.[5]

The Charter's commitment to democracy appears most strongly in its accompanying declaration, which asserts as the first goal of the Alliance the need "to improve and strengthen democratic institutions through application of the principle of self-determination by the people." It then affirms as the "basic principle" of the Alliance the conviction that "free men working through the institutions of representative democracy can best satisfy man's aspirations, including those for work, home and land, health and schools. No system can guarantee true progress unless it affirms the dignity of the individual which is the foundation of our civilization."

The Charter itself focuses solely on social and economic matters. Socially, it looks to improve medical care, housing, and education, with special attention to the needs of the poor. In economic terms, it seeks more equitable income distribution and growth through increasingly balanced, diversified, and industrialized national economic structures based on higher investment, monetary stability, and regional integration.

It is the Charter's insistence on land reform, however, that makes it appear so serious politically, indeed so radical. Never before or again would the United States put itself this squarely on the line with respect to transforming the socioeconomic character of Latin America. Earlier efforts—whether under Theodore Roosevelt or Woodrow Wilson—lacked a strong appreciation of the relationship between socioeconomic power and political democracy. Later programs, such as the Kissinger Commission Report or the related Caribbean Basin Initiative in the 1980s, were also vague in their linkages between socioeconomic and political reform.[6]

It is true, of course, that land reform alone is no guarantee that democracy will necessarily follow. The experiences of Taiwan and South Korea are evidence of that, even if it may be argued that over the long run the transition to democracy in these two countries in the late 1980s and early 1990s was facilitated by their earlier land reforms. But the contention that only industrialization and the emergence of a middle class can lay the socioeconomic basis of democracy is equally debatable. Not only may an emergent middle class fail to be the carrier of democratic demands and instead ally itself to established authoritarian groups in countries where the state is traditionally strong and the threat of revolution from below a real possibility, but, alternatively, land reform may facilitate the movement toward democracy in countries where concentrated ownership of the land typically not only creates vast disparities in wealth that feed class conflict, but also provides the basis for a narrow elite of ruling families whose attitudes and practices are usually profoundly antidemocratic. In these latter circumstances, political institutions are relatively simple in structure and few in number, and are dominated by the persons who hold office. The rule of law is difficult, if not impossible, to entrench in these agrarian settings for lack of an adequately complex set of institutions.

In short, effectively institutionalizing democratic government is no easy affair in countries with a simple division of labor where wealth, power, and prestige have historically accrued to the few. Yet to wait for economic development to occur and a middle class to arise and demand democracy may be unrealistic, either because of the amount of time involved and the threat of revolution, or because of the disinterest of the middle class in certain cultural or historical circumstances in democratic government.

As a result, the issue of land reform is more than an economic or social issue; it is chiefly political in character. It includes not only the distribution of land to family farms or village cooperatives; it also entails the formation of farmers' leagues or associations concerned with credit, markets, and related needs; the participation of the farmers in political life through parties that represent their interests; and the creation of institutions able to respond to a growing range of demands. Successful land reform may produce not only economic prosperity and social peace, but political development as well: the governmental institutions necessary to manage such a state of affairs—from party to bureaucratic structures—require a complexity and integrity of organizational forms that are the hallmark of modernity. Of course, personalism and clientelism remain characteristic of any political order. Yet political modernity and democracy call for a durable, neutral framework of political association governed by the rule of law, which includes the entire population and which rests on their consent. Whatever the economic and social appeal of land reform, its political and institutional consequences are what should most concern us when we think of its relationship to the prospects for democracy.

This relationship was certainly true in Latin America in the early 1960s. Land had to be the route to political reform, since in most areas over half the population earned its living in the countryside, while some 5–10 percent of the population owned 70–90 percent of the land. Such acute and widespread class (and often racial) polarization could only make the prospects for democracy dim indeed.[7]

An apt comparison can be made with the Philippines, where in nearly half a century of American rule, the United States successfully introduced the entire panoply of political mechanisms characteristic of democracy, yet left the social and economic structure untouched. Today, as a result, the major obstacle facing the durable consolidation of democracy remains the extended patronage systems of large families whose wealth and prestige rests on their estates, while some 60 percent of the agrarian population (itself at least half the national total) is landless.[8]

Appropriately enough, therefore, the Alliance insisted that "unjust structures and systems of land tenure and use" had to be replaced by "an equitable system of property" backed by "timely and adequate credit, technical assistance and improved marketing arrangements" such that "the land will become for the man who works it the basis of his economic stability, the foundation of his increasing welfare, and the guarantee of his freedom and dignity."

Radical as the suggestions for land reform surely were, the startling aspect of the Charter was that these socioeconomic changes would be accompanied by the simultaneous introduction of representative democratic government throughout the continent. As a result, the Alliance was not only a far more ambitious undertaking than the Marshall Plan launched in 1947, but also the civil rights legislation under consideration in the United States in the early 1960s.[9]

The American sponsorship of socioeconomic reform in Iran began at almost exactly the same time as the Alliance. While the case of Iran was introduced in the preceding chapter and will be returned to in the chapter that follows, it is appropriate to mention it in the context of the Alliance for Progress for the simple reason that in each respect the driving concern in Washington was the threat of the expansion of international communism to American national security, and the conviction that, if the shah or the elites in Latin America failed to bring about a more just social order and a government with deeper social roots, the price might well be the installation of a Leninist regime.

The case of Iran and Latin America are also worth noting in common given the reaction of elites in both regions to American pressures for reform. As we shall see, the dominant groups in most of Latin America reacted with skepticism or hostility to the Alliance for Progress. The shah also opposed Washington's efforts, seeing them "as more or less an American coup." He later referred to these years as "the worst period" of American interference, and denounced "your great American 'liberals' wanting to impose their way of 'democracy' on others, thinking their way is wonderful."[10] Were reforms to succeed, the vehicle for change was to be the new American-sponsored Iranian prime minister, Ali Amini, and the activist agriculture minister, Hassan Arsanjani. Both appeared open to ideas that could be seen as turning Iran in a liberal democratic direction. But in 1962, when the shah removed these ministers from power, the United States let itself be reassured—thanks in part to officials in the State Department hostile to these reforms—that viable reform was still under way because the monarch asserted his continued commitment to social and economic reform.[11]

Working with as little leverage in Latin America as in Iran, hoping for more than in civil rights reform in the United States, what reason was there to think a program as ambitious as the Alliance could ever be enacted?

THE REASONING IN WASHINGTON

The most important reason for the Kennedy administration to think their support for fundamental change in Latin America might bear fruit was that there were indigenous political movements that the Alliance could look to as examples and for support: Romulo Betancourt's Accion Democratica in Venezuela, Fernando Belaunde's Accion Popular in Peru, or Eduardo Frei's Christian Democrats in Chile, for instance, plus the democratic governments in Puerto Rico, Costa Rica, and Uruguay. In 1955, a year before he became president of Brazil, Juscelino Kubitschek laid out in some detail an ambitious assistance program for Latin America, and the idea had been seconded by other presidents of the region, including Alberto Lleras Camargo of Colombia. The proposal was institutionalized in 1959, when the multilateral Inter-American Development Bank opened. The following year the CIA opened the Institute for Political Education in Costa Rica (it later moved to the Dominican Republic) to study the prospects for democracy in the region: Betancourt, Jose Figueres of Costa Rica, and Juan Bosch of the Dominican Republic were among its teachers.

With these institutions in place, and thanks especially to the wide business and governmental connections in Latin America of Adolf Berle, who was instrumental in formulating the Alliance, Washington believed that the program the Charter proposed would meet with an enthusiastic reception from the region's political elite. These leaders, plus the military and trade union movement, would provide the critical mass needed to bring about basic change.[12] The Americans could then be what the Soviets claimed to be: midwives of history—though for democratic not communist systems.

Given its reliance on local actors, there seemed to be no compelling reason for Washington to spell out precisely what it meant by democracy. Washington did not want to prejudge the institutional shape governments might assume in the process of becoming democratic. It seemed obvious that democracy entailed such things as a decline in class polarization thanks to a growing middle class, land reform, and the incorporation of the working class into politics through an open, competitive electoral system run under constitutional procedures. To try to say more would be to force local events into a mold they surely would break. An additional reason not to trumpet the variety of options too loudly was that some might appear to smack of what Europeans called social democracy (involving state intervention to assure social welfare and income redistribution) rather than be the liberal democracy North Americans were more comfortable with. Better not to alarm Congress and to remain silent on the details.

What might make the appeal of democracy to Latin American regimes all the more automatic in the early 1960s, so Washington could assume, was the keenly felt sense that time was running out on the traditional elites. Their choice—or so it was believed at the time—was between democracy, however defined, and communist revolution. Presumably, enlightened Latin American leaders could be counted on to see the handwriting on the wall.

Washington's concern for political stability in Latin America as a way of keeping hostile foreign powers out of the Western Hemisphere was, of course, long standing. The Monroe Doctrine of 1823 was seen as a way of providing support to fledgling regimes in Latin America in the wake of their independence from Spain. The Roosevelt Corollary to the Doctrine in 1904 had been a way of insuring that foreign powers did not take advantage of the financial instability and frequent civil conflicts there to establish a direct presence in the hemisphere. The search for a stable political order in Latin America had been the preeminent national security concern of Washington in the region for well over a century before the Alliance of Progress came into being.[13]

By 1961 Washington's priority in foreign affairs was stopping the expansion of international communism. In lands as different as Greece, China, the Philippines, and Vietnam, the United States had taken upon itself the task of defeating local communist insurgencies. The Korean War had taken tens of thousands of American, and millions of Korean, lives. The Alliance was thus but one part of a global strategy; regionally it aimed to block a repetition of the Cuban Revolution.

Yet the course of the Cuban Revolution had presented special problems to the North Americans. Castro's genius had been to present himself as nothing more than an armed nationalist and so to avoid the most obvious trappings of communism—reliance on a Leninist party vanguard. The result, so the Cubans believed, was that an armed resistance (the *foco*) working through a series of united front organizations, could deceive both the local middle class and Washington as to its real nature. Only after the triumph of the revolution (as in Nicaragua in 1979), would Cuban-style communists reveal their true identity.[14]

The American response to communist insurgencies was to fight them on two fronts, the military and the social. The military challenge obliged the United States to conduct a new kind of antiguerrilla warfare (parallel to the British efforts in Kenya and Malaya and the French experience in Algeria) focused on mobility and featuring especially the helicopter and small, flexible fighting units such as the Green Berets. During the 1960s, these tactics were employed with the most force in Vietnam, but they were also practiced in Latin America, where the most notable success was the killing of the Castroite guerrilla leader Che Guevara in Bolivia in 1967. An unstated—but widely understood—first premise of the Alliance, therefore, was to accompany the olive branch of reform with a fist of steel.[15]

Yet Washington's commitment to the use of force was matched by a genuine commitment to reform on the social front, even if Americans seemed unsure exactly how to go about it. As the preceding chapter recounted, during the 1960s, North Americans talked about "winning the hearts and minds" of the Vietnamese people and so defeating Ho Chi Minh's bid for power. In Latin America, the idea was also to appeal to the masses. The exclusion of large numbers of lower class and racially oppressed groups from any effective political voice provided the social tinder that could be ignited by communists in revolution. So could economic expansion that did not directly address the needs of the poor. But to inoculate a population against the temptations of communism, change had to be effected socially and organized politically.

The problem with such thinking, however, was its simplistic assumption that economic development was the source of all good things: social reform, political stability and democracy, and friendship with the United States. In fact, of course, economic development can be an extremely destabilizing affair, shifting hierarchies of social power, upsetting governments with new demands, and fueling nationalist resentment against the United States. Nor is it apparent that historical transformation is either necessarily or primarily grounded in economic change. The forces that have unleashed mass participation in politics worldwide since the end of the eighteenth century have been as much cultural and political as they have been economic. In a word, armed with academic thinking on "development," "modernization," and "nation building" in the early 1960s, Washington was relying on intellectual arguments long on self-confidence but short on practical understanding.

With Kennedy's election, an administration was in office that felt communism had to be combatted politically through the establishment of a national government widely perceived as legitimate by the major class and ethnic elements that composed the country. Presumably, only democracy could fulfill this need, and it, in turn, depended on economic development. In the late 1950s, thanks to the influence of what Arthur Schlesinger, Jr., has called the Charles River School of "action intellectuals" in the Boston area, it had become current in some academic circles to believe that large-scale socioeconomic reform could lead to democratic government in the third world. Through the work of men like Max Millikan, pushing for the creation of the Agency for International Development, and presidential advisor W. W. Rostow, these ideas had special influence in the Kennedy administration.[16]

The Alliance thus amounted to a combination of Wilson's commitment to fostering democracy politically in the Americas with Roosevelt's concern for New Deal style reforms in the socioeconomic structure. By avoiding direct military intervention in favor of backing indigenous political movements, and by relying on a broad, integrated range of reforms, the Alliance could present itself as moving a clear step beyond Wilson's policies half a century earlier while preserving the liberal democratic conviction that the national interest and doing good for others might be overlapping goals. In short, the enthusiasm of the Kennedy Administration for democracy as a way of blocking the appeal of communism in Latin America seemed to amount to a serious program.

Why, then, did the Alliance fail?

THE FAILURE OF THE DEMOCRATIC PROMISE

If there is general agreement in academic circles that the cause of democracy was not noticeably advanced in Latin America in the 1960s by the Alliance for Progress, there are at least two objections to concluding therefrom that the program was a failure. One objection is that the Alliance contributed to a certain economic dynamism in the region; the upsurge of democracy there in the 1980s thus might be said to draw some of its inspiration from the experience of the 1960s.[17] The problem with this reading, however, is that there is good evidence that the Alliance may have actually strengthened the forces of the right; there were nine military coups against constitutional, civilian governments in the first five years of the Alliance, for example, and few of the figures on income distribution, land reform, and the like (as opposed to figures of gross economic growth) substantiate the idea that there were structural socioeconomic reforms of any significance. To link progressive developments in the 1980s or 1990s to calls for reform in the early 1960s appears quite unwarranted.

The second criticism of the notion that the Alliance was a failure also asserts that it was in reality a success, for the United States achieved its primary goal of blocking a recurrence of the Cuban Revolution in the hemisphere (until the Sandinista victory of 1979). From this perspective, the Alliance fully accomplished its primary mission.[18] The problem is that this argument discounts the complexity of American imperialism, making it appear a far more crude force than it actually was. To say that the Alliance in fact succeeded is to dismiss the American ambition as rhetorical window dressing for counterinsurgency rather than to see it as a serious Wilsonian effort to protect American interests by fostering a specific kind of domestic political reform in Latin America.

The question thus remains to explore more fully why the Alliance failed in its proclaimed goal of promoting democracy in Latin America. An important explanation comes from an examination of these ideas themselves, for it is difficult to deny that however committed Washington may have been to the notion of working on a broad range of issues at once, more precise concepts of how democracy related to social reform were abstract and vague. The actual implementation of the Alliance program lacked anything like an adequate theoretical framework from which to proceed.

The major shortcoming in Washington's blueprint for change was that it lacked an adequate conceptual model of the relationship between socioeconomic and political change. Moreover, the Alliance never clearly specified just what would or would not be considered steps toward democracy: how did proposed reforms explicitly relate to democratization? How were they to be attained? What kind of obstacles might be confronted and how should these be faced? None of these basic political matters was addressed. By comparison, the Americans were quite vocal as to what they expected from economic development, both as to the ends to be achieved and as to the indicators that would be used to evaluate performance.

It should scarcely come as a surprise that many later observers criticized not Alliance policy itself, but instead its implementation, as indecisive and self-contradictory. These criticisms often come from former members of the Kennedy administration trying to assign responsibility for the Alliance's failure to President Johnson. The origins of the problems lie, however, in the initial conception of the program itself.

Two major theoretical issues lay unresolved: how automatic was the link between socioeconomic and political reform, and what should the United States do if Latin American elites failed to assume the leadership in bringing reform about? A good part of the failure to ask what it might mean to institute democracy in the Latin American context lay in the presumption that socioeconomic reform would lead naturally to progressive political change. To their credit, the American leaders who had emerged from the New Deal era understood, as their predecessors had not, that promoting democracy abroad entailed much more than simply transplanting such political practices as free elections. Their mistake was to assume that reforms in the socioeconomic sector would easily breed democracy in the political sphere. The success of the reform movement in Venezuela—led by Bentancourt and helped by substantial oil revenues—would not be easily duplicated. To the contrary, reforms such as those called for by the Alliance were widely perceived by elites in Latin America as a threat to their power.[19]

However, the failure of the Alliance was not due solely, or even principally, to its overoptimism with respect to socioeconomic reform engendering political change, important as naivete may have been. To the contrary, the major failing came from Washington's inability to find Latin American leaders capable of democratizing their countries. Given the dynamics of the cold war, Washington was unwilling to push Latin American leaders too hard for fear that the crusade to prevent communism might engender the very communist takeover the Alliance was designed to forestall. In fact, the Americans knew no better than the leaders in the third world how to organize politically the vast changes that social and economic reforms would unleash. They too drew back when it came time to convert the outlines of their program into actual practice.

Two issues vividly illustrate America's retreat from the promise of the Charter: the failure to push land reform and the willingness to work with military governments that had overthrown constitutional, civilian governments. Reneging on the first implied abandonment of the heart of the program of socioeconomic reform; conspiring in the latter represented a clear break with the commitment to democratic government.

Land reform was the Alliance program best designed to help alleviate the economic problems of the poor while beginning to empower them politically. It attempted to incorporate the politically excluded masses into the governing structures of the region through the formation of peasant cooperatives and leagues capable of being linked to national political parties and government bureaucracies. In theory, the result would be a broadening of the political base, an increase in the number of grassroots and regional political organizations, and a growth in the institutional capacities of the state. Yet while perhaps a million peasant families benefited from land reform during this period, another 10–14 million families remained untouched. Worse, given the demographic increase, the ranks of the impoverished actually expanded.[20]

Why was Washington reluctant to interfere, to lend its full support to land reform, when the Alliance had singled it out as a major focus for its efforts? One reason was a policy debate over the relative merits of land redistribution versus expanded production. The belief was that redistribution might cut agricultural output, but an expansion of commerical agriculture would contribute immediately and directly to economic growth and so more benefit the poor as inflation was checked, exports were promoted, and the economy expanded with new jobs opening in other sectors.[21] Such a belief was buttressed by various American interests involved in agribusiness, who could point out the foreign exchange benefits they could bring to Latin America while cautioning that radical slogans such as "the land to those who till it" would depress the opportunities for investment in the agricultural sector.

Yet more than theoretical concerns or interest groups handicapped Washington's approach to land reform. The chief concerns were political, stemming from a growing fear that the kind of transformations called for in agriculture might well play into the hands of local communists (a worry vigorously fanned by the established Latin landed elite, who would not cooperate with Washington's initiatives). Not only were communists quite able to work clandestinely through united fronts in order to control the management of fledgling peasant associations, but the disruption of the established order in the countryside might well be followed by the increased influence of radical agitators.

Nowhere is the contradiction between theory and practice better expressed than in two of the most quoted phrases of the Kennedy presidency. "Those who make peaceful revolution impossible make violent revolution inevitable," John F. Kennedy said promoting the Alliance in 1961. But "evolutionary revolution" turned out to be a far easier process to manage in theory than in practice as the president himself is reported to have admitted in another of his classic remarks, this one on the death of Rafael Trujillo, long-time dictator of the Dominican Republic: "There are three possibilities in descending order of preference: a decent democratic regime, a continuation of the Trujillo regime, or a Castro regime. We ought to aim at the first, but we really can't renounce the second until we are sure we can avoid the third."

An illuminating account of American inconsistency in promoting Alliance goals appears in Riordan Roett's book analyzing United States involvement in agrarian reform in Brazil. In 1959 the Brazilian Congress created a special agency to promote the economic and social development of its Northeast, which was dominated by large sugar plantations and cattle ranches, and where a third of the country's population lived, most in severe poverty. An increasingly active Church, student organizations, and an independently formed peasant league complemented the agency's efforts, which itself was under the direction of a distinguished Brazilian economist and historian, Celso Furtado. However, in short order the Americans began to fear the leftist tendencies of the agency and its collaborators. The United States then opted to work instead through local state governments, bypassing the institutions that promised fundamental structural change, and in the process, so Roett reports, actually strengthening the dominant, traditional political order.[22] The support for land reform had given way to a higher priority: blocking communism. This concern, in turn, allied Washington with the Brazilian right.

As the United States backtracked on its commitment to land reform, so, despite their explicit commitment to fostering democracy, the Americans found a way to reconcile themselves to military coups against constitutional, civilian governments in the region. To be sure, when the Peruvian military launched a coup against what would presumably have been the Aprista government of Raul Haya de la Torre in 1962, President Kennedy took it as a direct assault on the principles of the Alliance. He ended economic and military aid, recalled the United States ambassador, and delayed recognition of the new government. Yet in due course Washington relented. Other Latin American governments had refused to follow Kennedy's example, which put Washington in the difficult position of actively intervening alone, and the military promised a return to civilian rule, which occurred in June 1963 with the election of Fernando Belaunde.

Thereafter, the United States' response to military takeovers in Latin America ranged from muted opposition (in the Dominican Republic and Honduras in 1963) to toleration (in Guatemala and Ecuador in 1963) to enthusiastic endorsement (in Brazil in 1964). Given this chain of events, it is not surprising that the United States itself finally launched a military intervention, if not against a constitutional government then against an undertaking that with some justification called itself a constitutionalist movement, in the Dominican Republic in 1965. In scarcely three years, from 1962 to 1965, Washington's policy had dramatically changed.

How could an Alliance fundamentally dedicated to the promotion of democratic government find itself not simply tolerating, but actually condoning, authoritarian government or military rule? The answer depends in part on the country in question, but the general pattern is clear. Joao Goulart's rule in Brazil appeared manifestly inept and dangerously involved with leftists, for example, and similar charges of civilian malfeasance could be claimed for other situations. Left-leaning incompetence then became the basis for justifying a military takeover. The promise of democratic government could be made to hang on the promise first of having good government. Such a conclusion was all the easier to reach given Washington's support for a military track to defeat communist insurgencies, and the role in "civic action" that it had already entrusted to the Latin American militaries in an effort to give them a grassroots political role.[23]

The result was yet another version of the classic debate about the relationship of means to ends. According to this logic, the successful establishment of democracy presupposes order and institutions; that is, a centralized state may organize the growing participation of the citizenry in politics through a managed increase of interest groups connected to the government by an expanded party system. Obviously, this is a major undertaking. If a high level of popular participation in independently formed associations predated a military takeover, institution building following the example of the Mexican (or the Turkish) model might prove impossible. Alternately, and more modestly, the military might preside over the economic expansion of a country while curtailing the participation of some groups (such as the communists) and favoring the activities of others (much as the Americans had done in the occupations after World War II) until the time an orderly transfer of power to a civilian government could be arranged. Such a program seemed to be the ambition of the Brazilian military after the coup of 1964. Either way, the United States could argue that the military was the necessary means for democracy, even if the Alliance had not originally intended to be party to such a process except in a subsidiary fashion through "civic action" programs.

The problem with such logic is familiar enough to the student of arguments about means and ends. More often than not, the means swallow the end they are supposed to serve. What is to be merely provisional instead becomes permanent; the detour becomes a road in its own right. Had the Americans forgotten that in the 1920s and 1930s they built up National Guards in the Dominican Republic and Nicaragua to serve as bulwarks of constitutional, civilian rule and watched instead as the Guards seized power and launched the careers of Somoza and Trujillo, two of the most infamous dictators in the region?

So too in the 1960s, when the military took power, it typically took it for itself. By imprisoning (and often killing) leftists, censoring the press, repressing the trade union movement, and banning peasant leagues (to list only the most flagrant violations of democratic norms and procedures), the military undermined the preconditions of democratic government. (Ironically, the one military government that had at least some promise for fulfilling the intentions of the Alliance found little favor in Washington. The Peruvian military coup of 1968 aimed to create a broad-based state thanks to land reform, education, and industrial reorganization, but it nationalized the North American International Petroleum Corporation and was hostile to the foreign private investment in Peru—positions the United States could not accept.)[24]

To examine the failure of the Alliance more closely, we cannot look solely at the evolution of thinking in Washington, however. Events in Latin America also played their part, as we can see in case studies of the Dominican Republic and Chile.

WASHINGTON'S LOSS OF NERVE: THE DOMINICAN REPUBLIC, 1961–1965

In 1924 American military forces ended eight years of occupation in the Dominican Republic designed to promote stability through democracy in that country (an experiment analyzed in chapter three). After a troubled period, Rafael Trujillo emerged in 1930 as the country's dictator thanks to his control of the National Guard. Under the terms of FDR's Good Neighbor Policy, Washington resigned itself to working with his government.

But in 1959 as the threat of Castroism became more worrisome and the inadequacies of Rafael Trujillo's dictatorship became ever more glaring, the Eisenhower administration began to study ways to oust the dictator. After Trujillo's assassination in May 1961 (with some American connivance), the United States (along with the Organization of American States) worked diligently to establish a reformist government for the country, immune both to communism and to a resurgence of Trujillism.[25]

How did conditions in the Dominican Republic affect the prospects for democracy? The problem dogging American policy in a variety of countries since 1945 had been the difficulty of finding or creating a "third force" between revolution and reaction. It might be argued that Trujillo's more than three decades of rule (1930–61) created certain conditions favorable to the eventual establishment of democracy in the country. The economy grew, a manufacturing sector coming to complement an agrarian order that itself increased many times over during these years. In addition, Trujillo's lower-middle class origins and his willingness to promote the poor in some commercial ventures and in the army eroded the hold of white Dominicans on power. Moreover, by centralizing and expanding government, the dictator in some ways contributed to its modernization. Most importantly, perhaps, Trujillo's unparalleled record of cruelty and corruption gave authoritarian government an irrevocably bad name.[26]

But more persuasive than that these developments encouraged the rise of democracy is the argument that the Trujillo period had laid the groundwork for a communist revolution. Under the tryant's rule, the concentration of land and wealth had actually worsened. The middle class remained small; the traditional elite, which Trujillo had marginalized, was depoliticized; those who were enriched by the dictator's actions were only active politically if they were in the armed forces, and even then in strictly subordinate roles.[27] In short, the social roots of the regime were quite shallow, there was no strong domestic social movement for reform, and there was a vacuum in terms of political institutions. Trujillo's death had the potential to be the prelude to a very different kind of political order for the country.

The communist movement in the Dominican Republic was quite weak, however, and no guerrilla units were operating. In theory the country was as vulnerable to a Castro-style revolution as Nicaragua, where a communist-controlled insurrection ultimately succeeded in coming to power in 1979, in the process deposing the Somoza family, which had similarly come to power on the basis of an American-created National Guard and then proceeded to rule cruelly and corruptly. Surely the Cubans must have been tempted to export their style of revolution to both countries thanks to their assessment of the sociopolitical weaknesses of personalistic rule.[28] But for historical reasons (explored in the next chapter), communism was relatively weak in the Dominican Republic.

In 1961, therefore, the revolutionary threat was not great. Neither, however, were the prospects for democracy very promising in a land where the traditional families had been depoliticized for over a generation and the middle class scarcely existed. For Trujillo to have been murdered (or executed, as many Dominicans prefer to put it) less than three months after the inauguration of the Alliance made it the obvious test case for the power of Kennedy's democratic vision. In a situation where communism was weak, but so were democratic forces, what would Washington do?

The terms of this study would suggest that the single most important factor determining the prospects for democracy after the Trujillo's death had to do with the disposition his family's huge estates. Estimates on Trujillo's wealth can only be approximations, but he seemed to have owned at least 1.4 million acres of land and one-third of the entire Dominican gross national product. In a country where more than half the population worked the land, and where a major part of the industry consisted in processing agricultural materials, the question of how Trujillo's properties would be transfered was obviously of critical political significance.[29]

Given the emphasis the Alliance put on the importance of land reform, the job might have appeared straightforward. No class of landed elites needed to be dispossessed; the Dominican poor could simply be given title (either individually or collectively as the productive character of the various estates suggested) to what had become vacant land. Properly handled (which is not to say it would have been easy), the result might have been to build up the socioeconomic infrastructure of democracy.

But there were obstacles to effective land reform. The established landed families and the officer corps in the military wanted the Trujillo holdings to add to their own. They opposed "giving them away" to the "unproductive" labor of the Dominican poor. And certainly the job of organizing the poor was a daunting undertaking.

At this critical moment in the history of the Dominican struggle for democracy, in December 1962, the reformist Juan Bosch was elected president. He proudly declared, "Agrarian reform *is* the Dominican Revolution."[30] In short order, Bosch set out to provide an integrated approach to the distribution of Trujillo's lands that would be both politically and economically progressive.

The story of Bosch's fate serves as a telling portrait of Kennedy and the Alliance. No one doubted Bosch's honesty or his commitment to social reform; working through his Dominican Revolutionary Party (PRD), he seemed in many respects to be the man who might do for the Dominican Republic what Betancourt had done for Venezuela. The problem, however, was that although Bosch failed quickly to mobilize his supporters, he did quickly antagonize both the Dominican upper class (which had hoped to replace Trujillo's rule with its own), the military, and the United States (which felt Bosch was far too "soft on communism"). Bosch thus gained enemies while failing to win friends. By September 1963, a military coup forced him from power. Washington protested, but none too vigorously.[31]

Nor does the story end here. When, in April 1965, Bosch's Constitutionalist movement appeared on the verge of regaining power by staging an insurrection in Santo Domingo, President Lyndon Johnson actually intervened militarily against him, worried that otherwise the communists might be the ultimate winners.[32]

Thus, by May 1965 at the latest, the prospects for socioeconomic changes that might have undergirded a nascent democracy had been effectively squelched, and this twice over—once in 1963, again in 1965—by the deliberate action of the United States. Perhaps Bosch would not have succeeded in any case. The officer corps of Trujillo's army and the land-grabbing traditional elite were serious forces to be reckoned with.[33] In such a politically polarized situation, the struggle would surely have been deadly without American intervention, so that Bosch's reformism might have been swept away for domestic reasons alone, either by the landed right and the army or by a sudden burst in strength of the communist left. Whatever Bosch's virtues, the social forces in place made the prospects for democracy dim in the years following Trujillo's death.

Still, one can speculate on how different the outcome of the struggle for democracy might have been had the Kennedy administration been more actively committed to its own program in the fatal period 1962–3 or had the Johnson administration held its fire in 1965. Earlier in the century, the Americans had created the National Guard, a force that necessarily opposed democratic government as a threat to its power and privileges. The Americans had also created the market for Dominican sugar, a form of agricultural exploitation that requires large tracts of land and outlays of capital and so is inherently antagonistic to the kinds of distribution of wealth and land that a democracy needs in an agrarian setting. Now a generation later, the United States had a second chance, but the commitments made under the terms of the Alliance were too fragile to survive doubts about Bosch. If the Alliance could not see its ambitions realized in the Dominican Republic, how seriously could its pledges be taken elsewhere?

The aftermath of the events of 1965 needs to be mentioned only briefly. The government that the Americans allowed to rule planned to hold elections in 1966. But it put a halt to land reform, in effect ratifying the takeover of Trujillo's property by army officers and the old families, *la gente de primera*. While the elections of 1966, which returned Joaquin Balaguer to the presidency, seemed to have been reasonably honest, Balaguer ruled without democratic accountability until 1978. The form of economic development he encouraged during these years favored his personal cronies and excluded the development of a vigorous middle class.

American policy did nothing to counter these trends. Instead it continued to pay a premium for the country's sugar, for example, without making any effort to change the terms of land ownership, just as its immigration policy drew to the United States many ambitious Dominicans who, in other circumstances, might have constituted that country's middle class.[34]

In the elections of 1978 the United States finally acted in an unquestionably positive manner so far as the prospects for Dominican democracy were concerned. President Jimmy Carter forcibly insisted that Antonio Guzman be inaugurated as president after an upset victory over Balaguer, who had ruled for the preceding twelve years (see the following chapter). Yet still today, the simple economic base of Dominican life and the concentration of wealth there indicate a socioeconomic structure where political life is highly personalistic and corrupt even as the formal requirements of political democracy are met. However much these problems must be understood in local Dominican terms, the American role in changing the structure of that country's government and economy after 1916, and its failure to rectify the problems it thereby had created after 1961, when Washington again had the ability to act, weigh far more heavily on the political identity of the Dominican Republic today than its brief incursion in favor of constitutional order in 1978.

THE POWER OF LATIN AMERICAN REACTION:
THE CASE OF CHILE

In fairness to the Kennedy administration, the task of economic, social, and political reform in the Dominican Republic was formidable. We can see this clearly by looking at Chile, a country where the preconditions for democracy were much stronger, yet the obstacles to success nonetheless enormous.

As early as 1833, constitutional government had been established in Chile, and a framework established after 1874 permitted the gradual incorporation of a wider stratum of the citizenry into an increasingly democratic polity. The country had the good fortune to be spared serious ethnic cleavages, and by the turn of the century the problem of Church-state relations had been settled in favor of secularism. A parliamentary system was established (at least in name), and middle class and socialist parties had begun to appear (though the latter only became significant politically in the 1930s).

The Constitution of 1925 established the framework for a multiparty, presidential system that endured until 1973. While the influence of the Chilean military should not be understated (it had played the leading role in the foundation of constitutional order in the nineteenth century), it was, by Latin American standards, of relatively marginal importance politically with the exception of the period 1924–32. Thereafter, the Constitution of 1925 came fully into its own, although the actual exercise of the franchise remained restricted. In 1949 women were enfranchised; however, a literacy test and landlords' control of rural voting still remained obstacles to universal suffrage. In 1958 new legislation ended landowner power over their workers' votes; in 1970 legislation terminated the literacy requirement. In 1961, when the Alliance for Progress was born, Chile was the most long-lived democracy in Latin America, with the well-established norms and procedures of democratic government.[35]

The alignment of political forces in the country had likewise moved in a direction favorable to implementing the goals of the Alliance. In 1957 a Christian Democratic party had appeared (though its roots extended back twenty years). Although more leftist than their namesakes in Europe, the Chilean Christian Democrats were nourished by their European connections, especially by the Catholic philosopher Jacques Maritain, to whom they owed their notions of "communitarianism."

As the extraordinary changes in the Catholic Church known as Vatican II were to demonstrate only a few years later, Chilean Christian Democracy was part of a growing wave of Catholic political activism. The party was unequivocal in its commitment to democracy and resolute in its determination to organize politics at the grass roots. Women and youth clubs and neighborhood committees were formed; the party announced its support for peasant cooperatives based on land reform and for workers' participation in management decisions in commerce; it called for the Chileanization of the country's natural resources. Finally, the party had the good fortune to have as its leader Eduardo Frei, a man of character and vision with solid connections throughout Latin America, in France, and in the United States.[36]

In 1964 Frei won the presidency of Chile with a resounding 56 percent of the vote. The next year, his party won a majority in the Chamber of Deputies, the first time this had occurred in a century. His plan was to embark on a "Revolution in Liberty." Yet despite Frei's successes in bringing about the beginnings of land reform and the extension of national control over Chile's natural resources, the pace was slow, the process incomplete, and the end calamitous. Part of the problem came from his party's early overconfidence, which meant that it did not look to build coalitions. Part of the problem came from the peculiarities of the Chilean constitution, which prevented presidents from succeeding themselves while allowing minority candidates to win office. But the most serious obstacles to reforms backed by the Christian Democrats arose as both the Chilean left and right solidified their positions and moved with utmost determination to oppose Frei's policies. Ultimately, although Frei's six years in office accomplished a great deal in terms of promoting growth, equitable distribution, and democracy, his efforts unleashed the fury of the opposition, so that he was unable to bring about the kind of durable changes that the Alliance called for even though Chile was perhaps the Latin American country best able to realize them.[37]

What the Chilean (like the Dominican and the Brazilian) experience obliges us to recognize is the depth of opposition to the Alliance that existed within Latin America itself. The point deserves emphasis since much of the literature on the Alliance concentrates on the shortcomings of Washington in the execution of the provisions of the Charter of Punta del Este. As we have already seen in the accounts of Washington's attitudes on the Dominican Republic, land reform and military governments, there is no reason to minimize its responsibility for the Alliance's failure. But as the case of Chile demonstrates, there is no reason to exaggerate it either. Washington was quite supportive of the Frei government (although the invasion of the Dominican Republic, the discovery of Project Camelot designed by the CIA to recruit Chilean academics to simulate counterinsurgency scenarios, and the suspicion by some United States observers around 1970 that the Christain Democrats were moving too far to the left did mar the relationship). The experience of Chile suggests, therefore, the need to appreciate the Latin American origins of the Alliance's failure. If reform failed in Chile, considered the showcase for the Alliance in Latin America, how distant the prospect must always have been during this period for Brazil, Nicaragua, or the Dominican Republic.[38]

CONCLUSION

Two matters become apparent as one reviews the American efforts to promote democracy in Latin America during the 1960s: Washington's unwillingness to play hardball with the Latin American right if there was any hint that such a tack would help communist organizers; and how critical it was, were the Alliance to prevail, that well-organized reformist movements exist in Latin America. If Washington wanted to do more through the Alliance than it was doing for blacks at home, if it wanted to achieve more than it had accomplished in nearly half a century of rule in the Philippines, in short, if it wanted to encourage the kinds of changes it had produced in Japan under General MacArthur, but without military intervention and assuming sovereign authority itself, then certainly its hope was illusory if its policy was wanting in either respect.

Does the failure of the Alliance provide yet more evidence that Wilsonianism (even in sophisticated form) is a mistaken way for the United States to protect its national security? Certainly it should caution Americans eager for idealistic reasons to promote democracy abroad about the chances of achieving long-term reformist goals. It should make Americans aware of the limits of their power and so more modest in what they presume they may easily accomplish abroad. In the literature on United States relations with Latin America, one frequently finds quoted the words of Secretary of State Richard Olney (1895–7): "The United States is practically sovereign in the Western hemisphere, and its fiat is law as to those subjects to which it confines its interposition." A belief such as this has never been true.

Yet these observations need not mean that the United States should forsake its support for reform. With the end of the cold war, it may be less important than in the past for Washingon to labor to see that stable, democratic governments exist throughout the region. Yet the arguments remain compelling that for national security even more than for economic reasons it is in the interest of the United States to see democratic governments consolidate their rule in the Western Hemisphere. Dedicated reformist forces committed to many of the goals for which the Alliance once stood exist today in Latin America, and their prospects may well be enhanced by timely support from Washington. Perhaps the next generation may witness Latin America solidly integrated into the democratic community of nations, with the economic, security, and psycho-cultural benefits such a transition could afford the United States in its century-old effort to bring about such a change.

But there are three caveats. First, the process of democratization requires that much of the old power structure be dissolved or converted to different forms of influence while elements of the new regime are created. Such a complex and subtle process cannot be mandated from without—as the Americans too easily assumed when they discussed "civic action" and "nation-building" during the Alliance period—unless a powerful array of local factors lend themselves fully to the undertaking. It is easier to wreck a constitutional order than to build one—which makes the damage the United States did to Guatemala by its intervention in 1954 so grievous. If Latin America consolidates the democratization process under way there since the early 1980s, it will essentially be the work of Latin Americans themselves establishing sociopolitical pacts that reinforce the legitimacy of democratic government. Second, there should be a strong presumption that undemocratic means will not result in democratic ends; military governments rarely beget democratic orders. A censored press, a broken trade union movement, a terrorized peasantry are not the material from which a democratic order is easily assembled. Finally, Washington must expect to counter determined opposition to socioeconomic reforms whatever direction they take: whether they favor the established interests and so provoke the outcry of the disadvantaged, or whether they favor the majority of the population and so arouse the opposition of the established elite and their American allies (as in the case of the International Petroleum Corporation in Peru in the 1960s). In such circumstances caution or indecisiveness can be fatal.

The challenge for a successor generation of liberal democratic internationalists is to learn from the mistakes of an earlier generation without discarding the original Wilsonian inspiration of linking the defense of American national security to the expansion of freedom and justice in the Western Hemisphere.[39]

PART IV

Liberal Democratic Internationalism and the Cold War, 1977–1989

Carter's Human Rights Campaign

> We have our democratic form of government which we feel is best.
> In everything that I do concerning domestic or foreign policy, I
> like to try to make other people realize that our system works, that
> freedom of elections, freedom from persecution, that basic human
> rights being preserved, that a move toward peace, reduction in
> weapons, prohibition against suffering from inadequate health care
> and so forth, are part of our national consciousness, and that we can
> demonstrate that it works in this country and serve as an example
> to others. I am sure the Soviet Union has always maintained that
> an ideological struggle was legitimate, and they have never
> refrained from doing so. I don't feel any inclination to refrain
> from doing it either.
>
> —Jimmy Carter, May 2, 1977

THE PROMOTION OF HUMAN RIGHTS ABROAD has not always been a central concern of American foreign policy. Although Washington officially pledged to defend this cause on December 10, 1948, when the United Nations adopted its Universal Declaration of Human Rights (drafted by a committee headed by Eleanor Roosevelt), it was not until the early 1970s that congressional leaders began actively to translate this statement of purpose into legislation. And it was not until the presidency of Jimmy Carter (1977–81) that an administration seriously attempted to implement the legislation passed. In the process, the Carter administration operationalized traditional American Wilsonianism in a novel and sometimes effective fashion by giving a relatively precise interpretation to what it meant by human rights and by connecting this purpose to a rather clear-cut set of political instruments. An abiding concern for human rights abroad is this presidency's finest legacy to the post–cold war world.

Under Henry Kissinger's stewardship, the Nixon and Ford administrations (1969–77) had conducted American foreign policy with respect to the dictates of "geopolitical realism" and evaluations of "the global balance of power"—approaches to world politics that specifically dismissed Wilsonian concerns to foster democratic governments abroad as naive, even dangerous ways of conducting international affairs. As this book has already indicated (and as a review of Carter's policy toward Iran will again demonstrate in this chapter), skepticism about how much concern to give to promoting democracy for others has often been well-founded in the history of American foreign policy. Whatever the merits of the debate between realists and Wilsonians, chapter seven suggested that the effects of a resurgence of unalloyed realism during the Nixon-Ford years could be felt from the Soviet Union to Latin America and the Far East, where Washington would work with whatever governments were cooperative without inquiring too closely into how they managed their domestic affairs. Washington was in retreat with Watergate, Vietnam, an apparent energy crisis, and the Soviet achievement of nuclear parity with the United States. It was no time to be weakening the country's position further with vain and potentially destabilizing notions that the world be redeemed through the ministry of the gospel of democracy.

Voices in the Congress and the public at large had long been criticizing Kissinger's "amoralism," but Jimmy Carter's inauguration as president in 1977 heralded a sharp reversal in the White House with regard to the role such principles might play in the conduct of American foreign policy. During the 1976 presidential campaign, Carter had discovered somewhat by accident the appeal a message of human rights might have for the American people. Yet such a crusade corresponded to his own predilections. A born-again Christian with an unquestioned commitment to the struggle for equality learned in the American civil rights movement was now in the White House. As the trials of black Americans so vividly demonstrated, the United States had its own share of shortcomings. But rather than stilling the American commitment to freedom and justice abroad, Carter could insist that these problems had made the American experience all the more relevant to others.

The Nixon-Ford days were over. The Soviet Union would be publicly criticized for its treatment of political dissidents; Vladimir Bukovsky would be invited to the White House and Andrei Sakharov receive a presidential letter. Washington would put South Africa on notice that its apartheid policy was abhorrent to American values. The repressive military dictatorships in Latin America would labor under no illusions that the United States saw their offenses as promoting what they styled "Western and Christian values" against a common communist enemy. In countries as diverse as South Korea, the Philippines and Iran, governments would also feel the winds of change. No longer would officials who championed reform be called soft and sentimental, their "idealism" responsible for the decline of American power and the expansion of Soviet influence. Now the argument was that reform would strengthen the national security of the United States by giving the country back its sense of purpose while correcting the manifest abuses of unjust and repressive regimes abroad, which so often gave the communist appeal its strength.

CARTER AND HUMAN RIGHTS

The Carter presidency's hallmark in foreign affairs, was its unabashed commitment to the cause of human rights worldwide. "Because we are free, we can never be indifferent to the fate of freedom elsewhere. . . . our commitment to human rights must be absolute," declared Carter in his Inaugural Address. At the end of nearly two years in office, he could repeat, "human rights is the soul of our foreign policy."[1] But what exactly did a commitment to human rights mean?

In its initial stages, these concerns translated largely into a defense of the rights of the individual: "Our most concentrated areas of concern have been violations of the integrity of the person—officially sanctioned murders, tortures, or detentions without trial," declared Secretary of State Cyrus Vance in March 1977.[2] The secretary was reflecting the congressional mood as well. During the activist Ninety-Fourth Congress especially (1974–5), liberal members of both the House and Senate were successful at eroding what they viewed as a policy of cynicism and immorality in Washington, culminating in President Nixon's resignation in August 1974, and the final American retreat from Saigon under humiliating circumstances in April 1975.

Since 1973, the most prominent advocate of human rights in the Congress had been Donald Fraser and his House Foreign Affairs Subcommittee on International Organizations and Movements. During the Ninety-Fourth Congress, it held forty hearings on the topic. Following the leadership of men like Fraser, Thomas Harkin, Edward Koch, George McGovern, Wayne Hays, James Abourezk, and Edward Kennedy, the Congress passed at different times a series of amendments to the Foreign Assistance Act of 1961. With only slightly different wording, the amendments restricted American economic and military assistance to countries engaged in what the amended act called "a consistent pattern of gross violations of internationally recognized human rights, including torture or cruel, inhuman, or degrading treatment or punishment, prolonged detention without charges, causing the disappearance of persons, or other flagrant denials of the right to life, liberty, and the security of persons, unless such assistance will directly benefit the needy people in such country."[3]

As such wording reveals, the campaign for human rights did not originally intend to promote the entire panoply of democracy in world affairs. Yet when all its implications were spelled out, it necessarily did so. In 1977, to show that Washington's concerns were not simply symbolic, the Agency for International Development and the United States Information Agency revamped their programs to reflect the heightened concern with human rights and democracy. Carter upgraded the recently created position as head of the human rights division of the State Department to that of an assistant secretary of state, and appointed a committed liberal activist, Patricia Derian, to the post. Annual State Department reports began publicly to document the human rights standards of any country receiving American foreign aid assistance.[4]

The checklist of concerns monitored by the State Department gives the best indication of what the Carter administration meant when it spoke of protecting human rights. Yearly reports enumerated three categories of rights: those of the individual, which might be called juridical; those pertaining to group activities, which were largely sociopolitical and hence the most explicitly concerned with democratization; and those covering economic matters, sometimes referred to at the time as "basic human needs." Ultimately, the volumes consisted of evaluations of all countries receiving American economic or military assistance under four rubrics:

> 1) respect for the integrity of the person, including freedom from torture, cruel, inhuman or degrading treatment of punishment; arbitrary arrest or imprisonment; denial of fair public trial; and invasion of the home; 2) government policies relating to the fulfillment of such vital needs as food, shelter, health care, and education; 3) respect for civil and political liberties, including freedom of thought, speech, press, religion, and assembly; freedom of movement within the country, foreign travel and emigration; freedom to participate in the political process; 4) government attitude and record regarding international and non-governmental investigation of alleged violations of human rights.[5]

Whatever the novelty of Carter's human rights campaign, care must be taken not to overstate its distinctiveness. Like the Kennedy administration, Carter made it clear that the United States would not directly intervene abroad to promote political reform. He left no doubt but that it was up to other peoples to work out their systems of government for themselves. America had learned from Vietnam the dangers of direct military involvement overseas. In this critical respect, Carter, like Kennedy, marked his distance from Woodrow Wilson.

Also like Kennedy, Carter understood that whatever his talk about making "an absolute commitment" to human rights, there could be circumstances where an overemphasis on these concerns might jeopardize American security interests; and if a conflict between competing ends arose, America's first priority was its self-defense. In the Philippines and Iran, for example, the administration acknowledged early on that despite human rights violations, the United States would continue its programs of military assistance designed to contain Soviet expansion, using if necessary provisions in the law specifying that the president had the authority to override human rights considerations in such instances. In the Philippines, human rights activists vigorously protested.[6]

With respect to South Korea and El Salvador, by contrast, the Carter administration walked a thin line. Despite the geostrategic importance of South Korea and the challenge posed by the North, Washington made statements in favor of imprisoned political leader Kim Dae Jung and did not flinch when the State Department published its annual report on human rights in the country. It also expressed its concern over the prospects for democracy after the assassination of Park Chung Hee in 1979, and expressed its disapproval the following year when hundreds of demonstrators against martial law were killed in Kwangju. So too in El Salvador, despite the imminent threat of a guerrilla "final offensive," Washington threatened to withhold military assistance in 1980 after that government failed to act to pursue the military killers of four American religious workers.[7]

Despite policy in South Korea and El Salvador, Carter was realistic enough to recognize that however much certain principles were "the soul of our foreign policy," other concerns might well take priority. The emphasis on human rights declined markedly in the final eighteen months of his presidency (following the setback of his efforts in Nicaragua and Iran and the Soviet invasion of Afghanistan), but Carter had earlier indicated "that this policy would not be painless, nor could it be based on a blind adherence to consistency. The world was too complex to respond to the application of a few simple principles."[8] Or as he had put it in 1977, after stressing the centrality of human rights in foreign affairs:

> This does not mean that we can conduct our foreign policy by rigid moral maxims. We live in a world that is imperfect, and which will always be imperfect; a world that is complex and confused, and which will always be complex and confused. I understand fully the limits of moral suasion. We have no illusion that changes will come easily or soon.[9]

Secretary Vance was equally clear-spoken on the United States' need to respect "the limits of our power and of our wisdom"; he warned against the belief that "a call to the banner of human rights will bring a sudden transformation in authoritarian societies. We have embarked on a long journey."[10] Given such reservations, skeptics could be forgiven for thinking not only that the Carter administration would fail to intervene directly on behalf of human rights, but that it might be reluctant to push them terribly hard by other means either.

The best comparison with Carter's human rights campaign is Kennedy's Alliance for Progress (reviewed in the preceding chapter). While Carter was like Kennedy in stressing the limits to an American commitment to furthering human rights abroad and in refusing to use force, he was considerably less ambitious than his predecessor by refusing to declare full-scale democratization to be his essential goal abroad and by his relative disregard of the need for socioeconomic reform. On occasion, of course, Carter might sound a Kennedyesque note: for example, he called for land reform in El Salvador to steal an important part of the communists' appeal. Where Carter did go beyond Kennedy was in his public condemnation of governments traditionally allied with Washington. But it was irresponsible partisan overkill of a kind that had blamed Truman for "losing" China to say, as Jeane Kirkpatrick did, that the "powerful inarticulate predisposition of the new [Carter] liberalism favored equality over liberty, and economic over political rights; socialism over capitalism, and communist dictatorship over traditional military regimes."[11]

Carter's human rights campaign got good press coverage. Criticisms of government-sanctioned kidnappings, tortures, and murders permitted the American public to follow foreign policy far more easily than had ever been possible with Kennedy's Alliance for Progress. But its salience in the annals of American foreign policy was due to Carter's contentious decision to apply his standards for proper government evenhandedly, to friends and foes alike. Aside from isolated cases such as Eisenhower and Kennedy's disapproval of Trujillo in the Dominican Republic, no administration since Wilson's had set out to reform regimes whose only crime was that they were internally repressive by publicly opposing them, especially when these governments were otherwise favorable to American interests. Since the time of FDR, liberals would play by the locally set rules of the political game.

The Good Neighbor Policy, begun in 1933 toward Latin America, had pledged the United States to leave domestic political affairs in the region to local forces. "Somoza is an SOB, but at least he's *our* SOB," Roosevelt is reputed to have declared (some attribute the remark to Acheson), expressing a sentiment that Kennedy liberals wholeheartedly endorsed in their dealings with the region a generation later. Accordingly, the Kennedy administration would introduce democracy where it could, but it would not endeavor to bring down pro-American dictatorships where democratic forces appeared weak.

In contrast, as his policy toward Somoza himself was to attest, Carter's brand of liberalism was far more willing to take chances, to push obstinate authoritarians to reform even at the risk of damaging other American interests that might be involved, and so to attack the premises of realistic thinking with its weary resignation to the SOB's of this world. While not oblivious to the counsels of prudence, Carter was far less persuaded than liberals since FDR's time had been that the limits of American power and the seriousness of the East-West struggle dictated a go-slow approach to authoritarian allies who were faithful in their opposition to Soviet expansion. After less than four months in office, Carter announced in one of the most cited phrases of his presidency, "We are now free of that inordinate fear of communism which once led us to embrace any dictator who joined us in that fear." Kennedy liberals with their ear for a catchy line might say no less, but they would never have acted on the statement as readily as Carter.[12]

Accordingly, after scarcely a month in office, Secretary of State Vance announced cuts in assistance to Argentina, Ethiopia, and Uruguay for human rights violations.[13] Similar cuts soon followed for El Salvador, Chile, and Nicaragua. Sensing impending humiliation, military governments in Guatemala and Brazil indignantly gave notice that they expected no further aid from Washington.

Cuts in aid for Latin America were dramatic. In fiscal year 1977, American foreign military assistance amounted to $2.6 billion, of which $210 million was to Latin America. In fiscal year 1979 (the first over which Carter's budgetary control was complete), total aid had dropped to $2.4 billion, but the Latin American component was only $54 million. Previous large recipients such as Argentina, Brazil, and Uruguay received no help at all, while sums disbursed to Bolivia, El Salvador, Guatemala, Mexico, Nicaragua, and Paraguay decreased substantially. Direct economic assistance and loans through multinational lending banks also declined precipitously to countries like Argentina and Chile as a result of their human rights record.[14]

Carter's policy toward Africa gave a good illustration of how forceful his commitment to principle might be. Since late 1974, Soviet influence had begun to increase in Ethiopia, where a revolution had toppled Emperor Haile Selassie in favor of a self-styled communist military junta headed by Colonel Mengistu Haile Meriam. A self-proclaimed Marxist-Leninist government also appeared in Benin (Dahomey). But the most serious issue had to do with Moscow's role in southern Africa, where the collapse of Portuguese control in 1975 (after a coup in Lisbon the preceding April) had opened the way for a Marxist-Leninist government to declare itself in Mozambique, at the very moment Cuban military and political advisers backed by the Soviet Union had established significant beachheads in Angola.

The effect of Cuban involvement in sub-Saharan Africa was of particular note. Under Castro's audacious leadership, some thirty-six thousand Cubans had crossed the ocean in late 1975 in World War II aircraft, fishing vessels, and merchant marine. By early 1976 these forces had halted a South African advance and secured in power in Luanda their Angolan communist comrades (the Popular Movement for the Liberation of Angola). In late 1977 they appeared in Ethiopia and saved the communist regime there from Somali attack. As a result Cuba was emerging as a warrior state, understandably proud of its achievements. Moscow rewarded this behavior with a dramatic increase of economic and military assistance to Havana.

The developments appeared ominous. Cuban troops, supported logistically by the Soviets, had scored resounding victories in two parts of Africa. The new Carter administration had good reason to fear further expansion of Soviet influence in Zimbabwe-Rhodesia, Namibia, and South Africa, where determined black nationalist forces, some quite favorable to Marxist-Leninist thinking (giving rise to the term *Afrocommunism*), were locked in combat with minority white regimes.[15]

While both the forces of Robert Mugabe in Zimbabwe-Rhodesia and the African National Congress in South Africa were known to be sympathetic to Marxism-Leninism and to have links to foreign communist governments, the Carter administration made it apparent that it would not bail out apartheid regimes simply because they were resolutely anticommunist. Accordingly, after less than two months in office, Carter had secured the repeal of the congressionally enacted Byrd Amendment, which had permitted American purchases of Rhodesian chrome, so joining the United States to the world boycott against the minority white government there. (In a turn around in his final months in power, Kissinger had called for the same action.) The president also gave his full support to the Sullivan Principles, a code of conduct earlier proposed by the African American pastor Leon Sullivan to monitor the treatment of black South Africans employed in American corporations there.[16]

After a well-publicized meeting between Vice President Walter Mondale and Prime Minister B. J. Vorster in May 1977, the South African leader denounced what he saw as Mondale's push for "one man, one vote" in his country. Mondale, speaking of the apartheid regime, made clear the differences that had surfaced in their deliberations:

> There is a fundamental and a profound disagreement. What we had hoped to do in these talks was to make it clear to the South African leadership the profound commitment that my nation has to human rights, to the elimination of discrimination, and to full political participation. . . . we believe that perpetuating an unjust system [in South Africa] is the surest incentive to increase Soviet influence. . . . They know we will not defend such a system. . . . I cannot rule out the possibility that the South African Government will not change, that our paths will diverge and our policies come into conflict. . . . In that event we would take steps true to our beliefs and values.[17]

Two months later, Secretary Vance reiterated this position, declaring that the United States would support "affirmative policies" that were "anticipatory" of the future and not "reactive," explicitly telling white South Africans that their obstinate refusal to reform was breeding the very communist threat they were seeking to allay.

To be sure, one may well ask whether the United States expected to see democracy flower under its calls for "majority rule" in southern Africa, for the two terms—*democracy* and *majority rule*—were not necessarily synonymous. African nationalism could block Soviet expansionism without giving root to democracy in the region. And the apartheid regime in Pretoria was not totally abandoned by the United States. With American support, it retained its seat in the United Nations and its access to various international lending agencies.[18] Nevertheless, while the Carter administration's liberalism may not have been entirely unadulterated, indications were that Washington did expect majority rule could result in stable democratic governments in the area. As the American refusal to recognize the white-backed government of Bishop Abel Muzorewa in Zimbabwe in mid-1979 attests, policy largely conformed to pronouncements.

Unsettling as Carter's policy was in southern Africa to many, it was setbacks to his approach in Iran and Nicaragua that occasioned the liveliest controversies. The disastrous year was 1979. In January, after having tried in vain to respond to Carter's talk about human rights, the shah of Iran lost his throne to a radical movement that labeled the United States "the Great Satan." In July, after two years of enduring sanctions attached to Carter's human rights campaign, Somoza fell from power in Nicaragua. The Sandinista force that ousted him in short order revealed its true colors as a Marxist-Leninist group friendly to Cuba, hostile to the United States, and bent on backing other left-wing guerrillas in the region.

Two other reversals occurred in 1979 as well. In March the communist New Jewel Movement took over in the tiny Caribbean island of Grenada. By September, when it was conclusively established at the Non-Aligned Summit hosted in Havana that the new Grenadian leaders were in league with Castro, there were shock waves throughout the British Commonwealth states in the region. And in December, the Soviet Union invaded Afghanistan. While Carter was criticizing governments loyal to the United States for their human rights abuses—some of which then collapsed—the Soviet Union and Cuba were adding strategic properties to what appeared to be their expanding international domain.

The obvious question is the extent to which Carter's brand of resurgent Wilsonianism was responsible for these threats to American security. Was the human rights campaign essentially a mistake, weakening authoritarian clients of the United States when they should have been shored up militarily? Or could a more skillful implementation of the human rights campaign somehow have saved the day for democracy and American interests in Iran and Nicaragua? Or finally, were the causes of these setbacks beyond the ability of either calls for reform or military determination to reverse? In short, what are the lessons of the Carter years for our understanding of liberalism's strengths and weaknesses in the conduct of American foreign policy?

THE DEBACLE IN NICARAGUA

The Somoza dictatorship that came crashing down in July 1979 had lasted since 1937, when Anastasio Somoza Garcia used the National Guard (put in place by the United States in 1927) to seize power from a civilian government elected under American-supervised balloting in 1932. Like other countries in the area except Costa Rica, Nicaragua was an agrarian land where rival caudillos, whose wealth was based on large landholdings, had long fought inconclusive civil wars. The resulting instability had been a constant cause for American concern. By 1909 not only were American lives and property in the country threatened, but Nicaragua President Jose Santos Zelaya's financial difficulties had led him to contemplate the sale of canal rights across his country to British or Japanese investors. The United States had thereupon intervened militarily, and except for a brief interval in the mid-1920s, stationed forces in the country until 1933. Despite ongoing efforts during this prolonged intervention to bring about stable, democratic (or at least constitutional) government, the United States was no more successful here than with its interventions in Haiti and the Dominican Republic at the same time and for the same purpose.[19]

As small, agrarian countries with long histories of civil war waged among rival caudillos, Nicaragua and the Dominican Republic (a country reviewed in chapters three and eight) had many similarities. But equally important were critical differences between the two lands. Racial cleavages were more important in the Dominican Republic than in Nicaragua, for example. Or again, Rafael Trujillo ruled uninterruptedly from 1930 to 1961, while from 1937 to 1979, three Somozas (Anastasio Somoza Garcia, 1937–56; his elder son Luis Somoza Debayle, 1956–67; his younger son Anastasio "Tachito" Somoza Debayle, 1967–79) were successively in power. More importantly, the Somozas had been better allies of the United States than Trujillo. While Somoza allowed Eisenhower and Kennedy to train Cuban refugees for the Bay of Pigs fiasco, and while he went through the motions of embracing the Alliance for Progress with plans for introducing land reform and a multiparty system in Nicaragua, the animosity between Santo Domingo and Washington was such that both Eisenhower and Kennedy had contemplated ways to get rid of Trujillo.

Another significant difference between the two countries had to do with the structure of political opposition to the dictator. Both countries had left-wing guerrilla groups inspired by the example of Cuba—the Sandinistas

(FSLN) in Nicaragua, and the Political Group Fourteenth of June (1J4) in the Dominican Republic. Ultimately, of course, the radicals took power in Nicaragua; in the Dominican Republic, they never were terribly strong. But the Dominican Republic had a powerful political movement in exile—the Revolutionary Dominican Party (PRD) founded by Juan Bosch in 1939 and pledged to democracy.

The oligarchic families that Trujillo and Somoza had displaced but not destroyed constituted yet another wing of the forces opposed to dictatorship. In the Dominican Republic these marginalized elites (for example, the powerful Vicini family) organized themselves in the National Civic Union. In Nicaragua, their counterparts grouped together in the Democratic Union of Liberation (Udel) founded by a member of the Chamorro family. There was a difference in how these oligarchic families related to the dictator, however. In the Dominican Republic, power had been closely held by Trujillo, and the great families were correspondingly weak politically. In Nicaragua, the "aristocrats" identified as Conservatives (in opposition to the Somozas, who were Liberals) had been permitted in a variety of ways to share power with the dictator. Elections may have been systematically rigged, but some legislative and town council seats would always be reserved for the Conservatives. Judgeships or lucrative contracts might be theirs. In general the Somoza in power would try to give the appearance of respecting constitutional forms, on occasion (though seldom without incident) even permitting figureheads to rule in his place.

The preservation of the Conservatives as a viable alternative of the Somozas was well illustrated in the history of the Chamorro family. Its prominence in Nicaraguan political life stretched back to the founding of the country in the first half of the nineteenth century. More recently, while some Chamorros sided with the Sandinistas and others with more moderate democrats, all of them opposed Somoza. The family paper *La Prensa* was the most outspoken critic of the regime in the country.

The most serious challenges to Somoza came in 1973, when it became apparent that the family had embezzled funds designated for the victims of a terrible earthquake that destroyed Managua in December 1972. Whatever accommodations existed between Somoza, the business community, and the traditional elites were now finished. The Church, under Archbishop Miguel Obando y Bravo, joined in proclaiming that his dictatorship must end.

Translating this conviction into a powerful political movement proved difficult. When in 1974 Somoza announced that he was rewriting the country's constitution so that he could run again for president, Pedro Joaquin Chamorro, editor and publisher of *La Prensa*, founded Udel. Backed by business and religious leaders, Udel promised to bring democracy to Nicaragua.

An equally determined source of opposition to Somoza, and one willing to use violence to remove him from power, was the Sandinista National Liberation Front (FSLN), founded by Nicaraguan radicals in Havana in 1961–2. They staged repeated armed attacks on the dictator (a strategy based on the Cuban-style tactics of Che Guevara and Regis Debray), but as late as December 1974, they were estimated to have only 150 men in arms. Following a crackdown in 1975, in which many Sandinistas were killed, the remainder of the movement seemed irreconcilably split into three factions.[20]

The murder of Pedro Joaquin Chamorro in January 1978 by persons close to Somoza (though the dictator's personal responsibility was not established) gave renewed determination to radicals and moderates alike in the struggle against Somoza. President Carlos Andres Perez of Venezuela called on the United States for direct action against Somoza and began preparations for his own armed intervention.

Early 1978 was the moment for President Carter to act. The obvious strategy—at least so knowledgeable observers sympathetic to Carter's position have argued persuasively since—was to remove Somoza under conditions that permitted a transfer of power to a provisional government dominated by moderates.[21] Somoza might be sensitive to either carrots or sticks: safe conduct to the United States, with the bulk of his foreign bank deposits intact, on the one hand, or clear threats to abandon him or force him from office if he did not agree to transfer power, on the other. Thereafter internal divisions among the moderates could perhaps be overcome by a transition plan backed not only by the United States, but also by Costa Rica, Panama, and Venezuela. Somoza would be out and the Sandinistas blocked from power unless they participated in democratic elections. Clarity, determination, speed: such were the necessities of policy.

What Carter was not prepared to do was to use force. He resolved to restrict American participation in the transition to organizing a mediation effort between a disparate group of Nicaraguan moderates and radicals (the Broad Opposition Front) and Somoza. The hope was that local forces could decide the modalities of the dictator's succession. Carter's position was consistent with his general stand on Latin American affairs: that the region needed to be treated in a less paternalistic way by the United States than in the past.[22]

What Carter had not reckoned with was Somoza's determination and cunning. The dictator interpreted a letter Carter sent him in July 1978, congratulating him on some superficial progress he had made toward liberalizing his regime, and a small amount of military aid released two months later as evidence that Washington would not intervene in force against his regime. Then, in the fall, Somoza agreed to negotiations with the moderate opposition under American auspices with the intention of dividing and discrediting its leaders. Many moderates would thereupon presumably join the FSLN united front, and Carter would be faced with the alternative of backing him or a communist front organization. Both FDR and Kennedy had counted on the Somozas to stop the communists, and Somoza counted on Carter to follow suit. In January 1979 the dictator deliberately torpedoed the talks.

Somoza's gamble did not pay off—in February, the Carter administration cut off all support to the dictator. Pro-Somoza forces in the U.S. Congress and elsewhere prophecized that if the United States did not immediately throw its weight behind Somoza, he would be driven out by a Marxist-Leninist united front that would be friendly to Moscow and Havana and serve as a center of sedition throughout Central America.

Somoza had been wrong to think that Carter would back him, but he was right that the only alternative to him was the FSLN. In August 1978 a daring Sandinista raid on the National Congress had resulted in fifteen hundred hostages, $500,000 in ransom payments, and the humiliation of the dictator. Thousands of new recruits joined the rebels. Moderate forces held demonstrations and launched strikes. Thanks to Castro's insistence, the FSLN closed ranks, its three factions becoming one party. Castro's other piece of advice was equally useful. He recommended that the FSLN placate the Nicaraguan moderates, inviting some of them to join its directorate and issuing pledges to hold elections within a year of taking power. With the collapse of negotiations with Somoza in January, many moderates joined the FSLN to bring the dictator down.

After suspending all aid to Somoza in February 1979, Washington kept its counsel. Then in June, at a conference of the Organization of American States, Secretary Vance cautiously proposed that an inter-American peace-keeping force supervise elections to determine Somoza's replacement. Nicaragua's neighbors objected. Mexico had never supported American leadership in the imbroglio. The Andean Pact countries, Costa Rica, and Panama all opposed an American-imposed settlement on the crisis. It was clear the FSLN had won.

Did Carter "lose" Nicaragua? As Jeane Kirkpatrick put it two years later in the most celebrated version of the indictment, the Carter administration first weakened Somoza by denying him military assistance, then assured his downfall by denouncing his human rights abuses and calling for his resignation. In short, Washington

> brought down the Somoza regime. [It] did not "lose" Nicaragua in the sense in which it was once charged Harry Truman has "lost" China, or Eisenhower Cuba, by failing to prevent a given outcome. In the case of Nicaragua, the State Department *acted* repeatedly and at some critical junctures to weaken the government of Anastasio Somoza and to strengthen his opponents.[23]

Given the multitude of forces arrayed against Somoza, the case that Washington alone brought the dictator down is no more persuasive than the argument that America alone could have kept him in power. Not only was he opposed by the FSLN, the Church, and most of the business class, but also by Venezuela, Panama, and Costa Rica. Carter's human rights policy may have emboldened Somoza's opponents and accelerated his fall. But the suggestion that singlehandedly Carter's policy overthrew Somoza fails to do justice to the power of local actors in Nicaragua in 1978–9.

If one wants to attach responsibility to someone in Washington for "losing" Nicaragua, a strong case can be made that it was done by President Nixon and Secretary Kissinger several years before Carter became president. In the critical twelve months from early 1973 to early 1974, when it became clear that Somoza had embezzled the earthquake-relief funds and that he intended to rewrite the Nicaraguan constitution yet again to perpetuate his control on power, Washington did nothing, despite a mobilized democratic opposition around Chamorro, strong relative to both Somoza and the FSLN. The American ambassador, Turner Shelton, continued to be a fervent admirer of Somoza, and Henry Kissinger's attention was elsewhere. As an indication of his well-known disdain for the third world, Kissinger's memoirs contain not a single reference to Nicaragua in all their 2,706 pages. In an important sense, then, Carter had the misfortune to inherit from his Republican predecessors a situation that could have been handled much more easily by them had their contempt for Wilsonianism and the promotion of democracy abroad not been so thoroughgoing.

It nonetheless remains true that Carter's policy was flawed. Acting early in 1978 with the help of countries like Venezuela and Costa Rica, Carter would have had an excellent chance of denying Nicaragua to the Sandinistas and insuring that democratic elections provided for a transition in power from Somoza. But this would have required using force, a tactic Carter was committed to avoiding both because it smacked of traditional American paternalism in the area and because he remembered Vietnam.

As a result of Washington's hesitation, Somoza's obstinacy, and the FSLN's flexibility, the Sandinistas took power in July 1979. Yet if there is good reason to be critical of Carter for this development, this need not mean that a policy of liberal democratic internationalism toward Nicaragua had been a mistake. Somoza's days were over not so much because of changes in Washington, but because of the evolution of political forces in his country and region in an era of nationalism and popular sovereignty. By hoping to channel Nicaraguan nationalism into democratic government, Carter was acting far more realistically than the so-called realists, who would have had him use force to keep the dictator in power. Nevertheless, the president needed to act more directly and aggressively in 1978, thereby securing national security while saving Central America a decade of terrible civil strife after the Sandinista victory.

THE DEBACLE IN IRAN

If the Nicaraguan case suggests that Carter should have put more teeth into his human rights campaign, the same assuredly cannot be said about his policy leading up to the fall of the shah of Iran. Here was a situation that was fundamentally misunderstood by those Americans who thought that efforts to democratize that country held any hope of bringing a stable, liberal, pro-Western government to power in Tehran. Iran represents the disaster that can occur when a policy of good intentions is ignorant of political reality.

As chapter seven recounted, a CIA-sponsored coup toppled the reformist, constitutional government of Iranian Prime Minister Mohammed Mosaddegh in 1953. Washington thereby conspired in the undoing of the most likely movement in that country's history to incorporate the excluded worker and peasant majority of the population into politics and to modernize Iranian politics in a democratic direction. The monarchy had been weak since World War II, while constitutionalist forces had roots going back to the Constitutional Revolution of 1905–7. When Washington and right-wing officers in Iran restored the shah to the throne in 1953, they were more than restoring his power—they were augmenting it significantly.[24]

It is nonetheless conceivable that an enlightened monarchy might have undertaken the changes necessary to introduce parliamentary government. It was widely believed that Shah Mohammed Reza Pahlavi had been reluctant to back the coup against Mossadegh in 1953, and responsibility for making oil concessions to the British and Americans could be laid at the feet of the coup leader, General Fazlollah Zahedi. Iranian nationalism and the shah were not yet completely at loggerheads.[25]

In the years following his restoration, the shah labored mightily to strengthen his authority; he gave no indication that he would introduce a broader sharing of governmental responsibilities through parliament and become a constitutional monarchy. Large-scale American assistance, initially accounting for some 60 percent of Iran's budget and including many technical advisers, permitted the shah to build up his army and secret police (the dreaded SAVAK). As American aid declined, Iranian oil revenues grew—from some $500 million in 1963 to $5 billion in 1973. Thanks to the combination of oil wealth, military power, and American support, the shah's power became virtually absolute.[26]

It might be argued that such a concentration of power did not inherently contradict eventual liberal reforms. Indeed, in 1961, just as Kennedy became president, the shah began what was to be a significant series of changes in the socioeconomic life of his country. He named a number of excellent ministers—especially Ali Amini as prime minister and Hassan Arsanjani as minister of agriculture. Women were enfranchised, popular education and health care were increased, and most importantly, in January 1963, a "White Revolution" was launched to bring land reform to the peasantry.[27]

The government also worked to improve economic output, the shah priding himself on his own technical understanding of issues surrounding energy and nuclear technology as well as military power. Figures on economic and social change indicate his reforms resulted in extensive progress. While there were dislocations, corruption, inequality in gains, and a growing Western presence, on balance the Shah's policies were having the intended results.[28]

The most critical question was political: would the shah share power with a parliament, gradually removing himself from center stage, agreeing to reign rather than rule? The monarch appeared determined to carry out political modernization and to expand Iran's civilian bureaucracy. And he was increasing popular participation in the political life of his country, although as the preceding chapter indicated, the shah opposed the Kennedy administration's suggestions as far too radical. Under the shah's tutelage, two political parties appeared in 1957; by 1960, both were discredited as agents of the throne, but in 1963, the talented Hassan Ali Mansur was named head of the Iran Novin party and in 1964 made prime minister. He was assassinated shortly thereafter.

The Iran Novin party went on to create a nationwide network of organizations, but it was controlled by the throne and opportunistic careerists. Its weakness was demonstrated in 1975, when the shah dissolved it overnight, to be replaced by the Rastakhiz party, a movement no better able to gain genuine popular backing than its predecessors. By 1977, this party claimed to have 5.4 million members, yet in fact it was little more than a letterhead organization, unable to mobilize popular forces and utterly lacking in institutional integrity. As one Iranian expert wrote me when I asked why no scholarly analyses existed on the vicissitudes of party life between 1957 and 1977: "It is quite obvious . . . they did not amount to anything, were a complete farce, and were led by cronies of the Shah's who had much better things to do than form parties."[29]

It is sometimes suggested that Mohammed Reza Pahlavi was weak and indecisive; at other times that he was a mystic out of touch with reality—in either case, that he was a poor leader and that his personality best accounts for the failure of political reform. History, however, provides few reports of absolute monarchs who have successfully arranged their own retreat from power. When they have turned into constitutional monarchs, it has been because other elements in their society, with far more clout, have been willing to tolerate their existence: the nobles in England, the French in Morocco, the Americans in Japan, the army in Thailand—these forces agreed to perpetuate a royal family for their own purposes. Even King Juan Carlos of Spain would have been fated for oblivion had he not rallied to the constitution when it was threatened by a right-wing military coup in 1981.

In short, absolute monarchs become constitutional not by some act of their own, but by a decision made by others. The shah had no intention of allowing this to happen. As he told Oriana Fallaci during a tempestuous interview in October 1973:

> If I've been able to do something, or rather a lot, for Iran, it's due to the small detail that I happen to be king. To get things done you need power, and to keep power you shouldn't have to ask permission or advice from anybody.... I wouldn't know what to do with [Western-style] democracy! It's all yours, you can have it! Your wonderful democracy! You'll see, in a few years, where your wonderful democracy leads.[30]

The crux of the problem of the transition from a ruling to a reigning monarch lay not so much in the nature of the shah's personality but in the character of his authority: using the vast powers at his disposal, the shah had launched a series of social reforms with political consequences that outdistanced the governmental means to control them. The economy, society, and his bureaucracy were becoming more complex, but politics remained in his pocket alone. This concentrated authority, which gave him success in pursuing socioeconomic change, proved his undoing in political matters. The shah was hoisted on his own petard.

Asked in 1961 why he was not preparing to become a constitutional monarch, the shah retorted, "When the Iranians learn to behave like Swedes, I will behave like the King of Sweden."[31] The quotation captures his dilemma. As social actors in Iran proliferated, their very dynamism fed the shah's determination to maintain his monopoly of power. Traditional landowners and the religious authorities understandably came to feel more and more threatened by the developments unleashed by modernization, as did those whom these rapid changes displaced physically or psychologically. The middle and poorer sectors of the population who had gained by these changes—the merchants of the bazaar, many peasants, and a new middle class of technocrats—began to turn against a political system that offered them no access to power. Despite the growing clamor against him, the shah insisted on preserving his authority, which he identified as indispensable to the reforms he had initiated.

Hence, the monarch refused to delegate responsibilities to able ministers or to devolve powers onto parties and a parliamentary government. He was convinced—in some instances correctly—that both popular ministers and ambitious generals had nearly been his undoing. Fearful that one might strike again, the shah either forced the resignation of leaders who were truly capable, or so divided the military and administrative channels that served him that they were unable to take a unified stand. Just as the parties outside government had become shallow mechanisms of co-optation and personal advancement, so the structure internal to the government was tightly centralized.

In short, it was not a responsible cabinet working with an increasingly powerful parliament controlled by effective parties that the shah was creating, but a government of paper institutions staffed by self-interested careerists. In such an institutional void, faced with the explosive changes his reforms had unleashed, and confronted by an economic downturn in late 1975, the shah turned ever more to his army, the secret police, and the American embassy for support. His military budget went from $1.4 billion in 1972 to $9.4 billion in 1977, reflecting the rise in oil prices (which gave him revenues of almost $20 billion in 1974) but also Henry Kissinger's willingness to sell him some $16 billion in arms from 1972 through 1977.[32] Small wonder that the Iranian clerics organized under Ayatollah Ruhollah Khomeini, whom Shiite tradition gave a special role as the scourge of secular government, should mobilize the masses to action against the monarch.

Throughout the process, the shah failed to grasp that the very process by which he tried to preserve his power was in fact undermining it. In his memoirs, he wrote:

> I am a great believer in a plurality of administrative channels and in having alternate channels always available. If through ignorance, laziness or self-interest one official refuses to bestir himself to vigorous action, then I turn to somebody else. . . . I do not employ advisers in the usual sense of the term. . . . I obtain information from many quarters and then try to strike a balance sincerely and solely in the light of the public interest.[33]

Indeed, the Shah was so blind to his own hand in his undoing that in 1978 he wondered whether it might not be the CIA that was conspiring against him.[34]

The shah's mood in November 1978 catches the pathos of the situation. During an interview with Secretary of the Treasury Michael Blumenthal and a group of congressmen, one visitor

> asked if the shah was still committed to moving Iran toward democracy. The shah said he saw no other way. In a monarchy like Iran's, he said, it was not possible to transfer full power and authority to your heir. Only institutions could be transferred. He wondered if he had not moved too fast in that direction. He said he was astonished by the reaction he was witnessing. A great many people who had benefited from his programs had now joined the opposition. He could not understand it. With this he fell into a long silence, staring dejectedly at the floor.[35]

Experts on Iran differ over when there was no longer any hope of creating a constitutional monarch or liberal democratic order in Iran. Some say such developments became impossible only after January 1978, when in response to religious disturbances, the army repressed demonstrations in Qum with heavy loss of life. They look to the round of reforms that the shah began in 1977 as his last missed opportunity to save the country from revolution. Then he released political prisoners, cut back on censorship, and renewed contact with moderate political leaders like Amini with a view to sharing power with them—all of this in some measure, it appears, as a reaction to Jimmy Carter's election as president. The opposition was once more emboldened to action, but (so this interpretation runs) the shah might have turned the ferment in a direction more favorable to domestic moderates and the United States had he taken more resolute steps toward change.

The problem with seeing any hope for the development of constitutional, much less democratic government at this late date, however, is that well before 1978, indeed probably no later than 1963, the shah had so alienated the politically important actors in his society and had so structured his own authoritarian rule, that democratizing reform under his command is difficult to envisage. By 1977, when the final round of reforms appeared, the obstacles to successful liberalization were far greater than they had been in the early 1960s. Repression had become more severe so that the shah was more hated, while groups on the left as well as the right had become far better organized and more determined to be done with him. Perhaps, had the shah abdicated in 1977, a civilian government might somehow have arranged to deny power to the ayatollah or to share it with him in a fashion that would have blunted his radicalism. I leave such debates to the experts, while registering my skepticism that such a transition, however much discussed in Washington late in 1978, had any basis of hope for being realized at that late hour.[36]

What, then, of solidifying the shah's control through introducing a fascistic government in Iran in the early 1970s, something along the lines of what Saddam Hussein in Iraq or Hafez al-Assad in Syria were institutionalizing at just this time? The requirements for such a regime are a demagogic and ruthless personality possessed of an ideology of national greatness and mission, a single party capable of mobilizing and controlling the most significant interest groups in society, and a strong military with a purpose. Assad and Hussein possessed all these characteristics and were secular nationalists to boot. Can a case be made that Mohammed Reza Pahlavi might have replicated their formulas in Iran?

Since the early 1960s, the shah had experimented with various forms of single party social mobilization on a secular nationalist basis reminiscent of the Ba'ath in neighboring Syria and Iraq. His military was unquestionably the most powerful Muslim force of the region, and the shah took a keen interest in honing its abilities. More, the monarch's sense of self-importance and of Iran's rightful place in history combined to give him many of the ingredients needed for demagogic leadership. Finally, there was a deep reservoir of anti-Western, nativist feeling to be mobilized in Iran, as the hatred of the Iranian people for the United States so amply demonstrated after 1978.

But for reasons that the scholarly literature on Iran has not yet explored, the shah showed as little ability to develop a variant of Iranian fascism as a school of Iranian democracy. Perhaps the problem was that he was too influenced by liberal Western ideas. For third world fascism to exist, it must be resolutely anti-Western, so as to fan the flames of nationalism to a fever pitch. However, the shah was so open to foreign influences that he gladly cooperated even in getting oil to Israel (and South Africa), despite the protests of his Muslim neighbors and Iranian Islamic authorities. By casting his lot with the West for the development of his country, he effectively precluded the fascist option.

Then there was his character. The shah had come to power by succession and the forcible acts of the Iranian military and the CIA. While the methods of his secret police were notoriously brutal, he nevertheless lacked that indispensable sense of the jugular necessary for the consolidation of a fascist government, the killer instinct that Assad and Hussein have demonstrated repeatedly. Finally, there was his health. By 1978 the shah knew he was terminally ill. He thus lacked the time and energy needed to militarize Iranian society.

By 1977, when Carter became president, the crisis in Iran clearly admitted of no easy solution favorable to American security interests. But what was Washington's perspective on the events?

The answer is sobering. A sense of the course of political development in Iran since 1953 might have indicated the hopelessness of keeping the shah in power. Aside from the military, the shah had no base of support. A broad-based nationalist movement centered on traditional religious leaders hostile to the United States was on the march. Yet so far as officialdom in Washington was concerned, no one was concerned about an orderly retreat. Instead, the debate was over whether the shah should try to co-opt his opposition through liberalization or whether the Iranian military should crack down on the insurgents. It was only in November 1978, just two months before the shah fell, that the weakness of both options was finally recognized. Even then, the third option—an opening to the ayatollah—was not actively explored. Fortunately, massive American military intervention received equally little consideration.

The dominant perspective in 1978—that of President Carter and Secretary Vance—was that liberalization might still hold the key to the shah's survival. In 1977 the shah had declared his firm intention to liberalize, and that was enough for Washington. "Iran, because of the great leadership of the Shah, is an island of stability," Carter announced in a New Year's toast in Tehran on December 31, 1977, only nine days before the violent events in Qum. "This is a great tribute to you, Your Majesty, and to your leadership and to the respect and the admiration and love which your people give you." The following September, hearing of serious violence in Iran—the Black Friday killings of some two hundred in Jaleh Square—Carter phoned the shah to reaffirm "the close and friendly relationship between Iran and the United States and the importance of Iran's continued alliance with the West," adding his "hope that the movement toward political liberalization would continue." Secretary Vance adopted the same line: "We fully support the efforts of the Shah to restore order while continuing his program of liberalization." The recommendation thus was to liberalize with an iron fist, a contradictory policy whose bankruptcy demoralized the shah, incited renewed anti-Americanism in Iran, and enraged Carter's conservative critics at home.[37]

For the United States, "the Shah was Iran and Iran was the Shah," remarks Gary Sick sarcastically of American understanding of that country.[38] Ambassador William Sullivan felt free to take extended home leave from Tehran from June through August 1978, and a CIA assessment at that time concluded Iran was not in a "prerevolutionary situation." It was not until early November 1978 that Ambassador Sullivan wrote his cable "Thinking the Unthinkable," in which he pronounced the shah a lost cause and suggested opening contacts with the ayatollah, who was then in France.[39]

Even at this late hour, Sullivan was virtually alone in his thinking. The president repeated on December 12, 1978, "I fully expect the Shah to maintain power in Iran. . . . the Shah has our support and he also has our confidence."[40] Secretary Vance could see that the military was "a paper tiger" and that the United States had been dealing with "evaporating institutions" as it struggled to block Khomeini's takeover. But his tardy decision to abandon the shah is apparent in the remark that "by late December [1978], I had little hope that even an English-style monarchy was possible."[41]

There were those in Washington who contemplated a military solution to the shah's dilemma. Three scenarios were possible: either the shah, a civilian prime minister, or the military alone could hold the country against the Ayatollah.[42] The head of this faction was National Security Adviser Zbigniew Brzezinski, who wrote after the fact: "I felt strongly that successful revolutions were historical rarities, that they were inevitable only after they had happened, and that an established leadership, by demonstrating both will and reason, could disarm the opposition through a timely combination of repression and concession."[43]

Yet for military intervention to have succeeded, the shah would have had to have been a strongman like Assad or Hussein. Since he was not, he had managed to keep order over his military by dividing the officer corps.

Meanwhile, the rank-and-file of the military had been heavily infiltrated by religious forces. The shah's expensive military establishment was essentially defenseless against an internal foe of Khomeini's sort.

Brzezinski's idea that somehow the religious nationalists could be stopped as late as December 1978 by military means was as groundless a conjecture as the president's belief that somehow liberal forces might still be found in Iran to rally to the shah's defense.[44] The relative virtue of the president's stance was that it did not call for the deadly use of force, which Brzezinski's "tough" approach (a term he uses repeatedly) would surely have involved. The desperate maneuvering to keep effective power in the hands of the pro-American, civilian prime minister Shapur Bakhtiar, who succeeded the shah, was the final chapter in the sad story of Washington's chimeras in Iran.

In fact, there was nothing to be done to stop the shah's overthrow short of a full-scale American invasion. America's experience in Vietnam indicated the enormous price of such a policy. It is unclear what American interest would have been served by such an extraordinary undertaking, and probable the Soviet Union's influence in the country would have expanded significantly.

Carter did not "lose" Iran anymore than he lost Nicaragua. By the time he entered office, the handwriting was on the wall for the shah, and given the history of American involvement in his regime there was probably no policy that could have saved American interests in that country. The choice was how best to minimize an unavoidable loss. Perhaps by establishing contact with the ayatollah much earlier, the Iranian people might have been saved a measure of the suffering they endured after 1979. But this is pure speculation. What is documentable is that Carter's campaign for human rights in Iran after 1977 made both the shah and the White House fail to adjust realistically to the changed political reality of that country, and so contributed to the ouster of the monarch on terms most unfavorable to American interests.

THE CARTER LEGACY

The virtue of the Carter years so far as liberal democratic internationalism was concerned was its unambiguous conviction that authoritarian governments were poor custodians of American security interests abroad. True to his insistence that power and principle could serve one another—that democratic morality and national security were mutually supportive—Carter used his human rights campaign to attempt to align the United States either with nationalist forces and their demands for popular sovereignty or with regimes that intended to develop a mass base of support. In his conviction that mass-based government was an inevitable development that the

United States should seek to shape, not to counter, Carter was unmistakably a Wilsonian.

Although Carter's policies toward Iran and Nicaragua were failures, there is no reason to conclude that Wilsonianism is necessarily a faulty framework to guide American foreign policy. From the experience in Nicaragua, Wilsonians might come to understand that the resolute exercise of American power may be necessary for the transition to democratic government. Good intentions are not enough. From the experience in Iran, Wilsonians might come to understand that there are limits to the appeal of democratic government abroad, and that in these cases Washington would be better advised to defend its interests in more traditional ways than trying to promote liberal reform.

The problem, however, is that the two lessons are to some extent contradictory. The Nicaraguan experience encourages policymakers to press ahead boldly; the Iranian situation teaches the value of prudence. What both cases illustrate is the importance of leaders having a clear sense of the political forces at play in the countries they hope to influence.

In southern Africa, Carter's principled approach was relatively successful in reaching its goals only in Zimbabwe-Rhodesia. Majority rule was obtained in Zimbabwe and the image of the United States improved among black nationalist leaders in the region, however distant the prospects for consolidating democratic government there might remain. By contrast, whatever the changes in South Africa, Carter's public diplomacy apparently had generated little change.

In Latin America, Asia, and Eastern Europe as well, thousands of individuals were helped—perhaps as many as thirty thousand political prisoners were released from jail in Indonesia alone—and many democratic movements emboldened by his human rights policy. In 1978 Carter could announce his policy a success in terms that future developments would confirm:

> In some countries, political prisoners have been released by the hundreds, even thousands. In others, the brutality of repression has been lessened. In still others, there's a movement toward democratic institutions or the rule of law when these movements were not previously detectable. To those who doubt the wisdom of our dedication, I say this: ask the victims. Ask the exiles. . . . From the prisons, from the camps, from the enforced exiles, we receive one message—speak up, persevere, let the voice of freedom be heard.[45]

Yet, despite the thousands helped by Carter's initiatives, and the impact this had on later political developments in Latin America especially, only one regime changed in a democratic direction under the influence of the human rights campaign during Carter's presidency. The country was the Dominican Republic. Here in 1978 President Joaquin Balaguer, who had ruled the country in a mild but nonetheless authoritarian manner since 1966, decided to stall on reporting election returns (a probable prelude to falsifying them) rather than be turned out of office.

American action was swift and, in the view of some observers, decisive. Monitors determined that the opposition Revolutionary Dominican Party candidate, Antonio Guzman, had won the balloting, and he was duly sworn in as president. At the ceremony, Guzman took advantage of his long acquaintance with visiting Secretary Vance to force the retirement of several Trujillista generals from the military.

Of course, other forces played their part in what is sometimes called "the democratic transition." The Dominican middle class had increased after more than a decade of uninterrupted high economic growth, and the Church, the Socialist International, and Venezuelan President Perez were all active in encouraging democratization, not to speak of those loyal to Guzman. Since then, the country has enjoyed regular democratic elections in which power alternated between parties—a development that in real measure reflects the continued dedication of Washington to democracy there.[46]

However, the decisive events of the Carter administration, so far as concrete American national security interests were affected by the human rights campaign, were the setbacks to American interests in Iran and Nicaragua, not the benefits that fell to political prisoners or the Dominican Republic. In the 1980 presidental elections, the Republicans leveled the charge against Carter that his Wilsonianism had undermined friendly governments in Tehran and Managua, which by 1979 had been replaced with illiberal regimes aggressively hostile to American security concerns. From the Republican perspective, the Soviet invasion of Afghanistan in December 1979 served as a final confirmation of the bankruptcy of Carter's policy, for they could allege his weakness had emboldened the Soviets to act in a way that menaced all the Middle East. At a time of growing tensions with Moscow, which since 1976 had begun targeting its new generation of intermediate-range nuclear weapons on Western Europe, Washington had been cutting the ground from under its own feet in country after country. Most-favored-nation commercial status had been extended to countries under Soviet domination, such as Hungary, while loyal friends such as in Chile and Argentina found their foreign assistance slashed. At the moment military preparedness needed to be shown, Washington had cut its military assistance to Latin America to a quarter of what it had been under Nixon and Ford. The time had come to reverse this dangerous policy in the name of the security of the free world.[47]

The Republican argument overstated the case against Carter by a long measure. While there can be little doubt that policy toward Iran and Nicaragua could have been better handled, there is no reason to think, as Republican criticism implied, that by sending in the Marines either Somoza or the shah would have been saved and American interests protected. By 1977 both dictators were lost. The question was not whether to save them or how, but instead how best to prepare for their succession by nationalist forces demanding governments rooted in the people that would not be hostile to American interests. If liberalism could not steer these countries in a direction favorable to American security, neither could the Marines.

It was not Carter's Wilsonianism, but his failure to size up the dynamic of political developments abroad, that was the source of his failures. A good part of the problem was that Carter seems never totally to have grasped that human rights could not be neatly confined to being a matter of protecting the integrity of the individual through a reinforcement of the rule of law. His appeal necessarily raised the greater question of citizenship and ultimately involved a call for democratic government. Indeed, the special effectiveness of Carter's human rights campaign was that by starting with a primary concern for the individual, new demands were soon forthcoming; a wedge had been found with which to open authoritarian political systems. By restricting government's power while enlarging the scope for citizen action, a genuine commitment to human rights may in fact spell the end to an established authoritarian system (though whether this be in favor of democracy as opposed to another authoritarian government of the right or the left remains to be determined). The selective and incremental character of the process set under way makes it all the more potent politically.

Hence the naivete in practice of ostensibly reasonable positions Carter held to in theory. "I was determined to combine support for our more authoritarian allies and friends with the effective promotion of human rights within their countries. By inducing them to change their repressive policies, we would be enhancing freedom and democracy, and helping to remove the reasons for revolution that often erupt among those who suffer from persecution."[48] Once implemented, however, such a policy could unleash the furies of the heavens, yet the president appears not to have anticipated the storm he could summon with his incantations about freedom and democracy.

The sharp negative reactions to this policy from a range of countries as different as Argentina, Brazil, and the Soviet Union attested to the sensitivity of regimes where American power was distinctly limited. From an idea that Carter had picked up only in 1976, and then because of its personal appeal given his character and background, and the reaction of the American public to it, the campaign for human rights came to be possessed of the potential to be a particularly sharp weapon in a renewed Wilsonian campaign in world affairs.[49]

Yet Carter appeared oblivious to the tiger he had uncaged. As he put it in 1977, "We have no wish to tell other nations what political or social systems they should have, but we want our own worldwide influence to reduce human suffering and not to increase it."[50] Hence, with respect to the Soviet Union:

> I am consistently and completely dedicated to the enhancement of human rights, not only as it deals with the Soviet Union but all other countries. I think this can legitimately be severed from . . . [efforts] in reducing dependence upon atomic weapons and also in seeking mutual and balanced force reductions in Europe. I don't want the two to be tied together. . . . The previous administration, under Secretary Kissinger, thought . . . that if you mentioned human rights or if you invited Mr. Solzhenitsyn to the White House that you might endanger the progress of the SALT talks. I don't feel that way. . . . We have got to be firm and we have got to be forceful. But I don't want to tie everything together in one package so that we are timid about insisting on human rights.[51]

Carter's naive failure to understand that one could not very easily "combine support for our more authoritarian allies and friends with the effective promotion of human rights within their countries" was evident especially in Iran and Nicaragua, where the United States had long been a major actor in domestic politics. In Nicaragua, Carter placed far too much trust in Somoza's willingess to participate in a transition to democratic government. The most stunning single example of Carter's shortcoming was the "secret" letter he wrote Somoza in July 1978, congratulating him on the small steps he had taken toward change and (characteristically) urging him on to more. In conjunction with some military aid released two months earlier, the letter could be seen as reassuring the Nicaraguan leader of Washington's support. Somoza immediately leaked the letter—first to Venezuelan President Perez—as proof that America would continue to stand beside him.[52]

The same naivete is evident in Carter's dealing with the shah. Thus, in a meeting with the Iranian leader in November 1977, Carter reports conveying sentiments that the poor shah may actually have taken to heart:

> You have heard of my statements about human rights. A growing number of your own citizens are claiming that these rights are not always honored in Iran. . . . Iran's reputation in the world is being damaged by their complaints. Is there anything that can be done to alleviate this problem by closer consultation with the dissident groups and be easing off on some of the strict policy policies?[53]

In the context of Iranian politics at the time, such advice was not simply supremely irrelevant; it was also misleading and ultimately damaging to all parties concerned.[54]

Perhaps the best explanation for Carter's naivete about political realities abroad is that his thinking originated in his experiences in the United States and his human rights campaign was in substantial measure directed to a domestic moral renewal. It is striking how deeply Carter had been moved personally and politically by the civil rights struggle at home, and how easily he seemed to assume that the lessons he had learned there had relevance for the distant climes of Nicaragua, Iran, southern Africa, and the Soviet Union.[55]

Carter also felt a need to restore America's self-confidence in its essential moral purpose in the aftermath of Watergate, Vietnam, and the rise of foreign dangers like the Organization of Petroleum Exporting Countries and the continued competition with the Soviet Union. Hence there was a domestic background to Carter's message that there could be a "new world," one where America could continue to be proud. A few lines (many more could be cited) from speeches in 1977 and 1978 convey the Wilsonian flavor of this conviction that a special providence had singled out the United States to be a beacon to others: "Throughout the world . . . there is a preoccupation with the subject of human freedom, human rights. . . . No other country is as well qualified as we to set an example." Or again: "The great democracies are not free because we are strong and prosperous. I believe we are strong and influential and prosperous because we are free." Once more: "We are confident that democracy's example will be compelling, and so we seek to bring that example closer to those from whom in the past few years we have been separated and who are not yet convinced about the advantages of our kind of life." Still again: "Uniquely, ours is a nation founded on an idea of human rights. From our own history we know how powerful that idea can be."[56]

The lessons of the Carter administration are not that Wilsonianism is futile or of only marginal importance to American national security so much as they are instructive about the need to operationalize carefully liberal democratic internationalism and to recognize what the limits of such a policy may be. Liberalism must know how to press its goals when appropriate and where there are limits to its appeal. When liberalism becomes moralism, substituting its wishes for realistic analysis of conditions abroad, it serves more as Fourth of July play to the grandstand than as an effective guide to policy. To be successful, Wilsonianism must be practiced selectively and with an understanding of the political context in which it is operating. Otherwise, as the examples of Nicaragua and Iran demonstrate, the price to be paid may well be high—for the peoples of the regions concerned even more than for the United States.

CHAPTER TEN

Reagan's Democratic Revolution

> Around the world today, the democratic revolution is gathering new strength. In India, a critical test has been passed. . . . In Africa, Nigeria is moving. . . . In the Caribbean and Central America, sixteen of twenty-four countries have freely elected governments. . . . In the communist world as well, man's instinctive desire for freedom and self-determination surfaces again and again. . . . optimism is in order, because day by day democracy is proving itself to be a not-at-all fragile flower. From Stettin on the Baltic to Varna on the Black Sea, the regimes planted by totalitarianism have had more than thirty years to establish their legitimacy. But none—not one regime—has yet been able to risk free elections. Regimes planted by bayonets do not take root.
>
> We must be staunch in our conviction that freedom is not the sole prerogative of a lucky few, but the inalienable and universal right of all human beings. . . . This is not cultural imperialism, it is providing the means for genuine self-determination and protection for diversity. Democracy already flourishes in countries with very different cultures and historical experiences. It would be cultural condescension, or worse, to say that any people prefer dictatorship to democracy.
>
> —Ronald Reagan, June 8, 1982

IN NOVEMBER 1989, with the fall of the Berlin Wall, the division of Europe was ended and the cold war was history. Changes in the Soviet Union had led the way. Mikhail Gorbachev became head of that country in 1985. In short order, the impact of his reforms (most of whose consequences were unanticipated) led to the disintegration first of the Soviet empire, then of the Soviet state. Soviet control over more than 100 million people in Eastern Europe came to an end in 1989–90, as Germany reunified alongside an upsurge of democratic reconstruction in Poland, Hungary, and Czechoslovakia. In 1991–2, Lenin's Communist party of the Soviet Union collapsed and the Soviet state ceased to exist. Democratic Baltic Republics emerged and for the moment democratic movements appeared predominant in the Ukraine, Belarus, and Russia itself. The contest between the Soviet Union and the United States, which at times had menaced the world with extinction, ended peacefully with a speed and a finality no one had anticipated.

When Soviet communism collapsed between 1989 and 1991, the terrible struggle over the character of the modern state had finally been resolved, at least in Europe. Fascism had been defeated in 1945; now Soviet communism had fallen. By 1992 democracy stood unchallenged as the only form of mass politics that offered itself as a model worldwide.

To be sure, there were limits to what this victory meant. In the United States in the early 1990s, recognition grew of serious internal social problems as economic growth faltered. In Western Europe, economic stagnation, unemployment, struggles over immigration, and the hesitations of the European Community to continue its integration raised concerns. In Eastern Europe, the disintegration of Yugoslavia, which led to bitter fighting—first in Croatia in 1991, then, beginning in 1992, in Bosnia—raised the question of whether the passions of ethnic hatred would result in similar death and destruction elsewhere in communism's wake. In Russia itself, right-wing militarist forces made a strong showing in the December 1993 parliamentary elections, gaining more than 40 percent of the votes. Despite these concerns, however, the precipitous decline of Soviet power removed for the while the threat of nuclear annihilation and meant that discord in Europe no longer threatened the peace of the world.

Outside Europe democracy was showing that its ways were not culture bound. In South Korea in 1987–8, another Confucian culture joined Japan as a democracy, and in 1989 forces in China tried to make that country follow suit. By the early 1990s, the prospects for democracy in Taiwan had turned brighter. In the Philippines and Malaysia, democratic forces appeared for the moment in ascendance, even if the process seemed open to reversal. But democracy's most significant successes outside Europe were in Latin America, where after more than 160 years of independence from Spain and Portugal, liberalism seemed finally to be sinking deep roots.

To some extent these gains in democracy were synchronized; to some extent they were independent. Democratic forces were weakest where, as in China in 1989, they were largely an imitation of events transpiring elsewhere. When democracy enjoyed strong indigenous bases in established political groups and procedures, as in most of Latin America (where the general movement toward democracy predated the end of the cold war and in some countries was generations old), its prospects were more promising.

Was it consequential or coincidental to these developments that, beginning in 1977, the United States was governed by administrations concerned with promoting democracy worldwide? We must be careful not to exaggerate the American contribution: many factors independent of American policy obviously played critical roles in this process, and to the extent Washington mattered, its program with respect to Germany and Japan in the

1940s surely weighed more heavily on the balance of history than anything accomplished after 1977.

Nevertheless, the sudden surge of democratic movements in the late 1980s and early 1990s did correspond to Washington's hopes at the time. To be sure, the first eighteen months of the Reagan presidency (1981–9) were in distinct contrast to the Carter years, whose emphasis on human rights and the democratization of authoritarian regimes the incoming Republicans had once roundly deplored. But conservative Republicans had never hesitated to call for democracy in Eastern Europe, and in short order many of them found it natural to encourage such developments in Latin America, the Far East, and Africa. However different these two administrations may have seemed in the early 1980s, today their continuity in foreign policy is more striking than their contrast.

Seen from the century-old perspective of American efforts to promote democracy abroad, no administration since the presidency of Woodrow Wilson [1913–21] has been so committed to the tenets of liberal democratic internationalism as that of Ronald Reagan. Reagan propounded the idealistic conviction that Washington had a duty to play a leadership role in world affairs by virtue not only of its power and but also of its moral example; he made repeated assertions that only democratic governments can be considered legitimate and trusted friends of the United States; he argued that a world order run by democratic states would be more prosperous, pacific, and morally superior to any other; he designed antistatist economic policies to reduce the strength of government relative to civil society; he unreservedly endorsed international open markets; and he indicated a willingness to use force for the defense of freedom worldwide.

Of course, Reagan himself would vehemently deny that he was a liberal. From the time he became prominent nationally by supporting Barry Goldwater's bid for the presidency in 1964, until his own election sixteen years later, the word *liberalism* was anathema to him. The issue is one of terminology, however, not of substance. Reagan was conservative by virtue of wanting to protect traditional family values, reduce the scope of government intervention in the economy, and rely on an expanded military capacity to defend America's interests abroad.[1] Nothing in this conservative creed necessarily contradicts nearly a century of American liberal practice in world affairs, however. When a president makes American leadership of a world community of democratic nations following free-market practices the core features of his foreign policy, then whatever he calls himself, he most certainly is a Wilsonian.[2]

Part of the difficulty in seeing Reagan as the liberal he was lies in what might be called his radical or born-again message, his insistent call for a new kind of world order, which harkened back to Woodrow Wilson, an approach to world politics that liberals since the time of FDR had thought of as too utopian, too idealistic, in fact, too dangerous. Especially after World War II, liberals had toned down their demands for a world order that matched their image of the way things should rightfully be in favor of a realistic acceptance of the necessity to work in the world as it was. From the late 1940s, in conjunction with policy toward such countries as Turkey and Iran, where the roots of democracy were weak, FDR-liberals had agreed that effectiveness might mean supporting authoritarian governments. And since the war in Vietnam, liberals had also been willing to seek an accommodation with the Soviet Union in world affairs, again because of a realistic understanding of the need for cooperation.

These FDR-liberals had long since abandoned Wilson's idea that Washington would only cooperate fully with democratic nations, that only a democratic community of states might preserve world order. Given the split between Wilsonians and Rooseveltians—between more idealistic and more realistic liberals, that is—Reagan emerges as a direct descendent of Wilson, for to an extent unmatched since Wilson's days, the promotion of democracy was both a means and an end in Reagan's foreign policy. There was far more to it, then, than William F. Buckley or George Will realized when they contemptuously dismissed the president as typically "sleep-walking" when he asked them: "Is it possible we conservatives are the real liberals and the liberals the real conservatives?"[3] In fact, Reagan was right.

The most obvious element in Reagan's Wilsonianism was his conviction, as he put it many times citing the pilgrim John Winthrop in 1630, that America was a "shining city on a hill. . . . the eyes of all the people are upon us."[4] Like Wilson before him, Reagan saw himself as moralist and a global populist: Reagan knew he was "lucky to be an American" and insisted that "America must successfully appeal to the sympathies of the world's peoples—the global electorate":

> By 1980, a national reawakening was underway—a reawakening that resulted in a new sense of responsibility, a new sense of confidence in America and the universal principles and ideals on which our free system is based. It is not an arrogant demand that others adopt our ways. It's a realistic belief in the relative and proven success of the American experiment.[5]

Reagan's populism was best expressed in his respect for individualism and in his deep-set liberal conviction that people know better than the state:

> Ours was the first revolution in the history of mankind that truly reversed the course of government, and with three little words: "We the people." "We the people" tell the government what to do, it doesn't tell us. . . . Almost all the world's constitutions are documents in which governments tell the people what their privileges are. Our Constitution is a document in which "We the people" tell the government what it is allowed to do. "We the people" are free.

Just as quintessentially Wilsonian was Reagan's conviction that a democratic world order would be peaceful:

> Free people, where governments rest upon the consent of the governed, do not wage war on their neighbors. Free people, blessed by economic opportunity and protected by laws that respect the dignity of the individual, are not driven toward the domination of others.[6]

In articulating this neo-Wilsonian view of the United States' place in the world, Reagan found especially effective support in his secretary of state, George Shultz (who took office in June 1982). In Shultz's words:

> Civilizations thrive when they believe in themselves. They decline when they lose this faith. All civilizations confront massive problems, but a society is more likely to master its challenges, rather than be overwhelmed by them, if it retains this bedrock self-confidence that its values are worth defending. This is the essence of the Reagan revolution and of the leadership the President has sought to provide in America. . . . As we head toward the 21st century, it is time for the democracies to celebrate their system, their beliefs, and their success. We face challenges, but we are well poised to master them. Opinions are being revised about which system is the wave of the future. The free nations, if they maintain their unity and their faith in themselves, have the advantage—economically, technologically, morally. History is on freedom's side.[7]

Like Wilson before them, Reagan and Shultz saw a community of democratic nations as the world's best hope for an enduring peace. During the course of his presidency, Reagan particularly liked to cite Truman:

> Harry Truman once said that ultimately our security and the world's hopes for peace and human progress "lie not in measures of defense or in the control of weapons but in the growth and expansion of freedom and self-government." And tonight, we declare anew to our fellow citizens of the world: freedom is not the sole prerogative of a chosen few; it is the universal right of all God's children. . . . Our mission is to nourish and defend freedom and democracy and to communicate these ideas everywhere we can.[8]

Arguing the "truly profound connection" among peace, economic progress, and democracy, the secretary insisted:

> It is no accident, for example, that America's closest and most lasting relationships are its alliances with its fellow democracies. These ties with the Atlantic Community, Japan, and other democratic friends have an enduring quality precisely because they rest on a moral base, not only a base of strategic interest.[9]

As Wilson's liberalism had its autocratic enemies abroad and its mission to spread the message of democracy, so too Reagan's. The United States' allies were democracies, its opponents the totalitarians of the "evil empire." The danger was clear and present. By their very nature, the Soviets were on the march. By its very nature, American values and institutions would put up a fight.[10] As Reagan put it in his famous speech of March 8, 1983, on the "evil empire": "There is sin and evil in the world, and we are enjoined by Scripture and the Lord Jesus to oppose it with all our might. . . . [Communists] are the focus of evil in the modern world."[11]

The hold of this reasoning was such that at first Reagan was reluctant to accept the normalization of relations with China begun by Nixon and confirmed by Carter. China was communist; Taiwan was not. A realistic accommodation to this fact was not easy. By the same logic, it seemed for a time that the United States could not negotiate an arms control agreement with the Soviet Union for the simple reason that it was not a democracy. As he prepared for his first summit with Mikhail Gorbachev, Reagan announced his reservations in unambiguous Wilsonian terms:

> True peace rests on the pillars of individual freedom, human rights, national self-determination, and respect for the rule of law. . . . Freedom and democracy are the best guarantors of peace. History has shown that democratic nations do not start wars. The rights of the individual and the rule of law are as fundamental to peace as arms control. A government which does not respect its citizens' rights and its international commitments to protect those rights is not likely to respect its other international undertakings.[12]

In conducting his crusade against communism, Reagan was not satisfied with containment. He deplored the traditional balance of power realism and the talk of detente that Nixon and Kissinger, and later Carter, had promoted, favoring instead what in the Eisenhower days had been called "rollback." The war in Vietnam had not been a mistake to undertake; it was lost, Reagan felt, by an unwillingness on Washington's part to press ahead, and by a strident liberal press and intelligentsia, more aware of what America had done wrong than what it had done right, and in their guilt and negativism emboldening Soviet expansionist designs. As the president put it in 1984 referring to the Carter years: "Gone are the days when the United States was perceived as a rudderless superpower, a helpless hostage to world events. American leadership is back. . . . we will not return to the days of handwringing, defeatism, decline, and despair."[13] This "new patriotism" was perhaps best summed up by Sylvester Stallone in a popular series of *Rambo* movies, wherein a tough, patriotic American soldier redeems the country's honor by fighting Washington and the Vietnamese communists alike for the sake of democracy's eventual triumph. Reagan thus became a president of patriotic slogans: "America is back." Exorcise the "Vietnam syndrome." "Stand tall." "It's morning in America."[14]

Once the United States had recovered its sense of purpose, Reagan intended to ignite a "democratic revolution" throughout the world. Just as

Woodrow Wilson declared America's intention to make the world safe for democracy, so President Reagan insisted on this country's global responsibility:

> Freedom in Nicaragua or Angola or Afghanistan or Cambodia or Eastern Europe or South Africa or anyplace else on the globe is not just an internal matter. . . . Vaclav Havel warned the world that "respect for human rights is the fundamental condition and the sole genuine guarantee of true peace." And Andrei Sakharov in his Nobel lecture said: "I am convinced that international confidence, mutual understanding, disarmament, and international security are inconceivable without an open society with freedom of information, freedom of conscience, the right to publish, and the right to travel and choose the country in which one wishes to live." Freedom serves peace; the quest for peace must serve the cause of freedom.[15]

Perhaps the greatest conundrum of the Reagan presidency in foreign affairs is how an administration so motivated by a born-again spirit of confrontation with the Soviet Union and so filled with a sense of the United States' democratizing mission could in practice be so relatively flexible and restrained. One usually expects ideological crusaders to be rigid and risk-taking; Reagan was not. Those military tasks that were undertaken were relatively risk-free: the invasion of Grenada in October 1983 and the attack on Libya in April 1986. Elsewhere, even when he seemed to have drawn a line in the sand, the president could retreat, as when he withdrew the Marines from Lebanon in 1984 after the devastating attack on their barracks there. So too with the Soviet Union, Reagan could offer an arms control agreement early on that alarmed some of his more bellicose followers.

One reason for the president's restraint had to do with the character of Reagan's thinking: while he held strongly to his convictions, some of them were contradictory and all of them were simple. Lacking a grand design that reconciled the inconsistencies in his thinking—reasoning (as Lou Cannon has put it) from anecdotes rather than from analysis—the president could be subject to surprising changes in attitude.

Thus, the Reagan who denounced the evil empire in March 1983, was the same Reagan who told an interviewer only nine months later, "I would not say that again," and by 1988 allowed, "I was talking about another time, another era." The Reagan who had said a few days after his inauguration that the Soviets "reserve unto themselves the right to commit any crime, to lie, to cheat" was the same Reagan who wrote a personal letter to Leonid Brezhnev less than three months later affirming their common humanity: "Is it possible that we have permitted ideology, political and economic philosophies, and governmental policies to keep us from considering the very real, everyday problems of people?"[16]

With respect to the arms race, Reagan could also be flexible. As he often said, he believed in "peace through strength," so for a while he deliberately avoided negotiating with the Soviets in order to increase the American arsenal. Yet he was able to talk about banning nuclear weapons completely by the end of the century at the Rekyjavik Summit in October 1986, and to sign a treaty removing most intermediate range nuclear missiles from Europe at the Washington Summit in December 1987, despite the criticisms of many of his fellow conservatives.[17]

If ambiguity in the principles Reagan endorsed is one explanation for the lack of a more militant foreign policy, another explanation may be found in the president's personality: unless there was virtual unanimity on a plan among his chief advisers, he was reluctant to endorse it. Accordingly, a clash of high level personalities was almost certain to delay, modify, or cancel policy initiatives. Since higher-risk operations typically generated deeper divisions, the administration's conduct remained relatively restrained. Hence, the United States would not "go to the source" and blockade Cuba, as Secretary of State Alexander Haig suggested in 1981 in order to bring a halt to communist insurgency in Central America, any more than it would invade Panama to punish Manuel Noriega in 1988. Reagan's advisers were divided, and the president declined to act.[18]

The restraint that was a matter of personality for the president was often put as a matter of principle by Secretary of State George Shultz. While Shultz was quite capable of calling for the use of force, he typically asked for clarity in the pursuit of ends and for judiciousness in the choice of means as well. Thus, in a major address in 1984, the secretary pointedly criticized as overly ambitious President Kennedy's famous statement that the United States would "pay any price, bear any burden, meet any hardship, support any friend, oppose any foe, in order to assure the survival and the success of liberty."[19]

Still another characteristic of Shultz's thinking was his respect for "history," as in his repeated observation that "history is on freedom's side," or his common metaphor that "the tide of history is with us." The view was picked up by the president who prophetically declared: "I have often said that the tide of the future is a freedom tide. If so, it is also a peace tide, for the surest guarantee we have of peace is national freedom and democratic government." When Reagan and Shultz spoke of history's tide, they meant that other forces would do some of the work of furthering human progress, so that as midwives of history they need not make every difficult decision. Hence the optimistic spirit of Reagan's statement in May 1981: "The years ahead are great ones for this country, for the cause of freedom and the spread of civilization. The West won't contain communism, it will transcend communism. . . . it will dismiss it as some bizarre chapter in human history whose last pages are even now being written." Nevertheless, both men also agreed that, in Shultz's words, "history will do us no special favors. A better future depends on our will, our leadership, our willingness to act decisively in moments of crisis. . . . we must be ready to engage ourselves where necessary throughout the world. We must be ready to use our diplomatic skills and our military strength in defense of our values and our interests."[20]

In short, activism in foreign affairs was one feature of the Reagan's foreign policy, but moderation was another. The resolution of this apparently contradictory prescription for promoting a global "democratic revolution" is apparent in its three key operational programs: "constructive engagement;" the push for antistatist, free markets abroad; and the Reagan Doctrine. In each case, as we shall see, Washington designed a strategy that called for minimal effort on its part to realize its vision of a world order dominated by democratic governments.

The Logic of Constructive Engagement

The term *constructive engagement* was first used in the Reagan administration by Chester A. Crocker, shortly before he became assistant secretary of state for African affairs in 1981.[21] Crocker applied the term to his proposal for proper American policy toward South Africa, intending it to indicate the character of American support for established governments seeking to democratize. By extension, it may be said that the Reagan administration practiced a policy of constructive engagement toward South Korea and El Salvador as well (although the military involvement with El Salvador was such that it could be analyzed in terms of the Reagan Doctrine).

Wherever it was applied, constructive engagement aimed at creating a climate of confidence, reassuring foreign governments of American commitment to their regime in the process of a difficult transition to democracy. Its implied formula was (a) to stress the common security interests of both governments (the Soviet menace), indicating that the United States recognized that it too would be threatened along with the incumbent government should local communists take over; (b) to mention collateral American concerns (usually economic) for continued stability in the region; and (c) to call for the established political elite to undertake a program of liberalization with American help as the necessary means to secure these jointly valued ends and to be assured membership in the club of democratic states.

On the face of it, there was nothing radically original about constructive engagement in terms of the traditions of American foreign policy. American policymakers trying to promote democracy in foreign countries during the twentieth century generally turned to local elites to effect change. The essential message was that these elites' principal interests could be secured with American help so long as they undertook a process of political reform.

Thus, as governor general of the Philippines, William Howard Taft exercised what he called "a policy of attraction" with respect to the oligarchs of that archipelago after the United States took power there in 1898. Their interests would be respected (indeed served) at the same time that the land would be democratized. So too in 1916, when the United States occupied the Dominican Republic, Washington's reforms were extensive in political affairs, but were carefully designed not to threaten the socioeconomic power structure of the country's elite. Again in the 1960s, the Alliance for Progress anticipated that democracy would come to Latin America through the efforts of local actors (although not necessarily the established power elite), without whose commitment nothing could be done. Seen from historical perspective, the policy of "constructive engagement," adopted first by the Reagan administration with respect to South Africa, was vintage American practice.

What made Crocker's formulation of constructive engagement distinctive was his battery of suggestions for micromanagement of the democratization process once a foreign elite appeared willing to experiment with reform. Crocker viewed the transition from several dimensions—economic, social, and political. Reforms in each arena were to proceed gradually and incrementally, one step preparing the way for the next.

Before becoming a template for policy in general, the strategy and tactics of constructive engagement had to be concretely articulated. In South Africa in 1980, some 17 million of a population of more than 25 million were black, held down by almost 5 million whites (another 3 million being coloureds and Asians). Enormous class differences were compounded by the South African government's policy of apartheid, a particularly offensive doctrine of racism practiced since 1948. Tensions were high: not only had the African National Congress party (ANC), representing a majority of the politically active blacks, called for the violent overthrow of the government, but a number of its leaders were communists who had contacts with Moscow. The fact that South Africa's two neighbors, Angola and Mozambique, had been ruled by Marxist-Leninist parties since the mid-1970s, and that black majority rule had been obtained in Zimbabwe under radical black leadership, only compounded anxiety among the whites. The Cuban-Soviet presence also meant that Washington's concern was with all of southern Africa, not simply with a single country.

The first step in implementing constructive engagement was to create a climate of ideological consensus between American and South African elites—specifically a mutual interest in stopping communism. The white South African community was menaced by the threat of Soviet expansion in southern Africa, while the United States was interested in the region because of its mineral resources, its geographic position on the Cape sea route, and America's general commitment to contain Soviet-Cuban expansion.[22] But to meet this challenge more than military force was called for; a political solution was needed. Aparthied had to be ended. South Africa had to become democratic.

Consensus on the need to democratize, or on how to achieve it, was not easy to achieve. Hardliners in Pretoria and antiapartheid activists in Washington were particularly unwilling to go along with the complicated, prolonged, and thus necessarily problematic process Crocker contemplated.[23] Nonetheless, Crocker proceeded to identify a credible democratizing force within South African ruling circles. This was the "modernizing autocracy" under President P. W. Botha, who since 1979, Crocker felt, was moving Afrikaner nationalist politics toward ending apartheid. While the conduct of the ruling elites was key (it should be emphasized that Washington expected to work with the Afrikaner, not the English part of the white population), Crocker could also point to recent developments that had "brought the black communities of South Africa to a new level of political awareness and ferment." This new political maturity on the part of both blacks and whites opened the door to American initiatives. Crocker was even daring enough to write in 1980, at a time when official Washington was refusing to meet with black radicals, "If the ANC were legalized now, a grand coalition, though fragile, might develop."[24]

To operationalize the reform movement, which would gradually dismantle apartheid while incrementally empowering blacks, Crocker made a critical tactical point:

> The innovative feature of constructive engagement is its insistence on serious thinking about the sequencing and interrelatedness of change. Priority ought to be given to those arenas of change that logically lead to and make possible further steps. We must avoid the trap of an indiscriminate attack on all aspects of the system—as though each were equally odious and none should be addressed first.[25]

Writing in 1980, Crocker was understandably vague about precisely what steps the new Reagan administration should take in South Africa "in the effort to recognize and support positive movement, and to engage credibly in addressing a complex agenda of change." Still, certain guidelines appeared clear. The United States should continue to honor international arms sanctions on South Africa. However, since "effective coercive influence is a rare commodity in foreign policy," he argued for continued economic ties with that country, working through them in a direction that was antistatist and favored the promotion of blacks. Foreign corporations should follow explicit guidelines like the Sullivan Principles on fair employment practices (named after an African American minister). Given the robustness of that country's economy and its need for more skilled and professional workers, there were solid reasons to think foreign trade and investment could contribute to positive political developments.[26]

Simultaneously, in the political realm, Crocker drew attention to a sequence of "power-sharing" reforms that would gradually draw the black community into a fully democratic process. Piecemeal power sharing steps deserved support if they were consistent with the goal of "expanded black political advancement." For example, the United States should oppose homeland settlements for blacks, but "support the devolution of real power to local and regional bodies" when it empowered blacks.[27]

A serious complicating factor was South Africa's relations with its neighbors. Angola and Mozambique had both fallen under communist rule since the departure of the Portuguese in 1975. Both harbored antiapartheid ANC guerrillas, but Angola represented by far the greater threat: its MPLA government (Movement for the Popular Liberation of Angola) had large-scale Cuban (and thus indirect Soviet) support, and it was bent on securing the independence of Namibia from South African rule. Accordingly, Pretoria felt the ANC's threat was dangerously compounded by foreign forces, a fear shared by Washington, which viewed Angola as the beachhead of Soviet influence throughout the region.

The international drama focused on Namibia, a territory assigned as a mandate to South Africa after World War I by the League of Nations. Washington's aim was to secure the independence of Namibia in return for the departure of Cuban troops from Angola. Angola and South Africa had the same concern: that each would fail to secure its goal while its adversary would gain its end. To reassure South Africa, and to pressure Angola, Washington lobbied Congress to repeal the Clark Amendment, which blocked American aid to forces fighting the MPLA government in Luanda. Congress agreed in mid-1985, and aid (estimated at only a few million dollars annually) was resumed to Jonas Savimbi and his National Union for the Total Independence of Angola (UNITA), fighting with South African support. Critics argued that South Africa was attempting to draw Washington more and more deeply into its military defense, so manuevering the United States into a major maelstrom of world affairs that could have serious repercussions on domestic American politics as well.

By 1984, however, constructive engagement seemed to show some progress. Crocker could maintain that the Nkomati accord between Mozambique and South Africa, and a South African–Angolan cease-fire agreement, paved the way for Pretoria to accept, rather than to try to replace, its communist neighbor states, so allowing domestic change within South Africa to proceed with minimal outside interference. More, domestic obstacles to South Africa's democratization seemed for a while to be diminishing. The government ended some of the measures of "petty apartheid" and announced the creation of a three-house Parliament (one each for whites, coloureds, and Asians) as part of a design that might lead to the eventual incorporation of the black majority into government.

Optimism was short-lived. In September 1984 violence shook the country as blacks reacted with anger to what they saw as the paltriness of the reforms Botha's government was offering them. In 1985, despite earlier agreements, South Africa again began to press its military advantages against Angola and Mozambique, and Botha in July declared a state of emergency. Reagan's critics pointed out how paltry Washington's concrete support for real change actually was. The Reagan administration was forced by Congress to respond by increasing economic sanctions—new banks loans, the export of nuclear technology, and the import of Kruger-rands were all banned.[28]

By 1986 the situation had worsened. Pretoria extended its state of emergency nationwide: by the end of the year there were some twenty-three thousand political prisoners (many under the age of sixteen), and some nine hundred had been killed in political violence. White commandoes struck in Zimbabwe, Zambia, and Mozambique. To charges that constructive engagement was dead and that it was only through "constructive disengagement" that the United States could hope to pressure South Africa to reform, President Reagan instead insisted that "active" constructive engagement now had to be contemplated. While he remained committed to an economic presence in South Africa, Reagan emphasized the need for political reforms, including the release of all political prisoners—especially of Nelson Mandela—and the legalization of all black political movements. In his words:

> The root cause of South Africa's disorder is apartheid, that rigid system of racial segregation, wherein black people have been treated as third-class citizens in a nation they helped to build. America's view of apartheid has been and remains clear. Apartheid is morally wrong and politically unacceptable. The United States cannot maintain cordial relations with a government whose power rests upon the denial of rights to a majority of its people based on race. If South Africa wishes to belong to the family of Western nations, an end to apartheid is a precondition.[29]

Despite the president's insistence and new reforms by the Botha government (permitting interracial marriages in 1985 and dropping the pass laws in 1986), the American Congress in October 1986 passed the Comprehensive Anti-Apartheid Act, imposing sanctions on South Africa that could only be lifted after significant progress had been made toward democratization. The act stayed in effect throughout the rest of the Reagan years until finally lifted at the end of the Bush presidency, indicating that constructive engagement as it had been conceived in 1980–1 was by 1986 a dead letter.

By 1988 the winding down of the cold war contributed to dramatic changes in the region. Exhausted by years of fighting, Angola and South Africa expressed interest in Washington's long-standing suggestion: that Angola promise a withdrawal of Cuban troops in exchange for South Africa granting Namibia's independence.[30]

International accords were soon followed by domestic reforms. In 1989 F. W. de Klerk replaced Botha as the country's president and in early 1990, Mandela was released from prison and the ANC legalized. Later that year, Namibia became independent and American and Soviet negotiators impressed upon their clients in Angola that they no longer would support armed confrontation there. In March 1992 the white South African electorate decisively rejected apartheid and negotiations began for a transition to full democracy. In October the ANC announced an internal purge of those of its members responsible for acts of torture and murder against prisoners taken by the organization. The announcement in September 1993 that an interim government including members of the ANC would rule the country until elections based on universal suffrage were held the following April, made South Africa a showcase of democratic reform in Africa, even if enormous difficulties lay ahead.

The debate over the extent to which American influence mattered, and which aspects of it mattered most, will continue for years and need not be resolved here. What the policy of the Reagan administration does demonstrate, however, is that a considered policy to promote democracy in South Africa did exist, and that it had at least some positive impact on the course of events. If constructive engagement appears in many respects to have been ineffectual to liberal aims, if one can suggest manifold ways in which it might have been more forcefully implemented, it nonetheless bears comparison with both Kennedy's Alliance for Progress in Latin America in the early 1960s and many chapters in Carter's human rights campaign in the late 1970s, where American policy was also hostage to local governments.[31] What all these cases indicate is that while Washington can make a difference in the transition to democracy, the most important actors are the local political elite for whose strength and commitment there can be no substitute.

Aspects of constructive engagement appear to have been adopted elsewhere during the Reagan years. In the case of South Korea, for example, the administration made clear its support for the Seoul government— lauding its economic successes and stressing mutual security concerns with respect to North Korea—before encouraging it to democratize. Thus, in a speech before the Korean National Assembly in 1982, Vice President George Bush congratulated the Koreans on their "economic miracle," saying that they had "one of the most dynamic economies of the 20th century," stressing that "the United States is, of course, a vital market for Korean goods and vice versa. President Reagan has made it clear that he will do all he can to keep the U.S. market open. There are few other advocates of free trade as ardent as he." He then turned to American hopes to see democracy eventually flower in South Korea:

> Against this background of extraordinary economic achievement, the opportunities for pluralism are strong. President Chun, the first head of state President Reagan received at the White House, spoke of a new era in the Republic of Korea . . . a "freer, more abundant, and democratic society in our midst." We support this philosophy with all our heart. And we look to President Chun and to this Assembly to build on such a commitment. In a democracy, legislatures are the only true means of determining the will of the people. Democracy, as President Abraham Lincoln defined it for us long ago, consists of "government of the people, by the people, for the people.". . . Some countries have a fear of pluralism, and only the preordained few control the destinies of many. . . . The United States . . . regrets the suppression of democratic practices in all countries, friend or foe. We see political diversity as a source of strength, not weakness.[32]

The extent to which American support for South Korean democratization mattered to the eventual emergence of democratic government in that country in 1987–8 is hard to evaluate. The process of ousting Chun was difficult; it depended largely on the determination of South Korea's leaders and internal political forces that Washington only indirectly and marginally affected.

During a delicate transition, however, even marginal and indirect influence may make a decisive difference. Washington was not only working with the government but also the democratic opposition to bring about change there. Under the auspices of the National Endowment for Democracy, started in 1982–3 as a bipartisan public agency to promote democracy abroad, Americans became active on behalf of South Korean groups genuinely interested in moving their country toward democracy. Washington's support for South Korea's eventual democratization was constant, however much human rights advocates on occasion may have hoped for more.

American involvement in the removal of Jean-Claude Duvalier from Haiti in 1986 and the democratic elections that made Jean-Bertrand Aristide president in 1990 should not be called a case of constructive engagement, however. Democratization was not the fruit of reform from above, and the record of American involvement in the ouster remains difficult to evaluate. It was popular protests against the corrupt and repressive government of Jean-Claude Duvalier ("Baby Doc," who had succeeded his father "Papa Doc" in 1971) that turned the country into chaos by late 1985, following an election that July, which confirmed Baby Doc as president-for-life by a 99.9 percent vote, and it was popular forces that made Aristide president of Haiti in December 1990.

Nevertheless, Washington steadily advocated liberalization and opposed military repression as a way to stability, finally arranging for the dictator to flee to exile in France in February 1986.[33] And it was American pressure on the Haitian military thereafter that was indispensable to the 1990 elections. But ten months later, in September 1991, Aristide was deposed by yet another military coup. Despite economic boycotts and the threat of joint action by the Organization of American States (OAS), the military authorities in Haiti remained firm in their opposition to a return to democracy. Neither Reagan nor his successor George Bush saw democratic government restored to Haiti.

Surely the Reagan and Bush administrations might have done more to guarantee the consolidation of democracy in Haiti than they did. In the critical days following Duvalier's departure in February 1986 or again after Aristide was deposed in 1991, Washington may have missed opportunities to make a difference. But as with South Africa, the question may not be so much to judge the effectiveness of Washington's policy, but rather whether it was genuinely committed to a democratic outcome.[34]

Nor was the ouster of Ferdinand Marcos from the Philippines in February 1986 an example of constructive engagement. The murder of the leading democratic activist Benigno Aquino in August 1983, after his return from exile in the United States, was the beginning of the process. In 1984 American Ambassador Stephen Bosworth bluntly declared that the Philippines was not a democracy and that Marcos's authoritarianism hurt both Filipino and American national interests. And the National Endowment for Democracy later worked for democratic elections there. But reforms were not initiated by Marcos, and Reagan was ambivalent about pressuring a man he considered a loyal ally of the United States with a communist insurgency facing him. Marcos could recall Vice President Bush's toast in Manila on the occasion of his inauguration as president following fraudulent elections: "We love your adherence to democratic principle and to the democratic processes. And we will not leave you in isolation to the degree we have any vibrant strength—it would be turning our backs on history if we did."[35]

The moment of truth came with the Filipino presidential elections of February 7, 1986. On February 1, President Reagan had dispatched his friend Senator Richard Lugar to the Philippines to observe the elections, saying that unless "the sovereign voice of the people" was heard "a totalitarian takeover" was likely. But on the tenth, after abundant evidence of electoral fraud had reached the White House, Reagan announced he would for the moment reserve judgment on the voting, noting only "the evidence for a strong two-party system in the islands." The next day, he retreated further, seeing "the appearance" but "no hard evidence" of fraud, which in any case "could have been that all of that was occurring on both sides" so that the United States was "going to wait. We're going to stay neutral."[36]

Conservatives around President Reagan had managed to persuade him that Corazon Aquino would be soft on the local communist insurgency and hard on pushing the United States to remove its military bases from the islands. As a result, the president hesitated in his commitment to democratic practices. Eventually, the administration came out clearly for a speedy departure of the dictator, but not before Reagan's anemic response had raised doubts about how genuine his commitment was to "constructive engagement" and the "democratic revolution."

Still another case of what might be called constructive engagement (though perhaps it would be better to consider it below as an element of the Reagan Doctrine) is that of El Salvador. Scarcely a month after Reagan's inauguration, the State Department released a White Paper on the the insurgency there, led by the Farabundo Marti National Liberation Front (FMLN). Its opening lines asserted there was

> definitive evidence of the clandestine military support given by the Soviet Union, Cuba, and their communist allies to Marxist-Leninist guerrillas now fighting to overthrow the established government of El Salvador. The evidence . . . underscores the central role played by Cuba and other communist countries beginning in 1979, in the political unification, military direction, and arming of insurgent forces in El Salvador.

It concluded that "the insurgency in El Salvador has been progressively transformed into a textbook case of indirect armed aggression by communist powers through Cuba."[37]

The reasoning behind President Reagan's policy on El Salvador sounded much like the domino theory President Eisenhower had once proposed: if a single country fell to communism, others would follow. Scarcely six weeks into his presidency, Reagan said:

> What we're doing, in going to the aid of a government . . . is to try to halt the infiltration into the Americas [of] terrorists . . . who aren't just aiming at El Salvador but, I think, are aiming at the whole of Central and possibly later South America—and I'm sure, eventually North America.[38]

Secretary of State Alexander Haig warned that the United States might "go to the source" of these troubles with a blockade of Cuba.[39] Similarly, in CIA Director William Casey's words: "This whole El Salvador insurgency is run out of Managua by professionals experienced in directing guerrilla wars. You've got to appreciate that Managua has become an international center. There are Cubans, Soviets, Bulgarians, East Germans, North Koreans, North Vietnamese, representatives of the PLO."[40] The arrival of Secretary of State Shultz in June 1982 did little to change Washington's interpretation:

> El Salvador provides a final example of [our] policy. The real moral question in Central America is not do we believe in military solutions, but do we believe in ourselves? Do we believe that our security and the security of our neighbors has moral validity? Do we have faith in our own democratic values? Do we believe that Marxist-Leninist solutions are antidemocratic and that we have a moral right to try to stop those who are trying to impose them by force. . . . The outcome of political competition will depend in large measure on the balance of military strength. In El Salvador, the United States is supporting moderates who believe in democracy and who are resisting the enemies of democracy on both the extreme right and the extreme left. If we withdrew our support, the moderates, caught in the crossfire, would be the first victims—as would be the cause of human rights. . . . Anyone who believes that military support for our friends isn't crucial to a just outcome is living in a dream world.[41]

United States policy to deal with the insurgency moved along two tracks. One was increased military and economic aid. Under President Carter, total economic assistance to El Salvador amounted over four years to $194 million ($114 in 1981 alone), while military assistance totaled $41 million ($36 million in 1981 alone). By contrast, during Reagan's first term in office, El Salvador received $1.1 billion in economic assistance, and $496 million in military aid, five times as much in these four years as that country had received in the previous thirty-five.[42] By the end of the Bush administration, El Salvador had received $6 billion from the United States over a twelve-year period.

But at the same time that it presided over a military response to the insurgency in El Salvador, Washington strongly endorsed elections there as a way to build up a stable centrist government. Skeptics charged that no such effort could be achieved and that all the talk of promoting democracy was only a smoke screen to deceive the United Nations and the U.S. Congress about the repression going on. Such may have been the intention of officials like Casey. But most in the administration agreed with the president:

> Despite all I and others have said, some people still seem to think that our concern for security assistance means that all we care about is a military solution. That's nonsense. Bullets are no answer to economic inequities, social tensions, or political disagreements. Democracy is what we want, and what we want is to enable Salvadorans to stop the killing and sabotage so that economic and political reforms can take root. The real solution can only be a political one.[43]

From Washington's perspective, the large turnout for the selection of representatives to a constituent assembly in March 1982 was encouraging. Given the local material it had to work with, what more could the Americans do were they not to turn the country over to the communists? Yes, right-wing death squads committed crimes in El Salvador, which were hushed up in Washington. Yet it was only in 1989 that the insurgency finally faced up to the fact that it could not win in El Salvador by force of arms and so made the concessions that eventually resulted in peace. From this perspective, the peace accords ultimately signed in January 1992, entrusting the future of the country to democracy, were the final vindication of yet another instance of constructive engagement, on balance the most difficult for the Reagan years to achieve practically or to justify morally.[44]

But surely the most celebrated case of what might with some justice be called constructive engagement was the personal link created between Ronald Reagan and Mikhail Gorbachev from the time of their first meeting at the Geneva summit in November 1985. To be sure, long after this date, Reagan was capable of warning Americans not to let their guard down as accommodation with the Soviet Union was reached (as in his continued commitment to the Strategic Defense Initiative). But the personal tie between the two men (as well as that between West German Chancellor Kohl and the Soviet leader) surely emboldened Gorbachev considerably as he contemplated the extraordinary range of economic, political, and especially military changes he proposed for the Soviet Union.

The heart of the Reagan-Gorbachev summits was concerned with arms control issues. The democratization of the Soviet Union and Eastern Europe was not an explicit goal of these negotiations. Nonetheless, human rights and democratic governance were constant themes of discussion, whether with respect to Soviet "refuseniks" or in terms of Moscow's support for antidemocratic governments in Warsaw or Managua. By 1987 Gorbachev was himself calling for the "democratization" of the Communist party of the Soviet Union and "self-government of the people." Reagan continued to push the matter. In a particularly striking venue, in front of the Berlin Wall in June 1987, for example, Reagan publicly questioned whether Gorbachev's reforms were "profound" or merely "token gestures":

> There is one sign the Soviets can make that would be unmistakable, that would advance dramatically the cause of freedom and peace. General Secretary Gorbachev, if you seek peace, if you seek prosperity for the Soviet Union and Eastern Europe, if you seek liberalization: Come here to this gate! Mr. Gorbachev, open this gate! Mr. Gorbachev, tear down this wall![45]

The essence of constructive engagement was its commitment to assist authoritarian regimes trying to democratize by aiding them through a difficult transition process. In this respect, the Reagan and Carter administrations represented a more Wilsonian brand of liberal democratic internationalism than had Roosevelt and Truman, who were indifferent to the prospects for promoting democracy in Africa, Asia, and Latin America. Republicans had shed even fewer tears—as the Nixon administration showed when it remained silent when authoritarian power grabs occurred on its watch in Nicaragua, the Philippines, and El Salvador in 1972. Indeed, during the Eisenhower years, even constitutional governments had been abandoned in Iran and Guatemala when they were not considered capable of resisting communist aggression.

Not so the Reagan administration. Instead, Washington stuck to its commitment to democratic reform, the novelty of which (in contrast to the Carter approach) was to work for the transition through authoritarian regimes rather than against them. Nowhere was this liberal democratic internationalism more apparent than in the rapprochement between the United States and the Soviet Union after 1985, a rapprochement based in Gorbachev's words on "new thinking," which in its attitudes toward peace in Europe (and thus in the world) based on arms control, economic reform, democratic government, international cooperation through multilateral institutions, and even possibly collective security sounded to all the world like the birth of Wilsonianism in Russia.

CONSTRUCTIVE ENGAGEMENT RECONSIDERED

The foregoing analysis is sure not to satisfy many of the critics of constructive engagement, who may insist that the policy only apparently promoted democracy in the countries where it was practiced, that in fact it was nothing other than a set of pious pronouncements designed to camouflage American support for the status quo, which, as in El Salvador, could only be maintained at a high price (a matter discussed below). They may maintain that the reason democracy began to flower in South Korea, the Philippines, Central America, and Eastern Europe in the late 1980s had little to do with policy in Washington, but depended instead on democratic activists in these regions. To the extent reformers abroad were influenced by Washington, their friends were congressional liberals and groups like the Free South Africa Movement—not the Reagan White House. So far as Eastern Europe and the Soviet Union is concerned, credit should go to Gorbachev and his foreign secretary, Eduard Shevardnadze, who backed down in the face of mounting American pressure rather than striking back as other empires in decline have elected to do. Similarly, credit is due in the Philippines to the Church and Corazon Aquino; in South Korea to democratic activists (as well as to individuals within Chun Doo Hwan's government); and in Central America to committed democrats like Costa Rican President Oscar Arias.

These points have merit. During at least its first eighteen months in office, the Reagan administration demonstrated repeatedly to authoritarian clients that it intended to turn its back on Carter's human rights policy and cooperate with them to oppose communist advances. On many occasions thereafter, Washington surely could have been more outspoken about the human rights abuses of governments it was supporting or more effective in its support of democracy. So too, it seems probable that in the hands of some policymakers, constructive engagement was at times nothing more than a smoke screen meant to deflect popular or congressional criticism of hardlines administration policies. And to date, the evidence indicates that rather than anticipate the success of democracy in the Philippines or the strength of the antiapartheid movement in South Africa, the Reagan White House was caught by surprise and in its confusion risked impeding the success of these developments. (In his memoirs, Shultz casts doubt on how serious constructive engagement ever was when he criticizes Reagan's emotional attachment to anticommunist authoritarians in South Africa, the Philippines, and Chile.)[46] Then there was luck. Military governments in countries like Argentina and Chile fell of their own accord, Soviet communism collapsed and democratic forces successfully mobilized in a range of countries for reasons that had little to do with policy in Washington, yet the Reagan administration took more credit than was its due.

These allowances made, the case for seeing constructive engagement as a serious approach to the democratization of authoritarian regimes remains persuasive, especially by 1982. Two sets of events made the second year of the Reagan administration critical. First, there was a change in personnel, especially at the State Department. Haig was replaced by Shultz, Robert McFarlane became national security adviser, and Elliott Abrams moved up within the State Department—all to join already established moderates like James Baker and George Bush. In the White House lingo of the times, the "one worlders" (as the hardliners called the moderates) were gaining on the "crazies" (as the moderates called the hardliners).[47]

An example of this liberal evolution comes from the experience of agencies entrusted with fostering democracy abroad. Initially, the position of assistant secretary of state for human rights was not taken seriously by the Reagan administration. Ernst Lefever, a man closely associated with Jeane Kirkpatrick, was nominated for the post, then rejected by a Republican-controlled Senate committee. By the time Elliott Abrams took the position, however, the utilitarian value of democracy had been become clearer, and this division of the State Department took on more prestige and became more effective.[48] Similarly, the National Endowment for Democracy (NED)—an idea discussed during the Carter years and created by the president and Congress in 1982–3—at first appeared little more than a propaganda tool in the cold war, but it quickly became an effective agent of democracy worldwide. Not only did the NED support Solidarity, it also worked for the Command for the No in Chile, against Marcos's attempts to engage in fraudulent elections in 1986, and for a democratic opening in South Korea in 1987.[49]

Second, and more importantly, by 1982, the White House could point to democratic movements in various parts of the world that it could work with. In Poland, Solidarity constantly reminded Washington of the passion democracy could arouse. In El Salvador, the elections of March 1982 indicated the viability of democracy and that the left could probably not emerge triumphantly from the voting boxes. The high voter turnout under difficult conditions, and the reelection as president in March 1984 of Jose Napoleon Duarte, a Christian Democrat, indicated that a democratic government free of both the communist insurgents and the right-wing death squads might be able to provide stable government to that long-suffering country. Finally, in Argentina, the Falklands War in the spring of 1982 demonstrated both how erratic military governments could be and the strength of long-suppressed democratic forces in that country.

To associate American interests with a transition to democracy in countries as different as Poland, Argentina, El Salvador, South Korea, South Africa, and the Philippines was therefore not a quixotic ambition. To see the political seriousness of constructive engagement as a framework for American policy, it can be contrasted to the ideas espoused at the time by Jeane Kirkpatrick, who for more than the first year of the Reagan administration was the leading conservative intellectual in Washington dealing with America's interest in promoting democracy abroad.

There is no question that Kirkpatrick was a committed democratic. Although she fell into the realist tradition by virtue of her skepticism that democracy was appropriate for all peoples, in her extensive writings one finds none of the gloomy reflections on democratic life that characterize the thinking of other realists, such as George Kennan, for example. Nor was her sense of how foreign affairs should be managed limited to cool appraisals of the balance of power and calculations of national security, such as characterizes Henry Kissinger's thinking. Instead, Kirkpatrick repeatedly asserts the importance of values guiding policy and the need to recall the preeminence of democracy as a system of government above all others.

Kirkpatrick's argument was essentially that of an FDR liberal: in those parts of the world where democracy had little immediate chance to take root and the communist danger was clear and present, America should be prepared to work with authoritarian regimes. Some of these partners might be unpleasant—she was particularly outspoken on the corrupt nature of the Somoza government in Nicaragua—but the fact that they were anticommunist and counted on American help, when America itself needed to prevent the expansion of Soviet influence, made it necessary to cooperate with them. To do otherwise courted disaster. Carter's policy was her negative example:

> Get rid of rightist dictators, support the democratic left, promote reform, preempt the radicals, build democracy and development: thus went the theory that gave us the Ayatollah Khomeini and the Ortega brothers. . . . good intentions and a mistaken theory produced results as destructive as they were unintended. Ideas have consequences, bad ideas have bad consequences.[50]

In Kirkpatrick's view, what Carter embodied was a naive projection of American values onto the world at large:

> Although most governments in the world are, as they always have been, autocracies of one kind or another, no idea holds greater sway in the mind of educated Americans than the belief that it is possible to democratize governments, anytime, anywhere, under any circumstances. This notion is belied by an enormous body of evidence.[51]

Wilsonians, Kirkpatrick believed, made typical and fateful errors:

> In the hope of strengthening a government [through liberalization] U.S. policymakers are led, mistake after mistake, to impose measures almost certain to weaken its authority. Hurried efforts to force complex and unfamiliar political practices on societies lacking the requisite political culture, tradition, and social structures not only fail to produce desired outcomes; if they are undertaken at a time when the traditional regime is under attack, they actually facilitate the job of the insurgents.[52]

More, as authoritarian rather than totalitarian regimes, Washington's partners might eventually reform and so come to embody the liberal values America favored:

> Generally speaking, traditional autocrats tolerate social inequities, brutality, and poverty, whereas revolutionary autocracies create them. Traditional autocrats leave in place existing allocations of wealth, power, status and other resources, which in most traditional societies favor an affluent few and maintain masses in poverty. But they worship traditional gods and observe traditional taboos. They do not disturb the habitual rhythms of work and leisure, habitual places of residence, habitual patterns of family and personal relations. . . .
>
> Precisely the opposite is true of revolutionary communist regimes. . . . the history of this century provides no grounds for expecting that radical totalitarian regimes will transform themselves. . . . Since many traditional autocracies permit limited contestation and participation, it is not impossible that U.S. policy could effectively encourage this process of liberalization and democratization, provided that the effort is not made at a time when the incumbent government is

fighting for its life against violent adversaries and that proposed reforms are aimed at producing gradual change rather than perfect democracy overnight.[53]

The immense popularity of Kirkpatrick's argument in Republican circles came from its cutting rhetorical style and its sharp refutation of Jimmy Carter's foreign policy. But as a general argument, it added nothing to the established American debate over the wisdom of promoting democracy abroad, and so could be criticized in traditional terms as well.

The flaw in Kirkpatrick's argument was its failure to specify how one correctly evaluates the prospects for democracy in a given country. She simply assumed democracy could not materialize, so that "realistically" Washington's range of choice was limited to helping authoritarian partners or allowing their totalitarian opponents to win. In effect, Kirkpatrick was projecting an argument current in the 1950s onto the 1980s, when events in short order were to make it hopelessly reactionary.

The first setbacks to the Kirkpatrick perspective were in Latin America, the area of the world she had professionally analyzed as an academic. Shortly after Reagan's inauguration, she visited the region, assuring leaders in Argentina and Chile that the Carter days were over. Washington would try to get Congress to approve economic and military aid packages, and closer collaboration could begin among the various capitals for the purpose of halting communist advances in the hemisphere.

Argentina had a special role to play in this new policy, for it would provide advisers to the contras the United States was training to bring pressure on the Sandinista government in Nicaragua. No longer would the military government in Buenos Aires be excoriated for its domestic abuses of human rights as it had been during Carter's time. Now it could expand its anticommunist mission from tracking down domestic subversives to uprooting them from the mountains of Central America.[54]

In the spring of 1982, however, Argentine leader General Leopoldo Galtieri engaged in a war with Great Britain with respect to sovereignty over the Falkland Islands. The Argentine forces were defeated and the military government collapsed shortly thereafter. By October 1983, a civilian government under Raul Alfonsin was in power, a regime none too favorably disposed to the rude treatment democratic forces in Argentina had suffered at the hands of Ambassador Kirkpatrick.

As in Argentina so in Chile: democratic forces felt abandoned by Washington during the days when Kirkpatrick's influence held sway. Here too the government of General Augusto Pinochet was reassured by her visit of August 1981. She proposed, "to normalize completely [American] relations with Chile." Arguing that Chile's record in human rights had improved since the late 1970s and that by contrast to other countries these violations were not too shocking, the Reagan administration began to lobby Congress to restore military and economic assistance. Chile's democratic movement got cold comfort from those who shared Kirkpatrick's view that in the mighty contest between East and West, centrist forces were to be disregarded. Shortly after her visit, Pinochet exiled human rights activists in the Christian Democratic party.[55]

By 1985 the mood had changed. Within Chile, democratic forces were showing more vigor. With the National Accord for Transition to Full Democracy signed by the leading political movements that August, the country's democratic leaders were beginning the difficult process of restoring Chile's historical commitment to democratic traditions.

By this time, Elliott Abrams had become assistant secretary of state for inter-American affairs, and Harry G. Barnes, Jr., had been named Ambassador to Chile—a combination favorable to Chilean redemocratization. From March 1986 to March 1988, the United States endorsed five UN resolutions critical of human rights in Chile and abstained on three others, while voting against only one.

Kirkpatrick was now out of office, but in her syndicated columns she maintained her illiberal positions. By 1986, her focus had changed to the Philippines, where she worried about the consequences of Marcos's fall from power.[56]

Kirkpatrick's approach was no more astute insofar as changes in the Soviet Union were concerned, for her analytical framework was certain to underestimate the pace and scope of change there. Anyone using her framework for analysis after 1985 would have badly misunderstood the character of events in Eastern Europe and the Soviet Union. Here especially, political reform was occurring much as constructive engagement anticipated: under the auspices of authoritarian rulers reassured by the United States of support in a difficult transition process (although it might be argued that it was not until the Bush presidency and the Malta summit of December 1989 that deliberate efforts to bolster the Gorbachev government concretely were first proposed by the Americans).

Kirkpatrick's views on the prospects for democracy in the third world were, then, fundamentally different from Crocker's call for "constructive engagement." Both insisted on the need to stop communist advances and both called for working with local governments to this end. But Crocker's position amounted to a serious effort to democratize the governments being supported, while Kirkpatrick's emphasis fell on how unrealistic, and at times dangerous, such efforts might be. Thus, Crocker, and the Reagan administration thereafter, identified the crux of the problem in southern Africa as apartheid, called for internal democratic reforms, and seemed prepared to accept Marxist-Leninist governments in Angola and Mozambique provided Cuban troops were removed from the region. How different this was from Kirkpatrick, who when asked why there were American sanctions against the Soviet Union but not against South Africa characteristically asserted, "Marxism is more dangerous than racism."[57]

DEMOCRACY AND THE FREE MARKET

One of the most effective tools adopted by the Reagan adminstration to further the "democratic revolution" is also one of the most difficult to evaluate precisely in terms of its impact abroad: the appeal for free-market economics. By getting the government out of the economy—by privatizing and deregulating business and by opening borders to the freer movement of goods and capital—the Reagan administration anticipated not just economic growth and general prosperity, but the strengthening of civil society and the emergence of democratic government as well.[58] The policy—sometimes called Reaganomics—was also important because, like constructive engagement, the United States could preach the virtues of democracy without being interventionist.

Of course, there had been attacks on government "taxing and spending" long before Reagan came into office. But the "supply side" economic theory that he advocated represented the most radical incarnation of such reasoning since Herbert Hoover had been turned out of office in 1932. The fact that it was complemented by economic thinking in Great Britain under Margaret Thatcher (who became prime minister in 1979), in Germany under Helmut Kohl (who became chancellor in 1982), in France under Francois Mitterrand (who as president radically redirected national economic policy in a liberal direction beginning in 1983), and in China (where Deng Xiaoping moved away from state control of the economy in the early 1980s) made Reagan's thinking all the more influential.

To communist countries, and in most of Latin America, Asia, and Africa, Reagan's message was clear: if they wanted prosperity, then they must introduce a free market, a necessary concomitant of which was political democracy. The populist utopianism of the rhetoric was old-time liberal religion as Reagan proselytized it:

Those who advocate statist solutions to development should take note: the free market is the other path to development and the one true path . . . where I believe we can find the map to the world's future: in the hearts of ordinary people, in their hopes for themselves and their children, in their prayers as they lay themselves and their families to rest each night. These simple people are the giants of the earth, the true builders of the world and shapers of the centuries to come. And if indeed they triumph, as I believe they will, we will at last know a world of peace and freedom, opportunity and hope, and, yes, of democracy—a world in which the spirit of mankind at last conquers the old familiar enemies of famine, disease, tyranny, and war. This is my vision—America's vision.[59]

Here is an important part of the answer to how a foreign policy as ideologically driven as Reagan's could at the same time be so restrained: namely, his belief that history was on the side of the democratic, free-market forces. America would lead, as the president once put it, by "example and persuasion."[60] Nothing interventionist was needed; others would follow or perish of their own foolishness. In the same tone, the president asserted his faith in an open international economic system: the World Bank, the International Monetary Fund, the General Agreement on Trade and Tariffs had managed an unprecedented increase in world trade, investment, and wealth through an emphasis on free-market practices that the rest of the world was well-advised to follow.

Again and again, the president and his secretary of state hammered away at the link between democracy and the free market. In the president's words:

It is the whole world where popular government might flourish and prosper. . . . Only a few years ago, this would have seemed the most outlandish and dreamiest of prospects. But consider for just a moment the striving for democracy that we have seen in places like the Philippines, Burma, Korea, Chile, Poland, South Africa—even places like China and the Soviet Union. . . . the democratic revolution has been accompanied by a change in economic thinking comparable to the Newtonian revolution in physics. . . .

These democratic and free-market revolutions are really the same revolution. They are based on the vital nexus between economic and political freedom. . . . government's attempt to encroach on that freedom—whether it be through political restrictions on the rights of assembly, speech, or publication or economic repression through high taxation and excessive bureaucracy—have been the principal institutional barrier to human progress.[61]

Accordingly, America could be a model and a magnet in virtually any foreign context. So in 1982 the White House announced its Caribbean Basin Initiative as an effort to improve prosperity in the Caribbean and Central America through free-market practices and improved access to American markets. Democracy would follow. As Shultz declared—distilling the experience of a life outside government spent as a professor of business and economics at MIT, Chicago, and Stanford—when he addressed the Organization of African Unity (OAU) in 1985: "The primacy accorded the state has hindered rather than furthered economic development."[62] With respect to South Africa, the president declared, "Capitalism is the natural enemy of such feudal institutions as apartheid."[63] In Mexico, he repeated:

History has demonstrated that time and again, in place after place, economic growth and human progress make their greatest strides in countries that encourage economic freedom. . . . this critical test is whether government is genuinely working to liberate individuals by creating incentives to work, invest, and succeed. Individual farmers, laborers, owners, and managers—they are the heart and soul of development. Trust them.[64]

So far as the communist world was concerned the same message rang true:

In an ironic sense Karl Marx was right. We are witnessing today a great revolutionary crisis, a crisis where the demands of the economic order are conflicting directly with those of the political order. But the crisis is happening not in the free, non-Marxist West, but in the home of Marxist-Leninism, the Soviet Union. It is the Soviet Union that runs against the tide of history by denying human freedom and human dignity to its citizens. It is also in deep economic difficulty. . . . the march of freedom and democracy . . . will leave Marxism-Leninism on the ash heap of history as it has left other tyrannies which stifle the freedom and muzzle the self-expression of the people.[65]

It is worth underscoring how automatic and natural the synergistic relationship between market forces and democracy seemed to the Reagan administration. Shultz was, if anything, even more emphatic on the political significance of the technological innovations of the 1970s and 1980s, explicitly linking them to the appeal "of the democratic idea" in the Philippines and Latin America. "There is a connection between freedom and economic progress," the secretary insisted:

This new information age has the potential to be *our* age—a period which plays to the great strengths of the West. The productivity and competitiveness of a nation will be far more dependent on how freely knowledge can be used and shared. . . . In this sort of environment, open societies such as our own will thrive; closed societies will fall behind.[66]

As the example of Chile demonstrates, the Reagan administration did understand that the relationship between the free market and democracy might not always be automatic. In the late 1970s, the so-called Chicago Boys (named after their education in liberal economics at the University of Chicago) oversaw a large-scale, free-market reordering of the Chilean economy. Rather than using this success to inaugurate a transition to a democratic order, the country's dictator, General Augusto Pinochet, cited their success as reason to stay in office. Washington nonetheless pushed for democratic government. In Abrams words in 1985, "U.S. Government policy toward Chile is straightforward and unequivocal: we support a transition to democracy." By 1987 Washington had become still more explicit, not only supporting the elections the following year (which ultimately turned Pinochet out), but specifying the kinds of civil liberties necessary to satisfy world opinion that democratic procedures were being observed there.[67]

As with many other cases, Washington's influence on Chile's transition to democracy was no more than marginal. Domestic forces and the activities of traditional Chilean institutions far better explain the course of events there. Nevertheless, the Reagan administration's liberal sympathies put it on the right side of history in a country sorely denied democracy by more than sixteen years of Pinochet's autocratic rule.

Of course, the most important question lies in the extent to which Mikhail Gorbachev rested his case for economic restructuring (*perestroika*) and a political opening (*glasnost*) on the kind of reasoning Reagan and Shultz articulated. By the mid-1980s, not only were the West Europeans in the midst of their own economic reforms, but China had also embarked quite successfully on an ambitious program of economic restructuring. All indicators showed that the Soviet Union was lagging far behind. Under the pressures of a renewed arms race after Reagan took office, Moscow began to contemplate the need for deep structural reforms in order to meet the challenge.[68]

Clearly, Gorbachev initially hoped to reinvigorate Communist party rule at home, not end it, when he introduced his package of reforms intended to modernize the Soviet Union economically. Apparently, he felt secure in the strength the Soviet Union had militarily and was willing to risk reform in Eastern Europe in a bid for better relations with the West, which in turn should help Soviet economic restructuring. Yet Gorbachev was compelled by the forces he unleashed with these economic changes to make political concessions of such magnitude that by 1989 the Soviet empire was lost; by 1991, the country itself had disintegrated.

The extent to which Reaganomics paved the way for these developments is impossible to specify exactly. On the one hand, Poland and the Czech Republic were obviously ready for democracy with or without the introduction of market economies. On the other, market forces have created problems in Eastern Europe and the former Soviet Union that have imperiled the consolidation of democratic governments there. Most importantly, it was not so much Gorbachev's economic reforms themselves that need to be understood, as it is their dramatic political consequences in international as well as domestic Soviet affairs as a rigid one-party system met an upsurge of repressed nationalist sentiment. Nonetheless, political reform in the Soviet empire was begun on the basis of calculations in Moscow designed to increase the economic strength of the Soviet Union, and it is apparent that the general tenor of these changes corresponded to the wave of economic opening endorsed by Reaganomics.

In sum, the antistatist, free-market economic doctrines espoused by the Reagan administration left a deep mark on the transitions to democracy in the 1980s. Such a conclusion does not require insisting that these ideas were an American monopoly, or even that they were necessarily as enlightened as they thought themselves to be. Yet here is an instance of a set of ideas on the proper economic organization unleashing profound political changes internationally as well as domestically, and in the process contributing directly and powerfully to democracy worldwide.

DEMOCRACY AND ECONOMIC LIBERALISM RECONSIDERED

It might plausibly be argued that the Reagan administration was mistaken to believe in a necessary correspondence between a reliance on free-market economics (embodied in deregulation, privatization, and open borders) and democracy. As Pinochet's experience showed in Chile, market forces could enrich a country without that amounting to an argument for democracy. In fact, where deregulation concentrates wealth, it might undermine democracy by polarizing political struggles. As governments practice the budgetary austerity mandated by supply-side thinking, social welfare programs are reduced and the poor suffer. The result can be the kind of outburst witnessed in Venezuela in February 1992, when popular passions against a government that failed to meet its social obligations triggered riots and an attempted military coup. Similarly, the "shock therapy" delivered to the Soviet Union after 1991 (so it might be argued) produced a voter backlash against Boris Yeltsin in the national parliamentary elections in Russia held in December 1993. But most fundamentally, one may question the foundation belief of free-market thinking—that antistatism is truly the best way to insure economic growth. There is abundant evidence from East Asia that a mix of market competition and government incentives to invest provides for a more dynamic economy than market forces left to their own devices. In short, it is not self-evident that to practice laissez-faire capitalism is the always the best, much less the only, way to encourage democracy.

The issues raised by these criticisms of the political impact of deregulation, privatization, and economic opening are difficult to evaluate in the abstract; we need a greater literature than now exists that comparatively analyzes concrete cases to see when and how opening a market facilitates or discourages democracy. Nevertheless, it does seem evident that in communist countries and third world lands like Kenya, Mexico, and the Dominican Republic, the state's ownership of corporations and its control of licensing monopolies and marketing boards has manifestly served as a means of personal enrichment and political patronage, which in turn has inhibited democratization. To reduce the role of government in these economies is indeed to empower civil society and so potentially to further democracy—provided, of course, that the standard of living does not fall dramatically for a substantial portion of the population so that they are driven to some new authoritarian solution in their desperation, as was witnessed in Russia at the end of 1993.

The problem is to distinguish between those times, places, and policies where antistatism fosters democracy and those where it impedes the popular control of government by concentrating wealth or by driving the desperate population into the hands of authoritarians. Surely by suggesting it was a universal remedy regardless of time or place, the Reagan administration exaggerated the extent to which adopting free-market practices would contribute to a country's democratization. In the United States during the Reagan years, for example, the richest 1 percent of the population so increased its share of the total net worth of the country from 31 percent to 37 percent, while the share of the poorest 90 percent slipped from 33 percent to 32 percent. It did not appear to be the case, as Reagan would have it, that "a rising tide lifts all ships." At the same time, the obstacles to addressing poverty compounded as programs to help the urban poor were cut with the blessing of another of the president's favorite sayings: "Government does not solve problems, it merely subsidizes them." Such a growing concentration of wealth, alongside increasing unemployment and poverty, underlay a deepening class and ethnic division in this country that could not be favorable for democratic stability.[69] One may debate the consequences of Thatcherism in Britain in these terms as well.

Nevertheless, whatever the problems facing Reagan's particular rendition of the proper form of a market economy, it was an undeniably liberal program of a vintage that predates the New Deal. Since the nineteenth century, liberalism has been associated with the market; indeed, the strongest economic variable predicting democratic government is the existence of a market economy.[70] The debate, then, is over variants of market orientation: how much state intervention in the economy is called for if democracy is to flourish?

Trends in economic thinking, when combined with concrete measures of reform, may have powerful political consequences. Just as the New Deal stabilized American democracy, so antistatist economic policies in some parts of the world (most notably in Latin America since the 1980s) may today encourage democratic governments by empowering various sectors of civil society. Given the range of circumstances to which such intricate experimentation may apply, however, it is prudent to be wary of grand generalizations. That said, the impact on antistatist economic thinking appears to have been profound on Soviet conduct as also in Latin America. It appears that one of the most powerful impetuses to democratization in the late 1980s was a form of economic argument that, while not unique to the United States, was articulated with special force by the Reagan administration.

THE REAGAN DOCTRINE

If any element of Reagan's foreign policy has been critically debated with respect to the promotion of democracy worldwide, it is the gambit of activities to support "freedom fighters" against communist regimes that became known as the Reagan Doctrine. Nothing more provoked Reagan's opposition than the notion that guerrilla forces bent on overthrowing communist regimes deserved to be seen, as the president once put it, as "the moral equivalent of the Founding Fathers."

The Reagan Doctrine was born late in 1981 with presidential approval to fund insurgents—the counterrevolutionaries or "contras"—against the Sandinista regime in Nicaragua. Eventually the Doctrine sanctioned funding for anticommunist insurgents in Cambodia, Angola, and Afghanistan (and perhaps other countries yet to be documented). Clandestine efforts to aid Solidarity in Poland through collaboration with the Vatican might be included in the same policy package, although here the use of force was ruled out.[71]

The relevance of the doctrine to traditional democratic liberalism was not immediately apparent; its principal purpose was to repeal the Brezhnev Doctrine, according to which Moscow had held, since the 1968 invasion of Czechoslovakia, that no country that became communist would ever leave the fold, even if it required Soviet military intervention to prevent such a development. Benefitting since the 1940s from the ability to select when, where, and how to move forward thanks to the tactics of guerrilla warfare, international communism had made noticeable gains. More recently, having gained nuclear parity with the United States and emboldened by Castro's successes, Moscow seemed to turn with renewed interest to the support of "wars of national liberation."[72]

Thanks to independent Cuban efforts, Moscow had growing influence in the horn of Africa and southern Africa after 1976, and in Central America after 1979. Its invasion of Afghanistan in December 1979 threatened to project Soviet power into the Middle East, where enormous petroleum reserves were of fundamental importance to the West and Japan. Finally, Moscow was enjoying a more privileged position in Southeast Asia, where by the late 1970s, it occupied bases originally opened by the United States in Vietnam, now a Soviet dependent with control over Laos and Cambodia.[73] Were this not bad enough, the balance sheet showed an important decline in American influence, as regimes friendly to the United States fell in Nicaragua and Iran in 1979. As the president noted in a nationally televised speech:

Guatemala, Honduras, El Salvador, and Costa Rica are all friendly and democratic. In their midst, however, lies a threat that could reverse the democratic tide and plunge the region into a cycle of chaos and subversion. That is the communist regime in Nicaragua called the Sandinistas, a regime whose allies range from communist dictator Fidel Castro of Cuba to terrorist-supporter Qadhafi of Libya. But their most important ally is the Soviet Union. With Cuban and Soviet-bloc aid, Nicaragua is being transformed into a beachhead of aggression against the United States. It is the first step in a strategy to dominate the entire region of Central America and threaten Mexico and the United States. That's why the cause of freedom in Central America is united with our national security. That is why the safety of democracy to our south so directly affects the safety of our own nation.[74]

Given the American arms buildup of the 1980s following the administration's sense of clear and present danger, its actual military interventions were relatively limited. In October 1983, American forces invaded the tiny island of Grenada, with a mission not only to remove the New Jewel communist government in power there, but to restore democracy to the country as well. In April 1986 Libya was bombed in retaliation for acts of Libyan state terrorism. Otherwise, the United States exerted much more restraint than many observers at the time expected.

The restraint reflected four concerns. The first was a reluctance to get involved in another quagmire reminiscent of Vietnam.[75] The second was domestic opinion, especially the fear of strong congressional opposition to direct American action in Central America. A third restraint was international opinion. Most West European capitals felt Washington was exaggerating the Sandinista threat, and as for Latin Americans, "It's the gringo problem: they don't want us down there," CIA Director William Casey acknowledged.[76]

Yet the chief explanation for American caution was the existence of freedom fighters, who could be used to roll back communism abroad without high-risk intervention by American forces. The administration was under no illusion that all the forces it proposed to back were democratic: neither Jonas Savimbi and his UNITA in Angola, nor the mujaheddin guerrillas in Afghanistan could pass muster in this respect. But in the words of Elliott Abrams:

> In the real world the choice is frequently not between good and bad but between bad and worse or, perhaps more accurately, bad but improvable or worse and permanent. . . . What this means is that the United States is at times reluctantly compelled to support regimes which abuse human rights, because we think that their replacements would be much worse for the cause of human rights, and because we think that American (and other) pressure can greatly improve these regimes over time.[77]

In short, freedom fighters who were not democrats could still be nationalists, and the United States would support their quest for national self-determination, an appeal that had mattered greatly to liberals of Wilson's era (and, indeed, could be traced back to the Monroe Doctrine). In clear Wilsonian terms, Secretary Shultz recognized the problem the Soviet Union was having with rebellious nationalist forces under its control:

> Peoples on every continent are insisting on their right to national independence and their right to choose their government free of coercion. The Soviets overreached in the 1970s. . . . In the 1980s, the Soviets and their clients are finding it difficult to consolidate these gains . . . mainly because of the courageous forces of indigenous resistance. Growing resistance movements now challenge communist regimes installed or maintained by the military power of the Soviet Union and its colonial agents—in Afghanistan, Angola, Cambodia, Ethiopia, and Nicaragua. We did not create this historical phenomenon, but we must not fail to respond to it.[78]

Eastern Europe, and especially Poland, was the most important seed ground for Reagan's conviction that the Wilsonian calls for democracy and self-determination could win out in the struggle with communism for the loyalty of nationalist passions. Since the beginning of his presidency, Reagan had supported the cause of Solidarity (the workers' and intellectuals' movement) and democracy in Poland, increasing American pressure late in 1981, when martial law was declared there by government of General Wojciech Jaruzelski.

As with earlier administrations, the United States made it clear it would not intervene militarily in Poland. In Secretary Shultz's words:

> In the final analysis, internal forces must be the major factors for democratization of communist states. Only the people of those countries can muster sufficient pressures for reform. Only they can seize opportunities to determine their own destinies. We do not seek to foment violent unrest or to undermine communist regimes.[79]

At the same time, Washington slapped sanctions on Warsaw, then on Moscow for dictating Jaruzelksi's program. An underground connection working through the Vatican and the Polish Church developed, putting Washington in touch with Solidarity. In 1982 the practice (begun in 1959) of remembering the "captive nations" was reestablished in emotional ceremonies in Washington, where the sixtieth anniversary of American recognition of the independence of the Baltic states was remembered and Solidarity saluted.[80] Even if the administration's effort to block the Soviet gas pipeline to Western Europe in retaliation for Moscow's crackdown was generally viewed as ill-conceived, there could be no doubt but that Reagan intended to give no quarter short of war in his opposition to the Soviet clampdown in Eastern Europe. "The current struggle and travails of the people of Poland are of truly historic import to the entire world," the president declared, and there is no reason to doubt he meant it.[81]

The most contentious arguments surrounding the Reagan Doctrine apply to Nicaragua. The Sandinistas were trying to export revolution to the rest of Central America and so seemed a direct threat to national security, justifying the expenditure of billions in counterinsurgency funds in the region and involving the death of perhaps 250,000 people, most of them peasants caught in the crossfire in Nicaragua, El Salvador, and Guatemala.

Washington's first goal was simply to contain Nicaragua—to end its ambition to promote insurgencies among its neighbors. But the goal soon expanded to include a demand that the government in Managua respect its 1979 pledges to hold free elections and become a democracy. To support its demands, Washington funded a band of what eventually was more than ten thousand contras—officially known as the Nicaraguan Democratic Resistance—to interdict arms exports from Nicaragua as well as to punish the Sandinista regime by destabilizing the country economically. At the same time, the Reagan Doctrine underwrote counterinsurgency efforts in El Salvador and Guatemala, which cost billions of dollars and took tens of thousands of lives.

Two major debates swirled around the contras: might they involve the United States in a ground war reminiscent of Vietnam, and could the future of democracy in the region justifiably be said to rest on their shoulders? On the first issue, the administration's position was unequivocal: short of specific belligerent acts by Nicaragua (such as the delivery of offensive aircraft incorrectly rumored to have been delivered by Moscow in November 1984), Washington had no intention of being drawn into a direct intervention in Central America. True, the White House rejected any analogies between Vietnam and Central America, insisting that, as in Grenada, it would win if it were obliged to act. But the administration's actual reluctance to get involved militarily was greater than its critics at the time recognized.

A more complicated debate was over the democratizing credentials of the contras. Could they credibly be thought to be harbingers of democracy in Nicaragua, either by the indispensable pressure they could bring to bear on the Sandinistas to live up to their promises to hold free elections, or by their own victory? Were they in fact at all as the president described them in a notable speech in 1985?

> They are our brothers, these freedom fighters, and we owe them our help. . . . You know the truth about them. You know who they're fighting and why. They are the moral equal of our Founding Fathers and the brave men and women of the French Resistance. We cannot turn away from them, for the struggle here is not right versus left; it is right versus wrong.[82]

To make its case, the administration had first to defend the contras from charges that they were for the most part former Somoza National Guardsmen who now spent a good deal of time running drugs. At the same time, Washington had to counter arguments that the shortcomings on democratic procedure in Nicaragua stemmed more from the state of siege the country was under thanks to the contras' attacks than from the intrinsic character of Sandinista rule. As one might expect, the White House was adamant on both counts, insisting that the National Guard was not preponderant in the Nicaraguan Democratic Force (FDN), and that whatever the momentary tactical concessions the Sandinistas might make, it was their nature as communists to be antidemocratic, as their repeated crackdowns at home demonstrated.[83]

Divisive as these two debates were, they were eventually preempted by yet a third controversy, one surrounding revelations in 1986 that a group of officials in the White House had arranged to fund the contras through covert, illegal means, including the sale of arms to Iran—in a way and to a degree that conceivably threatened the functioning of democratic government in the United States itself. As still later information revealed, the president and his closest advisers (including in all probability George Bush) knowingly and repeatedly overstepped the constitutional limitations on their power. The result, the Iran-contra scandal, was as great a challenge to the constitutional system of checks and balances as the United States has known in this century. And like McCarthyism in the early 1950s, the irony was that the threat to democratic government came in the name of defending democracy.[84]

Ultimately, the administration could claim that the Reagan Doctrine directly aided the expansion of democracy in Central America, by forcing the Sandinistas to hold elections in early 1990, which they lost. Moreover, by raising the costs of foreign intervention to the Soviet Union, in Afghanistan especially, the Reagan Doctrine pushed Moscow to reform by making it aware of its weaknesses. Because these reforms ultimately led to the disintegration of the Soviet empire, the Reagan Doctrine might claim a role in indirectly aiding nationalist and democratic forces throughout Eastern Europe.

THE REAGAN DOCTRINE RECONSIDERED

Arguments over the moral and practical justification of the Reagan Doctrine resolve themselves into the classic debate over means and ends. First, the end may be debated: was keeping El Salvador and Guatemala (the countries in the region most threatened by communist insurgencies after the Sandinista victory in Nicaragua in 1979) under the control of pro-American governments genuinely a critical security concern of the United States? As in Vietnam, so in this part of Central America, it might be argued, American security interests were simply not vital enough to justify involvement in a conflict in this region that took some 250,000 lives between 1981 and 1992, many if not most of them the casualties of brutal right-wing armies and some the victims of atrocities deliberately committed to intimidate the population by soldiers trained by American advisers.[85] Similarly, the deadly civil war in Afghanistan, which went on for years after the Soviet departure, might have been avoided had there been a more orderly transfer of power there. The Reagan Doctrine concentrated on the periphery of world politics. The cold war was settled where it began: in Europe, between Moscow and Washington. For tens of thousands of Latin American poor to die in this struggle, for civil disorder to become endemic in Afghanistan, was unjustified.

Second, the means adopted by Washington can be disputed. Neither backing thugs like the contras nor subverting the Constitution of the United States were necessary means to bringing democracy to Central America. Yes, there were free elections in Nicaragua in February 1990, and the candidate of the United Opposition (UNO), Violeta Chamorro, became president. Yes, a peace accord promising democracy was finally signed early in 1992 in El Salvador between the rebels and the government, while the reversal of the coup in Guatemala launched in May 1993 indicates healthy support for constitutional government there. But it was the efforts of local peacemakers like Costa Rican President Oscar Arias and the Guatemalan human rights activist Rigoberta Menchu (both winners of the Nobel Peace Prize) and the end of the cold war that brought peace and the promise of democracy to Central America, not the contras and their high-handed backers in Washington.

In their defense, supporters of the Reagan Doctrine claim that military action against communist forces in Central America must be understood in the context of its times. Cuban-backed movements had been on the rise since the mid-1970s, and here was the appropriate place to draw the line. By the time of Reagan's inauguration, about $100 million in American financial assistance had reached Managua, but the Sandinistas would not honor their pledges to introduce democracy or to leave their neighbors alone. To have failed to act would have been to lose much of the region to communism, so emboldening Moscow and discouraging our allies.

More, the Reagan Doctrine worked. Moscow was forced to evacuate Afghanistan by early 1989, a decision that stimulated first the economic, then the political, reform efforts in the Soviet Union even more by laying bare the need for change. The doctrine also contributed handily to election victory of Violeta Chamorro in February 1990 and to the strength of the democratization process in El Salvador and Guatemala thereafter, for what reason is there to think that the Sandinista government would have held elections had it not been to try to bring peace to the land? Doctrine supporters might cite the moral weight of deposed Haitian President Aristide's appeal that something like the contras be used to restore democracy in Haiti. On a visit to the United States in April 1992, Aristide implicitly criticized the relative passivity of the Bush administration when he declared, "We need you to fight with us in the same way we saw Americans fight in Nicaragua."[86] Presumably, many Nicaraguans would agree with him. Most importantly, by standing firm in Central America and causing so many problems for the Soviets in Afghanistan, Reagan signaled his determination to Moscow to be firm elsewhere, thereby lending credibility to his policy in Europe. In short, so its defenders could maintain, the doctrine contributed directly to the end of the cold war.[87]

From the perspective of a time still close to these events, it would appear that the Reagan Doctrine did indeed serve the end of bringing about democracy in Central America and ending the cold war (although this is not to justify many brutal aspects of the policy that appear to have been unnecessary). Certainly the use of force did not disqualify the Reagan Doctrine as an instrument of liberal democratic internationalism. Nor was the administration cynical about its support for democracy. In August 1987, when the United States gave its conditional approval to the peace agreement proposed by five Central American presidents, the provisions to ensure the democratization of Nicaragua were uppermost in Washington's thinking. Only later did Washington begin to worry about the distinct possibility that the Sandinistas might win the elections that were finally held in February 1990, after Bush had become president. Secretary Shultz's faith in 1987 was more simple: "The democratization provisions alone are, simply put, incompatible with a communist dictatorship . . . for no democratic government in Nicaragua would attack its neighbors or allow its territory to be used militarily by the Soviet Union."[88]

In keeping with his convictions, Shultz saw the triumph of democracy in Nicaragua as something of a panacea not only in Central America but throughout the continent. As he put it before the Organization of American States:

> Internal conflicts threaten to spill over borders, so each state should be encouraged to create processes by which internal adversaries can be reconciled, human rights respected, and political competition substituted for violent confrontation. Reconciliation leads to that fundamental value, democracy. We all know that in the end there is no enduring stability and legitimacy without it. We also know that democracies are far less likely to go to war than governments whose leaders need not obtain the consent of the people.[89]

So far as we now know, there was never a case of CIA intervention against a democratic government during the Reagan years. To the contrary, there was a steady drum beat of concern that democracy be promoted as the antidote to a variety of problems in a series of countries as varied as during the Carter years, and the refusal to countenance coups even when they would have been directed against leaders Washington disliked (as in 1988, when the Peruvian military aiming to oust President Alan Garcia sounded out Washington for its reaction).[90] Whether as a direct aid to democracy, as in Central America, or as an indirect aid through helping to undermine the Soviet empire, as in Afghanistan, the Reagan Doctrine appears to have been duly Wilsonian.

Conclusion

The main purpose of this chapter has been to establish the bona fides of Reagan's liberal democratic internationalism. On this score there should be no doubt. No administration since Wilson's has been as vigorous or as consistent in its dedication to the promotion of democracy abroad as that of Ronald Reagan. One may debate the effectiveness of constructive engagement, the morality of the Reagan Doctrine, the prudence of America's arms buildup, or the wisdom of aspects of Reagan's call for economic deregulation and privatization. What these debates cannot obscure is this administration's unparalleled Wilsonianism in its commitment to the promotion of democracy worldwide.

However, the fundamental question to be asked of Reagan's policy is today impossible to answer with any finality: how much did its initiatives actually matter to the gathering wave of democracy around the globe during the decade of the 1980s? The question is difficult because we are still so close to this momentous period. Time is needed to evaluate more fully the logic of these years—time for more evidence of what transpired in the 1980s to become available and especially time for the consequences of developments set in motion then more fully to reveal themselves so that we can better judge the past.

Nevertheless, the question of how to understand the collapse of Soviet communism and the succeeding prestige of democratic governance worldwide can be divided into three levels of analysis: the contribution of the Reagan administration's policies; the contribution of American impact on world affairs over the half century preceding the fall of the Berlin Wall; the contribution of global processes independent of American policy.

At the level of an analysis of the Reagan years, it would appear that, in conjunction with the Reagan administration's position on the fundamental issue of the arms control, the policies of constructive engagement (including relations with Moscow after 1985), of calling for a market economic system, and of force applied on Soviet clients at the periphery known as the Reagan Doctrine all moved the Soviet Union toward reform. A problem is to establish the relative importance of different policies of this administration. Presumably, for example, aid under the Reagan Doctrine to the Afghan resistance or Solidarity had more effect on Moscow than did aid to the contras in Central America, while the doctrine's effect on democracy may have been greater in Central America than in Afghanistan or Angola.

These considerations notwithstanding, the synergy of the various policies combined produced a greater effect than a simple sum of the parts. Thus, Moscow was put on notice by Washington's arms buildup and the Reagan Doctrine of the United States' competitive posture in world affairs, so heightening the Soviet sense of a need for economic reform, while Moscow was told in the language of antistatist economics and through the constructive engagement of bilateral talks beginning in Geneva in 1985 that the United States welcomed Soviet reform and would not exploit a difficult transition process for unilateral advantage. Without claiming that the Reagan administration ran no risks or made no mistakes, or that another less costly set of policies altogether might not have yielded similar results, the mark of this presidency on the upsurge of democracy worldwide in the 1980s seems undeniable.[91]

But a second level of analysis cautions against focusing overly on this decade and suggests that it is rather American policy since the 1940s that won the cold war. For example, if Latin American democratization beginning in the late 1970s seems to have reflected, on the one hand, that region's internal socioeconomic development and, on the other, its reaction to the experiences of Spain and Portugal with the European Community, the United States may nonetheless be seen as an important agent of change. For it was in the 1940s that Washington inaugurated an open international economic system and the process of European integration, developments that by the late 1970s were coming to have a substantial positive impact on the democratization of Latin America. To limit an investigation of American influence on Latin American democratization to the Carter and Reagan years would be to miss the most critical features (even if largely indirect) of America's role in the domestic affairs of its southern neighbors.

Similarly, much more needs to be known about the forces lying behind the collapse of Soviet communism. The primary agent of change was obviously Gorbachev, whose extraordinary policies must be considered in their own right. Moreover, as events unrolled there, it was the structure of the Communist party and the inability of the Soviet authorities to control nationalist opposition to their rule that proved Moscow's undoing (and not American policy).[92] But if we ask to what extent Gorbachev's effort to reform was a reaction to the Reagan challenge, to what extent it was a response to over four decades of competition that seemed to be turning to the West's advantage, the argument is persuasive that it was the liberal democratic United States, considered globally and as the work of fifty years and more, that triumphed in 1989. This consideration is important, for if it is the entire thrust of American power in the world over the preceding half century and more that explains the victory of the democracies in the 1980s, then a different Reagan administration (one less brutal than with the contras, more progressive than with constructive engagement, less confrontational militarily with the Soviet Union, and less bent on antistatist economic practices) would presumably also have won the cold war, perhaps at less risk and cost.

A third level of analysis cautions against exaggerating the American role in the collapse of Moscow's power in 1989–91 and the concurrent upsurge of democratic forces worldwide. It doubts the extent to which the United States was at the origin (or the center) of international trends favoring democratic government over the preceding half century, and it indicates that modesty is in order.

For example, by championing the self-determination of peoples since the early nineteenth century, but especially after World War I, for its own national security interests, the United States was putting itself on the right side of history by giving concrete aid to the nationalist forces which pulled apart the Austro-Hungarian, Ottoman, Russian, and West European colonial empires after 1918 (just as it had tried to preserve Latin American and Chinese independence in the nineteenth century with the Monroe Doctrine and the Open Door Notes respectively). But it would be an absurd exaggeration to say that the power of nationalism in world affairs over the last century and more was a product of American (or Anglo-American) international hegemony rather than the consequence of global political forces stemming from seemingly universal processes of change with roots in the eighteenth century, forces that in fact gave birth to the United States itself. Certainly the nationalist challenges bedeviling Moscow from all sides by the 1980s represented historical forces that the United States could influence only marginally.

Similarly, the kind of world economic order the United States established after World War II reflected not simply American power, but the interests of economic actors around the world, especially those in Western Europe, Canada, and Japan. Indeed, ultimately it may be argued that it was these classes and countries, even more than the United States, which benefited from the period of American international hegemony.[93] And they played their part in the conduct of the cold war, especially in their relative openness to working with Moscow, whether under Charles de Gaulle's inspiration from 1963 to 1968, or under the terms of Ostpolitik developed by Willy Brandt's Social Democratic party in Bonn in 1969, or again in their steadfastness to the Atlantic Alliance demonstrated with the decision to permit the deployment of Pershing and Cruise intermediate-range nuclear missiles in 1963. Hence the strength of democratic peoples at the end of the cold war should perhaps be best understood as reflecting global processes of economic, social, and political change rather than as a development reflective of American (and previously British) interest and power internationally.

Cogent as the argument of the third level of analysis may be, it is nonetheless important to insist upon the distinctive American contribution to the success of democratic government at the end of the twentieth century. For it was the United States that had the capacity to organize a winning coalition of economic and nationalist forces in the second half of the century, giving them indispensable military strength and political direction. Without ignoring the serious errors in American policy—as toward Guatemala and Iran in the 1950s or toward Vietnam in the 1960s—or denying the importance of global forces of economic development and nationalist self-consciousness that Washington could only hope to channel rather than to control, the case for assigning a preeminent importance to the United States in explaining the strength and prestige of democratic governments at the end of the century is compelling.

Let us then suggest that the American role in the spread of democracy worldwide in the late twentieth century was a necessary, but far from sufficient, cause for the current strength of democratic government. Let us suggest further that the appropriate level of analysis for the events of the late 1980s and early 1990s is not the decade of the 1980s so much as the preceding half century and more, and this for an understanding of the impact of American foreign policy as well as for an appreciation of the development of other international political forces.

To conclude in this manner is not to doubt the importance of the Reagan years. In fact such a conclusion might not surprise Reagan or Shultz. Their conviction was that communism was fated for oblivion by virtue of its own failed economic, political, and moral tenets. In these circumstances, Washington was riding (rather than creating) what these two men often referred to as a "tide of history." At the end of his eight years in office, Reagan offered a balanced assessment of his place in America's history and America's place in world affairs:

> Once you begin a great movement, there's no telling where it will end. We meant to change a nation, and instead, we changed a world. Countries across the globe are turning to free markets and free speech and turning away from the ideologies of the past. For them, the great rediscovery of the 1980s has been that, lo and behold, the moral way of government is the practical way of government: democracy, the profoundly good, is also the profoundly productive.[94]

PART V

Toward the Year 2000

CHAPTER ELEVEN

After the Cold War: Wilsonianism Resurgent?

History's lesson is clear. When a war-weary America withdrew from the international stage following World War I, the world spawned militarism, fascism, and aggression unchecked, plunging mankind into another devastating conflict. But in answering the call to lead after World War II, we built from the principles of democracy and the rule of law a new community of free nations, a community whose strength, perseverance, patience, and unity of purpose contained Soviet totalitarianism and kept the peace.

No society, no continent should be disqualified from sharing the ideals of human liberty. The community of democratic nations is more robust than ever, and it will gain strength as it grows. . . . abandonment of the worldwide democratic revolution could be disastrous for American security.

History is summoning us once again to lead.
—George Bush, December 15, 1992

In a new era of peril and opportunity, our overriding purpose must be to expand and strengthen the world's community of market-based democracies. During the Cold War, we fought to contain a threat to the survival of free institutions. Now we seek to enlarge the circle of nations that live under those free institutions, for our dream is that of a day when the opinions and energies of every person in the world will be given full expression in a world of thriving democracies that cooperate with each other and live in peace.
—Bill Clinton, September 27, 1993

GEORGE BUSH BECAME PRESIDENT at a watershed moment in twentieth-century history. Like 1918 and 1945, 1989 was a year when the old great-power order had collapsed and the United States stood preeminent in world affairs. At the conclusion of World War I, Woodrow Wilson had held forth a vision of American national security protected by a peaceful community of democratic nations, engaged in nondiscriminatory trade, and associated to resolve their conflicts in a covenant of collective security called the League of Nations. He presumed that the peace of the world depended on peace in Europe, which in turn depended on democracy in Germany, Franco-German rapprochement, stability in Eastern Europe based on the principle of national self-determination, and American leadership of the emerging new order.

At the conclusion of World War II, Franklin Roosevelt and then Harry Truman tried to promote an updated version of Wilsonianism. While relations with the Soviet Union were of fundamental importance, their proposals centered on the United Nations, on a set of accords creating the foundations for managing the world economy reached at Bretton Woods, on the democratization of Japan, Germany, and Eastern Europe, on European decolonization, and on a commitment to American leadership in world affairs. Once again, stability in Europe was seen as the centerpiece of world peace, although Washington understood that in the future the Far East would also weigh heavily in the balance.

George Bush took office as the Soviet empire in Eastern Europe was breaking up and Moscow was looking for a new framework of understanding with the West. How would he approach the question of establishing a world order favorable to the national security at this third moment of American supremacy, when, indeed, the military, economic, cultural, and political preeminence of the United States was greater than it had ever been in international affairs?

THE END OF THE COLD WAR AND A "NEW WORLD ORDER"

President Bush's response to the challenge of world leadership was appropriately Wilsonian. Given the legacy of the Reagan years and that of Wilson and Roosevelt before him at other watershed moments, how indeed could it have been otherwise? Approaches critical of liberalism in the conduct of world affairs were mooted, and deep disagreement might exist as to where and how to operationalize various aspects of its agenda. But to the extent the United States had an established doctrine in foreign policy, one that linked the definition of its national security to a particular structure of international relations, it was liberal democratic internationalism.

In the opinion of most analysts, Bush differed from Ronald Reagan by being less ideological and more pragmatic or opportunistic—a difference summed up when Bush confessed that he did not possess "the vision thing." Nevertheless, he had been vice president in an administration that had circled Jericho for eight full years trumpeting the virtues of democracy, and once the walls of the adversary had fallen, no other reliable formula seemingly existed for policymakers to help chart American policy in what was now a very different world.

Bush's rhetoric was akin to that of the Reagan years, but the substance of his policies had its intellectual provenance in ideas set in place by Wilson three quarters of a century earlier. As Bush put it in his Inaugural Address:

Great nations of the world are moving toward democracy through the door of freedom. Men and women of the world move toward free markets through the door to prosperity. The people of the world agitate for free expression and free thought through the door to the moral and intellectual satisfactions that only liberty allows. We know what works: freedom works. We know what's right: freedom is right. We know how to secure a more just and prosperous life for man on earth: through free markets, free speech, free elections, and the exercise of free will unhampered by the state.

America is never wholly herself unless she engages in high moral principle. We as a people have such a purpose today, to make kinder the face of the nation and gentler the face of the world.[1]

In implementing his program, Bush was assisted by Secretary of State James Baker, a man as close personally and philosophically to the president as any secretary had ever been in American history. While Baker was a consummate pragmatist and displayed enormous gifts as a diplomatic negotiator, he also declared himself to be a committed liberal democratic internationalist. As he put it at his Senate confirmation hearings early in 1989, "the only sure guide" for American foreign policy was "the compass of American ideals and values—freedom, democracy, equal rights, respect for human dignity, fair play—the principles to which I adhere:

I believe in freedom for the individual because it's a God-given right and the source of human creativity. The Founders of our country recognized that such freedom was preserved best by limited government—the checks and balances system that still provides the framework for our success. . . . economic freedom, the free market system, is an essential part of the framework. Finally and above all, I believe, like Lincoln, that the United States has a special role in this world, a special contribution to make—as he put it, "the last, best hope of earth."[2]

In 1989–90 the administration's principal concern was how to deal with the collapse of the Soviet empire in Eastern Europe; by the fall of 1991, it was how to respond to the disintegration of the Soviet Union itself. At first the administration seemed to hesitate, unsure how far to trust Mikhail Gorbachev. But by May 1989 Bush had been convinced in discussions with leaders of Solidarity and other democratic movements in Eastern Europe, as well as with West Europeans like Margaret Thatcher, Helmut Kohl, and Jacques Delors, that Gorbachev's "new thinking" for Eastern Europe constituted a genuine basis on which to end the cold war on terms long espoused by the West.[3]

Thanks to the terms of the Soviet leader's new thinking, the United States felt it might participate in the conversion of the Soviet Union and its East European empire to Western-style constitutional government. Late in 1989 the Congress passed the Support for East European Democracy

(SEED) Act, tying funds for Eastern Europe to explicit promotion of democracy.

> The President should ensure that the assistance provided to Eastern European countries pursuant to this Act is designed 1) to contribute to the development of democratic institutions and pluralism characterized by: a) the establishment of fully democratic and representative political systems based on free and fair elections; b) effective recognition of fundamental liberties and individual freedoms, including freedom of speech, religion, and association; c) termination of all laws and regulations which impede the operation of a free press and the formation of political parties; d) creation of an independent judiciary; and e) establishment of non-partisan military, security, and police forces.[4]

Strong in these convictions, Secretary Baker addressed a committee of the Supreme Soviet in Moscow in early 1990. Asserting that the birth of democracy in Eastern Europe and the Soviet Union represented the "taking root" of "universal democratic values," which were the basis of "a revolution in relations between nations and a revolution in human consciousness," the secretary foresaw the creation of "a Europe which is both whole and free."[5]

Baker's visit to Moscow came several months after Washington had already made it clear that its ambitions were not restricted solely to the democratization of the Soviet empire, enormous as that undertaking was. In a speech to the United Nations in September 1989, the president sounded three major themes of an American foreign policy aimed at the construction of a Wilsonian world order. First, democracy would expand worldwide:

> Make no mistake. Nothing can stand in the way of freedom's march. There will come a day when freedom is seen the world over to be a universal birthright of every man and woman, of every race and walk of life. . . . today is freedom's moment. You see, the possibility now exists for the creation of a true community of nations built on shared interests and ideals.

Second, the president repeated the traditional liberal presumption that "the power of commerce is a force for progress;" that is, open markets make for prosperity and promote democratic forces. Third, he emphasized, as liberal doctrine would suggest, an urgent need for disarmament—"we must move forward to limit and eliminate weapons of mass destruction"—while insisting that the way forward lay through more effective international institutions: "The United Nations can play a fundamental role in the central issue of our time . . . that the nations of the world might come to agree that law, not force, shall govern."[6]

The fourth and final element of traditional Wilsonianism appeared in Bush's conviction of the need for American leadership in world affairs to make sure these arrangements held. As he asserted in his State of the Union Address in January 1990:

> The anchor in our world today is freedom, holding us steady in times of change, a symbol of hope to all the world. And freedom is at the very heart of the idea that is America. . . .
>
> America, not just the nation, but an idea, alive in the minds of people everywhere. As this new world takes shape, America stands at the center of a widening circle of freedom—today, tomorrow, and into the next century. . . .
>
> This nation, this idea called America, was and always will be a new world—our new world.[7]

The Soviet Union was far from the only place where the American commitment to aid the transition to democracy was evident. In May 1989, in a major address on policy toward Latin America, Bush insisted: "The day of the dictator is over. The people's right to democracy must not be denied." In December he showed what he meant, first in the Philippines, then in Panama. In reaction to a military threat against Corazon Aquino in Manila, the United States stood by her government with a show of air power. Washington was explicit that the defense of her regime was based on its democratic credentials: "The United States is totally, absolutely, and completely committed to the Aquino government as a government that was elected in a free, fair, and open election. We don't like to see governments that are duly elected democratic governments overthrown by bullets and bayonets."[8]

In Panama the United States invoked the restoration of democracy as the principal justification for the American invasion and the extradition of the dictator Manuel Noriega to Miami to stand trial on charges of drug-running. Following the Panamanian incursion, Washington exerted even more pressure on the Organization of American States (OAS) to take a united stand in favor of democracy, leading to the Santiago Agreement of June 1991, pledging American states to act jointly to defend established democratic governments in the hemisphere from internal threats. Agreement on this principle represented the fulfillment of Woodrow Wilson's hopes, nearly eighty years old, to see a hemisphere united in this respect.[9]

The Bush administration's greatest triumph with respect to furthering democracy in Latin America came with the election of Violeta Chamorro as president of Nicaragua in February 1990, ending nearly eleven years of Sandinista rule. Bush had shown himself less wedded to the contras and more willing to stake the future of relations with the region on free elections. Chamorro's victory was a striking endorsement of this policy. "Beyond containment lies democracy," Secretary Baker declared dramatically, seemingly articulating a new framework for American foreign policy.

Meanwhile, in public forums the president began to speak of what Reagan had called "the democratic revolution" as "the Revolution of '89."

In the case of Nicaragua, Baker explained, Washington had stood firm throughout the 1980s on the necessity of a democratic transition. Leaders in Central America then agreed to back the American proposals for a peace based on democracy. Faced with a regional consensus, the European allies lent their support. Then Moscow listened. Now that democracy had come to Nicaragua the example would be contagious:

> For we have a broad vista—stretching from Guatemala to Panama—of new possibilities for democratization, demilitarization, and development which offers a bright future for all the peoples of the region. With our help and the help of other democracies, it can and will be done. . . .
>
> Democracy speaks to universal aspirations—to use those famous old American words, "regardless of race, creed, or color." I reject, and I hope America always rejects, the view that democracy is for certain societies but has no place in Africa or Asia or South America or even in the Middle East. . . . Because we trust the people, not only here or in Europe or in Central America but everywhere, we are using democracy and elections as valuable tools in helping end regional conflicts and to bring about national reconciliation.[10]

An important element in Washington's promotion of democracy abroad during the Reagan years had been encouragement to deregulate and privatize foreign markets and to open them to the world economy. Aside from the Caribbean Basin Initiative, however, little had been done to operationalize these ideas. But in June 1990, in order to give concrete force to Republican convictions that prosperity, the free market, and democracy went hand in hand, Bush announced his Enterprise for the Americas Initiative (EAI). Later that year, he saluted the Chileans and Venezuelans especially for sharing his belief in the link between liberal economics and democratic government.[11]

It was with respect to the promotion of democracy in Mexico that the effects of a new economic order in North America might have the greatest consequences for U.S. security interests. In 1988 Carlos Salinas de Gortari had been elected president of Mexico; in short order he introduced a package of economic reforms designed to deregulate, privatize, and open the Mexican economy. Aspects of Salinas's reforms were strictly Mexican; the state would presumably continue to play a large role in the macromanagement of the country's economy (as in Japan or South Korea, for example), and a "solidarity" fund would increase governmental expenditures on the infrastructure in order also to provide jobs for some Mexicans who might otherwise be hurt by the economic restructuring. But on the whole, the Salinas program corresponded well to the kind of thinking Washington had been promoting since the early 1980s.

Relations between the United States and Mexico had not been especially cordial during the Reagan years. Given the even longer history of strained relations (going back to the war of 1846–8), the Bush administration was careful to avoid any appearance of meddling in that country's political affairs, despite continued concern about drug-running and human rights abuses. Yet the effects of the trade and investment negotiations finally signed with President Salinas in December 1992 (the North American Free Trade Agreement [NAFTA], also including Canada, and ratified by the U.S. Congress in November 1993) may eventually contribute handily to Mexican democratization. Commentators in both countries tended at the time to focus their analyses on the relative costs and benefits Mexico and the United States might expect in strictly economic terms. But from a longer-term political perspective, the changes the NAFTA introduced might be even more significant for Mexico and for relations between the two countries. In short, by encouraging Mexico to privatize its statist economy and open it to foreign economic forces, the United States was assisting in what might well eventually be a domestic restructuring of power in Mexico unprecedented since the days of Lazaro Cardenas in the 1930s. Should the country ultimately become a stable democracy, the benefits for the United States would presumably be significant.[12]

The power of the single party that has ruled Mexico in the aftermath of the Revolution of 1910—the Institutional Revolutionary Party (PRI)—has in good measure rested on its control of the state and on the state's control, in turn, of the economy—through direct ownership, subsidies, exchange controls, and the domination of labor and peasant unions. Careful to avoid the pitfalls of the Soviet experience, Salinas restricted his program to efforts to restructure Mexico economically. While there are those who doubt that the PRI will ever willingly relinquish power, these socioeconomic reforms may eventually oblige it to democratize the country. Should this be the path of Mexican political development, presumably the NAFTA will have played a role in that country's democratization.

The common denominator to a wide range of policies adopted in Washington between the summers of 1989 and 1990 was their Wilsonianism: the Bush administration asserted that support for democracy abroad might reap handsome dividends for American security interests. In Nicaragua, Panama, Poland, Hungary, and Czechoslovakia, authoritarian regimes hostile to Washington were replaced with governments with democratic credentials that were staunchly pro-American. Germany would soon be reunited and securely anchored in NATO and the European Community. The OAS was committed for the first time to intervention for the sake of preserving democracy in the Western Hemisphere. With the EAI, Washington could look forward to helping to consolidate democracy in places like Chile while coaxing along democratization in Mexico. In the Philippines, the

United States had successfully aided a democratic government under siege. What was less evident to many at the time was how tentative and fragile many of these bids to establish democratic governments actually were.

In the midst of this apparent flood tide of democratization came the Iraqi invasion and annexation of Kuwait in August 1990. To be sure, democracy was not the issue; neither in Iraq nor in Kuwait could there be much hope of fostering so Western a style of government. Nevertheless, here was a challenge to regional stability in an area of special interest to the United States, so that in acting decisively, Bush might give still more shape to what he now called a "new world order" to be crafted by American leadership. The president's address to a Joint Session of Congress in September put the matter in Wilsonian tones:

> We stand today at a unique and extraordinary moment. The crisis in the Persian Gulf, as grave as it is, also offers a rare opportunity to move toward an historic period of cooperation. Out of these troubled times . . . a new world order can emerge: a new era—freer from the threat of terror, stronger in the pursuit of justice, and more secure in the quest for peace. An era in which the nations of the world, East and West, North and South, can prosper and live in harmony. A hundred generations have searched for the elusive peace, while a thousand wars raged across the span of human endeavor. Today that new world is struggling to be born, a world quite different from the one we've known. A world where the rule of law supplants the rule of the jungle. A world in which nations recognize the shared responsibility for freedom and justice.[13]

In mobilizing forces to combat Iraq, President Bush took a variety of initiatives that might be called Wilsonian. He asked the United Nations for its support to defend Kuwaiti sovereignty, and so showed his respect for the importance of international institutions. He involved the Soviet Union, and so seemed to be paving the way for a later collective security agreement with Moscow. And he affirmed the battle to be one to have lasting repercussions:

> The triumph of democratic ideas in Eastern Europe and Latin America and the continuing struggle for freedom elsewhere all around the world all confirm the wisdom of our nation's founders. . . . For two centuries, we've done the hard work of freedom. What is at stake is more than one small country; it is a big idea: a new world order, where diverse nations are drawn together in common cause to achieve the universal aspirations of mankind—peace and security, freedom, and the rule of law. Such is a world worthy of our struggle and worthy of our children's future.[14]

In retrospect, however, it appears that the Gulf War marked not only the zenith of Bush's liberal democratic internationalism but the beginning of its decline as a road map for American foreign policy as well. Saddam Hussein remained in power in Baghdad; the democratization process in Latin America began to appear reversible; the outbreak of bitter nationalist wars in the former Yugoslavia confronted Washington and the European Community with a conflict they could not manage; and an American electorate with growing concerns about economic problems at home started to tire of a presidency that only seemed concerned about questions of world order.

In fact, even before the victory over Iraq, the Bush administration had had to recognize the fragility of democratization efforts abroad and the limits on American power to do much about it. In the summer of 1989, after Chinese students and their supporters had erected a Goddess of Liberty modeled on the Statue of Liberty, demanded democratic reforms of their government, and had been crushed in Tiananmen Square, Washington did little to protest. Whatever the justifications for American reticence (there were many), they were not Wilsonian.

Again, by the winter of 1990–1, the Bush administration had become sensitive to the resistance to change within the Soviet Union. The resignation of Eduard Shevardnadze as foreign minister in December 1990, charging that Gorbachev was moving too far to the right, raised concerns about Gorbachev's ultimate intentions: perhaps he still was determined to reform Leninist party rule so as to preserve it, or perhaps he was preparing his own coup rather than moving toward democracy. As with Beijing, Washington had to recognize limits on its power to influence events in Moscow.

In short order Washington was to realize that its hopes for a new world order could be dashed by peoples less powerful than the Chinese and the Soviets. In retrospect, it appears that perhaps the most significant blow to the emergence of a new democratic world order was the failure of the administration and its European partners to act decisively with respect to Serbian assaults on Croatia beginning in June 1991. Critics of the administration's passivity lamented not only the high loss of life in the region, but also the wider political repercussions of inaction on civil strife in neighboring areas and the apparent inability of NATO (or the UN or the Conference on Security and Cooperation in Europe, the CSCE) to define its mission in a new way to control such threats to the peace. What had happened to hopes for collective security or to the promise of American leadership (even if Washington could blame the European Community for having claimed it could handle the crisis)?[15]

In September 1991 Washington reacted relatively passively to a military coup that overthrew Jean-Bertrand Aristide, Haiti's first democratically elected president. Neither Washington nor the OAS was able to prevent Aristide's followers from being delivered to the wolves. In a region where

American power was supreme, what had happened to the proud boast made only months earlier that the United States would work to establish "a world where the rule of law, not the law of the jungle, governs the conduct of nations?"

The Haitian case was the first of a series of setbacks for democracy in Latin America. The Venezuelan military attempted a coup against the democratic government of that country in February 1992, while in April the Peruvian President Alberto Fujimori arranged for his military to stage a coup on his behalf against his country's legislature. Washington remonstrated, but to no avail. Meanwhile, the prospects for consolidating democracy in Panama dimmed as drug trafficking, secret banking, and unaccountable government practices reasserted themselves.[16] The boost given to democratic forces in 1989–90 in Central America apparently was not to have its sequel in Latin America in 1991–2.

Even as conditions seemed to improve in Moscow, Washington continued to experience a sense of its own limits. Thus, in May 1991, when Shevardnadze visited Washington, the former Soviet foreign minister reassured the Bush administration that Gorbachev was now committed to democratic reform, but he also warned that the economic situation in his country was worsening and that the fate of democracy hung in the balance. The coup attempt against Gorbachev in August 1991 confirmed the fears of many. The problem (which has continued to bedevil American leaders ever since) is that even with committed democratizers in the Kremlin, it is not self-evident that the United States can do a great deal to aid their efforts. By March 1992 former President Richard Nixon was nonetheless publicly embarrassing Bush, calling aid provisions for the former Soviet Union "pathetically inadequate" and warning that the old question of "who lost China" might soon be replaced by the far more serious question "who lost Russia?" Several weeks later, the front-running Democratic challenger for the presidency, Bill Clinton, repeated the charge, formulating an agenda to promote democracy abroad as if in contradiction to Bush: "No national security issue is more urgent than securing democracy's triumph around the world. . . . It is time for America to lead a global alliance for democracy as united and steadfast as the global alliance that defeated communism."[17]

Here is a key to understanding American intervention in Somalia in December 1992. Faced with a loss in momentum for his new world order, Bush secured United Nations authorization to occupy that country for humanitarian relief. However, it was unclear how the American initiative amounted to more than an isolated instance of humanitarian service unrelated to any grand vision of the appropriate structure of international affairs. To many it appeared that precisely because Bush did not know how to act in a Wilsonian manner toward Haiti or the former Yugoslavia, toward China or Panama, toward the former Soviet Union or in the aftermath of the victory over Iraq, that he had looked for a low-cost, high profile action in the Horn of Africa. Yes, Somalia should be saved; but where was the new world order?

There are three different ways to evaluate the Bush years. One is to confirm Bush's assertion that a "new world order" was potentially in the making, but to argue that his faulty leadership prevented the United States from laying the groundwork for what would have been an enduring Pax Americana. From this perspective, the successes of 1989–91 might have been multiplied had Washington had a better operationalized vision.[18]

By contrast, a second judgment holds that the Wilsonian enthusiasm of the first half of the Bush administration was misplaced all along. The limits of the contemporary wave of democratization would eventually be reached; it was improvident of Washington not to have foreseen the inevitable flagging of the momentum for democracy. Whether it was Panama or the Philippines, the Soviet Union or elsewhere, the obstacles to the consolidation of democratic governments were simply too great for all the transitions following the fall of the Berlin Wall in November 1989 to be sustained. America may have won the Gulf War, but it was dangerous for the administration to conclude from this that it had the power to bend the forces of history to its will.[19]

A third judgment is more generous toward the Bush years, holding that its "selective" liberal democratic internationalism was an essentially realistic approach to world affairs. Where it reasonably could do so, Washington acted to support democracy or economic liberalism or to restore the peace—as in the Philippines, Mexico and Central America, Eastern Europe, the former Soviet Union, and the Gulf. But as the momentum halted, Washington prudently assessed the situation, showing the same caution that it had already demonstrated in China. To be sure, the administration's policies toward Panama, Haiti, and the former Yugoslavia were clearly wanting, and perhaps Washington should have understood earlier that there were more vigorous defenders of democracy in Moscow than Gorbachev. Nonetheless, on balance the record was unquestionably positive.

Such a defense of Bush's record suggests a comparison with Roosevelt or Kennedy. Thus, FDR had modified Wilsonianism with his Good Neighbor Policy as early as 1933 and was pragmatic in his approach to the world's dictators thereafter. Yet he worked for a liberal international economic order and hoped for the creation of international institutions to preserve the peace; and presumably he would have insisted as Truman did on the democratization of Japan and Germany during their occupation.

Kennedy also demonstrated a selective approach. Under the terms of the Alliance for Progress, Washington stood ready to act to promote democracy where conditions were favorable; but it would not move precipitously. The failure of the Alliance was at least as much due to the resistance of

Latin America elites to reform as to shortcomings in Washington's execution of policy.

The virtue of selective liberal democratic internationalism is that policymakers hold it to be in the United States' security interest for democracy to expand abroad, yet are aware that this country's power is too limited for it to promote such reforms imprudently, meaning that important stakes must be involved or that the likelihood of success is high before the United States commits itself. Saddled with these reservations, such an approach may fail to promote democracy to the extent it might and may then justifiably be criticized (as in Bush's policy toward the former Yugoslavia, Haiti, or Panama). Yet if we consider the assurance with which Wilson thought he could bring democracy to the Dominican Republic and Nicaragua, or Kennedy thought he might count on "nation-building" to stop communism in South Vietnam, or Carter imagined respect for human rights might reinforce the shah's authority in Iran, we may better appreciate the strengths of this more modest approach.

If the Bush administration refrained from a full-throttle campaign for democracy abroad, by no means did it ignore the importance of such developments for the national security in the manner of, say, the Johnson or Nixon administrations. For decades to come, debate is sure to swirl around the question of how effective Bush's policy actually was in promoting democracy in Eastern Europe and the former Soviet Union. Undoubtedly there were errors of judgment. What cannot be doubted, however, is that policy toward this region was the central foreign policy concern of the Bush administration. In its firm conviction that it mattered mightily to American national security whether democratic forces took power there, American policy was Wilsonian root and branch.

Hence, as the Soviet Union disintegrated in the aftermath of the August 1991 coup attempt in Moscow against Gorbachev's authority, Secretary Baker repeated the five principles governing American policy toward Eastern Europe and the USSR: that minority rights be considered sacrosanct; that human rights be respected; that borders were inviolable; that changes were to come through peaceful means; and that the Helsinki Final Act and the Charter of Paris confirming these norms and practices were to guide conduct. In his words:

> The opportunities are historic. We have the chance to anchor Russia, Ukraine, and other republics firmly into the Euro-Atlantic community and the democratic commonwealth of nations. We have the chance to bring democracy to lands that have little knowledge of it, an achievement that can transcend centuries of history. . . . This historic watershed, the collapse of communist power in Bolshevism's birthplace, marks the challenge that history has dealt us: to see the end of the Soviet empire turned into a beginning for democracy and economic freedom across the former Soviet empire.[20]

The president was of the same mind. In April 1992 he called the evolution of domestic forces in Eastern Europe and the former Soviet Union "a defining moment in history, with profound consequences for America's own national interest":

> The stakes are as high for us now as any that have faced us in this century. . . . the one nation that posed a worldwide threat to freedom and peace is now seeking to join the community of democratic nations. A victory for democracy and freedom in the former USSR creates the possibility of a new world of peace for our children and grandchildren. But if this democratic revolution is defeated, it could plunge us into a world more dangerous in some respects than the dark years of the Cold War.[21]

The most salient outcome of these dramatic statements was to increase significantly the amount of money to be made available to the former Soviet Union through the Freedom Support Act. Nevertheless, critics pointed out that compared to the $6 billion spent on El Salvador in the 1980s or the $3 billion spent annually on Israel, American assistance to Russia was paltry.

To conclude. Certainly there was something embarrassing about the heady rhetoric surrounding a new world order that never materialized: democratic forces remained weak in Panama; democracy was not restored in Haiti; the failure to manage the dismemberment of Yugoslavia was a blow to American leadership in Europe. Yet there is good reason to commend the administration for its policies toward the former Soviet Union, Eastern Europe, the Philippines, Mexico, and Nicaragua, and sound cause to give it credit for not pushing too hard in China. Later observers may find that Washington also acted constructively with respect to pushing African countries such as Kenya to democratize. And for all the criticism that arose for failing to depose Saddam Hussein, the objective difficulties facing the United States in the region—Iranian power, the ongoing Arab-Israeli dispute, and the rise of Islamic fundamentalism—meant that many other serious problems would have remained whatever Saddam's fate. There were clear limits to what American military capabilities in the region could achieve politically. Indeed, the success of the Israeli-PLO peace negotiations in September 1993 was a testimony to the skill and perseverance of Bush and Baker in navigating these difficult waters.[22]

Eighty years after Woodrow Wilson entered office in 1913, George Bush departed Washington. In this interval—spanning both World Wars and the cold war—much had changed, yet much remained the same with respect to liberal democratic internationalism's ability to defend American national security. Some, especially in the Wilson, Carter, and Reagan administrations, unequivocally affirmed the priority of fostering democracy abroad for the sake of American national security. Others, especially the "realists"

of the Johnson and Nixon years, doubted that promoting transitions to democracy abroad mattered much at all to national security, preferring to
ignore the internal character of states in favor of evaluating them by their
external behavior. A third approach advocated the selective promotion of
democracy abroad in the manner of Roosevelt, Truman, Kennedy, and
Bush.

During the 1992 presidential campaign, Bill Clinton called for an active
American defense of democracy and human rights with respect to Haiti,
China, and the former Yugoslavia, so appearing more in line with Carter
and Reagan than with Bush, whom Clinton criticized for his failure to promote these matters more vigorously. Yet once in office, Clinton adopted
Bush's policy in all of these cases—deciding against asking for trade sanctions against China for its human rights performance, backing down from
his threats against the Serbs, putting a limit on the American involvement
in Somalia, and failing to restore Aristide in Haiti. To be sure, in a series of
coordinated talks in September 1993 given by the president, Secretary of
State Warren Christopher, Ambassador to the UN Madelaine Albright, and
National Security Council Adviser Anthony Lake, the administration announced its primary commitment to the "enlargement of the family of free-
market democracies" (and the appropriate reorganization of foreign assistance as a consequence). But with respect to military intervention, Clinton
put clear limits on what could be expected of Washington when he said in
a major address to the UN in September 1993 that that organization "must
know when to say no." For example, with respect to eventual peacekeeping
operations in Bosnia:

> I would want a clear understanding what the command and control was. I would
> want the NATO commander in charge of the operation. I would want a clear
> timetable for the first review and ultimately for the right to terminate American
> involvement. I would want a clear political strategy along with a military strat-
> egy. . . . I would want a clear expression of support from the United States Con-
> gress. Now, there are 20 other operational things I would want, but those are the
> big policy issues.[23]

On other issues, Clinton was more assertive, although here too his policy
was in line with his predecessor's. Thus, Clinton pursued the NAFTA,
hoping that it would reinforce democratic trends in Mexico and using its
ratification in November 1993 as a source of influence at the Asian-Pacific
Economic Cooperation summit shortly thereafter. These successes in turn
enhanced his position at the concluding session of the Uruguay round of
the General Agreement on Tariffs and Trade (GATT) negotiations with the
Europeans in December. The result was considerably to strengthen a sometimes beleaguered American commitment to a liberal international economic order.[24]

Clinton also followed Bush in indicating that the first priority of American foreign policy was to foster to the extent possible democratic government in Russia. His unwavering support for Boris Yeltsin from their first meeting in April 1993, through Yeltsin's crackdown on the Russian parliament in October, and at the Moscow summit of January 1994 was premised on the conviction that Yeltsin alone represented the hope for democracy in that troubled land, and that democracy, in turn, was the sole form of government for Russia that would guarantee a stable peace in Europe.[25]

Working for Russian reform and cooperation did not come easily. The most enduring problem was deciding how to come to Moscow's assistance; through his first year in office, Clinton had no novel ideas on the matter. A new and more vexing issue was how to deal with proposals by Germany and various East European countries to expand NATO to the East. As the Czech President Vaclav Havel put it, several of these lands (notably the Czech Republic, Poland, Hungary, Lithuania, and Slovakia) felt that they belonged culturally to Western civilization. Hence, it was their sovereign right to ask for membership in its security arrangements, and it was a moral duty of the West to honor the request. A democratic Russia should have no trouble with such an arrangement, and an authoritarian Russia would be put on notice thereby to temper its foreign policy. The Wilsonian basis of the moral claim could not have been stronger.

However, true to the compromising tone of his presidency in domestic as well as foreign policy, Clinton declined to challenge Russia directly. No new cordon sanitaire would be set up in Europe, but instead Moscow would be encouraged to see itself as a leading guarantor of the peace in Europe by trying to include, rather than exclude, its participation in regional security pacts. The East Europeans were to be offered a "partnership for peace," an associate status with NATO whose meaning remained vague. Clinton recognized the size of the stakes. "If democracy in the East fails, then violence and disruption from the East will once again harm us and other democracies," he declared to a NATO meeting in January 1994. Nevertheless, how to secure democratic forces and so to preserve the peace appeared to elude this president as it had his predecessor. The most Wilsonian of answers to the security dilemma of Eastern Europe was not that given by President Clinton but instead that promoted by President Havel, who insisted on the moral and cultural oneness of Western civilization as he asked that Washington go beyond the partnership-for-peace proposals to an explicit plan incorporating countries like the Czech Republic into NATO.[26]

For the first year of his presidency, Clinton thus deserved to be called a selective liberal democratic internationalist. While he left no doubt in his public statements as to his administration's commitment to promoting democracy abroad, Clinton nevertheless had no grand design for how such a

326 · Chapter Eleven

program was to be advanced, and he steadfastly refused any direct intervention for the sake of human rights or democracy abroad (aside from an effort in Somalia, which badly backfired). As a result, although all four of the last administrations deserve to be called liberal in world affairs (and American policy to be called bipartisan), there has been more similarity in foreign affairs between Bush and Clinton in his first year in office and between Carter and Reagan than the labels Democrat and Republican might suggest.

The drawback of a selective approach, epitomized by Bush and Clinton, is that its circumspection may lose the moment by indecision. The need to judge each case by its merits while respecting the limits of American power is scarcely a receipe for boldness, as, for example, policy toward Haiti during both administrations illustrates. Nor is it likely to have much carry-through, as the failure to follow up on intervention in Panama after 1989 indicates. Moreover, as hesitation follows hesitation, American policy loses in credibility and prestige, which has clearly been the case for NATO after Clinton's contradictory pronouncements over Bosnia. As of this writing, the most critical failure of Wilsonianism has been Washington's striking inability to devise a new role for NATO after the cold war. Should American isolationism become more pronounced, here is the development later historians are most likely to pinpoint as the beginning of the end of American liberal democratic internationalism. Nevertheless, the advantage of selective liberal democratic internationalism is that (unlike antiliberalism) it clearly recognizes the concrete national security interests served by the expansion of democracy abroad, while (unlike unqualified liberalism) it has a realistic sense of the limits of American power and the need to work with the world as it is.

The difficulty of implementing a selective policy is that leaders must know where and how to act aggressively to promote democracy abroad and when prudently to remain silent. They must reconcile the contradiction that while American security is served by a successful liberal agenda, there are definite limits to the American ability to foster developments such as democracy abroad. Leaders must therefore not cloud their appreciation of what is possible by their beliefs as to what is desirable. But just as importantly, they must not forget what is desirable because of their fear of taking action.

THE DESIRABILITY OF MORE DEMOCRATIC GOVERNMENTS

In the 1890s Americans criticized what today would be called human rights abuses inflicted by the Spanish on valiant Cuban nationalists and speculated on whether a country so poor, so racially divided, and so influenced by Spanish authoritarianism and Catholic dogmatism could ever become a democracy, and on why it should matter to American interests if it did. In the 1990s much the same debate could be heard. Did it matter for the national security if democracy took root in places as different as Russia or China, Mexico or the Balkans; if it did, what might the United States do to influence the course of events there?

Earlier chapters in this book maintained that there were three legs to the American conception of national security defined as a liberal world order—one economic, a second political, the third military—each of which served concrete national interests, which in turn created the Wilsonian agenda for American national security. In combination these elements have created a distinctive American approach to world affairs, one premised on the notion that only a world that respects the right of democratic self-determination, fosters nondiscriminatory markets, and has institutional mechanisms to ensure the peace can be an international order ensuring the national security and so permitting liberty at home. Much as Lincoln doubted that the United States could be "half slave and half free," so since Wilson's time, the concern to "make the world safe for democracy" has expressed the conviction that militarism, mercantilism, and dictatorship abroad could eventually endanger the American way at home by forcing the regimentation of this country itself in its self-defense. Perhaps fear of the outside world was exaggerated; perhaps hope to change the character of other peoples was excessive; perhaps, indeed, there was something dangerous to the world's peace in the American insistence that world order conform to its definition of national security. Whatever the justice of the criticisms, the ambition of liberal democratic internationalism was to give rise to the attempt to form a particular kind of international system, with characteristics more congenial to the American way than mercantilism and military dictatorships could promise.

The idea that national security would be served by a liberal international trading system was characteristic of the United States since the Revolution of 1776. To be sure, free trade was not national policy until FDR's election, and liberalism did not prohibit the United States from acting aggressively toward weaker peoples to protect its economic interests. But the essential spirit of American international economic doctrine from 1776 through the Open Door Notes of 1899–1900 (and their repeated use to defend Chinese sovereignty against the Japanese in the 1930s), embodied in the Bretton Woods Agreements of 1944, and still in force today has been an antimercantilism dedicated to the peaceful resolution of economic competition among the great powers on terms that were better for weaker states than an international order of competitive imperialism would have been.[27]

That an open world economy has served American economic and national security interests is undeniable. When the country was young, mercantilistic systems limited its ability to trade. When the country was becoming the world's foremost industrial economy, great-power spheres of interest hindered its access to foreign markets. At each stage, a nondiscriminatory international economic order operating under most-favored nations agreements was official policy. Given the economic abundance at home, gaining market access abroad through military means and political control seldom was a profitable calculation (though both Japan and Korea were opened by such threats). Like Great Britain, the United States practiced an "imperialism of free trade," which implied the creation (through the deliberate use of influence—including force on occasion) of a world community of independent states bound together by an interdependent economic order.

The success of the international economic system born of this conviction encouraged a phenomenal growth in world trade. To be sure, there are vulnerabilities associated with this interdependent system as well—international financial forces lacking adequate political control, individual states taking unilateral advantage of such an order, or the system itself being jeopardized by the uneven pace of development within it. Nonetheless, in 1991 $2.5 trillion of the $3.4 trillion in world commerce consisted of exports from the United States and its twenty-one free-market, democratic trading partners. These countries also accounted for $376 billion of the $404 billion directly invested in the United States in 1990, while being the home of $276 billion of the $370 billion of direct American investments abroad. The consensus is that the prosperity and political harmony that characterizes these countries came in significant measure from liberal arrangements they had developed to handle their economic exchanges— reason enough that so many countries are now applying to join the institutions of this regime of trade and finance.[28]

But it is largely for its political effects on the national security that liberal economic practices are to be celebrated. On the one hand, such arrangements have dampened the appeal of militarism in countries that otherwise might feel themselves obliged to act forcibly to preserve their economic interests (like Japan and Germany for a half century prior to World War II), while to some extent insulating political relations among states from those that are more narrowly economic. On the other hand, such cooperation contributed directly to the defeat of Soviet communism by creating an international economic powerhouse whose relative strength could not be gainsaid by the leaders in the Kremlin.

As in economic relations so in those that are explicitly political: America's national security has been served by being liberal and supporting local nationalisms as a way of opposing great powers' efforts to expand by conquest, which could potentially have dangerous consequences for the United States. Part of these calculations were also economic: once freed of enforced participation in a preferential trading system, subject peoples might welcome ties with the United States. But given the small economic stakes involved, American calculations of the national security were usually premised on military and political reasoning. The United States feared that imperialist rivalries must eventually involve it too, while a plural world order assured this country a competitive advantage given its size, wealth, and location.[29]

Protected by mighty oceans, the United States at first defined its national security in terms of preventing a recurrence of European imperialism in the Western Hemisphere. Accordingly, the Monroe Doctrine of 1823 saluted the independence of Spanish America and affirmed an American commitment to preserve what Latin nationalism had won. Later, at the end of the nineteenth century, the Open Door Notes (which, although largely symbolic, were more political than economic in their effect) echoed the Monroe Doctrine by supporting the stirrings of Chinese nationalism against imperialist efforts to carve that country into great power spheres of influence. The Open Door thereafter became the basis of American policy in the Far East to block Japanese designs on China (especially as reaffirmed in the so called Stimson Doctrine, named after Secretary of State Henry Stimson, which protested Japan's 1931 occupation of Manchuria). Once again, the thinking behind backing a politically plural order was that of national security.

Because of its democratic government, its economic self-sufficiency, and its geostrategic isolation, the United States had no strong territorial drive once its continental shape had been concluded in the 1840s. Control over large foreign populations, much less their annexation, had no great appeal. American policy was to preserve a world order open to it economically and where no great foreign rival would amass through imperialist expansion the ability to threaten this country's existence. America's position was perforce liberal, evolving naturally over time into a support for democracy abroad, not for pietistic reasons but because it served national security.

In the twentieth century, the Monroe Doctrine was globalized as Woodrow Wilson helped to dispose of the fallen Russian, Austro-Hungarian, and Ottoman multinational empires by endorsing the self-determination of their subject peoples. As the United States had once interposed itself between Europe and Latin America, now it would help guarantee the survival of a host of new nation-states. This was also the moment when the United States explicitly defined democratic government as the proper embodiment of nationalist energies abroad. Once again the thinking was premised on preserving the national security of the United States.

Although he was less confident than Wilson that democratic government was likely to take root in many countries around the world, FDR followed Wilson's lead and insisted on promoting self-determination abroad after World War II as a way of securing the national interest. Nationalist forces unleashed in the aftermath of World War I had proved unable to establish stable governments, but Roosevelt nonetheless brought pressure to bear to end the West European empires in Asia and Africa and to prevent Soviet imperial expansion in Eastern Europe. As Wilson had counted on the League of Nations to protect this fragile new international political order, so Roosevelt counted on the United Nations. As in the 1820s, 1890s, and 1920s, American policy in the 1940s was once again consonant with the objectives of powerful nationalist movements abroad.

On occasion—as in the Philippines—the United States did act as a traditional imperialist power. And its liberal orientation did not prevent it from engaging in a "preemptive imperialism" of its own in regions like Central America and the Caribbean where anarchy prevailed, American security interests were involved, and rival powers might act. These interventions created their own problems. Faced with what to do with direct control over foreign peoples, the United States would seek to establish a stable government favorable to American values and interests and then leave. From FDR's Good Neighbor Policy after 1933 to events in Greece in 1947, however, it seemed apparent that Washington might have to content itself with a secure authoritarian order able to ward off instability or communist takeovers. Whatever the justifications for defending these authoritarian regimes, the rationales obviously contradicted the liberal premises on which American policy had been established.

While with FDR, liberal democrats found a way to make their peace with dictators, they remained committed to fostering democracy where they might. As a modern, stable form of government, democracy held out the prospect of ending civil strife and power vacuums in regions of strategic concern to the United States, such as Central America and the Caribbean. It also held the promise of creating regimes favorable to Washington by virtue of a common socioeconomic structure and set of political values, as in Eastern Europe. The strength of American relations with fellow democracies like Britain, Canada, and Japan, and the momentous changes that have occurred (thanks in good measure to American sponsorship) within Europe—first with the creation of the European Community, then with the collapse of the Soviet empire to the East—reflect the benefits of a shared community of democratic values and institutions that have always made relations with authoritarian governments somewhat suspect.

Corresponding to the economic and political aims of its liberal democratic internationalism, American ideas of world order have essentially been antimilitarist. As a young republic, the United States feared a standing army. As a bourgeois republic, it opposed large public expenditures. And as a major actor in world affairs after 1918, disarmament proposals were an obvious way to maintain this country's preeminent rank at a relatively low cost.

To be sure, when military force was needed after 1939, the United States mounted a massive call to arms, which it maintained for half a century thereafter. For good reason, President Eisenhower warned against the machinations of the "military-industrial complex," pointing to the growing role of war-fighting interests in this country's political life. And there were specific military doctrines (the Strategic Defense Initiative during the Reagan years, for example) that aroused concern about America's commitment to peace, just as the character of the country's intelligence community could raise questions about the preservation of democratic government. Nevertheless, the American military never has had the prestige or the political clout of the German and Japanese officer corps or the Russian and Chinese revolutionary armies. And vocal elements of the population, whether out of economic or political concerns, always opposed "excessive" military spending. From the League of Nations to the United Nations, the United States has promoted international law and organization as a way to keep the peace in the belief that such arrangements protected its internal democratic system from destablization better than military solutions might, by keeping government clearly subordinate to society.

Thus, American liberal democratic internationalism has contributed concretely to basic structures of international politics today, from the organization of the world's economy to the legitimacy of the nation-state as an international actor. Neither the timeless truths of human affairs (as suggested by those who write as if nothing has changed in this domain since Thucydides first wrote about it in the fifth century B.C.) nor the march of history accomplished without human agency (as suggested by those who talk of current affairs as if they express ineluctable universal stages in development) should disguise this fact. Democracy's current elevated status represents the effects of 175 years of Anglo-American international hegemony.

Take the consolidation of democracy in Germany after 1945. No doubt the Germans themselves were largely responsible for this achievement, helped by other occupying powers besides the United States. But without the sustained backing of American liberal democratic internationalism, not only the rapid democratization of Germany, but more especially its incorporation into a Western Europe bent on economic and political integration are difficult to imagine. As a result, European politics are fundamentally different from what they were in the period between German unification in 1871 and the collapse of the Third Reich in 1945. As Wilson first argued with only slight exaggeration, to change Germany internally was to change Europe, and to change Europe was to change the world.

Today the evolution of the struggle for democracy in Russia has the same meaning for world peace as the conversion of Germany had before. Hence the importance of Boris Yeltsin's declaration before a Joint Session of Congress in June 1992: "The world can sigh in relief—the idol of communism, which spread social strife, enmity, and unparalleled brutality everywhere, which instilled fear in humanity, has collapsed. It has collapsed never to rise again."[30]

Only weeks earlier, Mikhail Gorbachev had been even more explicit. In a talk at Fulton, Missouri, on the anniversary of Churchill's famous speech in 1946 warning that an Iron Curtain was falling across Europe, Gorbachev saluted the end of the cold war as "a victory for common sense, reason, democracy." Suggesting that the United Nations should "create structures . . . which are authorized to impose sanctions, to make use of other measures of compulsion especially when rights of minority groups especially are being violated," the former Soviet leader sounded every inch a Wilsonian, insisting on the "universality of human rights" and "the acceptability of international interference wherever human rights are violated." In Gorbachev's words: "Today democracy must prove that it can exist, not only as the antithesis of totalitarianism. This means that it must move from the national to the international arena. On today's agenda is not just a union of democratic states, but also a democratically organized world community."[31]

The argument that nothing serves American national security like the expansion of democracy worldwide can be made historically, empirically, and logically. In 1983 Professor Michael Doyle showed that the record of the last 150 years and more demonstrates that democracies are highly unlikely to fight with one another. He turned to classic writers like Kant and Mill promoting liberal democracy in the eighteenth and nineteen centuries in an effort to explain this regularity. Several suggestive conclusions emerge. Democracies may possess something of a self-denying ordinance that inhibits them from fighting other democratic states, which they see as inherently legitimate and so deserving of respect. Democracies also have established domestic procedures—embodied in institutions, values, and practices summed up as the rule of law—that can be transposed with relative ease to international forums for conflict adjudication. In combination these characteristics appear significantly to dampen tensions among democratic peoples.[32]

Other writers have added further arguments: that authoritarian states tend to be based on extorting revenues from their populations far more than democracies and hence are inherently bellicose; that liberal states favor limited government and so tend to dislike military expenditures and to distrust military establishments, making them inherently pacific; that the need to see oneself as the moral embodiment of "right" and one's opponent as less than human—what Erik Erickson has called "pseudospeciation" and has posited to be the psychological basis of racism as well as war—is reduced by democracy's secular toleration of diversity and is more difficult

when one's opponent is unquestionably like oneself; that as market economies, liberal democracies tend to absorb in entrepreneurial pursuits individual energies that might elsewhere be directed toward war; and that
under a liberal international economic order, the leading democratic countries provide for themselves an integrative mechanism for peaceful economic competition, which takes the edge off the imperialist scrambles for
economic advantage that might otherwise occur.[33]

These writers are often the first to acknowledge a major problem with the
direction in which their thinking points, however: despite two world wars
in this century and the end of the cold war, it appears unlikely that all the
leading states will soon become democracies, however desirable such an
evolution may seem to the West. China and the Muslim world (like Germany and Russia earlier in this century) continue to appear opposed to
democratization, essentially on nationalist grounds, as the imposition of
alien, unhealthy ways. Moreover, some of democracy's problems are internal. Without a clear and present danger from without, it is conceivable that
difficulties among democratic peoples will multiply in the years ahead,
making the adoption of democratic government by other peoples more
problematic. One can even imagine plausible scenarios by which countries
that are now democratic might eventually opt for another system of government. In short, what is desirable and what is attainable may be two quite
different things.

OBSTACLES TO THE EXPANSION OF DEMOCRATIC GOVERNMENT

Nationalism has been the dominant political force of our century. Its fury
contributed directly to World War I and to the disintegration of the Austro-
Hungarian, Ottoman, and Russian empires thereafter. Its energy exploded
again in World War II and fueled the subsequent process of European decolonization. It sapped the strength of the Soviet empire and destroyed the
Soviet Union.

The question, then, is how liberal democracy and nationalism are related. Can a world order led by liberal democratic states promise a more
durable peace than other kinds of international community? If it can,
how can these two forces be most successfully wedded? Can democratic
peoples live in harmony with those who embrace other forms of modern
government?[34]

The term nationalism may be defined as an ideologically formulated
sense of union among a people, giving rise to the call for a state to rule over
a specific territory in a way made legitimate by some concept of popular
sovereignty. A people's feeling of nationalism may be based on common
kinship and ethnicity, or on a communality created by religion, language,
territory, or shared history—factors that either alone or together establish

the boundaries of a group. However, these elements of social solidarity have held individuals together since time immemorial. It is the political demand for a state based on popular sovereignty that makes nationalism distinctively modern.[35]

Starting with the political upheavals in England in the seventeenth century and augmented by the combined force of the Industrial, American, and French Revolutions of a century later, a wave of demands for popular sovereignty led to momentous changes in the character of Western political life. No longer could individuals alone manage the political affairs of a people through personalistic followings, massive bureaucracies, and the blessings of religion. History was passing a sentence against authoritarian governments whose rulers might claim like Louis XIV, "I am the state," even though such regimes had dominated the world politically for thousands of years.

More flexible, decentralized, complex political structures were called for. On the one hand, modern political life required a state with institutions powerful enough to escape the whims of the momentary incumbent of office, states that were predictable and accountable for their actions, states run, in short, by the rule of law. On the other hand, such a system also needed party structures tying the state to a citizenry that itself was undergoing constant change in terms of its composition and interests. The result was a new conception of the state and the citizen, a redefinition of the proper relationship of government and society.

Liberalism and democracy were the first ideologies to reflect this epochal change in the basic structure of domestic politics. As noted in chapter one, in the late eighteenth century liberalism and democracy both envisioned the end of authoritarian government, though each was also hostile to the other. Neither doctrine was static. Each evolved over time, so that it was only around the time of World War I that they came to work together in association with democratic socialism.

Meanwhile rival ideologies reconceptualizing the citizen and the state had also come into existence, gaining mass followings and bidding for power. By the time of World War I, the leading revolutionary ideology was Marxism-Leninism; shortly thereafter a rival mass movement, fascism, appeared in reaction. As new concepts of citizenship and the state became international issues, liberalism and democracy with their socialist allies came to be identified, like fascism and communism, as political doctrines of specific states—Italy, Germany, and Japan as fascist; the Soviet Union as the homeland of communism; Britain and the United States as the leading liberal democratic powers. The rise of nationalism thus provoked a crisis at once domestic and international. Modernity was born in the threat of revolution, secession, and war.

Until the mid-nineteenth century, the growth of nationalism and the turmoil attending it was a political matter largely confined to Europe and the Western Hemisphere (including Latin America, whose separation from Spain was based on much the same mix of economic interests and demands for more popular representation that fueled the American Revolution). Soon thereafter, its appeal was evident in lands as diverse as Russia, the Balkans, China, Japan, and Turkey.

In the twentieth century the nationalist watchword became *self-determination*, and its power was most immediately evident in World War I, when nationalism contributed directly to the collapse of the Russian, Austro-Hungarian, and Ottoman multinational empires. Nationalism also changed the character of Mexico in the Revolution of 1910, and by the 1920s was felt with redoubled force in China and Japan while foreshadowing the eventual end of European empire in countries as different as India, Indochina, and Indonesia. In the aftermath of World War II, nationalist demands were global. By then the crisis of modernity—how to establish a state capable of expressing the popular will—had become a universal concern.

Granted that statesmen in the twentieth century recognized the power of nationalism—which, unfortunately, they often did not—the important question was how the upsurge of popular political participation would express itself institutionally in the new states being created, and how a world order of nation-states could then be most stably constituted. Nationalism might be a solvent of empire, a destroyer of monarchies; but what of its state-building capacities—what institutional form would it devise to handle diversity and conflict for the people who believed they were riding it to freedom, justice, and dignity?

To the extent that thinkers in the nineteenth century provided a reply to the political chaos caused by the rise of nationalism, they tended to believe in a natural affinity between the rise of popular sovereignty and the emergence of a liberal or social democratic state. Here was a principal reason liberals and democrats of the time viewed nationalism so positively, whether in Poland or in Greece. By the early 1930s, however, with the collapse of democracy in Germany and most of Eastern Europe, any notion that nationalism was inherently a progressive force was revealed to be profoundly mistaken.

World War I thus failed not only to settle traditional balance of power concerns in Europe—principally the question of how German power could be contained—but it also proved unable to give birth to a stable form of the modern state in the region, that is, to government based on some notion of popular sovereignty expressed through a system of political parties. Henceforth, rivial forms of nationalism were in competition—traditional authoritarians being challenged or replaced by democrats, fascists, and communists.

What each of these three rival creeds of modernism provided was a set of relatively explicit blueprints of governmental and popular organization to embody the nationalist sentiments let loose in the modern era, ideas far more concrete than the nationalist call for self-government alone could provide and embodied in political parties anxious to take power. In the process, the traditional competition among states in the international system was now complicated by the fact that the leading governments of the period espoused rival forms of domestic organization: the United States, Britain, France, and their allies calling for democracy; the Soviets and their comrades in the Comintern (the Third International) promoting communism through world revolution; and the Germans, Italians, Japanese, and their imitators championing some form of fascism. In effect, three kinds of rivalries overlapped one another: that of states, that of nationalisms, and that of ideologies.

As the Spanish Civil War (1936–9) was the first arena of combat to reveal, the differences among these rival political embodiments of nationalism were fundamental, concerning their definition of the national community and the character of world order. How inclusive would the "nation" be; could its concept of citizenship handle internal diversity in the name of broad principles of inclusion, or would it instead seek to exclude some categories of people (by race or class) from belonging to the collectivity by virtue of their apparently unassimilable character? How would the "nation" select its representatives; would a single party privy to the general will appoint the leaders, or was there to be some process of universal suffrage and representative government? How would the "nation" deal with the rest of the world: as one people among the many, willing to submit disputes to the binding arbitration of peers, or as a victimized or conquering group determined to remake world order on principles other than those of mutual respect and cooperation through international law and organization?

In a word, not all nationalisms were or are alike—nor in their mutual antagonisms did they pretend that they were. In their various ways during the interwar years, communists, fascists, and democrats proposed fundamentally opposed conceptions of citizenship and the state as well as of relations among peoples. As a result, the moral foundation of the state, the matter of its legitimacy, became as much a reason for individuals and groups to struggle internationally as domestically. Not only were "co-religionaries"—be they fellow communists, fascists, or liberal or social democrats—in a struggle literally for their lives abroad, but the agenda in world affairs of the state to be created by the victory of one of these parties would presumably reflect a worldview born of the values and interests possessed by the coalition that ultimately took power.

The greatness of Woodrow Wilson rests on his remarkable intuition of the importance of these matters in an era when communism had only recently come to power and fascism was just being born. Rather than struggling futilely against the storm, he sought to channel nascent nationalist forces in the direction of becoming democracies. His conviction was that a world composed of a community of democratic nation-states, which respected diversity and the rule of law internally, would contribute by the same token to a peaceful international order. Economic liberalism, democratic self-determination, and collective security served not only American national interests but also the quest for a principled foundation of international stability fair to all peoples. In the pursuit of such an order, American leadership was vital.

Whatever the power of Wilson's vision, the world of his time was most decidedly not ready to channel its nationalist passions into the niceties of liberal or social democracy with arrangements for universal suffrage, open debate, mutual respect, competitive parties, and states based on the rule of law. Some countries—such as those of Central America and the Caribbean—were prenationalistic, and thus Wilson's sermons quickly came to naught as anarchy and authoritarianism by turns gripped the region. Except for Czechoslovakia, nationalist forces in Eastern Europe turned to authoritarianism rather than to democracy within a few years of the Versailles Peace Settlement in 1919. Everywhere fascists and communists bid against democrats in the search for power. The United States retreated into isolationism.[36]

While World War II resulted in the destruction of fascism, it did not bequeath to the postwar world much more of an ability to foster stable state structures atop the demands of nationalism than had World War I. Of course, India, Ireland, and the Anglophone Caribbean were important exceptions to this generalization (and a tribute to London's governance, whatever the earlier trials of British imperialism), as was Israel, where Zionists created a democratic state. Another exception was China, whose Confucian communist revolution is best understood as part of this same wave of anti-Western nationalist fervor gaining in Asia in the early twentieth century and appearing in Africa after World War II. Elsewhere in Asia and Africa, however, the postcolonial period was largely a story of anarchy and authoritarianism, with no mass-based state able to secure its rule, just as in most of Latin America, too, party-based governments were fragile (but included Mexico, Costa Rica, Venezuela, Cuba after 1959, and Chile until 1973).

In these circumstances, where many peoples were casting about for a modern form of the state that could embody nationalist demands, the cold war was not simply the struggle between the United States and the Soviet Union acting as rival states in the world arena, but it was also the conflict waged within countries between two incompatible models of mass-based government, each claiming that its adoption better served the interests of the people. Although the central stake of struggle was for control of Europe, the primary arenas of tension were in the third world of Africa, Asia, and Latin America, where antagonistic nationalist groups were struggling among themselves and with traditional authoritarian elites to create political regimes based on popular participation. In the process they automatically looked to the rival superpowers for assistance.

By and large, neither great power was successful in securing imitators (as opposed to clients); communism seemed to have as hard a time sinking roots in these regions—even in Latin America where anti-Americanism was strong—as did democracy. In these circumstances, the dilemma for American policy was to decide when to act in terms of the traditional politics of international relations, where cooperation with whomever was available against mutual enemies mattered most, and when to act in terms of the new politics of the modern world, where promoting democratic governments abroad better served national security.

THE SHAPE OF THE CURRENT DISCONTENT

At the end of a terrible seventy-five years—from the outbreak of World War I in 1914 until the fall of the Berlin Wall in 1989—democracy, with its mixture of socialism and liberalism, has triumphed in the West. Its managed market economies and its welfare provisions, its empowerment of civic society through a range of civil liberties and competitive party systems, and the variety of its representative governmental structures have shown it to be effective economically and stable politically relative to alternative political systems. Most critically for this study, democratic governments have also demonstrated a historically unprecedented ability to serve as a basis for collective action on the part of like-minded states.

The triumph of democratic government over the rival regimes opposing it was no foregone conclusion. Its victory depended on nationalist commitment to an ideology that is not essentially belligerent as well as on its intrinsic abilities with respect to politics and the economy. Triumphalism should be restrained, however: the horrors of World War II might have been reduced had the democracies acted earlier against the rise of fascism, the United States surely overmilitarized the cold war, with cruel results for the peoples of Asia especially, and whatever the success of the peace based on "the balance of terror" of mutual nuclear annihilation, we should be thankful that no calamity occurred.

Nor has the defeat of Soviet communism meant that the furies of nationalism will everywhere finally be embodied in stable democratic government. Indeed, the end of the superpower contest has released nationalist inhibitions in large parts of the world where governments once dependent on foreign backing find this support ending and their regimes under siege from popular forces or rival states. In some instances, the failure of democratic government will probably be largely irrelevant to American security—as in Central Asia, South Asia, and most of Africa. Elsewhere, however, opposition to democratic government reflects an explicit hostility to the West by nations whose power matters. The irony of the United States' position in the mid-1990s is that the triumph of democracy notwithstanding, its ability to underwrite a new world order remains limited.[37]

In fact, in many parts of the world, authoritarian and totalitarian movements and governments may be gaining strength. If democracy appears to be healthy in some countries of Eastern Europe, it is prudent to reserve judgment on its eventual fate in several others. The critical question remains Russia. After a moment of optimism when the Soviet empire broke apart in 1989, followed by the Soviet Union itself in 1991–2, it became clear that there was no necessary natural affinity between the powerful force of Russian nationalism, with its demand for collective protection and its militaristic threats (embodied in individuals like Vladimir Zhirinovsky), and the more contingent appeal of democracy, with its claims for tolerance, compromise, and a state of limited powers in a world where Russian influence would be reduced.[38]

In Asia, too, the prospects for democracy are cloudy. In India despite a distinguished democratic history, some form of authoritarian rule seems likely eventually to prevail if the rise of Hindu fundamentalism continues. Only time can tell what political future awaits China once its aged leadership leaves power. There is no reason to be optimistic about democracy's prospects. China's nationalist self-confidence and insularity, its ethnic homogeneity, its economic vigor, and its interpretation of what happened to the Soviet Union when it experimented with Western ways all presumably combine to restrain its enthusiasm for adopting a form of government as foreign as democracy. One can only worry that its elite, increasingly unable to manage a diverse and rapidly changing society, may decide to militarize its foreign policy in order to bring about domestic unity.

From the perspective of the mid-1990s, the relationship of Islam to democracy appears problematic as well. To date only Iran has tried to institutionalize a modern, mass-based state, and it would be premature to judge the likely political development of the rest of the Muslim world by a single example. Nevertheless, even as it becomes more democratic (the will of the majority apparently being represented), the Iranian state does not appear much interested in liberalism (a state limited in its powers and responsible to a civil society politically empowered to protect its diversity). Although Muslim culture holds to the equality of all believers and is rigorously legalistic, and hence implicitly constitutional, in character, its dogmatism, authoritarianism, and long tradition of personalism explain why no Islamic country has ever had stable constitutional government (much less been a functioning liberal democracy). To the extent mass government appears, it seems based on a tyranny of the majority, closer to fascism than to democracy.[39]

Perhaps most importantly, Islamic culture tends to define itself by institutional arrangements that stand in opposition to Western practice. Those Muslim countries (Turkey, Tunisia, Jordan, Morocco, and Pakistan) that have traditionally declared themselves to be friendly to the West and its institutions (as opposed to states like Saudi Arabia, which have cooperated with the West without expressing an interest in change) have had secular leaders who have not yet succeeded in creating stable modern states. Time may now have run out. The poor masses of the population are increasingly being mobilized politically on the basis of a religious sentiment that is unlikely to inaugurate democratic government. In these circumstances, perhaps no issue is more critical for global, and not simply regional reasons, than the consolidation of the peace accord signed between Israel and the PLO in September 1993.

In sub-Saharan Africa there is also good reason to be skeptical of the prospects for democratic government. To be sure, at the local level many African villages practice forms of democratic governance; and if any way is finally to be found to bridge the numerous ethnic cleavages so common to the region, then surely it is through democracy. Nevertheless, the poverty of the continent, the lack of traditions of political unity, the competing claims on national loyalty that arise from tribal obligations, and the memories of still unsettled ancient grievances mean that one must be an optimist indeed to see how a vigorous democratic life expressing a clear nationalist identity will soon function there.[40]

Even where the democratic state appears well entrenched, there is cause for concern with respect to international cooperation. Critical Japanese-American trade disputes continue with no end in sight, feeding growing political concerns over the dangers of an arms race in the Far East. Neither NATO nor the Conference on Security and Cooperation in Europe (CSCE) has found a serious mission for itself in the aftermath of the cold war, despite the need for international action in the former Yugoslavia. And since 1992 progress on European integration has stalled: Franco-German relations, the heart of the European Community's undertaking, seem, momentarily at least, to have lost their capacity to increase the region's integration.

To be sure, it is difficult to believe that the many significant recent accomplishments of the European Community (especially the Single Act adopted in 1986–7 to enhance unity) are about to be reversed. Most importantly, the conversion of Germany to democracy appears to have put to rest the danger of German militarism.[41] Nevertheless, there are clear limitations on the probability of further integration before the end of the century. Whether it was the postponment of hopes for monetary integration in 1992–3, or the inability of the Community to take an effective stand on stopping the fighting in the former Yugoslavia after 1991, there was graphic demonstration of the Community's political immaturity.

In the mid-1990s, an era of optimism following the decline of Soviet communism has become more muted. The belief that with the collapse of Soviet communism "history has ended" is as mistaken as the notion that liberal democracy is due to be adopted worldwide.[42] The history of our age has been a struggle among classes, ethnic groups, and states over competing interpretations of how a nationalist state should be structured. That struggle is far from being resolved.

Of course the tidings of democracy are not all bleak.[43] In addition to the significant gains made for democracy in Eastern Europe, Latin America is more democratic than at any time in that region's history. Here a combination of forces appear at work. Industrial development has given a more complex socioeconomic profile to much of the continent over the last generation, disposing it to democracy (with its flexible, decentralized rule) in a way its more simple agrarian structure could not. The turn against statism in economic affairs has similarly encouraged the development of civil forces independent of the state by eroding the corporatist political structures of the region, which have for so long have impeded the advent of democracy.[44]

Some of these changes may be momentary—the military, strong men, or neocorporatism will surely reassert themselves in some instances, as one sees today in Peru and Argentina. But the external forces that played a critical, if not decisive, part in these developments may act to hold many of the changes in place. Thus, the conversion of the Iberian peninsula to democracy in the late 1970s, thanks in good measure to the European Community, as well as the end of the cold war, which has meant the decline of Marxist thought in the region, have been important in the evolution toward democracy. So too, the backing of the Roman Catholic Church for these changes has been a development of profound importance by altering the thinking of some of the more traditional elements in society.

The result has been a new era in relations between the United States and Latin America, wherein for the first time since the war with Mexico in the 1840s, Latin nationalism has begun to regard American power more as an ally than an enemy. Like Spain and Portugal, Latin America is being "Westernized" to an extent and at a pace unthinkable only twenty years ago. In Mexico, the Latin American country of most importance to the United States, the success not only of the NAFTA but also of democratic government may soon make it time to retire the celebrated expression "Poor Mexico, so far from God, so close to the United States."

In South Korea as well, the elections of December 1992 and the inauguration of Kim Young Sam as president in February 1993 appear to mark its transition from a fragile democracy to one having a government increasingly independent of the military. Similar developments are under way in Taiwan. The steadfast commitment of Japan to democratic government demonstrated again after the fall of the Liberal Democratic party from power late in 1993 suggests that democracy is not culture bound but may be adopted by Confucian peoples.

American foreign policy has traditionally emphasized the importance of Europe, Latin America, and the Far East to its national security. It is in these regions of the world that the current wave of democracy is now spreading. But Russia, China, and the Muslim world (to the extent one can speak of so many countries with hundreds of millions of citizens as a unit) still are all potentially capable of becoming profoundly hostile to Western ways. With the rise of a Hindu fundamentalism and with the apparent descent of Africa into war and starvation, the twenty-first century may be typified by rivalries of a sort different from those of communism, fascism, and democracy in the West.

The United States may be a *hegemonic* power today and the international system be *unipolar*, but these grand words should not disguise the difficulty Washington may have in bringing about stable constitutional governance in many parts of the world despite well-intentioned efforts—as in Haiti and Somalia. The truth with which Washington must live is that while the expansion of democracy worldwide is unquestionably in the interest of national security, and while America's role in world affairs has indeed been a principal cause of the expansion that has occurred in the last half century, there are definite limits on what America alone can expect to accomplish. Dare the United States make relations with a country as powerful as China dependent on its definition of human rights? Do good relations with the Muslim world necessarily presuppose the conversion of these countries to democratic government? Does anyone in the West have the answer on how outsiders should deal with Yeltsin's Russia so as to consolidate democracy's chances? When events in militarily weak countries like Haiti and Somalia defy liberal democratic influence, who can put much faith in foreign policies designed to promote reform in China, Russia, or the Muslim world?

Yet given the American security interest in the spread of democracy worldwide and its demonstrated success at certain moments, Washington would just as clearly be foolhardy not to act where conditions are favorable.[45] The United States is economically, militarily, and politically predominant in world affairs to a historically unprecedented degree. Perhaps the most important factor in Washington's success has been this country's relative strength and its powerful relations with its fellow democracies, reasons which have caused other countries to emulate the United States and seek membership in the democratic club. A weak and divided United States in decline, like a fractious Europe or a Japan that chooses to become authoritarian, would surely set back the trends favorable to democracy very considerably. Washington's first responsibility, then, is to keep its own house in order and maintain the links of solidarity among consolidated democratic states.

As a consequence of Washington's willingness to do what it can where the prospects for democracy remain problematic, a wide range of American governmental agencies have become involved on a hands-on basis with democratization efforts in foreign countries. Several branches of the State Department (most notably the U.S. Agency for International Development and the Human Rights Division) and the United States Information Agency are focusing increasingly on the kind of root-and-branch programs that might stimulate democratic development abroad. The nonpartisan (although government funded) National Endowment for Democracy fulfills similar objectives, funding movements and taking sides (in Chile, the Philippines, and South Korea in the late 1980s, for example) with democrats seeking to replace authoritarian regimes. Nongovernmental organizations (NGOs)—among them Freedom House, Human Rights Watch, Amnesty International, and former President Jimmy Carter's Democracy Project at Emory University—have also been positive influences on forces working for democracy in many parts of the world.

Practical efforts to move foreign societies toward democracy may be divided into two kinds: those dealing with social forces, and those working with the organization of government.[46] With respect to the former, the task is to help empower civil society through encouraging the independent formation of a variety of organizations such as women's groups, bar associations, student movements, labor unions, ethnic associations, the media, religious institutions, peasant leagues, and small business organizations. Obviously different countries need different tactics for democracy to succeed, but the single most effective reform from the point of view of promoting democracy may be the liberalization of market forces, which at one stroke curtails the patronage power of the state while freeing social groups to bargain independently.

However, the empowerment of society without thought to promoting a kind of social contract among these forces and backing it up with strong governmental institutions may result not in democracy, but in anarchy, followed by a return to authoritarianism. For the tyranny of the majority or the rich to be avoided, and for the people to be strong enough to preserve their freedoms against efforts by those who have lost their privileges under authoritarian rule and want to return to power, effective party systems and constitutional structures with legal codes adequate to provide the rule of

344 · Chapter Eleven

law must be instituted. In their enthusiastic promotion of popular participation, many democratizers forget how fundamental political agreements and institutions are to hold together what otherwise might be a fratricidal new order.

While there are, then, important ways the United States can act so as to promote democracy abroad, it should not exaggerate its role. Even where Washington has exercised sovereign control over other peoples and its influence has been essential for the creation of democratic institutions—as in the Philippines, Japan, and Germany—democratization necessarily required the full participation of local groups led by individuals of character and vision. It could not be otherwise; without agreement on the terms of a social contract decided by the consent of the governed, democracy could not come into existence. Washington cannot rewrite cultural histories or force social pacts on class or ethnic groups that would rather dominate or destroy one another than work together democratically.

Of course, the United States can also be part of the problem. The drug market in the United States, for example, draws as much in exports from Colombia as all the legal trade of that country with the world. Democratic order is threatened by drug traffickers grown rich on the American market in Ecuador, Peru, Bolivia, and Panama as well. Moreover, there may be a contradiction between the internationalization of trade, finance, and investment and democratic governments, as peoples around the globe react defensively to their lack of political protection from these self-interested and often brutal forces. Even in Western Europe, there was strong resistance in 1992 to increased economic integration under plans brought forward by technocrats in the European Commission in Brussels without what many felt was competent political oversight. One might also cite the rebellion in the Mexican state of Chiapas in 1994 against what many indigenous people there saw as the threat of the NAFTA to their already precarious existence. Even if the answer to these problems of economic liberalization is a reinforcement of international institutions linking democratic states, the practical obstacles to such political coordination are substantial (as the experience of the European Community illustrates).

These considerations help us to appreciate the enormous imponderables today facing American policymakers trying to encourage the consolidation of democratic governments in countries as important to national security as Mexico and Russia. Of course the United States can make a difference. Its support for market reforms and the rule of law, for human rights and basic civil liberties, and for international agreements that allow these countries to feel supported rather than challenged during the difficult transitions they are undertaking can be critical to the eventual success of democratization there. Yet no one doubts that it is ultimately Mexican and Russian leaders and social forces that will decide whether democratic government succeeds in these two lands, and that their actions will be predicated on their own reading of their individual and national interest.

At the end of the twentieth century, democracy has defied the doom-sayers and emerged triumphant over hostile forms of mass political organization. But if excessive pessimism was misplaced in the past, so too excessive optimism should be avoided today. Given the vital American security interests served by the expansion of democracy worldwide, Wilsonianism will continue to serve as a principal guide for policy. Yet given the established character of other peoples and the obvious limits on American power, Wilsonianism will not everywhere be a relevant framework for action.

The world is far too difficult and dangerous an environment to suppose that any single doctrine, especially one that looks forward to a relatively peaceful world order composed of free states, is likely to be one that is easily attained or that long endures, or that the effort to produce such a world order should always be the central concern of policymakers in Washington. However important the counsels of Wilsonianism, American leaders would do well also to keep in mind Machiavelli's remark in his *Discourses* (2, 27): "Men always commit the error of not knowing where to limit their hopes, and by trusting to these rather than to a just measure of their resources, they are generally ruined." What the historical record nonetheless shows is that this country's greatest triumphs in foreign affairs have been the result of its liberal democratic internationalism, and that American national security would surely suffer were this vision to be forgotten today, when nationalist and religious extremism are breeding anarchy and militarism in a world whose increasing political fragmentation calls for determined American leadership.

Notes on the Study of the
International Origins of Democracy

> More matter, with less art.
> —Gertrude to Polonius in Shakespeare's *Hamlet*

GIVEN THE ABUNDANT LITERATURE analyzing the character of democracy on the one hand and the nature of American foreign policy on the other, why has so little been written on the vast range of efforts the United States has engaged in during the past century to promote democratic government abroad? For the student of comparative politics, there are a variety of individual cases waiting to be analyzed in terms of a general framework; for the student of international relations, there is the history of the twentieth century to be reviewed in terms of the expansion of democracy worldwide; for the student of American foreign policy, there is the investigation of arguably the most important theme of the country's history in the twentieth century.

Yet most writing on the origins of democratic government has considered countries individually, in domestic terms, as if international influences were relatively extraneous. There are lengthy academic debates of a comparative, historical sort on the relationship between democracy and a people's level or structure of economic development. Books exist on the cultural characteristics that predispose a country to democracy, and social systems that appear favorable to democratic rule have come under close scrutiny. Scholars have argued at length about the stages of historical development that may lead to the emergence of democratic rule. However, aside from cases of settlement, such as in Canada or Australia, or with respect to individual countries exposed to sustained efforts from abroad (like Japan during the American occupation), nothing comprehensive has been written on the international origins of democracy; that is, on how and with what effect powers like the United States or Great Britain have sought to foster democracy abroad.[1]

When I began this study late in 1988, I assumed that I had somehow missed this literature. I started with the most obvious of cases, the occupations of Japan and Germany in 1945. What I found was that no comparative study existed on the subject of American efforts to remake these two militaristic socities in the aftermath of World War II, although the undertaking was an ambition of enormous importance to world affairs and the greatest peacetime achievement in the history of American foreign policy.[2]

It soon became evident that the problem was not limited to postwar American occupation policy. There was no adequate study of the American impact on democracy in the Philippines—a country held by the United States for nearly fifty years and where its first announced intention was to prepare the Filipinos for democratic self-government. Writing in 1965, Harry J. Benda noted:

> It is surprising that half a century of American involvement with Philippine affairs has, on the whole, yielded so meager a scholarly harvest. . . . Philippine democracy, one of the most fascinating but hitherto inadequately explored polities in postwar Southeast Asia, emerges clearly as a rare example of successful adaptation to an Asian environment of imported Western institutions.[3]

The scholarly record has not noticeably improved on this count in the ensuing generation.

Or again, despite the legion of competent scholars working on Latin America, only in 1992 did an edited volume appear covering a range of various episodes of American efforts—during the Wilson, Kennedy, and Reagan administrations particularly—to try to promote democracy in that region. Abraham Lowenthal, the book's editor, remarked on the "collective amnesia that affects both academia and contemporary Washington" with respect to the American impact on democracy in Latin America:

> No systematic and comparative study of past U.S. attempts to promote Latin American democracy has ever been published. Nor does the Washington policy community seem aware of this long history. Policies are fashioned and discussed, instruments are designed and implemented—all with little consciousness of the legacy of previous U.S. attempts to export democracy in the Americas.[4]

What is true of the study of U.S. policy toward individual countries holds equally for the study of the international system. In the hands of Wilson, Roosevelt, Truman, and Reagan especially, Washington attempted to construct a world order favorable to American security by promoting the establishment of democratic government worldwide. Prior to the late 1980s, however, the academic commentary tended to scoff at these pretensions, seeing them either as a hypocritical cover for American imperialism (as in Dulles's excuses for CIA-sponsored coups in Iran and Guatemala) or as a dangerous case of self-deception wherein the United States risked forgetting the limits on its power (as in Kennedy's initial position on South Vietnam).[5] Yet the course of events in the second half of this century demonstrated that American support for democracy abroad could be an effective way to truly serve the national interest. The conversion of Germany and Japan to democracy, the magnetic pull of democracy in the European

Community, and the influence of the Roman Catholic Church as it shifted its weight to support democratic government meant not only an enormous net gain to the United States in the cold war, but subsequently have pulled Southern and Eastern Europe (including much of the former Soviet Union), Latin America, Africa, and parts of the Far East toward democratic government and thus better relations with the United States.

The examples could be multiplied, but the point should be clear. Until the late 1980s, American scholarship neglected to investigate with any comparative framework or historical depth the consequences for foreign peoples and for the international system of the greatest ambition of United States foreign policy over the past century: to foster democracy abroad as a way of ensuring national security.

Why such inattention? Part of the answer may lie in the intrinsicially difficult nature of conducting so broad a study. Given the segmented life of the social sciences in the United States—where not only is economics separated from politics and history, but even within disciplines subdivisions with rigid barriers occur (as between international relations and comparative politics within political science)—the sharpest intellectual tools have been honed to examine questions that can be more precisely formulated, often through quantitative procedures, than the issues surrounding such a complex process as the American impact on democratization abroad over the past century. Whatever the praise in the social sciences for being "interdisciplinary," most leading professional reputations today are made by pursuing "elegant" formal hypotheses as "parsimoniously" as possible (as one hears at conference after conference). Whatever the professional and intellectual advantages of such highly focused pursuits, they cannot mount a study as vast as is needed to explore the international origins of democracy since the late nineteenth century.

What, then, of collaborative efforts, where different scholars contribute separate pieces to a composite understanding of a topic? These are familiar stuff in the study of topics in history, comparative politics, and international relations; indeed, in the last few years a number of excellent group studies on democratization around the globe have appeared. Why not earlier?

The central reason lies in the character of the paradigms that leading schools of social analysis in the United States have been using over the last fifty years. We may define a paradigm as a reasoned ordering of evidence used to establish a general framework of understanding. Work in the social sciences precedes on the basis of assumptions about the logic of social action that are affirmed in a theoretical literature (usually in the form of rather abstract models) and then illustrated (or proved, typically through the means of testable hypotheses) with respect to closer empirical investigations. (Perhaps the most succinct example of such a general historical model is Marx and Engel's assertion in *The Communist Manifesto* that "all history is the history of class conflict.")

Paradigms of analysis are usually the creation of individual thinkers of distinction: Marx, Weber, Durkheim, and Freud come to mind. In the United States, paradigms tend to be set by schools of analysis, where teams of scholars collaborate on specific research agendas where theoretical and empirical work are conducted in tandem. Occasionally, thinkers of note may stand apart from these team efforts: the pragmatist tradition of thinkers like William James and John Dewey, and the socioeconomic theories of Thorstein Veblen, for example. But American work is primarily recognizable in terms of the school to which it belongs.

The virtue and inevitability of paradigmatic thinking in the social sciences are undeniable. Issues of a social nature are invariably so complex that a theoretical framework is needed to order the relationship among the multiple factors to be analyzed. Once a cluster of empirically verifiable questions has been assembled and the framework has demonstrated its utility as an explanatory device, the paradigm is set. The way is now clear for refinements, for comparisons to become broader or finer—in short, for the theory itself to become enriched by studying the very reality it seeks to comprehend.

But if the virtues of paradigms are evident, so too are their drawbacks. Paradigms often dictate the questions that can be asked of social life or the answers that can be recognized. Certain topics or conclusions may be ruled out as irrelevant and therefore as illegitimate because their inclusion would threaten the integrity of a paradigm. Alternatively, a paradigm may distort the apparent logic of evidence in the process of molding it to its framework of explanation. The more highly articulated the paradigm, the more likely these strictures to apply.

For example, Marxist and realist understandings of the logic of a state's foreign policy are fundamentally incompatible. For the Marxist, the state is the executive agent of the ruling class; foreign policy will be inner-directed, the expression of class interest. Hence, domestic affairs bear directly on a country's foreign policy; if capitalists control the state, they will dictate a foreign policy the working class would not support. By contrast, for the realist, states must be primarily concerned about the prospects for war and the need to survive; their first order of action will be comprehensible not in terms of domestic politics but with respect to an evaluation of their relative positions in the international arena. For the realist, it is of relatively little importance whether Russia is czarist, communist, or democratic, for example; its foreign policy is essentially outer-directed, reflecting its place in a world of competitive states.

Of course, with some imagination (or simple common sense), it is possible to synthesize these two viewpoints. But it is a hallmark of contemporary social science literature that such hybrid work is an unstable element, unlikely to extend beyond individual maverick writers unless their work is of such genius that they can formulate their own paradigm. Ultimately, it is the integrity of the paradigm that prevails over the influence of the possibility of dispersion. Certainly the fundamental incompatibility of the Marxist and realist framework for the study of international affairs is evident if we look at the literature exponents of these schools have produced. Each paradigm is monotheistic, home to a jealous god.

The staying power of a paradigm comes from more than its strictly intellectual authority, however. The reigning paradigms with relevance to this study were all born of particular intellectual struggles: realism of the battle against Wilsonianism and liberalism in the 1930s and 1940s; postwar Marxism as a tool to bring about the union of nationalism with communism in the third world especially, in the effort to block the expansion of U.S. power; comparative politics as a deliberate effort to provide a unified school of historical understanding the equivalent to that set up by rival Marxist theory. To forget the historical origins of the way we think, to suppose that social science paradigms represent no more than disinterested intellectual frameworks is to miss an important explanation of their blindspots and staying power.

What we shall see from this review may be stated now in capsule form. Since World War II, realism has been the dominant academic paradigm in the United States for the study of world affairs. By virtue of its structure of analysis, realism argues that America has no important interest to be served by promoting democracy worldwide. Indeed, a single-minded drive in this direction, such as happened under Woodrow Wilson, fosters "idealistic" or "utopian" thinking that makes American foreign policy "ideological" and hence forgetful of the essential needs of national security defined in terms of power for the sake of the country's survival.

The second paradigm is that of non-Marxist comparative political development, which, like realism, came to maturity in the United States shortly after World War II. Its models of social interaction predispose it to study the evolution of political life in terms of domestic dynamics, which it sees as a dense and powerful interactive network where the role of international actors can have only marginal influence. To be sure, some comparativists have fervently hoped to promote democracy abroad. Nonetheless, the major tenets of the comparative approach implicitly argue against such undertakings.

The third paradigm derives from Marxism. Unlike realism, which studies world affairs, and comparative analysis, which focuses on domestic matters, Marxism has the advantage of possessing a unified theory of domestic and international politics. Nevertheless, Marxism reduces political action to economic interests and maintains that authoritarianism, not democracy, is the most likely outcome of American influence in the world.

Whatever the differences among them, then, these three paradigms agree on one matter: democracy should seldom (realist theory), can seldom (comparative theory), will seldom (Marxism) be fostered abroad by American foreign policy. The attempt to investigate the impact overseas of American liberal democratic internationalism in terms either of specific countries or with respect to the international system is thus not what a serious person (read exponent of these schools) would choose to do.

In respecting the strictures of their paradigms, American academics have neglected to study one of the great themes of American foreign policy and twentieth-century history.

International Relations Theory: The Realist Tradition

Realism holds that the major actors in world affairs are states, and that their actions will primarily be based on calculations having to do with their power relative to that of other states. Given the anarchy of the international order, war is an ever-present possibility; hence, the first duty of states is to ensure their own survival by evaluating the needs of the national security. From this perspective, *world order* may be understood as any stable distribution of power that inhibits war, while the term *the balance of power* can be used to refer to those configurations of states—whether in multipolar, bipolar, or hegemonic systems—that achieve this end.

Realists hold that their insights have been true of the human condition since time immemorial. A line they often quote comes from Thucydides' *History of the Peloponnesian War* written in the fifth century B.C.: "What made war inevitable was the growth of Athenian power and the fear which this aroused in Sparta." Or again, they cite as timeless a phrase from Machiavelli's *The Prince*, written in the sixteenth century:

> A man who wishes to make a profession of goodness in everything must necessarily come to grief among the many who are not good. Therefore, it is necessary for a prince, who wishes to maintain himself, to learn how not to be good and to use this knowledge or not to use it, according to the necessity of the case.

To bring the lessons up to date, realists may cite Henry Kissinger's hardnosed affirmation on the first page of *A World Restored*:

> Those ages which in retrospect seem most peaceful were least in search of peace. Those whose quest for it seems unending appear least able to achieve tranquillity. Whenever peace—conceived as the avoidance of war—has been the primary objective of a power or a group of powers, the international system has been at the mercy of the most ruthless member of the international community.

Based on their conviction that it is states that matter in world affairs, and that the primary focus of the state's considerations will be rational assessments of how to optimize its power position given the shape of the international system, realists' principal concerns are matters of military strategy and diplomatic negotiation as well as the logic of state action in terms of the existing configuration of power internationally. Other domains, such as economic relations, become the stuff of "high politics" only when they impinge directly on the state's power.

Realism does not deny that states may engage in mutually beneficial collaborative endeavors (military alliances, for example), that some states follow more civilized codes of conduct than others, or that the international order may not be more or less stable depending on how power in it is organized. But states, in Lord Palmerston's celebrated phrase, have interests, not friends, and this fundamental reality circumscribes all their activities. So long as world government has not become a reality, so long as states cannot know with full assurance how other states will behave and this uncertainty matters to their survival, then so long will the basic existential dilemma of international politics prevail.[6]

While the value of realism's insights should not be doubted, its recommendations come at a price. Its very analytical sharpness has led to a disregard for aspects of world affairs whose importance is devalued by its paradigm: for example, the study of international law and ethics. The reasons for this spring obviously enough from the rationale of the realist paradigm. Faced with the law of the jungle, nice distinctions of legal or ethical theory are not compelling discourses. Neither Immanuel Kant's disquisitions on categorial imperatives universally common for ethical action nor Hugo Grotius's inquiries into the character of natural law binding on all states stir much interest, for example. Moreover, realists argue that the world system is composed of a collection of states of vastly different moral codes. It would be unrealistic to expect that a universal standard of ethical behavior could be erected with equal authority for them all.[7]

Realism has shown interest in the impact of individual leaders on world affairs—for these are the people who interpret the logic of power in international politics and must be dealt with diplomatically. Nevertheless, rational leadership is more comprehensible to them than chiliastic men like Hitler or Mao, for states are better understood when they act predictably in terms of their relative power position, not when they have plans totally to reorder world affairs in a way incommensurate with their "objective" capacities.

By the same token that it discounts ethics and the role of the irrational in world affairs, realism likewise accords little importance to the domestic base of the state in its concern to explain the pattern of international relations. Hence, the tremendous change in the structure of domestic politics that has swept over the world in the last two centuries with the rise of nationalism and corresponding changes in the structure of the state, matters which are the subject of this book, would necessarily be of no more than secondary interest to realists, any more than such issues as whether a country were capitalist or Christian would matter.

What might concern the realist, however, is the danger that nationalism and its attendant ideology poses to the proper calculation of a state's place in the international system. So long as leaders are not deluded by their own rhetoric into irrational acts (as FDR was careful not to be, for example), realists can accept a modicum of ideological cant to justify reasons of state. They recognize Lenin's call for "world revolution" or Wilson's appeal for a "world made safe for democracy" as ideological masks assumed by imperialists, who imagine that once their way of life is made universal, global harmony will ensue.[8] When vacuums develop, or changes in the relative strength of the powerful occur, or the system itself alters its polarity, the result may well be bellicose language like Lenin's or Wilson's or Hitler's. But for the realist it is not rhetoric that is the goad to action, so much as shifts in the underlying structure of world power. As the Marxists reduce ideology to class interest, so the realists reduce it to state interest.

Since the twentieth century has been a period particularly rife with ideological pronouncements, realism may be willing to accord this era its distinctiveness. But it is not willing to take seriously the study of the massive transformations of domestic politics brought about by nationalism and the rival demands for popular sovereignty as critical elements in the study of world politics. A book that studies the rhetoric of liberal democratic internationalism in order to reveal its basic cynicism or to discover its inherent dangers may be welcomed. A book that looks at how this effort at international reform has reshaped domestic political systems and the character of world affairs itself in the twentieth century is not.

The reason should be evident. Like Marxists, ironically enough, realists are drawn by the assumptions of their paradigms of political analysis to see the United States' liberal democratic internationalism as an ideological mask for the projection of state power. Whereas Marxists see through the heat of nationalist debate and the claims of liberal democracy to the reality of class interests, realists see through them to the eternal quest of the state for power. Neither realism nor Marxism takes nationalist emotion or its ideological message seriously, except by reducing them to a "deeper" meaning. For realists, the danger comes when statesmen forget that their rhetoric is only intended for mass consumption and try to subsitute utopian ideals for the realities of power politics, in the manner of Woodrow Wilson (whence their visceral dislike of "Wilsonianism").

The degree to which realists are led by the logic of their own thinking is surprising to common sense, perhaps, but not to those who feel they have found a key to history across the ages. Thus, for the realist the struggles of our century have been among the major states: Britain, the United States, Germany, Japan, Russia, and China. The rise of nationalism; the modernizing imperative that a great state be based on popular support; and the ensuing struggle among traditional authoritarians, fascists, communists, and democrats—the forces, in short, which have been the fundamental and distinctive dynamic to world politics in the twentieth century—are incidental to them.

While political science has been the citadel of realism, its practitioners have included historians. Robert Dallek, for example, describes the American penchant to remake domestic orders abroad "the product of emotional displacement," "the impulse to make overseas affairs a vehicle for expressing unresolved internal tensions," "an irrational extension of internal hopes and fears." Similarly, William Pfaff, in reviewing American foreign policy from Wilson's time through Reagan's in a book sarcastically entitled *Barbarian Sentiments*, finds that whatever the presidency "the United States still is aggressively described as a model for mankind, source of idealism, seat of justice. . . . The unspoken but unmistakable assumption behind all of this was that the world would be a safe place for America only when the world was made very much like America." Americans should know, Pfaff continues, that "their language is false and their ideas are sentimental and self-aggrandizing. . . . America's problem is how to free itself from the grip of its exhausted ideas . . . an ambition sure to fail." Even John Lewis Gaddis at one point writes that Woodrow Wilson

> created in the minds of Americans an unfortunate association between the form and the behavior of governments. . . . But the most egregious example of this American tendency to confuse forms of goverment with the behavior of governments was the nation's long-standing misunderstanding of international communism. . . . There was, in all of this, a curious myopia. Whether in dealing with the Kaiser's Germany, Lenin's Russia, Nazi Germany, Imperial Japan, Stalinist Russia, Communist China, North Vietnam, Castro's Cuba, or even Nicaragua under the Sandinistas, the United States tended to equate internal form with external behavior. It assumed an "inner-directed" quality to these regimes that neglected the impact of external circumstances on what they actually did.[9]

The common denominator of these judgments is that they fail to take seriously legitimate American concerns with the outcome abroad of basic transformations in the organization of the state in the twentieth century. Ironically, Dallek and Gaddis are examples of the American insularity they deplore, while Pfaff serves to demonstrate the self-righteous moralism he debunks as quintessentially American.

To see the full strength of the realist resistance to the study of the American promotion of democracy abroad, we must understand realism not only as a social science paradigm but also as a historically constructed political position in its own right. As chapter three indicated, Walter Lippmann in the early 1940s, then George Kennan, Hans Morgenthau, and Reinhold Niebhur, used Wilson as a negative example in their reviews of the history of American foreign policy. Wilson's preoccupation with promoting democracy, they alleged, had obscured the real challenge to America in the 1930s, the threat of German domination of Europe. Thereafter, the United States was to keep its focus clearly on what mattered: namely, that no state, whatever its domestic base, achieve effective control of the Eurasian land mass, for that would create a power of such magnitude relative to the United States that this country's own freedom would be in doubt. The form of power in terms of its objective disposition was the critical matter, not its domestic organization.

The influence of these men on thinking about U.S. foreign policy thereafter is difficult to exaggerate. To be sure, realism split and evolved during the cold war. There were those (predominant in the 1950s especially) who "realistically" sanctioned support for authoritarian regimes in the third world in the name of stopping communism; and those (predominant by the 1970s) who—again in the name of "realism"—called for accommodation with the Soviet Union and insisted that superpower competition in the third world be downgraded. Yet whatever the changes and divisions, no realist could stomach "utopian" and "idealistic" thinking about the appropriateness of democracy for others.

On occasion, the realists' antipathy toward Wilsonianism served them well. They could approve of the instrumental use of democratic rhetoric by Roosevelt or Eisenhower with respect to Eastern Europe; they could criticize Kennedy for talking about Vietnam as "a laboratory for democracy"; and they might shake their heads over Carter's democratic sermons to the shah of Iran.

But in more important respects, the realists' rejection of the appeal of liberal democratic internationalism undermined their ability to comprehend international relations in this century. Lacking a theory of domestic politics, realism could not perceive the stakes involved in world affairs with the rise of mass-based states. They therefore could not appreciate the importance of the efforts to remake Japan and Germany domestically after the war, the practical seriousness of Kennedy's Alliance for Progress in the early 1960s, the political dynamic of European integration long sponsored by the United States, the depth of the appeal generated by Carter's human rights campaign in the late 1970s, or the political effectiveness of the enduring claims of Wilsonianism put forth by Reagan in the 1980s. Nor did their own paradigm save many realists from supporting American involvement in Vietnam or backing the shah, for they were quite able to argue "realistically" that the loss of these countries to movements hostile to the United States compromised the basic tenets of containment and so should be resisted for the sake of national security.

Still, satisfied by the points they had scored on a number of foreign policy failures, comforted by the record of FDR, a president whom they admired, and convinced of their wisdom in disdaining "ideology" by the seamless logic of the paradigm from which they operated, realists could dominate American academic life for over half a century and never inquire into the consequences either for foreign countries or for world politics of American liberal democratic internationalism.

COMPARATIVE POLITICS AND UNITED STATES FOREIGN POLICY

The failure of the dominant school of international relations theory to investigate the impact of American policy on democracy abroad need not necessarily have inhibited students of other disciplines from exploring the matter. Indeed, the field of comparative politics might be considered the most appropriate field for such work, given its ambition to establish general patterns of social development by studying the varied reactions among different peoples to similar developments. A topic such as the impact of American efforts to promote democracy in foreign lands would appear tailor-made to suit its agenda.

To determine why comparativists have not successfully pursued the subject, we must turn to the evolution of comparative study as a paradigm of analysis since World War II. What we find is a combination of two levels of analysis to the study of society: *macro*, or *grand theory*, which tries to see the large patterns ordering social life; and *micro*, or *middle range theory*, which looks for testable hypotheses to sustain or disprove grand theory. As we shall see, neither of these modes of study was terribly encouraging to an investigation of the international origins of democracy. When to these considerations we add the political agenda of mainstream comparativist thinking in the 1950s and its political divisions in the 1960s, the failure of the field to address the subject of this book becomes understandable.

Grand comparative theory strives to provide a comprehensive analytical framework to make sense of the basic dynamics of universal history. Writers like Marx, Weber, and Durkheim give comparative political analysis a classical tradition, where all-encompassing theories of analysis make claims to account for most features of social life in a unified manner. No single paradigm dominates the field of comparative political development, however, in the manner that realism dominates the professional study of world affairs, although it is certainly Weberian analysis that comes the closest to filling this role, thanks in good measure to the efforts of Talcott Parsons, Reinhard Bendix, and Clifford Geertz to introduce Max Weber's writing in the United States after World War II.

Comparative theorists share the working assumption that societies are complex organisms composed of inherited values and practices, where organized socioeconomic interests and political institutions interact in a historically dense manner largely resistant to foreign influence. Thus, they study the internal dynamic of societies across time, largely as if they exist in a world unto themselves (except as one people may try to emulate the achievements of another). It is almost as if the international space inter-relating states no longer exists. If one consults the offerings in virtually any university course catalog, or books dealing comparatively with different societies in terms of similar topics, the point will be clearly illustrated: comparative political study almost always leaves the analysis of inter-national relations to those who concern themselves directly with such matters.[10]

Instead of discussing foreign influences on the genesis of democracy, comparativists link its prospects to some combination of forces that can be tracked internally: to a society's path of economic development, its class and ethnic structure, its cultural values, and its political traditions. Take economic considerations, for example. Some comparativists point out that modern democracy is associated with industrial society, a form of organi-zation that necessitates an urbanized, educated, specialized citizenry. Since such a socioeconomic order undergoes constant interaction and change, it appears to mandate freedom of information and a political order capable of decentralized as well as centralized decision-making, with publicly ac-countable officeholders. Democracy and economic development hence have a pronounced affinity for one another.[11]

Others interested in the origins of democracy stress not simply the fact of industrialization but the development of a market economy and the strength it gave to civil society relative to the state. Here debates become historical, involving questions of whether the bourgeoisie is the bearer of democracy or whether one might better study the process of the incorpora-tion of labor into the political system. What matters is how various classes enter into coalition or opposition to one another during the industrialization process. Depending on the road chosen, fascism or communism may pre-vail over democracy.[12]

Whatever the differences among these analyses, what they have in com-mon is their relative disregard of the international origins of democracy. While the argument has been made that a high degree of involvement with the world market stimulates economic growth (thereby satisfying the re-quirement that a certain threshhold of economic development is necessary for democracy), this point simply does not provide an adequate foundation from which to launch a full-scale investigation of the larger role of interna-tional forces in sponsoring democracy worldwide.[13]

Some writers explicitly attack any such ambition, as, for example, Robert Dahl in *Polyarchy*, published in 1971. Probably no work on democ-ratization is cited more frequently in the vast literature on the subject. The book's opening line poses an obviously important question: "Given a re-gime in which opponents of the government cannot openly and legally organize into political parties to oppose the government in free and fair elections, what conditions favor or impede a transformation into a regime in which they can?" Dahl devotes a short chapter to "foreign control" in the birth of democratic regimes and acknowledges that in lands as different as Japan and Jamaica, American or British imperialism made for important differences. Yet at the point where one would expect a discussion of how these democratic grafts onto foreign cultures occurred, we find a warning that such efforts should be avoided. Thus, when Dahl asks under what conditions foreign domination is most favorable to the emergence of democracy, he reports that "weak or temporary" control rather than "strong and persistent" rule is more likely to succeed, although it should be evident that precisely the opposite case is more persuasive. Dahl concludes by arguing against efforts to promote democracy abroad:

> The whole burden of this book, I believe, argues against the rationality of such a policy. For the process of transformation is too complex and too poorly understood to justify it. The failure of the American foreign aid program to produce any transformations of this kind over two decades gives additional weight to this negative conclusion.

Writing eighteen years later, in 1989, Dahl's position had not changed. He continued to caution that "the capacity of democratic countries to bring democracy about in other countries will remain rather limited."[14]

To be sure, this book has repeatedly pointed out the limits on American power with respect to the ambition to foster democracy abroad. Perhaps no pattern has emerged more clearly in this study than the persistence of country-specific socioeconomic power structures and their ability to dominate local political systems, even those largely created by outside powers. India and Jamaica may have been British for generations, just as the Philippines and (to a lesser extent) Japan and the Dominican Republic bear the marks of extensive American influence. But no one doubts for an instant that these countries are quite themselves when social policies or practices are analyzed today.

Yet though India is Indian and the Philippines is Filipino, the hand of British and American rule is nonetheless still visible in both countries. Since the Philippines was American it adopted a presidential not a parliamentary form of government. Parties created there resembled in structure the open parties in the United States (with their relatively easy penetration by interest groups and control by local forces) rather than those in Britain (with their far more centralized and disciplined structures). Or again, the civil service bred by American rule was far more open to control by local Filipino interests than was the case under the British in India, who prided themselves on the bureaucratic "steel frame" they left behind in Delhi. Still again, the Americans had no political theory similar to Fabianism that the Filipino elite might borrow, as the Indian elite around Nehru did. Finally, the Americans were reluctant to reform the socioeconomic power structure of the Philippines; they promoted basic political change without addressing the question of the country's land tenure system, whose concentrated ownership was reinforced by American-sponsored international trade networks. The British were equally concerned to make allies of the Indian landed elite, part of which they deliberately created for the purpose. But as early as the 1920s, they were confronted by a principled nationalist struggle under Gandhi and the Indian National Congress party (founded in 1885, in part under British auspices), whose complex democratic organization established links with the agrarian poor, the working class, and the Untouchables in a way without the faintest parallel in the Philippines. Land reform followed Indian independence. In short, American and British efforts to bring democratic government to India and the Philippines continue to mark the political life of these two countries in profound ways half a century after their independence.

Part of the reason comparativists have failed to deal with these international forces is due to decisions made in the 1940s and 1950s, when this field of study was young in the United States. At the time, the challenge was to arrive at a "general theory of social action," motivated largely by a hope to counter Marxist claims to having the sole "science of history" that could fully comprehend the character of world affairs. The cold war globally was thus joined in the university as well.

Rather than working deductively from a single established paradigm in the manner of the realists or traditional comparative grand theory, however, American comparativists sought to create an understanding of society by merging the insights of economics, sociology, anthropology, and political science. Comparative studies increasingly became the preserve of "middle range" theorists, striving to propose testable generalizations about social life. It was not that grand theory was abandoned; rather it was to be reconstituted as the sum of parts studied independently in an empirical or inductive fashion and then carefully integrated.[15]

Ironically, the rich heterogeneity of perspectives was not the solution it thought itself to be; instead, it proved to be its own problem. Some writers had the temerity to say that a "developed" or "modern" polity was perforce democratic; others doubted this, speculating instead that alternative kinds of authority systems might provide political legitimacy, social stability, and economic growth in the late twentieth century. Analysts argued over whether democracy and modernity were synonymous, and disagreed yet again on how democracy might be achieved: some felt it must emerge gradually, as both the scope of political participation and the complexity of political institutions grew (the British or Swedish model, for example); others felt that a period of revolutionary or military government might serve as a necessary prelude to the inauguration of democracy. Only a few insisted that the United States could be instrumental in the process.[16]

The problem was that this variety of viewpoints failed to come together in an integrated fashion to produce a coherent statement either on the process of development in general or on the topic of democratization in particular. Middle range comparative theory did not live up to its promise. What began as separate enterprises in a joint venture ended up being an increasingly fragmented field unable to deal with issues of broad concern.

A concrete case illustrates the fragmentation. In 1963, Gabriel Almond and Sidney Verba published *The Civic Culture: Political Attitudes and Democracy in Five Nations*, a widely read study that sought to establish the social-psychological profile of individual democrats. According to the authors, "The central question of public policy in the next decades is what content [an] emerging world culture will have . . . [which in turn has] raised questions of the future of democracy on a world scale." The "contemporary historical challenge," they felt, was the contest between democracy and totalitarianism so that "understanding the problems of the diffusion of democratic culture" was a prime responsibility of the West. While the authors recognized that it still remained a "mystery" how democracy, "a set of arrangements and attitudes . . . so fragile, so intricate, and so subtle" could be "transplanted out of historical and cultural context," they nonetheless concluded: "we hope to contribute to the development of a scientific theory of democracy" for precisely such a purpose.[17]

For many, the *Civic Culture* represented a breakthrough for political science, the ability to formulate transnational psychological surveys of the basis of modern citizenship. New courses were taught, books published, journals enriched, and professional careers established. For our purposes, however, the shortcoming of the *Civic Culture* is its striking inability to see the establishment of democracy in more than a partial way—from the viewpoint of social psychology with a conservative bias against militant social reform. What good could such lessons be unless they were integrated into a more comprehensive understanding of the nature of democratic government?

The ready answer might be that studies of the civic culture were intended to be but one aspect of just such a greater enterprise. The trouble was that the general theory these writers awaited, like the holy grail, never materialized from their efforts. Significant work was done by writers in a variety of fields, except that once the search for a general theory was implicitly abandoned, the comparative study tended to fragment into distinct fields, each with its specialized hypotheses and literature. A complex issue like the emergence of democracy at the behest of foreign forces simply could not be studied.

Even works dealing explicitly with the organization of the state suffer from this limitation. Consider, for example, the book generally considered to be the best comparative framework for the study of political institutions:

Samuel Huntington's *Political Order in Changing Societies* (1968). The power of Huntington's work comes from the singular emphasis he gives to the autonomy and importance of political institutions in a people's history. But the book neglects—and at times explicitly dismisses—a battery of other issues including a country's pattern of ethnic splits, cultural values, or foreign influences.[18]

A quarter of a century later, little has changed. Illuminating as more recent literature is on the "transition" to democracy, its "consolidation" or its "breakdown," today's writing still typically lacks a sufficiently comprehensive framework of analysis to explore socioeconomic factors that promote democracy. Much less does it consider as more than incidental the impact of foreign actors on the process.[19]

To conclude: neither grand nor middle range comparative political theorists concerned themselves more than marginally with the international sources of domestic politics. In the hands of its American exponents such as Parsons, classical theory stayed in the stratosphere of lofty formalism—too abstract for the purpose, too rigidly wedded to general propositions that did relatively little to illuminate actual historical processes, too committed to the idea that each country had to be studied on its own terms. By contrast, middle range theory, which was out there in the trenches dealing with a wide variety of facts, never was able to overcome its forces of dispersion, unleashed after 1945, when each of the social science disciplines began more self-consciously to till its own field.

The historical origins of the decision by social scientists in the 1940s and 1950s to engender "a general theory of social action" lay in the effort to counter Marxism's unified theory of historical change. As its origins were historical, so its decline was related to Washington's failures in the 1960s in the Alliance for Progress and Vietnam to quell the appeal of communism. Demoralized by the failure, comparative studies—and the search for a general theory—became "area studies," where guilds of professors and students labored on common themes whose specialized nature made a common field of political development an increasingly distant prospect.

THE MARXIST STUDY OF AMERICAN FOREIGN POLICY

For decades now the disagreements among historians over the dynamics of American foreign policy in this century has centered on the origins of the cold war—the period from planning for the postwar order after the victory over Germany and Japan through the early stages of the Korean War in 1950. Why did the bitter contest between Washington and Moscow begin? Might it have been avoided altogether, or ended earlier, or kept from expanding to Asia had sounder counsels prevailed in Washington? Or did its origins lie instead in Moscow? Or was it perhaps the bipolar structure of postwar relations with a power vacuum in Europe after 1945 that made the cold war almost inevitable (and, on balance, far less deadly than it might have been—whatever the carnage in Vietnam and Afghanistan—had leaders not been as prudent as they were)?

While Marxism has never found much favor in mainstream American intellectual life, it can provide a contrasting perspective from dominant modes of study in a way that has consistently invigorated scholarly investigations. This is certainly true of the topic at hand, for after 1945 Marxism had a unified theory of domestic and international politics, which afforded it a strong framework from which to investigate the logic of American foreign policy. It thus was spared the handicaps of its "bourgeois" rivals, whose efforts to conceptualize world politics were split among international relations, which preferred to study the international system independently of domestic politics; comparative theory, which did exactly the reverse; and traditional American diplomatic historians, who were bedeviled by their own lack of a cogent theoretical framework providing unity to their studies and a compelling answer to the Marxists.[20]

Until the early twentieth century, Marxism was a theory of comparative politics; that is, it essentially dealt with countries in terms of their internal class dynamics. So far as the study of a country's foreign policy in the nineteenth century was concerned, it was axiomatic that it served the interests of the bourgeoisie. However, with its various studies of imperialism that appeared in the second decade of this century (approaches that were improved upon during the 1920s by intellectuals within the Communist International), Marxism came to have a theory of world affairs as well.

By the 1960s, Marxists (many of whom were Americans for the first time) had added further refinements to their argument. Some writers investigated splits within the capitalist class (as opposed to stressing the interests of this class as a whole) and speculated on the repercussions this might have on the conduct of the state. Others wrote of the "world system" as constituted by the relative needs and capacities of the leading capitalist states, while analyzing through concepts of "dependency" the political vicissitudes of the weaker states on the "periphery" of world affairs, which were subjected to the tides of fortune emanating from the "core" capitalist countries. Although there might be rough edges and disagreements within this school of analysis, Marxism found itself armed with a unified concept of history able to see domestic political developments and international affairs in terms of one another. As a result, Marxism became a formidable ideological weapon during the cold war, turning the nationalist convictions of many intellectuals in Latin America, Asia, and Africa especially in the direction of communism.[21]

A brief review of the Marxist approach cannot do justice to the variety of arguments it has advanced, perhaps, but the common denominator of this large literature has been its single-minded insistence on changes in economic structure and class interest as the basis of the behavior of capitalist states and the evolution of world affairs. So far as Africa, Asia, and Latin America are concerned, for example, these analysts claim that, thanks to British activity since the early nineteenth century and U.S. foreign policy after 1898, Washington found weaker countries ready for its leadership. Collaborating classes, dependent on import-export concerns, took over the governments of the weaker peoples, running them for their own interest and that of their foreign bourgeois benefactors. Economic development in Africa, Asia, and Latin America therefore occurred quite differently than in Europe, producing particularly weak states (because of shallow bases in terms of local social alliances) that tended to be authoritarian since they relied heavily on outside support rather than domestic coalitions to stay in power. Rivalries among the powerful, or alterations in the structure of economic production, might modify the character of the dependent state, to be sure, but the nature of its development predisposed these regions to remain poor and undemocratic. From this perspective, it would be preposterous that students of American foreign policy should take the democratizing elements of Wilsonianism seriously when repressive regimes were its far more likely consequence.

For Marxists looking at Washington rather than the periphery, by contrast, changes in capitalism and the state in the twentieth century corresponded nicely to the rhetoric of liberal democratic internationalism, but that assuredly did not mean that democracy would in fact be the product of the global expansion of American power. Seen from this perspective, Wilson was the harbinger of a new American activism in world affairs based on the changing character of American capitalism and its relative power in the international arena. His ambition to make the world safe for democracy was best understood as an effort to contain the Bolshevik Revolution while preparing as much of the world as possible for American trade and investment. Although his efforts failed, they corresponded with American interests, so that with World War II and the Roosevelt presidency, America was primed to follow his lead again in its effort to create a world order subservient to its economic agenda. Given the character of the world system, such a drive led to the cold war and the ruthless supression of nationalist movements in Asia and Latin America.

Since the Marxist approach stressed the strictly class nature of state action, American attempts to foster democracy abroad could only be interpreted as an effort to protect the interests of American capitalism by associating it with complementary forces abroad. Instead of making the world safe for democracy, the United States' first ambition was to make the world safe for corporate profit. Washington might use the rhetoric of democracy and might even come to believe it (after all, effective exploitation requires a self-righteous frame of mind). But if in some few instances the political impact of American power was indeed democracy, elsewhere it was sure to be dictatorship; everywhere it would be hypocritical.

Given these working assumptions, Marxism mistook both the deepest wellsprings of American foreign policy and the most lasting character of its consequences abroad. So far as Marxism was concerned, neither Soviet behavior, nor the concerns automatically raised by the structure of a bipolar world order, nor legitimate considerations of national security dating back to the Monroe Doctrine determined American policy, but rather its capitalist dynamics. The Marxist paradigm was thus yet another obstacle to a serious investigation of American liberal democratic internationalism.

The problem with the Marxist perspective may be put simply: it lacks a theory of politics. Take the issue of national security. In international relations, where there is no common sovereign, where anarchy prevails, each state must look first to its own resources for survival. As realist theory has long held, this issue is the basic existential preoccupation of every government in a world arena where war is an ever-present possibility. Hence, states are universally vigilant that a hostile power or coalition not have the ability to limit its action in some critical way or to subordinate it completely. Such concerns are necessarily political, even when they focus on economic, psycho-cultural, or geostrategic matters, for they are preoccupied with the organization and use of power as the ultimate question on which all these other issues have bearing.

But for Marxists, this dimension of reality simply does not register as an analytically significant feature of world affairs; they find other ways to explain the conduct of a capitalist country's foreign policy or the evolution of world affairs. Reducing all behavior to economic interest, they cannot accord either autonomy or importance to political considerations having to do with calculations of national security or the balance of power. It is this theoretically induced blindness of Marxism, in combination with its conviction that its own insight is the riddle of history solved, that makes it so rigid and doctrinaire.

As a consequence, Marxists could not grasp the rationale in national security terms for the American effort to influence the nationalist political dynamic of other peoples; instead, they had to deconstruct the ambition to find its economic roots. In doing so, these writers may have been satisfied that they had demonstrated that things were not as they seemed and that they were telling harsh truths to a cruel and hypocritical world. Yet whatever the occasional insight Marxism generated, in fact much more than class interest and class power determine human relations. In its failure to grasp the character of these other forces, Marxism failed altogether to appreciate either the political origins and reasoning of American liberal democratic internationalism in national security calculations or its impact on world affairs.

Thus, Marxism could not see the Monroe Doctrine as an essentially strategic defense of the Western Hemisphere grounded in national security considerations any more than it could credit the Open Door with being a political agenda whose major aim through the 1930s was to preserve China from Japanese aggression. Woodrow Wilson in Paris was seen as bungling the interests of American capitalism rather than dealing seriously with the political character of nationalism in his hopes for expanding democratic government. FDR's effort to keep the Soviets out of Eastern Europe and promote West European decolonization in Africa and Asia had its deepest meaning in terms of the economic, not geopolitical, calculations of Washington's leaders. Even the wars in Korea and Vietnam, distant as they might be from concrete economic concerns, could be explained by Marxist assumptions. Indeed everywhere in the third world, Marxists saw Washington shoring up authoritarian regimes, not out of national security concerns but for the sake of economic exploitation. As for the force of nationalism in world affairs, the Marxists appealed to it ceaselessly (ironically enough) with arguments that should it give in to Washington it would be betraying the integrity of its people, while in analytical terms failing altogether to grasp its strength (as the Soviet Union was to discover when it began its political reforms in 1987).

THE WAY FORWARD

Three kinds of analytical tools are necessary in order to take American liberal democratic internationalism seriously. First, students of U.S. foreign policy need a sense of the historical formulation of such a doctrine in terms of an articulation of American national security concerns shared by a wide segment of the American population. Such a study would show how across time—going from the Monroe Doctrine to Reagan's democratic revolution, for example—the United States developed a security doctrine promoting a politically plural world order, a design for the proper organization of international affairs that reflected a combination of distinctively American ways of being whose identity included a relatively self-sufficient economic base; a capitalist class largely independent of the state; geographic isolation from the centers of world power; a socially and politically weak military establishment; a stable political democracy; and a culturally specific way of perceiving and arguing about the logic of world events.

The problem in developing such a perspective in formal, theoretical terms has been that while international relations theory has articulated a persuasive argument as to the critical importance of thinking politically about national security, it has done so on the basis of the analysis of strictly international forces and so has failed to deal with the internal dynamic of the formation of the American agenda. Students of American foreign policy would thus be well advised to borrow from the Marxists a sense of the internally generated, historical development of a security perspective, though to depart from this school in its single-minded pursuit of economic explanations in favor of the kinds of arguments found in international relations theory, which correctly stress the primacy of the political. The result should be a theoretical basis for a unified approach to the study of American foreign policy that is capable of respecting the various elements entering into play (of which economic considerations is certainly one) in the course of establishing the meaning of national security understood as the political matter of ultimate importance in the articulation of American foreign policy.

Second, students of American foreign policy must develop a sense of the evolution of international history in terms allowing American security doctrine to be evaluated as a force with resonance in world affairs. Once again, realism has failed in this task because of its ahistorical approach to international relations, which deliberately slights the study of domestic politics. By contrast, Marxism with its world system approach indicates a path to follow, although again with the priviso that the single-minded study of economic forces be superseded by a discussion of international political development. The result should be a far richer understanding of the global importance of nationalism and the worldwide search for stable political order in the twentieth century; that is, an appreciation of the fierce contests—at once cultural, ideological, class based, and ethnically conceptualized—to redefine the meaning of citizenship and state legitimacy in an era when the modern state requires broad-based mass support. It is in the context of this historically specific, global struggle that American liberal democratic internationalism must be viewed, not only in terms of its economic interest and appeal, as Marxists would have it, but also for its influence on matters of ethnic and gender identity, class relations, cultural expression, domestic political organization and state-society relations, and the national stance toward questions of war and peace.

Third, the student of American foreign policy needs the analytical tools to understand the political development of specific countries in terms of the evolution of their state structures in correspondence with the forces impinging on them from the international system. No amount of study of U.S. foreign policy or the logic of the international system can adequately prepare one for the unique constellation of forces at the level of a specific country to be considered in terms of its prospects for democratic government. Comparative politics is the undisputed home of such studies, except that its variables of change have tended systematically to disregard international influences on domestic developments. Here again, the exception is the Marxists, who in their work on "dependency" have sought to explain the persistence of authoritarian state structures in Africa, Asia, and Latin America through an analysis of the place of these countries in the international division of labor. Once more, the task is to break free of the single-factor Marxist analysis of economic forces and its preconceived bias against democratic government being positively promoted by outside influences to a perspective that admits more factors at work linking the external to the internal, more variability in the outcomes of these foreign influences, and more weight to things properly political.

As we have seen, the dominant paradigms of the social sciences in the United States were formed in league with their times: realism as an attack on Wilson and a determination never again to let a menace such as Hitler's arise unopposed; comparative political development as a response to the cold war, especially to American concern to block communism's appeal to the Third World; Marxism as an ideological tool of the Third International designed to make Leninism the choice of nationalists around the world. Although they remained marked by the historical engagements that had been present at their birth, these concerns subsequently came to take on a life of their own through the paradigms of analysis they engendered and the professional establishments they created.

What, then, of social science paradigms today? With the end of the cold war, when both international and domestic politics have changed dramatically, new problems emerge, and new light is shed on past matters. Questions about entire historical epochs wait to be answered through recombinations of methods of analysis taken from Marxist, international, and comparative theory. The result should be a period of eclectic hybridization in which Marxist arguments as to the existence of a world system and the historically generated character of an American foreign policy congruent with domestic interest groups is grafted onto arguments stressing the primacy of political considerations—that is, onto realism and its understanding of the compelling logic of national security considerations; and onto comparative theory with its appreciation of the modern concern for stable massed-based states capable of possessing a nationalist legitimacy. The field of study known as international political economy has been especially fruitful in combining history, economics, and politics in a meaningful way. (Of particular note is the journal *International Organization*, whose role in sponsoring interdisciplinary studies of a sort that integrates comparative and international studies at the political as well as economic level became especially noteworthy after Robert O. Keohane became its editor.)

Let me conclude by mentioning studies that might grow from the specific concerns of this book. Cases not analyzed here include the American impact on political life in Panama, Liberia, Taiwan, and South Korea.

More importantly, major work remains to be done on the British impact on democracy in India and the Anglophone Caribbean. Why were the British successful there but not in Africa? Why were the British more likely than the Dutch or the French to leave democratic government behind them? Why were they more successful in agrarian lands than the Americans (Jamaica compared to the Dominican Republic, for example, or India compared to the Philippines)?

The focus should not be exclusively on democracy. There is no adequate work on fascism as an international movement (including its emergence in Asia, the Middle East, and Latin America in the interwar years). And what of the strength of neo-fascism today, as various countries struggle to build legitimate mass-based states? Here, I suspect, lies (unfortunately) fertile ground indeed for comparative, international study in the years ahead. In addition, we need to know far more about the diffusion of other political systems at earlier historical moments (or again today)—Confucian and Muslim especially. In all these cases, we need a more explicit sense of historical periods and of specific modes of international influences as they grafted themselves onto local political and social forces.

The end of the cold war is the beginning of a new configuration of power in the international system, ushering in a variety of profound domestic political changes as well. Old jealousies and rivalries will also fade in the academic world, to be replaced by others. The next generation of social scientists will surely find that established paradigms of analysis are in many respects ill-suited to an analysis of the world they behold. If charting the way forward is difficult, it is nonetheless an exciting time for meaningful work. What better indication of the new era for Western social science can there be than in the successful mating of Marxism, with its historical breadth of vision, to a politically centered study of American foreign policy and world affairs?

Notes

CHAPTER ONE

1. On Jefferson, see Robert W. Tucker, "The Triumph of Wilsonianism?" *World Policy Journal* 10, no. 4 (Winter 1993/1994); and Drew R. McCoy, *The Elusive Republic: Political Economy in Jeffersonian America* (W.W. Norton, 1982). Also Felix Gilbert, *To the Farewell Address: Ideas of Early American Foreign Policy* (Princeton University Press, 1961); and Tony Smith, *The Pattern of Imperialism: The United States, Great Britain and the Late-Industrializing World since 1815* (Cambridge University Press, 1981), chap. 4.

2. A controversial recent book is Francis Fukuyama, *The End of History and the Last Man* (Free Press, 1992), which maintains that successful peoples will converge on liberalism and democracy as the sole form of effective government in the modern era. Interesting as the book is, especially in its speculations on the psychological basis of liberal democracy's appeal, Fukuyama's book has two major shortcomings so far as this work is concerned: despite his pretentious claims to perceive the logic of the march of "universal history," he does not appreciate the concrete Anglo-American contributions to liberal democracy's victory today, and he far too cavalierly dismisses the likelihood that rival forms of government may one day supersede liberal democracy. See instead, Thomas M. Franck, "The Emerging Right to Democratic Governance," *The American Journal of International Law* 86, no. 1 (January 1992).

3. Lucian W. Pye, *Asian Power and Politics: The Cultural Dimensions of Authority* (Harvard University Press, 1985).

4. See the account in Ernest R. May, *American Imperialism: A Speculative Essay* (Atheneum, 1968), 120ff.

5. It is generally agreed that the "classic" definition of modern democracy is found in Joseph A. Schumpeter, *Capitalism, Socialism and Democracy* (Harper and Row, 1942), chaps. 21–23. However, the most commonly cited book today is Robert Dahl, *Polyarchy: Participation and Opposition* (Yale University Press, 1971). For current examples showing the influence of Schumpeter and Dahl, see Larry Diamond et al., *Democracy in Developing Countries: Latin America* (Lynne Rienner, 1989), xvi; and Guillermo O'Donnell and Philippe C. Schmitter, *Transitions for Authoritarian Rule: Tentative Conclusions about Uncertain Democracies* (Johns Hopkins University Press, 1986), 8.

6. Giovanni Sartori, *The Theory of Democracy Revisited* (Chatham House, 1987), 380; see also his chap. 13.

7. Harold J. Laski, *The Rise of European Liberalism: An Essay in Interpretation* (1936; Unwin, 1962); R. R. Palmer, *The Age of Democratic Revolution: A Political History of Europe and America, 1760–1800* (Princeton University Press, 1959, 1964), vols. 1–2. See also Brian M. Downing, *The Military Revolution and Political Change: Origins of Democracy and Autocracy in Early Modern Europe* (Princeton University Press, 1992).

8. Louis Hartz, *The Liberal Tradition in America: An Interpretation of American Political Thought since the Revolution* (Harcourt, Brace, 1955).

9. Alexis De Toqueville, *Democracy in America* (Harper and Row, 1966), pt. 1, chaps. 2–3. For a modern restatement of Toqueville's insistence on American egalitarianism, see Gordon S. Wood, *The Radicalism of the American Revolution* (Knopf, 1992).

10. On Reconstruction see especially Eric Foner, *Reconstruction: America's Unfinished Revolution, 1863–1867* (Harper and Row, 1988); also, Barrington Moore, Jr., *Social Origins of Dictatorship and Democracy: Lord and Peasant in the Making of the Modern World* (Beacon Press, 1966), chap. 3; Kenneth M. Stampp, *The Era of Reconstruction, 1865–1877* (Knopf, 1965); and C. Vann Woodward, *The Strange Career of Jim Crow*, 3d rev. ed. (Oxford University Press, 1974).

11. *The Federalist Papers* (Bantam Books, 1982), nos. 3, 6, 7.

12. Annual Message to Congress, December 1, 1862, *The Collected Works of Abraham Lincoln* (Rutgers University Press, 1953), 2:537.

13. *The Collected Works of Lincoln*, 2:461f.

14. Texts reproduced in Mario M. Cuomo and Harold Holzer, eds., *Lincoln on Democracy* (HarperCollins, 1990), April 6, 1859; August 22, 1862; Woodward, *Strange Career*, 21.

15. *Collected Works of Lincoln*, 7:53ff.

16. *Collected Works of Lincoln*, 8:403. See also Peyton McCrary, *Abraham Lincoln and Reconstruction: The Louisiana Experiment* (Princeton University Press, 1978).

17. Cited in Foner, *Reconstruction*, 36.

18. On Johnson, see Foner, *Reconstruction*, chap. 5.

19. Foner, *Reconstruction*, 142ff.

20. Foner, *Reconstruction*, 51ff, 69ff.

21. W. E. B. DuBois, *Black Reconstruction in America* (1935; Atheneum, 1992), 219.

22. Roger L. Ransom and Richard Sutch, *One Kind of Freedom: The Economic Consequences of Emancipation* (Cambridge University Press, 1985), 85, chaps. 4–5; Foner, *Reconstruction*, 45ff, 159ff; population figures from *Historical Statistics of the United States: Colonial Times to 1970* (U.S. Department of Commerce, Bureau of the Census, 1976), 1:26.

23. Woodward, *Strange Career*, 85; population figures, *Historical Statistics*, 1:28.

24. Moore, *Social Origins*, 115, 153.

25. Woodrow Wilson, *Division and Reunion, 1829–1889* (1893; Longmans, Green, 1897), 273.

CHAPTER TWO

1. Woodrow Wilson, "The Ideals of America," *Atlantic Monthly*, December 1902, reprinted in Ray Stannard Baker and William E. Dodd, eds., *The Public Papers of Woodrow Wilson: College and State: 1875–1913* (Harper and Brothers, 1925), 427.

2. See among others the discussion in Thomas G. Paterson and Stephen G. Rabe,

eds., *Imperial Surge: The United States Abroad, the 1890s–Early 1900s* (D. C. Heath, 1992); and Thomas G. Paterson et al., *American Foreign Policy: A History to 1914*, 2d ed. (D. C. Heath, 1983), chap. 6.

3. See, for example, the discussion in Lester D. Langley, *The Cuban Policy of the United States: A Brief History* (John Wiley and Sons, 1968), chap. 5.

4. I have paraphrased President McKinley's deliberations, reprinted in Alexander DeConde, *A History of American Foreign Policy*, 2d ed. (Charles Scribner's Sons, 1971), 351. For a discussion of the debate in the United States, see Ernest R. May, *Imperial Democracy: The Emergence of America as a Great Power* (Harcourt, Brace, and World, 1961), especially pt. 6; and Ernest R. May, *American Imperialism: A Speculative Essay* (Atheneum, 1968), especially chaps. 6–8; also James C. Thomson, Jr., et al., *Sentimental Imperialists: The American Experience in East Asia* (Harper and Row, 1981), chap. 8. Lodge is cited in Henry F. Graff, *American Imperialism and the Philippine Insurrection* (Little, Brown, 1969), xv.

5. On the economic basis of American imperialism in the Philippines, see Walter LaFeber, *The Cambridge History of American Foreign Relations II: The American Search for Opportunity, 1865–1913* (Cambridge University Press, 1993), chap. 8; also William J. Pomeroy, *American Neo-colonialism: Its Emergence in the Philippines and Asia* (International Publishers, 1970). On other motivations, see May, *Imperial Democracy* and *American Imperialism*; Julius W. Pratt, *Expansionists of 1898: The Acquisition of Hawaii and the Spanish Islands* (Johns Hopkins Press, 1936), especially chaps. 6–7; Tony Smith, *The Pattern of Imperialism: The United States, Great Britain and the Late-Industrializing World since 1815* (Cambridge University Press, 1981), chap. 4; and John M. Dobson, *America's Ascent: The United States Becomes a Great Power, 1880–1914* (Northern Illinois University Press, 1978).

6. Roosevelt is cited in Stanley Karnow, *In Our Image: America's Empire in the Philippines* (Random House, 1989), 85. Beveridge is cited in Louis J. Halle, *The United States Acquires the Philippines: Consensus vs. Reality* (University Press of America, 1985), 16; and on Beveridge see also Karnow, *Image*, 109. For a political and psychological approach to the study of American imperialism at this time, see May, *American Imperialism*.

7. Daniel B. Schirmer, *Republic or Empire: American Resistance to the Philippine War* (Shenkman, 1972).

8. Taft is cited in Peter W. Stanley, *A Nation in the Making: The Philippines and the United States, 1899–1921* (Harvard University Press, 1974), 65; Glenn Anthony May, *Social Engineering in the Philippines: The Aims, Execution and Impact of American Colonial Policy, 1900–1913* (Greenwood Press, 1980), 9; testimony in Graff, *American Imperialism*, 48, 39.

9. Root cited in Theodore Friend, *Between Two Empires: The Ordeal of the Philippines, 1929–1946* (Yale University Press, 1965), 35.

10. Lewis E. Gleeck, *American Institutions in the Philippines, 1898–1941* (Historical Conservation Society, Manila, 1976), 131. See also May, *Social Engineering*.

11. On village government, see John Leddy Phelan, *The Hispanization of the Philippines: Spanish Aims and Filipino Response, 1565–1700* (University of Wisconsin Press, 1959), especially chap. 2; May, *Social Engineering*, chap. 3; Stanley,

Nation, 37ff; Nicholas P. Cushner, *Landed Estates in the Colonial Philippines*, Southeast Asia Studies Monograph Series, no. 20 (Yale University, 1976); Norman G. Owen, "The Principalia in Philippine History: Kabikolan, 1790–1898," *Philippine Studies* 22 (1974). These studies do not all agree with one another and are incomplete on many vital questions of social organization.

12. For a discussion of Philippine social structure in comparative perspective, see Lucian W. Pye, *Asian Power and Politics: The Cultural Dimensions of Authority* (Harvard University Press, 1985), 127ff; 299ff.

13. See the description in Stanley, *Nation*, 52ff; and Karnow, *Image*, 131f.

14. Cited in Karnow, *Image*, 175. On Pardo, see also Stanley, *Nation*, 72. On the cultural adaptation of Filipino ways to American institutions, see Carl H. Lande, *Leaders, Factions, and Parties: The Structure of Philippine Politics* (Yale University Press, 1965). For comparison of American policy in the Philippines with contemporary practices toward Alaska, Hawaii, and Puerto Rico, see Julius W. Pratt, *America's Colonial Experiment: How the United States Gained, Governed, and in Part Gave Away a Colonial Empire* (Prentice-Hall, 1950), chaps. 5–7.

15. Karnow, *Image*, 60. See also, Benedict Anderson, "Cacique Democracy in the Philippines: Origins and Dreams," *New Left Review* 169 (1988).

16. Edgar Wickberg, *The Chinese in Philippine Life, 1850–1898*, Southeast Asia Studies Monograph Series (Yale University, 1965).

17. David Joel Steinberg, *Philippine Collaboration in World War II* (University of Michigan Press, 1967), 9. See also Ferdinand E. Marcos, *The New Philippine Republic: A Third World Approach to Democracy* (Manila: n.p., 1982), 5. Marcos gives a population of 2.5 million in 1810, of whom 119,000 were Chinese mestizos, 4,000 Spanish, and 7,000 Chinese.

18. The notion of the collaboration of the Filipino elite with the Americans is discussed by Steinberg, *Collaboration*, chap. 2.

19. Karnow, *Image*, 272. See also United States government's, *Area Handbook for the Philippines*, in two editions, 1969, 253ff., and 1976, 284ff. Francisco Lara, Jr., and Horacio R. Morales, Jr., "The Peasant Movement and the Challenge of Rural Democratisation in the Philippines," *The Journal of Development Studies*, July 1990.

20. *Area Handbook for the Philippines*, 1969, 298, 293. For further discussion, see the comparison of the Philippines with the Dominican Republic in the following chapter.

21. Onofre D. Corpuz, *The Philippines* (Prentice Hall, 1965), chap. 4.

22. Aquino is cited by Karnow, *Image*, p. 177; see also Karnow, *Image*, 22, on the "sixty families"; and Corpuz, *Philippines*, chap. 4.

23. John Foreman, *The Philippine Islands* (1906; Manila: Filippina Book Guild, 1980), 601f; Dean C. Worcester, *The Philippines Past and Present*, ed. by Ralston Hayden (Macmillan, 1930), chap. 28; W. Cameron Forbes, *The Philippine Islands* (Houghton Mifflin, 1928), 1:323ff, 2:89ff; and Alejandro M. Fernandez, *The Philippines and the United States: The Forging of New Relations* (Quezon City: NSDB-UP Integrated Research Program, 1977), 142f.

24. An example of American thinking at the time is chap. 28 of Worcester, *Philippines*. Worcester was secretary of the interior of the Philippines and a member of the Philippine Commission from 1901–1913.

25. Stanley, *Nation*, 236ff.

26. On MacArthur, see Karnow, *Image*, chap. 12; also Steinberg, *Collaboration*, chap. 6; and William Manchester, *American Caesar* (Dell, 1978), especially chap. 7, 439f, 487ff.

27. Friend, *Between*, 248f. When MacArthur refused, Ickes insisted that anyone above level of school teacher who had held civil office be deprived of the right to vote or hold office for a period of one election. His suggestion was ignored.

28. See Carol Morris Petillo, *Douglas MacArthur: The Philippine Years* (Indiana University Press, 1981), chap. 6.

29. Karnow, *Image*, 345f.

30. Benedict J. Kerkvliet, *The Huk Rebellion: A Study of Peasant Revolution in the Philippines* (University of California Press, 1977); and Richard J. Kessler, *Rebellion and Repression in the Philippines* (Yale University Press, 1989).

31. *Area Handbook for the Philippines*, 1976. See also Lara and Morales, "The Peasant Movement."

32. On the agrarian question, see David Wurfel, *Filipino Politics: Development and Decay* (Cornell University Press, 1988), 165ff; also Karl D. Jackson, "The Philippines: The Search for a Suitable Democratic Solution, 1946–86," in Larry Diamond et al., *Democracy in Developing Countries: Asia* (Lynne Rienner, 1989). On Marcos's "weak authoritarianism," see Stephan Haggard, "The Political Economy of the Philippine Debt Crisis," in Joan Nelson, ed., *Economic Crisis and Policy Choice: The Politics of Adjustment in Developing Countries* (Princeton University Press, 1990); also, David A. Rosenberg, ed., *Marcos and Martial Law in the Philippines* (Cornell University Press, 1979).

33. Cited in Karnow, *Image*, 350, 390.

34. Cited in Jose Veloso Abueva, "Ideology and Practice in the 'New Society,'" in Rosenberg, *Marcos*, 33.

35. Anderson, "Cacique Democracy."

36. Students of the "export" of democracy can see from this account of the United States in the Philippines that the character of the socioeconomic power structure of the people to be democratized is of basic importance. Thus, the lack of an indigenous reformist political history in the Philippines marks that country off from, say, India, where the British during the interwar period were also attempting to lay the foundations for a democratic state. Here the development of a principled nationalist struggle under the influence of Gandhi especially, and the organization of the Indian National Congress party (founded in 1885) as early as 1920 into a complex institution able to run its internal affairs democratically while establishing links with the agrarian poor, the working class, and the Untouchables is a record of accomplishment without the faintest parallel in the Philippines.

At the same time, the distinctive mark of the imperial power needs to be paid its due. Because of the Americans, the Philippines adopted a presidential, not a parliamentary, form of government. In addition, political parties there corresponded to the open structure of parties in the United States, with their relatively easy penetration by interest groups (rather than to the more centralized and disciplined British party structures). The civil service bred by American rule was also far more open to control (i.e., corruption) by local Filipino interests than would have been the case under the British, who prided themselves on the bureaucratic "steel frame" they left behind in India. Still again, the Americans had no political theory akin to Fabianism that the Filipino elite might borrow. In all, it would appear that the British approach was superior to that of the Americans.

CHAPTER THREE

1. On Wilson's domestic struggles, see Arthur S. Link, *Woodrow Wilson and the Progressive Era, 1910–1917* (Harper and Brothers, 1954), chaps. 1–3, and Link, *Wilson: The New Freedom* (Princeton University Press, 1959), chaps. 5–8.

2. Speech of April 2, 1917, reprinted in Albert Shaw, ed., *The Messages and Papers of Woodrow Wilson* (George H. Doran, 1924), 1:372ff. His remarks on Mexico are reprinted in "A Conversation with President Wilson," in Ray Stannard Baker and William E. Dodd, *The New Democracy: Presidential Messages, Addresses, and Other Papers, 1913–1917* (Harper and Brothers, 1926), 1:111f. Wilson went so far as to endorse the land reform proposals of Pancho Villa and Emiliano Zapata. On Wilson and social reform in Mexico, see Alan Knight, *U.S.-Mexican Relations, 1910–1940: An Interpretation*, monograph series 28 (San Diego: University of California, Center for US-Mexican Studies, 1987), chaps. 7–8; Thomas J. Knock, *To End All Wars: Woodrow Wilson and the Quest for a New World Order* (Oxford University Press, 1992), 25ff; and the interesting material in Arthur S. Link, ed., *The Papers of Woodrow Wilson* (Princeton University Press, 1979), 30:39ff, 186ff.

3. Wilson, "A New Latin American Policy," the so-called Mobile speech, reprinted in Baker and Dodd, *The New Democracy*, 68.

4. "Democracy and Efficiency," *Atlantic Monthly*, March 1901, and "The Ideals of America," *Atlantic Monthly*, December 1902, reprinted in Ray Stannard Baker and William E. Dodd, *The Public Papers of Woodrow Wilson: College and State: Education, Literary and Political Papers, 1875–1913* (Harper and Brothers, 1925), 427, 436, 412.

5. Wilson, "The Ideals of America," 434, 436ff.

6. On efforts to promote constitutional democracy before Wilson, see Philip C. Jessup, *Elihu Root* (Dodd, Mead and Co., 1938), vol. 1, especially chaps. 14, 15, 17, 25; and Theodore Paul Wright, Jr., *American Support of Free Elections Abroad* (Public Affairs Press, 1964), especially chaps. 1–3.

7. Reacting to events from China to South Africa, Great Britain began to scale down its presence in the Caribbean after 1900. For the rise of a perceived German threat in the area, see the remarks by Samuel Flagg Bemis, *The Latin American Policy of the United States: An Interpretation* (Harcourt, Brace, 1943), 191; Dana G. Munro, *Intervention and Dollar Diplomacy in the Caribbean, 1900–1921* (1964; Greenwood Press, 1980), 270, 326f; and P. Edward Haley, *Revolution and Intervention: The Diplomacy of Taft and Wilson with Mexico, 1910–1917* (MIT Press, 1970), chap. 11.

8. Arnold Bauer, "Rural Spanish America, 1870–1930," in Leslie Bethell, ed., *The Cambridge History of Latin America* (Cambridge University Press, 1981), chaps. 1–2.

9. Wilson's most frequently cited statement to this effect was made on March 18, 1913, when he ended American participation in the six-power loan to China: "The conditions of this loan seem to us to touch very nearly the administrative indepen-

dence of China itself, and this administration does not feel that it ought, even by implication, to be a party to those conditions." See Link, *Wilson: The New Freedom*, 285. For Wilson's position on low interest loans to Latin America, see Link, *Wilson: The New Freedom*, 337f.

10. Buchanan is cited in Howard F. Cline, *The United States and Mexico*, rev. ed. (Harvard University Press, 1963), 141. See also Bemis, *Latin American Policy*, 160f.

11. "A Statement on Relations with Latin America," in Arthur S. Link, ed., *The Papers of Woodrow Wilson*, (Princeton University Press, 1978), 27:172.

12. For a fuller account, see Link, *The New Freedom*, chaps. 11–12. This discussion also draws on Knight, *U.S.-Mexican Relations*; Knock, *To End All Wars*; Kendrick A. Clements, *The Presidency of Woodrow Wilson* (University Press of Kansas, 1992), 99f; John S. D. Eisenhower, *Intervention! The United States and the Mexican Revolution, 1913–1917* (W. W. Norton, 1993); and for economic issues especially, Lorenzo Meyer, *Mexico and the United States in the Oil Controversy, 1917–1942* (University of Texas Press, 1977), 34ff, chap 4.

13. Cited in Link, *The New Freedom*, 379, 386f.

14. Wilson in Baker and Dodd, *New Democracy*, 119. On Wilson in Mexico see also Knight, *US-Mexican Relations*, chaps. 7–8, and on economic matters, chaps. 5, 8.

15. The classic account remains Sumner Welles, *Naboth's Vineyard: The Dominican Republic, 1844–1924* (Payson & Clarke, 1928), vol. 2, chaps. 13–15. Other excellent reviews are Munro, *Intervention*, chap. 7; and Arthur S. Link, *Wilson: The Struggle for Neutrality, 1914–1915* (Princeton University Press, 1960), chap. 15.

16. Bruce Calder, *The Impact of Intervention: The Dominican Republic during the U.S. Occupation of 1916–1924* (University of Texas Press, 1984), chaps. 2–4.

17. Marvin Goldwert, *The Constabulary in the Dominican Republic and Nicaragua* monograph 17 (University of Florida, School of Inter-American Studies, 1961).

18. See Munro, *Intervention*, chaps 8–10.

19. An exception is Bemis, *Latin America Policy*, 191, which may well be the reason his own critics have dubbed him "U.S. Flagg Bemis." For the first of the unsparing criticisms of Wilson, see Welles, *Naboth's Vineyard*.

20. Thus, in both Guatemala and Costa Rica, Wilson blamed United Fruit for initiatives that unsettled constitutional rule there. On Costa Rica, see Munro, *Intervention*, 428ff, 447ff. Again, with respect to Mexico, the president repeatedly denounced selfish North American economic interests that tried to compromise Mexican sovereignty; see e.g., Wilson, "The Mexican Problem Again: An Interview," in Baker and Dodd, *The New Democracy*, 2:339ff.

21. See Samuel P. Huntington, *Political Order in Changing Societies* (Yale University Press, 1968), chap. 1.

22. For an overview of the distinctively Latin American model of political behavior, see Howard J. Wiarda, *The Democratic Revolution in Latin America* (Basic Books, 1992).

23. Calder, *Impact of Intervention*, introduction. See also Howard J. Wiarda, "The Dominican Republic: Mirror Legacies of Democracy and Authoritarianism," in Larry Diamond et al., *Democracy in Developing Countries: Latin America* (Lynne Rienner, 1989).

24. Cited in Welles, *Naboth's Vineyard*, 918.

25. See Calder, *Impact of Intervention*, chaps. 2–4. On sugar, see Manuel Moreno Fraginals, "Plantation Economies and Societies in the Spanish Caribbean, 1860–1930," in Leslie Bethell, ed., *The Cambridge History of Latin America*, vol. 4. On foreign involvement see also Catherine M. Conaghan and Rosario Espinal, "Unlikely Transitions to Uncertain Regimes: Democracy without Compromise in the Dominican Republic and Ecuador," *Journal of Latin American Studies* 22, (1990): 556.

26. See Wilson's views on economic justice and land reform in his interview of May 1914; also Knight, *U.S.-Mexican Relations*, chap. 7.

27. Wilson continued (in words that could also be used to criticize his own later policy): "Misled by our own splendid initial advantage in the matter of self-government, we have suffered ourselves to misunderstand self-government itself. . . . The people of the United States have forgotten the discipline which preceded the founding of the colonies, the long drill in order and in obedience to law, the long subjection to kings and to parliaments which were not in fact of the people's choosing. They have forgotten how many generations were once in tutelage in order that the generations which discovered and settled the coasts of America might be mature and free. No thoughtful student of history or observer of affairs needs to be told the necessary conditions precedent to self-government: the slow growth of the sense of law; the equally slow growth of the sense of community and of fellowship in every general interest; the habit of organization, the habit of discipline and obedience to those intrusted with authority, the self-restraint of give and take; the allegiance to ideals, the consciousness of mutual obligation; the patience and intelligence which are content with a slow and universal growth." Wilson, "Democracy and Efficiency," 396f, 406f.

28. On Wilson, the Civil War, and African-Americans, see August Heckscher, *Woodrow Wilson* (Charles Scribner's Son, 1991), 1ff, 11ff, 16ff, 290ff.

29. Woodrow Wilson, "The Reconstruction of the Southern States," January 1901, in Baker and Dodd, *Woodrow Wilson*, 377f.

30. John Maynard Keynes, *Essays in Biography* (Horizon Books, 1951), 21f. See also Garry Wills, "The Presbyterian Nietzsche," *New York Review of Books*, January 16, 1992.

CHAPTER FOUR

1. Thomas J. Knock labels Wilson's New Diplomacy "progressive internationalism." See Knock, *To End All Wars: Woodrow Wilson and the Quest for a New World Order* (Oxford University Press, 1992). On the traditions of American foreign policy from which Wilson could draw, see Tony Smith, *The Pattern of Imperialism: The United States, Great Britain, and the Late-Industrializing World since 1815* (Cambridge University Press, 1981), chap. 4.

2. The point deserves qualification. In the Fourteen Points, Wilson tried to alleviate Russian territorial concerns. In addition, Wilson was initially reluctant to agree to the dismemberment of the Austro-Hungarian empire, hoping that internal reforms could preserve it. See Wilson's request to Congress for a declaration of war against Austria-Hungary, December 4, 1917, in Albert Bushnell Hart, ed., *Selected*

Addresses and Public Papers of Woodrow Wilson (Boni and Liveright, 1918), 235; Arthur S. Link, *Woodrow Wilson: Revolution, War, and Peace* (Harlan Davidson, 1979); Francois Fejto, *Requiem pour un empire defunt: Histoire de la destruction de l'Autriche-Hongrie* (Lieu Commun, 1988), chap. 27.

3. Wilson in Saint Louis, September 5, 1919, in Albert Shaw, ed., *The Messages and Papers of Woodrow Wilson* (George H. Doran, 1924), 2:757.

4. Wilson in San Diego, September 19, 1919, in Shaw, *Messages and Papers*, 2:1015.

5. Wilson to the United States Senate, January 22, 1917, in Shaw, *Messages and Papers*, 1:353, 355.

6. Woodrow Wilson, *The State: Elements of Historical and Practical Politics* (D. C. Heath, 1898), 494.

7. Wilson cited in Klaus Schwabe, *Woodrow Wilson, Revolutionary Germany, and Peacemaking, 1918–1919* (University of North Carolina Press, 1985), 18. For an informed discussion of Wilson and self-determination, see Betty Miller Unterberger, *The United States, Revolutionary Russia, and the Rise of Czechoslovakia* (University of North Carolina Press, 1989), chap. 7.

8. Wilson before Congress, April 2, 1917, in Hart, *Addresses and Papers*, p. 193.

9. Wilson before Congress, December 4, 1917, in Hart, *Addresses and Papers*, 237.

10. Kay Lundgreen-Nielsen, "Woodrow Wilson and the Rebirth of Poland," in Arthur S. Link, ed., *Woodrow Wilson and a Revolutionary World, 1913–1921* (University of North Carolina Press, 1982).

11. Wilson before Congress, April 2, 1917, in Hart, *Addresses and Papers*, 194.

12. Wilson on June 14, 1917, in Hart, *Addresses and Papers*, 212.

13. Bowman cited in Charles Seymour, *Intimate Papers of Colonel House: The Ending of the War* (Houghton Mifflin, 1928), 4:282.

14. Wilson cited in Lloyd Gardner, *The Anglo-American Response to Revolution, 1913–1923* (Oxford University Press, 1984), 1.

15. Wilson in San Diego, September 19, 1919, in Shaw, *Messages and Papers*, 2:1017. On the British origins of Wilson's liberalism and his affinities with radical liberals during World War I, see Laurence W. Martin, *Peace without Victory: Woodrow Wilson and the British Liberals* (Yale University Press, 1958).

16. Wilson on September 25, 1916, in Hart, *Addresses and Papers*, 161f.

17. Wilson on November 12, 1917, in Shaw, *Messages and Papers*, 1:436–8.

18. Wilson in Arthur S. Link, ed., *The Papers of Woodrow Wilson* (Princeton University Press, 1977), 24:204; Wilson, "The Road away from Revolution," in Shaw, *Messages and Papers*, 1230f.

19. For accounts of Wilson's economic thinking that stress his concern with creating an international system favorable to American economic interests, see William Appleman Williams, 2d revised ed. *The Tragedy of American Diplomacy* (Dell, 1972), chaps. 2–3; N. Gordon Levin, Jr., *Woodrow Wilson and World Politics: America's Response to War and Revolution* (Oxford University Press, 1968); and Carl P. Parrini, *Heir to Empire: United States Economic Diplomacy, 1916–1923* (University of Pittsburgh Press, 1969).

20. For accounts that stress Wilson's relative lack of understanding of economic questions, see Richard Hofstadter, *The American Political Tradition and the Men*

Who Made It (Alfred A. Knopf, 1948), 269ff; William Diamond, *The Economic Thought of Woodrow Wilson* (Johns Hopkins Press, 1943), 175ff; and John Maynard Keynes, *The Economic Consequences of the Peace* (Harcourt, Brace, 1920).

21. On the thinking behind the League, see F. S. Northedge, *The League of Nations: Its Life and Times, 1920–1948* (Holmes and Meier, 1986); Lloyd E. Ambrosius, *Woodrow Wilson and the American Diplomatic Tradition: The Treaty Fight in Perspective* (Cambridge University Press, 1987); Inis L. Claude, Jr., *Swords into Plowshares: The Problems and Progress of International Organization*, 4th ed. (Random House, 1971), chap. 3; August Heckscher, *Woodrow Wilson* (Charles Scribner's Sons, 1991), 529ff; and Robert W. Tucker, "Brave New World Orders," *New Republic*, February 24, 1992, 29ff.

22. Wilson in Boston, February 24, 1919, in Shaw, *Messages and Papers*, 2:645; see also 757f.

23. Wilson to the Senate, January 22, 1917, in Shaw, *Messages and Papers*, 1:351.

24. Wilson before the Congress, April 2, 1917, in Shaw, *Messages and Papers*, 1:379.

25. Northedge, *The League*, 328f.

26. Wilson to the Daughters of the American Revolution, October 11, 1915, in Shaw, *Messages and Papers*, 1:123f.

27. Ambrosius, *Woodrow Wilson*, 39f.

28. Wilson to the Senate, January 22, 1917, in Shaw, *Messages and Papers*, 1:351.

29. Northedge, *The League*, 51f.

30. Keynes, *Economic Consequences*, 35, 37. See also Harold Nicolson, *Peacemaking 1919* (Harcourt, Brace, 1939); and Ronald Steel, *Walter Lippmann and the American Century* (Little, Brown, 1980), chaps. 9–13. The British were for the most part strongly biased against Wilson before arriving at the conference. See Arthur S. Link, "President Wilson and His English Critics: Survey and Interpretation," in Link, *The Higher Realism of Woodrow Wilson and Other Essays* (Vanderbilt University Press, 1971).

31. Wilson to the Senate, January 22, 1917, in Shaw, *Messages and Papers*, 1:352.

32. Edwin Weinstein, *Woodrow Wilson: A Medical and Psychological Biography* (Princeton University Press, 1981), chaps. 19–21. See also John Milton Cooper, *The Warrior and the Priest: Woodrow Wilson and Theodore Roosevelt* (Harvard University Press, 1983), 337ff; and Jeffrey Tulis, *The Rhetorical Presidency* (Princeton University Press, 1987), 147ff.

33. On the paramount importance of French security concerns, see Winston S. Churchill, *The Aftermath* (Charles Scribner's Sons, 1929), especially 222ff; Link, *Woodrow Wilson: Revolution, War, and, Peace*, 89; and Keynes, *Economic Consequences*.

34. For an account of the territorial deliberations, see Edward Mandell House and Charles Seymour, eds., *What Really Happened at Paris: The Story of the Peace Conference, 1918–1919, by American Delegates* (Charles Scribner's Sons, 1921).

35. The classic account is offered by Keynes, *Economic Consequences*. See also Thomas William Lamont, "Reparations," Allyn Abbott Young, "The Economic

Settlement," Edward Mandell House, "The Versailles Peace in Retrospect," all in House and Seymour, *Paris*; Heckscher, *Wilson*, 544ff.

36. The strain of the conference is well captured in Nicolson, *Peacemaking*; the alternatives for Wilson should he have walked away are well analyzed in Schwabe, *Wilson*, 295ff, 395ff.

37. Paul Mantoux, *The Deliberations of the Council of Four (March 24–June 28, 1919)* (Princeton University Press, 1992), 1:47; 2:119.

38. See Churchill, *The Aftermath*, 197ff.

39. Schwabe, *Wilson*, chap. 6. The German statement is reprinted in Alma Luckau, *The German Delegation at the Paris Peace Conference* (Columbia University Press, 1941), 112.

40. On the continued power of agrarian based antidemocratic, quasi-feudal forces, see Arno J. Mayer, *The Persistence of the Old Regime: Europe to the Great War* (Pantheon Books, 1981). On the reconstitution of rightist politics after 1918, see Charles S. Maier, *Recasting Bourgeois Europe: Stabilization in France, Germany, and Italy in the Decade after World War I* (Princeton University Press, 1975). On the ultimate collapse of German liberalism, see Larry Eugene Jones, *German Liberalism and the Dissolution of the Weimar Party System, 1918–1933* (University of North Carolina Press, 1988).

41. For a clear, brief account, see Felix Gilbert, *The End of the European Era, 1890 to the Present* (W. W. Norton, 1979), chap. 6. For a more detailed review, see Hugh Seton-Watson, *Eastern Europe between the Wars, 1918–1941* (Cambridge University Press, 1945; Archon Books, 1962), Seton-Watson, *The East European Revolution* (Praeger, 1951), chaps. 1–2; Joseph Rothschild, *East Central Europe between the Two World Wars* (University of Washington Press, 1974); C. A. Macartney and A. W. Palmer, *Independent Eastern Europe: A History* (Macmillan, 1962).

42. Rothschild, *East Central Europe*; Seton-Watson, *Eastern Europe*, chaps. 3–5, and 6, pt. 2; and Seton-Watson, *East European Revolution*, chaps. 1–2.

43. Masaryk is quoted by Arthur Walworth, *America's Moment: 1918: American Diplomacy at the End of World War I* (W. W. Norton, 1977), 1.

44. George F. Kennan, *American Diplomacy*, expanded ed. (University of Chicago Press, 1984), 69.

45. Hans J. Morgenthau, *In Defense of the National Interest: A Critical Examination of American Foreign Policy* (Alfred A. Knopf, 1952), 27.

46. Walter Lippmann, *U.S. War Aims* (Little, Brown, 1944), 180f.

47. Walter Lippmann, *U.S. Foreign Policy: Shield of the Republic* (Little, Brown, 1943), 6ff.

48. Morgenthau, *The National Interest*, 4.

49. Lippmann, *U.S. Foreign Policy*, 37. For similar views held by Morgenthau, see *The National Interest*, 26.

50. Thomas J. Knock has demonstrated that in later years, George Kennan seemed to move closer to a Wilsonian view of foreign affairs. Kennan then remarked on Knock's observation: "I now view Wilson . . . as a man who like so many other people of broad vision and acute sensitivities, was ahead of his time, and did not live long enough to know what great and commanding relevance many of his ideas would acquire before this century was out. In this sense, I have to correct or

modify, at this stage of my own life, many of the impressions I had about him at an earlier stage." See Knock, "Kennan Versus Wilson," and Kennan, "Comments," in John Milton Cooper, Jr., and Charles E. Neu, *The Wilson Era: Essays in Honor of Arthur S. Link* (Harlan Davidson, 1991), 330. For other arguments in favor of taking Wilson more seriously in terms of his times, see Link, *Higher Realism*; Levin, *Woodrow Wilson*; and Arno J. Mayer, *Politics and Diplomacy of the Peacemaking: Containment and Counterrevolution at Versailles, 1918–1919* (Alfred A. Knopf, 1967). However, Mayer and Levin make Wilson out to be far more the spokesman of international capitalism than I believe is warranted.

51. On the continuity between the Marshall Plan and American thinking after World War I, see Michael J. Hogan, *The Marshall Plan: America, Britain, and the Reconstruction of Western Europe, 1947–1952* (Cambridge University Press, 1987), introduction.

52. *New York Times*, February 22, 1990; see also Havel, "The Future of Central Europe," in *New York Review of Books*, March 20, 1990. In Wilson's words, "Do not think . . . that questions of the day are mere questions of policy and diplomacy. They are shot through with the principles of life. We dare not turn from the principle that morality and not expediency is the thing that must guide us and that we will never condone iniquity because it is most convenient to do so." Wilson, October 27, 1913, in Hart, *Addresses and Papers*, 16ff.

53. Victor S. Mamatey, *The United States and East Central Europe, 1914–1918: A Study in Wilsonian Diplomacy and Propaganda* (Princeton University Press, 1957). See also Thomas Garrigue Masaryk, *The Making of a State* (Frederick A. Stokes, 1927), chap. 7; and Eduard Benes, *Democracy Today and Tomorrow* (Macmillan, 1939), 33ff.

54. Wilson cited in Charles Seymour, "Wilson and His Contributions," in Arthur S. Link, ed., *Woodrow Wilson: A Profile* (Hill and Wang, 1968), 162. See also Akira Iriye, *The Globalizing of America, 1913–1945*, vol. 3 of *The Cambridge History of American Foreign Policy* (Cambridge University Press, 1993), 68ff.

CHAPTER FIVE

1. On American economic policy in the mid-1940s, see especially Cordell Hull, *The Memoirs of Cordell Hull* (Macmillan, 1948), 364ff. An excellent account of Hull's worldview may be found in Richard Gardner, *Sterling-Dollar Diplomacy in Current Perspective: The Origins and the Prospects of Our International Economic Order*, 2d ed. (Columbia University Press, 1980), chap. 1. Roosevelt's words of February 15, 1945, appear in Samuel I. Rosenman, ed., *The Public Papers and Addresses of Franklin D. Roosevelt* (hereafter *PPA*) (Random House, 1938–50), 13:554. On American security policy in the mid-1940s, see especially George F. Kennan, *Memoirs, 1925–1950* (Pantheon Books, 1967), chap. 15; and John Lewis Gaddis, *Strategies of Containment: A Critical Appraisal of Postwar American National Security Policy* (Oxford University Press, 1982). The Truman Doctrine is reprinted in Joseph Marion Jones, *The Fifteen Weeks: An Inside Account of the Genesis of the Marshall Plan* (Harcourt, Brace, and World, 1955), 269ff.

2. Marshall's speech appears in Jones, *Fifteen Weeks*. On the plan's origins in New Deal thinking, see Michael J. Hogan, *The Marshall Plan: America, Britain,*

and the Reconstruction of Western Europe, 1947–1952 (Cambridge University Press, 1987); also Melvyn P. Leffler, *A Preponderance of Power: National Security, the Truman Administration and the Cold War* (Stanford University Press, 1992), 159ff; and Charles S. Maier, "The Two Postwar Eras and the Conditions for Stability in Twentieth-Century Western Europe," *American Historical Review* 86, no. 2 (April 1981).

3. On the shift from the FDR's "multilateralism" to containment, see Henry Nau, *The Myth of America's Decline: Leading the World Economy into the 1990s* (Oxford University Press, 1990), pt. 2; and G. John Ikenberry, "Rethinking the Origins of American Hegemony," *Political Science Quarterly* 104, no. 3 (Fall 1989).

4. The text of the Atlantic Charter is *PPA*, 10:314ff. See also Winston S. Churchill, *The Second World War: The Grand Alliance* (Houghton Mifflin, 1950), 393f.

5. *PPA*, 13:441f. On Roosevelt's mixture of realism and idealism, see Robert Dallek, *Franklin D. Roosevelt and American Foreign Policy, 1932–1945* (Oxford University Press, 1979), 12ff, 538.

6. December 24, 1943, *PPA*, 12:138; February 19, 1943, *PPA*, 12:101. On American attitudes toward Chiang Kai-shek, see Warren I. Cohen, *America's Response to China: An Interpretative History of Sino-American Relations* (John Wiley and Sons, 1971), 158f.

7. State Department, "Background Briefing Paper on Turkey," *Foreign Relations of the United States (hereafter FRUS)*, The Conference of Berlin (The Potsdam Conference), 1945 (GPO, 1960), 1:1015.

8. Hull, *Memoirs*, 976; Gaddis, *Strategies*, 3.

9. *PPA*, 2:130, 544f.

10. Cited in Julius W. Pratt, *Cordell Hull* (Cooper Square, 1964), 162.

11. See Franklin D. Roosevelt, "Our Foreign Policy: A Democratic View," *Foreign Affairs* 6, no. 4 (July 1928): 584f; and *PPA*, 2:544ff.

12. Irwin F. Gellman, *Good Neighbor Diplomacy: United States Policies in Latin America, 1933–1945* (Johns Hopkins Press, 1979) 31ff.

13. On Roosevelt's relations with Mexico under Cardenas, see Lorenzo Meyer, *Mexico and the United States in the Oil Controversy, 1917–1942* (University of Texas Press, 1977), chaps. 8–9; on Hull, see April 7, 1935, *FRUS, 1935*, 4:623.

14. Hull, *Memoirs*, chaps. 24–27. See also, Paul A. Varg, "The Economic Side of the Good Neighbor Policy: The Reciprocal Trade Program and South America," *Pacific Historical Review*, 95 (1976). Unfortunately, no study has yet been undertaken of the markedly different political reactions of the various Central American and Caribbean countries that hereby entered into closer economic association with the United States. Such an investigation would offer an excellent opportunity to compare varied political consequences of a common economic stimulus, and at the same time to analyze an important moment of Washington's thinking with respect to the ties between economic and political matters in foreign affairs.

15. On the question of sugar in Cuba, see Robert F. Smith, *The United States and Cuba: Business and Diplomacy, 1917–1960* (College and University Press, 1960), chaps. 2, 10.

16. *PPA*, 5:211f, 438. See also 5:232f.

17. *PPA*, 10:255, 399, 474.

382 · Notes to Chapter Five

382 · Notes to Chapter Five

18. Two excellent studies on Anglo-American relations during the war are Christopher Thorne, *Allies of a Kind: The United States, Britain and the War against Japan, 1941–1945* (Oxford University Press, 1978); and William Roger Louis, *Imperialism at Bay: The United States and the Decolonization of the British Empire, 1941–1945* (Oxford University Press, 1978). See also the interesting observations in John Lewis Gaddis, "Spheres of Influences: The United States and Europe, 1945–1949," in Gaddis, *The Long Peace: Inquiries into the History of the Cold War* (Oxford University Press, 1987).

19. Hull cited in Gardner, *Sterling-Dollar*, 19; Hull, *Memoirs*, 520.

20. See Churchill, *The Grand Alliance*, chap. 24, and Hull, *Memoirs*, 975f.

21. Cited in Terry H. Anderson, *The United States, Great Britain, and the Cold War, 1944–1947* (University of Missouri Press, 1981), 187.

22. *FRUS, 1945: The Conferences at Malta and Yalta*, (GPO, 1955), 844f.

23. Dallek, *Roosevelt*, 511; and John D. Sbrega, "The Anticolonial Views of Franklin D. Roosevelt, 1941–1945," in Herbert D. Rosenbaum and Elizabeth Barteleme, eds., *Franklin D. Roosevelt: The Man, the Myth, the Era, 1882–1945* (Greenwood Press, 1987), 195.

24. Hull, *Memoirs*, 1599.

25. On India, *FRUS, 1941* (GPO, 1959), 3:176f, 191ff; Hull, *Memoirs*, 1600f.

26. Cited in Akira Iriye, *The Cold War in Asia: A Historical Introduction* (Prentice-Hall, 1974), 87.

27. Cited in Sbrega, "Anticolonial Views," 195.

28. On de Gaulle's colonial policy after 1945, see Tony Smith, *The French Stake in Algeria* (Cornell University Press, 1978), chaps. 2–3.

29. The topic arose frequently; see, for example, *FRUS, 1942* (GPO, 1961), 3:580f; *FRUS, 1943: The Conferences at Cairo and Tehran*, 484f.

30. Charles de Gaulle, *The Complete War Memoirs* (Di Capo Press, 1967), 573f.

31. *FRUS, Malta and Yalta*, 234f; *FRUS, Potsdam*, 1:262; Gabriel Kolko, *The Politics of War: The World and United States Foreign Policy, 1943–1945* (Random House, 1968), 470ff; Gaddis, "Spheres of Influence," 53; Dallek, *Roosevelt*, pp. 507f, 524f.

32. *FRUS, 1942*, 3:538ff.

33. *FRUS, Tehran*, 594f.

34. *FRUS, Malta and Yalta*, 104ff.

35. *FRUS, 1944* (GPO, 1965), 5:119ff.

36. *FRUS, Malta and Yalta*, 971ff.

37. *FRUS, Potsdam*, 1:358f, 381.

38. *FRUS, Potsdam*, 1:724. See also, Harry S. Truman, *Memoirs* (Doubleday, 1955), vol. 1, chap. 6.

39. *FRUS, Malta and Yalta*, 250ff; also *FRUS, Potsdam*, 1:826f.

40. *FRUS, Potsdam*, 2:1171ff. See also Stanley G. Payne, *The Franco Regime, 1936–1975* (University of Wisconsin Press, 1987), chap. 15.

41. *FRUS, Potsdam*, 1:681.

42. See the discussion in Tony Smith, *The Pattern of Imperialism: The United States, Great Britain and the Late-Industrializing World since 1815* (Cambridge University Press, 1981), 162ff.

43. See the lengthy memorandum on the threat of international communism in *FRUS, Potsdam*, 1:267ff.

44. *FRUS, Potsdam*, 1:688f. See also Gianfranco Pasquino, "The Demise of the First Fascist Regime and Italy's Transition to Democracy: 1943–1948," in Guillermo O'Donnell et al., *Transitions from Authoritarian Rule: Southern Europe* (Johns Hopkins University Press, 1986).

45. See Joseph Rothschild, *Return to Diversity: A Political History of East Central Europe since World War II* (Oxford University Press, 1989), 23, also 26ff, 79ff; and Kennan, *Memoirs*, chap. 8. See also, Sarah Meiklejohn Terry, *Poland's Place in Europe: General Sikorski and the Origin of the Oder-Neisse Line, 1939–1940* (Princeton University Press, 1983).

46. For a different interpretation, see John Lewis Gaddis, *The United States and the Origins of the Cold War, 1941–1947* (Columbia University Press, 1972), chap. 5. See also Leffler, *Preponderance of Power*, 49ff.

47. June 7, 1944, *PPA*, 13:161.

48. *FRUS, Yalta*, 854.

49. Winston S. Churchill, *The Second World War: Triumph and Tragedy* (Houghton Mifflin, 1953), chaps. 18–19.

50. See Nicos P. Mouzelis, *Modern Greece: Facets of Underdevelopment* (Holmes and Meier, 1978); also sections on Greece in his *Politics in the Semi-Periphery: Early Parliamentarism and Late Industrialisation in the Balkans and Latin America* (Macmillan, 1986).

51. John O. Iatrides, ed., *Ambassador MacVeagh Reports: Greece, 1933–1947* (Princeton University Press, 1980), 661.

52. *FRUS, 1946* (GPO, 1969), 7:92.

53. *FRUS, 1946*, 7:206. See also George Th. Mavrogordatos, "The 1946 Election and Plebiscite: Prelude to Civil War," in John O. Iatrides, ed., *Greece in the 1940s: A Nation in Crisis* (University Press of New England, 1981); Constantine Tsoucalas, *The Greek Tragedy* (Penguin Books, 1969); and P. Nikiforos Diamandouros, "Regime Change and the Prospects for Democracy in Greece: 1974–1983," in O'Donnell, *Transitions*.

54. Iatrides, *MacVeagh Reports*, 697f.

55. Toward the end of the war, Churchill may have told King Peter of Yugoslavia that "the three great powers will not lift one finger to put any king back on any throne in Europe," but in Greece, Italy, and Japan, it was the Americans who proved more skeptical of a continued political role for royal families. Churchill in *FRUS, 1945*, 5:1175f; on Greece, Iatrides, *MacVeagh Reports*, letters to FDR of December 8, 1944, and January 5, 1945, 659ff; on Italy, John Edward Miller, *The United States and Italy, 1940–1950* (University of North Carolina Press, 1986), 24ff, 35f, 50ff; on Japan, see the comparison of American and British terms for surrender, *FRUS, Potsdam*, 2:1277.

56. John O. Iatrides, "Reviewing American Policy toward Greece: The Modern Cassandras," in Iatrides and Theodore A. Couloumbis, eds., *Greek-American Relations: A Critical Review* (Pella, 1980), 13. See also Theodore A. Couloumbis et al., *Foreign Interference in Greek Politics: An Historical Perspective* (Pella, 1976).

57. Lawrence S. Wittner, *American Intervention in Greece, 1943–1949* (Columbia University Press, 1982).

58. On the historiography of the cold war, see Arthur M. Schlesinger, Jr., "The Cold War Revisited," *New York Review of Books* 26, no. 16 (October 25, 1979); and Lynn Eden, "The End of U.S. Cold War History?" *International Security* 18, no. 1 (Summer 1993). On the structural basis of the confrontation, see A. W. Deporte, *Europe between the Superpowers: The Enduring Balance*, 2d ed. (Yale University Press, 1986); and Warren I. Cohen, *America in the Age of Soviet Power, 1945–1991*, vol. 4 of *The Cambridge History of American Foreign Relations* (Cambridge University Press, 1993), chap. 2. Recent examples of revisionism include Thomas J. McCormick, *America's Half-Century: United States Foreign Policy in the Cold War* (Johns Hopkins University Press, 1989); and Bruce Cumings, "Revising Post-revisionism," *Diplomatic History* 17, no. 4 (Fall 1993). On postrevisionism, see John Lewis Gaddis, "The Emerging Post-Revisionist Synthesis on the Origins of the Cold War," *Diplomatic History* 7, no. 3 (Summer 1983); Gaddis "The Cold War, the Long Peace, and the Future" in Michael J. Hogan, ed., *The End of the Cold War: Its Meaning and Implications* (Cambridge University Press, 1992), 23ff; Gaddis, *Strategies*; and Gaddis, *The Long Peace*, 18.

59. John Lewis Gaddis, "The Tragedy of the Cold War," *Foreign Affairs* 73, no. 1 (January/February 1994), 146f.

60. An excellent synthesis of economic and political considerations which gives primacy to the latter is Leffler, *Preponderance of Power*, 10ff. See also Leffler, "National Security," in Michael J. Hogan and Thomas G. Paterson, *Explaining the History of American Foreign Relations* (Cambridge University Press, 1991); John Lewis Gaddis, "The Insecurities of Victory: The United States and the Perception of the Soviet Threat after World War II," in Gaddis, *The Long Peace*; and James Chace and Caleb Carr, *America Invulnerable: The Quest for Absolute Security from 1812 to Star Wars* (Summit Books, 1988).

61. On economic thinking see Robert J. Pollard, *Economic Security and the Origins of the Cold War, 1945–1950* (Columbia University Press, 1985), 144: "The original impulse behind American multilateralism was neither anti-communism nor a need to sustain world capitalism. Instead, American officials . . . were largely determined to prevent a revival of the closed autarkic systems that had contributed to world depression and split the world into competing blocs before the war."

62. On the reaction to fascism in terms of geopolitical thinking in Washington, see Akira Iriye, *The Globalizing of America, 1913–1945*, vol. 3 of *The Cambridge History of American Foreign Relations* (Cambridge University Press, 1993), chaps. 9–10; and on Roosevelt, Leffler, *Preponderance of Power*, 21f.

63. Truman cited in Leffler, *Preponderance of Power*, 13.

64. See Robert Jervis, "The Impact of the Korean War on the Cold War," *Journal of Conflict Resolution* 24 (December 1980); Cohen, *America in an Age of Soviet Power*, chap. 3.

CHAPTER SIX

1. See George F. Kennan, *American Diplomacy*, expanded ed. (University of Chicago Press, 1984), chap. 4; and A. W. DePorte, *Europe between the Superpowers: The Enduring Balance*, 2d ed. (Yale University Press, 1986), chaps. 1–4.

These authors locate the reasons for the German problem in the structure of international relations, rather than in the domestic character of German politics.

2. A seminal comparative perspective on conservative authoritarian versus liberal democratic modernization is Barrington Moore, Jr., *Social Origins of Dictatorship and Democracy: Lord and Peasant in the Making of the Modern World* (Beacon Press, 1966), chaps. 5, 7, 8. On Japan, see also Kentaro Hayashi, "Japan and Germany in the Interwar Period," R. P. Dore and Tsutomu Ouchi, "Rural Origins of Japanese Fascism," and Edwin O. Reischauer, "What Went Wrong?" all in James William Morley, ed., *Dilemmas of Growth in Prewar Japan* (Princeton University Press, 1971); John W. Dower, "E. H. Norman, Japan, and the Uses of History," in E. H. Norman, *Origins of the Modern Japanese State: Selected Writings of E. H. Norman* (Pantheon Books, 1975); Masao Maruyama, *Thought and Behavior in Modern Japanese Politics* (Oxford University Press, 1963); and Carol Gluck, *Japan's Modern Myth: Ideology in the Late Meiji Period* (Princeton University Press, 1985). On Germany, the most important debate surrounds David Blackbourn and Geoff Eley, *The Peculiarities of German History: Bourgeois Society and Politics in Nineteenth-Century Germany* (Oxford University Press, 1984). See also, Ralf Dahrendorf, *Society and Democracy in Germany* (W. W. Norton, 1984); Richard J. Evans, *Rethinking German History: Nineteenth Century Germany and the Origins of the Third Reich* (Allen and Unwin, 1987); Konrad H. Jarausch and Larry Eugene Jones, "German Liberalism Reconsidered," in Jarausch and Jones eds., *In Search of a Liberal Germany: Studies in the History of German Liberalism from 1789 to the Present* (Berg, 1990); V. R. Berghahn, *Germany and the Approach of War in 1914* (St. Martin's Press, 1973); Fritz Stern, *The Failure of Illiberalism: Essays on the Political Culture of Modern Germany* (Knopf, 1972), introduction; Jeffrey Herf, *Reactionary Modernism: Technology, Culture, and Politics in Weimar and the Third Reich* (Cambridge University Press, 1984); and Gordon A. Craig, "The German Mystery Case," *New York Review of Books*, January 30, 1986. Indeed, it would seem from a broader historical comparison that the triumph of democracy might be the historical exception, the *Sonderweg*, not the developmental path followed by Germany and Japan. For in many other countries (as still today in China and part of the Arab world, for example), nationalist sentiment insisted that Western technical accomplishments could be adopted without borrowing from the West culturally or politically. Consequently, for second or third generation industrializing countries, an authoritarian state-centered development process, preserving the power of the traditional elites while co-opting the emerging middle class, appeared a more likely model for others to follow—as in Japan, Russia, and the Ottoman Empire—than did democracy in its British or American form.

3. Ian Kershaw, ed., *Weimar: Why Did German Democracy Fail?* (St. Martin's Press, 1990). See also Franz Neumann, *Behemoth: The Structure and Practice of National Socialism, 1933–1944* (Octagon Books, 1972), introduction; Henry Ashby Turner, *German Big Business and the Rise of Hitler* (Oxford University Press, 1985); Eberhard Kolb, *The Weimar Republic* (Unwin Hyman, 1988).

4. Robert A. Scalapino, *Democracy and the Party Movement in Prewar Japan* (University of California Press, 1953), and Scalapino "Elections and Political Modernization in Prewar Japan," in Robert E. Ward, ed., *Political Development in Mod-*

ern Japan (Princeton University Press, 1978); Harry Wray and Hilary Conroy, eds., *Japan Examined: Perspectives on Modern Japanese History* (University of Hawaii Press, 1983), pts. 7, 9; Edwin O. Reischauer, *The Japanese Today: Change and Continuity*, 2d ed. (Harvard University Press, 1988), chaps. 7–9; Akira Iriye, *Power and Culture: The Japanese-American War, 1941–1945* (Harvard University Press, 1981), chap. 1.

5. Richard J. Smethurst, *A Social Basis for Prewar Japanese Militarism: The Army and the Rural Community* (University of California Press, 1974); Michael A. Barnhart, *Japan Prepares for Total War: The Search for Economic Security, 1918–1941* (Cornell University Press, 1987).

6. Two comparisons that point to the differences between Japan and Germany are Smethurst, *A Social Basis*, 180ff, and Hayashi, "Japan and Germany."

7. There is an extensive debate on whether to place the generic label of *fascism* on Germany and Japan (and yet another as to whether they were *totalitarian*). I use *fascism* to apply to both regimes in order to stress the many similarities in their origin and program, but am quite willing to admit their differences. Although he does not discuss Japan, a particularly good essay in an abundant literature is Juan Linz, "Totalitarian and Authoritarian Regimes," in Fred I. Greenstein and Nelson W. Polsby, eds., *Macropolitical Theory*, vol. 3 of *Handbook of Political Science* (Addison-Wesley, 1975). See also Stein Ugelvik Larsen et al., *Who Were the Fascists: Social Roots of European Fascism* (Columbia University Press, 1982). An important book that does call Japan fascist is Maruyama, *Thought and Behavior*.

8. Moore, *Social Origins*, chap. 7, stresses the timing and economic path of industrialization chosen by Germany and Japan relative to Britain and the United States. He does not discuss the relatively independent and very important role of the military in politics in these two quite different pairs of countries. See especially, Brian M. Downing, *The Military Revolution and Political Change: Origins of Democracy and Autocracy in Early Modern Europe* (Princeton University Press, 1992), chaps. 1, 10. On the United States, figures on the American military can be found in *Historical Statistics of the United States: Colonial Times to 1970* (U.S. Department of Commerce, Bureau of the Census, 1975), 2:1141; and comparative numbers appear in Quincy Wright, *A Study of War* (University of Chicago Press, 1942), 670ff. See also, Robert W. Tucker and David C. Hendrickson, *Empire of Liberty: The Statecraft of Thomas Jefferson* (Oxford University Press, 1982), 9, 41f, 50, 225, 266 n. 48. On Germany, in addition to sources cited in note 2 above, see Gordon A. Craig, *The Politics of the Prussian Army, 1640–1945* (Oxford University Press, 1956), chaps. 6–7; Otto Hinzte, "Military Organization and State Organization" (1906), in Felix Gilbert, ed., *The Historical Essays of Otto Hintze* (Oxford University Press, 1975). On Japan, see sources cited in note 5 above.

9. Michael Schaller, *The American Occupation of Japan: The Origins of the Cold War in Asia* (Oxford University Press, 1985), 3f.

10. *Foreign Relations of the United States* (hereafter *FRUS*): *The Conferences at Cairo and Tehran, 1943* (GPO, 1961), 600ff.

11. Roosevelt cited in Cordell Hull, *The Memoirs of Cordell Hull* (Macmillan, 1948), 2:1603.

12. November 22, 1944, *FRUS, Yalta* (GPO, 1955), 173.

13. *FRUS, 1945*, (GPO, 1968), 3:487, 493.

14. George F. Kennan, *Sketches from a Life* (Pantheon, 1989), 125. And see the discussion in John Lewis Gaddis, *Strategies of Containment: A Critical Appraisal of Postwar American National Security Policy* (Oxford University Press, 1982), chaps. 2–3.

15. Godfrey Hodgson, *The Colonel: The Life and Wars of Henry Stimson, 1867–1950* (Knopf, 1990); Jean Edward Smith, *Lucius D. Clay: An American Life* (Holt, 1990); Thomas Alan Schwartz, *America's Germany: John J. McCloy and the Federal Republic of Germany* (Harvard University Press, 1991).

16. George F. Kennan, *Memoirs, 1925–1950* (Little, Brown, 1967), 375ff.

17. *FRUS, 1945*, 3:487.

18. *FRUS, Potsdam*, 2:1503.

19. JCS 1779 is reprinted in United States State Department, *Documents on Germany, 1944–1985* (GPO, 1985), 124ff.

20. *FRUS, Potsdam*, 2:1476.

21. United States Initial Post-Surrender Policy for Japan, August 29, 1945, in *Political Reorientation of Japan* (1948; Scholarly Press, 1968), 2:423.

22. John Gimbel, *The American Occupation of Germany: Politics and the Military, 1945–1953* (Stanford University Press, 1973); Hans W. Gatzke, *Germany and the United States: A Special Relationship?* (Harvard University Press, 1980); John H. Backer, *Winds of History: The German Years of Lucius Dubignon Clay* (Van Nostrand Rheinhold, 1983); Kazuo Kawai, *Japan's American Interlude* (University of Chicago Press, 1960).

23. *FRUS, 1945*, 3:488.

24. JCS 1779, *Documents on Germany*, 126. See also *FRUS, 1945*, 3:488ff.

25. An early account is still among the most vivid: John D. Montgomery, *Forced to Be Free: The Artificial Revolution in Germany and Japan* (University of Chicago Press, 1957). See also, on Germany, Dennis L. Bark and David R. Gress, *From Shadow to Substance, 1945–1963,* vol. 1 of *A History of West Germany* (Basil Blackwell, 1989), chaps. 8–9; and John H. Herz, "Denazification and Related Policies," in Herz, ed., *From Dictatorship to Democracy: Coping with the Legacies of Authoritarianism and Totalitarianism* (Greenwood Press, 1982). On Japan, see Edwin O. Reischauer, *The United States and Japan*, 3d ed. (Harvard University Press, 1965), chap. 10; and the official American report in *Political Reorientation of Japan*, 1:8ff, 2:479ff.

26. See JCS, 1779, *Documents on Germany*, 125: "Your Government does not wish to impose its own historically developed forms of democracy and social organization and Germany. . . . the ultimate constitutional form of German political life should be left to the decision of the German people made freely in accordance with democratic processes." See also the discussion in Carl J. Friedrich, "The Legacies of the Occupation in Germany," *Public Policy* 17 (1968).

27. Gimbel, *American Occupation*, and Bark and Gress, *Shadow to Substance*, pts. 2–3. For tables summarizing election results from 1920–33 and from 1949–87, see Volker Berghahn, *Modern Germany: Society, Economy, and Politics in the Twentieth Century*, 2d ed. (Cambridge University Press, 1987), 301f.

28. Arthur E. Tiedemann, "Japan Sheds Dictatorship," in Herz, *Dictatorship to Democracy*; Reischauer, *The United States and Japan*, chap. 10; D. Clayton James, *Triumph and Disaster, 1945–1964*, vol. 3 of *The Years of MacArthur* (Houghton

Mifflin, 1985), chap. 4; and for copies of the constitution at its various stages, see *Political Reorientation of Japan*, 1:82ff, 2:586ff.

29. JCS 1779, *Documents on Germany*, 132.

30. MacArthur, statement of February 1, 1948, in *Political Reorientation of Japan*, 2:780.

31. Clay cited in Frank Ninkovich, *Germany and the United States: The Transformation of the German Question since 1945* (Twayne, 1988), 27, 40.

32. James, *Years of MacArthur*, chaps. 7–8; Howard B. Schonberger, *Aftermath of War: Americans and the Remaking of Japan, 1945–1952* (Kent State University Press, 1989), chaps. 6–7; Theodore Cohen, *Remaking Japan: The American Occupation as New Deal* (Free Press, 1987). See also Chalmers Johnson, *MITI and the Japanese Miracle: The Growth of Industrial Policy, 1925–1975* (Stanford University Press, 1982).

33. While it is sometimes suggested that zaibatsu ownership was concentrated in elite former samurai or daimyo families, in fact merchant families, who were not part of the traditional elite, were predominant. Access to politics by these families was thus through economic power or the Diet. See Yamamura Kozo, *A Study of Samurai Income and Entrepreneurship: Quantitative Analyses of Economic and Social Aspects of the Samurai in Tokugawa and Meijii Japan* (Harvard University Press, 1974); references to various individuals and zaibatsu in Janet Hunter, *Concise Dictionary of Modern Japanese History* (University of California Press, 1984); Reischauer, *United States and Japan*, 93ff, 198ff; Ronald P. Dore, *Land Reform in Japan* (Oxford University Press, 1959), 118; and Arthur E. Tiedemann, "Big Business and Politics in Prewar Japan," in Morley, *Dilemmas*.

34. Lucius D. Clay, *Decision in Germany* (Doubleday, 1950), 281.

35. See Moore, *Social Origins*, chap. 5; Dore, *Land Reform*, pt. 2.

36. In MacArthur's words, the intent was to "remove economic obstacles to the revival and strengthening of democratic tendencies, establish respect for the dignity of man, and destroy the economic bondage which has enslaved the Japanese farmer to centuries of feudal oppression . . . to exterminate those pernicious ills which have long blighted the agrarian structure of land." *Political Reorientation of Japan*, 2:752.

37. W. I. Ladejinsky, "Agriculture," in Hugh Borton, ed., *Japan* (Cornell University Press, 1951). Douglas MacArthur, *Reminiscences* (McGraw-Hill, 1964), 313f; MacArthur's statement of February 1, 1948, in *Political Reorientation of Japan*, 2:780.

38. Tony Smith, *The Pattern of Imperialism: The United States, Great Britain, and the Late-Industrializing World since 1815* (Cambridge University Press, 1981), chap. 1.

39. See the discussion in Charles S. Maier, "The Two Postwar Eras and the Conditions for Stability in Twentieth-Century Western Europe," *American Historical Review* 86, no. 2 (April 1981); and Herman Van Der Wee, *Prosperity and Upheaval: The World Economy, 1945–1980* (University of California Press, 1987), chaps. 2, 9.

40. John Gillingham, *Coal, Steel, and the Rebirth of Europe, 1945–1955: The German and French from Ruhr Conflict to Economic Community* (Cambridge University Press, 1991); Volker Berghahn, *Modern Germany*, 183ff, 197f, 201ff; and

Volker Berghahn, *The Americanization of West German Industry, 1945–1973* (Berg, 1986).

41. September 29, 1944, *FRUS, Yalta*, 157f. See also, John Gimbel, *The Origins of the Marshall Plan* (Stanford University Press, 1976).

42. November 10, 1944, *FRUS, Yalta*, 170.

43. Akira Iriye, "The Failure of Military Expansionism," in Morley, ed., *Dilemmas*, 107, 138; see also Barnhart, *Japan Prepares* 5.

44. Hull, *Memoirs*, chaps. 71, 78–9.

45. *FRUS, Potsdam*, 1:891. MacArthur, *Reminiscences*, 276.

46. Montgomery, *Forced to Be Free*, 106f.

47. Samuel I. Rosenman, ed. *The Public Papers and Addresses of Franklin D. Roosevelt* (Random House, 1950), 13:554, February 15, 1945. See also, Henry Nau, *The Myth of America's Decline: Leading the World Economy into the 1990s* (Oxford University Press, 1990).

48. Clay, *Decision*, 281.

49. MacArthur, *Reminiscences*, 283f.

50. Clay, *Decision*, 287.

51. MacArthur, *Reminiscences*, 276, 283f, 310.

52. JCS 1779, *Documents on Germany*, 133f.

53. MacArthur, *Reminiscences*, 276.

54. JCS 1067, *FRUS, 1945*, 3:492f. On Japan, see Reischauer, *Japanese Today*, chap. 18; on Germany see Gimbel, *American Occupation*, chap. 14; and Jutta-B. Lange-Quassowski, "Coming to Terms with the Nazi Past: Schools, Media, and the Formation of Opinion," in Herz, *Dictatorship to Democracy*, 90ff.

55. JCS 1779, *Documents on Germany*, 134.

56. William Manchester, *American Caeser* (Dell, 1978), 578f, 591f, 603f. Clay, *Decision*, 283ff. By contrast, on American failures with film, see Ian Buruma, "Americainerie," *New York Review of Books*, March 25, 1993.

57. Anne J. Merritt and Richard L. Merritt, *Public Opinion in Occupied Germany: The Omgus Surveys, 1945–9* (University of Illionis Press, 1970), 30ff.

58. David B. Conradt, "Changing German Political Culture," in Gabriel A. Almond and Sidney Verba, *The Civic Culture Revisited* (Little, Brown, 1980), 226.

59. Herbert Passin, "Changing Values: Work and Growth in Japan," *Asian Survey* 15, no. 10 (October 1975): 837. See similar findings in *Japan Quarterly* 26, no. 4 (October–December 1979), 565f; and *Japan Echo* 5 (1978): 74ff.

60. Figures on Japan from James, *Years of MacArthur*, 307; on Germany in Peter H. Merkl, "Allied Strategies of Effecting Political Change and Their Reception in Occupied Germany," *Public Policy* 17 (1968): 60f.

61. Robert E. Ward, "Conclusion," in Ward and Sakamoto Yoshikazu, *Democratizing Japan: The Allied Occupation* (University of Hawaii Press, 1987), 397.

62. Murphy cited in Backer, *Winds of History*, 31

63. Consider the political profile of Henry Stimson, FDR's secretary of war. As a conservative Republican, Stimson had been a personal friend of President Theodore Roosevelt, Secretary of War Elihu Root, and General Leonard Wood, who was military governor of Cuba, then governor general of the Philippines—in their manner, liberal imperialists all. Stimson supported Wilson's ideas for the League of Nations and approved of an open international economic system. He was secretary

of state under President Calvin Coolidge, secretary of war under President Herbert Hoover, and governor general of the Philippines (1937–9). His influence did not end when he finally left public life in 1945: Dean Acheson, Robert Lovett, John McCloy, and McGeorge Bundy were among his younger followers.

64. In addition, as a Catholic and a Rhinelander, Konrad Adenauer was pro-French. On Adenauer, see his *Memoirs* (Weidenfeld and Nicholson, 1966); Jeffrey Herf, *War by Other Means: Soviet Power, West German Resistance, and the Battle of the Euromissiles* (Free Press, 1991), 4ff, chap. 2. On German economic thinking see also Peter J. Katzenstein, *Policy and Process in West Germany: The Growth of a Semisovereign State* (Temple University Press, 1987), chap. 2.

65. Maier, "Two Eras."

66. John Lewis Gaddis, "The Insecurities of Victory: The United States and the Perception of the Soviet Threat after World War II," in Gaddis, *The Long Peace: Inquiries into the History of the Cold War* (Oxford University Press, 1987), 45f.

67. Schwartz, *America's Germany*, 50ff, 295ff; Herf, *War by Other Means*, chap. 2.

68. As George Kennan later wrote about the Marshall Plan, "We hoped to force the Europeans to begin to think like Europeans, and not like nationalists, in their approach to the economic problems of the continent." Under-Secretary of State for Economic Affairs Will Clayton described the Marshall Plan in words that Secretary of State Dean Acheson approvingly repeated, "Surely the plan would be a European plan and come, or, at any rate, appear to come from Europe. But the United States must run the show. And it must start running it now." Kennan, *Memoirs*, 337; Dean Acheson, *Present at the Creation: My Years in the State Department* (Norton, 1969), 232. On the importance of the American role, see also Melvyn P. Leffler, *A Preponderance of Power: National Security, the Truman Administration, and the Cold War* (Stanford University Press, 1992), 116ff, 151ff, 233f.

69. Yoshida Shigeru, *The Yoshida Memoirs: The Story of Japan in Crisis* (Houghton, Mifflin, 1962), 286ff. See also W. G. Beasley, *The Rise of Modern Japan* (St. Martin's Press, 1990), 218.

70. The fiftieth anniversary of Pearl Harbor proved an outlet for multiple warnings about Japan in the United States. For example, see George Friedman and Meredith LeBard, *The Coming War with Japan* (St. Martin's Press, 1991); Steven R. Weisman, "Pearl Harbor in the Mind of Japan," *New York Times*, November 11, 1991; and the three special essays that appeared in the *New York Times* entitled "Fifty Years Later," December 3, 4, 5, 1991. For a range of opinion on the question of the challenge posed by Japan to the United States, see Samuel P. Huntington, "Why International Primacy Matters," Peter J. Katzenstein and Nobuo Okawara, "Japan's National Security: Structures, Norms, and Policies," and Thomas U. Berger, "From Sword to Chrysanthemum: Japan's Culture of Anti-Militarism," all in *International Security* 17, no. 4 (Spring 1993).

71. Clay cited in Smith, *Clay*, 244.

72. *FRUS, Yalta*, 185f.

73. McCloy cited in Schwartz, *America's Germany*, 306f. For an assessment that differs from mine, see John J. Mearsheimer, "Back to the Future: Instability in Europe after the Cold War," *International Security*, 15, no. 1 (Summer 1990). For an assessment that confirms the importance of the changes in Germany, see Stephen

Van Evera, "Primed for Peace: Europe after the Cold War," *International Security* 15, no. 3 (Winter 1990/91).

74. MacArthur on September 2, 1947, in *Political Reorientation of Japan*, 2:775.

CHAPTER SEVEN

1. Department of State, *Bulletin* 13 (December 2, 1945): 892. Larreta's note is reprinted in the same volume, pp. 864ff. See also Charles D. Ameringer, *The Democratic Left in Exile: The Anti-Dictatorial Struggle in the Caribbean, 1945–1959* (University of Miami Press, 1974).

2. On early postwar policy toward Latin America, see Stephen G. Rabe, *Eisenhower and Latin America: The Foreign Policy of Anticommunism* (University of North Carolina Press, 1988); Leslie Bethell, "From the Second World War to the Cold War, 1944–1954," and Carlos Escude, "Argentina: The Costs of Contradiction," both in Abraham F. Lowenthal, ed., *Exporting Democracy: The United States and Latin America* (Johns Hopkins University Press, 1991). On the 1954 Caracas Conference, see Richard H. Immerman, *The CIA in Guatemala: The Foreign Policy of Intervention* (University of Texas Press, 1982), 144ff.

3. Dean Acheson, *Present at the Creation: My Years in the State Department* (Norton, 1969), 501ff. On the militarization of American policy, see figures on American arms transfers from 1950 to 1970 to be found in the Stockholm International Peace Research Institute, *The Arms Trade with the Third World* (Humanities Press, 1971). See also, United States Arms Control and Disarmament Agency, *World Military Expenditures* (various years).

4. Citations may be found in Jane Degras, ed., *The Communist International*: vol. 2, *1923–1928* (Oxford University Press, 1960) 25f. See also Tony Smith, *Thinking Like a Communist: State and Legitimacy in the Soviet Union, China, and Cuba* (W. W. Norton, 1987); and Robert V. Daniels, *Communism and the World*, vol. 2 of *A Documentary History of Communism*, rev. ed. (University Press of New England, 1984). See also Adam B. Ulam, *Expansion and Coexistence: Soviet Foreign Policy, 1917–1973*, 2d ed. (Praeger, 1974).

5. John Foster Dulles, "A Policy of Boldness," *Life*, May 19, 1952, 154; and Dulles cited in Louis L. Gerson, *John Foster Dulles* (Cooper Square, 1967), 87f.

6. Interview of October 21, 1956, reprinted in Robert L. Branyan and Lawrence H. Larsen, eds., *The Eisenhower Administration, 1953–1956: A Documentary History* (Random House, 1971), 670.

7. Dulles, "Boldness," 157.

8. Dulles, November 1953 speech reprinted in the Department of State *Bulletin* 29 (December 14, 1953): 755. See also John Lewis Gaddis, "The Unexpected John Foster Dulles," in Gaddis, *The United States and the End of the Cold War: Implications, Reconsiderations, Provocations* (Oxford University Press, 1992).

9. *Public Papers of the Presidents of the United States: Dwight D. Eisenhower, 1956* (GPO, 1960), 1022, 1052, 1096. For a general discussion, see Bennett Kovrig, *Of Walls and Bridges: The United States and Eastern Europe* (New York University Press, 1991), chap. 2.

10. See Robert Divine, *Eisenhower and the Cold War* (Oxford University Press,

1981); see also, Richard H. Immerman, ed., *John Foster Dulles and the Diplomacy of the Cold War* (Princeton University Press, 1990); Richard A. Melanson and David Mayers, eds., *Reevaluating Eisenhower: American Foreign Policy in the 1950s* (University of Illinois Press, 1987); Robert J. McMahon, "Eisenhower and Third World Nationalism: A Critique of the Revisionists," *Political Science Quarterly* 101, no. 3 (1986); and John Lukacs, "Ike, Winston, and the Russians," *New York Times Book Review*, February 10, 1991.

11. February 17, 1955, *Foreign Relations of the United States* (hereafter *FRUS*), *1955–1957* (GPO, 1987) 6:4f.

12. Mossadegh is cited in Fakhreddin Azimi, "The Reconciliation of Politics and Ethics, Nationalism and Democracy: An Overview of the Political Career of Dr. Muhammad Musaddiq," in James A. Bill and William Roger Louis, eds., *Musaddiq, Iranian Nationalism, and Oil* (University of Texas Press, 1988), 62. In this volume see also, Richard Cottam, "Nationalism in Twentieth Century Iran and Dr. Muhammad Musaddiq," and James A. Bill, "America, Iran, and the Politics of Intervention, 1951–1953."

13. See Mark J. Gasiorowski, *U.S. Foreign Policy and the Shah: Building a Client State in Iran* (Cornell University Press, 1991), 44, 85ff.

14. Piero Gleijeses, *Shattered Hope: The Guatemalan Revolution and the United States, 1944–1954* (Princeton University Press, 1991), 147.

15. Fearful of Soviet intentions on Iran, Eisenhower warned his advisers that the United States might "have to face . . . the question of going to full mobilization. . . . [Otherwise] the United States would descend to the status of a second-rate power." *FRUS, 1952–1954* (GPO, 1989), 10:698.

16. On the case against United Fruit and the government's decision not to prosecute, see *FRUS, 1952–1954*, 4:191ff. On the Justice Department and the international oil cartel, see Bill, "Politics of Intervention," in Bill and Lewis, *Musaddiq*, 276f, and in the same volume, Irvine H. Anderson, "The American Oil Industry and the Fifty-Fifty Agreement of 1950," and Ronald W. Ferrier, "The Anglo-Iranian Oil Dispute: A Triangular Relationship." Two interesting studies on the general matter of U.S. protection of foreign investments are Stephen D. Krasner, *Defending the National Interest: Raw Materials Investments and U.S. Foreign Policy* (Princeton University Press, 1978); and Charles Lipson, *Standing Guard: Protecting Foreign Capital in the Nineteenth and Twentieth Centuries* (University of California Press, 1985).

17. Dulles cited in Christopher Mitchell, "Dominance and Fragmentation in U.S. Latin American Foreign Policy," in Julio Cotler and Richard R. Fagen, eds., *Latin America and the United States: The Changing Political Realities* (Stanford University Press, 1974), 183.

18. See the various reports in *FRUS, 1952–1954*, vol. 10; also the essays by Bill and Cottam cited in note 12 above, and Gasiorowski, *Policy*, 79ff.

19. *FRUS, 1952–1954*, 4:1031ff, 1066ff; Cole Blasier, *The Hovering Giant: U.S. Response to Revolutionary Change in Latin America* (University of Pittsburgh Press, 1976), 151ff; and Gleijeses, *Shattered Hope*, chap. 8.

20. Post-coup American and Iranian positions are reported in *FRUS, 1952–1954*, 10:870, 1068ff. Dwight D. Eisenhower, *The White House Years: Mandate for Change, 1953–1956* (Doubleday, 1963), 437.

21. Rabe, *Eisenhower*, chaps. 8–9.

22. *Public Papers: Eisenhower, 1957* (GPO, 1958), 203. Dwight D. Eisenhower, *Waging Peace, 1956–1961: The White House Years* (Doubleday, 1965), 621, 624, 627.

23. See George C. Herring, *America's Longest War: The United States and Vietnam, 1950–1975* (John Wiley and Sons, 1979); George McTurnan Kahin, *Intervention: How America Became Involved in Vietnam* (Knopf, 1986); and Guenter Lewy, *America in Vietnam* (Oxford University Press, 1978).

24. *Public Papers: Truman, 1950* (GPO, 1965), 674ff.

25. *FRUS, 1952–1954*, 13:83f.

26. Eisenhower, *Mandate*, 347, 363, 373.

27. John F. Kennedy, *The Strategy of Peace* (Harper and Row, 1960), 60.

28. Part of the speech is quoted in Kennedy, *Strategy*, 62ff, but see other parts in Lewy, *America*, 12f.

29. *FRUS, 1955–1957*, 1:3ff.

30. On Diem, see George McTurnan Kahin and John W. Lewis, *The United States in Vietnam*, rev. ed. (Dell Publishing, 1979), chaps. 5–6. On Johnson, see Stanley Karnow, *Vietnam: A History* (Penguin Books, 1983), 230.

31. For an account of the thinking of the Kennedy administration, see Arthur M. Schlesinger, Jr., *A Thousand Days: John F. Kennedy in the White House* (Fawcett, 1965), chaps. 10, 13–15, 20. See also the description in Frances Fitzgerald, *Fire in the Lake: The Vietnamese and the Americans in Vietnam* (Random House, 1972), pt. 2; and D. Michael Shafer, *Deadly Paradigms: The Failure of U.S. Counterinsurgency Policy* (Princeton University Press, 1988).

32. Kennedy, *Strategy*, 61.

33. September 2, 1963, *Public Papers: Kennedy, 1963* (GPO, 1964), 340, and September 14, 1963, p. 459. For testimony as to how blind high officials could be about Diem, see the memoirs of former Secretary of State Dean Rusk by Richard Rusk, *As I Saw It* (Norton, 1990), and of former Ambassador to South Vietnam Frederick Nolting, *From Trust to Tragedy: The Political Memoirs of Frederick Nolting, Kennedy's Ambassador to Diem's Vietnam* (Prager, 1988). An important and often overlooked consideration was the concern of Kennedy and Johnson that Mao Zedong had invented a form of subversion going under the name "people's war," wherein a small nucleus of guerrillas could seize power in a politically immature and militarily weak country, a strategy for insurgents that had to be faced down here once and for all. See Douglas S. Blaufarb, *The Counterinsurgency Era: U.S. Doctrine and Performance, 1950 to the Present* (Free Press, 1977). For an argument that Kennedy would have withdrawn American troops in 1965, see John M. Newman, *JFK and Vietnam: Deception, Intrigue, and the Struggle for Power* (Warner Books, 1991). In a letter to me dated March 1, 1994, Arthur Schlesinger, Jr., insists that after Kennedy became president, he did not think about Vietnam as he had in 1956: "We were all a little naive in 1956. Bill Douglas and Mike Mansfield, exemplary liberals both, were Diem's big sponsors then; Joe Buttinger was hopeful about him; and Norman Thomas and others, including me, were so relieved by the French withdrawal that we went happily along with Douglas and Mansfield. We all . . . learned better soon enough." By contrast, Henry Kissinger cites Kennedy's emphasis on the necessity and feasibility of internal political reform in South Vietnam to

stop communism as evidence that Wilsonian thinking was basic to the Kennedy administration's commitment in Vietnam. See Henry Kissinger, *Diplomacy* (Simon and Schuster, 1994), 647ff.

34. In addition to the uniformly bleak assessments of land reform discussed in the works cited in note 23 above, see Roy L. Prosterman and Jeffrey M. Riedinger, *Land Reform and Democratic Development* (Johns Hopkins University Press, 1987), chap. 5; and various reports in *FRUS*, for example the report from Ladejinsky, June 7, 1955, in the series *1955–1957*, 1:456ff; 721ff; *1958–1960* (GPO, 1986), 1:516ff.

35. Reports from government sources, cited in Noam Chomsky, "Vietnam: How Government Became Wolves," *New York Review of Books* 18, no. 11 (June 15, 1972): 26.

36. For a discussion of the strength of communism in Vietnam before 1954, see Tony Smith, *The Pattern of Imperialism: The United States, Great Britain, and the Late-Industrializing World since 1815* (Cambridge University Press, 1981), 125ff.

37. January 20, 1961, *Public Papers: Kennedy, 1961* (GPO, 1962), 1.

38. For a nuanced discussion on the place of democracy in American foreign policy, see Henry A. Kissinger, *The Necessity for Choice: Prospects of American Foreign Policy* (Harper and Brothers, 1960), 308ff. On Jackson-Vanik, see Walter Isaacson, *Kissinger: A Biography* (Simon and Schuster, 1992), 611ff; Henry A. Kissinger, *Years of Upheaval* (Little, Brown, 1982), chap. 22; and Kissinger, *Diplomacy*, 747ff.

39. Henry A. Kissinger, *American Foreign Policy*, 3d ed. (Norton, 1977), speech of February 3, 1976, pp. 317ff.

40. Kissinger, *Years of Upheaval*, 50; on geopolitical thinking see also p. 239. In *Diplomacy*, chaps. 1–2, and 31, Kissinger tries to synthesize what he calls the European penchant for thinking in terms of the national interest and the balance of power with Wilsonianism. Thus, Kissinger asserts that "every American president" since Wilson has been a Wilsonian; indeed that even Nixon believed himself to be "a disciple of Wilson's internationalism," although in reality he was not; and that "a country with America's idealistic tradition cannot base its policy on the balance of power as the sole criterion for a new world order." However, by reducing Wilsonianism to "moral convictions" and "exalted sentiments," it is apparent that Kissinger has no understanding of Wilsonianism's relevance to the national security based on its concerns for the process of development of mass-based states abroad. Hence his attempt at a synthesis ends in failure.

41. Isaacson, *Kissinger*, 657ff; and Kissinger, *American Foreign Policy*, speech of July 15, 1975, pp. 195ff. Kissinger appears to concrede his critics' point in *Diplomacy*, 758.

42. Henry A. Kissinger, *White House Years* (Little, Brown, 1979), 655–7. On Chile, see also Seymour M. Hersh, *The Price of Power: Kissinger in the Nixon White House* (Summit Books, 1983), chaps. 21–2; and Isaacson, *Kissinger*, chap. 14.

43. Kissinger, *Years of Upheaval*, 672.

44. Kissinger, *American Foreign Policy*, speech of April 27, 1976, p. 369; Isaacson, *Kissinger*, 685ff; and Christopher Coker, *The United States and South Africa*,

1968–1985 (Duke University Press, 1986), chaps. 2–6 and pp. 127ff. See also the discussion in John Lewis Gaddis, "Rescuing Choice from Circumstance: The State-craft of Henry Kissinger," in Gordon A. Craig and Francis L. Loewenheim, eds., *The Diplomats, 1939–1979* (Princeton University Press, 1994).

CHAPTER EIGHT

1. Jerome Levinson and Juan de Onis, eds., *The Alliance That Lost Its Way* (Quadrangle Books, 1970). This book remains the best general survey of the Alliance.

2. L. Ronald Scheman, ed., *The Alliance for Progress: A Retrospective* (Praeger, 1988), 10f.

3. Theodore Paul Wright, Jr., *American Support of Free Elections Abroad* (Public Affairs Press, 1964); also various essays in Abraham F. Lowenthal, ed., *The United States and Latin American Democracy: Essays from History* (Johns Hopkins University Press, 1991).

4. On Wilson and socioeconomic reform in Mexico, for example, see note 2 in "Notes to Chapter Two," above. On Wilson in the Philippines, see Peter W. Stanley, *A Nation in the Making; The Philippines and the United States, 1899–1921* (Harvard University Press, 1974), 196ff.

5. The Charter and other official pronouncements are reprinted in the United States Department of State *Bulletin* 45, no. 1159 (September 11, 1961).

6. The Kissinger Commission Report spends far more time discussing matters such as education and housing than land reform, which receives only perfunctory mention. The Caribbean Basin Initiative concentrates on stimulating gross economic output and may be read as an encouragement for agribusiness. See Henry Kissinger et al., *Report of the National Bipartisan Commission on Central America* (GPO, 1984).

7. Subcommittee on American Republics Affairs, U.S. Senate Committee on Foreign Relations, *Survey of the Alliance for Progress*, Doc. 91–17, 91st Cong., 1st sess., 1969, 12844–2, p. 181. Interesting testimony is provided herein by William C. Thiesenhusen, Marion R. Brown, T. Lynn Smith, and Peter Dorner.

8. David Wurfel, *Filipino Politics: Development and Decay* (Cornell University Press, 1988), chaps. 3, 6.

9. Of course, the question of the degree to which the struggle against racial discrimination involves the need to reshape economic practices in the United States is an old one. Dr. King was killed when he sought to broaden his campaign and make economic issues central.

10. James A. Bill, *The Eagle and the Lion: The Tragedy of American-Iranian Relations* (Yale University Press, 1988), chap. 4.

11. James Goode, "Reforming Iran during the Kennedy Years," *Diplomatic History* 15, no. 1 (Winter 1991).

12. On the role of Berle, see Levinson and Onis, *Alliance*, 52ff. In a letter to me of October 18, 1989, Arthur Schlesinger, Jr., writes "There is no question that we saw Betancourt's Venezuela as the model for democratic development; the future of Latin America, it seemed to us, lay between the Castro road and the Betancourt road." On the role of various Latin Americans and the Institute for Political Educa-

tion, see Howard J. Wiarda, *The Democratic Revolution in Latin America* (Holmes and Meier, 1990), chap. 5.

13. An excellent account remains Samuel Flagg Bemis, *The Latin American Policy of the United States: An Interpretation* (Harcourt, Brace, 1943). See also Tony Smith, *The Pattern of Imperialism: The United States, Great Britain, and the Late-Industrializing World since 1815* (Cambridge University Press, 1981), chap. 4.

14. Tony Smith, *Thinking Like a Communist: State and Legitimacy in the Soviet Union, China, and Cuba* (Norton, 1987), chap. 5.

15. On military matters, see Subcommittee on American Republics Affairs, *Survey of the Alliance*, statements by Edwin Lieuwen and David Burks. A good discussion on counterinsurgency tactics, but without reference to U.S. policy in Latin America, is D. Michael Shafer, *Deadly Paradigms: The Failure of U.S. Counterinsurgency Policy* (Princeton University Press, 1988).

16. On social programs, see Arthur M. Schlesinger, Jr., *A Thousand Days: John F. Kennedy in the White House* (Fawcett, 1965), 176ff; also the review by Robert Packenham, *Liberal America and the Third World: Political Development Ideas in Foreign Aid and Social Science* (Princeton University Press, 1973), chap. 2. In an interview with me on October 18, 1989, Lucian Pye, an active member of the Charles River School, stressed the influence these intellectuals came to have in Washington within the State Department and the White House (thanks to W. W. Rostow) and at the Agency for International Development (thanks to Max Millikan). For an example of how simplistic their thinking could be, see especially Max F. Millikan and W. W. Rostow, *A Proposal: Key to an Effective Foreign Policy* (Harper and Row, 1957). The most influential book published by members of this group was surely Rostow's *Stages of Economic Growth* (MIT Press, 1960).

17. Such is the general tenor of most contributions to Scheman, *Alliance*. See also Richard N. Goodwin, *A Voice from the Sixties* (Little, Brown, 1988), chap. 8 and pp. 244ff.

18. See the challenge issued by Che Guevara at the Punta del Este Conference, "The Alliance for Progress," in *Che: Selected Works of Ernesto Guevara* (MIT Press, 1969), 265ff. For a more extended discussion and references, see Abraham F. Lowenthal, "'Liberal,' 'Radical,' and 'Bureaucratic' Perspectives on US Latin American Policy: The Alliance for Progress," in Julio Cotler and Richard R. Fagen, eds., *Latin America and the United States: The Changing Realities* (Stanford University Press, 1974), 221ff.

19. The opposition of many Latin American elites to the goals of the Alliance is described repeatedly in Subcommittee on American Republics Affairs, *Survey of the Alliance* (especially testimony by Holt, Lieuwen, and Halperin).

20. See Levinson and Onis, *Alliance*, 60ff, 216.

21. An overall review of what might be called the mindset of official Washington can be found in Lars Schoultz, *National Security and United States Policy toward Latin America* (Princeton University Press, 1987). See also, Levinson and Onis, *Alliance*, 200ff.

22. Riordan Roett, *The Politics of Foreign Aid in the Brazilian Northeast* (Vanderbilt University Press, 1974), especially chap. 9. Similar, if less pointed, observa-

tions are made by the Senate staff of the Committee on Foreign Relations in its study of land reform in Colombia, in Subcommittee on American Republics Affairs, *Survey of the Alliance*.

23. See Samuel P. Huntington, *Political Order in Changing Societies* (Yale University Press, 1968), chap. 4. Under the terms of the Alliance, Latin American armies were to undertake "civic action" to bring reform to the countryside. See the testimony of Field Haviland in Subcommittee on American Republics Affairs, *Survey of the Alliance*. For a study that explicitly pits the promise of the Alliance against the reality, see Edwin Lieuwen, *Generals vs. Presidents: Neomilitarism in Latin America* (Praeger, 1964). See also Alfred Stepan, "The New Professionalism of Internal Warfare and Military Role Expansion," in Stepan, ed., *Authoritarian Brazil: Origins, Policies, and Future* (Yale University Press, 1973); and Douglas S. Blaufarb, *The Counterinsurgency Era: U.S. Doctrine and Performance* (Free Press, 1977), chap. 9.

24. On Peru, see Levinson and Onis, *Alliance*, 80ff, 98ff, 146ff. Also, essays by Julio Cotler, Peter S. Cleaves, and Henry Pease Garcia in Cynthia McClintock and Abraham F. Lowenthal, eds., *The Peruvian Experiment Reconsidered* (Princeton University Press, 1983).

25. Robert Crassweller, *Trujillo: The Life and Times of a Caribbean Dictator* (Macmillan, 1966), chap. 29; also, Bernardo Vega, *Eisenhower y Trujillo* (Fundacion Cultural Dominicana, 1991); and Jonathan Hartlyn, "The United States and Latin American Democracy: The Dominican Republic, 1916–1990," in Lowenthal, *United States*.

26. Frank Moya Pons, "The Dominican Republic since 1930," in Leslie Bethell, ed., *The Cambridge History of Latin America* (Cambridge University Press, 1990), vol. 7; Piero Gleijeses, *The Dominican Crisis: The 1965 Constitutionalist Revolt and American Intervention* (Johns Hopkins University Press, 1978), chap. 11; and Howard J. Wiarda, "The Dominican Republic: Mirror Legacies of Democracy and Authoritarianism," in Larry Diamond et al., *Democracy in Developing Countries: Latin America* (Lynne Rienner, 1989).

27. Howard J. Wiarda, *Dictatorship, Development and Disintegration* (Ann Arbor, Mich., Xerox University Microfilms, 1975), vol. 3, chpt. 19.

28. See Smith, *Thinking*, chap. 5 and note 18 above.

29. See Wiarda, *Dictatorship*, chap. 19; Pons, "Dominican Republic"; and Jonathan Hartlyn, "The Dominican Republic: Contemporary Problems and Challenges," in Jorge Dominguez et al., *The Caribbean Prepares for the Twenty-First Century* (Johns Hopkins Press, 1992).

30. Wiarda, *Dictatorship*, 1535. In an interview I had with Bosch on March 10, 1992, he reiterated that the "first priority" of his administration was land reform combined with a "massive campaign" including the registration of deeds and the provision of credit to see that it worked.

31. John Bartlow Martin, *Overtaken by Events: The Dominican Crisis from the Fall of Trujillo to the Civil War* (Doubleday, 1965), chaps. 25, 28.

32. Jerome Slater, *Intervention and Negotiation: The United States and the Dominican Revolution* (Harper and Row, 1970); Abraham F. Lowenthal, *The Dominican Intervention* (Harvard University Press, 1972); and Gleijeses, *Dominican Cri-*

sis. In my visit with Bosch, he lauded Castro, denounced current efforts to overthrow his regime in Havana, and talked about the need for the Dominican Republic of a "cadre party." But I was told repeatedly that he did not think in such terms in the 1960s.

33. Wiarda, *Dictatorship*, chap. 19. This point was made as well by Bernardo Vega in an interview with me on March 9, 1992. On the Dominican Republic today, see Hartlyn, "Dominican Republic."

34. Wiarda, *Dictatorship*, chap. 11; also Hartlyn, "United States."

35. Arturo Valenzuela, "Chile: Origins, Consolidation and Breakdown of a Democratic Regime," in Larry Diamond et al., *Democracy in Developing Countries* (Lynne Rienner, 1989); and Brian Loveman, *Chile: The Legacy of Hispanic Capitalism* (Oxford University Press, 1979).

36. Ernst Halperin, *Nationalism and Communism in Chile* (MIT Press, 1965), chap. 5; Leonard Gross, *The Last, Best Hope: Eduardo Frei and Chilean Democracy* (Random House, 1967).

37. See especially, Paul E. Sigmund, *The United States and Democracy in Chile* (Johns Hopkins University Press, 1993), chap. 2; also Loveman, *Chile*, chaps. 8–9; Eduardo Frei, "The Alliance that Lost Its Way," *Foreign Affairs* 45, no. 3 (April 1967); Staff Report of the Select Committee to Study Governmental Operations with Respect to Intelligence Activities, U.S. Senate, *Covert Action in Chile, 1963–1973*, 94th Cong., 1st sess., December 18, 1975.

38. Howard J. Wiarda, "Did the Alliance 'Lose Its Way,' or Were Its Assumptions All Wrong from the Beginning and Are Those Assumptions Still with Us?" in Scheman, *Alliance*; also Joseph Maier and Richard W. Weatherhead, eds., *The Future of Democracy in Latin America: Essays by Frank Tannenbuam* (Knopf, 1974).

39. The Alliance's advocates avoided connecting their ambitions to Wilson. Milton Eisenhower, who first alerted his brother's administration to the depth of the social problems in Latin America, endorsed the Alliance, but condemned Wilson in favor of FDR's Good Neighbor Policy. See his *The Wine Is Bitter: The United States and Latin America* (Doubleday, 1963), 175ff. Robert F. Kennedy also salutes FDR, but neglects Wilson in his introduction to William D. Rogers, *The Twilight Struggle: The Alliance for Progress and the Politics of Development in Latin America* (Random House, 1967). Lincoln Gordon is similarly discreet in his volume *A New Deal for Latin America: The Alliance for Progress* (Harvard University Press, 1963). Nor do the contributors to Scheman, *Alliance*, many of whom were architects of the Alliance, refer to Wilson. In his letter of October 1989, Arthur Schlesinger writes that no one thought of Wilson in the early 1960s; that instead their inspiration was FDR. In subsequent discussions, Schlesinger told me he was thinking of the reforms of the New Deal as characteristic of Roosevelt and armed intervention as Wilson's hallmark; he had forgotten how hostile the Good Neighbor Policy was to the notion of sponsoring democracy in the hemisphere.

CHAPTER NINE

1. Speech of January 20, 1977, *Public Papers of the Presidents of the United States: Jimmy Carter, 1977* (GPO, 1978), 1:2f; speech of December 6, 1978, Department of State, *Bulletin* 79, no. 2022 (January 1979):2. For earlier statements on

human rights, see Jimmy Carter, *A Government as Good as Its People* (Simon and Schuster, 1977), 125ff, 172ff.

2. March 7, 1977, Department of State, *American Foreign Policy: Current Documents, 1977–1981* (GPO, 1983), 408.

3. The various amendments are reprinted as appendices in David P. Forsythe, *Human Rights and U.S. Foreign Policy: Congress Reconsidered* (University of Florida Press, 1988). See also Lars Schoultz, *Human Rights and United States Policy toward Latin America* (Princeton University Press, 1981), 194ff.

4. Schoultz, *Human Rights*, 120ff; Joshua Muravchik, *The Uncertain Crusade: Jimmy Carter and the Dilemmas of Human Rights Policy* (Hamilton Press, 1986), 9ff, 40ff.

5. See the breakdown of the various countries in *Country Reports on Human Rights Practices* (GPO, 1977 and annually thereafter).

6. See the March 10, 1977, testimony of Richard Holbrooke, assistant secretary of state for East Asia and Pacific affairs, *Current Documents, 1977–1981*, 3f. Also Raymond Bonner, *Waltzing with a Dictator: The Marcoses and the Making of American Policy* (Times Books, 1987), 250f, 255f.

7. Cyrus Vance, *Hard Choices: Critical Years in Amercia's Foreign Policy* (Simon and Schuster, 1983), 32, 127f; and A. Glenn Mower, Jr., *Human Rights and American Foreign Policy: The Carter and Reagan Experiences* (Greenwood Press, 1987), 139ff. On Korea, see the State Department's June 19, 1989, reply to a request from the South Korean National Assembly on American policy toward civil rights abuses in 1979–80, reprinted in *Current Documents, 1989* (GPO, 1990), 554ff. On El Salvador, see Robert A. Pastor, "The Carter Administration and Latin America: A Test of Principle," Carter Center of Emory University, Occasional Paper Series 2, no. 3 (1992): 31, 36.

8. Jimmy Carter, *Keeping Faith: Memoirs of a President* (Bantam Books, 1982), 143. On changes in Carter's emphases over time, see Raymond L. Gartoff, *Detente and Confrontation: American-Soviet Relations from Nixon to Reagan* (Brookings Institution, 1985), chap. 27; also Jerel A. Rosati, *The Carter Administration's Quest for Global Community* (University of South Carolina Press, 1987). On El Salvador, for example, see Thomas Carothers, *In the Name of Democracy: U.S. Policy toward Latin America in the Reagan Years* (University of California Press, 1991), 14f.

9. Speech of May 22, 1977, *Bulletin* 76, no. 1981 (June 13, 1977).

10. Cyrus Vance speech of April 30, 1977, *Current Documents, 1977–1981*, 410, 412.

11. Jeane Kirkpatrick, "Human Rights and American Foreign Policy," *Commentary* 72, no. 5 (November 1981): 43.

12. Speech of May 22, 1977, *Bulletin* 76, no. 1981 (June 13, 1977). As an example of the nervousness of Kennedy liberals with this kind of talk, see Arthur Schlesinger, Jr., "Human Rights and the American Tradition," *Foreign Affairs* 57, no. 3 (1979).

13. Schoultz, *Human Rights*, 114.

14. Schoultz, *Human Rights*, 203ff, 265, 292ff.

15. See David and Marina Ottaway, *Afrocommunism* (Africana, 1981); and Central Intelligence Agency, *Communist Aid to Less Developed Countries of the Free World, 1977* (National Foreign Assessment Center, 1978).

16. Carter, *Keeping Faith*, 146ff; *Current Policy*, 181 (May 13, 1980); Christopher Coker, *The United States and South Africa, 1968–1985* (Duke University Press, 1986), chap. 7.

17. Mondale cited, *Current Documents, 1977–1981*, 1172.

18. Mower, *Human Rights*, 124ff.

19. The discussion of Nicaragua relies especially on Robert A. Pastor, *Condemned to Repetition: The United States and Nicaragua* (Princeton University Press, 1987); and also on Shirley Christian, *Nicaragua: Revolution in the Family* (Vintage, 1985); James Chace, *Endless War: How We Got Involved in Central America and What Can Be Done* (Vintage, 1984); Walter LaFeber, *Inevitable Revolutions: The United States in Central America*, expanded ed. (W. W. Norton, 1984); and Joseph Tulchin and Knut Walter, "Nicaragua: The Limits of Intervention," in Abraham F. Lowenthal, *Exporting Democracy: The United States and Latin America* (Johns Hopkins Press, 1991).

20. See Tony Smith, *Thinking Like a Communist: State and Legitimacy in the Soviet Union, China, and Cuba* (W. W. Norton, 1987), chap. 5; and Jiri Valenta and Esperanza Duran, eds., *Conflict in Nicaragua: A Multidimensional Perspective* (Allen and Unwin, 1987).

21. Pastor, *Condemned to Repetition* 19; and Anthony Lake, *Somoza Falling: A Case Study of Washington at Work* (University of Massachusetts, 1989).

22. See Vance, *Hard Choices*, chap. 8; Carter, *Keeping Faith*, 152ff.

23. Jeane J. Kirkpatrick, "U.S. Security Interests and Latin America" (1981), in Kirkpatrick, ed., *Dictatorships and Double Standards: Rationalism and Reason in Politics* (Simon and Schuster, 1982), 72 (emphasis in original).

24. H. E. Chehabi, *Iranian Politics and Religious Modernism: The Liberation Movement of Iran under the Shah and Khomeini* (Cornell University Press, 1990), chaps. 1, 3, pp. 183ff, 224ff; Richard W. Cottam, *Iran and the United States: A Cold War Case Study* (University of Pittsburgh Press, 1988), chaps. 1–3; James A. Bill, *The Eagle and the Lion: The Tragedy of American-Iranian Relations* (Yale University Press, 1988), chaps. 1–3.

25. Cottam, *Iran*, 113ff; James F. Goode, *The United States and Iran, 1946–1951* (Macmillan, 1989).

26. Cottam, *Iran*, 112; Mark J. Gasiorowski, *U.S. Foreign Policy and the Shah: Building a Client State in Iran* (Cornell University Press, 1991), chap. 4.

27. Assistant Secretary of State Alfred L. Atherton, Jr., "Human Rights in Iran," testimony before the Subcommittee on International Organizations of the House Committee on International Relations, 94th Cong., 2d sess., September 8, 1976; Mohammed G. Majd, "Land Reform Policies in Iran," *American Journal of Agricultural Economics* 69, no. 4 (November 1967).

28. Julian Bharier, *Economic Development in Iran, 1900–1971* (Oxford University Press, 1971), chap. 3; Shaul Bakhash, "Fall and Decline," *New York Review of Books*, December 2, 1981.

29. Chehabi, *Iranian Politics*, chap. 4; Cottam, *Iran*, 122ff; Gasiorowski, *Foreign Policy*, 160ff; letter to the author from Houchang Chehabi, September 24, 1991.

30. Oriana Fallaci, *Interview with History* (Houghton Mifflin, 1976), 266, 274. In his own writings, the shah is much more pro-Western: see Mohammed Reza

Pahlavi, *Mission for My Country* (McGraw-Hill, 1961), chaps. 7–8. But see the shah's often-expressed dislike of Americans in Asadollah Alam, *The Shah and I: The Confidential Diary of Iran's Royal Court, 1969–1977* (St. Martin's Press, 1991).

31. Cited in Samuel P. Huntington, *Political Order in Changing Societies* (Yale University Press, 1968), 179; see also the analysis in *Political Order*, chap. 3.

32. Estimates vary a bit. See Bill, *Eagle and Lion*, 202; and Gary Sick, *All Fall Down: America's Tragic Encounter with Iran* (Random House, 1985), 15.

33. Pahlavi, *Mission*, 321f.

34. William H. Sullivan, *Mission to Iran* (W. W. Norton, 1981), 156ff.

35. Sick, *All Fall Down*, 97.

36. Sullivan, *Mission*, 186ff; Bakhash, "Fall and Decline."

37. *Current Documents, 1977–1981*, 723, 725; Sick, *All Fall Down*, 31f; Cottam, *Iran*, 156ff.

38. Sick, *All Fall Down*, 31. See also Cottam, *Iran*, 172; Chehabi, *Iranian Politics*, 246ff.

39. Vance, *Hard Choices*, fn. 7, chpt. 14; Carter, *Keeping Faith*, fn. 8, p. 438.

40. Statement of December 12, 1978, *Bulletin* 79, no. 2022 (January 1979), 12.

41. Vance, *Hard Choices*, 331.

42. Sick, *All Fall Down*, 96ff; Zbigniew Brzezinski, *Power and Principle: Memoirs of the National Security Adviser, 1977–1981* (Farrar, Straus, Giroux, 1983), chap. 10.

43. Brzezinski, *Power*, 355. On November 11, 1978, Brzezinski confided to his journal this farfetched notion: "We have to concentrate on longer-term and more basic reforms. The Shah needs to develop a pertinent and relevant concept of modernization which will enable the people to identify progress with the system and effective political organization to absorb the shocks of modernization. He has so far been able to do neither. Unless he accomplishes both, his regime and particularly his personal role will be finished" (*Power*, 370).

44. For an analysis that agrees with Brzezinski, see Michael Ledeen and William Lewis, *Debacle: The American Failure in Iran* (Knopf, 1981), and Marvin Zonis, *Majestic Failure: The Fall of the Shah* (University of Chicago Press, 1991), chap. 10. For the Shah's unwillingness to use force against his own people, see Mohammed Reza Pahlavi, *Answer to History* (Stein and Day, 1982), 165ff; also Shaul Bakhash, "Who Lost Iran?" *New York Review of Books*, May 14, 1981.

45. Speech of December 6, 1978, *Bulletin* 79, no. 2022 (January 1979) 1ff.

46. Jonathan Hartlyn, "The Dominican Republic: The Legacy of Intermittent Engagement," in Lowenthal, *Exporting Democracy*; Rosario Espinal, "Between Authoritarianism and Crisis-Prone Democracy: The Dominican Republic after Trujillo," in Colin Clarke, ed., *Society and Politics in the Caribbean* (Macmillan, 1991); and Howard J. Wiarda and Michael J. Kryzanck, *The Politics of External Influence in the Dominican Republic* (Praeger, 1988).

47. Muravchik, *Uncertain Crusade*, chap. 5.

48. Carter, *Keeping Faith*, 143; see also Gaddis Smith, *Morality, Reason, and Power: American Diplomacy in the Carter Years* (Hill and Wang, 1986).

49. On the Soviet Union, see Raymond L. Garthoff, *Detente and Confrontation: American-Soviet Relations from Nixon to Reagan* (Brookings Institution, 1985),

402   ·   Notes to Chapter Nine

567ff, 1123f; on Argentina, see Joseph S. Tulchin, *Argentina and the United States: A Conflicted Relationship* (Twayne, 1990), 145ff; on Brazil, see Thomas E. Skidmore, "Brazil's Slow Road to Democratization: 1974–1985," in Alfred Stepan, ed., *Democratizing Brazil: Problems of Transition and Consolidation* (Oxford University Press, 1989), 15ff.

50. December 15, 1977, *Current Documents, 1977–1981*, 418; Carter, *Keeping Faith*, 144. Robert Pastor insists in a letter to the author dated April 14, 1992, that Carter knew very well that his human rights approach was a way of "getting his nose under the tent" and was intended as a prelude to more extensive democratization later. Pastor therefore objects to calling Carter naive.

51. February 8, 1977, *Current Documents, 1977–1981*, 558f. The unconsciously competitive nature of Carter's approach is also apparent in further comments about the Soviet Union: "Detente between our two countries is central to world peace. . . . Both nations must exercise restraint in trouble areas and in troubled times . . . [yet] the Soviet Union attempts to export a totalitarian and repressive form of government, resulting in a closed society. . . . [For the Soviets] detente seems to mean a continuing aggressive struggle for political advantage and increased influence in a variety of ways. . . . [By contrast, America is in a] much more favorable position. Our industrial base and our productivity are unmatched; our scientific and technological capability is superior to all others; our alliances with other free nations are strong and growing stronger; and our military capability is now and will be second to none. . . . Our democratic way of life warrants the admiration and emulation by other people throughout the world. Our work for human rights makes us part of an international tide, growing in force." See also June 7, 1988, *Current Documents, 1977–1981*, 565ff; and *Bulletin* 77, no. 1994 (September 12, 1977), 357.

52. On the secret letter, see Lake, *Somoza Falling*, 82ff.

53. Carter, *Keeping Faith*, 436. For the shah's general reaction, see Pahlavi, *Answer*.

54. Still another example of Carter personalizing foreign affairs and failing to see how radical his hopes for having human rights respected might be comes from his experience with Panama. Carter considered the conclusion of the Panama Canal Treaty (begun before he came to office and intended to turn the property over to the Panamanians on December 31, 1999) as the finest accomplishment of his presidency with respect to Latin America. The treaty was signed with Omar Torrijos, a populist Panamanian leader who had come to power by military coup in 1968 and who had staked his reformist government on securing local control over the Panama Canal.

Carter tells how on the occasion of signing the treaty, "our conversation was primarily about two subjects: human rights and the relationship between the rich and poor nations of the world." Carter describes as "the most impressive aspect of the evening" the moment the general "broke down and sobbed as his wife held him" shortly before the signing ceremony took place. This display of patriotic seriousness cemented Carter's "respect and affection" for the "quiet and courageous" general, although true to form Carter later "was pushing him hard to further democratize his government."

In light of what we now know about the general's trafficking in drugs and arms—

and what Carter could surely have known if he had thought to find out before his June 1978 visit to Panama, a decade after the general took power—the American president's undoubtedly heart-felt feelings are best seen as yet another symptom of his heart substituting for his mind. It is true that the general had many progressive admirers for his efforts with respect to the poor in Panama. Moreover, he had promised a transition to democracy, pledging later to hold national elections in 1984. In light of Torrijos's efforts at reform, Carter's determination to begin the process of turning the canal over to Panamanian authorities was indeed an important act. Yet, it should not be forgotten that the banking system that has worked so remarkably well over the last quarter century in handling illegal arms and drugs shipments was significantly expanded and modernized by General Torrijos; that the head of Panamanian intelligence, a man whom Torrijos had promoted through the ranks and who was to succeed him within two years of his death in 1981, was none other than Manuel Antonio Noriega; and that whatever the noble promises about eventual elections in 1984—sixteen years after he had seized power—the government Torrijos actually created and ran for thirteen years ultimately proved far more conducive at promoting dictatorship than democracy. See Carter, *Keeping Faith*, 161, 178f; Andrew Zimbalist and John Weeks, *Panama at the Crossroads: Economic Development and Political Change in the Twentieth Century* (University of California Press, 1991), 30ff, 51ff; Frederick Kempe, *Divorcing the Dictator: America's Bungled Affair with Noriega* (G. P. Putnam, 1990), chap. 7; John Dinges, *Our Man in Panama: How General Noriega Used the United States—and Made Millions in Drugs and Arms* (Random House, 1990), 61ff; and Steve C. Ropp, "Explaining the Long-Term Maintenance of a Military Regime: Panama before the U.S. Invasion," *World Politics* 44, no. 2 (January 1992).

55. See, for example, Carter's speech of October 5, 1977, in *Current Documents, 1977–1981*, 417f; of May 22, 1977, in *Bulletin*, 76, no. 1981 (June 13, 1977), 621ff.

56. Speech of May 22, 1977, in *Bulletin* 76, no. 1981 (June 13, 1977), 621ff; speech of December 6, 1978, in *Bulletin* 79, no. 2022 (January 1979), 1ff.

CHAPTER TEN

1. See Ronald Reagan, "What Is a Conservative?" (1977) in Reagan, *A Time for Choosing: The Speeches of Ronald Reagan, 1961–1982* (Regnery Gateway, 1983), 181ff.

2. Liberals might disagree among themselves without ceasing all the while to be liberals. With the New Deal, FDR introduced the state into economic relations in the United States, worrying particularly about the welfare of the poor and claiming that without government's action, democracy was in peril. That was modern liberalism. But nineteenth century liberalism had originally opposed such a role for the state, insisting on the primacy of civil society and the workings of the market—a view to which Reagan wholeheartedly subscribed, once again in the name of preserving democratic government. Two of Reagan's supporters who recognized his liberalism in the historical sense of the term were Jeane J. Kirkpatrick, "The Reagan Phenomenon and the Liberal Tradition" (1981), in Kirkpatrick, *The Reagan Phenomenon and Other Speeches on Foreign Policy* (American Enterprise Institute, 1983); and

Charles Krauthammer, "The Poverty of Realism," *New Republic*, February 17, 1986. See also Milton Friedman, *Capitalism and Freedom* (University of Chicago Press, 1962), 5f.

3. Cited in Lou Cannon, *President Reagan: The Role of a Lifetime* (Simon and Schuster, 1992), 133. I have borrowed the term *sleepwalking* from Haynes Johnson, *Sleepwalking through History: America in the Reagan Years* (W. W. Norton, 1991).

4. Reagan, "What is a Conservative," 201; Reagan, *Speaking My Mind: Selected Speeches* (Simon and Schuster, 1989), 44, 417.

5. *American Foreign Policy: Current Documents* (hereafter *Current Documents*), (GPO, 1985), February 22, 1983, pp. 1ff.

6. Reagan, January 11, 1989, in *Speaking My Mind*, 414; *Current Documents, 1985*, October 24, 1985, p. 13. On Reagan's individualism and populism, see also Cannon, *President Reagan*, 792ff.

7. *Current Documents, 1985* (GPO, 1986), January 31, 1985, pp. 7f.

8. *Public Papers of Presidents of the United States: Ronald Reagan* (hereafter *Public Papers*), *1985* (GPO, 1988), 1:134f.

9. *Current Documents, 1985*, January 31, 1985, p. 7.

10. See Ronald Reagan, "United States Foreign Policy and World Realities," (1977), in Reagan, *A Time for Choosing*; also Caspar Weinberger, *Current Documents, 1985*, July 25, 1985, pp. 59ff. The differences between the two systems are laid out by Jeane Kirkpatrick, whose writings were the most important theoretical documents circulated at the beginning of the new administration. See especially, "Reflections on Totalitarianism" and "Sources of Stability in the American Tradition," in Kirkpatrick, ed., *Dictatorships and Double Standards: Rationalism and Reason in Politics* (Simon and Schuster, 1982); and "The Reagan Reassertion of Western Values," in *Reagan Phenomenon*; also various statements in Kirkpatrick, *Political and Moral Dimensions*, vol. 1 of *Legitimacy and Force* (Transaction Books, 1988).

11. The speech is reprinted in Reagan, *Speaking My Mind*, but improvised remarks are included in the report in *New York Times*, May 9, 1983. See also, Cannon, *President Reagan*, 281ff; *Speaking My Mind*, January 11, 1989, p. 414; and Reagan, "What is a Conservative?" 186.

12. Reagan, "An American Citizen Views the Republic of China," *Vital Speeches of the Day* 44, no. 18 (July 1, 1978): 554; Reagan, *Public Papers, 1985*, 2:1388f.

13. Carter's policy changed dramatically in the last fourteen months he was in office, paving the way for many of the positions later taken by Reagan. See Zbigniew Brzezinski, "The Cold War and Its Aftermath," *Foreign Affairs* 71, no. 4 (Fall 1992): 41ff. For Reagan, see *Current Documents, 1984* (GPO, 1986), April 6, 1984, p. 8.

14. On the "new patriotism" see Kirkpatrick, "The Reagan Reassertion."

15. *Current Documents, 1987* (GPO, 1988), September 21, 1987, p. 10. On the "democratic revolution," see Reagan's important speech before the British Parliament, June 8, 1982, in *Speaking My Mind*, 115; *Current Documents, 1988* (GPO, 1989), December 16, 1988, pp. 7ff; and George Shultz, speech of February 22, 1985, in the State Department, *Bulletin* 85, no. 2097 (April 1985), 16ff.

16. Cannon, *President Reagan*, 291f, 297ff. See also, Henry Kissinger, *Diplomacy* (Simon & Schuster, 1994), 764f.

17. Don Oberdorfer, *The Turn: From the Cold War to a New Era, the United States and the Soviet Union, 1983–1990* (Poseidon Press, 1991).

18. Cannon, *President Reagan*, 339ff, 373f; Thomas Carothers, *In the Name of Democracy: U.S. Policy toward Latin America in the Reagan Years* (University of California Press, 1991), 174f.

19. *Current Documents, 1984*, April 3, 1984, p. 1ff (see also his speech of February 22, 1984, pp. 279ff). Shultz's memoirs lack an extended statement of his philosophy of power. See George P. Shultz, *Turmoil and Triumph: My Years as Secretary of State* (Charles Scribner's Sons, 1993).

20. *Current Documents, 1984*, April 6, 1984, p. 12; September 20, 1984, pp. 62f; *1986* (GPO, 1987), March 14, 1986, p. 8; *Public Papers, 1981* (GPO, 1982), May 1, 1981, p. 434. See also Coral Bell, *The Reagan Paradox: American Foreign Policy in the 1980s* (Rutgers University Press, 1989), vii.

21. Christopher Coker uses the term *constructive engagement* to refer to an approach initiated during Nixon years. See Coker, *The United States and South Africa, 1968–1985* (Duke University Press, 1986). While Chester Crocker appeared before numerous congressional committees to update his ideas, his key statement remains, "South Africa: Strategy for Change," *Foreign Affairs* 59, no. 2 (Winter 1980–1). See also Crocker, *High Noon in Southern Africa: Making Peace in a Rough Neighborhood* (W. W. Norton, 1992), 74ff.

22. Crocker in *Current Documents, 1981* (GPO, 1984), August 29, 1981, p. 1113; 1982, March 22, 1982, pp. 1172ff.

23. Crocker, *High Noon*, chap. 19.

24. Crocker, "South Africa," 337, 341, 343.

25. Crocker, "South Africa," 346f.

26. Crocker, "South Africa," 325, 328, 349.

27. Crocker, "South Africa," pp. 347f.

28. On this period, see Coker, *The United States and South Africa*, chaps. 8–13; and Sanford J. Ungar and Peter Vale, "South Africa: Why Constructive Engagement Failed," *Foreign Affairs* 64, no. 2 (Winter 1985–6).

29. *Current Documents, 1986*, July 22, 1986, pp. 652f. See also Shultz's testimony before the Senate Foreign Relations Committee, *Current Documents, 1986*, July 23, 1986, p. 656.

30. See Shultz, *Turmoil and Triumph*, 1124ff.

31. For opposing opinions, see Crocker, *High Noon*, chap. 19; and Michael Clough, *Free at Last? U.S. Policy toward Africa and the End of the Cold War* (Council on Foreign Relations, 1992), 103ff.

32. *Current Documents, 1982* (GPO, 1985), April 26, 1982, pp. 1102ff. In 1988 Shultz doubtlessly jarred Confucian sensibilities even more when he said, "Democracy is a rough and tumble process of give-and-take, debate, and compromise. . . . even in the midst of vigorous public debate and societal change, democratic governments can remain strong because they have a structure of consent behind them—elections, a free press, open institutions." *Current Documents, 1988*, July 18, 1988, pp. 561ff. See also Shultz, *Turmoil and Triumph*, 975ff. Reagan offered the same

advice, "I have faith in the Korean people's ability to find a political system meeting their democratic aspirations, even in the face of the heavy security challenge presented by the North." *Current Documents, 1983*, November 12, 1983, p. 1068. See also Sung-joo Han, "South Korea: Politics in Transition," in Larry Diamond et al., eds., *Democracy in Developing Countries: Asia* (Lynne Rienner, 1989).

33. *New York Times*, January 30–1, 1986.

34. Carothers, *In the Name of Democracy*, 182ff; Georges Fauriol, "The Duvaliers and Haiti," *Orbis* 32, no. 4 (Fall 1988); Anthony P. Maingot, "Haiti and Aristide: The Legacy of History," *Current History*, February 1992.

35. *Current Documents, 1981*, June 1, 1981, p. 1049 (Bush); *1984*, October 24, 1984, pp. 759ff (Bosworth).

36. *New York Times*, February 2, 9–11, 1986. Theodore Friend, "Marcos and the Philippines," *Orbis* 32, no. 4 (Fall 1988); Raymond Bonner, *Waltzing with a Dictator: The Marcoses and the Making of American Policy* (Times Books, 1987), chaps. 15–17. See also, David G. Timberman, *A Changeless Land: Continuity and Change in Philippine Politics* (M. E. Sharpe, 1991), 139f, 148; W. Scott Thompson, *The Philippines in Crisis: Development and Security in the Aquino Era, 1986–1992* (St. Martin's Press, 1992), chap. 3; and Shultz, *Turmoil and Triumph*, 615ff, 626ff.

37. *Bulletin* 81, no. 2048 (March 1981): 1, 7.

38. *Current Documents, 1981*, March 6, 1981, p. 1284.

39. *Bulletin*, 81, no. 2050 (May 1981): 2050; *Current Documents, 1981*, February 27, 1981, pp. 1274f; also, Alexander M. Haig, Jr., *Caveat: Realism, Reagan and Foreign Policy* (Macmillan, 1984), 107.

40. *Current Documents, 1982*, March 8, 1982, p. 1404.

41. *Current Documents, 1984*, April 3, 1984, p. 5.

42. Calculated from the Agency for International Development, *U.S. Overseas Loans and Grants*, various years.

43. See Carothers, *In the Name of Democracy*; also Benjamin C. Schwartz, *American Counterinsurgency Doctrine and El Salvador: The Frustrations of Reform and the Illusions of Nation Building* (Rand, 1991). For the Bush Presidency see *Human Rights Watch World Report, 1992* (Human Rights Watch, 1992), 12ff. On Reagan see, *Current Documents 1983*, March 10, 1983, p. 1288; (also December 1, 1983, p. 1389); Reagan, April 27, 1983, *Speaking My Mind*, 145ff; also *Current Documents, 1981*, 1326ff; *1982*, 1373ff.

44. Schwarz, *Counterinsurgency*; and Terry Lynn Karl, "El Salvador's Negotiated Revolution," *Foreign Affairs* 71, no. 2 (Spring 1992).

45. See Mikhail Gorbachev's speech of January 27, 1987, "On Restructuring the Party's Personnel Policy: Report to the Plenary Meeting of the CPSU Central Committee," in Gorbachev, *M.S. Gorbachov: Speeches and Writings* (Pergamon Press, 1987), 1:118ff; Gorbachev, *Perestroika: New Thinking for Our Country and the World* (Harper and Row, 1987), chap. 2, sec. 3; Reagan cited in Cannon, *President Reagan*, 774. See also Cannon's chap. 21, Oberdorfer, *Turn*, 139ff; and Seweryn Bialer and Michael Mandelbaum, eds., *Gorbachev's Russia and American Foreign Policy* (Westview Press, 1988).

46. See Shultz's criticism of Reagan for his failure to push hard enough against antidemocrats in *Turmoil and Triumph*, 615ff, 626ff, 820, 1115f.

47. Cannon, *President Reagan*, 305ff.

48. See Ernst Lefever "The Trivialization of Human Rights," *Policy Review* 3 (Winter 1978); Tamar Jacoby, "The Reagan Turnaround on Human Rights," *Foreign Affairs* 64, no. 5 (Summer 1986).

49. For the opening charter of the NED, see *Current Documents, 1984*, December 1984, pp. 324ff; for a discussion see Carothers, *In the Name of Democracy*, 199ff; and Joshua Muravchik, *Exporting Democracy: Fulfilling America's Destiny* (American Enterprise Institute, 1991), chap. 13.

50. Kirkpatrick, *Dictatorships and Double Standards*, introduction, 8.

51. Kirkpatrick, "Dictatorships and Double Standards," in *Dictatorships and Double Standards*, 30f.

52. Kirkpatrick, "Dictatorships and Double Standards," 34.

53. Kirkpatrick, "Dictatorships and Double Standards," 49ff.

54. See Carothers, *In the Name of Democracy*, 124f; Joseph S. Tulchin, *Argentina and the United States: A Conflicted Relationship* (Twayne, 1990), 150ff; A. Glenn Mower, Jr., *Human Rights and American Foreign Policy: The Carter and Reagan Experiences* (Greenwood Press, 1987), 32ff.

55. Paul E. Sigmund, *The United States and Democracy in Chile* (Johns Hopkins University Press, 1993), chaps. 6–7.

56. Pamela Constable and Arturo Valenzuela, *A Nation of Enemies: Chile under Pinochet* (W. W. Norton, 1991), 289ff; Carothers, *In the Name of Democracy*, 153ff. Bonner, *Waltzing with a Dictator*, 404f.

57. Cited in Mower, *Human Rights*, 135.

58. Reagan, *Speaking My Mind*, 212f.

59. *Current Documents, 1987*, September 21, 1987, p. 8.

60. *Current Documents, 1988*, December 16, 1988, p. 7.

61. *Current Documents, 1988*, December 16, 1988, pp. 7f.

62. *Bulletin*, 83 no. 2072 (December 22, 1982): 36; *Current Documents, 1984*, December 6, 1984, pp. 1116ff; *Current Documents, 1987*, January 8, 1987, p. 614.

63. *Current Documents, 1986*, July 22, 1986, p. 654.

64. *Current Documents, 1981*, October 22, 1981, p. 282.

65. *Current Documents, 1987*, September 21, 1987, pp. 7f; also, Reagan, *Speaking My Mind*, June 8, 1982, pp. 112, 118.

66. *Current Documents, 1987*, February 20, 1987, p. 2; *1986*, 9ff; see also *Current Documents, 1983*, February 22, 1983, p. 2.

67. *Current Documents, 1985*, December 5, 1985, p. 1087; *1987*, 823ff; also Shultz, *Turmoil and Triumph*, 969.

68. The economic issues seem foremost in Gorbachev's mind in his *Perestroika*, 45ff; see also John B. Dunlop, *The Rise of Russia and the Fall of the Soviet Empire* (Princeton University Press, 1993), chap. 1; and Francis Fukuyama, "The Modernizing Imperative: The USSR as an Ordinary Country," *The National Interest*, Spring 1993, 15ff.

69. Federal Reserve, *Survey of Consumer Finance*, as reported in the *New York Times*, April 21, 1992; also Andrew Hacker, "Paradise Lost," *New York Review of Books*, May 13, 1993. The Los Angeles riots of April 1992 are linked in the same fashion to Reagan's economic practices.

70. Charles G. Lindblom, *Politics and Markets: The World's Political-Economic Systems* (Basic Books, 1977), pt. 5.

71. See the discussion in Cannon, *President Reagan*, chap. 14; also Carl Bernstein, "The Holy Alliance," *Time*, February 24, 1992.

72. On the matter of overall defense thinking, see *Current Documents, 1981*, January 9, 1981; March 18, 1981, p. 32; *1982*, April 20, 1982, p. 4. See also Barry R. Posen and Stephen Van Evera, "Reagan Administration Defense Policy: Departure from Containment," in Kenneth Oye et al., *Eagle Resurgent? The Reagan Era in American Foreign Policy* (Little, Brown, 1987). The result was a rise in defense spending in the first Reagan administration of 51 percent (excluding inflation) with additional requests for continued buildup thereafter. See also Raymond L. Gartoff, *Detente and Confrontation: American-Soviet Relations from Nixon to Reagan* (Brookings Institution, 1985), 1009ff; Fareed Zakaria, "The Reagan Strategy of Containment," *Political Science Quarterly* 105, no. 3 (1990). On Carter's shift toward a more militant posture, see *Bulletin* 80, 2035, pp. 58, 60; 2036, p. 29; and *American Foreign Policy: Basic Documents, 1977–1981*, (GPO, 1983), 53ff.

73. Weinberger, *Current Documents 1982*, April 20, 1982, p. 5; Casey, March 8, 1982, p. 1403; Reagan, *A Time for Choosing*, 213.

74. *Current Documents, 1988*, February 2, 1988, p. 733.

75. Cannon, *President Reagan*, 338f, 346ff.

76. Casey, *Current Documents, 1982*, March 8, 1982, p. 1405. For Reagan, see *Current Documents, 1981*, 1277ff.

77. *Current Documents, 1983*, April 19, 1983, p. 329. See also the introduction to the first edition under Abrams of the State Department's annual *Country Reports on Human Rights Practices for 1982* (GPO, 1983). See too, Kirkpatrick, *Current Documents, 1981*, November 24, 1981, pp. 379ff.

78. *Current Documents, 1986*, March 14, 1986, p. 4.

79. *Current Documents, 1982*, October 18, 1982, p. 379.

80. *Current Documents, 1982*, July 19, 1982, pp. 665ff; see also Bernstein, "Holy Alliance."

81. *Current Documents, 1983*, May 1, 1983, p. 505.

82. *Current Documents, 1985*, March 1, 1985, p. 973.

83. *Current Documents, 1983*, March 23, 1983, pp. 1291ff; *1986*, February 24, 1983, pp. 735ff.

84. Theodore Draper, *A Very Thin Line: The Iran-Contra Affairs* (Hill and Wang, 1991); and Draper, "The Iran-Contra Secrets," *New York Review of Books*, May 27, 1993, June 3, 1993. See also Johnson, *Sleepwalking*, chaps. 20–26.

85. The UN Truth Commission investigating killings in El Salvador pointed to the brutality of the military-backed death squads and American trained combat battalions as well as U.S. knowledge of the atrocities. *New York Times*, March 15, March 21, November 9, 1993; and Mark Danner, "The Truth of El Mozote," *New Yorker*, December 6, 1993.

86. *New York Times*, April 28, 1992.

87. Roy Gutman, *Banana Diplomacy: The Making of American Policy in Nicaragua, 1981–1987* (Simon and Schuster, 1988), chap. 11. By contrast, see Robert F. Turner, *Nicaragua vs. the United States: A Look at the Facts* (Pergamon-Brassey's, 1987). See also Bruce W. Jentleson, "The Reagan Administration and Coercive Diplomacy: Restraining More than Remaking Governments," *Political Science Quarterly* 106, no. 1 (1991): pp. 66ff, 74; and Robert H. Johnson, "Misguided Mo-

rality: Ethics and the Reagan Doctrine," *Political Science Quarterly* 103, no. 2 (1988).

88. *Current Documents, 1987*, September 10, 1987, p. 759. See also Shultz, "New Realities and New Ways of Thinking," *Foreign Affairs*, 63, no. 4 (1985); and *Current Documents, 1984*, February 8, 1984, pp. 967ff.

89. *Current Documents, 1982*, November 17, 1982, p. 1284. See also Reagan, *Current Documents, 1984*, May 8, 1984, pp. 970ff.

90. Carothers, *In the Name of Democracy*, 135.

91. Stephen Sestanovich, "Did the West Undo the East?" *National Interest*, Spring 1993; Kissinger, *Diplomacy*, chap. 30.

92. Theodore Draper, "Who Killed Soviet Communism?" *New York Review of Books*, June 11, 1992; Michael Mandelbaum, "The Fall of the House of Lenin," *World Policy Journal*, Fall 1993; and Andrew C. Janos, "Social Science, Communism, and the Dynamics of Political Change." *World Politics* 44, no. 1 (October 1991).

93. See the argument about "imperial overstretch" in Paul Kennedy, *The Rise and Fall of the Great Powers: Economic Change and Military Conflict from 1500 to 2000* (Random House, 1987).

94. Reagan, *Speaking My Mind*, 413.

CHAPTER ELEVEN

1. *American Foreign Policy: Current Documents* (hereafter *Current Documents*), *1989)* (GPO, 1990), January 20, 1989, p. 4.

2. *Current Documents, 1989*, 2.

3. Arnold L. Horelick, "U.S.-Soviet Relations: A New Era," *Foreign Affairs* 69, no. 1 (Winter 1989–90); Michael Mandelbaum, "The Bush Foreign Policy," *Foreign Affairs* 70, no. 1 (1991); and Michael R. Beschloss and Strobe Talbott, *At the Highest Levels: The Inside Story of the End of the Cold War* (Little, Brown, 1993), chap. 4.

4. Support for East European Democracy Act, H.R. 3402, 101st Cong., 1st sess., November 17, 1989, p. 3.

5. *Current Documents, 1990* (GPO, 1991), February 10, 1990, pp. 371ff.

6. *Current Documents, 1989*, September 25, 1989, pp. 12f.

7. *Current Documents, 1990*, January 31, 1990, pp. 1f.

8. Bush speaking on May 2, 1989, reprinted in the U. S. Department of State, *Bulletin* 89, no. 2147 (June 1989); Baker in *Current Documents, 1989*, December 10, 1989, p. 577.

9. *Current Documents, 1989*, November 13, 1989 (on the OAS), 678ff; and (on Panama), 712ff.

10. *Current Documents, 1990*, March 30, 1990, pp. 12ff.

11. *Current Documents, 1990*, June 27, 1990, pp. 813ff; also 844ff.

12. For a negative assessment of the likely influence of the NAFTA on the political organization of Mexico, see Jorge G. Castaneda, "Can NAFTA Change Mexico?" *Foreign Affairs* 72, no. 4 (September–October 1993); for contending, but largely positive, assessments see Riordan Roett, ed., *Political and Economic Liberalization in Mexico: At a Critical Juncture?* (Lynne Rienner, 1993); and Sidney

Weintraub and Delal Baer, "The Interplay Between Economic and Political Opening: The Sequence in Mexico," *Washington Quarterly* 15 (Spring 1992).

13. *Public Papers of the Presidents of the United States* (hereafter *Public Papers: George Bush, 1990*): (GPO, 1991), September 11, 1990, p. 1219.

14. *Public Papers Bush, 1991* (GPO, 1992), January 16, 1991, p. 44. On relations with the Soviet Union and the UN at this juncture, see Beschloss and Talbott, *Highest Levels*, chaps. 12–13.

15. John Newhouse, "No Exit, No Entrance," *New Yorker*, June 28, 1993.

16. Among the many reports, see Alma Guillermoprieto, "Letter from Panama," *New Yorker*, August 17, 1992; and Richard H. Shultz, Jr., "The Post-Conflict Use of Military Forces: Lessons from Panama, 1989–91," *Journal of Strategic Studies* 16, no. 2 (June 1993).

17. See Beschloss and Talbott, *Highest Levels*, chap. 18 and pp. 469ff; *New York Times*, May 7, 1991; March 11, 1992; April 2, 1992.

18. Charles Krauthammer, "The Unipolar Moment," *Foreign Affairs* 70, no. 1 (1991).

19. Richard W. Tucker and David C. Hendrickson, *The Imperial Temptation: The New World Order and America's Purpose* (Council on Foreign Relations Press, 1992).

20. *New York Times*, December 13, 1991. As Baker warned, "Great empires rarely go quietly into extinction. . . . No one can dismiss the possibility that darker political forces lurk in the wings, representing the remnants of Stalinism or the birth of nationalist extremism or even fascism, ready to exploit the frustrations of a proud but exhausted people in their hour of despair."

21. *New York Times*, April 2, 1992.

22. See Raymond Bonner, "African Democracy," *New Yorker*, September 3, 1990; and "Africa Watch," *World Report 1992* (Human Rights Watch, 1991). Bush's last statement on the principles of a sound foreign policy were markedly restrained in what he felt the United States could accomplish. See *New York Times*, January 6, 1993.

23. The Clinton foreign policy team's collective position is reviewed by Thomas L. Friedman in *New York Times*, October 1, 1993; see also *New York Times*, September 22, 1993. Clinton's speech before the UN is reprinted in *New York Times*, September 28, 1993. For the on-going contradictions of American policy toward China, see *Wall Street Journal*, March 22, 1994.

24. Vice President Albert Gore strongly implied the importance of democratization to Mexico on a trip there reported in *New York Times*, December 2, 1993.

25. Speech on Russia by Warren Christopher, *New York Times*, March 23, 1993; by Bill Clinton, April 2, 1993.

26. Clinton in *New York Times*, January 16, 1994; Havel in "The Post-Communist Nightmare," *New York Review of Books*, May 27, 1993, and "A Call for Sacrifice," *Foreign Affairs* 73, no. 2 (March–April 1994).

27. In 1785, the United States signed a reciprocal most-favored nation commercial treaty with Prussia and in 1789 enacted nondiscriminatory Tariff and Tonnage Acts. See *Treaties and Conventions Concluded between the United States of America and Other Powers since July 4, 1776* (GPO, 1889), 907; Tony Smith, *The Pattern of Imperialism: The United States, Great Britain, and the Late-Industrializing*

World since 1815 (Cambridge University Press, 1981), 142ff; Felix Gilbert, *To the Farewell Address: Ideas of Early American Foreign Policy* (Princeton University Press, 1961), 49ff, 69ff; Drew R. McCoy, *The Elusive Republic: Political Economy in Jeffersonian America* (W. W. Norton, 1982), chaps. 2–3; Cecil V. Crabb, Jr., *The Doctrines of American Foreign Policy: Their Meaning, Role, and Future*, (Louisiana State University Press, 1982), chap. 2; David A. Lake, *Power, Protection, and Free Trade: International Sources of U.S. Commercial Strategy, 1887–1939* (Cornell University Press, 1988); and the debate over free trade imperialism William Roger Louis, *Imperialism: The Robinson and Gallagher Controversy* (Franklin Watts, 1976).

28. Angus Maddison, *The World Economy in the 20th Century* (Organization of Economic Cooperation and Development, 1989); Herman Van Der Wee, *Prosperity and Upheaval: The World Economy, 1945–1980* (University of California Press, 1987); Paul Kennedy, *The Rise and Fall of the Great Powers: Economic Change and Military Conflict from 1500 to 2000* (Random House, 1987), 413ff; and Richard N. Gardner, "The Comeback of Liberal Internationalism," *Washington Quarterly* 13 (Winter 1990). For figures, see the International Monetary Fund, *Direction of Trade*, December 1992, p. 2: and U.S. Department of Commerce, *Survey of Current Business*, June 1991, pp. 29, 32.

29. For an effort to distinguish the political from the economic motivations of U.S. foreign policy, see Smith, *Pattern*, 182ff. For an interesting book on early thinking about America in world affairs, see Robert W. Tucker and David C. Hendrickson, *The Empire of Liberty: The Statecraft of Thomas Jefferson* (Oxford University Press, 1990).

30. *International Herald Tribune*, June 18, 1992.

31. *New York Times*, May 7, 1992.

32. Michael Doyle, "Kant, Liberal Legacies, and Foreign Affairs," *Philosophy and Public Affairs* 12, pts. 1 and 2 (Summer and Fall 1983); Doyle, "Liberalism and World Politics," *American Political Science Review* 80, no. 4 (1986); and Doyle, "An International Liberal Community," in Graham Allison and Gregory F. Treverton, eds., *Rethinking America's Security: Beyond Cold War to New World Order* (W. W. Norton, 1991).

33. Bruce Russett, *Grasping the Democratic Peace: Principles for a Post–Cold War World* (Princeton University Press, 1993); David A. Lake, "Powerful Pacifists: Democratic States and War," *American Political Science Review* 86, no. 1 (March 1992); Randall L. Schweller, "Domestic Structures and Preventive War: Are Democracies More Pacific?" *World Politics* 44, no. 2 (January 1992); Tony Smith, "Social Violence and Conservative Social Psychology: The Case of Erik Erikson," *Journal of Peace Research* 13 (January 1976); Bruno J. Bueno de Mesquita et al., "Democracy and Foreign Policy: Community and Constraint," *Journal of Conflict Resolution* 35 (June 1991); William J. Dixon, "Democracy and the Management of International Conflict," *Journal of Conflict Resolution* 37 (March 1993); Dixon, "Democracy and the Peaceful Settlement of International Conflict," *American Political Science Review* 88, no. 1 (March 1994); Jack Snyder, *Myths of Empire: Domestic Politics and International Ambition* (Cornell University Press, 1991); Stephen Van Evera, "Primed for Peace: Europe after the Cold War," *International Security* 15, no. 3 (Winter 1990–91); Thomas M. Franck, "The Emerging Right to

Democratic Governance," *American Journal of International Law* 86, no. 1 (January 1992). For statements on how the United States might actively encourage democracy abroad, see Graham T. Allison, Jr., and Robert P. Beschel, Jr., "Can the United States Promote Democracy?" *Political Science Quarterly* 107 (Spring 1992); Larry Diamond, "Beyond Authoritarianism and Totalitarianism: Strategies for Democratization," *Washington Quarterly* 12 (Winter 1989); Diamond and Marc F. Plattner, eds., *The Global Resurgence of Democracy* (Johns Hopkins University Press, 1993); Diamond, "The Global Imperative: Building a Democratic World Order," *Current History* 93, no. 579 (January 1994); and Giuseppe Di Palma, *To Craft Democracies: An Essay on Democratic Transitions* (University of California Press, 1991).

34. Samuel P. Huntington, "A Clash of Civilizations?" *Foreign Affairs* 72, no. 3 (Summer 1993).

35. Benedict Anderson, *Imagined Communities: Reflections on the Origin and Spread of Nationalism*, rev. ed. (Verso, 1991); Liah Greenfeld, *Nationalism: Five Roads to Modernity* (Harvard University Press, 1992); Anthony D. Smith, *Theories of Nationalism* (Holmes and Meier, 1983); Ernest Gellner, *Nations and Nationalism* (Basil Blackwell, 1983); Nathan Gardels, "Two Concepts of Nationalism: An Interview with Isaiah Berlin," *New York Review of Books*, November 21, 1991; and Stanley Hoffmann, "The Passion of Modernity," *The Atlantic*, August 1993.

36. F. L. Carsten, *The Rise of Fascism*, 2d ed. (University of California, 1980); Tony Smith, *Thinking Like a Communist: State and Legitimacy in the Soviet Union, China, and Cuba* (W. W. Norton, 1987).

37. For reflections on these matters, see John Lukacs, *The End of the Twentieth Century and the End of the Modern Age* (Ticknor and Fields, 1993), chap. 9; and Paul Kennedy, *Preparing for the Twenty-First Century* (Random House, 1993), pt. 1.

38. Walter Laqueur, *Black Hundred: The Rise of the Extreme Right in Russia* (HarperCollins, 1993).

39. For opposing views, see Robin Wright, "Islam, Democracy, and the West" *Foreign Affairs* 71, no. 2 (Summer 1992); Judith Miller, "The Challenge of Radical Islam," *Foreign Affairs* 72, no. 1 (Spring 1993); and Bernard Lewis, "Islam and Liberal Democracy," *The Atlantic*, February 1993.

40. The fortunes of democracy in Africa are followed in *Africa Demos*, published by the African Governance Program of the Carter Center at Emory University.

41. On the decline of militarism in European thanks to the spread of democracy, see Van Evera "Primed for Peace."

42. Francis Fukuyama, *The End of History and the Last Man* (Free Press, 1992). For an enduring critique of this kind of thinking see Herbert Butterfield, *The Whig Interpretation of History* (S. Bell and Sons, 1931).

43. Since 1978, the varying fortunes of democracy worldwide have been followed by the annual publication *Freedom in the World* (Freedom House). A historical survey of democracy's fortunes is Samuel P. Huntington, *The Third Wave: Democratization in the Late Twentieth Century* (University of Okalahoma Press, 1991).

44. Terry Lynn Karl, "Dilemmas of Democratization in Latin America," *Com-*

parative Politics 25 (October 1992); Frances Hagopian, "After Regime Change: Authoritarian Legacies, Political Representation, and the Democratic Future of South America," *World Politics* 45 (April 1993); Scott Mainwaring et al., *Issues in Democratic Consolidation: The New South American Democracies in Comparative Perspective* (Notre Dame University Press, 1992); and Jorge G. Castenada, *Utopia Unarmed: The Latin American Left after the Cold War* (Knopf, 1993).

45. Allison, and Beschel, "Can the United States Promote Democracy?"; Larry Diamond, "Promoting Democracy," *Foreign Policy* 87 (Summer 1992); Di Palma, *To Craft Democracies;* Franck, "Emerging Right." By contrast, see the warning on the limits to the current wave of democratic transitions in Huntington, *Third Wave,* chap. 6. While the United States has obviously been more successful promoting democracy in industrial rather than agrarian countries, this record may reflect as much the character of American policy as the nature of the countries in question. The reader is reminded of the American reluctance to address the socioeconomic power structure in the defeated Confederacy, the Philippines, or the Dominican Republic. By contrast, the British did leave behind stable democratic governments in the Anglophone Caribbean and India. For a more extended comparison of the U.S. in the Philippines and the British in India, see note 36 in "Notes to Chapter Two" above. On Jamaica, see Jorge I. Dominguez et al., *Democracy in the Caribbean: Political, Economic, and Social Perspectives* (Johns Hopkins University Press, 1993); and Carl Stone, "Decolonization and the Caribbean State System: The Case of Jamaica," and "Democracy and Socialism in Jamaica, 1972–1979," in Paget Henry and Carl Stone, eds., *The Newer Caribbean: Decolonization, Democracy, and Development* (Institute for the Study of Human Relations, 1983). On India, see Om P. Gautam, *The Indian National Congress* (Delhi: B.R. Publishing, 1985); and Robert L. Hardgrave, Jr., and Stanley A. Kochanek, eds., *India: Government and Politics in a Developing Nation*, 4th ed. (Harcourt Brace Jovanovich, 1986), chap. 2. For a statement opposing American efforts to try to foster democracy in the agrarian world, see Stephen Van Evera, "The United States and the Third World: When to Intervene?" in Kenneth A. Oye et al., *Eagle in a New World: American Grand Strategy in the Post–Cold War Era* (HarperCollins, 1992).

46. For more theoretical literature on the transition to democracy, see Dankwart A. Rustow, "Transitions to Democracy," *Comparative Politics*, 2, no. 3 (April 1970); Guillermo O'Donnell et al., *Transitions from Authoritarian Rule*, 4 vols. (Johns Hopkins University Press, 1986); Herbert Kitschelt, "Political Regime Change: Structure and Process-Driven Explanations," *American Political Science Review* 86, no. 4 (December 1992); Robert D. Putnam, *Making Democracy Work: Civic Traditions in Modern Italy* (Princeton University Press, 1993); and Joan M. Nelson, *Encouraging Democracy: What Role for Conditional Aid?* (Overseas Development Council, 1992).

APPENDIX

1. But see Samuel P. Huntington, *American Politics: The Promise of Disharmony* (Yale University Press, 1984), 246ff; Laurence Whitehead, "International Aspects of Democratization," in Guillermo O'Donnell et al., *Transitions from Authoritarian Rule: Comparative Perspectives* (Johns Hopkins University Press,

1986); and Robert A. Dahl, *Polyarchy: Participation and Opposition* (Yale University Press, 1971), chaps. 9–11.

2. But see John Montgomery, *Forced to Be Free: The Artificial Revolution in Germany and Japan* (University of Chicago Press, 1957).

3. Harry J. Benda, preface to Carl H. Lande, *Leaders, Factions, and Parties: The Structure of Philippine Politics,* Southeast Asia Studies Monograph Series no. 6 (Yale University, 1965).

4. Abraham Lowenthal, ed., *Exporting Democracy: The United States and Latin America* (Johns Hopkins University Press, 1991), viii.

5. But see Michael Doyle, "Kant, Liberal Legacies, and Foreign Affairs," 2 pts., *Philosophy and Public Affairs* 12 (Summer and Fall 1983).

6. The work most cited in the field of realism is Kenneth Waltz, *Theory of International Relations* (Addison-Wesley, 1979). For current analyses following Waltz's formulations and that debunk the liberal democratic internationalist perspective today, see John J. Mearsheimer, "Back to the Future: Instability in Europe after the Cold War," *International Security* 15, no. 1 (Summer 1990); and Christopher Layne, "The Unipolar Illusion: Why New Great Powers Will Arise," *International Security,* 17, no. 4 (Spring 1993).

7. See Charles Beitz, *Political Theory and International Relations* (Princeton University Press, 1979), pt. 1, p. 1; and Stanley Hoffmann, *Duties beyond Borders: On the Limits and Possibilities of Ethical International Politics* (Syracuse University Press, 1981).

8. Hans Morgenthau, introduction to David Mitrany, *A Working Peace System* (Quadrangle Books, 1966), 8, where Morgenthau describes as similar manifestations of "nationalistic universalism," "Wilson's crusade for democracy, the 'new order' of German fascism, the universal mission of Russia and Chinese Bolshevism, and the American response to protect the 'free world' from it." See also E. H. Carr, *The Twenty Years' Crisis, 1919–1939: An Introduction to the Study of International Relations,* rev. ed. (Harper and Row, 1946), 85ff. For skepticism that a community of democratic states would much matter in world affairs, see also Raymond Aron, *Peace and War: A Theory of International Relations* (Doubleday, 1966), 99ff; Henry Kissinger, "Domestic Structure and Foreign Policy" in *American Foreign Policy,* expanded ed. (W. W. Norton, 1977). For a sense of the evolution of liberal institutional ideas over time and their accommodation with realism, see Joseph S. Nye, Jr., "Neorealism and Neoliberalism," *World Politics* 40, no. 2 (January 1988). For an earlier effort to effect the union of realism and liberalism, see John H. Herz, *Political Realism and Political Idealism: A Study in Theories and Realities* (University of Chicago Press, 1951), chaps. 4–6. For a recent failed attempt to blend realism with liberalism, see Henry Kissinger, *Diplomacy* (Simon and Schuster, 1994), chaps. 1, 2, and 31. For an excellent study of competing explanations for the conduct of American foreign policy that nonetheless, inexplicably but tellingly, fails to investigate the logic or force of liberal democratic internationalism, see Michael J. Hogan and Thomas G. Paterson, eds., *Explaining the History of American Foreign Relations* (Cambridge University Press, 1991).

9. William Pfaff, *Barbarian Sentiments: How the American Century Ends* (Hill and Wang, 1989), 9–13; Robert Dallek, *The American Style of Foreign Policy: Cultural Politics and Foreign Affairs* (Oxford University Press, 1983), xiif; and

John Lewis Gaddis, *The United States and the End of the Cold War: Implications, Reconsiderations, Provocations* (Oxford University Press, 1992), 11ff. (For what appears to be a retreat from this position, see Gaddis, "The Tragedy of Cold War History," *Foreign Affairs* 73, no. 1 (January–February 1994.)

10. Tony Smith, "Requiem or New Agenda for Third World Studies?" *World Politics* 37, no. 4 (July 1985).

11. See Seymour Martin Lipset, *Political Man: The Social Basis of Politics* (Doubleday, 1960), chap. 2; also Talcott Parsons, "Evolutionary Universals," *American Sociological Review* 29, no. 5 (June 1964).

12. See Barrington Moore, Jr., *Social Origins of Dictatorship and Democracy: Lord and Peasant in the Making of the Modern World* (Beacon Press, 1966); Gregory M. Luebbert, *Liberalism, Fascism, or Social Democracy: Social Class and the Political Origins of Regimes in Interwar Europe* (Oxford University Press, 1991); and Dietrich Rueschemeyer et al., *Capitalist Development and Democracy* (University of Chicago, 1992).

13. The relationship between the international system, rapid economic growth, and the emergence of democracy is most often discussed with respect to South Korea and Taiwan. See also Edward N. Muller, "Dependent Economic Development, Aid Dependence on the United States, and Democratic Breakdown in the Third World," *International Studies Quarterly* 29 (1985).

14. Dahl, *Polyarchy*, 203, 214; and Dahl, *Democracy and Its Critics* (Yale University Press, 1989), 317.

15. See Smith, "Requiem or New Agenda."

16. The literature is voluminous. For an example of the assumption that development and democracy are synonymous, see Parsons, "Evolutionary Universals"; Leonard Binder, "Crises of Political Development," in Binder et al., *Crises and Sequences in Political Development* (Princeton University Press, 1971), 56–7; and Daniel Lerner, *The Passing of Traditional Societies: Modernizing the Middle East* (Free Press, 1958). For an argument that democracy and development may go together but need not, see Lucian Pye, *Aspects of Political Development* (Little, Brown, 1964), chap. 4; Pye "The Concept of Political Development," *Annals of the American Academy of Political and Social Science* 358 (March 1985); and S. N. Eisenstadt, "Varieties of Political Development: The Theoretical Challenge," in Eisenstadt and Stein Rokkan, *Building States and Nations: Models and Data Resources* (Sage Publications, 1973). For revolutionary preconditions to democracy, see Moore, *Social Origins*, chap. 7; for military preconditions, see Samuel P. Huntington, *Political Order in Changing Societies* (Yale University Press, 1968), chap. 4. As an example of literature that promoted U.S. involvement for the sake of democracy, see Max F. Millikan and W. W. Rostow, *A Proposal: Key to an Effective Foreign Policy* (Harper and Brothers, 1957), especially chaps. 3, 14; Millikan and Donald L. M. Blackmer, *The Emerging Nations: Their Growth and United States Policy* (Little, Brown, 1961); Edwin O. Reischauer, *Wanted: An Asian Policy* (Knopf, 1955), chap. 9. For work critical of this approach, see Howard J. Wiarda, *Ethnocentrism in Foreign Policy: Can We Understand the Third World?* (American Enterprise Institute, 1985). On American academic involvement with the CIA, see Pierre Gremion, *Le congres pour la liberte de la culture en Europe, 1950–1967* (Centre Nationale de Recherche Scientifique, 1988).

17. Gabriel A. Almond and Sidney Verba, *The Civic Culture: Political Attitudes and Democracy in Five Nations* (1963; Little, Brown, 1965), chap. 1.

18. Huntington, *Political Order*, fn. 16. It is an overstatement to say that no books attempting to meet the original ambition of development studies appeared. See, e.g., David E. Apter, *The Politics of Modernization* (University of Chicago Press, 1965).

19. Juan J. Linz and Alfred Stepan, eds., *The Breakdown of Democratic Regimes: Crisis, Breakdown, and Reequilibration* (Johns Hopkins University Press, 1978); Guillermo O'Donnell et al., *Transitions from Authoritarian Rule: Tentative Conclusions about Uncertain Democracies*, 4 vols. (Johns Hopkins University Press, 1986); Larry Diamond et al., *Democracy in Developing Countries*, 3 vols. (Lynne Rienner, 1989–90); and Giuseppe Di Palma, *To Craft Democracies: An Essay on Democratic Transitions* (University of California Press, 1991). See also Linz, "Transitions to Democracy," *Washington Quarterly*, Summer 1990; Diamond, "Beyond Authoritarianism and Totalitarianism: Strategies for Democratization," *Washington Quarterly*, Winter 1989; and Terry Lynn Karl, "Dilemmas of Democratization in Latin America," *Comparative Politics* 23, no. 1 (October 1990).

20. An excellent statement on the dilemma of writing American diplomatic history is Robert J. McMahon, "The Study of American Foreign Relations: National History or International History?" in Hogan and Paterson, *American Foreign Relations*.

21. For examples of interesting work I would call Marxist, see, on the character of U.S. foreign policy, William Appleman Williams, *The Tragedy of American Diplomacy*, 2d ed. (Dell, 1959); Arno Mayer, *Politics and Diplomacy of the Peacemaking: Containment and Counterrevolution at Versailles, 1918–1919* (Alfred A. Knopf, 1967); N. Gordon Levin, Jr., *Woodrow Wilson and World Politics: America's Response to War and Revolution* (Oxford University Press, 1968); Gabriel Kolko, *The Politics of War: The World and United States Foreign Policy, 1943–1945* (Random House, 1968); Gabriel Kolko and Joyce Kolko, *The Limits of Power: The World and United States Foreign Policy, 1945–1954* (Harper and Row, 1972); Fred L. Block, *The Origins of International Economic Disorder: A Study of United States International Monetary Policy from World War II to the Present* (University of California Press, 1977); Bruce Cumings, *The Roaring of the Cataract, 1945–1950*, vol. 2 of *The Origins of the Korean War* (Princeton University Press, 1990), chap. 1; and Cumings, "Revising Postrevisionism," *Diplomatic History* 17, no. 4 (Fall 1993). On world system analysis, see among Immanuel Wallerstein's many publications, *The Capitalist World-Economy* (Cambridge University Press, 1979); and Thomas J. McCormick, "World Systems," in Hogan and Paterson, *Explaining*, and McCormick, *America's Half Century: United States Foreign Policy in the Cold War* (Johns Hopkins University Press, 1989). On the character of the state-capitalist relations, see Nicos Poulantzas, *State, Power, Socialism* (Verso, 1978). On dependency, see Fernando Henrique Cardoso and Enzo Faletto, *Dependency and Development in Latin America* (University of California Press, 1979); Cardoso, "Dependent Capitalist Development in Latin America," *New Left Review* 74 (July–August 1972); Louis A. Perez, Jr., "Dependency" in Hogan and Paterson, *Explaining*; and Peter Evans, *Dependent Development: The Alliance of Multinational, State, and Local Capital in Brazil* (Princeton University Press, 1972). For a more

extended critique of these viewpoints, see Tony Smith, *The Pattern of Imperialism: The United States, Great Britain, and the Late-Industrializing World since 1815* (Cambridge University Press, 1981), chaps. 2, 4; and Smith, *Thinking Like a Communist: State and Legitimacy in the Soviet Union, China, and Cuba* (W.W. Norton, 1987), 43ff, 90ff, 167ff. See also, Theda Skocpol, "Wallerstein's World Capitalist System: A Theoretical and Historical Critique," *American Journal of Sociology* 82, no. 5 (March 1977); and Skocpol, *State and Social Revolutions: A Comparative Analytsis of France, Russia, and China* (Cambridge University Press, 1979).

Bibliography

PRIMARY SOURCES

Department of Commerce, Bureau of the Census. *Historical Statistics of the United States: Colonial Times to 1970.*
Department of State. *Bulletin.* Government Printing Office.
Department of State. *Country Reports on Human Rights Practices.* Annual from 1977.
Department of State. *Foreign Relations of the United States.* Government Printing Office.
Office of the Federal Register, National Archives and Records Administration. *Public Papers of the Presidents of the United States.* Government Printing Office.

SECONDARY SOURCES

Acheson, Dean. *Present at the Creation: My Years in the State Department.* Norton, 1969.
Adenauer, Konrad. *Memoirs.* Weidenfield and Nicholson, 1966.
African Demos. African Governance Program. Carter Center, Emory University.
Alam, Asadollah. *The Shah and I: The Confidential Diary of Iran's Royal Court, 1969–1977.* St. Martin's Press, 1991.
Allison, Graham T., Jr., and Robert P. Beschel, Jr. "Can the United States Promote Democracy?" *Political Science Quarterly* 197 (Spring 1992).
Almond, Gabriel A., and Sidney Verba. *The Civic Culture: Political Attitudes and Democracy in Five Nations.* Little, Brown, 1965.
Alsop, Joseph. *FDR: A Centenary Remembrance.* Viking Press, 1982.
Ambrose, Stephen E. *Eisenhower.* Simon and Schuster, 1983.
Ambrosious, Lloyd E. *Woodrow Wilson and the American Diplomatic Tradition: The Treaty Fight in Perspective.* Cambridge University Press, 1987.
Ameringer, Charles D. *The Democratic Left in Exile: The Anti-Dictatorial Struggle in the Caribbean, 1945–1959.* University of Miami Press, 1974.
Anderson, Benedict. *Imagined Communities: Reflections on the Origin and Spread of Nationalism.* Rev. ed. Verso, 1991.
Anderson, Terry H. *The United States, Great Britain, and the Cold War, 1944–1947.* University of Missouri Press, 1981.
Apter, David E. *The Politics of Modernization.* University of Chicago Press, 1965.
Aron, Raymond. *Peace and War: A Theory of International Relations.* Doubleday, 1966.
Azimi, Fakhreddin. "The Reconciliation of Politics and Ethics, Nationalism and Democracy: An Overview of the Political Career of Dr. Muhammad Musaddiq." In James A. Bill and William Roger Louis, eds., *Musaddiq, Iranian Nationalism, and Oil.* University of Texas Press, 1988.

Backer, John H. *Winds of History: The German Years of Lucius Dubignon Clay.* Van Nostrand Rheinhold, 1983.

Baker, Ray Stannard, and William E. Dodd, eds. *The New Democracy: Presidential Messages, Addresses, and Other Papers, 1913–1917.* Harper and Brothers, 1926.

———. *The Public Papers of Woodrow Wilson: College and State Education, Literary and Political Papers, 1875–1913.* Harper and Brothers, 1925.

Bakhash, Shaul. "Fall and Decline." *New York Review of Books,* December 2, 1981.

———. "Who Lost Iran?" *New York Review of Books,* May 14, 1981.

Bark, Dennis L., and David R. Gress. *From Shadow to Substance, 1945–1963.* Vol. 1 of *A History of West Germany.* Basil Blackwell, 1989.

Bauer, Arnold. "Rural Spanish America, 1870–1930." In Leslie Bethell, ed., *The Cambridge History of Latin America.* Cambridge University Press, 1984.

Beasley, W. G. *The Rise of Modern Japan.* St. Martin's Press, 1990.

Beitz, Charles. *Political Theory and International Relations.* Princeton University Press, 1979.

Bemis, Samuel Flagg. *The Latin American Policy of the United States: An Interpretation.* Harcourt, Brace, 1943.

Bendix, Reinhard. "Tradition and Modernity Reconsidered." *Comparative Studies in Society and History* 9, no. 3 (April 1967).

Benes, Eduard. *Democracy Today and Tomorrow.* Macmillan, 1939.

Berghahn, Volker. *The Americanization of West German Industry, 1945–1973.* Berg, 1986.

———. *Germany and the Approach of War in 1914.* St. Martin's Press, 1973.

———. *Modern Germany: Society, Economy, and Politics in the Twentieth Century.* 2d ed. Cambridge University Press, 1987.

Beschloss, Michael R., and Strobe Talbott. *At the Highest Levels: The Inside Story of the End of the Cold War.* Little, Brown, 1993.

Bharier, Julian. *Economic Development in Iran, 1900–1971.* Oxford University Press, 1971.

Bialer, Seweryn, and Michael Mandelbaum, eds. *Gorbachev's Russia and American Foreign Policy.* Westview Press, 1988.

Bill, James A. "America, Iran, and the Politics of Intervention, 1951–1953." In James A. Bill and William Roger Louis, eds., *Musaddiq, Iranian Nationalism, and Oil.* University of Texas Press, 1988.

———. *The Eagle and the Lion: The Tragedy of American-Iranian Relations.* Yale University Press, 1988.

Binder, Leonard, et al. *Crises and Sequences in Political Development.* Princeton University Press, 1971.

Blackbourn, David, and Goeff Eley. *The Peculiarities of German History: Bourgeois Society and Politics in Nineteenth-Century Germany.* Oxford University Press, 1984.

Blasier, Cole. *The Hovering Giant: U.S. Response to Revolutionary Change in Latin America.* University of Pittsburg Press, 1976.

Blaufarb, Douglas S. *The Counterinsurgency Era: U.S. Doctrine and Performance, 1950 to the Present.* Free Press, 1977.

Block, Fred L. *The Origins of International Economic Disorder: A Study of United*

States International Monetary Policy from World War II to the Present. University of California Press, 1977.

Bonner, Raymond. "African Democracy." *New Yorker*, September 3, 1990.

————. *Waltzing with a Dictator: The Marcoses and the Making of American Policy.* Times Books, 1987.

Borton, Hugh, ed. *Japan.* Cornell University Press, 1951.

Branyan, Robert L., and Lawrence H. Larson, eds. *The Eisenhower Administration, 1953–1956: A Documentary History.* Random House, 1971.

Brzezinski, Zbigniew. "The Cold War and Its Aftermath." *Foreign Affairs* 71, no. 4 (Fall 1992).

————. *Power and Principle: Memoirs of the National Security Adviser, 1977– 1981.* Farrar, Straus, Giroux, 1983.

Bueno de Mesquita, Bruno J. "Democracy and Foreign Policy: Community and Constraint." *Journal of Conflict Resolution* 35 (June 1991).

Buruma, Ian. "Americainerie." *New York Review of Books*, March 25, 1993.

Butterfield, Herbert. *The Whig Interpretation of History.* S. Bell and Sons, 1931.

Calder, Bruce. *The Impact of Intervention: The Dominican Republic during the U.S. Occupation of 1916–1924.* University of Texas Press, 1984.

Cannon, Lou. *President Reagan: The Role of a Lifetime.* Simon and Schuster, 1992.

Cardoso, Ciro F. "Central America: The Liberal Era, ca. 1870–1930." In Leslie Bethell, ed., *The Cambridge History of Latin America.* Cambridge University Press, 1984.

Cardoso, Fernando Henrique, and Enzo Faletto. *Dependency and Development in Latin America.* University of California Press, 1978.

Carothers, Thomas. *In the Name of Democracy: U.S. Policy toward Latin America in the Reagan Years.* University of California Press, 1991.

Carr, E. H. *International Relations between the Two World Wars, 1919–1939*, Harper and Row, 1947.

————. *The Twenty Years' Crisis, 1919–1939: An Introduction to the Study of International Relations.* Rev. ed. Harper and Row, 1946.

Carsten, F. L. *The Rise of Fascism.* 2d ed. University of California, 1980.

Carter, Jimmy. *A Government as Good as Its People.* Simon and Schuster, 1977.

————. *Keeping Faith: Memoirs of a President.* Bantam Books, 1982.

Castaneda, Jorge G. "Can NAFTA Change Mexico?" *Foreign Affairs* 72, no. 4 (September–October 1993).

————. *Utopia Unarmed. The Latin American Left after the Cold War.* Alfred A. Knopf, 1993.

Chace, James. *Endless War: How We Got Involved in Central America and What Can Be Done.* Vintage, 1984.

Chace, James, and Caleb Carr. *America Invulnerable: The Quest for Absolute Security from 1812 to Star Wars.* Summit Books, 1988.

Chehabi, H. E. *Iranian Politics and Religious Modernism: The Liberation Movement of Iran under the Shah and Khomeini.* Cornell University Press, 1990.

Christian, Shirley. *Nicaragua: Revolution in the Family.* Vintage, 1985.

Chomsky, Noam. "Vietnam: How Government Became Wolves." *New York Review of Books*, June 15, 1972.

Churchill, Winston S. *The Aftermath.* Charles Scribner's Sons, 1929.

Churchill, Winston S. *The Second World War: The Grand Alliance*. Houghton Mifflin, 1950.

———. *The Second World War: Triumph and Tragedy*. Houghton Mifflin, 1953.

Claude, Inis L., Jr. *Power and International Relations*. Random House, 1962.

———. *Swords into Plowshares: The Problems and Progress of International Organization*. 4th ed. Random House, 1971.

Clay, Lucius D. *Decision in Germany*. Doubleday, 1950.

Clements, Kendrick A. *The Presidency of Woodrow Wilson*. University Press of Kansas, 1992.

Cline, Howard F. *The United States and Mexico*. Rev. ed. Harvard University Press, 1963.

Clough, Michael. *Free at Last? U.S. Policy toward Africa and the End of the Cold War*. Council on Foreign Relations, 1992.

Cohen, Theodore. *Remaking Japan: The American Occupation as New Deal*. Free Press, 1987.

Cohen, Warren I. *America in the Age of Soviet Power, 1945–1991*. Vol. 4 of *The Cambridge History of American Foreign Relations*. Cambridge University Press, 1993.

———. *America's Response to China: An Interpretative History of Sino-American Relations*. John Wiley and Sons, 1971.

Coker, Christopher. *The United States and South Africa, 1968–1985*. Duke University Press, 1986.

The Collected Works of Abraham Lincoln. Vols. 2, 7, 8. Rutgers University Press, 1953.

Conradt, David B. "Changing German Political Culture." In Gabriel A. Almond and Sidney Verba, eds., *The Civic Culture Revisited*. Little, Brown, 1980.

Cooper, John Milton. *The Warrior and the Priest: Woodrow Wilson and Theodore Roosevelt*. Harvard University Press, 1983.

Corpuz, Onofre D. *The Philippines*. Prentice Hall, 1965.

Cotler, Julio, and Richard R. Fagen, eds. *Latin America and the United States: The Changing Realities*. Stanford University Press, 1974.

Cottam, Richard W. *Iran and the United States: A Cold War Case Study*. University of Pittsburgh Press, 1988.

———. "Nationalism in Twentieth Century Iran and Dr. Muhammad Musaddiq." In James A. Bill and William Roger Louis, eds., *Musaddiq, Iranian Nationalism, and Oil*. University of Texas Press, 1988.

Couloumbis, Theodore A., et al. *Foreign Interference in Greek Politics: An Historical Perspective*. Pella, 1976.

Crabb, Cecil V., Jr. *The Doctrines of American Foreign Policy: Their Meaning, Role, and Future*. Louisiana State University Press, 1982.

Craig, Gordon A., "The German Mystery Case." *New York Review of Books*, January 30, 1986.

———. The Politics of the Prussian Army, 1640–1945. Oxford University Press, 1956.

Crocker, Chester A. *High Noon in Southern Africa: Making Peace in a Rough Neighborhood*. W. W. Norton, 1992.

———. "South Africa: Strategy for Change." *Foreign Affairs* 59, no. 2 (Winter 1980–1).

Cumings, Bruce. "Revising Postrevisionism." *Diplomatic History* 17, no. 4 (Fall 1993).

———. *The Roaring of the Cataract, 1947–1950.* Vol. 2 of *The Origins of the Korean War.* Princeton University Press, 1990.

Cushner, Nicholas P. *Landed Estates in the Colonial Philippines.* Southeast Asia Studies Monograph Series, no. 20. Yale University, 1976.

Dahl, Robert A. *Democracy and Its Critics.* Yale University Press, 1989.

———. *Polyarchy: Participation and Opposition.* Yale University Press, 1971.

Dahrendorf, Ralf. *Society and Democracy in Germany.* W. W. Norton, 1984.

Dallek, Robert. *The American Style of Foreign Policy: Cultural Politics and Foreign Affairs.* Oxford University Press, 1983.

———. *Franklin D. Roosevelt and American Foreign Policy, 1932–1945.* Oxford University Press, 1979.

Danner, Mark. "The Truth of El Mozote." *New Yorker*, December 6, 1993.

DeConde, Alexander. *A History of American Foreign Policy.* 2d ed. Charles Scribner's Sons, 1971.

De Gaulle, Charles. *The Complete War Memoirs.* Di Capo Press, 1967.

DePorte, A. W. *Europe between the Superpowers: The Enduring Balance.* 2d ed. Yale University Press, 1986.

De Tocqueville, Alexis. *Democracy in America.* Harper and Row, 1961.

Diamandouros, P. Nikiforos. "Regime Change and the Prospects for Democracy in Greece: 1974–1983." In Guillermo O'Donnell et al., *Transitions from Authoritarian Rule: Southern Europe.* Johns Hopkins University Press, 1986.

Diamond, Larry. "Beyond Authoritarianism and Totalitarianism: Strategies for Democratization." *Washington Quarterly* 12 (Winter 1989).

———. "The Global Imperative: Building a Democratic World Order." *Current History* 93, no. 579 (January 1994).

———, "Promoting Democracy." *Foreign Affairs* 87 (Summer 1992).

Diamond, Larry, et. al. *Democracy in Developing Countries.* 3 vols. Lynne Rienner, 1989–90.

Diamond, Larry, and Marc F. Plattner, eds. *The Global Resurgence of Democracy.* Johns Hopkins University Press, 1993.

Diamond, William. *The Economic Thought of Woodrow Wilson.* Johns Hopkins University Press, 1943.

Dinges, John. *Our Man in Panama: How General Noriega Used the United States—and Made Millions in Drugs and Arms.* Random House, 1990.

Di Palma, Giuseppe. *To Craft Democracies: An Essay on Democratic Transitions.* University of California Press, 1991.

Divine, Robert. *Eisenhower and the Cold War.* Oxford University Press, 1981.

Dixon, William J. "Democracy and the Management of International Conflict." *Journal of Conflict Resolution* 37 (March 1993).

———. "Democracy and the Peaceful Settlement of International Conflict." *American Political Science Review* 88, no. 1 (March 1994).

Dominguez, Jorge I., et al. *Democracy in the Caribbean: Political, Economic and Social Perspectives.* Johns Hopkins University Press, 1993.

Dore, Ronald P. *Land Reform in Japan.* Oxford University Press, 1959.

Dore, Ronald P., and Tsutomu Ouchi. "Rural Origins of Japanese Fascism," In

James William Morely, ed., *Dilemmas of Growth in Prewar Japan*. Princeton University Press, 1971.

Dower, John W. "E. H. Norman, Japan, and the Uses of History," In E. H. Norman, ed., *Origins of the Modern Japanese State: Selected Writings of E. H. Norman*. Pantheon Books, 1975.

Downing, Brian M. *The Military Revolution and Political Change: Origins of Democracy and Autocracy in Early Modern Europe*. Princeton University Press, 1992.

Doyle, Michael. "An International Liberal Community." In Graham Allison and Gregory F. Treverton, eds., *Rethinking America's Security: Beyond the Cold War to New World Order*. W. W. Norton, 1991.

———. "Kant, Liberal Legacies, and Foreign Affairs." 2 parts. *Philosophy and Public Affairs* 12 Summer and Fall 1983.

———. "Liberalism and World Politics." *The American Political Science Review* 80, no. 4 (1986).

Draper, Theodore. *A Very Thin Line: The Iran-Contra Affairs*. Hill and Wang, 1991.

———. "Who Killed Soviet Communism?" *New York Review of Books*. June 11, 1992.

Dulles, John Foster. "A Policy of Boldness." *Life*, May 19, 1952.

Dunlop, John B. *The Rise of Russia and the Fall of the Soviet Empire*. Princeton University Press, 1993.

Eden, Lynn. "The End of U.S. Cold War History?" *International Security* 18, no. 1 (Summer 1993).

Eisenhower, Dwight D. *Mandate for Change, 1953–1956: The White House Years*. Doubleday, 1963.

———. *Waging Peace, 1956–1961: The White House Years*. Doubleday, 1965.

Eisenhower, John S. D. *Intervention! The United States and the Mexican Revolution, 1913–1917*. W. W. Norton, 1993.

Eisenhower, Milton. *The Wine Is Bitter: The United States and Latin America*. Doubleday, 1963.

Eisenstadt, S. N., and Stein Rokkan. *Building States and Nations: Models and Data Resources*. Sage Publications, 1973.

Evans, Peter. *Dependent Development: The Alliance of Multinational, State, and Local Capital in Brazil*. Princeton University Press, 1972.

Evans, Richard J. *Rethinking German History: Nineteenth Century Germany and the Origins of the Third Reich*. Allen and Unwin, 1987.

Fallaci, Oriana. *Interview with History*. Houghton Mifflin, 1976.

The Federalist Papers. Bantam Books, 1982.

Fejto, Francois. *Requiem pour un empire defunt: Histoire de la destruction de l'Autriche-Hongrie*. Lieu Commun, 1988.

Fitzgerald, Frances. *Fire in the Lake: The Vietnamese and the Americans in Vietnam*. Random House, 1972.

Floto, Inga. "Woodrow Wilson: War Aims, Peace Strategy, and the European Left." In Arthur S. Link, ed., *Woodrow Wilson and a Revolutionary World, 1913–1921*. University of North Carolina Press, 1982.

Foner, Eric. *Reconstruction: America's Unfinished Revolution, 1863–1867*. Harper and Row, 1988.

Forbes, W. Cameron. *The Philippine Islands*. Houghton Mifflin, 1928.

Forsythe, David P. *Human Rights and U.S. Foreign Policy: Congress Reconsidered.* University of Florida Press, 1988.

Fraginals, Manuel Moreno. "Plantation Economies and Societies in the Spanish Caribbean, 1860–1930." In Leslie Bethell, ed. *The Cambridge History of Latin America.* Vol. 4. Cambridge University Press, 1984.

Franck, Thomas M. "The Emerging Right to Democratic Governance." *American Journal of International Law,* 86, no. 1 (January 1992).

Freedom in the World. Annual. Freedom House.

Frei, Eduardo. "The Alliance that Lost Its Way." *Foreign Affairs* 45, no. 3 (April 1967).

Friedman, George, and Meredith LeBard. *The Coming War with Japan.* St. Martin's Press, 1991.

Friedman, Milton. *Capitalism and Freedom.* University of Chicago Press, 1962.

Friedrich, Carl J. "The Legacies of the Occupation in Germany." *Public Policy* 17 (1968).

Friend, Theodore. *Between Two Empires: The Ordeal of the Philippines, 1929–1946.* Yale University Press, 1965.

———. "Marcos and the Philippines." *Orbis* 32, no. 4 (Fall 1988).

Fukuyama, Francis. *The End of History and the Last Man.* Free Press, 1992.

———. "The Modernizing Imperative: The USSR as an Ordinary Country." *National Interest,* Spring 1993.

Fulbright, William, and Seth P. Tillmans. *The Price of Empire.* Pantheon, 1989.

Gaddis, John Lewis. "The Emerging Post-Revisionist Synthesis on the Origins of the Cold War." *Diplomatic History* 7, no. 3 (Summer 1983).

———. *The Long Peace: Inquiries into the History of the Cold War.* Oxford University Press, 1987.

———. "Rescuing Choice from Circumstance: The Statecraft of Henry Kissinger. In Gordon A. Craig and Francis L. Loewenheim, eds., *The Diplomats, 1939–1979.* Princeton University Press, 1994.

———. *Strategies of Containment: A Critical Appraisal of Postwar American National Security Policy.* Oxford University Press, 1982.

———. "The Tragedy of Cold War History." *Foreign Affairs* 73, no. 1 (January–February 1994).

———. *The United States and the Origins of the Cold War, 1941–1947.* Columbia University Press, 1972.

Gardels, Nathan. "Two Concepts of Nationalism: An Interview with Isaiah Berlin." *New York Review of Books,* November 21, 1991.

Gardner, Lloyd. *The Anglo-American Response to Revolution, 1913–1923.* Oxford University Press, 1984.

Gardner, Richard. "The Comeback of Liberal Internationalism." *Washington Quarterly* 13 (Winter 1990).

———. *Sterling-Dollar Diplomacy in Current Perspective: The Origins and the Prospects of Our International Economic Order.* 2d ed. Columbia University Press, 1980.

Garthoff, Raymond L. *Detente and Confrontation: American-Soviet Relations from Nixon to Reagan.* Brookings Institution, 1985.

Gasiorowski, Mark J. *U.S. Foreign Policy and the Shah: Building a Client State in Iran.* Cornell University Press, 1991.

Gatzke, Hans W. *Germany and the United States: A Special Relationship?* Harvard University Press, 1980.

Gautam, Om P. *The Indian National Congress.* Delhi: B.R. Publishing, 1985.

Gellman, Irwin F. *Good Neighbor Diplomacy: United States Policies in Latin America, 1933–1945.* Johns Hopkins University Press, 1979.

Gellner, Ernest. *Nations and Nationalism.* Basil Blackwell, 1983.

Gilbert, Felix. *The End of the European Era, 1890 to the Present.* W. W. Norton, 1979.

———. *To the Farewell Address: Ideas of Early American Foreign Policy.* Princeton University Press, 1961.

———, ed. *The Historical Essays of Otto Hintze.* Oxford University Press, 1975.

Gillingham, John. *Coal, Steel, and the Rebirth of Europe, 1945–1955: The German and French from Ruhr Conflict to Economic Community.* Cambridge University Press, 1991.

Gilpin, Robert. *The Political Economy of International Relations.* Princeton University Press, 1987.

———. *War and Change in World Politics.* Cambridge University Press, 1981.

Gimbel, John. *The American Occupation of Germany: Politics and the Military, 1945–1953.* Stanford University Press, 1973.

———. *The Origins of the Marshall Plan.* Stanford University Press, 1976.

Gleeck, Lewis E. *American Institutions in the Philippines, 1898–1941.* Historical Conservation Society, Manila, vol. 28, 1976.

Gleijeses, Piero. *The Dominican Crisis: The 1965 Constitutionalist Revolt and American Intervention.* Johns Hopkins University Press, 1978.

———. *Shattered Hope: The Guatemalan Revolution and the United States, 1944–1954.* Princeton University Press, 1991.

Gluck, Carol. *Japan's Modern Myths: Ideology in the Late Meiji Period.* Princeton University Press, 1985.

Goldman, Eric F. "Woodrow Wilson: The Test of War." In Arthur S. Link, ed., *Woodrow Wilson and the World of Today.* University of Pennsylvania Press, 1957.

Goldwert, Marvin. *The Constabulary in the Dominican Republic and Nicaragua.* University of Florida, School of Inter-American Studies, 1961.

Goode, James. "Reforming Iran during the Kennedy Years." *Diplomatic History* 15, no. 1 (Winter 1991).

Goode, James F. *The United States and Iran, 1946–1951.* Macmillan, 1989.

Goodwin, Richard N. *A Voice from the Sixties.* Little, Brown, 1988.

Gorbachev, Mikhail. *M.S. Gorbachov: Speeches and Writings.* 2 vols. Pergamon Press, 1987.

———. *Perestroika: New Thinking for Our Country and the World.* Harper and Row, 1987.

Gordon, Lincoln. *A New Deal for Latin America: The Alliance for Progress.* Harvard University Press, 1963.

Graff, Henry F. *American Imperialism and the Philippine Insurrection.* Little, Brown, 1969.

Greenfeld, Liah. *Nationalism: Five Roads to Modernity.* Harvard University Press, 1992.

Gremion, Pierre. *Le congres pour la liberte de la culture en Europe, 1950–1967.* Centre Nationale de Recherche Scientifique, 1988.

Gross, Leonard. *The Last, Best Hope: Eduardo Frei and Chilean Democracy.* Random House, 1967.

Guevara, Che. "The Alliance for Progress." In *Che: Selected Works of Ernesto Guevara.* MIT Press, 1969.

Guillermoprieto, Alma. "Letter from Panama." *New Yorker,* August 17, 1992.

Gutman, Roy. *Banana Diplomacy: The Making of American Policy in Nicaragua, 1981–1987.* Simon and Schuster, 1988.

Haas, Ernst. *The Uniting of Europe: Political, Social and Economic Forces, 1950–1957.* Stanford University Press, 1958.

Hacker, Andrew. "Paradise Lost." *New York Review of Books,* May 13, 1993.

Haggard, Stephan. "The Political Economy of the Philippine Debt Crisis." In Joan Nelson, ed., *Economic Crisis and Policy Choice: The Politics of Adjustment in Developing Countries.* Princeton University Press, 1990.

Haggard, Stephen, and Beth A. Simmons. "Theories of International Regimes." *International Organization* 41, no. 3 (Summer 1987).

Hagopian, Frances. "After Regime Change: Authoritarian Legacies, Political Representation, and the Democratic Future of South America." *World Politics* 45 (April 1993).

Haig, Alexander M., Jr. *Caveat: Realism, Reagan and Foreign Policy.* Macmillan, 1984.

Haley, P. Edward. *Revolution and Intervention: The Diplomacy of Taft and Wilson with Mexico, 1910–1917.* MIT Press, 1970.

Hall, Charles A. "Political and Social Ideas in Latin America, 1870–1930." In Leslie Bethell, ed. *The Cambridge History of Latin America.* Cambridge University Press, 1985.

Halle, Louis J. *The United States Acquires the Philippines: Consensus vs. Reality.* University Press of America, 1985.

Halperin, Ernst. *Nationalism and Communism in Chile.* MIT Press, 1965.

Han, Sung-joo. "South Korea: Politics in Transition." In Larry Diamond et al. *Democracy in Developing Countries: Asia.* Lynne Rienner, 1989–90.

Hardgrave, Robert L., Jr., and Stanley A. Kochanek, eds. *India: Government and Politics in a Developing Nation.* 4th ed. Harcourt Brace Jovanovich, 1986.

Hart, Albert Bushnell, ed. *Selected Addresses and Public Papers of Woodrow Wilson.* Boni and Liveright, 1918.

Hartlyn, Jonathan. "The Dominican Republic: Contemporary Problems and Challenges." In Jorge Dominguez et al. *The Caribbean Prepares for the Twenty-First Century.* Johns Hopkins University Press, 1992.

Hartz, Louis. *The Liberal Tradition in America: An Interpretation of American Political Thought Since the Revolution.* Harcourt Brace, 1955.

Havel, Vaclav. "A Call for Sacrifice." *Foreign Affairs* 73, no. 2 (March–April 1994).

———. "The Future of Central Europe." *New York Review of Books,* March 20, 1990.

———. "The Post-Communist Nightmare." *New York Review of Books,* May 27, 1993.

Hayashi, Kentaro. "Japan and Germany in the Interwar Period." In James William Morely, ed., *Dilemmas of Growth in Prewar Japan*. Princeton University Press, 1971.

Heckscher, August. *Woodrow Wilson*. Charles Scribner's Sons, 1991.

Henry, Paget, and Carl Stone, eds. *The Newer Caribbean: Decolonization, Democracy, and Development*. Institute for the Study of Human Relations, 1983.

Herf, Jeffrey. *Reactionary Modernism: Technology, Culture, and Politics in Weimar and the Third Reich*. Cambridge University Press, 1984.

———. *War by Other Means: Soviet Power, West German Resistance, and the Battle of the Euromissiles*. Free Press, 1991.

Herring, George C. *America's Longest War: The United States and Vietnam, 1950–1975*. John Wiley and Sons, 1979.

Hersh, Seymour M. *The Price of Power: Kissinger in the Nixon White House*. Summit Books, 1983.

Herz, John H., ed. *From Dictatorship to Democracy: Coping with the Legacies of Authoritarianism and Totalitarianism*. Greenwood Press, 1982.

———. *Political Realism and Political Idealism: A Study in Theories and Realities*. University of Chicago Press, 1951.

Hodgson, Godfrey. *The Colonel: The Life and Wars of Henry Stimson, 1867–1950*. Knopf, 1990.

Hoffmann, Stanley. *Duties beyond Borders: On the Limits and Possibilities of Ethical International Politics*. Syracuse University Press, 1981.

———. "Liberalism and International Relations." In Stanley Hoffmann, *Janus and Minerva: Essays in the Theory and Practice of International Politics*. Westview Press, 1987.

———. "The Passion of Modernity." *The Atlantic*, August 1993.

Hofstadter, Richard. *The American Political Tradition and the Men Who Made It*. Alfred A. Knopf, 1948.

Hogan, Michael J. *The Marshall Plan: America, Britain, and the Reconstruction of Western Europe, 1947–1952*. Cambridge University Press, 1987.

Hogan, Michael J., ed. *The End of the Cold War: Its Meaning and Implications*. Cambridge University Press, 1992.

Hogan, Michael J., and Thomas G. Paterson, eds. *Explaining the History of American Foreign Relations*. Cambridge University Press, 1991.

Horelick, Arnold L. "U.S.-Soviet Relations: A New Era." *Foreign Affairs* 69, no. 1 (1989–90).

House, Edward Mandell, and Charles Seymour, eds. *What Really Happened at Paris: The Story of the Peace Conference, 1918–1919, by American Delegates*. Charles Scribner's Sons, 1921.

Hull, Cordell. *The Memoirs of Cordell Hull*. Macmillan, 1948.

Hunt, Michael H. *Ideology and U.S. foreign Policy*. Yale University Press, 1987.

Hunter, Janet. *Concise Dictionary of Modern Japanese History*. University of California Press, 1984.

Huntington, Samuel P. *American Politics: The Promise of Disharmony*. Yale University Press, 1984.

———. "A Clash of Civilizations?" *Foreign Affairs* 72, no. 3 (Summer 1993).

———. *Political Order in Changing Societies*. Yale University Press, 1968.

———. *The Third Wave: Democratization in the Late Twentieth Century.* University of Oklahoma Press, 1991.

Iatrides, John O. *Ambassador MacVeagh Reports: Greece, 1933–1947.* Princeton University Press, 1980.

———. "Reviewing American Policy toward Greece: The Modern Cassandras." In John O. Iatrides and Theodore Couloumbis, eds., *Greek-American Relations: A Critical Review.* Pella, 1980.

Iatrides, John O., ed. *Greece in the 1940s: A Nation in Crisis.* University Press of New England, 1981.

Ikenberry, G. John. "Rethinking the Origins of American Hegemony." *Political Science Quarterly* 104, no. 3 (Fall 1989).

Ikenberry, G. John, and Charles A. Kupchan. "Socialization and Hegemonic Power." *International Organization* 44, no. 3 Summer 1990.

Immerman, Richard H. *The CIA in Guatemala: The Foreign Policy of Intervention.* University of Texas Press, 1982.

Iriye, Akira. *The Cold War in Asia: A Historical Introduction.* Prentice-Hall, 1974.

———. "The Failure of Military Expansionism," In James William Morely, ed., *Dilemmas of Growth in Prewar Japan.* Princeton University Press, 1971.

———. *The Globalizing of America, 1913–1945.* Vol. 3 of *The Cambridge History of American Foreign Relations.* Cambridge University Press, 1993.

———. *Power and Culture: The Japanese-American War, 1941–1945.* Harvard University Press, 1981.

Isaacson, Walter. *Kissinger: A Biography.* Simon and Schuster, 1992.

Jackson, Karl D. "The Philippines: The Search for a Suitable Democratic Solution." In Larry Diamond et al., *Democracy in Developing Countries: Asia.* Lynne Reinner, 1989.

Jacoby, Tamar. "The Reagan Turnaround on Human Rights." *Foreign Affairs* 64, no. 5 (Summer 1986).

James, D. Clayton. *Triumph and Disaster, 1945–1964.* Vol. 3 of *The Years of MacArthur.* Houghton Mifflin, 1985.

Janos, Andrew C. "Social Science, Communism, and the Dynamics of Political Change." *World Politics* 44, no. 1 (October 1991).

Jarausch, Konrad H., and Larry Eugene Jones, eds. *In Search of a Liberal Germany: Studies in the History of German Liberalism from 1789 to the Present.* Berg, 1990.

Jentleson, Bruce W. "The Reagan Administration and Coercive Diplomacy: Restraining More than Remaking Governments." *Political Science Quarterly* 106, no. 1 (1991).

Jervis, Robert. "The Impact of the Korean War on the Cold War." *Journal of Conflict Resolution* 24 (December 1980).

Jessup, Philip C. *Elihu Root.* Dodd, Mead and Co., 1938.

Johnson, Haynes. *Sleepwalking through History: America in the Reagan Years.* W. W. Norton, 1991.

Johnson, Robert H. "Misguided Morality: Ethics and the Reagan Doctrine." *Political Science Quarterly* 103, no. 2 (1988).

Jones, Joseph Marion. *The Fifteen Weeks: An Inside Account of the Genesis of the Marshall Plan.* Harcourt, Brace, and World, 1955.

Jones, Larry Eugene. *German Liberalism and the Dissolution of the Weimar Party System, 1918–1933.* University of North Carolina Press, 1988.

Kahin, George McTurnan. *Intervention: How America Became Involved in Vietnam.* Knopf, 1986.

Kahin, George McTurnan and John W. Lewis. Rev. ed. *The United States in Vietnam.* Dell, 1979.

Kahler, Miles, and Jeffrey A. Frankel. *Regionalism and Rivalry: Japan and the United States in Pacific Asia.* University of Chicago Press, 1993.

Karl, Terry Lynn. "Dilemmas of Democratization in Latin America." *Comparative Politics* 23, no. 1 (October 1992).

———. "El Salvador's Negotiated Revolution." *Foreign Affairs* 71, no. 2 (Spring 1992).

Karnow, Stanley. *In Our Image: America's Empire in the Philippines.* Random House, 1989.

———. *Vietnam: A History.* Penguin Books, 1983.

Katzenstein, Peter. *Policy and Process in West Germany: The Growth of a Semisovereign State.* Temple University Press, 1987.

———. "The Small European State in the International Economy: Economic Dependence and Corporatist Politics." In John Gerard Ruggie, ed., *The Antinomies of Interdependence: National Welfare and the International Division of Labor.* Columbia University Press, 1983.

Kempe, Frederick. *Divorcing the Dictator: America's Bungled Affair with Noriega.* G. P. Putnam, 1990.

Kennan, George F. *American Diplomacy.* Expanded ed. 1951; University of Chicago Press, 1984.

———. *Memoirs, 1925–1950.* Pantheon, 1967.

———. *Sketches from a Life.* Pantheon, 1989.

Kennedy, John F. *The Strategy of Peace.* Harper and Row, 1960.

Kennedy, Paul. *Preparing for the Twenty-first Century.* Random House, 1993.

———. *The Rise and Fall of the Great Powers: Economic Change and Military Conflict from 1500 to 2000.* Random House, 1987.

Keohane, Robert O. *After Hegemony: Cooperation and Discord in the World Political Economy.* Princeton University Press, 1984.

Keohane, Robert O., and Joseph Nye. *Power and Interdependence: World Politics in Transition.* Little, Brown, 1977.

Kerkvliet, Benedict J. *The Huk Rebellion: A Study of Peasant Revolution in the Philippines.* University of California Press, 1977.

Kershaw, Ian. *Weimar: Why Did German Democracy Fail?* St. Martin's Press, 1990.

Keynes, John Maynard. *The Economic Consequences of the Peace.* Harcourt, Brace, 1920.

———. *Essays in Biography.* Horizon Books, 1951.

Kirkpatrick, Jeane. *The Reagan Phenomenon and Other Speeches on Foreign Policy.* American Enterprise Institute, 1983.

———. "U.S. Security Interests and Latin America" (1981). In Kirkpatrick, ed. *Dictatorships and Double Standards: Rationalism and Reason in Politics.* Simon and Schuster, 1982.

Kissinger, Henry. *American Foreign Policy*. 3d ed. Norton, 1977.

———. *Diplomacy*. Simon and Schuster, 1994.

———. "Domestic Structure and Foreign Policy." In *American Foreign Policy*. Expanded ed. W. W. Norton, 1977.

———. *The Necessity for Choice: Prospects of American Foreign Policy*. Harper and Brothers, 1960.

———. *White House Years*. Little, Brown, 1979.

———. *Years of Upheaval*. Little, Brown, 1982.

———. Kissinger, Henry, et al. *Report of the President's National Bipartisan Commission on Central America*. Government Printing Office, 1984.

Kitschelt, Herbert. "Political Regime Change: Structure and Process-Driven Explanations." *American Political Science Review*, 86, no. 4 (December 1992).

Knight, Alan. *U.S.-Mexican Relations, 1910–1940: An Interpretation*. Monograph Series 28. University of California, San Diego, Center for U.S.-Mexican Studies, 1987.

Knock, Thomas J. "Kennan Versus Wilson." In John Milton Cooper, Jr., and Charles E. Neu, eds., *The Wilson Era: Essays in Honor of Arthur S. Link*. Harlan Davidson, 1991.

———. *To End All Wars: Woodrow Wilson and the Quest for a New World Order*. Oxford University Press, 1992.

Kolko, Gabriel. *The Politics of War: The World and United States Foreign Policy, 1943–1945*. Random House, 1968.

Kolko, Gabriel, and Joyce Kolko. *The Limits of Power: The World and United States Foreign Policy, 1945–1954*. Harper and Row, 1972.

Kovrig, Bennett. *Of Walls and Bridges: The United States and Eastern Europe*. New York University Press, 1991.

Krasner, Stephen D. *Defending the National Interest: Raw Materials Investments and U.S. Foreign Policy*. Princeton University Press, 1978.

———. *International Regimes*. Cornell University Press, 1983.

Krauthammer, Charles. "The Poverty of Realism." *New Republic*, February 17, 1986.

———. "The Unipolar Moment." *Foreign Affairs* 70, no. 1 (1991).

Ladejinsky, W. I. "Agriculture," In Hugh Borton, ed., *Japan*. Cornell University Press, 1951.

LaFeber, Walter. *The American Search for Opportunity, 1865–1913*. Vol. 2 of *The Cambridge History of American Foreign Relations*. Cambridge University Press, 1993.

———. *Inevitable Revolutions: The United States in Central America*. Expanded ed. W. W. Norton, 1984.

Lake, Anthony. *Somoza Falling: A Case Study of Washington at Work*. University of Massachusetts, 1989.

Lake, David A. *Power, Protection, and Free Trade: International Sources of U.S. Commercial Strategy, 1887–1939*. Cornell University Press, 1988.

———. "Powerful Pacifists: Democratic States and War." *American Political Science Review* 86, no. 1 (March 1992).

Lande, Carl H. *Leaders, Factions, and Parties: The Structure of Philippine Politics*. Southeast Asia Studies Monograph Series, no. 6. Yale University, 1965.

Langer, William F. "Peace in the New World Order." In Arthur S. Link, ed., *Woodrow Wilson and the World of Today*. University of Pennsylvania Press, 1957.

Lange-Quassowski, Jutta B. "Coming to Terms with the Nazi Past: Schools, Media, and the Formation of Opinion." In John H. Herz, ed., *From Dictatorship to Democracy: Coping with the Legacies of Authoritarianism and Totalitarianism*. Greenwood Press, 1982.

Langley, Lester D. *The Cuban Policy of the United States: A Brief History*. John Wiley and Sons, 1968.

Lansing, Robert. *The Peace Negotiations: A Personal Narrative*. Houghton Mifflin, 1921.

Laqueur, Walter. *Black Hundred: The Rise of the Extreme Right in Russia*. Harper-Collins, 1993.

Larsen, Stein Ugelvik, et al. *Who Were the Fascists: Social Roots of European Fascism*. Columbia University Press, 1982.

Laski, Harold. *The Rise of European Liberalism*. An Essay in Interpretation. Unwin, 1962.

Layne, Christopher. "The Unipolar Illusion: Why Great New Powers Will Arise." *International Security* 17, no. 4 (Spring 1993).

Ledeen, Michael, and William Lewis. *Debacle: The American Failure in Iran*. Alfred A. Knopf, 1981.

Lefever, Ernst. "The Trivialization of Human Rights." *Policy Review* 3 (Winter 1978).

Leffler, Melvyn P. *A Preponderance of Power: National Security, the Truman Administration and the Cold War*. Stanford University Press, 1992.

Legvold, Robert. "The Revolution of Soviet Foreign Policy." *Foreign Affairs* 68, no. 1 (1988).

Levin, N. Gordon, Jr. *Woodrow Wilson and World Politics: America's Response to War and Revolution*. Oxford University Press, 1968.

Levinson, Jerome, and Juan de Onis, eds. *The Alliance That Lost Its Way*. Quadrangle Books, 1970.

Lewis, Bernard. "The Enemies of God." *New York Review of Books*, March 25, 1993.

———. "Islam and Liberal Democracy." *The Atlantic*, February 1993.

Lewy, Guenter. *America in Vietnam*. Oxford University Press, 1978.

Lieuwin, Edwin. *Generals vs. Presidents: Neomilitarism in Latin America*. Praeger, 1964.

Lindblom, Charles G. *Politics and Markets: The World's Political-Economic Systems*. Basic Books, 1977.

Link, Arthur S. *The Higher Realism of Woodrow Wilson and Other Essays*. Vanderbilt University Press, 1971.

———. *Woodrow Wilson and the Progressive Era, 1910–1917*. Harper and Brothers, 1954.

———. *Woodrow Wilson: Revolution, War, and Peace*. Harlan Davidson, 1979.

———. *Wilson: The Diplomatist: A Look at His Major Foreign Policies*. Johns Hopkins University Press, 1957.

———. *Wilson: The New Freedom*. Princeton University Press, 1959.

———. *Wilson: The Struggle for Neutrality, 1914–1915*. Princeton University Press, 1960.

Link, Arthur S., ed. *Woodrow Wilson and a Revolutionary World, 1913–1921*. University of North Carolina Press, 1982.

———. *Woodrow Wilson and the World of Today*. University of Pennsylvania Press, 1957.

———. *Woodrow Wilson: A Profile*. Hill and Wang, 1968.

Linz, Juan J. "Totalitarian and Authoritarian Regimes," In Fred I. Greenstein and Nelson W. Polsby, eds., *Macropolitical Theory*. Vol. 3 of *Handbook of Political Science*. Addison-Wesley, 1975.

———. "Transitions to Democracy." *The Washington Quarterly*, Summer 1990.

Linz, Juan J., and Alfred Stepan, eds. *The Breakdown of Democratic Regimes: Crisis, Breakdown, and Reequilibration*. Johns Hopkins University Press, 1978.

Lippmann, Walter. *U.S. Foreign Policy: Shield of the Republic*. Little, Brown, 1943.

———. *U.S. War Aims*. Little, Brown, 1944.

Lipset, Seymour Martin. *Political Man: The Social Basis of Politics*. Doubleday, 1960.

Lipson, Charles. *Standing Guard: Protecting Foreign Capital in the Nineteenth and Twentieth Centuries*. University of California Press, 1985.

Louis, William Roger. *Imperialism at Bay: The United States and the Decolonization of the British Empire, 1941–1945*. Oxford University Press, 1978.

———, ed. *Imperialism: The Robinson and Gallagher Controversy*. Franklin Watts, 1976.

Loveman, Brian. *Chile: The Legacy of Hispanic Capitalism*. Oxford University Press, 1979.

Lowenthal, Abraham F. *The Dominican Intervention*. Harvard University Press, 1972.

———, ed. *Exporting Democracy: The United States and Latin America*. John Hopkins University Press, 1991.

———. "'Liberal,' 'Radical,' and 'Bureaucratic' Perspectives on US Latin American Policy: The Alliance for Progress." In Julio Cotler and Richard R. Fagen, eds., *Latin America and the United States: The Changing Realities*. Stanford University Press, 1974.

Luckau, Alma. *The German Delegation at the Paris Peace Conference*. Columbia University Press, 1941.

Luebbert, Gregory M. *Liberalism, Fascism, or Social Democracy: Social Classes and the Political Origins of Regimes in Interwar Europe*. Oxford University Press, 1991.

Lukacs, John. *The End of the Twentieth Century and the End of the Modern Age*. Ticknor and Fields, 1993.

———. "Ike, Winston, and the Russians." *New York Times Book Review*, February 10, 1991.

MacArthur, Douglas. *Reminiscences*. McGraw-Hill, 1964.

Macartney, C. A., and A. W. Palmer. *Independent Eastern Europe: A History*. Macmillan, 1962.

Maddison, Angus. *The World Economy in the 20th Century.* Organization of Economic Cooperation and Development, 1989.

Maier, Charles S. *Recasting Bourgeois Europe: Stabilization in France, Germany, and Italy in the Decade after World War I.* Princeton University Press, 1975.

———. "The Two Postwar Eras and the Conditions for Stability in Twentieth-Century Western Europe." *American Historical Review* 86, no. 2 (April 1981).

Maier, Joseph, and Richard W. Weatherhead, eds. *The Future of Democracy in Latin America: Essays by Frank Tannenbaum.* Alfred A. Knopf, 1974.

Majd, Mohammed G. "Land Reform Policies in Iran." *American Journal of Agricultural Economics* 69, 4 (November 1967).

Mamatey, Victor S. *The United States and East Central Europe, 1914–1918: A Study in Wilsonian Diplomacy and Propaganda.* Princeton University Press, 1957.

Manchester, William. *American Caesar.* Dell, 1978.

Mandelbaum, Michael. "The Bush Foreign Policy." *Foreign Affairs* 70, no. 1, (1991).

———. "The Fall of the House of Lenin." *World Policy Journal* 10, no. 3 (Fall 1993).

———. "The Luck of the President." *Foreign Affairs* 64, no. 3 (Winter 1986).

Mantoux, Paul. *The Deliberations of the Council of Four, March 24–June 28, 1919.* 2 vols. Princeton University Press, 1992.

Marcos, Ferdinand E. *The New Philippine Republic: A Third World Approach to Democracy.* Manila: n.p., 1982.

Martin, Laurence W. *Peace without Victory: Woodrow Wilson and the British Liberals.* Yale University Press, 1958.

Maruyama, Masao. *Thought and Behavior in Modern Japanese Politics.* Oxford University Press, 1963.

Masaryk, Thomas Garrigue. *The Making of a State.* Frederick A. Stokes, 1927.

Mavrogordatos, George T. "The 1946 Election and Plebiscite: Prelude to Civil War." In John O. Iatrides, ed., *Greece in the 1940s: A Nation in Crisis.* University Press of New England, 1981.

May, Ernest R. *American Imperialism: A Speculative Essay.* Atheneum, 1968.

———. *Imperial Democracy: The Emergence of America as a Great Power.* Harcourt, Brace, and World, 1961.

May, Glenn Anthony. *Social Engineering in the Philippines: The Aims, Execution and Impact of American Colonial Policy, 1900–1913.* Greenwood Press, 1980.

Mayer, Arno J. *The Persistence of The Old Regime: Europe to the Great War.* Pantheon Books, 1981.

———. *Politics and Diplomacy of the Peacemaking: Containment and Counterrevolution at Versailles, 1918–1919.* Alfred A. Knopf, 1967.

McClintock, Cynthia, and Abraham F. Lowenthal, eds. *The Peruvian Experiment Reconsidered.* Princeton University Press, 1983.

McCormick, Thomas J. *America's Half-Century: United States Foreign Policy in the Cold War.* Johns Hopkins University Press, 1989.

McCoy, Drew R. *The Elusive Republic: Political Economy in Jeffersonian America*. W. W. Norton, 1982.

McCrary, Peyton. *Abraham Lincoln and Reconstruction: The Louisiana Experiment*. Princeton University Press, 1978.

McMahon, Robert J. "Eisenhower and Third World Nationalism: A Critique of the Revisionists." *Political Science Quarterly* 101, 3 (1986).

Melanson, Richard A., and Mayers, David, eds. *Reevaluating Eisenhower: American Foreign Policy in the 1950s*. University of Illinois Press, 1987.

Merkl, Peter H. "Allied Strategies of Effecting Political Change and Their Reception in Occupied Germany." *Public Policy* 17 (1968): 60f.

Merritt, Anne J., and Richard L. *Public Opinion in Occupied Germany: The Omgus Surveys, 1945–49*. University of Illinois Press, 1970.

Meyer, Lorenzo. *Mexico and the United States in the Oil Controversy, 1917–1942*. University of Texas Press, 1977.

Miller, John Edward. *The United States and Italy, 1940–1950*. University of North Carolina Press, 1986.

Miller, Judith. "The Challenge of Radical Islam." *Foreign Affairs* 72, no. 1 (Spring 1993).

Millikan, Max F., and Donald L. M. Blackmer. *The Emerging Nations: Their Growth and United States Policy*. Little, Brown, 1961.

Millikan, Max F., and W. W. Rostow. *A Proposal: Key to an Effective Foreign Policy*. Harper and Brothers, 1957.

Mitchell, Christopher. "Dominance and Fragmentation in U.S. Latin American Foreign Policy." In Julio Cotler and Richard R. Fagan, eds., *Latin America and the United States: The Changing Political Realities*. Stanford University Press, 1974.

Mitrany, David. *A Working Peace System*. Quadrangle Books, 1966.

Montgomery, John. *Forced to Be Free: The Artificial Revolution in Germany and Japan*. University of Chicago Press, 1957.

Moore, Barrington, Jr. *Social Origins of Dictatorship and Democracy: Lord and Peasant in the Making of the Modern World*. Beacon Press, 1966.

Morgenthau, Hans J. *In Defense of the National Interest: A Critical Examination of American Foreign Policy*. Alfred A. Knopf, 1952.

Morley, James William. *Dilemmas of Growth in Prewar Japan*. Princeton University Press, 1971.

Morse, Edward L. *Modernization and the Transformation of International Relations*. Free Press, 1976.

Mouzelis, Nicos P. *Modern Greece: Facets of Underdevelopment*. Holmes and Meier, 1978.

———. *Politics in the Semi-Periphery: Early Parlimentarianism and Late Industrialisation in the Balkans and Latin America*. Macmillan, 1986.

Mower, A. Glenn, Jr. *Human Rights and American Foreign Policy: The Carter and Reagan Experiences*. Greenwood Press, 1987.

Munro, Dana G. *Intervention and Dollar Diplomacy in the Caribbean, 1900–1921*. Princeton University Press, 1964; Greenwood Press, 1980.

Muravchik, Joshua. *Exporting Democracy: Fulfilling America's Destiny*. American Enterprise Institute, 1991.

Muravchik, Joshua. *The Uncertain Crusade: Jimmy Carter and the Dilemmas of Human Rights Policy.* Hamilton Press, 1986.

Nau, Henry. *The Myth of America's Decline: Leading the World Economy into the 1990s.* Oxford University Press, 1990.

Nelson, Joan M. *Encouraging Democracy: What Role for Conditional Aid?* Overseas Development Council, 1992.

Nelson, Joan, ed. *Economic Crisis and Policy Choice: The Politics of Adjustment in Developing Countries.* Princeton University Press, 1990.

Neumann, Franz. *Behemoth: The Structure and Practice of National Socialism, 1933–1944.* Octagon Books, 1972.

Newhouse, John. "No Exit, No Entrance." *New Yorker,* June 28, 1993.

Newman, John M. *JFK and Vietnam: Deception, Intrigue, and the Struggle for Power.* Warner Books, 1991.

Nicolson, Harold. *Peacemaking 1919.* Harcourt, Brace, 1939.

Niebuhr, Reinhold. *The Irony of American Diplomacy.* Charles Scribner's Sons, 1952.

Ninkovich, Frank. *Germany and the United States: The Transformation of the German Question since 1945.* Twayne Publishers, 1988.

Nolting, Frederick. *From Trust to Tragedy: The Political Memoirs of Frederick Nolting, Kennedy's Ambassador to Diem's Vietnam.* Prager, 1988.

Norman, E. H. *Origins of the Modern Japanese State: Selected Writings of E. H. Norman.* Pantheon Books, 1975.

Nye, Joseph S., Jr. *Bound to Lead: The Changing Nature of American Power.* Basic Books, 1990.

———. "Neorealism and Neoliberalism." *World Politics,* 40, no. 2 (January 1988).

Oberdorfer, Don. *The Turn: From the Cold War to a New Era, the United States and the Soviet Union, 1983–1990.* Poseidon Press, 1991.

O'Donnell, Guillermo, Philippe C. Schmitter, and Laurence Whitehead, eds. *Transitions from Authoritarian Rule.* 4 vols. Johns Hopkins University Press, 1986.

Owen, Norman G. "The Principalia in Philippine History: Kabikolan, 1790–1898." *Philippine Studies* 22 nos. 3–4 (1974).

Packenham, Robert. *Liberal America and the Third World: Political Development Ideas in Foreign Aid and Social Science.* Princeton University Press, 1973.

Pahlavi, Mohammed Reza. *Answer to History.* Stein and Day, 1982.

———. *Mission for My Country.* McGraw-Hill, 1961.

Palmer, R. R. *The Age of Democratic Revolution: A Political History of Europe and America, 1760–1800.* Princeton University Press, 2 vols., 1959, 1964.

Parrini, Carl. *Heir to Empire: United States Economic Diplomacy, 1916–1923.* University of Pittsburgh Press, 1969.

Parsons, Talcott. "Evolutionary Universals." *American Sociological Review* 29, no. 5 (June 1964).

Pasquino, Gianfranco. "The Demise of the First Fascist Regime and Italy's Transition to Democracy." In Guillermo O'Donnell et al., *Transitions from Authoritarian Rule: Southern Europe.* Johns Hopkins University Press, 1986.

Passin, Herbert. "Changing Values: Work and Growth in Japan." *Asian Survey* 15, no. 10 (October 1975): 565f.

Pastor, Robert A. "The Carter Administration and Latin America: A Test of Principle." Carter Center of Emory University, Occasional Paper Series, 1992.

———. *Condemned to Repetition: The United States and Nicaragua.* Princeton University Press, 1987.

Pastor, Robert A., ed. *Democracy in the Americas: Stopping the Pendulum.* Holmes and Meier, 1989.

Paterson, Thomas G., et al. *American Foreign Policy: A History to 1914.* 2d. ed. D. C. Heath, 1983.

Paterson, Thomas G., and Stephen G. Rabe, eds. *Imperial Surge: The United States Abroad, the 1890s–Early 1900s.* D. C. Heath, 1992.

Payne, Stanley G. *The Franco Regime, 1936–1975.* University of Wisconsin Press, 1987.

Petillo, Carol Morris. *Douglas MacArthur: The Philippine Years.* Indiana University Press, 1981.

Pfaff, William. *Barbarian Sentiments: How the American Century Ends.* Hill and Wang, 1989.

Phelan, John Leddy. *The Hispanization of the Philippines: Spanish Aims and Filipino Response, 1565–1700.* University of Wisconsin Press, 1959.

Pollard, Robert A. *Economic Security and the Origins of the Cold War, 1945–1950.* Columbia University Press, 1985.

Posen, Barry R., and Stephen W. Van Evera. "Reagan Administration Defense Policy: Departure from Containment." In Kenneth Oye et al., *Eagle Resurgent? The Reagan Era in American Foreign Policy.* Little, Brown, 1987.

Poulantzas, Nicos. *State, Power, Socialism.* Verso, 1978.

Pratt, Julius W. *Cordell Hull.* Cooper Square, 1964.

Prosterman, Roy L., and Riedinger, Jeffrey M. *Land Reform and Democratic Development.* Johns Hopkins University Press, 1987.

Putnam, Robert D. *Making Democracy Work: Civic Traditions in Modern Italy.* Princeton University Press, 1993.

Pye, Lucian W. *Asian Power and Politics: The Cultural Dimensions of Authority.* Harvard University Press, 1985.

———. *Aspects of Political Development.* Little, Brown, 1964.

———. "The Concept of Political Development." *Annals of the American Academy of Political and Social Science* no. 358 (March 1985).

Rabe, Stephen G. *Eisenhower and Latin America: The Foreign Policy of Anticommunism.* University of North Carolina Press, 1988.

Reagan, Ronald. *Speaking My Mind: Selected Speeches.* Simon and Schuster, 1989.

———. *A Time for Choosing: The Speeches of Ronald Reagan, 1961–1982.* Regnery Gateway, 1983.

Reischauer, Edwin O. *The Japanese Today: Change and Continuity.* 2d ed. Harvard University Press, 1988.

———. *The United States and Japan.* 3d ed. Harvard University Press, 1965.

———. "What Went Wrong?" In James William Morely, ed., *Dilemmas of Growth in Prewar Japan.* Princeton University Press, 1971.

Roberts, Brad, ed. *The New Democracies: Global Change and U.S. Foreign Policy.* MIT Press, 1990.

Roett, Riordan. *The Politics of Foreign Aid in the Brazilian Northeast.* Vanderbilt University Press, 1974.

Roett, Riordan, ed. *Political and Economic Liberalization in Mexico: At a Critical Juncture?* Lynne Rienner. 1993.

Roosevelt, Franklin Delano. "Our Foreign Policy: A Democratic View." *Foreign Affairs* 6, no. 4 (July 1928).

Ropp, Steve C. "Explaining the Long-Term Maintenance of a Military Regime: Panama before the U.S. Invasion." *World Politics* 44, no. 2 (January 1992).

Rosati, Jerel A. *The Carter Administration's Quest for Global Community.* University of South Carolina Press, 1987.

Rosenbaum, Herbert D., and Elizabeth Barteleme, eds. *Franklin D. Roosevelt: The Man, the Myth, the Era, 1882–1945.* Greenwood Press, 1987.

Rosenman, Samuel I., ed. *The Public Papers and Addresses of Franklin D. Roosevelt.* 13 vols. Random House, 1938–1950.

Rostow, W. W. *Stages of Economic Growth.* MIT Press, 1960.

Rothschild, Joseph. *East Central Europe between the Two World Wars.* University of Washington Press, 1974.

————. *Return to Diversity: A Political History of East Central Europe since World War II.* Oxford University Press, 1989.

Rudolph, Susanne Hoeber, and Lloyd I. Rudolph. "Modern Hate." *New Republic,* March 22, 1993.

Rueschemeyer, Dietrich, et al. *Capitalist Development and Democracy.* University of Chicago Press, 1992.

Ruggie, John Gerard, ed. *The Antimonies of Interdependence: National Welfare and the International Division of Labor.* Columbia University Press, 1983.

Russett, Bruce. *Controlling the Sword: The Democratic Governance of National Security.* Harvard University Press, 1990.

————. *Grasping the Democratic Peace: Principles for a Post–Cold War World.* Princeton University Press, 1993.

Rustow, Dankwart A. "Transitions to Democracy." *Comparative Politics* 2, no. 3 (April 1970).

Sartori, Giovanni. *The Theory of Democracy Revisited.* Chatham House, 1987.

Sbrega, John D. "The Anticolonial Views of Franklin D. Roosevelt, 1941–1945." In Herbert D. Rosenbaum and Elizabeth Barteleme, eds., *Franklin D. Roosevelt: The Man, the Myth, the Era, 1882–1945.* Greenwood Press, 1987.

Scalapino, Robert A. *Democracy and the Party Movement in Prewar Japan.* University of California Press, 1953.

————. "Elections and Political Modernization in Prewar Japan." In Robert E. Ward, ed., *Political Development in Modern Japan.* Princeton University Press, 1978.

Schaller, Michael. *The American Occupation of Japan: The Origins of the Cold War in Asia.* Oxford University Press, 1985.

Schemen, L. Ronald, ed. *The Alliance for Progress: A Retrospective.* Praeger, 1988.

Schirmer, Daniel B. *Republic or Empire: American Resistance to the Philippine War.* Shenkman, 1972.

Schlesinger, Arthur M., "The Cold War Revisited." *New York Review of Books* 26, no. 16 (October 25, 1979).

―――. "A Democrat Looks at Foreign Policy." *Foreign Affairs* 62, no. 2 (Winter 1987–8).

―――. *A Thousand Days: John F. Kennedy in the White House*. Fawcett, 1965.

Schonberger, Howard B. *Aftermath of War: Americans and the Remaking of Japan, 1945–1952*. Kent State University Press, 1989.

Schoultz, Lars. *Human Rights and United States Policy toward Latin America*. Princeton University Press, 1981.

―――. *National Security and United States Policy toward Latin America*. Princeton University Press, 1987.

Schumpeter, Joseph Alois. *Capitalism, Socialism and Democracy*. Harper and Row, 1942.

―――. *Imperialism and Social Classes*. A. M. Kelly, 1951.

Schwabe, Klaus. *Woodrow Wilson, Revolutionary Germany, and Peacemaking, 1918–1919*. University of North Carolina Press, 1985.

Schwartz, Benjamin C. *American Counterinsurgency Doctrine and El Salvador: The Frustrations of Reform and the Illusions of Nation Building*. Rand, 1991.

Schwartz, Thomas Alan. *America's Germany: John McCloy and the Federal Republic of Germany*. Harvard University Press, 1991.

Schwarzenberger, Georg. *Power Politics: A Study of International Society*. 2d ed. Praeger, 1951.

Schweller, Randall L. "Domestic Structures and Preventive War: Are Democracies More Pacific?" *World Politics* 44, no. 2 (January 1992).

Sestanovich, Stephen. "Did the West Undo the East?" *National Interest*, Spring 1993.

Seton-Watson, Hugh. *Eastern Europe between the Wars, 1918–1941*. Cambridge University Press, 1945; Archon Books, 1962.

―――. *The East European Revolution*. Praeger, 1951.

Seymour, Charles. *Intimate Papers of Colonel House: The Ending of the War*. Houghton Mifflin, 1928.

―――. "Wilson and His Contributions." In Arthur S. Link, ed., *Woodrow Wilson: A Profile*. Hill and Wang, 1968.

Shafer, D. Michael. *Deadly Paradigms: The Failure of U.S. Counterinsurgency Policy*. Princeton University Press, 1988.

Shaw, Albert, ed. *The Messages and Papers of Woodrow Wilson*. 2 vols. George H. Doran, 1924.

Shultz, George P. *Turmoil and Triumph: My Years as Secretary of State*. Charles Scribner's Sons, 1993.

Shultz, Richard H., Jr. "The Post-Conflict Use of Military Forces: Lessons from Panama, 1989–1991. *Journal of Strategic Studies* 16, no. 2 (June 1993).

Sick, Gary. *All Fall Down: America's Tragic Encounter with Iran*. Random House, 1985.

Sigmund, Paul E. *The Overthrow of Allende and the Politics of Chile, 1964–1976*. University of Pittsburgh Press, 1977.

―――. *The United States and Democracy in Chile*. Johns Hopkins University Press, 1993.

Skidmore, Thomas E. "Brazil's Slow Road to Democratization: 1974–1985." In Alfred Stepan, ed., *Democratizing Brazil: Problems of Transition and Consolidation*. Oxford University Press, 1989.

Skocpol, Theda. *State and Social Revolutions: A Comparative Analysis of France, Russia, and China*. Cambridge University Press, 1979.

———. "Wallerstein's World Capitalist System: A Theoretical and historical Critique." *American Journal of Sociology* 82, no. 5, March 1977.

Slater, Jerome. *Intervention and Negotiation: The United States and the Dominican Revolution*. Harper and Row, 1970.

Slater, Jerome, and Terry Nardin. "Nonintervention and Human Rights." *Journal of Politics* 48, no. 1 (February 1986).

Smethurst, Richard J. *A Social Basis for Prewar Japanese Militarism: The Army and the Rural Community*. University of California Press, 1974.

Smith, Anthony D. *Theories of Nationalism*. Holmes and Meier, 1983.

Smith, Gaddis. *Morality, Reason, and Power: American Diplomacy in the Carter Years*. Hill and Wang, 1986.

Smith, Jean Edward. *Lucius D. Clay: An American Life*. Holt, 1990.

Smith, Robert F. *The United States and Cuba: Business and Diplomacy, 1917–1960*. College and University Press, 1960.

Smith, Tony. *The French Stake in Algeria*. Cornell University Press, 1978.

———. *The Pattern of Imperialism: The United States, Great Britain, and the Late-Industrializing World since 1815*. Cambridge University Press, 1981.

———. "Requiem or New Agenda for Third World Studies?" *World Politics* 37, no. 4 (July 1985).

———. "Social Violence and Conservative Social Psychology: The Case of Erik Erikson." *Journal of Peace Research* 13 (January 1976).

———. *Thinking Like a Communist: State and Legitimacy in the Soviet Union, China, and Cuba*. W. W. Norton, 1987.

———. "The Underdevelopment of Development Literature: The Case of Dependency Theory." *World Politics*, January 1979.

Smith, Wayne S. *The Closest of Enemies: A Personal and Diplomatic Account of U.S.-Cuban Relations since 1957*. W.W. Norton, 1987.

Snyder, Jack. *Myths of Empire: Domestic Politics and International Ambition*. Cornell University Press, 1991.

Stampp, Kenneth M. *The Era of Reconstruction, 1865–1877*. Alfred A. Knopf, 1965.

Stanley, Peter W. *A Nation in the Making: The Philippines and the United States, 1899–1921*. Harvard University Press, 1974.

Steel, Ronald. *Walter Lippmann and the American Century*. Little, Brown, 1980.

Steinberg, David Joel. *Philippine Collaboration in World War II*. University of Michigan Press, 1967.

Stepan, Alfred. "The New Professionalism of Internal Warfare and Military Role Expansion." In Alfred Stepan, ed., *Authoritarian Brazil: Origins, Policies, and Future*. Yale University Press, 1973.

Stern, Fritz. *The Failure of Illiberalism: Essays on the Political Culture of Modern Germany*. Knopf, 1972.

Stevenson, David. *The First World War and International Politics.* Oxford University Press, 1988.

Stone, Carl. "Decolonization and the Caribbean State System: The Case of Jamaica," and "Democracy and Socialism in Jamaica, 1972–1979." In Paget Henry and Carl Stone, eds., *The Newer Caribbean: Decolonization, Democracy, and Development.* Institute for the Study of Human Relations, 1983.

Sullivan, William H. *Mission to Iran.* W. W. Norton, 1981.

"Support for East European Democracy Act." H.R. 3402, 101st Congress, 1st sess., November 17, 1989.

Talbott, Strobe. *Master of the Game: Paul Nitze and the Nuclear Peace.* Alfred A. Knopf, 1988.

Terry, Sarah Meiklejohn. *Poland's Place in Europe: General Sikorski and the Origin of the Oder-Neisse Line, 1939–1940.* Princeton University Press, 1983.

Thompson, W. Scott. *The Philippines in Crisis: Development and Security in the Aquino Era, 1986–1992.* St. Martin's Press, 1992.

Thomson, James C., Jr., et al. *Sentimental Imperialists: The American Experience in East Asia.* Harper and Row, 1981.

Thorne, Christopher. *Allies of a Kind: The United States, Britain and the War against Japan, 1941–1945.* Oxford University Press, 1978.

Tiedemann, Arthur E. "Big Business and Politics in Prewar Japan." In James William Morely, ed., *Dilemmas of Growth in Prewar Japan.* Princeton University Press, 1971.

———. "Japan Sheds Dictatorship." In John H. Herz, ed., *From Dictatorship to Democracy: Coping with the Legacies of Authoritarianism and Totalitarianism.* Greenwood Press, 1982.

Timberman, David G. *A Changeless Land: Continuity and Change in Philippines Politics.* M. E. Sharpe, 1991.

Truman, Harry S. *Memoirs.* Doubleday, 1955.

Tsoucalas, Constantine. *The Greek Tragedy.* Penguin Books, 1969.

Tucker, Richard W. "Brave New World Orders." *New Republic*, February 24, 1992.

———. "The Triumph of Wilsonianism?" *World Policy Journal* 10, no. 4 (Winter 1993–4).

Tucker, Richard W., and David C. Hendrickson. *The Empire of Liberty: The Statecraft of Thomas Jefferson.* Oxford University Press, 1990.

———. *The Imperial Temptation: The New World Order and America's Purpose.* Council on Foreign Relations, 1992.

Tulchin, Joseph S. *Argentina and the United States: A Conflicted Relationship.* Twayne, 1990.

Tulchin, Joseph, and Walter Knut. "Nicaragua: The Limits of Intervention." In Lowenthal, Abraham F., *Exporting Democracy: The United States and Latin America.* Johns Hopkins University Press, 1991.

Tulis, Jeffrey. *The Rhetorical Presidency.* Princeton University Press, 1987.

Turner, Henry Ashby. *German Big Business and the Rise of Hitler.* Oxford University Press, 1985.

Turner, Robert. *Nicaragua vs. the United States: A Look at the Facts.* Pergamon-Brassey's, 1987.

Ungar, Sanford J., and Peter Vales. "South Africa: Why Constructive Engagement Failed." *Foreign Affairs* 64, no. 2 (Winter 1985–6).

U.S. Senate. Committee on Foreign Relations, Subcommittee on American Republics Affairs. *Survey of the Alliance for Progress.* Document 91-17, 91st Cong., 1st sess., 1969.

―――. Select Committee to Study Governmental Operations with Respect to Intelligence Activities. *Covert Action in Chile, 1963–1973,* 94th Cong., 1st sess. December 18, 1975.

Unterberger, Betty Miller. *The United States, Revolutionary Russia, and the Rise of Czechoslovakia.* University of North Carolina Press, 1989.

―――. "Woodrow Wilson and the Russian Revolution." In Arthur S. Link, ed., *Woodrow Wilson and a Revolutionary World, 1913–1921.* University of North Carolina Press, 1982.

Valenta, Jiri, and Esperanza Duran. eds. *Conflict in Nicaragua: A Multidimensional Perspective.* Allen and Unwin, 1987.

Valenzuela, Arturo. "Chile: Origins, Consolidation and Breakdown of a Democratic Regime." In Larry Diamond et al., *Democracy in Developing Countries.* Lynne Rienner, 1989.

―――. *A Nation of Enemies: Chile under Pinochet.* W. W. Norton, 1991.

Van Der Wee, Herman. *Prosperity and Upheaval: The World Economy, 1945–1980.* University of California Press, 1987.

Van Evera, Stephen. "Primed for Peace: Europe after the Cold War." *International Security* 15, no. 3 (Winter 1990–1).

―――. "The United States and the Third World: When to Intervene?" In Kenneth A. Oye et al., *Eagle in a New World: American Grand Strategy in the Post-Cold War Era.* HarperCollins, 1992.

Vance, Cyrus. *Hard Choices: Critical Years in America's Foreign Policy.* Simon and Schuster, 1983.

Varg, Paul A. "The Economic Side of the Good Neighbor Policy: The Reciprocal Trade Program and South America." *Pacific Historical Review* 45, no. 1 (February 1976).

Vega, Bernardo. *Eisenhower y Trujillo.* Fundacion Cultural Dominicana, 1991.

Wallerstein, Immanuel. *The Capitalist World-Economy.* Cambridge University Press, 1979.

Waltz, Kenneth. *Theory of International Relations.* Addison-Wesley, 1979.

Walworth, Arthur. *America's Moment: 1918, American Diplomacy at the End of World War I.* W. W. Norton, 1977.

Walzer, Michael. *Just and Unjust Wars: A Moral Argument with Historical Illustrations.* Basic Books, 1977.

Ward, Robert E., *Political Development in Modern Japan.* Princeton University Press, 1978.

Ward, Robert E., and Sakamoto Yoshikazu. *Democratizing Japan: The Allied Occupation.* University of Hawaii Press, 1987.

Weinstein, Edwin. *Woodrow Wilson: A Medical and Psychological Biography.* Princeton University Press, 1981.

Weintraub, Sidney, and Delal Baer. "The Interplay between Economic and Political Opening: The Sequence in Mexico." *Washington Quarterly,* 15 (Spring 1992).

Welles, Sumner. *Naboth's Vineyard: The Dominican Republic, 1844–1924*. Payson & Clarke, 1928.

Whitehead, Laurence. "International Aspects of Democratization." In Guillermo O'Donnell et al., *Transitions from Authoritarian Rule: Comparative Perspectives*. Johns Hopkins University Press, 1986.

Wiarda, Howard J. *The Democratic Revolution in Latin America*. Holmes and Meier, 1990.

————. "Did the Alliance 'Lose Its Way,' or Were Its Assumptions All Wrong in the Beginning and Are Those Assumptions Still with Us?" In Ronald Scheman, ed., *The Alliance for Progress: A Retrospective*. Praeger, 1988.

————. "The Dominican Republic: Mirror Legacies of Democracy and Authoritarianism." In Larry Diamond et al., *Democracy in Developing Countries: Latin America*. Lynne Rienner, 1989.

————. *Ethnocentrism in Foreign Policy: Can We Understand the Third World?* American Enterprise Institute, 1985.

————. "Rethinking Political Development: A Look Backward over Thirty Years, and a Look Ahead." *Studies in Comparative International Development* 24 no. 4 (Winter 1989–90).

Wiarda, Howard J., and Michael J. Kryzanck. *The Politics of External Influence in the Dominican Republic*. Praeger, 1988.

Wickberg, Edgar. *The Chinese in Philippine Life, 1850–1898*. Southeast Asia Studies Monograph Series. Yale University, 1965.

Williams, William Appleman. 2d ed. *The Tragedy of American Diplomacy*. Dell, 1972.

Wills, Garry. "The Presbyterian Nietzsche." *New York Review of Books*, January 16, 1992.

Wilson, Woodrow. *The State: Elements of Historical and Practical Politics*. D. C. Heath, 1898.

Wittner, Lawrence S. *American Intervention in Greece, 1943–1949*. Columbia University Press, 1982.

Wolfers, Arnold, and Laurence W. Martin, eds. *The Anglo-American Tradition in Foreign Affairs*. Yale University Press, 1956.

Wood, Gordon S. *The Radicalism of the American Revolution*. Knopf, 1992.

Woodward, C. Vann. *The Strange Career of Jim Crow*. 3d rev. ed. Oxford University Press, 1974.

Wray, Harry, and Hilary Conroy, eds. *Japan Examined: Perspectives on Modern Japanese History*. University of Hawaii Press, 1983.

Wright, Quincy. *A Study of War*. University of Chicago Press, 1942.

Wright, Robin. "Islam, Democracy, and the West." *Foreign Affairs* 71, no. 2 (Summer 1992).

Wright, Theodore Paul, Jr. *American Support of Free Elections Abroad*. Public Affairs Press, 1964.

Wurfel, David. *Filipino Politics: Development and Decay*. Cornell University Press, 1988.

Yamamura Kozo. *A Study of Samurai Income and Entrepreneurship: Quantitative Analyses of Economic and Social Aspects of the Samurai in Tokugawa and Meijii, Japan*. Harvard University Press, 1974.

Yoshida Shigeru. *The Yoshida Memoirs: The Story of Japan in Crisis.* Houghton, Mifflin, 1962.

Zakaria, Fareed. "The Reagan Strategy of Containment." *Political Science Quarterly* 105, no. 3 (1990).

Zimbalist, Andrew, and John Weeks. *Panama at the Crossroads: Economic Development and Political Change in the Twentieth Century.* University of California Press, 1991.

Zonis, Marvin. *Majestic Failure: The Fall of the Shah.* University of Chicago Press, 1991.

Index

Abrahms, Elliott, 286, 290, 293, 298

Acheson, Dean, 57, 183, 390n.63

Adenauer, Konrad, 159, 160, 171, 172, 173

Afghanistan, Soviet invasion of, 243, 247, 262, 297; U.S. involvement in, 301, 302, 303

Africa, 8, 9, 163, 211, 216; prospects for democracy in, 4, 247, 340. *See also individual countries*

African-Americans, 19–27, 80–81, 234, 240

African National Congress (ANC), 275, 276, 279

Agency for International Development, 214, 222, 241, 343

Aguinaldo, Emilio, 48, 51, 63

Allende, Salvador, 210

Alliance for Progress, 6, 18, 27, 180, 198, 213, 214–34, 335, 361; anti-communism of, 215–16, 221–22, 223, 225–26; and Chile, 323–34; commitment to democracy of, 214, 217; as compared to policies by other presidents, 78, 214–16, 217, 223, 243–44, 321; and the Dominican Republic, 229–32; land reform and, 217–19, 225–26; lessons of, 234–36; military takeovers and, 226–28, 235; view of Latin America and, 220–21; view of reform process and, 224; U.S. national security and, 221; Wilsonianism of, 82, 216, 223, 234–36, 398n.39. *See also* J. Kennedy; Latin America

Almond, Gabriel A., 360–61

American foreign policy, as academic study, 32, 139–44, 346–49, 362–67. *See also* international relations theory; liberal democratic internationalism

American Revolution, 7, 8, 19, 85, 334

Amnesty International, 4, 343

ANC, *see* African National Congress

Anglo-Iranian Oil Company, 183, 192, 195, 197

Angola, 209, 245; relations with South Africa, 277, 278, 279. *See also* Cuba, in Africa

apartheid, *see* race

Aquinaldo, Emilio, 48, 51

Aquino, Benigno, 53, 58, 281

Aquino, Corazon, 39–40, 58, 282, 315

Arbenz, Jacobo, 192, 193–94, 197

Argentina, 183, 185, 210, 243, 262, 287, 289

Arias, Oscar, 285, 302

Aristide, Jean-Bertrand, 280–81, 303, 319

arms race, 105, 139, 141, 297, 338. *See also* militarism; R. Reagan, arms control; United States, support for militaries

Atlantic Charter, 5, 113, 118–19, 125, 129, 130–31, 190

Austro-Hungarian empire, 85, 87, 97, 100, 105, 306

Ba'ath party, 185, 257

Baker, James, 286, 323; and Central America, 316; and Europe, 314, 332; and the Soviet Union, 314, 332, 410n.20; as a Wilsonian, 313

Balaguer, Joaquin, 231–32, 261

Baltic states, 4, 129–30, 190, 266, 299

Barnes, Harry G., 290

Benda, Harry J., 347

Berle, Adolf, 129, 220

Betancourt, Romulo, 220, 230, 395n.12

Bosch, Juan, 220, 230–31, 249, 397n.30, 397–98n.32

Bosnia, 324, 326

Bosworth, Stephen, 281

Botha, P. W., 276, 278

Brandt, Willy, 306

Brazil, 216, 220, 226, 227

Bretton Woods Agreements, 10, 108, 114, 115, 128, 164, 327

Brezhnev, Leonid, 272

Brezhnev Doctrine, 210, 297

Brzezinski, Zbigniew, 259, 260, 401n.43

Bulgaria, 130, 131

Bunker, Ellsworth, 205

Bush, George, 83, 286; and Central America, 316, 320; and China, 319; as compared to other presidents, 312, 321–22, 323–24; and Eastern Europe, 313–14;

sonianism. *See also* League of Nations; Paris Peace Conference; F. Roosevelt, Wilson

Wilsonianism, 12–13, 84–86, 134; British influence on, 328; critics of, 102–9, 288, 354–55, 363–64; defined, 6–7, 85–86, 327; and economic liberalism, 87, 90–93, 140; evolution in thinking, 71, 117–18, 311–12; in Latin America, 32–33, 67, 74, 82–83, 120–21; limits and problems of, 180, 234–35, 261, 341; and nationalism, 8–9, 10, 88, 139, 168, 306, 333; and national security, xv, 78–80, 85–86, 103–9, 200; 236, 327; in practice, 95–102; and realism, 32–33, 181, 211–13, 240, 355; resurgence of, 108, 247, 312; in theory, 84–95. *See also* democracy; M. Gorbachev; V. Havel; liberal democratic internationalism; *specific presidents*

World War I, 8, 74, 140, 145, 147, 306, 311, 333, 334, 335, 338. *See also* Paris Peace Conference; *specific countries*

World War II, 8, 108, 140, 146–47, 186, 306, 333, 335, 338. *See also specific countries*; *specific presidents*; Yalta Conference

Yalta Conference, 119, 125–26, 130, 134, 135, 153, 207, 210. *See also* Declaration on Liberated Europe

Yeltsin, Boris, 295, 325, 331–32, 342

Yoshida Shigeru, 160, 173

Yugoslavia, 93, 108, 130, 131, 138, 140, 189–90; disintegration of, 267, 319, 323, 340, 341. *See also* G. Bush, Yugoslavia; Bosnia; J. Tito

Zaire, 12

Zhirinovsky, Vladimir, 339

Zimbabwe, 246, 247, 261, 278